MASTERPLOTS II

SHORT STORY
SERIES

MASTERPLOTS II

SHORT STORY SERIES

3

Gre-Lod

Edited by

FRANK N. MAGILL

SALEM PRESS

Pasadena, California   Englewood Cliffs, New Jersey

Library of Congress Cataloging-in-Publication Data
Masterplots II: Short story series.
    Bibliography: p.
    Includes index.
    Summary: Examines the theme, characters,
plot, style and technique of more than 700 nine-
teenth- and twentieth-century works by prominent
authors from around the world.
    1. Fiction—19th century—Stories, plots, etc. 2.
Fiction—19th century—History and criticism. 3.
Fiction—20th century—Stories, plots, etc. 4. Fic-
tion—20th century—History and criticism. 5.
Short story. [1. Short stories—Stories, plots, etc. 2.
Short story] I. Magill, Frank Northen, 1907-   .
II. Title: Masterplots 2. III. Title: Masterplots two.
PN3326.M27 1986   809.3   86-22025
ISBN 0-89356-461-3 (set)
ISBN 0-89356-464-8 (volume 3)

LIST OF TITLES IN VOLUME 3

page

Greasy Lake—*T. Coraghessan Boyle* 925

Great Good Place, The—*Henry James* 929

Great Wall of China, The—*Franz Kafka* 932

Greek Interpreter, The—*Arthur Conan Doyle* 936

Green Tea— *Joseph Sheridan Le Fanu* 940

Greenleaf—*Flannery O'Connor* 944

Greyhound People—*Alice Adams* 948

Guest, The—*Albert Camus* 952

Guests of the Nation—*Frank O'Connor* 956

Gun Shop, The—*John Updike* 959

Gusev—*Anton Chekhov* 962

Guy de Maupassant—*Isaac Babel* 966

Haircut—*Ring Lardner* 970

Hamlet of the Shchigrovsky District—*Ivan Turgenev* 973

Handsomest Drowned Man in the World, The—
  Gabriel García Márquez 977

Happy August the Tenth—*Tennessee Williams* 981

Happy Autumn Fields, The—*Elizabeth Bowen* 985

Harmony—*Ring Lardner* 989

Headless Hawk, The—*Truman Capote* 993

Her First Ball—*Katherine Mansfield* 997

Her Table Spread—Elizabeth Bowen 1000

Herakleitos—*Guy Davenport* 1003

Herodias—*Gustave Flaubert* 1007

Heroes in the Dark House, The—*Benedict Kiely* 1011

Higgler, The—*A. E. Coppard* 1014

Hills Like White Elephants—*Ernest Hemingway* 1018

His Son, in His Arms, in Light, Aloft—*Harold Brodkey* 1022

Hitchhiking Game, The—*Milan Kundera* 1026

Hodel—*Sholom Aleichem* 1029

Home—*Jayne Anne Phillips* 1033

Horse and Two Goats, A—*R. K. Narayan* 1037

Horse Dealer's Daughter, The—*D. H. Lawrence* ....1041 page

House in Turk Street, The—*Dashiell Hammett* 1045
House with the Grape-vine, The—*H. E. Bates* 1049
Housebreaker of Shady Hill, The—*John Cheever* 1052
How Claeys Died—*William Sansom* 1056
How I contemplated the world from the Detroit House of Correction
  and began my life over again—*Joyce Carol Oates* 1060
How I Finally Lost My Heart—*Doris Lessing* 1064
How It Was Done in Odessa—*Isaac Babel* 1067
How Much Land Does a Man Need?—*Leo Tolstoy* 1070
How the Devil Came Down Division Street—*Nelson Algren* 1073
Hunger Artist, A—*Franz Kafka* 1077
Hunter Gracchus, The—*Franz Kafka* 1081
Hunting Season—*Joanne Greenberg* 1085

I Look Out for Ed Wolfe—*Stanley Elkin* 1088
I Stand Here Ironing—*Tillie Olsen* 1091
I Want to Know Why—*Sherwood Anderson* 1095
Ice House, The—*Caroline Gordon* 1099
Ice Wagon Going Down the Street, The—*Mavis Gallant* 1103
Icicle, The—*Abram Tertz* 1106
Idiots First—*Bernard Malamud* 1109
Idle Days on the Yann—*Lord Dunsany* 1112
I'm a Fool—*Sherwood Anderson* 1116
Imagination Dead Imagine—*Samuel Beckett* 1119
Imagined Scenes—*Ann Beattie* 1122
Impulse—*Conrad Aiken* 1126
In Another Country—*Ernest Hemingway* 1130
In Dreams Begin Responsibilities—*Delmore Schwartz* 1134
In Greenwich There Are Many Gravelled Walks—
  Hortense Calisher 1137
In the Cage—*Henry James* 1141
In the Garden of the North American Martyrs—*Tobias Wolff* 1146
In the Heart of the Heart of the Country—*William H. Gass* 1150
In the Penal Colony—*Franz Kafka* 1154
In the White Night—*Ann Beattie* 1158
Indian Camp—*Ernest Hemingway* 1162
Indian Uprising, The—*Donald Barthelme* 1165
Indissoluble Matrimony—*Rebecca West* 1169
Infant Prodigy, The—*Thomas Mann* 1173
Innocence—*Seán O'Faoláin* 1176
Instructions for John Howell—*Julio Cortázar* 1180
Interest in Life, An—*Grace Paley* 1184

LIST OF TITLES IN VOLUME 3

page

Interlopers, The—*Saki* 1187
Invisible Man, The—*G. K. Chesterton* 1191
It May Never Happen—*V. S. Pritchett* 1194
Ivy Day in the Committee Room—*James Joyce* 1197
Ivy Gripped the Steps—*Elizabeth Bowen* 1201

Jackals and Arabs—*Franz Kafka* 1205
Jacklighting—*Ann Beattie* 1208
Japanese Quince, The—*John Galsworthy* 1211
Jean-ah Poquelin—*George Washington Cable* 1214
Jewbird, The—*Bernard Malamud* 1218
Jim Baker's Bluejay Yarn—*Mark Twain* 1222
John Napper Sailing Through the Universe—*John Gardner* 1226
Jolly Corner, The—*Henry James* 1230
Jordan's End—*Ellen Glasgow* 1234
Jorinda and Jorindel—*Mavis Gallant* 1237
Josephine the Singer—*Franz Kafka* 1241
Julia and the Bazooka—*Anna Kavan* 1245

Keela, the Outcast Indian Maiden—*Eudora Welty* 1248
Kepi, The—*Colette* 1252
Kerchief, The—*Shmuel Yosef Agnon* 1255
Killers, The—*Ernest Hemingway* 1259
King Solomon—*Isaac Rosenfeld* 1262
King's Indian, The—*John Gardner* 1265
Kiss, The—*Anton Chekhov* 1270
Kleist in Thun—*Robert Walser* 1273
Kugelmass Episode, The—*Woody Allen* 1276

Lady Macbeth of the Mtsensk District—*Nikolai Leskov* 1280
Lady or the Tiger?, The—*Frank R. Stockton* 1284
Lady with the Dog, The—*Anton Chekhov* 1288
Lagoon, The—*Joseph Conrad* 1292
Lamb to the Slaughter—*Roald Dahl* 1295
Last Class, The—*Alphonse Daudet* 1298
Last Mohican, The—*Bernard Malamud* 1302
Laura—*Saki* 1305
Leaning Tower, The—*Katherine Anne Porter* 1309
Leaves—*John Updike* 1313
Leaving the Yellow House—*Saul Bellow* 1317
Lefty—*Nikolai Leskov* 1320
Legal Aid—*Frank O'Connor* 1325

page

Legend of St. Julian, Hospitaler, The—*Gustave Flaubert* 1328
Legend of Sleepy Hollow, The—*Washington Irving* 1331
Lenz—*Georg Büchner* 1335
Lesson of the Master, The—*Henry James* 1339
Library of Babel, The—*Jorge Luis Borges* 1342
Lifeguard—*John Updike* 1345
Life-Story—*John Barth* 1348
Ligeia—*Edgar Allan Poe* 1352
Lightning—*Donald Barthelme* 1355
Like the Night—*Alejo Carpentier* 1359
Lions, Harts, Leaping Does—*J. F. Powers* 1363
Lispeth—*Rudyard Kipling* 1367
Little Cloud, A—*James Joyce* 1371
Little Herr Friedemann—*Thomas Mann* 1375
Living Relic, A—*Ivan Turgenev* 1379
Livingstone's Companions—*Nadine Gordimer* 1383
Lodging for the Night, A—*Robert Louis Stevenson* 1387

MASTERPLOTS II

SHORT STORY
SERIES

GREASY LAKE

Author: T. Coraghessan Boyle (1948-   )
Type of plot: Adventure
Time of plot: The 1960's
Locale: A small American town and its environs
First published: 1982

> *Principal characters:*
> THE NARRATOR, an unnamed teenage boy
> DIGBY, the narrator's teenage friend
> JEFF, another friend
> BOBBY, a rough character, also a teenager
> AL, a "biker," who is found dead
> A YOUNG WOMAN, unnamed, who is looking for Al

The Story

"Greasy Lake" is, on the surface at least, a teenage adventure story replete with high jinks, slapstick, and a good brawl. The good times go decidedly sour before the story is over, however, and the reader realizes that something more serious has been at issue all along.

The story is divided into three major sections. The first introduces the narrator and his two friends, just out of school for the summer, who cruise the streets of their small hometown, drinking, sniffing glue, and in general being what they consider "bad characters."

The longer second section of the story begins when the three drive out to scum- and refuse-clotted Greasy Lake in search of "action." A "chopper" (motorcycle) is parked on one side of the lot next to the lake, no owner in sight. A 1957 Chevy with the inevitable teenage lovers inside is parked on the other. The three friends mistake the car for that of an acquaintance; the narrator pulls his car behind the Chevy and, for a joke, flashes his headlights and honks the horn. Unfortunately, the owner of the car (Bobby) is not their friend after all. A fight ensues. The narrator and his friends are routed, comically so, by Bobby, who is in truth the "bad character" they believe themselves to be.

The relatively harmless fun now begins to sour. The narrator, humiliated by a kick to the mouth, hits Bobby over the head with a tire iron, perhaps hurting him seriously. Bobby's girl emerges screaming from the car, half-clothed, and the three, impassioned and heedless from the recent violence, attempt to rape her. They are stopped not by their consciences but by the headlights of an approaching car. This fresh carload of "bad characters" rescues the girl and chases narrator and friends into the brush surrounding the lake. Dodging rocks hurled into the darkness, the narrator dives into the lake and bumps into a true horror—a floating corpse. The second section ends as the narrator staggers out of the water and hears Bobby (recovered) and his friends battering the narrator's car.

The third section begins as dawn allows the narrator, Digby, and Jeff to survey the damage. It is some consolation, though not much, that the tires were not slashed and the car is still drivable. As they are about to leave, another car pulls into the lot. In it are two young women in their mid-twenties. One approaches and asks if the boys have seen Al, the owner of the "chopper" across the lake. Al, the narrator realizes, is the corpse he splashed into in the lake, but he denies having seen anyone. The woman takes a good look at the three of them—cut, bruised, and filthy—and says, "Hey, you guys look like some pretty bad characters." The three would have considered this high praise at the beginning of the story, but now they are too stunned by events to react. They decline when she offers them drugs, and the story ends as they drive away from the lake.

Themes and Meanings

Were it not for the story's obvious dual point of view—an older, mature narrator looking back at his foolish younger self—the reader could be for-given for dismissing "Greasy Lake" as a sordid and superficial teenage "thriller." The very fact that the mature narrator isolates this one night out of all of his youth for dramatization implies its importance. His experience amounts, in fact, to a harrowing "initiation ritual," in anthropological terms, or a "dark night of the soul," in religious terms. By the end he has taken one large step toward maturity.

The principal theme of the story could be summarized quite well in the old Greek saying, "Through suffering comes wisdom." Several details support this reading. Much of the action turns on mistakes that the narrator must rec-ognize as such and atone for—above all, his belief that he and his friends are "bad characters." They attempt to bolster this self-image by "razzing" their friend in the Chevy—another mistake, which is followed by yet another when the narrator drops his car key and cannot flee the enraged Bobby. The narrator, however, becomes "bad" in a moral sense when he hits Bobby with the tire iron, then tries to rape the girl. When he flees into the brush at the approach of the car, he is more shaken by guilt than by fear that Bobby's friends will hurt him. He is, in fact, later overjoyed to hear the sound of Bobby's voice. His punishment comes in several forms: He is kicked in the mouth and then hit on the knee by a rock; he splashes up against the horrible corpse in the lake; he watches his mother's car being demolished (and one can only guess what further punishment awaits him at home).

Two patterns of symbolism support the story's theme. One centers on the lake itself. The narrator's submersion in the lake, in his fear and guilt, amounts to a ritual baptism; the fetid waters are appropriate to his "filthy" moral condition. In the water he encounters what teenagers are generally heedless of but what life and sin inevitably lead one to: the corpse, death. The second pattern of symbolism involves the car key. The lost key is the narrator's "grail and . . . salvation," religious images that prepare the reader for the baptism in the lake. The second time he thinks of the key is after bumping into the corpse—he wants to flee, obviously—but such "nasty little epiphanies" cannot simply be driven away from. He does not find the key until his dark night of the soul is over; dawn reveals the key shining like a "jewel" just where he had dropped it.

Having confronted his own sin (his "bad character") and his mortality (the corpse), the narrator has earned the right to face the dawn (the light of truth) and take up the key (to understanding). In rejecting the offer of drugs at the end he is not merely rejecting a dangerous life-style but is accepting, by implication, the responsibilities of adulthood. The end is hardly a joyful one, but then, as the Greeks well knew, the price of wisdom is suffering.

Style and Technique

The dual point of view is obviously crucial to the story's theme, but it is also the most important technical feature, and Boyle wields the dual perspective to interesting effects, especially in tone and imagery. In fact, the careful reader will note how often the tone and imagery seem to break into contrasting halves, mirroring the contrasting levels of understanding exhibited by the older narrator and his younger self.

It is the narrator as a nineteen-year-old, for example, who considers his friend Digby a "dangerous character" and who is impressed by the gold star Digby wears in his right ear; the older narrator, however, notes ironically that this dangerous Digby "allowed his father to pay his tuition at Cornell." The boy thinks that it will be a great joke to "razz" their friend in the Chevy; the older narrator casts all this in an ironic light, reflected in his inflated rhetoric, when he speculates that after the joke the friends will "go on to new heights of adventure and daring." The reader would do well, in fact, to remember the difference between "atmosphere" and "tone" throughout the story. "Atmosphere" is the mood evoked by setting and events. "Tone" is the author's (narrator's) perceived attitude toward the story. These may be nearly identical or greatly at variance—the latter in "Greasy Lake."

The dichotomy between tone and atmosphere is supported by contrasting images—between past and present, between nature and civilization, between horror and humor, but most importantly between the "tough guy" images nurtured by the teenagers and contrasting images of immaturity. The friends assert their toughness by rolling marijuana cigarettes, for example, but the "joints" are "compact as a Tootsie Roll Pop stick." In the fight with Bobby, Digby's karate maneuvers are far less effective than Jeff's more elementary tactics: jumping on Bobby's back and biting his ear. To underscore the childishness of the scene, the narrator immediately recalls that he had not been in a fight since the sixth grade. After bumping into the corpse in the lake, the narrator realizes, "I was nineteen, a mere child, an infant. . . ." At the end, when the young woman says that the three look like "pretty bad characters," the narrator's reaction is hardly one of pride: "I thought I was going to cry."

In this last section, the distance between tone and atmosphere is radically reduced and the use of contrasting images largely abandoned, all of which is appropriate; after his painful learning experience, the nineteen-year-old is much closer to the maturity of the older narrator than to his childish self of only a few hours before.

Dennis Vannatta

THE GREAT GOOD PLACE

Author: Henry James (1843-1916)
Type of plot: Dream fantasy
Time of plot: Late nineteenth century
Locale: London
First published: 1900

> *Principal characters:*
> GEORGE DANE, an elderly, successful author
> BROWN, his manservant
> A WRITER, an unnamed, unsuccessful young man
> TWO BROTHERS, shadowy figures within the dream

The Story

George Dane, a writer whose success has brought with it a tremendous amount of responsibility in the form of increasingly more reading and writing to be done, wakes up one morning feeling overwhelmed by all the paperwork on his desk. The rain during the night has not washed away the work waiting to be done, the sentence waiting to be completed. Brown, his servant, enters the study to remind him of an engagement and inquire about his luncheon plans. Dane would rather not be bothered. Brown's distractedness leads them to talk at cross-purposes until Dane intones, "There is a happy land— far far away!" Brown is concerned that Dane is not well. Upon Dane's reassurance, Brown introduces a young man, whose name Dane does not catch, into the room. The story's first scene ends as they shake hands.

The remaining four scenes take place within Dane's dream until he wakes up for the story's last few paragraphs. The second scene begins with Dane feeling as if he is experiencing the rebirth of consciousness in a place of infinite charm, peace, and freshness: the "great good place" of the title. Author Henry James dramatizes the growth of Dane's consciousness through the successive scenes until Dane awakens to the everyday world. Within the dream, Dane is first vaguely aware of a place defined as "such an abyss of negatives, such an absence of everything." Out of a general feeling of peace and contentment, he develops self-consciousness as he become aware of a shadowy, humanlike figure who seems to be sharing a bath with him. This figure is a "Brother," one who shares Dane's sense of ease, serenity, and security in this place that appears to be a combination of monastery and health spa: a retreat from the world that will invigorate the self. The pleasant sound of bells introduces times and the orders of spatial form and perspective. Dane and the Brother discuss the finding of the place and what it means to them. Dane names it "The Great Good Place." For the Brother it is "The Great Want Met." They agree that to get to there, the burden of the world had to be dropped. Dane tells how the young man who showed up in his study that morning became his "substitute in the world" by assuming all of his obligations. As the young man took over the identity of Dane, Dane gained the freedom of becoming nobody.

After what seems like three weeks to Dane, he believes that he has regained his vision, his genius, his way of ordering and understanding the world. Instead of appearing amorphous, everything now seems crystal clear, the creation of a wise consciousness exactly like his own. He is able to analyze the situation. The place has a library containing all the books he has always wanted to read but did not have the time to read. His comparisons become more aesthetic, including references to painting and music. He feels the pleasure of detachment in combination with the impression that everything was a result of his desires and vision. In the company of another, apparently younger, Brother, he comes to believe that he has found what he wanted.

As the final scene commences, it seems to be raining, indicating an element of change which has heretofore been absent in the place. Dane and the Brother compare the place to a convalescent home and a kindergarten, institutions that imply process or development. With this comes a concern that the place will not always be available. They decide that it will. They realize that they must return to life itself. As Dane shakes the hand of the Brother in farewell, he wakes up to find his hand being held by the manservant Brown. He has been sleeping all day while the young visitor has taken care of all of his correspondence.

Themes and Meanings

The theme of the story, the importance of consciousness, is the primary theme of James's fiction as a whole. The "great good place" is consciousness. The scenes in the study provide the frame for the dramatization of the process of a developing consciousness, which constitutes the dream sequence. George Dane's literary correspondence and obligations have diminished his contact with his own consciousness, the source of his creative abilities and of his sense of identity. Dane's despair and rejection of the work of his everyday life, his distraction, his overall feeling of being overwhelmed by the details of his life brought about by his success, result from this lack of nurturing contact with his consciousness. Dane's withdrawal from the world into his dream is the vehicle for reunification with that inner life of which the principal component is consciousness itself.

The conjunction of "the great good place" with "the great want met" signifies that Dane has come to the right place to fulfill his desire to regain contact with himself even though he does not yet realize exactly what this means. The place is, in effect, consciousness unadulterated by the facts of the world. The "blessed fact of consciousness" antedates all values or perceptions. From being conscious, Dane moves through stages of becoming self-conscious to awareness of the significant patterns of the world of both the inner and outer life. He wakes from his dream with the realization that through consciousness, inner and outer worlds are united.

Style and Technique

Through the device of the dream story, James is able to render the theme of consciousness more directly than he normally does. He dispenses with the exigencies of plot, characterization, and the defining details necessary for verisimilitude. Within the dream, George Dane is nothing but consciousness. He is what he is aware of being. He encounters nothing but himself in the process of becoming aware of himself. Even those shadowy figures, the Brothers, are merely projections of his desire to communicate with those aspects of himself that validate his work as an author and his vision of life. There is no boundary between inner life and outer world. Within some vaguely defined limits, Dane's consciousness is free to reconstruct itself and the world at the same time, and James is free to dramatize this process. Of "The Great Good Place," Henry James himself wrote that "any gloss or comment would be a tactless challenge." The unity of story and theme validates his assertion.

William J. McDonald

THE GREAT WALL OF CHINA

Author: Franz Kafka (1883-1924)
Type of plot: Allegory
Time of plot: After the construction of the Wall
Locale: China
First published: "Beim Bau der chinesischen Mauer," 1931 (English translation, 1933)

> *Principal characters:*
> THE NARRATOR, anonymous, apparently an official in the imperial bureaucracy
> THE EMPEROR OF CHINA
> THE STAFF OF THE HIGH COMMAND, in charge of the construction of the Wall

The Story

The anonymous speaker of this quasi-historical report on the Great Wall of China speculates not only about the peculiar method of the Wall's construction but also about the motives behind the project and the authorities upon whose decision it was undertaken. The speaker's focus gradually expands to consider the larger matters of relationship between the Emperor and his people, between the Empire and the barbarians beyond it, and, ultimately, between the real and the imagined meanings of all these various shapers of the speaker's world.

At the outset, the speaker points out a conspicuous peculiarity in the construction of the Wall: Rather than being built continuously from one end to the other, the Wall was assembled piecemeal in sections of about a thousand yards each. Isolated from other workers and usually not even in sight of another section of the Wall, two crews, beginning at opposite ends of the thousand-yard stretch, would spend as much as five years laboring to make their respective sections meet; after appropriate ceremonies, they would then be dismissed to their homes. After such a lengthy absence, their return would be celebrated in their native villages, which were very often many miles from the borders upon which their section of the Wall had been constructed. After a period of rest and rejuvenation, the workers would be dispatched again to join others with whom they had not worked before and to begin a new section of the Wall in some other remote corner of the Empire, far from home.

Such a method of construction left many gaps in the Wall over the long period of its building, some of which were not closed until after the Wall was officially declared complete. This fact, coupled with the apparent motive for the Wall itself—namely, to provide security against the barbarian hordes that threatened invasion—gives the speaker the problem that he sets out to resolve by considering the history and development of this imperial project.

Among the considerations that he entertains is the evidence of a central and all-encompassing plan designed by the "high command" in charge of the project, even though—as he remarks—the whereabouts and staff of the high command remain veiled in mystery. Nevertheless, so large a project and so peculiar a method of construction force him to assume that the high command existed and had direct control. Otherwise, he says, how can one account for the long period of preparation before the first stone was laid? for the emphasis upon architecture as the greatest of sciences? for the schoolyard games of building pebble-walls? or for the rigorous training and high culture possessed by a mere supervisor of even four workers on the Wall? Then, too, the expense of the project, not only material but also psychological, suggests that some greater power and design were at work than even the most advanced and intelligent individual could comprehend. The high command must have all human designs and all human wishes within its purview, and the Wall must therefore represent the cryptic but necessary working out of this truly benevolent design. Or, as the speaker finally admits, it is perhaps not useful or safe to dwell too much upon the greater design, or to attempt a complete understanding on one's own; better by far to repose one's trust in the plans of the high command and to submit to its decrees.

Although the speaker confesses this maxim of resignation as useful, it is clear that he is unable to apply it fully. He insists that he is pursuing an inquiry that is historical, not critical or philosophical, but his attempts to reconcile the evidence of the great plan with the experience of his own life nag him into broader considerations. Why should he, for example, whose home is far down in the southeast of China, be involved in the project—or indeed, why should he care about the northern barbarians, who could never penetrate so far into the Empire? He questions whether the barbarians exist, because (apart from the frightening pictures that sometimes appeared in children's books) no other representation of the great enemy exists. At its root, therefore, the grand design of the high command must predate even the decree of the Emperor that establishes the project, and in that grand design, the actions of the northern barbarians and of the Emperor himself have their appropriate place, acquiring meaning only in relation to the design of the high command, eternal, mysterious, and finally unknowable. These things, says the speaker, only those who have meditated upon the history of the Wall can know.

In the second half of the story, the speaker works out the consequences of this idea about the division between the nominal authority of the Emperor and the real authority of the high command. As before, his speculation revolves around the disparity between perception and explanation. The Empire is too vast for the Emperor's authority to reach all of his subjects: A messenger dispatched from the Emperor's bedside could not even struggle through the concentric rings of the palace or reach the surrounding imperial city—to say nothing of the remote provinces—before both the Emperor and the one to whom the message was sent had crumbled into dust. There can be no news from the capital because all news becomes obsolete, owing to the long period of its transmission. Although the living Emperor and his provincial subjects depend upon each other for their mutual existence, their relationship is unreal because of their remoteness from each other. The Emperor must therefore imagine his people, and the people must construct in their imagination the figure and the authority of the Emperor whom they will not and cannot ever know. As a result, even the Empire must remain largely in the imagination of its subjects, giving them a kind of freedom—since no actual external authority interferes with their lives—but only at the cost of depriving them of the security that these fictions still provide. Having gone so far, the speaker declines to pursue his inquiry further.

Themes and Meanings

As a fictional and indeed allegorical work, Franz Kafka's story is not really concerned with the Great Wall of China or the process of its building, but with the relationship between the abstract structures that give human life its meaning and the quality of life that human beings lead as a result. The only absolutes in the story are the absolutes of experiences: that some sections of the Wall have been completed; that many stand in isolation from others, defeating the nominal defensive purpose of the project; that workers come and go; that the daily life of villages, although remote from the Wall itself, is nevertheless affected by it in the absence of the workers and, more positively, in the brief but happy celebrations of the workers' return. Against these absolutes of experience, which are the actual shaping forces of the villagers' (and the speaker's) lives, stand the great abstracts, which all the subjects can only imagine to exist: the Emperor, the Empire, the high command, even the Wall itself, now officially declared to be complete. The principal theme of the story is thus the dissociation of modern life: that the realities of experience are in fact too little associated with the abstract ideals and forces (whether economic, social, political, or religious) which modern humanity uses as an explanation of its actions, or as a veil for the essential meaninglessness of many modern concerns. The inset tale of the Emperor's messenger hints that the possibility for meaning still exists, if only connections between abstractions and experiences could be made explicit, but the fate of the message, the Emperor, and the receiver shows that such a hope is finally futile. The refusal of the speaker to pursue his inquiry about the Wall is thus a representation of a similar modern refusal to question the apparent motives by which actions and circumstances are directed and shaped: For the world, as for the Empire, it is better to accept the specious security of illusory ideals than to question their reality and significance.

Style and Technique

Many of the characteristic marks of Kafka's short-story style appear here. First-person narration from an unnamed narrator, exotic or peculiar locales, and the general tendency to weave together an integrated metaphor—an allegory—for some larger issue are all typical of his general handling of story materials. By far the most conspicuous of Kafka's stylistic markers is the tone of the story as a whole: the flat, quasi-historical, apparently calm and reasonable but clearly single-minded opening masks the much more disturbing, less rational, and finally almost frightening voice of a speaker confronting an unthinkable gap in the order of his experience. The accumulation of subtle but important contradictory details, especially in the mass of obsessively collected and apparently objective data about the Wall, leads the reader to question the accuracy of the report that the speaker gives. While at the outset the speaker seems both lucid and authoritative, this lucidity and authority are quickly obscured by the weight of information not given, so that even the anonymity of the speaker and the proposition of an all-knowing, eternal high command become finally threatening. Kafka's control of tone, so that in the apparently reasonable monologue of the speaker one can discern the shrill overtones of mania, is an indication of his mastery of that anxious and ominous style that is so distinctively his own.

Dale B. Billingsley

THE GREEK INTERPRETER

Author: Arthur Conan Doyle (1859-1930)
Type of plot: Detective story
Time of plot: The mid-1880's
Locale: London, England
First published: 1893

> *Principal characters:*
> SHERLOCK HOLMES, the world's greatest detective
> DR. JOHN H. WATSON, his friend and biographer
> MR. MELAS, the Greek interpreter
> MYCROFT HOLMES, Sherlock Holmes's elder brother

The Story

The story opens in the familiar quarters of Sherlock Holmes and Dr. Watson at 221-B Baker Street in London. It is a warm summer evening, and their conversation wanders from subject to subject until Holmes mentions his family. Despite Watson's sharing the apartment for several years, he has never known Holmes to speak much of his background, and Watson is surprised to hear that Holmes has an elder brother, Mycroft, whom the detective describes as a reasoner even greater than himself. Yet Mycroft, Holmes explains, has an absolute aversion to interrupting his daily routine for the sometimes vigorous activity needed to solve crimes.

Holmes has a purpose in mentioning Mycroft precisely at this time, because his corpulent brother has summoned him to what Holmes characterizes as one of the strangest clubs in London. Holmes and Watson, therefore, stroll to the Diogenes Club for Watson's first sight of this strangest member of the city's strangest club. The Diogenes Club was founded for gentlemen who desired the refuge of a club and the privacy of their homes: Conversation is forbidden except in the Strangers' Room, in which Holmes and Watson are joined by Mycroft.

Mycroft sets before Holmes the mystery of the story: A neighbor of his, a Mr. Melas, has come to him with the tale of a very strange experience. Thinking at once of his younger brother, Mycroft has asked Melas to join them at the club so that Holmes may pursue the problem. Melas, a Greek, works as a translator in London, and his adventure began when he was hired for that purpose by a Mr. Latimer. Latimer asked Melas to accompany him to his house; when they entered their carriage, Latimer closed the window shades so that Melas could not see where they were going. Latimer then drew out a blackjack and threatened Melas so effectively that the interpreter made no protest during their ride of almost two hours.

Because night had fallen, Melas was unable to identify his surroundings when the carriage stopped. He was shown into a house and introduced first to a small, mean-looking man, and then to an emaciated figure whose head was crisscrossed and whose mouth was sealed with adhesive tape. The man, obviously a prisoner, was given a slate, and Melas was instructed to ask him questions (in Greek), to which the man would write his replies.

During the questioning, the captors insisted that the taped figure sign some papers, an act which he absolutely refused to do. After a session of several hours, Melas was taken back to town in the same furtive manner and warned to tell no one.

Melas immediately went to the police, who refused to credit his story, and he then turned to Mycroft Holmes. The stage is now set, and Sherlock Holmes's work begins. They have a few clues: Melas had been able during his questioning to find out that the captive's name was Paul Kratides, and, during an unexpected intrusion, that the man's young sister was also in the house, although she was unaware that her brother was under the same roof. Unfortunately for Holmes (and for Melas, too, eventually), Mycroft has run an advertisement in the papers for anyone knowing anything about a Paul Kratides or his sister. As Holmes points out, this notice will inform Latimer and his confederate that Melas has talked about their actions.

After leaving the Diogenes Club, Holmes and Watson send some telegrams to some possible sources of information, but when they enter their flat at Baker Street, Mycroft is already there. He says that an answer to his advertisement has identified the house in question. Mycroft wants to interview the writer of the letter, but Holmes rightly observes that the captive man is being starved to death and that they should head immediately for the house.

Watson suggests that they pick up Melas on the way, should they need an interpreter, but when they arrive at Melas' address, he has already gone off with the mean-looking little man he had described to them earlier that day. Knowing that Melas is now in mortal danger as well, Holmes rushes to Scotland Yard to appeal for a warrant to force entry into the sinister house. After a worrisome delay, they receive the warrant and reach the house in question only to find that the captors have escaped. They hear a groan from upstairs and rush up to find two prostrate figures in a room with a burning charcoal fire—the taped man, already suffocated, and Melas, whom they are able to save.

In the quiet aftermath of the action, Holmes pieces together the story of a young Greek woman, obviously with prospects of inheriting some wealth, who fell in love with the Englishman Latimer. When her brother arrived in England, he was taken by Latimer and his confederate, who attempted to force him to sign over the girl's property; keeping his arrival a secret from his sister, they had taped the brother's face so that she would not recognize him should she see him being moved about the house. The story ends with a notice in a European paper that the two Englishmen have been found stabbed, and that the woman with whom they were traveling has vanished. The girl has avenged her brother's death.

Themes and Meanings

One will not find philosophical themes in "The Greek Interpreter." When Arthur Conan Doyle first wrote of Sherlock Holmes, he was interested only in giving the readers of *Strand Magazine* an exciting, well-written story. Yet he soon found that he had created in Holmes something of a Frankenstein's monster: The public took the detective to its collective heart. Perhaps it was the detective's lucid intelligence: Through the power of the mind, the world could be seen to make sense. Holmes lives and moves among the most emotional of people, but his clear sight and keen study of detail allow him (almost always) to help reason to triumph.

Some of Holmes's quirks became set pieces, little bits of introduction that the audience came to expect, such as the detective's revelations about a client from details of the client's appearance. Yet even a good thing can be overdone, and Doyle must have felt a need from time to time to get Holmes and Watson out of their flat at Baker Street in order to expand the cast of continuing characters. Something like this may have been the motive behind "The Greek Interpreter." The story's main charm lies in its details about Holmes's life, in particular about his fascinating older brother, Mycroft. Mycroft gives Doyle a chance for one of the set pieces of observation noted above, and the further chance to show in Mycroft someone who is even better at it than Holmes is. The story furnishes a deeper, more detailed history for the detective. As one of the first continuing characters in short fiction, Holmes needed more depth, more solidity, than would normally be supplied for a character in a short story.

This was an entirely new method—to round out a fictional character through a number of works: One story might demonstrate Holmes's love of music, another his moods of depression, and another his deep friendship with Watson. This story focuses on, one might say, his heredity, through the equally remarkable powers of his brother.

Style and Technique

"The Greek Interpreter" is certainly an unusual representative of the sixty-odd stories of Sherlock Holmes written by Doyle. The story contains no mystery whatsoever to display the singular intellect of the great detective: Melas tells Holmes almost everything that he ever learns about the captive man, and almost anyone could guess at the rest, given Melas' account. The mystery of the location of the house is solved in a very prosy way, by Mycroft's placing an advertisement in the newspapers, a notice that at the same time tips off the kidnapers and very conveniently supplies the one piece of information that the rescuers need. Holmes knows this and complains about it to Mycroft.

There are other inconsistencies in the story, too: Holmes knows that both the mysterious, taped man and Melas are in danger of being murdered, yet he waits for a long while until he can obtain a proper search warrant for the house in which they are being held. In other stories Holmes has not strictly observed the laws against breaking and entering when the stake was someone's life.

Many of the Holmes stories that Doyle wrote are better as *detective* stories; that is, they have a tighter plot, a deeper mystery, or require real imagination and daring on the part of the famous detective. By 1893, however, the character of Sherlock Holmes had come so vividly to life that details of the detective's life were as pleasing to the public as any merely puzzling plot. It is in that characterization of Holmes that the enduring interest of "The Greek Interpreter" lies.

Walter E. Meyers

GREEN TEA

Author: Joseph Sheridan Le Fanu (1814-1873)
Type of plot: Horror
Time of plot: c. 1805 and c. 1869
Locale: London, rural Warwickshire, and Richmond, England
First published: 1869

> *Principal characters:*
> THE ANONYMOUS NARRATOR
> DR. MARTIN HESSELIUS, a physician and author of medical
> works
> LADY MARY HEYDUKE, a society woman and friend of Dr.
> Hesselius and Mr. Jennings
> THE REVEREND MR. ROBERT LYNDER JENNINGS, the vicar of a
> rural parish in Warwickshire
> JONES, Mr. Jennings' servant

The Story

The anonymous narrator, who was trained as a surgeon, has been arranging the papers of his deceased mentor, Dr. Martin Hesselius. One case in particular, from about sixty-four years before, draws his attention; forthwith the narrator presents a set of letters, with a memorandum, that discuss the doctor's efforts to treat a particularly insidious and vexing complaint.

One evening, Dr. Hesselius meets the Reverend M. Robert Lynder Jennings at the house of a mutual friend, Lady Mary Heyduke. In an aside, the hostess informs the doctor of Mr. Jennings' probity and good standing in the community; nevertheless, the clergyman's health is uncertain and he seems subject to sudden and mysterious collapses. With some evident embarrassment, the clergyman engages Dr. Hesselius in a discussion of Metaphysical Medicine, and evinces an active interest in the doctor's publications on the subject. Later, Lady Mary mentions that Mr. Jennings' late father had seen and spoken with a ghost. On the following evening, the clergyman sends his calling card with a note requesting a consultation with Dr. Hesselius.

At Mr. Jennings' house in Richmond, the doctor is received by Jones, the vicar's servant; the clergyman has been detained by work in his parish. While waiting in his host's library, Dr. Hesselius comes upon a set of the complete works, in Latin, of Emanuel Swedenborg, the Swedish mystical philosopher; perusal indicates that Mr. Jennings has underscored such passages as "May God compassionate me." As Dr. Hesselius continues, he realizes with a start that "four eyes were reading the passage." Mr. Jennings' unannounced return is revealed by his features reflected in an overhanging mirror. He abruptly embarks on a conversation about the origins of illness, and he confounds the doctor with his spirited denunciation of materialism in medical thought. Dr. Hesselius is taken aback particularly by the abrupt fluctuations of unchecked gloom and brisk gaiety in his host's demeanor.

After five weeks, Mr. Jennings again summons the doctor to his home, and there sets forth his own diagnosis of the maladies which have taken possession of him. Already he has been described as having once been an inveterate tea drinker. Mr. Jennings now maintains that his nervous sensibilities have been upset by the consumption first of black and then, gradually and more insidiously, of green tea. Even a change in his habits has not improved his condition. More than that, he is stalked by a creature that, whether imagined or real, relentlessly insinuates itself into his field of vision at every turn. Once while riding on an omnibus, he endeavored to push a small monkey out of his way; his umbrella actually seemed to pierce the animal. Since that time this small, jet-black primate has followed him, its eyes ever animated with burning malevolence; in the dark, it is enveloped in a glowing reddish aura. Inexplicably it has been absent for fifteen days, but the clergyman suspects it will return. He fears that it will induce a cataleptic state, rendering powerless his own will, and lead him to crime or self-destruction. After this exposition, the first he has made to anyone, Mr. Jennings asks Dr. Hesselius whether the quantities of tea he has taken could have affected his inner eye, the cerebral tissue alongside the optic nerve. He increasingly has become conscious of the monkey's singing speech, which would seem to have entered his mind through some degeneration of his faculties.

Rather soon after his second visit, the doctor receives another, and unmistakably urgent, appeal from the clergyman. It is all in vain. When he arrives, Dr. Hesselius is met by Jones, who leads him to his master's body; Mr. Jennings has opened a deep gash in his neck and left a vast pool of blood on his bedroom floor. During his last night on earth, Mr. Jennings asked his servant whether he could hear the monkey's cursing; evidently he then did away with himself during the early morning hours.

In his concluding statement, Dr. Hesselius expounds his belief that Mr. Jennings was persistently affected by hereditary suicidal mania. The doctor contends that the optic nerve is the channel by which the inner eye establishes contact with the external world. Prolonged abuse of chemical agents—such as those found in tea—upsets the mental equilibrium and renders those affected vulnerable to innate weaknesses. Dr. Hesselius maintains finally that this combination of predisposed melancholia and morbid overstimulation of the nervous system led Mr. Jennings to take his own life.

Themes and Meanings

Victorian writers were markedly prone to ascribe their characters' complaints to brain fever or other, equally vague, maladies. The effects of opium, morphine, and other such agents were also explored in fiction, sometimes with (to the modern mind) extraordinary and indeed implausible results. At first, some readers may regard as preposterous, if not laughable, the notion that drinking strong tea could produce prolonged visions and ultimately death. This story manifestly does not elicit that reaction, although the Reverend Mr. Jennings' green tea figures prominently in it from the title to the conclusion. The active properties in tea are never really demonstrated. At one time, Lady Mary had almost quarreled with the clergyman on this subject; during his longest consultation with the doctor, Mr. Jennings cites green tea specifically as the source of his visions. Evidently the effect is cumulative and possibly irreversible; even abstention cannot dispel the specter that haunts Mr. Jennings. Both he and Dr. Hesselius regard this complaint as much more than mere dyspepsia. Neither believes, however, that his malady may be understood through medical materialism alone.

This curious ambivalence, where neither spiritual nor chemical origins may be established with certainty, is heightened by Le Fanu's presentation of several characters' points of view; the author does not explicitly endorse any of them. The narrator, who introduces the story, regards Dr. Hesselius as highly gifted, but one who alternately takes the standpoints of an intelligent layman or a medical philosopher. In several places the doctor somewhat ponderously expounds his theory that man is a spiritual being, and that the body is merely a material expression of his essential and ideal nature. He can explain Mr. Jennings' affliction only by referring to "a poison which excites the reciprocal action of spirit and nerve." Mr. Jennings himself originally found green tea pleasant and almost soporific in its effects; though later he withdraws from it in horror, he admits candidly that his medical reasoning against it is speculative. The notion of hereditary trauma, which Lady Mary and the doctor accept in part, is not much discussed by Mr. Jennings; this factor remains lurking in the background, putting in occasional appearances at particularly murky junctures. The peculiarly horrific atmosphere of "Green Tea" is derived in part from the separate explanations which leading characters offer for Mr. Jennings' malevolent visions, none of which needs to be accepted entirely.

Style and Technique

In its turn, this studied ambiguity is amplified by those stylistic qualities which distinguished Le Fanu from other horror writers of his era. There is no omniscient narrator, only a series of admittedly subjective accounts from the various characters. Trappings that are often featured in ghost stories appear, but are not thrust upon the reader. The aged volumes of Emanuel Swedenborg and of German medical-philosophical cogitations are shown discreetly; gloomy scenes of the doctor's crepuscular visits to Mr. Jennings' house are presented quite in passing, as part of the larger scheme of Dr. Hesselius' narrative. Some effects are achieved obliquely, as when the doctor realizes that

Mr. Jennings is watching him from beyond a mirror. The spectral monkey itself is presented only as the clergyman seems to have perceived it, in colors and outlines; ultimately it becomes a hissing sound that appears to emanate from within Mr. Jennings' very ears.

In other respects the narrative style is understated but forthright, both in the introduction and in the ten letters of Dr. Hesselius. Most sentences are simple and direct, with the exception of a few convoluted passages wherein Dr. Hesselius holds forth on medicine and spiritualism. Very few words are emphasized, and then generally from the characters' direct discourse; there are few exclamations or questions, save for when the characters themselves utter them. The effect, though seemingly subdued and understated, actually intensifies the unfolding sense of approaching doom that imbues this work.

J. R. Broadus

GREENLEAF

Author: Flannery O'Connor (1925-1964)
Type of plot: Comic with mythological overtones
Time of plot: The 1950's
Locale: The rural South
First published: 1956

> *Principal characters:*
> MRS. MAY, the protagonist and the owner of a dairy farm
> MR. GREENLEAF, her hired man
> WESLEY, one of Mrs. May's sons, a teacher
> SCOFIELD, her other son, an insurance salesman
> O.T. and
> E.T., Mr. Greenleaf's sons, successful dairy farmers
> MRS. GREENLEAF, the wife of the hired man

The Story

Mrs. May, the owner of a dairy farm, awakes in the night from a strange dream in which something was eating everything she owned, herself, her house, her sons, her farm, all except the home of Mr. Greenleaf, her hired man. She looks out the window and discovers a stray scrub bull chewing on the hedge below her window. She considers dressing and driving down the road to Greenleaf's place to get him to catch the bull, lest it get into the pasture with her cows and corrupt the breeding schedule of her purebred cattle. She decides to put it off until morning, not because she is averse to bothering Mr. Greenleaf in the night but because she anticipates his uncomplimentary remarks about her two grown sons, who should be able to help their mother in such emergencies.

One of the long-standing rivalries between Mrs. May and Mr. Greenleaf during the fifteen years of their association has been the relative merits of their sons. Mr. Greenleaf's twins, O.T. and E.T., married two French girls of good family during the war when they were in the army. As Mrs. May rationalizes their good fortune, "disguised in their uniforms, they could not be told from other people's children. You could tell, of course, when they opened their mouths but they did that seldom." They both "managed to get wounded," so they received pensions and went to agricultural school on veterans' benefits. They had become the owners of a prosperous dairy farm nearby and the heads of flourishing bilingual families. As Mrs. May bleakly predicts, in twenty years their children will be *"society!"*

Mrs. May is secretly envious of such productive sons, since her own give her little satisfaction. Wesley has a heart condition, commutes to a teaching job, and has a vile disposition. Mrs. May pretends that he is an "intellectual."

Scofield is loud and vulgar, has gained nothing from his two years as a private during the war, and now sells insurance to blacks. He is what the blacks call the "policy man," a position of considerable mortification to his mother. Neither has married, and they both refuse to lift a hand to help with the farm work.

The next day, Mrs. May finds out that the scrub bull belongs to Mr. Greenleaf's sons, that it can apparently escape from almost any confinement, and that it hates trucks and cars. It has already attacked the twins' pickup, causing considerable damage. Mrs. May drives to the twins' house and delivers an ultimatum: Either they pick up the bull or she will have Mr. Greenleaf shoot it the next day. It is no comfort to her to learn that the twins probably do not want it and will be happy that she must destroy it for them.

The bull visits her again that night, munching away under her window. The sound of the bull tearing at the hedge enters her sleeping consciousness as a menacing dream about the sun piercing through the vegetation that surrounds her cultivated fields. The burning sun seems to burst through the trees and is racing toward her. She wakes in panic.

The next morning, she orders the reluctant Mr. Greenleaf to get his gun; they are going to shoot the bull. Mr. Greenleaf is angry, but he finally gets his weapon and joins her in the truck. They drive into the pasture, where Mrs. May has seen the animal in the distance. Mrs. May thinks with some satisfaction, "He'd like to shoot me instead of the bull." They drive into the pasture. Mrs. May waits at the truck while Greenleaf looks for the bull in the grove of trees at the edge of the pasture.

After a considerable wait, during which Mrs. May dozes as she sits on the bumper of the truck, the bull emerges from the wood, but Mr. Greenleaf is nowhere to be seen. She had been vaguely fantasizing about the bull attacking Mr. Greenleaf in the wood. The situation is curiously like her dream. She is standing in the middle of the pasture ringed by trees, a natural amphitheater, and the bull is racing toward her. She seems mesmerized, unable to move, until the bull has "buried his head in her lap like a wild tormented lover." One horn pierces her heart and the other encircles her waist: ". . . and she had the look of a person whose sight has been suddenly restored but who finds the light unbearable." Mr. Greenleaf, running toward her now from the side, pumps four bullets into the eye of the bull.

Themes and Meanings

The Greenleafs are members of the social class that was once called "poor white trash." Mrs. May, as a landowner, a user of "correct" English, and the widow of an urban businessman, considers herself socially superior to the Greenleafs in many ways. She is described as a "country woman only by persuasion." The farm, bought as an investment when land was cheap, is the only legacy that her husband left her. She has exported the urban business orientation to the countryside, determined to wrest a living from nature by sheer strength of will, despising the careless ease with which the Greenleafs exist in that environment. Yet the conflict between Mrs. May and her sometimes incompetent hired man is only partially sociological. It suggests a more elemental difficulty with Mrs. May, which may be called philosophical or even religious.

What the Greenleafs unself-consciously possess that Mrs. May lacks is a sacramental view of nature. Religiously suggestive metaphors, as well as the comic description of Mrs. Greenleaf's grotesque religious rituals, convey this difference. Mrs. May insists on taking credit for whatever success and well-being the Greenleafs enjoy. "They lived like the lilies of the field, off the fat that she struggled to put into the land." She is extremely annoyed when Greenleaf drawls, in one of their several discussions about their sons, "I thank Gawd for ever-thang." Mrs. May obviously believes that she should get the credit, not the Lord. When her city friends visit, Mrs. May complains that everything—the weather, the dirt, the hired help—are in league against her. "There's nothing for it but an iron hand!" The insensitive Scofield holds up her arm mockingly to display "Momma's iron hand," which would "dangle from her wrist like the head of a broken lily."

Mrs. Greenleaf, whom Mrs. May despises even more than she does Mr. Greenleaf, is a "prayer healer." She cuts morbid stories out of the newspaper—accidents, murders, rapes, even divorces of film stars—takes them all out in the woods, and buries them. Then she mumbles and groans and calls upon Jesus over them, usually ending up sprawled facedown in the dirt in her earnestness to win redemption for the miserable and sinful. Mrs. May is appalled at this vulgar display of piety; she is described as "a good Christian woman with a large respect for religion, though she did not, of course, believe any of it was true."

One remembers Mrs. Greenleaf's shriek as she grovels in the dirt: "Oh, Jesus, stab me in the heart!" The image receives a wildly ironic echo when Mrs. May bends over the horn of the unruly scrub bull that stabs her in the heart. There is also a curious irony in the fact that Greenleaf, who once mistakenly planted a field in clover when she had ordered rye, pierces the bull's eye four times, while running. Yet his surprising competence in this crisis comes too late.

Style and Technique

The names May and Greenleaf, both suggestive of springtime, the symbolic dreams, and especially the suggestive imagery and diction used in the confrontations between Mrs. May and the bull, give this sardonic tale a cast of archetypal myth. In the initial scene, the bull stands in the moonlight under her window "like some patient god come down to woo her." He has ripped loose some of the hedge, which encircles his horns, presumably making him even more like a garlanded Dionysus in his bull form. Later he is likened to "an uncouth country suitor." Moreover, Mrs. May's first words are addressed to the bull in curiously anthropomorphic terms: "Get away from here, Sir!" Before the disappointed lover leaves, he has shaken his head so that the vines have slipped down to the base of the horns, now looking like a "menacing prickly crown," suggesting perhaps the sacrificial role that she imposes on him.

When he comes again to her window, her dream is more menacing; the noise of the bull becomes associated with the sun, which burns through the trees and races toward her. Is the reader to remember the ancient pairing of the sun bull with the moon cow? When Mrs. May wakes and looks out the window, however, she sees the bull only as an "iron shadow," a suggestive echo of the "iron hand" with which she attempted to fight the forces of nature and Greenleaf.

In the last scene, the bull, rejected twice in his nocturnal visits, emerges like a "black heavy shadow" from the trees and starts toward her at a slow gallop, "a gay almost rocking gait as if he were overjoyed to find her again." Soon, however, he becomes the "violent black streak" that pierces and embraces her with his horns. She has the appearance of having a blinding vision. As the bull crumbles to the earth, Mrs. May seems to be bent over, "whispering some last discovery" into the bull's ear.

The tale has many of the distinctive qualities that make Flannery O'Connor one of the most original of American short-story writers: the combination of humor and violence with ironic overtones of revelation. Ordinary, small-minded, and often mean-spirited mortals find out that they have dissipated their lives without recognizing their responsibilities for transcendence. Unusual literary symbols point to some other dimension or interpretation of reality: a scrub bull, or, in other stories, a peacock, a clubfoot, an absurd hat, tattoos, even pigs. Whether such emblems actually induce wisdom or bring about redemption for O'Connor's spiritual cripples is often ambiguous.

Katherine Snipes

GREYHOUND PEOPLE

Author: Alice Adams (1926-   )
Type of plot: Psychological realism
Time of plot: The 1970's
Locale: Northern California
First published: 1981

> *Principal characters:*
> THE NARRATOR, the unnamed protagonist, a government
>   statistician
> HORTENSE, an older woman with whom the narrator lives

The Story

Nothing extraordinary happens on the first or any of the subsequent bus rides that the narrator takes between her home in San Francisco and her job in Sacramento, a fact that makes her attitude toward buses and the people on them even more puzzling and interesting. She is never accosted or threatened. Her worst experience is being asked, on her first ride, to move out of a seat claimed by a burly black man: She moves, and the incident is over.

Yet the narrator is a study in paranoia. In the first of the eleven unnumbered sections of the story, the narrator is afraid that she has gotten on the wrong bus. Her fellow passengers look strange, intimidating. She puts her briefcase on the adjoining seat so that no one can sit next to her. The bus driver apparently takes the incorrect number of coupons from her ticket book, a circumstance she regards as "mysterious"; a retarded boy makes a "senseless" racket in the back; and so on. Yet the narrator's exposure to this apparently hostile environment seems to work a healthy change in her, noticeable even by the end of the first section, where she "yearns to," but does not, join in the general applause for the black woman who has the last word in an argument.

In the second and very brief section of the story, the narrator describes her "situation." She is recently divorced and living with an older woman, Hortense. She lives with Hortense not because of any lesbian tendency, she assures the reader, but out of "sheer dependency." After this brief meditation, the narrator is back on the bus completing the journey to San Francisco. On one leg of the trip she makes friends with a young black woman who works with retarded children. The narrator feels guilty about siding with the black woman against the mother of the retarded boy until her new acquaintance assures her that retarded children have not only rights but also obligations. The narrator is relieved to find that she was right to be resentful of the noisy child.

In the fourth section, the narrator finally reaches San Francisco, and Hortense's agitation at her late arrival—she had indeed taken the wrong bus, the "local" rather than the express—rekindles her fears concerning the "types" who frequent the bus station.

Whatever slight understanding of and rapport with her fellow passengers the narrator seemed to be moving toward at the end of the first bus trip dissipates after contact with Hortense. Once more, she sits by herself on the trip back to Sacramento. Even the scenery seems duller than before. Later, she sits next to a girl who comes from the same part of upstate New York as she, who even works in the same building. Rather than regarding such a coincidence as grounds for enlivening the conversation, however, the narrator sees it as "ominous." Nearing Sacramento, she sees a profusion of pink and white oleanders along the road; they strike her as "unnaturally hardy" and make her uneasy.

The story's turning point takes place in the seventh section, in which the narrator—deliberately or accidentally (even she is not sure)—once more takes the wrong bus: the "local" upon which all the dangerous black people ride. Taking the local will force her to be late once more, she well knows, and force another confrontation with Hortense. Suddenly, however, it occurs to the narrator that such worries are "silly," since both she and Hortense are adults. This realization leads indirectly to a second: that she shares a certain camaraderie with the passengers. All, including her, are in one sense or another "poor people."

The last four sections of the story show the consequences of these realizations. The narrator admires a handsome young man on the bus, her first notice of a man, in "that" way, since her divorce. She tells Hortense that she need not bother picking her up at the bus station anymore, then makes plans to move out of Hortense's apartment altogether. In the last section, the black man who had so intimidated her on the first bus ride greets her, and she returns the greeting with confidence. At the very end, she has decided to purchase a "California pass," which will allow her to travel anywhere in the state. "I could meet anyone at all," she concludes in the story's final line.

Themes and Meanings

Although the title seems to indicate that the story will be a sociological dramatization of the lives of a certain segment of society, "Greyhound People" is really a psychological study, a "rite of passage" in which the narrator learns to engage the world as a mature adult.

Although an adult in age at the beginning of the story, in many other ways the narrator is a child. Her fear of riding the bus, of associating with strangers is more childish than cautious. Like a child, she requires approval from a more knowledgeable adult before she feels right about siding with the black woman in her dispute with the mother of the retarded boy. Ironically, it is the retarded boy whom the narrator most resembles early in the story. He, too, is trying to understand the world around him—hence his irritating questions. Like the retarded boy, the narrator lives in "sheer dependency" with a mother figure, Hortense, who worries over and scolds the narrator for her late arrival.

The narrator's childishness and dependency, despite her adult age, are explained by a fact given little emphasis until late in the story: her recent divorce. The reader can conjecture that she moved from being dependent on her actual parents to being dependent upon her husband to being dependent upon her parent substitute, Hortense.

Thus, her growing camaraderie with the "Greyhound people"—the independent, functioning adults of the working world—and her estrangement from Hortense occur simultaneously. At the end, she can fearlessly exchange greetings with a black man, can look yearningly at a male other than her husband, and can buy a bus ticket that will allow her to go anywhere that her will and maturity take her.

Style and Technique

The surface simplicity of "Greyhound People"—its plain prose style and lack of flamboyant characters and action—should not conceal the fact that the author is an artful and sophisticated storyteller. Her skill is noticeable especially in word choice and narrative structure.

Two related examples may serve to illustrate Adams' skillful use of language. The first two pages of the story are filled with nouns and modifiers—"frightened," "anxiety," "fear," "angry," "scared," "apprehensively," "mysterious," "senseless"—that convey not the quality of her surroundings so much as the narrator's fearfulness and lack of confidence. Three sections later, the same sort of diction appears, but with a difference. In one paragraph persons in the bus station are described as being "frightened-*looking*," "belligerent-*looking*," and "dangerous-*looking*" (emphasis added), the "looking" implying that the narrator has realized by this point—subconsciously, to be sure—that these are impressions only, as dependent upon the attitude of the observer as upon the actual qualities of the observed. By the end of the story, the use of such "fearful" word choice is almost totally absent from the prose.

Noting how the diction changes over the course of the story emphasizes how artful is the story's structure. In general, two types of rhythms are evident in the structure: the interplay between the narrator's experiences with the bus people and her experience with Hortense, and the interplay between her *meditation* on the bus people—not only her experiences with them but also her understanding of them—and her meditation upon her own condition. The two rhythms move toward two climaxes: one in which the bus people "win out" over Hortense, so to speak, and one in which the narrator concludes that her own condition is related to her understanding of the bus people. Ultimately, the two rhythms and their two climaxes are interrelated, both showing the narrator's growth toward maturity and independence.

Dennis Vannatta

THE GUEST

Author: Albert Camus (1913-1960)
Type of plot: Social and psychological realism
Time of plot: 1952
Locale: French Algeria
First published: "L'Hôte," 1957 (English translation, 1958)

> *Principal characters:*
> DARU, the protagonist, a young teacher
> BALDUCCI, an old gendarme
> AN UNNAMED ARAB, the prisoner of Balducci and then of
> Daru

The Story

A young Frenchman named Daru sees two men climbing toward the schoolhouse where he teaches and resides in the desert mountains of French Algeria. One man, the old Corsican gendarme Balducci, rides on horseback and holds a rope tethered to his prisoner, an unnamed Arab, who proceeds on foot. Balducci informs Daru that he is to receive the prisoner (who has killed a cousin of his in a fight over some grain) and deliver him to police headquarters at Tinguit, some fifteen kilometers away. At first Daru refuses Balducci's order, then relents and takes the prisoner in; having been offended by Daru's reluctance, Balducci leaves in a sullen mood.

As the story progresses, it becomes clear to the reader that Daru would welcome the escape of the prisoner: It would relieve Daru of the demands thrust upon him against his will. It is a time of uprising, the Arabs against the French government. The Arab prisoner asks Daru to join him and the other rebels, but it is unlike Daru to make an active commitment to anything. In the inscrutable world in which he lives it would make no difference anyhow, for actions are misconstrued over and over again. Still, one must do what one must do, in spite of the absurd interpretations society might make: This is a central message which runs throughout Albert Camus' work. Daru, after a restless night, walks with his prisoner to a point between two directions, one of which leads to the French administration and the police, the other of which leads to the nomads. Having given the Arab dates, bread, sugar, and a thousand francs, he leaves the choice of directions to him. The Arab remains motionless in indecision as Daru turns his back on him and walks away; when, after a time, Daru turns around, he sees that the Arab is walking on the road to prison.

A little later, as Daru stands before the window of the classroom, he watches, but hardly sees, the panorama of the plateau; behind him, on the blackboard, are written the words: "You handed over our brother. You will pay for this." Daru feels alone.

Themes and Meanings

The original French title of this story, "L'Hôte," means not only "the guest" but also "the host." There is no English word which conveys the double meaning of the French word. Distinctions are leveled, done away with, in order to show a common humanity between Daru and the Arab; still further opposed meanings suggested by the title (amity and hospitality on the one hand, enmity and hostility on the other) add to the ambiguity.

The author is deliberately ambiguous because the circumstances of Daru and his Arab guest are. There is no absolute action that can completely satisfy either character. Daru can neither accept European justice nor ignore the crime for which his guest is guilty. The Arab can neither give himself up to his own people nor go to the nomads. To do the former would be to invite severer penalties upon himself; to do the latter would be to surrender his identity in a self-imposed exile.

Because he is opposed to the denial of personal freedom but also respectful of law, Daru does not release his prisoner outright; he does, however, leave to him the choice of directions. It can never be clear to the reader why the Arab prisoner elects to go in the direction of the jail. It may be that he is the victim of conditioning; it may be that, from a sense of guilt, he invites condemnation; it may be that, since his crime has cut him off from his own people, he expects European criminal justice to be less harsh and more sober. One view seems as likely as any other: The Arab merely does what Daru does—that is, surrenders to others the determination of his fate. A noble action, Camus seems to say, cannot always be counted on to bring about a favorable end.

It is ironic that Daru, who has chosen to cut himself off from society, is representative of the best sense of humanity that any society can offer. He is both Everyman and Christ figure, suffering as a citizen of the world and suffering for the world, providing sustenance and comfort and promoting tolerance and understanding. A measure of his tolerance is that he reserves ultimate judgments and generously sees more than one side of any question. His charitable reasonableness does not suffice, though, to counter the cruelties and unreasonableness in the Algerian situation.

For Camus, however, the act of confrontation with absurdity, with the meaninglessness and the contradictoriness of experiences in life, is the duty of the heroic type; it is perpetual, as is the struggle of Sisyphus, the mythological figure who passes eternity pushing a huge rock up a mountain only to have it fall again once he has arrived at the top with it. The confrontation is undertaken by the conscious hero with the understanding that there can be for him no divine hope to sustain him in his struggle. He knows that he is inevitably bound for extinction, but he brings a dignity, a grandness, to his task that sustains him and that lends to his existence the only meaningfulness it can have. Daru is no conscious hero, certainly, but he is representative of the noble person who confronts existence and, usually, ends by having to suffer, and sometimes die, for it.

Style and Technique

The style of the story is taut, concise, stripped of inessentials. One sees in this the influence of Ernest Hemingway, whom Camus admired very much. All that is there is there for a reason; accepting that truth, all the reader has to do is relate the making of the story to its meaning. The reader has already seen how the title, with its ambiguity, sets the stage for various reversals, displacements, and contradictions. From the beginning to the end of the story, for example, the two main characters shift roles unexpectedly or do, or have done to them, unexpected things. Daru is a host to the Arab but is a guest in the Arab's homeland, making the Arab Daru's host. Received by Daru as a prisoner, the Arab is set free, made his own host; received in hostility, he is accepted in hospitality and amity. Though he is a gracious host, Daru is treated as, at the very least, an unwelcome guest and, at the end of the story, is condemned to a solitude that is absolute.

The description of solitude and isolation at the beginning of the story prepares the reader for the theme of alienation. Daru is alone at the top of a mountain whose ascent is steep and rocky. The difficulty in scaling the heights (reminiscent, incidentally, of the plight of Sisyphus) defines the difficulty of communication. Daru is far from society. He has no vehicle for transportation and has no significant contact with his family, colleagues, or friends. His only acquaintance (except with his very young students, who have been away for a time because of severe climatic conditions) is with the military. He has tried to put behind him, from not many years before, his war experience; thus, such association as he may have is with those with whom he has no spiritual identity. With one of them, Balducci, he has an immediate falling-out. He is an exile in his own homeland.

He and the Arab speak, literally, different languages. This fact further alienates the two men, when the political situation has already made a breach between them. If human beings cannot communicate on one level, they cannot be expected to communicate very easily on another; misunderstanding is bound to be, in such an event, profound and perpetual. Like Meursault, the central character in Camus' *L'Étranger* (1942; *The Stranger*, 1946), Daru is utterly cut off—as much from himself as from the world around him. He is a stranger. Camus is uncharacteristically clear on this point. Almost every line of his story underlines it, artistic structure conveying meanings and themes. The sterile plateau, the steep mountain, the self-imposed apartness, the impossibility of understanding, the cruel ironies—all serve as images or symbols evoking the theme of alienation.

From the evils of human nature one may find consolation in nature; nature—in the usual sense of the word, the natural world of rocks and flowers and trees—is not as unkind as human beings. The author of "The Guest" shows through a technique of contrasts that nature is, at worst, indifferent.

David Powell

GUESTS OF THE NATION

Author: Frank O'Connor (Michael Francis O'Donovan, 1903-1966)
Type of plot: Social criticism
Time of plot: The first third of the twentieth century
Locale: Ireland
First published: 1931

> *Principal characters:*
> BONAPARTE, the narrator, a common young IRA soldier
> lacking in formal education
> NOBLE, Bonaparte's fellow youthful IRA jailer of the two
> British captives, who is religious and has a brother serving
> in the priesthood
> JEREMIAH DONOVAN, the immediate superior officer over
> Bonaparte and Noble, and a dogmatic patriot
> HAWKINS, a British common soldier, both Communistic and
> atheistic
> BELCHER, a British soldier also held captive with Hawkins,
> whose large stature and taciturnity belie his sensitive
> nature
> AN IRISH WOMAN, an old rustic at whose cottage the British
> captives are kept

The Story

In the first of the four numbered sections of "Guests of the Nation," the main characters are introduced. Though Ireland and the Irish Republican Army (IRA) are not named explicitly, through mention of names such as Claregalway, reference to the British as foreigners, and dialectal expressions such as "divil" (devil), the implicit premise is established that two ordinary British soldiers have been abducted by the IRA and have been held on a rural farm for a period of several days or weeks. Just as the British soldiers got on well with their prior IRA captors in the Second Battalion, even attending Battalion dances, so they play cards with their present captors and are on friendly terms with them and the somewhat peevish old woman who owns the farm where they are being kept, largely because of Belcher's considerate actions toward her.

The tempo of the plot, which takes place in only two days, quickens in the second through fourth sections. In the second section, after the description of yet another nocturnal argument about religion and capitalism between the devout Irishman Noble and his contentious, atheistic captive Hawkins, Bonaparte discovers (as does the reader) from his superior Donovan that their British prisoners are actually hostages, who soon may be shot in retaliation for the threatened execution of imprisoned IRA members. Indeed, as narrated in the third section, the next evening Donovan calls at the farm to implement the retaliation for the execution that day of four of the Irish "lads" (one of whom was only sixteen years old). With the reluctant help of Noble and Bonaparte, who have grown fond of them, the prisoners are taken out into the marshes near the farm, Hawkins arguing all the way, once he has learned what is in store for him and Belcher.

Finally, in the fourth section, a little later in the evening at the bog, Hawkins—despite his vehement arguments and objections and offering to desert and turn renegade—is suddenly shot by Donovan and then again minutes later (at Belcher's behest) by the disinclined narrator in order to hasten the lingering death caused by Donovan's poor aim. After Bonaparte and Donovan help Belcher with a blindfold, the group listens to a surprising outburst of talk about his life from the usually taciturn soldier. Obviously moved, Noble seems about to intercede when Donovan hastily executes the second prisoner. After Bonaparte and Noble return to the farmhouse that night, they and the old woman have powerful feelings of regret or remorse, which the narrator says forever affected and altered his subsequent experience of life.

Themes and Meanings

The main theme of the story, the conflict between duty and humanitarianism, is clearly enunciated in two signature passages (technically, places in which the author explicitly articulates his theme). The first is in section 3 in the interchange between Donovan and Bonaparte about duty; the second, in section 4, in the interchange between Donovan and Belcher about the same subject. In these and other passages, the story shows that unlike Donovan, Bonaparte and Belcher, as well as Noble, Hawkins, and the old woman, move beyond a circumscribed conception of nationalistic duty to a sympathy and compassion for their fellow human beings that transcend the borders and politics of separate countries. Thus, unlike Donovan, the other major characters feel that harming another human being who is both friendly and innocent is wrong, even in the name of patriotic duty. The Englishmen's "peculiar" expression "chums," picked up by Bonaparte and Noble and repeated seventeen times in the story, embodies the idea of the paramount importance of friendship or humanitarian sympathy. So, too, does the biblical genealogy that Hawkins scorns as "silly" in one of his arguments with Noble. Hawkins does not realize that Old Testament genealogies suggest by way of descent from a common ancestor the brotherhood of mankind, making mankind a nation that surmounts individual countries—a belief that would have saved his life, which is instead sacrificed because of the conflict between the two countries of England and Ireland.

Hawkins' twice disparaging the "fairytale" about Adam and Eve picking the forbidden fruit highlights an implied moral theme relating to the conflict of duty and humanitarianism. Reinforced by constant explicit references to religion in the story, largely in Bonaparte's description of the arguments between Hawkins and Noble on the subject, the Adam and Eve incident recalls the key concept of God's prohibition against sinful acts, including murder—an issue of central importance in the killings that are contemplated by Donovan and his superiors. Even the old woman's apparent non sequitur in referring to Jupiter Pluvius early in the story has a bearing on the theme by recalling that the planned killings would have been a moral wrong in the ancient classical religions, since foreigners and strangers were under the protection of Zeus or Jupiter, who was patron god of hospitality. Because of a larger sense of duty as moral obligation, these two British soldiers, the story implies, deserve to be "guests of the nation" (the story's title) in a true sense rather than as a euphemism for "prisoners."

One of the story's many fine insights into human nature and behavior derives from its portrayal of the conflict between conscience and conformity. Bonaparte and Noble go along with the plan for the execution, despite serious reservations. What overrides their moral objection is the pressure exerted by peers (Donovan and Feeney, the local intelligence officer) and by social situation. Many instances from real life, as in the Holocaust of World War II, demonstrate the applicability of this theme.

Style and Technique

One of the most important components of technique in "Guests of the Nation" is O'Connor's masterful use of irony. An early instance of irony, apart from the story's title and the repetition of the word "chum" (underlining the failure of friendship in the plot), is the reference to the Irish dances that Belcher and Hawkins have learned, whose titles ("The Walls of Limerick," "The Siege of Ennis") allude to divisiveness, violence, and war, which undercut the harmony of the social occasion. Further, the narrator's word to describe the timbre of Belcher's speech, "peaceable," ironically contrasts with the reason the British soldiers are kept captive, as well as their fate.

Indeed, ironies run throughout the story: The two soldiers executed are among the most congenial to the country and its culture; the religious doubter Hawkins is the first to discover the truths about the afterlife (by being the first killed); Belcher is so considerate of his executioners that just before he is shot he asks their forgiveness for his sudden outpouring of talk, explains his thoughtful wish to speed things up because he knows the delay is painful to them, and finally absolves them all with consoling words. Finally Belcher's blindfold, made by knotting his handkerchief with Bonaparte's, ironically symbolizes the union that should have prevented Belcher's pitiful death, while it is also connected to the story's motif of blindness—to human community and to the twists of fate, summarized in the repeated key word "unforeseen."

Norman Prinsky

THE GUN SHOP

Author: John Updike (1932-   )
Type of plot: Realism
Time of plot: The early 1970's
Locale: Pennsylvania
First published: 1972

> *Principal characters:*
> BEN TRUPP, the protagonist, who with his family is visiting his parents for Thanksgiving
> SALLY, his wife
> YOUNG MURRAY, his fourteen-year-old son
> MURRAY, his father

The Story

Ben and Sally Trupp, their two daughters, and their fourteen-year-old son, Murray, are visiting Ben's parents in Pennsylvania for Thanksgiving. A highlight of the annual trek from the Trupps' home in Boston is the opportunity for Murray to shoot his father's old Remington .22, a gun given to Ben when he was about Murray's age. As the father and son go out to a field to shoot the rifle, Ben remembers his son's last birthday, when he tapped Murray's head to quiet him and the boy, holding the cake knife, threatened to kill him if he were hit again. Sally agreed that Murray was too old to be hit, but Ben, watching his son carrying the rifle, thinks he looks very young.

In the field, the gun does not fire, and Murray curses and throws a tantrum. Ben, unable to help, remembers how his father, also named Murray, taught him to shoot this same gun. The two return to the house, where old Murray, to calm his grandson, promises action and calls Dutch, a local gunsmith. That evening, Ben, his father, and young Murray drive to the gun shop—actually the crowded cellar of Dutch's home.

Ben realizes that neither he nor his son has ever been in such a place, that it is only his father who would have stumbled upon it. He reflects on his own cautious and prescribed life as against his father's disorderly but somehow more real one. Old Murray introduces his grandson to Dutch as a perfectionist, a boy with drive, and then extols Dutch's talents to the others. Ben interrupts to explain the gun's malfunction to Dutch, and old Murray praises Ben's conciseness, an ability, he says, which he did not inherit from his father.

As Dutch works on the gun, old Murray begins to tell another customer, Reiner, of young Murray's prowess at sailing, golfing, and skiing. His grandson loves competition, he states, a trait he did not get either from his father or from his grandfather. He voices regret that he could not teach Ben the ability to work with his hands and adds that Ben should have had Dutch as his father. Reiner, a gun lover, tells young Murray bloody stories of Vietnam and of bullets which could tear a man to pieces. Dutch finishes his repair and asks two dollars for the job. Ben protests that it is too little, but his father intervenes, saying that no amount of money can pay for the kind of talent Dutch has.

In the car on the way home, old Murray mentions that Reiner had been in the Navy but, like himself, had not seem combat. As he talks, his voice sounds tired and Ben hopes they have not exhausted his father. Old Murray replies that that is what he is for. Once home, Ben tries to explain the evening to Sally and tells her the shop "smelled of death." He thinks it may have frightened young Murray. In bed, he dreams of himself as a boy killing a bird and awakes to realize it had occurred exactly as he dreamed. He thinks that he has never forgiven himself for the bird's death.

That morning, he and young Murray again take the gun to the field. There, the story states, the dream continues. Although Ben concentrates fully, he cannot hit the cans and bottles used as targets. The bullets seem to go right through them. When young Murray fires, however, the cans leap and the bottles break. Ben yells, "You're killing me!" and then laughs in "pride and relief."

Themes and Meanings

A familiar theme of John Updike's work is the relationship between generations, particularly the ambivalent feelings of fathers and sons: the combination of guilt, pride, rivalry, and inadequacy. It is clear that Ben feels inadequate both as a father and as a son. In his role as son, he has not been quite what he thinks his father wanted: He does not work with his hands and he does not have the drive that his father sees in young Murray. He has led a cautious, orderly life, never exposing himself in the way his father does. He recognizes that the traits his father praises in young Murray are not inherited from him. As a father, he feels he has not done his job: "to impart the taste of the world" to his son. In paying for Murray's golf lessons or skiing instruction, he has simply purchased amusements for the boy. It is his father, not he, who finds a way to get the rifle fixed on Thanksgiving day. Similarly, old Murray feels inadequate in his role as a father. He thinks Dutch would have given Ben something more.

On the other hand, although fathers and sons may feel inadequate, they also have a sense of rivalry. Young Murray's threat to kill his father may have been the result of a childish tantrum, but it also expresses the resentment of the younger generation toward the domination of the older one. Sally frequently sides with young Murray, telling Ben that he is too hard on the boy, a suggestion that the hostility young Murray feels may be more than childishness. This rivalry, though, can bring about guilt. When Sally warns Ben to be easier on their son, he replies that his father was nice to him and it only gained old Murray "chest pains. A pain in the old bazoo."

There is a sense, however, in which the rivalry is natural and right. When Ben asks his father if they have worn him out, old Murray says, "That's what I'm here for. . . . We aim to serve." Sons should surpass fathers, and it is the job of fathers to make that possible. Thus, at the end of the story, when Ben shouts that young Murray is killing him, he refers not only to his son's marksmanship but to the larger rivalry as well. The relief he feels may come partly from the fact that the killing is metaphoric, that he is being beaten in a contest. The mingling of pride and relief suggests, however, that he is joyful that young Murray can defeat him. He is proud and relieved that his son is a better man than he.

Style and Technique

As in his other stories and novels, Updike here uses images and scenes that are literal and evoke a strong sense of physical reality while at the same time having symbolic resonance. The gun shop itself is particularized with its "cardboard cartons, old chairs and sofas from the Goodwill, a refrigerator, stacked newspapers, shoot posters, and rifle racks. . . ." It is also, however, a symbol of adventure and death. Going down into the cellar gun shop, Ben moves into a world that seems more disorderly and less safe than his own, but also one closer to reality. Dutch, he views as a man who can "descend into the hard heart of things." While both Ben and his father are sorry that young Murray has heard Reiner's gory tales, this knowledge of mortality seems necessary for growth and success. In the images used at the end of the story, Ben cannot hit the targets even though he "aimed so carefully his open eye burned." On the other hand, the boy's success comes through his "murderous concentration."

The dialogue is natural and realistic while also conveying more than characters sometimes know. Talking to Dutch, old Murray says of Ben, "My biggest regret is I couldn't teach him the pleasure of working with your hands." The change of person represented by "your" is a typical linguistic error, but it also suggests Murray's wish that his son had Dutch's hands. Throughout the story, Updike draws out the deeper meanings of a realistic surface texture.

Larry L. Stewart

GUSEV

Author: Anton Chekhov (1860-1904)
Type of plot: Character sketch
Time of plot: 1890
Locale: A ship at sea
First published: 1890 (English translation, 1917)

>*Principal characters:*
>PAVEL IVANYCH, an intellectual civilian
>GUSEV, a peasant soldier

The Story

Anton Chekhov's brief tale traces the thoughts and interactions of two sick men being transported in a ship infirmary from the Far East back to their native Russia. The first, an intellectual named Pavel Ivanych, delivers several angry speeches in which he criticizes injustice in Russian society. The second, a peasant soldier on an indefinite leave resulting from a severe case of consumption, listens only intermittently to Pavel Ivanych, preferring to think of life in his native village.

With these two characters, Chekhov presents two differing approaches to life. Pavel Ivanych is acutely sensitive to the way that defenseless or unsuspecting individuals can be mistreated by the authorities in Russia. In particular, he rails against the military, finding it disheartening that a man can be uprooted from his home and family and sent thousands of miles away to serve as a mere orderly for some petty officer. He also criticizes the Russian masses themselves, calling them dark, blind, and crushed, too willing to accept whatever they are told. He considers himself, on the other hand, to be "protest personified." Claiming that he always tells people the truth to their faces, he states that he is not afraid of anything, and that he would continue to protest even if he were to be walled up in a cellar. He asserts that he is proud of his reputation as an insufferable person, and he considers this relentless zeal for protest to be real life.

Yet while Pavel Ivanych rants on, Gusev ceases to listen to him. Indeed, as Pavel Ivanych concludes one of his fiercer lectures, Gusev pays no attention, but rather looks out a porthole and watches Chinese merchants in small boats selling canaries in cages and shouting "It sings! It sings!" This image serves as an ironic commentary on Pavel Ivanych's ineffectual monologue: He, like the caged canaries, seems merely to be singing an empty song. Shortly thereafter, he succumbs to his illness and dies, and his body is buried at sea.

With the death of Pavel Ivanych, Chekhov's focus swings to Gusev. Unlike Pavel Ivanych, Gusev does not concern himself with social injustice. A simple man, he believes folk myths about the natural world: Storms arise, he thinks, because the world has broken loose from its chains. As for his military service, he believes that he has fulfilled his duty without undue hardship, and he finds such a life to be a decent existence. Returning to his homeland, he thinks only of his family and of village life, and he dreams of driving his sleigh across the snowy landscape. Yet he too, like Pavel Ivanych, is destined never to reach his homeland. He also dies and is buried at sea. Chekhov describes the process by which Gusev's body is wrapped in canvas and thrown into the water. He follows the corpse as it sinks into the depths, and he notes how a large shark approaches the body and cautiously rips the canvas wrapping from head to toe. Chekhov then turns away from this scene and concludes his tale with a description of the natural landscape, noting how the sky and the sea merge harmoniously in joyous colors with the setting of the sun. In this final scene, the power and majesty of the natural world dwarf the petty concerns of ordinary humans.

Themes and Meanings

In "Gusev," Chekhov offers two radically opposed views of life and of possible ways to deal with its hardships. He wrote the story on his return voyage from a visit to the Russian penal colony on the Siberian island of Sakhalin, where he had encountered a series of disturbing scenes of human degradation and cruelty. Pavel Ivanych's indignant criticism of social injustice undoubtedly reflects something of Chekhov's own dismay at the prevalence of brutality and evil in the world. Yet Pavel Ivanych's protests are strikingly ineffectual. Gusev pays little attention to his words and does not understand very much of what he hears. For his part, Pavel Ivanych does not try very hard to find the appropriate words with which to make an impression on such listeners as Gusev. One wonders whether he would be capable of transforming his negative words into positive deeds; he appears to be content with his role as an insufferable individual—"protest personified." Such an attitude significantly undermines his validity as a spokesman for Chekhov.

In Gusev's character Chekhov presents a potential alternative to Pavel Ivanych's stance of irritated protest: Gusev humbly accepts all that comes his way and appears content with his lot. His calm complacency recalls the positive heroes depicted by Leo Tolstoy in his fiction, and it is likely that Chekhov intended the character to embody, at least in part, the Tolstoyan ideal of passive acceptance. Yet the character of Gusev, like that of Pavel Ivanych, contains evident flaws. In his passivity he appears almost subhuman or animalistic; one detects a penchant for mindless violence beneath his veneer of stolid placidity. When looking out the porthole, Gusev sees a corpulent Chinese man in a boat and thinks of bashing the fat man in the neck. Earlier, he had recounted an episode in which he beat four such men simply because they had come into his courtyard.

Neither Pavel Ivanych's posture of angry protest nor Gusev's manner of blind actions strikes the reader as completely satisfying or worthy of emulation. No character in the story serves as ideal role model for the reader. Instead Chekhov provides a more elusive or suggestive vision of the proper relationship between the human world and the cosmos at large. Shortly before his death, Gusev had looked out at the sea and sky. In the sky he saw bright stars, peace, and quiet, while below lurked darkness and disorder. After Gusev's death, Chekhov notes the beautiful play of light that occurs at sunset, and he concludes "Looking at the magnificent, enchanting sky, the ocean at first frowns, but soon it also takes on tender, joyful, and passionate colors that are difficult even to name with human words." These scenes carry symbolic implications. Like the realm of the sea, the human realm—the world "below"—is dark and disordered. Neither vehement protest nor dull resignation holds out the promise of lasting fulfillment. Rather, one must observe and absorb the mute lessons of nature. Only through a kind of wordless communion with the natural world can one transcend the limitations of the self and attain a measure of peace and joy.

Style and Technique

As the final scene of "Gusev" indicates, Chekhov often utilizes symbolic descriptions to convey implicit messages to his reader. Nature descriptions in particular play an important role in shaping the reader's understanding of the author's designs. The vastness of the natural world and its indifference to the everyday travails of human life are evoked by Chekhov's choice of the sea as the setting for his story and his inclusion of the scene in which the shark casually tears open the canvas sack containing Gusev's body. Similarly, the recurring image of a huge bull's head without eyes that Gusev sees in his daydreams of home serves to underscore his own primitive and animalistic character.

The recurring image of the bull's head itself points to another distinctive feature of Chekhov's narrative technique in "Gusev." His portrait of the peasant provides an interesting blend of internal psychology and external sensory stimuli. To convey the mental state of a man stricken with fever, Chekhov skillfully interweaves Gusev's reveries about his village life with the sounds and sights of his shipboard passage. Things happen on the ship around Gusev without his full knowledge or comprehension. As these sights or sounds penetrate into his consciousness, they at times seem curiously relevant, while at other times they seem chaotic or meaningless. Through this flow of apparently random yet meaningful events, Chekhov highlights the unpredictability and mysteriousness of human existence.

In "Gusev," as in many of his other tales, Chekhov doe not overtly preach to his readers. As he explores possible approaches to life, he creates two characters with contrasting attitudes, and he allows his readers to judge for themselves the merits and drawbacks of each. Avoiding melodrama or bold gestures, he constructs his tale out of small incidents and thereby subtly shapes the readers' perception of events. A master of understatement, Chekhov manages to create a portrait of human experience as nuanced and moving as life itself.

Julian W. Connolly

GUY DE MAUPASSANT

Author: Isaac Babel (1894-1941)
Type of plot: Impressionistic realism
Time of plot: Winter, 1916-1917
Locale: St. Petersburg
First published: "Giui de Mopassan," 1932 (English translation, 1955)

> *Principal characters:*
> THE NARRATOR, the protagonist, a free-lance journalist and
>   story writer, twenty years old
> RAISA BENDERSKY, a woman attempting to translate the
>   works of Guy de Maupassant into Russian and requiring
>   the assistance of the narrator
> BENDERSKY, the husband of Raisa, a converted Jew and a
>   lawyer, banker, and owner of a publishing house

The Story

   Although unnamed, the protagonist is approximately identical with the author, as the latter was in the winter of 1916-1917: a young Jewish writer from Odessa who has moved to the capital illegally, on the eve of the February Revolution.

   The young writer, though poverty-stricken and selling almost nothing he has written, is so supremely confident that he spurns an offer of a job as a clerk. He sees himself as superior to Leo Tolstoy, whose religion was "all fear. He was frightened by the cold, by old age, by death. . . ."

   The narrator finds acceptable employment when Bendersky's publishing house decides to bring out a new edition of Maupassant's works; Bendersky's wife, Raisa, has begun some translations, but they are flat and lifeless. The narrator is summoned to assist Raisa; he meets her at the Bendersky mansion on Nevsky Prospect—a habitation decorated in profoundly poor taste. The Benderskys are converted Jews, in consequence of which they have been allowed to grow rich.

   The narrator would despise Raisa as he does her husband—"a yellow-faced Jew with a bald skull"—were it not for the fact that he finds her ravishing on first sight (although, it must be admitted, the young man finds all women ravishing, including his forty-year-old washerwoman, Katya). The fact that Raisa is enfolded in pink layers of fat is all to the good—precisely Babel's type, as the readers know from his other stories.

   The narrator meets Raisa daily to go over her translations and to instruct her in literary style. Although Raisa has almost no feeling for style, her redeeming feature is that she recognizes that fact. Furthermore, additionally to her credit, she declares that Maupassant is the only passion of her life.

Gradually it becomes apparent that the basic plot line of Babel's story centers on the attempted seduction of Raisa by her new young assistant, who is probably only half her age. As the two become acquainted, the narrator tells stories of his childhood that, to his "amazement," turned out to be "very sordid." He frightens Raisa and moves her to pity.

Babel's continuing discussion of Maupassant throughout the story contributes to an ongoing instruction in art and literary style that is central to the work. Maupassant also becomes an element in the plot, however, in that his story "L'Aveau" ("The Confession"), which Raisa and the narrator work on together for a very long time, is retold in some detail. The reader learns that Monsieur Polyte the coachman, who drives red-haired Céleste to market twice a week, continually attempts to seduce Céleste through innuendo and coarse suggestion. Finally, after two years, he succeeds: "What about having some fun today, Mamselle Céleste?" She replies, "I am at your disposal, Monsieur Polyte." It is interesting that Babel describes Céleste, with her "mighty calves in red stockings," almost as he does Raisa, with her "strong soft calves . . . planted wide apart on the carpet." He mentions also that the cart in which Polyte and Céleste make love is pulled by a white mare that keeps on moving forward at a walking pace.

At this point in the narrative, the young writer is full of wine and is alone with Raisa in her big house. He clumsily kisses her, and she recoils. She pushes him into a faraway chair, but he suddenly lunges for her, knocking all twenty-nine volumes of Maupassant off a shelf.

The reader is not told explicitly what happens next. After the books fall to the floor, however, the narrator remarks, " . . . and the white mare of my fate went on at a walking pace"—an obvious reference to "The Confession." The reader also learns that the young man has spent enough additional time at the Bendersky house to become sober. He leaves for home near midnight, wonderfully happy, swaying from side to side (though sober) and singing in a language that he has "just invented." It is impossible not to conclude from this joyful epiphany (added to the earlier evidence) that the seduction has occurred.

The story requires this seduction so that the conclusion, presented as contrast, may be better appreciated. The young man spends the rest of the night reading a biography of Maupassant; he learns that the great writer died insane, from syphilis, at age forty-two, crawling on his hands and knees and "devouring his own excrement." The young writer looks out the window at the morning fog, perceiving that the world is hidden from him and realizing that there is much more for him to learn in life.

Themes and Meanings

The ending of "Guy de Maupassant" is significant for several reasons. First, it marks the transition of the young writer from a state of cockiness and overconfidence (recall his disdain as a "young genius" for Tolstoy) to one of doubt and anxiety. The author writes, "My heart contracted as the foreboding of some essential truth touched me with light fingers." This truth includes the understanding that great art is seldom achieved without great suffering: The young man now realizes the full implication of his choice of writing as a career.

In general, the story treats the theme of illusion seen against the truth of life. The narrator's roommate, Kazantsev, lives in an imaginary Spain—his permanent escape from the St. Petersburg snows. Raisa's one passion is Maupassant. Though Babel "forgives" Raisa this, he has little use for the whole Bendersky clan, who have deceived themselves into believing that by worshiping Jesus they will escape Russian anti-Semitism and get to keep their money, too. Babel's disdain for such converted Jews is nicely contained in the narrator's remark about Raisa after she has pressed herself against the wall and "stretched out her arms": "Of all the gods ever put on the crucifix, this was the most ravishing."

The theme of illusion contrasted with truth also occurs in the dream of the young writer about Katya, the washerwoman: In the dream they do "god-awful things together" and almost "destroyed each other with kisses." In the morning, however, he sees a "wan woman" with "ash-gray hair" and "labor-worn" hands. The young man also has sexual fantasies about Raisa's maid. Probably the treatment of sex in this story is meant to be positive: Sex, passion, and love are essential to life and must be seized with zest and joy. This is not all of life, however: hence, the somber ending. Yet the ending should not be read as a puritanical, Tolstoyan castigation of Maupassant (or the narrator) for sexual promiscuity.

"Guy de Maupassant" is famous for its observations on literary style. The narrator (clearly speaking for the mature Babel) declares: "A phrase is born into the world both good and bad at the same time. The secret lies in a slight, an almost invisible twist. The lever should rest in your hand, getting warm, and you can only turn it once, not twice." Then, in speaking of style to Raisa, the young writer asserts, "No iron can stab the heart with such force as a period put just at the right place."

Style and Technique

The remarks on style quoted above reflect the author's attitude toward his own writing. His story is like an icon painted with perfect phrases.

In describing the stairway of the Bendersky mansion, Babel writes: "On the landings, upon their hind legs, stood plush bears. Crystal lamps burned in their open mouths." Avoiding all authorial commentary, Babel gives the reader in seventeen words a perfect description of nouveau-riche bad taste. (The word for this in Russian is *poshlost'*; in German, *kitsch*.) Babel's effectiveness as a writer owes much to his laconism and detachment.

The author's treatment of the sexual theme is enhanced by repetition, until the whole story seems suffused with sexual imagery—as is the inside of the young writer's head. Three times a Bendersky servant is described as "the high-breasted maid." "In her open gray eyes," writes Babel, "one saw a petrified lewdness." The narrator imagines that she makes love with an "unheard-of agility." There is often exaggeration, humor, and vivid color in Babel's images: The narrator and his friends get "as drunk as a flock of drugged geese." The dinners at the Bendersky house are always noisy: "It was a Jewish noise, rolling and tripping and ending up on a melodious sing-song note."

Maupassant and the narrator's tale are linked by a motif using images of the sun. In referring to the twenty-nine volumes of Maupassant's collected works, Babel writes: "The sun with its fingers of melting dissolution touched the morocco backs of the books—the magnificent grave of a human heart." When the story "The Confession" is retold, Babel informs the reader that "the sun is the hero of this story": Molten drops of it patter on the red-haired Céleste. When she and Polyte make love, "the gay sun of France pours down on the ancient coach."

Although the closing summary of Maupassant's life is both frightening and repellent, one must balance it against a compelling image of the writer's greatness: Earlier, the narrator refers to the set of Maupassant's works as "twenty-nine bombs stuffed with pity, genius and passion."

Donald M. Fiene

HAIRCUT

Author: Ring Lardner (1885-1933)
Type of plot: Social realism
Time of plot: The 1920's
Locale: A small, unnamed town in Michigan
First published: 1925

> *Principal characters:*
> DICK, the barber and narrator
> DOC RALPH STAIR, a doctor and coroner
> JIM KENDALL, the town practical joker
> PAUL DICKSON, a mentally retarded boy
> JULIE GREGG, a young, sophisticated woman in love with Doc
> Stair

The Story

"Haircut" takes its title from the frame story, in which a barber is talking to a stranger in town as he cuts his hair. The barber is a naïve narrator who does not grasp the full impact of the story that he is telling. His narration concerns the town practical joker, Jim Kendall, who was recently killed in what everyone supposes was an accident.

The barber is a typical resident of a small, unnamed Michigan town near Carterville, who is telling the newcomer how, in his opinion, the liveliness of the town has diminished since the demise of Jim Kendall, whose shaving mug the barber still keeps on the shelf. He begins to illustrate Jim's sense of humor by relating some of the practical jokes that Jim played, such as sending letters to men whose names he would see on signs of establishments in the towns that he passed through on the train. In the letters, he hinted that their wives were being unfaithful. The barber then fills in Jim's background, describing how Jim lost his sales job and was reduced to taking odd jobs around town, spending most of what he earned on drink. Then, when his wife began trying to collect his salary before he got to it, he began borrowing against his wages in order to foil her plan, and, the barber adds, Jim punished her by inviting her and their two children to the circus, where he left them waiting at the tent entrance and never appeared with the tickets.

At this point in the narrative, the barber tells of how Doc Stair, a new doctor in the town, saw them and paid their way into the circus, thus incurring the enmity of Jim. The barber then describes how Doc Stair came to town and gradually built up a good practice, and how he was very lenient with those who could not pay their bills. He relates how the doctor became coroner when the old coroner died, because he was the type of person who could not refuse when asked to do a favor.

He then relates the background of another town resident, Paul Dickson, who received a head injury when he was ten years old and is slightly retarded, and who was a frequent butt of Jim Kendall's practical jokes. Because of these jokes, the barber says, Paul has nothing to do with most people except Doc Stair and Julie Gregg, the only two residents of the town who show him kindness. This thought leads him to relate how Julie Gregg fell in love with Doc Stair when she took her invalid mother in to see him.

The plot of the central incident begins as the barber tells of Jim Kendall's attempt to rape Julie. After she called the marshal, Jim decided to revenge himself on her by playing one of his tricks. At a time when he knew that Doc Stair was out of town, he phoned her, disguising his voice as the doctor's, and asked her to come and see him. When she arrived at the doctor's office and called for him, Jim and all of his friends, who were hiding under the stairs, came out, shouting and ridiculing her.

The barber says that later, when Jim came looking for someone with whom to go duck shooting, Paul Dickson volunteered to join him. According to the barber, Paul accidentally shot Jim in the boat while handling a gun for the first time in his life. He ends his tale by saying that it was probably Jim's fault for letting a "half-wit" use a gun with which he was not familiar, but he adds that the town certainly misses Jim Kendall. The barber has ignored the fact that Paul acted deliberately after Doc Stair had told Paul that a person who would play such a trick on a person such as Julie "ought not to be let live."

Themes and Meanings

The real meaning of "Haircut" is conveyed as the reader begins to understand the situation in the small town as told, but not understood, by the barber. The barber is insensitive and imperceptive. His recounting of the crude jokes told in his barbershop, which are the counterparts of the cruel tricks played by Jim Kendall, and his appreciation of those jokes, shows his insensitivity. He speaks of Jim as being the life of the town who is sorely missed rather than as the sadistic, violent, and insensitive bully he really was.

Ring Lardner is satirizing the smug values of people who live in isolated, small communities (and, by extension, any closed community in which evil is condoned). While the barber seems to believe that his town is unique in having an entertaining practical joker, he is unaware of how typical a character such as Jim Kendall is, and how many other towns are populated by Jim Kendalls. By not recognizing the cruelty that lurked beneath the surface of the tricks played by Jim Kendall, the barber, in a sense, is vicariously participating in it. His appreciation of Jim Kendall's not-so-amusing stories and practical jokes stems from his own insensitivity, ignorance, and latent cruelty.

The theme is conveyed by the dramatic irony of the narrator's thickheaded obliviousness to the cruelty perpetrated by Kendall, and the shock at the end when it becomes apparent that Paul Dickson deliberately killed Kendall. The barber, although he has access to all the facts, fails to put these details together or to realize that the shooting was anything but accidental.

The primary effect of the story is to shock the reader with the realization of what has been called "the banality of evil." Jim Kendall, who is in reality a sadistic personality, is described by the barber as being "all right at heart, but just bubblin' over with mischief." Evil can often be ignored or rationalized, especially when it is condoned or explained away by "good" people.

Style and Technique

The primary technique employed in this story is the use of irony in having an imperceptive, naïve narrator relate a story, the impact of which he fails to understand himself. This frame story maintains some subtlety in what would otherwise be a fairly obvious tale about a cruel, mean-spirited character who gets the punishment that he deserves.

Lardner's story is related through the use of a dramatic monologue; the barber is the only character who speaks. The full setting and the understanding that the customer in his chair is a stranger in town become clear entirely through the barber's conversation. Through his speech, the barber shows himself to be a rather crude, unintelligent, and insensitive observer. He narrates the events in a fashion sympathetic to the jokester, without analyzing or commenting on them except to indicate how amusing he thought all of Jim Kendall's jokes were.

The entire narration is in a consistent conversational tone typifying a small-town man. The diction, syntax, and pronunciation show the narrator to be provincial and uneducated. For example, he says, "I bet they was more laughin' done here than any town its size in America," and "he'd be settin' in this chair part of the time," and "she'd of divorced him only they wasn't no chance to get alimony and she didn't have no way to take care of herself and the kids. She couldn't never understand Jim." Such language (at which Lardner was especially skilled), along with the observations and interpretations of the barber, and juxtaposed to the obvious cruelty of the tricks played, make the reader aware of the unreliability of the speaker and heighten the impact of the events narrated.

Roger Geimer

HAMLET OF THE SHCHIGROVSKY DISTRICT

Author: Ivan Turgenev (1818-1883)
Type of plot: Sketch
Time of plot: The 1840's
Locale: A backwater village in the Shchigrovsky District of Russia
First published: "Gamlet Shchigrovskogo uezda," 1849 (English translation, 1855)

Principal characters:

THE SPORTSMAN, the narrator and assumed voice of the writer, a traveling hunter

VASILY VASILYCH, the main character, an embittered, poor landowner

PYOTR PETROVICH LUPIKHIN, the sharp-tongued village wit

The Story

The first-person narrator begins this story by establishing a frank and straightforward camaraderie with his audience. A well-mannered, cultured, and polite man, the narrator informs his readers that he had, on one of his hunting trips, been invited to a dinner party that was given by one Alexander Mikhailych G. G.'s surname is unimportant. A minor character, he is a representative of his class: a small-minded, provincial landowner who nearly starves his guests because he must wait for the arrival of an important dignitary.

Using the party as a vehicle to satirize provincial aristocracy, the narrator gives a blow-by-blow account of the evening's festivities: when he arrived, how he was greeted, who was there and what was said. He minutely details how he watched the provincials playing cards, their stomachs drooping over the tables; how he nearly fell asleep; and how he was first whisked away by Voinitsyn, a college failure, and then by Pyotr Lupikhin, the local satirist. This traveling hunter is far too reserved and polished to direct more than a subtle, pointed attack on what he witnessed. In this story he uses first Lupikhin and then Vasily Vasilych as mouthpieces for broad, virulent satire.

Lupikhin mocks the pageant of landowners who parade in front of him: They are a fat, ignorant lot, and Lupikhin sees them as so many animals. One is said to be "as stupid as a couple of merchants' horses"; another is described as a sly predator, "stealing along by the wall, glancing all around him like a veritable wolf."

While pleading disgust and claiming that it is hardly necessary for him to describe such a dinner, the narrator, humorously enough, describes it anyway. He captures snapshots of hypocritical stances: The boorish landowners, attempting to appear sophisticated, wear French manners as one wears a tight girdle. The tardy dignitary graces his fellow guests with a high-sounding after-dinner speech; this high official's remarks are as fatuous as the philosophizing of William Shakespeare's Polonius.

The party described, the narrator slowly moves toward the core of his story. Something happened that evening, he tells his readers, that made the party worth mentioning: He met "a certain remarkable person." This is where the story-within-a-story begins. In a thoroughly unappealing room, the narrator meets one Vasily Vasilych. The latter, seeing that the narrator cannot sleep just as he cannot, begins a long dramatic monologue on the story of his life: the circumstances of his birth; his mama's efforts to educate her boy of the steppes; his foolish boyhood. What Vasily Vasilych reiterates, in this confessional tirade, is his awareness of his mediocrity. He knows that, like everyone else, he lacks originality. He differs from those pretentious party guests only in that he knows that he is common; he suffers, Vasily Vasilych tells the narrator (and the narrator retells his readers), because he is sensitive to his condition.

Who knows what one will say in the middle of the night, in a strange house, to a bedfellow who is a complete stranger whom one will never see again? The narrator, merely acting as a drum upon which Vasily Vasilych beats, documents a moment in time. It is a moment in which he is placed in a situation wherein he hears the most pitiful of stories from a man who really is not remarkable. Really, the narrator implies, Vasily Vasilych is a man of his time, a man of his place, a representative of his generation.

Vasily Vasilych recounts how he came to be fully repulsed by his very being. One day he was accosted by a local inspector for not repairing his bridge. A conversation ensued, in which the poor landowner derided a certain party who was running for office. The inspector chided Vasily Vasilych, saying that persons of no consequence such as the two of them have no business passing judgment on the higher-ups. Vasily Vasilych, a man who is consumed by self-hatred and an abject sense of smallness, relates how he retreated into his room, scrutinized his face in the mirror, then, slowly, stuck out his tongue at his own reflection.

Interrupted by a sleepy, irritated neighbor, the main character sheepishly hides beneath the bedding. When the narrator presses him at least to state his full name, he alludes to another self-absorbed man, a man who is fated to live and die in a rotten world: the prince in Shakespeare's *Hamlet*:

> But if you earnestly want to give me some kind of title, then call me . . . call me Hamlet of the Shchigrovsky District. There are many such Hamlets in every district. . . .

Themes and Meanings

Hamletism, both in the Russian people and in an individual's personality, was an issue which Ivan Turgenev explored, initially in his early sketches and later in his novels. In 1860, Turgenev actually gave a lecture entitled "Hamlet and Don Quixote," in which he delineated two basic personality types. In "Hamlet of the Shchigrovsky District," Vasily Vasilych utters what became the subtext for some of the author's later characters: those highly sensitive, cultured intellectuals who cry out against the petty conventions of their fathers yet ultimately succumb to these very same conventions because of a kind of spinelessness—a lack of will. Turgenev's Hamlets, feeling themselves alone in a hostile, corrupt world, rail not only against society but also against themselves. They berate themselves for doing nothing, and they persist in doing nothing. They wear themselves out with philosophical talk, yet they are afraid to act on their words. Perhaps they despair that action will ever do any good. Perhaps they lack a kind of faith in human nature. They are cynical, self-deprecating men who thrive on self-pity and who, like Vasily Vasilych, "become reconciled" to their meaninglessness. They will make no mark on their world; they will change nothing; they will blame fate for their failure. They are, according to Turgenev, "superfluous" men.

Turgenev first introduced this type of character into his works because he believed that the youth of Russia was falling into Hamletism. In 1849, the date when "Hamlet of the Shchigrovsky District" was published in a Russian journal called *The Contemporary*, Russia was a country caught between two modes of being. It could no longer remain isolated from Western influence. Napolean had done the unthinkable: He and his horses and his men had marched on Moscow; whether Russians liked it or not, they felt the imprint of Western ideas. Yet Russia, in 1849, was still operating under feudal codes. Twelve more years would pass before the emancipation of the serfs. The younger generation revolted against the feudal hierarchy. Turgenev, a man influenced by Western ideas, sometimes more at home in Paris than in Russia, advocated change: a slow process of change. He decried the horror of a caste system in which capricious, petty landowners had full power over their serfs. Yet he believed that his country's youth were not strong enough to move Russia into a modern age. A man who saw people as either Hamlets (passive intellectuals) or Don Quixotes (blind idealists), Turgenev attacked the younger generation through his creation of these types. The self-pitying Vasily Vasilych is Turgenev's indictment of Russian youth; the petty landowners at the party are caricatures of these youths' fathers.

Style and Technique

Written more as a character study than a short story, "Hamlet of the Shchigrovsky District" is one of twenty-five sketches that Turgenev wrote between 1847 and 1851. It was included in Turgenev's first published work, a collection of the most important of these sketches, entitled *Zapiski okhotnika* (1852; *A Sportman's Sketches*, 1855). Each sketch is a minutely detailed portrait of a Russian type: a representative of the kinds of people whom Turgenev met while he hunted through the Russian countryside. The sketches are linked by an objective narrator, a discerning hunter who is able to hear the voices of provincial landowners and peasants, who is able to hear the land and its peasant boys speak; yet this huntsman cannot answer. He is a nearly mute narrator, an instrument upon which the people he encounters play a uniquely poignant Russian tune.

While the role of the narrator in this story is typical of the collection, in other ways this is an atypical piece. It is one of Turgenev's broadest satires; whereas some of Turgenev's sketches, such as "Bezhin Meadow," are poetically descriptive and capture the beauty of the Russian countryside, and others, such as "Khos and Kalinych," document peasant life, this piece concentrates on the landowning class. Dialogue is minimal. Vasily Vasilych's speech, imitative of Hamlet's soliloquies, indicates how form fits meaning: The dramatic monologue is an ideal form for this self-absorbed, overly sensitive man. While Hamlet directs his words to his audience, Vasily Vasilych uses the narrator (and consequently the reader) as an audience. Not only is he a Hamlet-type, but also he acts Hamlet; the tiny, damp bedroom becomes his stage.

This particular sketch is like the others in Turgenev's first published work, however, in that it captures and holds a moment in time. All the sketches, enduring works of art in their own right, allowed Turgenev a means to perfect his craft.

Miriam Bat-Ami

THE HANDSOMEST DROWNED MAN IN THE WORLD

Author: Gabriel García Márquez (1928-   )
Type of plot: Symbolic realism
Time of plot: Unspecified, but perhaps colonial South America
Locale: A small, barren fishing village
First published: "El ahogado más hermoso del mundo," 1968 (English translation, 1971)

Principal characters:
THE HANDSOME DROWNED MAN, named Esteban by the villagers
THE VILLAGERS, grouped by children, women, and men
THE OLDEST WOMAN, who leads the villagers' reactions toward the drowned man

The Story

Significantly, "The Handsomest Drowned Man in the World" begins with the children of the seaside fishing village. They see the drowned man floating ashore; at first they think he is an enemy ship, then a whale. The discovery that he is a drowned man does not dampen their sense of play at all: They proceed, in the beach sand, to bury and dig him up repeatedly.

Responsible adults see the drowned man and take over. The village men carry the body to the village, noting that the drowned man is enormously heavy, tall, and encrusted with ocean debris. Even though his face is covered, they know he is a stranger because no man in the village is missing. Instead of going fishing that night, the men leave the body with the women and visit neighboring villages to check if the drowned man belongs to one of them.

The women prepare the body for burial. As they clean off the encrusted vegetation, they observe that the material comes from faraway places. The man's shredded clothes also indicate a long ocean voyage. The most astounding thing about him, however, once the crust is removed, is his handsome appearance: "Not only was he the tallest, strongest, most virile, and best built man they had ever seen, but even though they were looking at him there was no room for him in their imagination."

As they sit through the evening sewing new clothes for him and admiring his body, the village women fantasize about the drowned man. They imagine the disturbed sea outside roaring in his honor. They imagine him as the village's leading man, who has the best house, who makes fish leap out of the sea, and who digs springs and makes the barren cliffs bloom. Most of all, they fantasize about the happiness of his wife, and in their secret thoughts they compare the drowned man with their own men, who seem like "the weakest, meanest, and most useless creatures on earth."

Their thoughts are redirected by the oldest woman, who feels "more compassion than passion" for the drowned man and who announces around midnight that his name must be Esteban. Another school of thought among the youngest women is that his name is Lautaro. This romantic notion is dispelled by the ill-fitting new clothes, however, which make it clear that he is Esteban. Once his name is settled, the women launch into compassionate fantasies, imagining Esteban suffering through life with his huge body, so ill-suited for parlor visits. When dawn breaks and they cover his face with a handkerchief, the women begin identifying Esteban with their own men, and finally they break into an orgy of weeping.

The village men find the women thus when they return from the neighboring villages. The women's weeping turns to delight, though, when they learn that the drowned man does not belong to the other villages: He is theirs. They start making a fuss about him, adorning him for burial. The men cannot understand the women's behavoir, until the handkerchief is taken off the drowned man's face. Then the men, stunned, also see that he is Esteban, the handsomest drowned man in the world. They give the drowned man a fabulous funeral. The women go to the neighboring villages for flowers, and other women return with them. Soon the village is overrun with flowers and people. Rather than let Esteban remain "an orphan," the villagers choose relatives for him from among themselves, "so that through him all the inhabitants of the village became kinsmen." Bearing his handsome corpse to the cliffs to toss it back to the sea, the grief-stricken villagers become "aware for the first time of the desolation of their streets, the dryness of their courtyards, the narrowness of their dreams." Yet from now on, things are going to be "different": Through their hard work, they are going to make the barren village prosper and bloom. It will become so famous that passing ocean travelers, overcome by the wafting fragrance, will point to "the promontory of roses on the horizon" and say "yes, over there, that's Esteban's village."

Themes and Meanings

It is easy, in a cynical fashion, to make fun of the villagers in this little story, which Gabriel García Márquez wrote shortly after finishing his great masterpiece, *Cien años de soledad* (1967; *One Hundred Years of Solitude,* 1970). *One Hundred Years of Solitude* chronicles the rise and decline of Macondo, a mythical city representing Latin American society in the period of independence. In some ways, the fishing village in this story is a stripped-down Macondo: The villagers are even more backward, provincial, ignorant, and gullible than the inhabitants of Macondo. Their village is the center of the universe, so instead of moving to a more promising location, they resolve to "break their backs" to turn a rocky promontory into a rose garden. They are inspired by a waterlogged corpse and led by emotional women. For all they know, the drowned man was a scoundrel, and there is no guarantee that their resolutions will ever lead to anything, that the rose garden will become a reality. If *One Hundred Years of Solitude* mirrors the history of Latin America's big hopes and bigger failures, is this story a boiled-down version of how the historical cycle begins?

The answer is no—enough of the devil's advocate. "The Handsomest Drowned Man in the World" is not so much a repetition of *One Hundred Years of Solitude* as a coda with a counterpoint theme. The story takes an even more unpromising situation than the one in Macondo and proposes a solution. The solution is the imagination, which might be circumscribed by circumstances but can be stimulated by outside influences, represented by the drowned man. In *One Hundred Years of Solitude*, an obsession with incest suggests cultural inbreeding and degeneracy; here, the villagers become kinsmen only through their imagined relationships with the corpse. What does it matter that the corpse is waterlogged, possibly a former scoundrel? He still inspires the villagers to see their desolate lives and to aspire to fill them with beauty. The drowned man is the poor villagers' Grecian urn.

As a story about the imagination, "The Handsomest Drowned Man in the World" has some powerful undercurrents appealing to the unconscious. The drowned man's long journey through the ocean deeps suggests the mysterious workings of the imagination. The drowned man is also an old motif in literature, where he frequently has positive associations, representing the preferred form of death (with overtones of baptism and spiritual rebirth, as in T. S. Eliot's poem *The Waste Land*, 1922) or even the triumph of the imagination over death (as in William Shakespeare's play *The Tempest*, 1611: "Those are pearls that were his eyes"). Here the drowned man's handsome looks symbolize such a triumph, as does his effect on the villagers. The story is a reminder that most of the people who inspire the world are dead. For García Márquez, much concerned in his fiction with death, whether cultural death or personal death, the story catches a particularly optimistic mood.

Finally, one does not have to know anything about Latin American history, *One Hundred Years of Solitude*, the unconscious, or García Márquez in order to appreciate "The Handsomest Drowned Man in the World." The reader can readily enjoy this story without these outside references, which merely provide its rich context. It is, at heart, a fable of the imagination. The English version of the story is appropriately subtitled "A Tale for Children," just as it is appropriate that the village children should discover the drowned man. They show the most imagination among the villagers, followed by the women, though ultimately everyone's imagination is sparked.

Style and Technique

Whether children could grasp the occasionally long Faulknerian sentences in this story is debatable, but they could probably follow the switches of voice within the sentences better than adults. The switches of voice reflect the villagers' thoughts, including what they think the corpse is thinking; this complexity is all subsumed and remarkably controlled by the humorous voice of the omniscient narrator, who makes it seem like child's play. The style is known as García Márquez' "magical realism," made famous in *One Hundred Years of Solitude*. The style also features exaggeration (as in the size of the corpse here) and imaginative thrusts ("the men began to feel mistrust in their livers") that now and then verge into fantasy.

It is certainly fantasy that the drowned man's corpse does not stink, a fantasy which enables García Márquez to construct a symbolism of smells reminiscent of the one in William Faulkner's "A Rose for Emily" (1930). Although Faulkner is perhaps the greatest influence on García Márquez, here the pupil reverses the master. Whereas Faulkner's story begins with a strong smell and ends with a decayed corpse, García Márquez' story begins with a remarkably preserved corpse and ends up smelling like roses. The symbolism typifies García Márquez' style, his gift to the world.

Harold Branam

HAPPY AUGUST THE TENTH

Author: Tennessee Williams (1911-1983)
Type of plot: Psychological realism
Time of plot: The 1960's
Locale: New York City and rural Connecticut
First published: 1971

> *Principal characters:*
> ELPHINSTONE, a self-employed genealogist
> HORNE, Elphinstone's apartment mate, employed as a
>   researcher for the *National Journal of Social Commentary*
> ELPHINSTONE'S MOTHER, unnamed

The Story

For ten years, Elphinstone and Horne, two unmarried women in their forties, have shared a small apartment on the fifth floor of a brownstone on East Sixty-first Street. They have abided by their original agreement to swap bedrooms during the dog days of August and September every year so that Elphinstone will have the one air-conditioned bedroom during the hottest time of the year. The story opens on the morning of August tenth with Horne popping her head into Elphinstone's cool bedroom and shrieking, "Happy August the Tenth!" at her apartment mate, waking her from her sleep.

Horne leaves the house every day to go to her job in the research department of the *National Journal of Social Commentary*. Elphinstone works at home as a free-lance genealogist. She awaits the death of her decrepit mother, who lives in Connecticut attended by servants. She worries about whether her mother will, upon her death, leave her estate equally to her and her sister, or whether she will leave the bulk of it to the sister, who is married and has three children.

Horne's genuine concern for Elphinstone is apparent. She urges Elphinstone to have a polio shot, and, although they have some unpleasant words about that matter, it is clear that Horne cares about Elphinstone's welfare and that Elphinstone, who regularly visits a psychiatrist, Dr. Schreiber, realizes that Horne is truly concerned about her and, in her own way, appreciates that concern.

Horne has the temerity to waken Elphinstone early on this particular morning because she knows that Dr. Schreiber has scheduled her for a nine o'clock appointment "in order," she relates, "to observe your state of mind in the morning." Elphinstone, nevertheless, is annoyed at having her sleep disturbed. She and Horne bicker, and it soon becomes evident that bickering is an established pattern in their relationship. Elphinstone, whose social circle is confined to a small group of other alumnae of Sarah Lawrence College, does not approve of Horne's friends. Although Horne wants to include her in social gatherings, Elphinstone, who has behaved badly at one such affair, resists her efforts, and the two have quite separate social lives.

Elphinstone casually reveals that she has talked with Dr. Schreiber about Horne's friends, whom she considers Village hippies, and that he has called them "instinctively destructive." Horne is outraged not only that Elphinstone has discussed her friends with the psychiatrist but also that he has made judgments about her friends, whom he does not know. She considers Dr. Schreiber's conduct unprofessional. Elphinstone upbraids Horne for her compulsion to use shocking language, and also reveals to her that Dr. Schreiber has described her as sick because she considers the buildings of New York to be giant tombstones that mark a city of the dead.

Much of the furniture in the apartment is Elphinstone's and has been handed down to her through her family. Horne lets it be known that she feels crowded by all the family relics that Elphinstone has crammed into their small apartment. She tells Elphinstone that she is going to check into the Chelsea Hotel for the weekend and then move out. She needs to assert herself as an individual.

By noon, Elphinstone has come to regret the unpleasantness of the morning. She calls Horne at work to apologize. They have a civilized conversation in which Elphinstone, without any additional prodding from Horne, agrees to go for her polio shot, even though she dreads "the prick of the needle." They both weep before they say good-bye. Elphinstone sees Dr. Schreiber that afternoon. He dismisses her after only twenty minutes of the hour she is paying for. On an impulse she decides to go to Connecticut to see her mother, and on another quite cruel impulse, she packs Horne's bags and puts them at the door where Horne will see them the minute she comes home.

In Connecticut, Elphinstone begins to regret her treatment of Horne. She spends eighty dollars—less than half of the cost of two sessions with Dr. Schreiber, she tells herself—to rush back to Horne by taxicab. When she gets home, she finds Horne asleep before the television set. She sinks to the floor, hugs Horne's knees, wishes her a happy August the eleventh, and promises to go for her polio shot the first thing on Monday morning.

In the end, the two women are probably back where they started. The bickering will continue, but the interdependence of the relationship will keep them together, as will the fear of being alone.

Themes and Meanings

"Happy August the Tenth" was written during a crucial period in Tennessee Williams' own life, and Elphinstone clearly represents Williams, who had himself been in psychoanalysis. Williams had broken up with Frank Merlo, his lover of several years. After the breakup, which was caused in part by Williams' flagrant infidelities, Merlo became seriously ill and finally died. Williams, who spent much of his time at Merlo's bedside during the fi- nal months of Merlo's life, felt great guilt about his treatment of Merlo, whom he loved deeply.

In many respects, "Happy August the Tenth" provides insights into Wil- liams' relationship with Merlo. More important, the story points to what might have been. It suggests that they could have gone on together, although in the continuation of their relationship they would have been quite unlikely to find peace or even what most people would regard as happiness.

The story suggests that people are essentially in a trap. They engage regu- larly in love-hate relationships, but interdependence keeps these relation- ships together in spite of the incredible cruelty that frequently character- izes them. If this story is a comment on the nature of people, it suggests that people feel very much alone, very much excluded, and that they reach out for any kind of relationship that will make them feel a part of something.

A naturalistic determinism pervades most of Williams' major dramas, and that determinism is also a part of this story. When Horne views New York City as a great necropolis, when she views its tall buildings as tombstones, she is essentially suggesting that people have little control over their own des- tinies. She is better resigned to this reality than Elphinstone is. Elphinstone wants more from life—she searches genealogies, ferrets out past greatness. Horne more realistically works for a journal that deals with social com- mentary, that deals with the here and the now. Elements of the kind of nihil- ism that pervades the work of Jean-Paul Sartre, Albert Camus, Edward Albee, and Samuel Beckett are present in this story and in much of Williams' other work.

Style and Technique

In "Happy August the Tenth," Williams shows through the use of carefully selected details that it is the small things in one's day-to-day existence that lead to immediate tensions among people. The story also suggests that it is elemental anger rather than the small occurrences that precipitate the bicker- ing that most people have to deal with essentially. The bickering is a symp- tom of deep anger. Perhaps this realization has led Elphinstone to go to the psychiatrist, but even the psychiatrist has his limits. In Elphinstone's August the tenth session with him, he dismisses her when they are not even halfway through the session. On the mundane level, this act has economic implica- tions because Elphinstone is paying for the hour; on a different level, it sug- gests that there are times when people cannot even pay a professional to put up with them.

Williams understood tension and depicted it with an accuracy that helps to define him as a literary master. For example, during the bickering between Elphinstone and Horne, "another pause occurred in the conversation. Both of them made little noises in their throats and took little sips of coffee and didn't glance at each other; the warm air trembled between them." Williams makes optimal use of every prop available to him. The heat of August, the futility of August, a time when many people have abandoned the city to go on holiday, work for him as the heat of New Orleans in the summer worked for him in *A Streetcar Named Desire* (1947).

Elphinstone and Horne have a parrot, Lorita, which is permitted to move about the apartment at will, but which apparently does not know that it can fly. During the story, it confines itself voluntarily to its "summer palace," its cage out on the balcony. Elphinstone and Horne are just as able to get out of their confining situation as Lorita is, but they apparently do not know that they, too, are free. Indeed, their freedom is merely physical. They are not free in spirit, and as the story ends, it is clear that they never will be. The best they can hope for is that they will have each other, that their interdependence will keep them in their little brownstone cage, bickering with each other just as Lorita, in her summer palace, makes clucking sounds and little musical whistles.

R. Baird Shuman

THE HAPPY AUTUMN FIELDS

Author: Elizabeth Bowen (1899-1973)
Type of plot: Psychological realism
Time of plot: The late 1800's and early 1940's
Locale: The English countryside and London
First published: 1944

Principal characters:
SARAH and
HENRIETTA, young sisters in Victorian England
THEIR FAMILY, their parents and their seven brothers and
    sisters
EUGENE, a suitor to Sarah
MARY, a young woman in London during World War II
TRAVIS, her fiancé

The Story

The story is told in four parts, sharply divided, differing in time, place, and characters and alternating between a Victorian country estate and a bombed-out London house during World War II. The focus of the whole is on the perception of a London woman, Mary, who learns about (or dreams) the experiences of the Victorian family and strongly identifies with Sarah, one of the daughters.

In the first episode, Papa and his family form a walking party to stroll through the stubbled autumn fields of his extensive land. The gathering honors three of his sons, who will leave the next day for boarding school. There is a sense of order and stability in their procession, a feeling of permanence. Details of action and conversation emphasize the extraordinary closeness between the two younger sisters, Henrietta and Sarah; they have shared all of their thoughts and all of their lives, and nothing, says Sarah, "can touch one without touching the other."

The walkers are joined by two horseback riders, Papa's eldest son and his friend Eugene. It is clear that the initiative to dismount and stroll with the others is Eugene's, and it is clear that he is in love with Sarah. Leading his horse, he walks beside Sarah, separating her from Henrietta. Henrietta, thus isolated, begins a plaintive song which pierces her sister's heart and makes Sarah long to call out her sister's name and to restore the old sense of communion.

There is a sudden break. The name Henrietta is spoken not by her sister but by Mary, waking from sleep in a half-destroyed London house, in about 1942. The reader becomes aware that reality lies not in the happy autumn fields but in Mary's mind. Somehow, perhaps through a box of old letters that she has found, Mary knows about and empathizes with Sarah's conflicting emotions, her established love for Henrietta fighting against her awakening love for Eugene; Mary identifies with Sarah. More important, she finds the world of fifty years ago a better place to be than the present world, and she resists the effort of her fiancé, Travis, to get her out of the dangerously damaged house. They compromise: She will have two hours alone with her house and her dreams. Travis, however, takes the box with him as he leaves.

The dreamworld returns. Papa's family is now gathered in the drawing room at the end of the day. Eugene is there, his love evident and still unspoken. When he says, "I shall be back to-morrow," both sisters understand that he will speak then, and both are frightened of impending change. Sarah has an ominous sense that "something terrible" might happen. Henrietta promises to stay with her and protect her, and she tells Eugene imperiously, "Whatever tries to come between me and Sarah becomes nothing." She begs Sarah to confirm that, but Sarah cannot speak.

As before, Sarah's unspoken word awakens Mary's consciousness; in her London world, she is aroused by a bomb falling nearby. Travis returns, anxious about her, and as she slowly returns to the war world, she speaks of the other: "I am left with a fragment torn out of a day, a day I don't even know where or when; and now how am I to help laying that like a pattern against the poor stuff of everything else?" She wonders if she is descended from Sarah, which might explain her close identification. Yet Travis has spent the two hours reading letters from the box, and he finds such a kinship impossible; the letters soon cease to mention Henrietta and Sarah, suggesting that they died young and unmarried. Another letter, written by a brother in his old age, mentions a friend who, in his youth, was killed when his horse threw him on an autumn evening after a visit to their home. In the last line of the story, as Mary and Travis leave the London house, Travis says that the brother had always wondered "what made the horse shy in those empty fields."

Themes and Meanings

The title is taken from Alfred, Lord Tennyson's poem "Tears, Idle Tears":

> Tears from the depth of some divine despair
> Rise in the heart, and gather to the eyes,
> In looking on the happy autumn fields,
> And thinking of the days that are no more.

Many stories have been told about people who yearn for bygone days. What is unusual about Elizabeth Bowen's story is that her central character yearns not for her own more peaceful past but for that of people she has never known, in a place and time she has never known. This kind of hallucinatory experience appears in other stories in *Ivy Gripped the Steps* (1946), and Bowen uses it as a unifying factor in her preface to the collection. The hallucinations, she says, "are an unconscious, instinctive, saving resort. . . . [L]ife, mechanised by the controls of wartime, and emotionally torn and impoverished by changes, had to complete itself in some other way."

Thus Mary completes herself through Sarah. When the reader first sees her and hears her cry out for Henrietta, Mary is lying on a bare mattress in a room covered with gritty white dust, in a house that she has loved and in which she can no longer stay. The destruction and loss incurred by the blitz make Sarah's long-ago, long-resolved emotional crisis—even with its tragic end—seem a thing of peace and permanence compared with the unending crisis and change of the war. Travis tells her, "You don't like it here. . . . Your will keeps driving your self, but it can't be driven the whole way—it makes its own get-out: sleep." Sleep—perchance to dream. It is Travis and London that seem unreal to her.

The meaning of the story for Mary is a desperate search for stability amid constant, uncontrollable change; the theme involved in the relationship of Henrietta and Sarah is a response to impending change. Eugene's courtship will force Sarah to grow up; she is not sure that she wants to, and Henrietta is certainly opposed. The passing of childhood, the beginning of life's inevitable mutations, is unwelcome and frightening. Is it possible that the story's final question—What made the horse shy?—has an answer involving Henrietta's white handkerchief?

Style and Technique

There is considerable ambiguity in the telling of "The Happy Autumn Fields," made possible by the use of an omniscient narrator. Had the story been told in Mary's voice, the details about Sarah's family would have been solidified by Mary's interpretation and the ambiguity lost. The omniscient narrator, however, instead of explaining overtly, drops hints from which the reader may draw interpretations—sometimes slightly differing ones.

The most cogent example is the final question and its possible connection with the flying flag of Henrietta's white handkerchief. The latter is mentioned once a fourth of the way into the story and alluded to once again; yet in the last lines, in another place and time and a different context, the reader may remember it and may remember Henrietta's determination never to lose her sister.

The most all-encompassing example involves Mary's consciousness. The narrator never says explicitly how Mary came to know Sarah's family—whether the detailed impressions of the Victorian afternoon are dreams or imaginative waking reconstructions. Both times when the story shifts to Mary, there are hints that she has wakened from sleep, but she might well have been seeking refuge in daydreams of happy autumn fields. Similarly, the box of letters and pictures is never explained; the reader may assume that it was shaken out of the house's walls or closets by an explosion, but how it came to London and to Mary's attention is never said.

Bowen uses much impressionistic detail as well as dialogue; these techniques, like the voice of the narrator, set up echoes which the reader may interpret. Impressionistic details inform and fill out setting and character. Henrietta, too young for floor-length skirts, is "still ankle-free" and free also from other burdens of maturity. The youngest boy's hand is a "twisting prisoner" in the restraint of his father's hand. Smoke from a cottage chimney is the "colour of valediction." In London, Mary sees that her watch has stopped and "through the torn window appeared the timelessness of an impermeably clouded late summer afternoon."

Dialogue, even more than detail, encourages the reader's interpretation. When Henrietta pauses during the afternoon stroll, Sarah says to her, "We cannot stay here forever." Sarah means that they must join the others, but the reader knows that it is their childhood that cannot stay. Eugene, on the point of leaving for his last ride, says gravely, "There cannot fail to be to-morrow," and Henrietta answers, "*I* will see that there is to-morrow." When Travis comments on the junk in the old leather box, Mary says, "Everything one unburies seems the same age." Thus the two women, Mary and Sarah, and the two time periods, fifty years apart, are one.

Rosamond Putzel

HARMONY

Author: Ring Lardner (1885-1933)
Type of plot: Comic realism
Time of plot: The 1920's
Locale: A train en route to Boston
First published: 1915

Principal characters:
THE NARRATOR, a baseball writer
WALDRON, a new outfielder and a tenor
ART GRAHAM, an outfielder who has a passion for quartet
  singing
BILL COLE, a pitcher and a member of Waldron's quartet
LEFTY PARKS, the fourth member of the quartet
RYAN, the baseball club manager

The Story

"Harmony" is both a baseball story and a mystery story. The setting is a train full of baseball players on their way east to a game in Boston; the narrator is a baseball writer; the mystery which the writer is trying to solve through talking to the manager and to various players is how the club recruited Waldron, the unknown player whose batting has put the team in first place.

Lardner's structure is fairly complex, involving stories within stories. There are five people who contribute information about the mystery: the narrator, who begins and ends "Harmony"; Ryan, who gives the first account but who disagrees with the narrator's final version; Dick Hodges, the Jackson coach, who originally acquired Waldron and who is quoted by Ryan; Art Graham, who recruited Waldron but who is secretive about the details; and Bill Cole, whose story the narrator accepts as the truth.

The story begins on a train moving east toward Springfield, Massachusetts, where the narrator must file a story about the team with which he is traveling. The hottest news is the new outfielder, Waldron, who is setting records at bat. The only story about him which has not been told, however, is how Ryan, the club manager, found him. According to Ryan, there is no mystery. Art Graham spotted Waldron and recommended him even though both men were outfielders, and Waldron might well take Graham's place. Ryan accepted Graham's explanation that his motive was the good of the club and drafted Waldron.

Yet the Jackson coach, Hodges, is still puzzled. Ryan quotes a conversation with him in which Hodges described his plan to conceal Waldron for a season and insisted that Graham could not possibly have been impressed with his single performance when Waldron batted under a false name and popped out, at that. Did a Jackson player tell Graham about Waldron? Or could Graham spot a great batter, as he insists, simply by the way he swung?

Although there are still some loose ends, the narrator files his story at Springfield and does not inquire further until he encounters Graham at dinnertime. Graham is noncommittal, and it is not until the narrator finds himself in the diner with Cole that he hears what Cole insists is the true story. Graham had never gone to the ballpark in Jackson, it seems. He had recruited Waldron not for his ball-playing abilities but for his fine tenor voice. Graham's great passion is barbershop quartet harmony, Cole says, and the happiest times in Graham's life have been those periods when the team included three other good singers, one of them the essential tenor, who were willing to sing with Graham for the long hours which he demanded. To keep his quartet going, Graham was willing to do almost anything. He had talked Lefty Parks out of a romantic involvement, which Graham thought was taking too much time away from his singing; he had rallied the team around Mike McCann, his tenor, in an attempt to keep McCann from being shipped out after his pitching deteriorated; in fact, he had been so concerned about McCann that he missed a fly he should have caught, thus ensuring the pitcher's departure.

With such an obsession, it is no wonder, says Cole, that Graham decided to get Waldron on his team after he heard him sing during a casual meeting on the fateful day in Jackson. Graham had no idea that Waldron would turn out to be a star player. He only hoped to keep a good tenor for a season. That, says Cole, is the real story, but it must not be published until Graham is off the team.

Two years later, after Graham has been let out, the narrator does tell Ryan the story that Cole had told him, but Ryan refuses to believe it. He cannot think that anyone would be so obsessed by quartet harmony. The narrator, however, does believe Cole, and concludes that despite Waldron's fine playing, the team is not doing as well in baseball as it had done during the great days of musical harmony before Graham, Cole, and Parks were retired.

Themes and Meanings

The theme of "Harmony" is indicated both by the title and by the narrator's final comment. The story involves two kinds of group effort: baseball and close-harmony singing. To most of the characters in the story, singing is a spare-time activity, while baseball is their primary interest, even though they know that their big-league careers will be over when their skills decline. To Graham, however, the quartet makes life worthwhile, and baseball is simply a necessary adjunct to the quartet. The comedy in "Harmony" comes from Graham's attempts to use the baseball system for the purposes

of his quartet, attempts which are doomed by the perishable nature of baseball talent.

In keeping his quartet together, Graham must always battle the clock and
the calendar. He fights for the players' time, hurrying them out of bed on the
train, gathering them from the dining car, resenting their leisure activities,
even breaking up Parks's romance. He would, if he could, put quartet practice ahead of baseball practice. Though he must let the players stop singing
long enough to play ball, however, Graham has considerable success in domi-
nating the rest of their time. It is the calendar which defeats him, first taking
McCann from him and finally removing Graham himself, who probably
leaves the team sooner because the tenor he scouted happens to play Graham's own position.

Although the story is built on Graham's attempt to serve the needs of his
quartet while seeming to live for his sport, an attempt in which the victories
are necessarily temporary, in his conclusion the narrator suggests that the
harmonizing of the quartet may have resulted in better play on the ball field.
One recalls Graham's insistence that he could not be a scout because he
would be too lonely. Perhaps the same spirit which brings the quartet
together, sometimes half unwilling, but submitting to Graham's demands in
part simply to make him happy, is the spirit which took the team to first
place. Somehow, once the habit of musical harmony has gone with three of
the harmonizers, says the narrator, the baseball team itself is not the same.

Style and Technique

The realism for which Lardner was praised is evident in "Harmony." The
setting is everyday and undramatic—a train running behind schedule, a
diner with good minced ham and inferior asparagus. The ball players talk,
sing, and eat. The talk itself is both matter-of-fact in tone and authentic in
detail, revealing Lardner's ear for slang, baseball jargon, and the peculiarities of spoken English. Talking about Mike McCann, for example, Cole
says, "You know what a pitcher Mike was. He could go in there stone cold
and stick ten out o' twelve over that old plate with somethin' on 'em." The
passage rings true, and it is typical. The asparagus, says Cole, for example, is
"tougher'n a doubleheader in St. Louis." When McCann's pitching fails, Cole
says, "I'll swear that what he throwed up there didn't have no more on it than
September Morning." The beauty of Lardner's language is that it seems tran-
scribed rather than invented.

Lardner has been criticized for his objectivity, which it has been argued
indicates a dislike of his own characters. In his satiric stories, the dislike is
justifiable, and Lardner should not be faulted for letting the characters condemn themselves as they talk. Lardner, however, is also capable of tenderness, of an appreciation of the human condition in a story more poignant
because it is told objectively, perhaps, as in "Harmony," by a number of tell-

ers. In Art Graham, a middling ball player and a fair singer, Lardner has drawn his portrait of the artist.

Rosemary M. Canfield-Reisman

THE HEADLESS HAWK

Author: Truman Capote (1924-1984)
Type of plot: Fantasy
Time of plot: The 1940's
Locale: New York City
First published: 1946

Principal characters:
VINCENT WATERS, the manager of an art gallery
D. J., an odd young woman

The Story

Considered one of the most complex of the author's stories, "The Headless Hawk" resembles several of Truman Capote's other pieces in its use of flashback. In the first part, the protagonist, Vincent Waters, is followed home by an unusual-looking girl; the middle section flashes back to their earlier meeting, romance, and separation; and the ending of the story returns to the beginning—the present—and accentuates the stasis of the situation, the impossibility of any resolution short of violence.

Vincent is shown in the first and last segments in a state of disintegration, uncertain about everything, as if he has lost contact with reality. When he leaves his art gallery one hot July evening, he begins to look for and soon notices the young woman whom he expects to see. Neither speaks to the other, yet there appears to be a pattern to the encounter: First she walks and he follows; she waits, he catches up, they pause, and then he sets off with her trailing behind him as he makes his way to his apartment. There she stands outside, always waiting.

At that point the story flashes back to their first meeting, the previous winter. A peculiarly dressed young woman, with unusual eyes and haircut, appears in the gallery to sell Vincent a strange self-portrait. In it, her severed head lies alongside her body, and in the background is a headless hawk. Although the girl tells Vincent a few things about herself, mentioning a Mr. Destronelli, a name that will become very familiar to him in the future, she is also curiously remote.

Impressed by the power of the painting and by the affinity that he feels for it, Vincent decides to buy it. He is also attracted by the girl herself, though he recognizes that he has a history of falling in love with eccentrics for brief periods. He knows that ultimately he will dislike the very quality that draws him to her.

When he is distracted by a phone call, the girl disappears, leaving behind on a piece of paper only her initials, D. J., and an open-ended address, the

Y.W.C.A. Because of that, Vincent cannot trace her. He spends lonely nights speaking to the painting, confessing his feelings about himself, his sense of failure and incompleteness.

Several months pass, during which Vincent is disturbed and upset. Then, one April evening as he wanders through the streets of New York City, he encounters D. J. Frightened of him at first, it is not long before she agrees to go home with him. They become lovers, and occasionally D. J. tells Vincent a little about her past, always invoking the name of the mysterious Mr. Destronelli. When Vincent wants to know more about Destronelli, he learns only that the man resembles everybody.

The affair ends in a month, after the two have celebrated D. J.'s birthday. That night Vincent has a terrifying dream, in which he sees himself at a party, carrying the burden of another self, a horrible old man. Lovers whom he has betrayed also appear in the dream. When he dances with D. J., he floats away from her. At that moment, he is attacked by a headless hawk, which the freakish host has been holding. With that he knows there can be neither love nor freedom from his fate.

Awakening from his dream, Vincent finds D. J. outside in the neglected garden, behaving in a way that leads him to question her sanity. As soon as he does that, he realizes that he has destroyed his love for her. The next day, sick in body and spirit, he cuts up her painting and puts her suitcase out in the hall.

The story returns to the present and ends quickly with a scene in front of the apartment house. Vincent, ill and indecisive, stands for a moment next to a lamppost. The rain that has been threatening all day comes, and, as everyone else goes indoors, D. J. walks up to Vincent and waits in the silence and the rain.

Themes and Meanings

Vincent is a solitary figure who cannot escape from himself any more than he can flee from D. J. All of his previous love affairs have been failures, and he has abandoned everyone with whom he has been intimate. Like all mortals, each of his lovers had some imperfection; Vincent, in spite of his brief infatuation with each, grew to despise them, both male and female. Although he has escaped from all of them, he knows, or suspects, that he has injured them beyond healing. Until his affair with D. J., however, he evaded the responsibility for their destruction. Yet D. J. is not to be eluded. She remains his waking reminder that he is a destroyer, a victimizer, a Mr. Destronelli, the one who has pursued D. J. throughout her life, the stranger who looks like everyone.

Vincent has also destroyed himself, though, becoming his own victim. Before meeting D. J., he was able to exist in his usual way, to work, to spend some time with friends, and to avoid examining his behavior too closely. Yet when he sees her painting of the headless hawk, two things happen to him: He has the sensation that the artist must know and understand his inner being, and he finds that he identifies with the hawk itself. Lacking its head, the hawk is without direction. Vincent recognizes his own directionless self, a man who has talents and abilities that have never been utilized, a man who has never really loved anyone. If, then, the hawk is a representation of Vincent, his dream in which the hawk assaults him reveals Vincent to be his own victim. Furthermore, his attack on the painting suggests self-destruction.

As to D. J.'s knowing his secret self even before she meets him, Vincent is only partly right.The deception and betrayal that she has experienced, and which she attributes to Mr. Destronelli, are characteristic of Vincent. That D. J. is an innocent, an eternal child, is shown through Vincent's dream. She is also his last opportunity for love, for she is symbolically his last dancing partner in his dream. On awakening from his dream, however, Vincent speaks the terrible words that bring about the death of love. Instead of accepting D. J. as she is, he rejects her.

Style and Technique

In writing "The Headless Hawk," Capote worked with many of the same components that he used in other short stories of the same period, as well as in his first novel: dreams, nightmares, distortions, all characteristic of the gothic mode that is typical of much of his work. The intent of this style is to reveal psychological states that cannot be portrayed in other ways, to show fear and horror within the inner core of many lives.

The dreams, the painting, and the fantasy of Mr. Destronelli compose the major symbols of the story, but there are many more, in addition to multiple images. Directionlessness, for example, is seen not only in the symbol of the headless hawk but also in other phases of the story: in Vincent's dream of waltzing; in his uncertainty as he walks the street; in his use of an umbrella, which makes the tapping sound of a blind man with a cane.

Images of imprisonment, entrapment, and death recur throughout the story. The word "locked" appears in several places, and at the end it is clear that the two characters are locked together figuratively, imprisoned in their lives, bound to their individual selves and to each other. A fan that turns around and around in a store window is still another emblem of the inescapable circularity of their lives.

The separation of Vincent and D. J. from the ordinary world is shown through nightmarish images. The people on a New York avenue appear to Vincent as underwater creatures in a green sea. D. J. appears in a green raincoat; her reflection in a store window is green; her eyes are green; the popcorn she buys is put into a green bag. The emphasis on the color green simultaneously suggests distortion and unreality; it symbolizes a lack of connection with human existence; and, most important, it serves as an image of drowning and death. The use of the color green is representative of Capote's style.

Light, dark, and shadow are utilized not only for setting but also to symbolize states of mind. Reflections are distorted; mirrors are either blank or hazy, or they give false images. Nothing is dependable; everything shifts and changes. Only the relationship of Vincent and D. J. seems fixed, like the fan in its endless turnings. In the final scene, they stand together yet separated by the rain that falls between them as if it were an uncrossable barrier.

Helen S. Garson

HER FIRST BALL

Author: Katherine Mansfield (Kathleen Mansfield Beauchamp, 1888-1923)
Type of plot: Romantic realism
Time of plot: Early nineteenth century
Locale: England
First published: 1921

> *Principal characters:*
> LEILA, the protagonist, a girl attending her first ball
> THE FAT MAN, one of Leila's dancing partners, a jaded cynic

The Story

Leila, the young protagonist of "Her First Ball," is thrilled though extremely self-conscious at the prospect of attending her first formal ball. Every detail, from the shared cab which takes her there to the coach bolster, which feels like the sleeve of an escort's dress suit, contributes to her pleasure. Not even the Sheridan girls, amazed that she has never been to a ball before, can dampen her enthusiasm. She does feel less sophisticated than her companions; after all, she has been reared in the country, fifteen miles from the nearest neighbor, and her friends have had such evenings before.

She admires the easy gallantry of her cousin Laurie when he arranges, as usual, to have the third and ninth dances with his sister Laura. Though sad almost to the point of tears that she herself does not have a brother to make such casual agreements with her ("no brother had ever said 'Twig?' to her"), the whole experience is so overwhelming that Leila seems almost lifted past the big golden lantern, and the couples seem to float through the air: Their "little satin shoes chased each other like birds."

Leila acts with instinctive grace and is courteous even to the boorish fat man who presumptuously compares his program with hers to schedule a dance. The fat man asks himself aloud whether he remembers Leila's "bright little face," whether he had known it "of yore," but his condescension does not faze her. She dances beautifully, even though she learned to dance in "a little corrugated iron mission hall" near her boarding school. Indeed, Leila has a series of partners, and Jose's wink tells the reader, though apparently not Leila, that her exuberance, grace, and beauty have quickly made Leila the "belle of the ball." Her partners, aware of her instinctive elegance and grace, try with varying degrees of success to appear nonchalant and to make the usual small talk. Leila herself seems unaware of the splendid impression that she is making; she knows only that she is enjoying herself immensely and that the evening is passing very quickly.

Then the fat man reappears for the dance he himself had scheduled, and the tone of the story changes completely. To this point, the words have flown by in a series of vignettes, almost a catalog of Leila's quick, vivid impressions of the scene. Instead of the expected awkward pleasantries about the quick and slippery dance floor, the fat man tells Leila that she "can't hope to last," that "long before that you'll be sitting up there on the stage, looking on, in your nice black velvet," that her "pretty arms will have turned to short fat ones," and that her fan will be "a black bony one."

Leila laughs at the fat man's words, though they bother her inwardly because she realizes that they are essentially true. One day she will grow old; then no one will dance with her, and she will become one of the chaperons. The music, which had seemed gay, suddenly seems sad to her. For a moment, Leila feels like a little girl wanting to throw her pinafore over her head and sob. Even so, she never loses her composure; she tells the fat man that she does not take his words seriously.

Leila's gloomy mood does not last. When the couples parade for the next dance and a new partner, "a young man with curly hair," escorts her to the center of the dance floor, Leila's feet "glided, glided," and she even smiles radiantly and without recognition when her next partner accidently bumps her into the fat man.

Themes and Meanings

Leila's first ball is her first social triumph, even as it is her first disillusionment. She knows, even before she dances with the fat man, that time will take her beauty, that she will not always be *la belle du bal*; even so, these are things that she need not consider on the evening of her first formal. What bothers her is not so much the fat man's words as his callousness in saying them. Indeed, what Leila discovers at the ball is human cruelty, that it is usually aimed at the naïvely innocent for the perverse pleasure it gives to its wicked agent. She also discovers how brief and fragile periods of absolute happiness are. Fortunately, however, youth is buoyant, and the fat man's remarks, though noted and stored away, do not mar Leila's perfect evening.

Since she has been reared in an isolated place and as an only child, Leila's sensitivity is more acute than that of others her age. This gives her greater capacity for joy, even as it makes her vulnerable to greater pain. One moment, the lanterns, the azaleas, the gowns, the music make her float on air; the next, an aging cynic's cruelty punctures all of her joy, and Leila wishes that she were at home listening to the baby owls in their nest near the veranda. In short, Katherine Mansfield's story, for all its brevity, encapsulates the bittersweetness of growing up.

Style and Technique

When scholars pored over Katherine Mansfield's autograph manuscripts and journals, they were struck by her poor spelling and her eccentric grammar. Even so, Mansfield's style is geared to pictorial rather than verbal vividness. For example, "Her First Ball," though narrated in the third person, re-creates the ball as Leila sees it: vivid colors, swift movements, ravishing music. It presents an important moment, perceived with the intensity possible only for a sensitive and impressionable young person. Indeed, the story is told with the manic mood swings of an adolescent. Like a musical composition, its tempos vary from allegro (the quickly narrated sections of Leila's arrival and first dances) to maestoso (the melancholy sadness following the fat man's words) to allegro vivace (when Leila dances with the curly haired young man). Often the words reproduce a waltz rhythm: " . . . in one minute, in one turn, her feet glided, glided. The lights, the azaleas, the dresses, the pink faces, the velvet chairs, all became one beautiful flying wheel."

Mansfield was born Kathleen Beauchamp in Wellington, New Zealand. When she became nineteen she changed her name to Katherine Mansfield, joining an altered first name to her mother's maiden name. She was not an only child, but she was lonely, and her early trip to Europe made her bloom as surely as Leila at her first ball. Mansfield's pictorial intensity is the single most distinguishing element of her technique; it brought her to the notice of the Bloomsbury writers and caused Virginia Woolf to say, "I was jealous of her writing. The only writing I have ever been jealous of."

Robert J. Forman

HER TABLE SPREAD

Author: Elizabeth Bowen (1899-1973)
Type of plot: Psychological realism
Time of plot: Early twentieth century
Locale: The coast of Ireland
First published: 1930

> *Principal characters:*
> VALERIA CUFFE, an heiress and owner of the Castle
> MRS. TREYE, her aunt
> ROBERT ROSSITER, Mrs. Treye's uncle
> MISS CARBIN, a friend of Mrs. Treye
> MR. ALBAN, a guest from London

The Story

"Her Table Spread" is the account of the events of one evening in an Irish castle. The title suggests the purpose of the lavish dinner party which has been staged by Valeria Cuffe, the young heiress who is also the owner of the Castle. She is twenty-five; it is time that she married. Mr. Alban is aware that he may be a likely candidate. What he discovers only gradually is that he is not the primary prospect for whom the Castle and Valeria are waiting.

As the story begins, the hostess and the guests come down to dinner. With the assurance of a guest of honor and a courted prospective husband, Alban observes the simple Valeria, to whom he is not particularly drawn. Alban's self-satisfaction diminishes, however, when he discovers that the ladies are hoping for a visit from the officers of a destroyer which is anchored in the estuary, perhaps the same destroyer whose officers, a Mr. Garrett and a Mr. Graves, visited at the Castle previously and were entertained at the Castle by friends living there during the absence of Valeria and her dependents.

After dinner, Alban's discontent increases. Although he plays the piano, he is ignored. Indeed, Valeria is not even present, but is racing about in the rain, careless of her satin evening dress, hoping to attract the officers, even if she must row out to their ship. Although she considered marrying Alban, she has now decided that her husband must be one of the officers; she assumes that the destroyer is the one on which Garrett and Graves serve, and she tries to choose between them, remembering her friends' descriptions.

Fearing that Valeria will come for a boat, Robert Rossiter, an uncle of hers, and Alban guard the boathouse until Alban is frightened out by a bat. On his way back to the Castle, he hears sobbing in the darkness and realizes that it is Valeria. She is certain that it is Garrett, the tall young officer, and she calls joyfully, "Mr. Garrett has landed." Suddenly Alban is touched by emotion; he feels himself a man desired by women. The next morning the destroyer leaves.

Themes and Meanings

Although Elizabeth Bowen penetrates the minds of both Alban and Valeria, it is the change in Alban which involves the theme of the story. Valeria is immature, childish, ruled by whims, perhaps a bit simple, but she is at least fully alive. Although her dreams of a visit from the naval officers are based on the flimsiest of chances, both her initial joy and her later grief indicate that she is certainly a woman.

On the other hand, Alban is aware that he is not fully a man, but he blames his lack of feeling on the other sex. In the first sentence of "Her Table Spread," Bowen points out that Alban dislikes women. The reason for his dislike becomes clear after he discovers that the candles, the delayed dinner, the air of expectation are all evidence that the guests to be truly honored are the officers who Valeria hopes will come to the Castle. Evidently, Alban is generally ignored by women. As a result, he dislikes them. Surely, he feels, some woman could have caused him to love her and, thus, could have cured his emptiness.

Bowen makes it clear, however, that Alban's unattractiveness to women is not their fault. When he plays the piano, he swings around on the stool "rather fussily"; later, in the boathouse, he runs away from the bat; he worries about his evening pumps, which are soaked by the rain. Clearly he projects the image of a male spinster, waiting for life to come to him, but only on his terms. His loneliness is his own doing.

When Valeria mistakes him for Garrett, when at her cry the other women come out onto the lamplit terrace, suddenly the magic touches Alban. He responds to the bare shoulders of the two women on the terrace above him; hearing Valeria's laughter, he thinks of her as the princess she imagines herself. For a moment he feels like a man, to whom all the women are reaching out. In a sense, he becomes the desired Garrett.

There the story ends. The destroyer leaves the next morning; the Castle is "extinguished," and Valeria's arms are empty. Bowen does not trace the results of the strange evening episode. With the destroyer fortuitously gone, will Valeria turn to Alban? Will he be able to become the prince of her dreams? In the daylight, will her eccentricities drive him away? The questions are left unanswered, and in a sense they are irrelevant. For Alban, there has been a difference. At the beginning of "Her Table Spread," he is alone, dead to feeling, unmanly and therefore inhuman. At the end of the story, he has, if only briefly, responded to women's beauty with manly strength; he has felt desired.

Style and Technique

In her spare, carefully crafted narratives, Bowen utilizes every character and every image to develop her theme. In "Her Table Spread," only five characters appear. Every one of them is important to the author's theme. For example, Mrs. Treye and Miss Carbin represent the dependents, to whom the marriage of the heiress is of practical importance. Should she not establish a permanent home and continue the line, their own security will be imperiled. In contrast, Valeria Cuffe herself wishes to marry for more romantic reasons. Even though she has not selected the man, she imagines an exciting life; childish though she is, she wisely understands her need for someone with whom to spend her life. Similarly, the elderly Robert Rossiter contrasts with young Alban. Old though he is, Rossiter is still part of life, chasing the parlormaid, drinking in the boathouse, despite the bats. His participation in life underlines Alban's flight from it.

In this story, the dominant symbols are light and darkness. The women may almost be said to be the carriers of light; from the gleam of Valeria's red satin dress to the sparkle of the other ladies' beaded dresses, feminine garb is intended to entice men into liveliness. Valeria deliberately uses light to attract her naval officers. The candles are lit so that they will be seen from the ship; later, the lantern Valeria carries is as much a signal as a light for her wanderings outdoors. On the other hand, though he is in the lamplit drawing room, Alban, at the piano, muses that he is "fixed in the dark rain."

At the end of the story, the light-dark symbolism becomes more complex. Valeria's lantern goes out, and she encounters Alban in the darkness. Although light streams from the terrace, Alban sees the beauty of the three women without seeing their faces; transformed in the darkness, he stands in the "flame" of their warmth toward him, or, indeed, toward the supposed Garrett. The fact that the Castle is "extinguished" in the morning leaves the issue in doubt; perhaps, having felt warmth, Alban will not be extinguished so easily.

Rosemary M. Canfield-Reisman

HERAKLEITOS

Author: Guy Davenport (1927-   )
Type of plot: Mythologized history
Time of plot: 500-400 B.C.
Locale: Ephesos
First published: 1974

> *Principal characters:*
> HERAKLEITOS, the Greek philospher
> KNAPS, Herakleitos' visitor and student
> SELENA, Herakleitos' female housekeeper
> TMOLOS, a mute slave of Herakleitos

The Story

Knaps, stranger to Ephesos, materializes one late summer morning at the home of Herakleitos, the thinker, whom Knaps presumes to visit without asking first. Knaps receives a gracious welcome from Herakleitos and his two companions, housekeeper Selena and slave Tmolos. Propriety and proper measure are important to Herakleitos; accordingly, Knaps, after sharing their breakfast, will be expected to observe the usual morning routine, including music and dancing performed by the three, the strangeness and intricacy of which Knaps can only gape at. Herakleitos explains: "Were I to visit you in your rocky Arkadia, I should not expect you to discompose your day." The philospher of flux and perpetual change silently observes and relishes the barbaric fashion of Knaps's hairstyle. Each is strange to the other, the difference being Herakleitos' at-homeness with contrariness and variety, out of which he has fashioned his famous thoughts.

Knaps's first impression of Herakleitos is of a man blending the exotic and the conventional. The strange musical performance is then followed by a session of philosophy, which Herakleitos initiates by crushing a leaf of sage and smelling his fingers, a religious observance. Herakleitos' "prayers"— whether before a session of thinking or at dinner—Knaps finds beside the point. When asked by the philosopher about the honor given Artemis in Arkadia, Knaps's home, the grave young man politely debunks the goddess: "There are country people who shout at the full of the moon. . . ." He admits to finding Artemis no more than a comfort for dull minds and women.

Knaps's secularity serves as a springboard for Herakleitos. Knaps is so philosophical that he has dismissed all customary acknowledgment of the mysterious or magical—Herakleitos pointing out the cosmic significance of Knaps's name he dismisses as a whim of his parents. Because Knaps is skeptical, and gently so, rather than cynical, he is no match for Herakleitos, whose penetrating vision repeatedly exposes the strangeness and harmony hiding beneath the obvious surface of nearly everything about which a mind can think. The old thinker's sense of paradox in nature, and in the way a mind works, soon reduces Knaps to a silent secretary, papyrus and quill at the ready. Herakleitos' utterances he records with proverblike succinctness. Asked if he does not find it remarkable that a thread drawn absolutely tight should still be composed of curly fibers, Knaps writes: "*Spun wool, . . . straight thread.*" For the duration of the story Knaps is an auditor, and gradually a disciple. He dances with Herakleitos, Selena, and Tmolos in the morning music rituals, even teaching the three new friends a wild partridge dance from his home region.

As summer changes to fall, Knaps accumulates a load of the sage's statements, which Herakleitos seems never at a loss to deliver while keeping each one in tune with his central theme: That which seems to be is often the opposite of what is. Thus, he intuits the motion in stone without the benefit of modern physics. Herakleitos' science is oracular, poetic, and very moving to Knaps's sense of wonder. Mesmerized, Knaps records:

> *Justice is contention.*
> *War is the father of all that is.*
> *Ephesians, be rich! I cannot wish you worse.*
> *Pigs wash in mud, chickens in dust.*
> *Even sleeping men are doing the world's business.*
> *The river we stepped into is not the river in which we stand.*

At the end of the story, Knaps accompanies Herakleitos, Selena, and Tmolos to the temple of Artemis. As Herakleitos offers his book of philosophy to the multibreasted image whose garmets are adorned with bears, cows, lions, bees, flowers, and frogs, Knaps offers a carved wooden horse. The secular Knaps is born again to the awe of nature through the witness to her by the philospher, whose concentrated attention is the most convincing kind of worship.

Themes and Meanings

"When Herakleitos finished his book on nature and the mind, he put it on the altar of the Artemis of Ephesos, for whatever nature is, we know it first through her knowing eyes, her knowing hands." These words are spoken by a character in another story in the same book (*Tatlin!*, 1974) which contains "Herakleitos." The speaker is also a philosopher, though living in the twentieth century. Guy Davenport, the author, has provided this "footnote" in the later story to emphasize the theme of knowledge. The archaic Herakleitos saw human knowing as a response to the signs, the *logos*, which nature offers to a man's senses. For Davenport, what is most crucial is Herakleitos' ability to have seen and interpreted the world with a clarity and rightness which the most current modern science only restates, albeit with more complexity and an array of technological "proof." This *logos*, the speech of the universe, is a constant down through the centuries.

Hence, Knaps's initiation by Herakleitos proceeds from the master's first official philosophical pronouncement: "Let us begin by noting that understanding is common to all men." Why, Herakleitos asks Knaps, should a man act as if his intelligence were private, an extension of his inner self, belonging to him alone? The eyes, nose, ears, hands, nervous system, and brain he uses to know things together constitute an organic structure, marvelous when attuned to the universe of which it is part, but tending frequently to forget its basis in process, the flow of miraculous creation for which the Greeks worshiped Artemis, the giver and sustainer of life's rich bounty. Whenever a thinker breaks his connection with the *logos*, Artemis' voice, he becomes less intelligent, for, as Herakleitos instructs Knaps, "Men are not intelligent . . . the gods are intelligent."

Style and Technique

The reader of this story will likely feel that he is experiencing something of the "real Herakleitos." That Herakleitos' life is a subject for conjecture, eluding documentation, matters not; Davenport's specificity in descriptions conjures the veritable. When Knaps first sees Herakleitos, the philosopher is "sprinkling crushed herbs into his wine, basil, tarragon and sage." The story's first three pages are crowded with sensuousness, from the fragrances mentioned to mouths "full of figs and spiced wine," to the sounds of barbitos, lyre, and a "chittering of sticks" accompanying the dance, a wild kinetic performance by Tmolos, the slave. Davenport's theme of knowing is played forte from the story's opening sentences, where the sensations of a rooster responding to sunrise and remembering other sunrises are conveyed through bright omniscience: "When he closed his eyes he sometimes saw a mare nursing her foal under the yellow leaves of a gingko, and heard the *tap tap* of the horseskin drum. . . ."

The author's language is applied to the page as if it were paint. The words call attention to themselves as words, as sounds. Selena walks around with her sandals "slapping the stone floor." Weather is frequently mentioned, the brightness of the sun on the sea. Sentences become paintings, imagistic and bright: "Herakleitos and Knaps stood in wild wheat above the olive groves, the royal blue of thistles beside the fluting of their cloaks." Davenport registers his vision by driving the language into the realm of iconography, the characters appearing in a visual stateliness, like figures drawn in frozen movement on an urn or carved in stone. The sentence rhythms create this "felt sense" as well, adding a weightiness and gonglike resonance to the description of Artemis in the temple: "Her golden hands were open in solicitude and blessing. A citadel crowned her neatly bound hair." The style makes the reader think about the artifice, which is the ordered language, at the same time as he is dazzled by the images—appropriate dilemma for someone reading a story about the man whose name is now trite with its association with the perception that everything perceived is something other than what it appears, and is constantly moving even though standing still.

Bruce Wiebe

HERODIAS

Author: Gustave Flaubert (1821-1880)
Type of plot: Historical and psychological realism
Time of plot: c. A.D. 30
Locale: Machaerous citadel, on the outskirts of ancient Jerusalem
First published: 1877 (English translation, 1903)

> *Principal characters:*
> HEROD ANTIPAS, the tetrarch of Jerusalem
> MANNAËI, a Samaritan, jailer, and executioner
> HERODIAS, Herod's wife, once his sister-in-law
> IAOKANANN (JOHN THE BAPTIST), a prisoner and prophet
> LUCIUS VITELLIUS, a Roman proconsul
> AULUS VITELLIUS, his son, a favorite of Tiberius
> SALOME, the daughter of Herodias by her first marriage

The Story

"Herodias" opens with a harsh and unsparing landscape, the powerful citadel of Machaerous as it looms over the desert, no city of men but an incarnation of power, a huge, pointed crown suspended over an abyss. Great forces are at work in this unforgiving land, against whose barren geometry of forms human figures are dwarfed. Herod Antipas and his wife, Herodias, dominate the foreground of the opening scene. He is surrounded by political factions and wracked by doubts, shaken by the voice of his prisoner Iaokanann. She is engaged in a remorseless pursuit of power, a pursuit furthered for her by Herod's love, at the expense of divorce and the loss of her daughter. Herod's love has died, but she still works to further his power, because she may yet rule through him. Thus she arranges the death of her own brother in prison; such intrafamilial killings are as commonplace to her as they are to Herod. Their very marriage is founded on her divorce from Herod's own brother. In Rome, such machinations are taken for granted, but to the peoples they rule, the marriage of Herodias and Herod is incestuous, an abomination.

Iaokanann, whose last day this story chronicles from rising sun to rising sun, is the opposite of Herodias; he denounces her as a Jezebel and threatens her power, his voice cuts off her breath, and she desires nothing so much as his death. All of her wiles are bent to this end from the moment that she appears on the scene. Since Herod is now dead to her charms, she does not hesitate to use other means: The first hint of the arrival of Salome comes through Herodias' reproaches to Herod. In Herod's mind, Iaokanann is still valuable in bargaining with the many sects that he must manipulate to control Jerusalem. Locked deep in the bowels of the citadel, the prisoner seems harmless, though the rumble of his voice arises at times to trouble the already troubled ruler.

Herod is preparing to celebrate his birthday. The most important leaders of Jerusalem, religious and secular, the Roman proconsul Lucius Vitellius and his son, and the most important of his allies and political opponents are invited. Outside the citadel the King of the Arabs, Herod's insulted first father-in-law, gathers forces for an attack. The progression of the day sees the interplay of these political forces as Herod attempts to maneuver himself into a position of safety and strength. There has even been a prophecy: Someone important will die in the citadel this day.

The arrival of various guests, especially of Lucius Vitellius and his son Aulus Vitellius, swamps the reader with names and a catalog of warring political and religious interests. Herod must meet and propitiate Samaritans, Essenes, Galileans, Pharisees, Nazarenes, Sadducees, Romans, and publicans, each of whom clamors for attention. Lucius Vitellius, representing the power of Tiberius Caesar, insists on inspecting the citadel and is led into all the storage rooms, the great beehive of the hollowed cliff under the fortress. Here armaments of all kinds are stockpiled, enough for forty thousand men. There is even a subterranean stable with a hundred white war-horses, trained and groomed by a Babylonian. During this inspection, the underground cell of Iaokanann is discovered and opened. The powerful voice, rising from darkness into a scene where sunlight glints from armor and jewels, blasts Herod and his wife. The leaders of the Jewish sects are set abuzz; the Romans find Iaokanann's accusations of adultery and incest against their host amusing but are more troubled to hear that he opposes paying taxes to Rome. So passes the afternoon of confusion and bargaining, in preparation for the evening's feast. In the course of the afternoon, Herod twice catches a glimpse of a young girl—a stranger, but very beautiful—first from a distance, then in the rooms of Herodias herself.

The feast is described in the most lavish of terms, a heaping up of all the excesses of Roman orgiastic cuisine for the benefit of the young Aulus Vitellius, who is already renowned as a glutton. The two cultures, Roman and Jewish, clash, and there are many conflicts of interest, both political and religious. Lucius Vitellius affects an interpreter but can understand the language of the people surrounding him; he hears them speak of a Messiah in connection with Iaokanann, one Jesus Christ, and must ask the definition of the term from the priests. The climax of the evening is reached with the entrance of the lovely Salome, glimpsed earlier in the day. At her mother's orders, Salome dances in such a seductive manner that she arouses all the men at the feast, and Herod, seeing in her the beauty that Herodias has lost, offers her any reward she wishes. Her answer? The head of Iaokanann.

The actual execution is not described. Mannaëi brings the severed head on a platter to Salome, then displays it to the guests. The banquet ends, and

Herod remains, staring at the head and weeping. Phanuel, an Essene who had delivered the prophecy of death to Herod and had pleaded for the life of Iaokanann, prays.

At dawn the next day, Phanuel leaves the citadel with the head still on its platter. He meets two men, messengers returning to Iaokanann. The three continue together on the road to Galilee, carrying the heavy load by turns.

Themes and Meanings

The late nineteenth and early twentieth centuries saw many adaptations of the biblical story of John the Baptist and Salome. Notable examples are the verse drama *Hérodias* (1940) by Stéphane Mallarmé and Richard Strauss's opera *Salome* (1905), which was based on a play of the same name by Oscar Wilde. In "Herodias," Gustave Flaubert focuses on the struggle between the worldly Herodias and the righteous Iaokanann. The swirl of political and religious interests which surrounds Herod Antipas and his wife is the antithesis of the simple yet terrible preaching of the Baptist. Herodias' power is doubled in the person of the young Salome, the incarnation of the sensuous life, while Iaokanann effaces himself as a double for Jesus, the Messiah. Iaokanann speaks from the shadows, a powerful voice whose echoes rock the citadel, while Herodias strikes the reader visually; she stands in the light, bright in color, sharp-edged. The pivotal point in this struggle is reached in the familiar scene of Salome's dance, the trap for the wavering Herod, who finds a kind of relief in seeing his decision made for him by Herodias' ruse. The execution of her enemy seems a victory for Herodias, yet it is only through the death of Iaokanann that Jesus can rise; the personal diminishment of the Baptist contributes to the eventual triumph of the Messiah.

Style and Technique

Flaubert is said to have done extensive historical research before writing the opening words of "Herodias." His arid painting of a geometric and empty world, where a great fortress stares across the desert to Jerusalem, expresses the spiritual vacuum behind the power of Herod's house. As the story progresses, the author continues to make every word count. His descriptions pile up, proliferating details on the fortress itself and the people who pass through its gates on this fateful day. Tribes are named and individuals listed and described in all their exotic and sometimes grotesque detail. In Herod's subterranean storerooms are a confusion of numbers and an exhaustive listing of armaments, such as the hundred blue-maned war-horses, gentle as sheep yet trained to eviscerate the enemy and fight all day. Against this world of proliferating detail is set Iaokanann, little more than a shadow with a voice, but this voice speaks in biblical phrases and rocks the foundations of the worldly power of the captors. During the banquet, Flaubert again heaps up details of food, arguments, personalities, adding to the masculine political world the raw sensuality of Salome and her dancing. This dance is the climax of all that has gone before. The execution of Iaokanann is anticlimactic; his head is presented to the reader in the flattest and simplest of terms. Absent are the lavish descriptions and listings, absent the lyric sensuality of Salome's dance. Iaokanann, deprived of his voice, has given way to a story yet to be told, that of the Messiah. The last glimpse of him is of his head, reduced to an object remarkable mainly for its weight, being carried toward Galilee. Flaubert does not mention Herodias again after the Baptist's death is assured; her place in the stylistic considerations of the story, as in thematic development, lies in descriptions of excess. There is no room for her in the cool and understated phrases that end the narration.

It is interesting to note that Flaubert has divided his action into three main parts and that he stays within the limits of the three classical unities of French tragedy: time (within the space of twenty-four hours), place (all action is in or about the fortress), and action (the story is devoted to the development of one narrative line, and it does not deviate from it.) Within these strict formal limitations, the author produces a story of remarkable power.

Anne W. Sienkewicz

THE HEROES IN THE DARK HOUSE

Author: Benedict Kiely (1919-   )
Type of plot: Story-within-a-story framed by ancient Irish bardic tradition
Time of plot: 1944
Locale: Northern Ireland
First published: 1963

Principal characters:
ARTHUR BRODERICK, an elderly folktale collector and
    storyteller
A YOUNG SCHOLAR, unnamed, interested in Broderick's tales
PATRICK, a village public house keeper
AMERICAN SOLDIERS, stationed briefly in Northern Ireland

The Story

Benedict Kiely's short story "The Heroes in the Dark House" is both a story of the sudden arrival and disappearance of modern-day heroes and the story of the narrator's visit with a young admirer who would hear one of his best Irish tales. Its dramatic impact comes from the juxtaposition of the exploits of ancient heroes such as Shawn of Kinsale with those of ordinary American G.I.'s stationed for a time in a Northern Irish village.

The story begins with Arthur Broderick, a collector of stories dealing with heroes, ending his tale about the American soldiers. The third-person narrator of the story indicates that Broderick has enthralled his young listener with an account of how dashing, even gallant Americans forever transformed the life of his village, then were gone to fight in France without any good-byes. Like true heroes, they went into the realm of myth and left behind no physical trace of their visitation. A bulldozer smashed everything they cast off, from bicycles to bayonets.

Most of the tales which Broderick collects from old people with long memories deal with events set in pre-Christian Ireland, but he insists to his scholar-visitor that the story of the American soldiers is a genuine folktale in its own right.

The "dark house" of the title is Broderick's old dwelling, which is both reminiscent of the smoke-filled castles of ancient Irish warriors and a reminder of the rebellion of 1798, when the house was used as a gathering place for conspirators against the Crown. Broderick makes much of the fact that the handsome oak table in front of the scholar was fashioned from a bellows in a smithy which was destroyed by British redcoats, who feared that it would be used to fashion the deadly Irish rebels' pikes. His mentioning the "men of '98" reemphasizes the heroic motif introduced when he spoke of the deeds of Shawn of Kinsale, who battled seven mile-high crags and seven miles of angry sea to gain the hand of his love.

The presence of departed heroes, the narrator notes, hangs about Broderick's house like smoke. Smoke and darkness are used throughout the story to establish the continuity of past and present.

After letting the reader know something about Broderick's house, the narrator then discusses some of the sources of his tales, people such as Peader Haughey of Creggan Cross, a wizened man recalling the struggles of the King of Antua and the tyranny of the giant of Reibhlean, and an eighty-year-old woman named Maire John who remembers the tale of the three princesses and a wishing chair.

The narrator emphasizes that such tales grow spontaneously in Ireland. Whenever a magical event occurs, it is transformed into a folk story by someone and thereafter is polished and reworked by tellers down the ages.

Next, the narrator is taken on a walk with Broderick during which he enters into the recent past and sees soldiers waving as they casually pass by and the dust clouds announce their passing. They stand out against the life of the village as the heroes of the past would have done; they are larger-than-life figures invigorating the world with their youth and vitality.

Patrick the pub keeper, a local trickster and character, cannot understand the Americans' lack of decorum and discipline, nor can he figure out why one large Texan would stoop so low as to assist a local prostitute struggling with a milk pail. Broderick counters that perhaps what every Irishwoman needs is a bit of chivalry.

A few days later, the shouting, friendly, gallant men are gone off to battle in Normandy to encounter the mighty and terrible weapons of Adolf Hitler's German army and air force. Broderick lets his listener know that the tests the American soldiers would face in Normandy would be as terrible as those faced by heroes of ancient times. Instead of mountains of fire, they would have to contend with mortars, rockets, and grenades. The story ends as it began: with an empty barracks and a quiet village.

Themes and Meanings

One of the central themes of "The Heroes in the Dark House" is that heroes are found whenever there is a monstrous evil in the world which must be overcome. The hero's characteristics remain unchanged throughout the ages. Cheerfulness despite the threat of injury and death, a compelling love for others which allows one to fight for their well-being, a bold resolution to act: These traits always have been those of the hero. The heroes of the story, for all their collective importance, are not given individual identities, a fact which points to another trait of the hero: Often he is not a three-dimensional personality, but rather a kind of ennobled Everyman, one to whom everyone can relate.

A second theme is that history is cyclic, and because it is, tyranny, though it takes many forms, is a recurring phenomenon in human affairs which demands either total submission to it or total defiance of it.

The heroes conjured forth in Broderick's dark house are giant-slayers, witch-destroyers, fighters against tyrannical kings, and the antagonists of evil, monstrous regimes. Because of them, civilization survives. Certainly, all about them is a magical, supernatural quality that comes from their ability to suspend their fear of death and fight for liberty.

If tyranny is cyclic and the nations of the world never see the end of it, so, too, hope is never-ending. At every challenge to civilization, heroes will come forth, often from the most unexpected quarters.

Style and Technique

By using the story-within-a-story technique to create a certain distance between the author/narrator and Arthur Broderick, teller of tales, Benedict Kiely expands upon the historic and mythic meaning of Broderick's dark house and Broderick's resemblance to a bard and a wizard, while allowing the old man to tell a spellbinding story. Thus, Broderick becomes as important a figure as the subjects of his account, and the reader discovers how significant is the local storyteller's contribution to his culture. By recording the great tales in written form, he assures their continued life.

In a large sense, then, this is a story not only about American soldiers in Ulster province but also about the storyteller's art. By extension, it is about the soul of Ireland, for storytellers have been fashioning a bold enchanted Ireland from stories for centuries. To Kiely, the Brodericks of Ireland weave together the past and the present into one remarkable tapestry, the very chronicle of everything heroic and sublime.

John D. Raymer

THE HIGGLER

Author: A. E. Coppard (1878-1957)
Type of plot: Realism
Time of plot: Shortly after World War I
Locale: Rural England
First published: 1924

> *Principal characters:*
> HARVEY WITLOW, the main character, an attractive young
>   higgler
> ELIZABETH SADGROVE, a prosperous widow
> MARY SADGROVE, her daughter

The Story

As the story opens, Harvey Witlow, the higgler, is driving his cart along a road on a remote moor. (A higgler is an itinerant dealer who buys poultry and dairy products from farms and supplies them with small items from the shops in town.) An attractive young man, Harvey is described as "shrewd . . . hard but not cold, crafty but not at all unkind." Harvey has recently been discharged from the army and is meeting with little success in his business. His financial situation is getting worse, but it is generally expected in his village that he will marry Sophy Dawson, the daughter of a gamekeeper. Although they are not formally engaged, Sophy clearly expects the marriage to take place soon.

Just when he is wishing that his affairs will "take a turn," he comes to the neatly maintained and obviously prosperous farm owned by Elizabeth Sadgrove. After some brief negotiations with Mrs. Sadgrove, he buys fifteen score eggs and some pullets from her. It is evident that the hoped-for turn for the better has occurred. Mrs. Sadgrove, a widow, also has a beautiful red-haired daughter named Mary, who has "the hands of a lady." Although Mary says almost nothing to the higgler, she appears to be impressed by him. For his part, Harvey momentarily forgets all—"his errand, her mother . . . Sophy"—at the sight of Mary.

Harvey begins to call regularly at Mrs. Sadgrove's farm, and his business flourishes. He discovers that Mrs. Sadgrove, who has the reputation of driving a hard bargain, is quite well-to-do. Mary has attended a "seminary for gentlefolks' females," and her superior education seems to have spoiled her for the work for a farm. When, for example, she goes out, heavily veiled, to collect a swarm of bees into a hive, her movements are tentative and ineffectual; Harvey, without protective clothing, comes to her rescue and confidently collects the swarm. Harvey is attracted to Mary, but he is puzzled by her quietness in his presence. They spend an entire day in the orchard, where

Harvey is picking cherries and Mary is walking back and forth with a clapper to frighten away the birds, but she never speaks to him. On the occasions when Harvey takes tea with the Sadgroves, her responses to his conversational overtures are brief and confused. Harvey wonders if there is anything wrong with her.

Harvey's doubts are increased when Mrs. Sadgrove invites him to have Sunday dinner with them. He dresses gallantly, putting a pink rose, which he plans to give to Mary, in his buttonhole. During dinner, he talks volubly about his war experiences, but Mary says almost nothing. After the meal, Mary withdraws and Mrs. Sadgrove invites Harvey to take a walk in the meadow. To his consternation, she asks if he has a sweetheart and then pointedly says that she wants to see Mary married before she dies. She estimates the worth of her farm at three thousand pounds and reveals that Mary will inherit five hundred pounds of her own when she is twenty-five. She describes Mary as healthy, quiet, and sensible, but declares that she has "a strong will of her own, though you might not think it or believe it." Although she does not press him for an immediate answer, she says that she is not a "long-living woman." Astonished by Mrs. Sadgrove's businesslike proposal, Harvey remembers as he drives away with the rose still in his buttonhole that he did not ask if Mary were willing to marry him.

When Harvey tells his mother, who also has the reputation of shrewdness, about Mrs. Sadgrove's proposition, Mrs. Witlow is surprised at her son's hesitation but asks if there is anything wrong with Mary. Harvey maintains that there is no problem with Mary, but he assumes that there must be a catch somewhere. On his subsequent visits to the farm, Mary does not even look at him; for his part, Harvey is now so inhibited in her presence that he can say nothing to her. He is powerfully attracted to Mary, but his "native cunning" persuades him that she is unaware of her mother's "queer project." Convinced that there is a trick somewhere, he makes up his mind to marry Sophy and stops calling at the Sadgrove farm altogether.

Harvey and Sophy's wedding is a rather strange affair, partly because Sophy's grandmother, who has come to the wedding with her aged third husband, takes this occasion to reveal that she was begotten by a wealthy gentleman who was having an affair with her mother. The couple cannot afford a honeymoon, but move in with Mrs. Witlow. Within four or five months after his marriage, Harvey's affairs have again declined. Sophy and his mother quarrel continually; Sophy wants a home of her own, but Harvey cannot afford to buy a separate cottage for his mother. Without the rich produce of the Sadgrove farm, his higgling business declines drastically. His horse has died, and he is compelled to "hire at fabulous cost a decrepit nag that ate like a good one." He needs desperately to borrow money but knows no one who can lend him any.

Finally, his desperation impels him to call again at the Sadgrove farm, hoping that Mrs. Sadgrove will make him a loan. When he arrives at the farm just at evening on a wildly windy day, Mary meets him at the door. She tells him that her mother died the previous night. The doctor that she sent for has not arrived, and Mary has been attempting all day to wash her mother's body and dress it for burial, a task that is now almost impossible because of rigor mortis. Harvey takes over and, although he has to tie one stiffened arm in place, succeeds in preparing Mrs. Sadgrove' body for burial. Harvey then inquires in a kindly way about Mary's circumstances. She has no other relatives, but she has been left well-off financially. She plans to get a working bailiff to look after her farm. Rather impetuously, Harvey asks if Mary knew that her mother had once asked him to marry her and wonders why she did. Mary reveals that her mother had actually opposed the marriage, but had made the request only because Mary had insisted that she do so since, as Mary says, "I was fond of you—then."

As Harvey drives away in the wind and darkness, his thoughts are "strange and bitter" as he realizes that he has thrown away both love and a fortune. He recollects that he has even forgotten to ask about the loan. He decides that he must give up higgling and take on some other job; a job as a working bailiff, he concludes, would suit him. Yet, he recalls, there is still Sophy.

Themes and Meanings

This story is a variation on the familiar motif of the trickster tricked, a plot pattern that can be traced back to dozens of folktales, in which a person with a reputation for shrewd bargaining outsmarts himself and loses everything. A successful higgler must be able to recognize a bargain and must be willing to extract advantageous terms from the person with whom he higgles. (Mrs. Witlow, also a higgler, is "perhaps more enlightened" than Harvey; it is "almost a misfortune to get into her clutches.") Yet Harvey, who is presented with the opportunity of marrying a beautiful, well-educated girl who not only cares about him but also is heir to a prosperous farm and a cash legacy, misses the opportunity because he suspects that there is a trick where there really is none. It is small wonder that he is not successful as a higgler except when he can draw on the resources of the Sadgrove farm.

As the trickster-tricked motif is usually developed, the reader delights to see the trickster outsmarted, or, better yet, outsmart himself by being too shrewd. In this story, however, the reader's sympathies lie with Harvey, who is clearly a decent young man, but one who misses a great bargain by suspecting a catch where there is none.

Style and Technique

In the foreword to the American edition of *The Collected Tales of A. E. Coppard* (1948), Coppard states that one of the two principles of storytelling is "that unity, verisimilitude, and completeness of contour are best obtained by plotting your story through the mind or consciousness of only one of your characters." Clearly, for the particular effect of this story, it is essential that the point of view be handled in such a way that the events are seen through the mind of Harvey. For one thing, plotting the story through Harvey's mind tends to persuade the reader to sympathize with him, since his are the only thoughts revealed to the reader. It is equally important that neither Harvey nor the reader know what Mrs. Sadgrove and Mary are thinking. Since Coppard carefully establishes the fact that Mrs. Sadgrove has a reputation for driving a hard bargain and since Mary's reserve seems almost pathological, the reader is likely to agree with Harvey that there is a catch somewhere in Mrs. Sadgrove's offer. The fact that Mrs. Witlow favors the marriage to Mary only contributes to the reader's suspicions, because Mrs. Witlow herself seems excessively hard and materialistic. Mary's revelation that she was fond of Harvey—then—is almost as much of a surprise to the reader as to Harvey, but like all good "surprise" endings, it has been carefully prepared for. The reader can only admire Coppard's skill in misdirection.

Erwin Hester

HILLS LIKE WHITE ELEPHANTS

Author: Ernest Hemingway (1899-1961)
Type of plot: Ironic vignette
Time of plot: c. 1920
Locale: A train station in rural Spain
First published: 1927

> *Principal characters:*
> AN UNNAMED MAN, an American
> JIG, his young female companion and lover, perhaps his wife

The Story

"Hills Like White Elephants" is an uneventful story; there is very little action, and little is said. Yet as with much of Hemingway's fiction, it is not so much what does happen or is said as what does not happen or is left unsaid that is important.

An unnamed American man and a young woman, Jig, are waiting for the express train from Barcelona; they are on the terrace of a small station-bar and seem to be on their way to Madrid. The story consists entirely of a seemingly objective documentation of their words and actions during their forty-minute wait for the train. The surface events are very simple. The woman looks at the hills across the valley of the Ebro, suggests that they order a drink, tries to engage the man in light conversation, responds briefly and unhappily to his assertion that an operation which she is to have is "really not anything . . . it's all perfectly natural"; she then stands up, walks to the end of the station, looks at the hills again, speaks angrily, sits back down, demands that he "stop talking," drinks in silence, and finally assures him that she feels "fine." The only actions of the man not accounted for in this detailing of the woman's movements occur after she asks him to "stop talking" and before she asserts that she is "fine." During that brief period, he carries their bags "around the station to the other tracks" and stops to drink an anisette at the bar alone.

Clearly, little happens and not much is said, but just beneath the surface of these spare and dull events, a quiet but crucial struggle between these two characters has been resolved. The future course of their relationship appears to have been charted in these moments, and the fate of their unborn child determined. Their very first words not only reveal tension between these two but also suggest that there are perhaps fundamental differences between them. The woman is interested in the world around her, concerned with being friendly, vital, and imaginative; the man, on the other hand, is self-involved, phlegmatic, and literal.

"They look like white elephants," she said.
"I've never seen one," the man drank his beer.
"No, you wouldn't have."
"I might have," the man said.

What is critical in this story, as in Hemingway's fiction generally, is the ironic gap between appearance and reality. The seemingly petty conversation here about hills and drinks and an unspecified operation is in actuality an unarticulated but decisive struggle over whether they continue to live the sterile, self-indulgent, decadent life preferred by the man or elect to have the child which Jig is carrying and settle down to a conventional but, in Jig's view, rewarding, fruitful, and peaceful life.

In spite of his transparent assertions to the contrary ("I don't want you to do it if you don't really want to"), it is clear that the man wants Jig to have an abortion so that they can be "just like we were before." Their life together up to this point seems to have been composed primarily of travel and aimless self-gratification: "That's all we do, isn't it—look at things and try new drinks?" "I guess so." The woman apparently yields to his unacknowledged insistence that she get an abortion; in order to do so, however, she must give up her self-respect and her dreams of a fruitful life: "I'll do it. Because I don't care about me." She does not seem to have the strength to resist his demands, but she is aware of the significance of her capitulation. She looks at the beauty, the life, the bounty across the tracks—fields of grain, trees, the river, mountains. "'We could have all this,' she said. 'And we could have everything and everyday we make it more impossible.'" The abortion is not merely a "perfectly natural" or "simple operation" to her; it is a symbolic act as well, which will cut her off irrevocably from what is good and alive in the world: "It isn't ours any more." The man takes exception to her powerfully negative vision of their situation, but she has heard enough: "Would you please please please please please please please stop talking?" He desists, moves their bags, wonders, while he drinks his anisette, why she cannot act "reasonably" like other people, and then returns to her as if nothing had happened. Perhaps Jig's perception that their lives are sterile and that the man does not truly love, or know, or care for her will enable her to leave him and struggle alone to live a meaningful life; yet Hemingway gives the reader no solid reason to believe that she will do so. The story ends with an apparent lie: "There's nothing wrong with me. I feel fine." Presumably they board the train; she has the abortion; and their relationship continues its downward drift into emptiness and hypocrisy.

Themes and Meanings

"Hills Like White Elephants" calls to mind the "A Game of Chess" section of T. S. Eliot's *The Waste Land* (1922); like Eliot's masterpiece, Hemingway's story deals with the sterility and vacuity of the modern world. The boredom of the man and the desperation of the girl reveal the emptiness of the postwar generation and the crucial necessity of taking responsibility for the quality of one's own life. Both Eliot's poetry and Hemingway's fiction are filled with a sense of missed opportunities and failed love, of a fullness of life lost and never to be regained: "Once they take it away, you never get it back." As in Eliot's poem, the landscape takes on powerful symbolic dimensions here. On the side of the tracks, where the couple is waiting, the country is "brown and dry"; "on the other side, were fields of grain and trees . . . the river . . . mountains." The girl calls attention to the symbolic value of the setting and indicates that in choosing to have an abortion and to continue to drift through life they are choosing emotional and spiritual desiccation.

Hemingway's characters seem to live in a world without a God, without traditions or clear and established values; they are, in Jean-Paul Satre's words, "condemned to be free" and consequently are responsible for their own meaning. The man here is unequal to the challenge; he is a bored and listless fragment of a human being. He resolutely refuses to speak truthfully, to acknowledge his own hypocrisy. His unwillingness to be honest—and, by extension, modern man's refusal to live honestly—is a consistent motif of this sketch. The girl is, at least, profoundly distressed by the aimless and sterile nature of their existence and does not give in to vacuity without a struggle.

One particularly interesting aspect of Hemingway's uncompromising dissection of the poverty of the modern world in this story is the juxtaposition of reason and emotion or imagination. The man is perfectly reasonable. He lives in a senseless and violent world; he has the financial resources to do as he pleases; he reasonably concludes that he should enjoy his life, not encumber himself with unnecessary conflicts or responsibilities, certainly not trouble himself with relationships which are demanding or in the least unpleasant. He is quite literal-minded, quite pragmatic, quite unemotional: an admirable fellow by modern patriarchal standards. The woman, on the other hand, is unreasonable enough to imagine that hills look like white elephants and that there might be some virtue to having a child who would surely be like a "white elephant," a sacred beast in some cultures, but in Europe and America something which is only apparently valuable and is in actuality more trouble than it is worth. Reason here is associated with dissimulation, death, nonmeaning; emotion with life, imagination, growth. Hemingway suggests that reason (the God of modern man) is an insufficient standard by which to live. The reasonable male here is a cipher, a man of straw who declines to acknowledge the necessity of making his every moment intense, honest, full.

Another interesting facet of this story in the context of Hemingway's fiction is the clear superiority of the woman to the man. Hemingway is not particularly kind to women generally, certainly not to women who want to have children. Usually such women are interested in asserting their sexual power over men and in depriving men of their freedom and their maleness. This girl may prove to be angry and frustrated enough to evolve into a castrating harridan; in this story, however, she is a tragic figure seemingly driven into a barren and empty existence by her love for this man.

Hemingway's brief and seemingly objective story is a powerful condemnation of the aimlessness, hypocrisy, and moral and spiritual poverty of the modern world.

Style and Technique

The impassive, documentary style of "Hills Like White Elephants" is typical of much of Hemingway's fiction. It manifests the care, restraint, intensity, and control, the economy and precision which characterize his best prose. The author seems to be indifferent both to the characters and to the reader; he pretends to be merely an objective observer content to report without comment the words and actions of these two people. He has virtually no access to their thoughts and does not even interpret the emotional quality of their words or movements by using adverbs; he simply records. Hemingway believed in a precise, naturalistic rendering of the surface; he insisted on presenting things truly.

As was indicated earlier, Hemingway's ironic technique plays an important role in this story. The very use of a clear and economical style to reveal a relationship which is troubled and complex is ironic. The story seems to be void of artifice and emotion yet is carefully fashioned and powerfully felt. The dispassionate style appears to be absolutely appropriate to the cold, sophisticated, literal-minded, modern sensibility of the protagonist, yet in fact the man is revealed to be disingenuous and destructive. The deeper levels of this story are disclosed by examining not only what is implied through the irony but also what is indicated by symbolism and repetition.

The symbolism has already been remarked, and only one other observation seems necessary here. It is important to note that anything which can be said to operate symbolically does so without violating the realism of the story in any way. Hemingway uses banal repetition quite effectively here. The insincerity of the man is apparent in his dependence on empty phrases: "it's perfectly simple"; "if you don't want to you don't have to." Both the man's duplicity and the girl's perceptiveness, anger, and despair are evident in the way in which she echoes his transparent lies: "And afterward they were all so happy. . . . I don't care about me. . . . Yes, you know it's perfectly simple."

In terms of style and technique, "Hills Like White Elephants" is a quintessential early Hemingway story. The use of the language of speech as the basis for the story, the insistence on presentation rather than commentary, the condensation, and the intensity are all basic elements of his theory of fiction.

Hal Holladay

HIS SON, IN HIS ARMS, IN LIGHT, ALOFT

Author: Harold Brodkey (1930-   )
Type of plot: Psychological realism
Time of plot: c. 1975
Locale: An unspecified Midwestern American city
First published: 1975

Principal characters:
THE NARRATOR
THE NARRATOR'S FATHER
THE NARRATOR'S MOTHER
THE NARRATOR'S SISTER

The Story

This story has no plot in the conventional sense; its narrator does not tell a tale with sequential events. Rather, he recalls from his childhood various sensations, emotions, and incidents arising from his relationship at that time with his father. The story is not solely about what he felt as a child; it is, more important, also a presentation of the sensations and emotions that his recollections arouse in him as he dredges them up from the past. The story is, then, in part a study of an emotional state in a man who is recalling and interpreting emotional states experienced in his childhood.

The narrator is an adult of unspecified age; the events that he describes happened when he was quite young, probably about six or seven. Among a far more extensive exploration of psychological states, his narrative includes several incidents from his childhood. Often, he recalls, he would be dispatched by his mother to cheer up his father, an exceedingly moody man. Once, when the narrator, as a young boy, was upset, his father came out onto the porch of the family home to reassure him. On another occasion, the father came home with several thousand dollars in bank notes and was chastised by his wife, whom he accused of being a spoilsport. He took his son and daughter outside, but when he was confronted with what he perceived as materialism in his daughter, he returned to the house to blame his wife for teaching that vice to her daughter.

These keys to the kind of family life that the narrator had are not told sequentially and are not even a framework on which the psychological exploration is based, but they do provide the backdrop for an investigation of more shifting, elusive emotions. That exploration is halting, detailed, and very introspective. While the few details of the domestic incidents are remembered relatively clearly and described briefly, the narrator's recollection of the emotions surrounding them is expressed less decisively; each element of the emotions is inspected, each conclusion reinspected and refined.

The narrator's descriptions and development of his recollections depend only in part on what actually occurred in his childhood. More important is what he can now make of what happened: "Some memories huddle in a grainy light. What it is is a number of similar events bunching themselves, superimposing themselves, to make a false memory, a collage, a mental artifact." The narrator is aware that he may well be reinventing, as in fiction—he likens what he is doing to the creation of fiction.

The most important category of "mental artifact" constructed by the narrator consists of several instances of being lifted into the air by his father. This is the central motif of the story, and the most emotionally charged recollection. In recalling such instances of fatherly affection or protection, the narrator experiences, as the title suggests, an exultant emotional state, a mixture of the sublime and the awestruck.

The first such instance is at the beginning of the story. The narrator remembers his father chasing him; he describes it as if it were happening at the moment he recalls it. In a sense, it is: He is compelled to remember and interpret the influence that his father has had on him, and this makes him feel it again now. At the story's opening, he is being chased by his father; he recalls all the childlike emotions that the event aroused in him. His father is enormous; his hands are giant; even his breath, the narrator recalls, seemed overwhelming: He feels "the huge ramming increment of his breath as he draws near."

Being lifted by his father has, each time it happens, the effect of profoundly moving the boy emotionally. Sometimes he is liberated or deeply reassured; each time he is awestruck and feels physically or emotionally helpless in the face of his father's physical force and force of personality. On the first occasion, the boy has been running from his father, who snatches him up and carries him home. Lifted aloft in his father's arms, the boy senses a oneness with his father: "I feel myself attached by my heated-by-running dampness to him: we are attached, there are binding oval stains of warmth." As the narrator recalls the event, details of the setting come to him, enriching his recollections; he sees—remembers—a path, a bed of flowers, and other very distinct features of his childhood world.

As memories come to him, he attributes various characteristics to his father: He has a distinct smell, which the narrator imagines changed to indicate his mood. His mood changes often and erratically. Even when in a dark mood, he adopts easily a protective, paternal demeanor if he sees that his son is suffering too. He is strong where the boy is defenseless. He is a sentimentalist, and when his sentimentality is engaged, he is profligate; the narrator explains that on one occasion, his father gave a car to a financially troubled man. The narrator also suggests the nature of the father-son relationship. It was a mutually dependent one, the son considering the father massively powerful, the father turning to the son for refuge from the animosity he feels toward his wife and daughter, and toward life itself.

Another instance of being lifted high in his father's arms, the narrator recalls, came after the father had tried to console the son, who had been overwhelmed by a characteristic, fretful insecurity. Again the son experiences a liberating sensation, heightened on this occasion by his being placed on top of a stone wall that overlooks a bluff and that he is usually forbidden to climb. The experience engages all the boy's senses: Wind flicks in his face; the view is so panoramic that he imagines it is audible, that he can hear it buzzing. All of his doubts and fears evaporate, and he senses a mixture of pleasure and "oblivion."

Themes and Meanings

The unifying characteristic of this highly idiosyncratic story is the way that it relates the nature of memory to particular memories involving a particular person. At the beginning of the story, the narrator says that he is being chased: The counterpart to his urgency as a child as he fled his father is the urgency that he feels as an adult to recall what his relationship with his father was, and in this way to make that relationship real again.

The narrator's attention returns repeatedly to the power of his father: "He kneeled—a mountain of shirt-front and trousers." That he feels unworthy of his father's doting attention, and at times even feels that he is blackmailing his father, is explained by his father's erratic personality, by his "disorderly massiveness." Just as the narrator describes his urgency to recall the past, he recalls the feelings of urgency that his father provoked in him. What he felt was not a sense of physical danger, although his father clearly was a physically overwhelming presence for the young boy; rather, he felt the danger of being bereft of the protection and identity that a father provides: "I could not live without the pride and belonging-to-himness of being that man's consolation." The father is recalled as far more than a mere life-sustaining force. He was able to transport his son into a heightened state: "I understood that he was proffering me oblivion plus pleasure."

Brodkey accords these recollections a lofty status. At the end of the story, that narrator says that as his father lifts him up in the early morning light, the sights and sensations that make their mark on his senses and mind have "the aliveness of myth." Under the influence of his father's hoisting him up in his arms, he experiences a transcendence expressed through images of bright, hot, alien light, one which is "not really friendly, yet reassuring." There was a "luminousness all around us." Such imagery of light is central to the story. Light is the essence of seeing and recollecting, of making the past actual: "I can, if I concentrate, whiten the light—or yellow-whiten it, actually—and when the graininess goes, it is suddenly one afternoon."

Although it is the father who triggers and sustains the narrator's sensation, the narrator certainly depicts his father as far from divine or even humanly ideal. He attributes to him an almost supernatural stature, but he also recalls that his father was very erratic in his behavior. At the end of the story, his face bathed in early morning sunlight, the father gains, not an unadulterated, divine glory, but "an accidental glory."

Style and Technique

Virtually all of Brodkey's writing involves the extremely involved investigation of memories of his own life. Memories are excavated from the past with a precision and sensitivity that is indulged and then indulged further. In this story, as elsewhere, his style suggests a process of profound, persistent reflection and constant refinement of memory.

In order to suggest, for example, that the past occurrences, when recalled by the narrator, produce in him elaborate emotional responses, Brodkey moves repeatedly from past to present tense, blurring the distinction between what happened in the past and what happens as the narrator explores his love for his father.

Brodkey's highly idiosyncratic, fragmented style expresses the way in which the act of remembering intensifies the past for the narrator and transports him to euphoria. Brodkey prevents this euphoria from appearing merely indulgent, nostalgic, facile, or incredible by underpinning it with more mundane elements. For example, at the end of the story, in a skillful touch of bathos, he writes that the luminousness that surrounds the narrator and his father has an effect like that of wearing a simple woolen cap—it is "very dimly sweaty; and it grew, it spread: this light turned into a knitted cap of light, fuzzy, warm, woven, itchy."

Peter Monaghan

THE HITCHHIKING GAME

Author: Milan Kundera (1929-   )
Type of plot: Psychological realism
Time of plot: The 1960's
Locale: Czechoslovakia
First published: "Falešný autostop," 1969 (English translation, 1974)

> *Principal characters:*
> A YOUNG MAN, who is on a vacation
> A YOUNG WOMAN, also on a vacation

The Story

Having been lovers for a year, a girl and a man embark on a two-week vacation, but by the end of the first day they discover more about themselves than most couples discover in a lifetime. The mechanism of discovery is the hitchhiking game, a game in which role-playing takes on a dangerous and irreversible intensity.

The "girl" is twenty-two, shy, jealous, uncomfortable with her body, and embarrassed by her need to use the bathroom. Yet she trusts her lover "wholly," because "he never separated her body from her soul." When she pretends to be a hitchhiker whom her lover picks up, she leaves behind her shy, embarrassed self, and takes on a role "out of trashy literature." She becomes a seductress and slips into "this silly, romantic part with an ease that astonished her and held her spellbound."

The twenty-eight-year-old man is not only older but also considerably more worldly than the girl. A former playboy who believes that he knows "everything that a man could know about women," this man admires his current lover for what his previous lovers have lacked: purity. He is, therefore, surprised and angry when the girl assumes her new role; he is furious with her for "refusing to be herself when that was what he wanted." His anger, in turn, makes him adopt the role of "a heartless tough guy," and he becomes willfull, sarcastic, and mean. In an act of defiance directed at both his Communistic country and his girl, he deviates from their original travel route and heads for an unfamiliar city, an action which makes him feel like "a free man."

Once in Nove Zamky, the girl continues her role-playing, and her lover becomes increasingly irritated at "how *well able* the girl was to become the lascivious miss." Their conversation becomes more brazen; she even exclaims that she has to "piss," a word the girl would have been too embarrassed to use at the beginning of the story. She is pleased with how astounded her lover is at her new vocabulary, and on the way to the bathroom, she notices how the other men in the hotel look at her. No longer self-conscious about her body, she thrusts out her breasts and sways her hips. She is even accosted as a prostitute, but she does not mind.

This freedom, however, has its price. The game, after all, is a "trap"; the more involved the girl becomes in the game, "the more obediently she would have to play it." When her lover decides that they will act out the roles of customer and prostitute, she plays along. In the hotel room, when her lover actually humiliates her by forcing her to strip and take obscene poses, she obliges, though she is frightened and confused. She does not realize that, for the man, the game has "merged with life," and that he "simply hated the woman standing in front of him." It is not until after their passionate but emotionless lovemaking that the game ends. In the aftermath of the game, the girl begins to sob, "I am me, I am me," and though he does not understand her plea and is reluctant to respond to it, the man eventually does console her.

Themes and Meanings

Who is the true person, the real "me"? When, at the end of the story, the girl hysterically asserts, "I am me, I am me, I am me," she asserts that she is both naughty and nice, both whore and madonna, capable of, as her lover discovers, "everything." Her lover, however, cannot accept this to be his girl. He wants her to remain a "nice" girl, a pure girl, a girl who fulfills an unambiguous role. For the most part, she plays her role beautifully; she is shy, pure, and frequently embarrassed by her body. She does not question this role, for it is the one that Western society expects most of its women to play; as soon as she has an opportunity to act other than shy and pure, however, she does so with great zeal. In her new role, the girl becomes sexually assertive and positively aware of her body; she becomes a powerful female. Her lover, however, is threatened by her, and in order to maintain his male dominance, he must frighten and humiliate her.

The most telling moment in the story regarding the male need to dominate a threatening female is the scene in the hotel room when the man makes the girl get up on a table. This is an ironic comment on the image of woman on a pedestal. Before she climbs on the table—which is not only the proverbial pedestal but also the go-go dancer's platform, the beauty contestant's runway, the bride-to-be's church aisle—the girl stops "playing the game." Stripped naked before her lover, she believes nothing else remains of herself to be exposed. She is "now herself." Yet a provocative and powerfully naked woman is not what the man wants; therefore, he longs to "treat her like a whore." He needs to treat her this way, and manipulates her through various postures, because this is the only way he can control and objectify her. Up on the wobbly table, squatting and wiggling, she is an object, something which has been purchased and is soon to be used.

This story presents other ironies: the subtle but important difference between worship and love; the need, especially for women, to romanticize their physical passions; the uncomfortable fact that personal growth is always attended by pain; and, the recognition of how limiting and debilitating fixed gender roles are for both sexes.

Kundera, however, does not want the reader to dismiss roles altogether as negative and unnecessary. He strongly suggests that only through such role-playing does the young woman discover how to assert her true self. Similarly, the man's closing gesture of compassion, albeit weak, suggests that he has learned to look behind a given role and to accept the ambiguity of character which is inherent in all human beings, male and female.

Style and Technique

Kundera's story is gamelike in a fundamental way: Two players take turns until the game is over. Since the story is divided into twelve sections, each player has six turns. Each section identifies and focuses on its particular player. Like any good omniscient narrator, Kundera's does not play favorites: The sections are equally divided between the male and female points of view. The reader gets to know the characters, both their past and present selves, in equal doses.

Since the story zigzags back and forth between the man and the woman, the reader experiences a strange kind of suspense as one role dissolves and another is shaped. The reader is also asked to identify alternately with first the male and then the female, a request that, perforce, requires of the reader a rapid and frequent modulation of roles. The more involved the reader becomes in the story, the closer he or she comes to being one of the players. Kundera seems to suggest that reading itself, then, is a game, a game in which all readers knowingly or unknowingly participate.

Sylvia G. O'Sullivan

HODEL

Author: Sholom Aleichem (Sholom Rabinowitz, 1859-1916)
Type of plot: Comic monologue
Time of plot: The late 1800's
Locale: Anatevka, a fictitious village in Russia, and environs
First published: 1894 (English translation, 1949)

> *Principal characters:*
> SHOLOM ALEICHEM, the listener-recorder and primary
>   narrator, an author
> TEVYE THE MILKMAN, the story's secondary narrator
> HODEL, Tevye's second eldest daughter
> PERTSCHIK (known as FEFEREL), Hodel's teacher and
>   husband, a revolutionary-minded socialist student
> GOLDE, Tevye's wife

The Story

After some time of not meeting him, Tevye the Milkman meets Sholom Aleichem, the story's primary narrator as well as its author, and begins to tell of the troubles which have come upon him (turning his hair gray) because of his gullibility, fatalism, and obedience to God, which make him an easy target for misfortune.

His latest trouble, as most always, involves marrying off his daughters by means of the traditional arrangements. Hodel, like many young people of her age, is thirsty for an education and has learned to read both Yiddish and Russian from a young university student, Pertschik (known as Feferel). Hodel met Feferel because of a chance happening in which her father played a part. One day, on his way home from delivering his dairy goods to the nearby summer vacation spot for the well-to-do of Boiberik (Aleichem's fictional name for the town of Boira), Tevye sees Feferel and offers the young man a ride.

Tevye's conversation with the sharp-tongued youth (as they ride together) reveals the latter's socialistic sentiments; the son of a local cigarette maker, Feferel expresses contempt for his own class for not sharing their possessions with the poor. Impressed by the lad's talkativeness, Tevye invites him for dinner, which henceforth precipitates Feferel's daily return visits. In return for his meals, the young man agrees to provide Tevye's daughters (six are left now) with lessons.

The only fault which Tevye finds in Feferel is his tendency to vanish suddenly, only to return several days later venting his anger toward the wealthy classes—possessors of money, the root of all evil on earth—while extolling the simple virtues of the poor.

Along with their "philosophical" conversations, Tevye soon learns of Feferel's admiration for his daughter Hodel. On the following day, while in Boiberik, Tevye happens upon Ephraim the matchmaker, who offers him an ideal match with a man from a fine family, educated in the holy books of Judaism—and rich. Although not a spring chicken, the prospective groom's credentials intrigue Tevye sufficiently so that he agrees to bring his daughter Hodel with him on his next week's journey.

Driving home, daydreaming about becoming a wealthy and influential man through the marriage of Hodel, Tevye recognizes Feferel walking out of the woods with her. Confronting them, Tevye soon realizes that his new hopes are about to be shattered, for Feferel and Hodel have become engaged without going through the traditional procedures of matchmaking, contract, or parental blessing. Tevye, accustomed by now to the modern notion of love, still cannot accept the young couple's decision to marry outside the traditional customs. Furthermore, Feferel's intention to leave immediately after the wedding, and leave Hodel behind, confounds Tevye. Adding to his consternation, Hodel and Feferel declare their plans to dispense with the prematrimonial customs; they want only a modest ceremony. That is how things happen, while Tevye placates his wife Golde with lies about Feferel's rich inheritance. After the wedding, while driving the young couple to the railroad station to see Feferel off, Tevye is still uncertain about Feferel's reasons for leaving; Hodel tells her father that he would not understand even if she were to tell him.

Some months later—after Tevye's worries bring him closer to Hodel's plight—news arrives for Hodel of Feferel's arrest. Thereupon she confides to Tevye her decision to follow Feferel to his distant place of exile, perhaps never again to see her mother, father, and sisters. Tevye, whose heart grieves over the news, feigns a cheerful expression and controls his emotions, knowing that no amount of pleading or anger can sway one of his daughters once her mind is made up. He thus becomes resigned to the differences in their views and values (as different as a hen is from a duck, they agree) and reluctantly agrees to help her.

To conceal the truth from Golde, Tevye fabricates a tale about an inheritance to justify Hodel's need to pack some bedding and belongings and depart on the following morning on a long journey. While the women cry, Tevye maintains a cool, sober exterior until he and Hodel arrive at the railroad station, where Hodel breaks down, crying on her father's shoulder, and he too appears to lose his composure.

Cutting his narrative at this point, Tevye asks Sholom Aleichem's forgiveness for becoming so emotional about his daughter (whose letters continue to arrive) and asks to talk about more cheerful things, such as the recent outbreak of cholera in Odessa.

Themes and Meanings

"Hodel" is the third in a cycle of stories concerning, and narrated by, Tevye the Milkman, one of Sholom Aleichem's most famous characters. In these tales, Tevye undergoes a series of educational and tragic encounters with life. The account of Hodel, the second eldest of his seven daughters, represents only a partial loss in Tevye's values, whereas most of the subsequent episodes are marked by more tragic events, as one daughter converts, another dies, and others lead lives of misery.

The incremental fragmentation and destruction of Tevye's family evokes the biblical archetype of Job, the man of patience, suffering in faith. Although juxtaposed against the story of Job, Sholom Aleichem's Tevye also departs from the biblical analogue. Whereas both Job and Tevye appear to maintain their faith in the Creator, it is Tevye who copes better with his world by laughing his fate away and adopting a humorous stance against all that befalls him. By doing so, Tevye seems to reject the past's hold on him. The stories consist of largely tragic events related in a humorous tone, and the reader becomes witness to the hero's cyclic downfall and recovery.

This central theme of Tevye's fall and recovery is what characterizes the core of this story (and the others in the cycle). It is Tevye who is the story's main protagonist, the man who weathers the onslaught of events, revolutions, social upheavals, and personal calamities. His ability to remain standing in face of these adversities is a demonstration of the human capacity to affirm life despite all of its miseries.

Tevye's perseverance is in part attributable to his flexibility, his capacity to adapt to the changes of the times. Among these are the recognition of the notion of romantic love as a precursor to marriage and the shifting regard each generation has for material possessions, dress, and government. Thus, Tevye's ability to accept Hodel's departure is a mark of his strength.

"Hodel" is also an account of the changes in the status of the father in the Jewish family. Whereas in the past the father was invested with nearly absolute authority, Aleichem depicts in Tevye one who most readily abdicates this role not only out of a love for his family but also out of a realization that a new world is about to dawn upon him and that he must accept it and its ways in order to survive.

The very fact that Tevye has seven daughters and not a single son (in a society favoring sons over daughters) is significant: His contentment with this circumstance provides further evidence of his broadmindedness, his flexibility, his ability to live in the modern world.

Thus, the story is a call by Sholom Aleichem for understanding, compassion, and compromise. As a document—as well a work of fiction— it stands at the threshold of the process of modernization (and Westernization) of a large segment of East European Jewry.

Style and Technique

The narrative technique of this story, as in all the Tevye stories, is that of the first-person, dramatic monologue. In using this technique, Sholom Aleichem implies the existence of a certain distance, emotional and temporal, between the events recounted and the present mind-set of Tevye, narrator of these events. The effect is that of a measure of objectivity and aesthetic organization. In "Hodel," Tevye's relatively cool, unemotional, and cheerful posture is maintained until the tearful moment at the railroad station; the heightened emotionalism at this point furnishes the motive for the story's closing while underscoring the lasting emotional impact which these events have had on Tevye.

"Hodel" also demonstrates some of the devices of humor and comedy which have made the Tevye stories—regardless of their ominous message concerning the disintegration and downfall of a Jewish way of life—among the most popular works by this author.

Particularly notable are the comic effects of Tevye's narrative style. Tevye tells his story in a torrent of words interspersed with references and allusions to traditional Jewish sources, particularly the Bible, to lend credence to his views. Tevye thus imitates the manner of a Talmudic scholar's discourse, where every assertion is supported with scriptural citations. Tevye's accounts, however, do not involve study, but rather his day-to-day affairs. Comical juxtapositions are thereby established between the traditional and the modern, the lofty and the everyday, the sacred and the profane.

Furthermore, Tevye makes himself the target of the reader's laughter by his use of biblical verses out of their appropriate context. One such instance in "Hodel" occurs when Tevye compares his daughter's beauty to that of Queen Esther; clearly, Hodel's fate is not as glorious as that of the biblical heroine, but Tevye is unaware of the irony. Furthermore, the citation is slightly off in that the biblical words (in the original Hebrew, while the story was written in Yiddish), from Esther 1:11, refer to Queen Vashti and not to Esther.

The biblical narrative, wherein the beauty of Vashti is noted, also tells of her refusal to appear before her king. According to one Jewish legend, her refusal to show her face in public was because of a horn which sprouted on her forehead, making her features hideous and grotesque. Describing Hodel in the words meant for Vashti, a Gentile woman, Tevye is again the unwitting victim of Aleichem's irony.

Stephen Katz

HOME

Author: Jayne Anne Phillips (1952-   )
Type of plot: Domestic realism
Time of plot: The mid-1970's
Locale: A small town in America
First published: 1978

Principal characters:

THE NARRATOR, the protagonist, a young woman returned
   home
HER MOTHER, a local school administrator, divorced
HER FATHER, whom the narrator no longer sees
JASON, her high school boyfriend
DANIEL, one of her more recent boyfriends

The Story

The unnamed twenty-three-year-old narrator/protagonist, finding herself
"out of money" and not "in love," returns home to live temporarily with her
mother, who gets for her a tutoring job. Her mother, a divorced school administrator, leads a quiet life in a small town resembling the author's West
Virginia hometown. The mother spends evenings knitting and watching television; the closest she comes to a man is watching Walter Cronkite, television's grandfatherly news anchorman, who she fears has cancer. After a liberated life in college and later in California, the narrator finds the home
routine incredibly dull. Rather than watch television, she starts going to her
room at night to read and think. She offers her mother "a subscription to
something mildly informative: *Ms., Rolling Stone, Scientific American*." The
mother declines.

One subject which the narrator thinks about is her mother's early life,
recalled in old photographs. The mother attended college, then became a
cadet nurse, but World War II ended before she finished her nurse's training.
She came home to care for her sick mother and eventually to marry the narrator's father: "She married him in two weeks. It took twenty years to
divorce him." The mother, it appears, married him for strictly practical purposes: "He was older, she said. He had a job and a car. And Mother was so
sick." Perhaps a related reason for the marriage's failure was sex—or the
lack thereof. After reading in her mother's *Reader's Digest* about a girl carried off by a grizzly bear, the narrator dreams that her father approaches her
sexually: "I think to myself, It's been years since he's had an erection. . . . " In
the final years of their marriage, the mother refused to have sex with the
father.

On weekends, the narrator gets away from home by attending rummage sales, but these, too, recall the past and raise the specter of sexuality. An old football sweater for sale reminds the narrator of Jason, her high school boyfriend who "made All-State but . . . hated football." They would park and try to make love on his sweater, but she was evidently so inhibited that their futile efforts only caused her pain. The narrator does not buy the sweater, but she does purchase "an old robe to wear in the mornings" because "it upsets my mother to see me naked. . . ." She also buys her mother an old record, *The Sound of Music*, but the record reminds them both of Jason. In a "ridiculous" high school production of the musical, handsome Jason stole the show as "a threatening Nazi colonel."

The subject of Jason and sex finally causes the differences between mother and daughter to erupt in an argument. It begins when they see Hubert Humphrey, the former vice president, now shockingly old and frail, on television. The mother immediately cries "cancer," but the daughter disagrees:

> All Hubert needs, I tell her, is a good roll in the hay.
> You think that's what everyone needs.
> Everyone does need it.
> They do not. . . . I seem to manage perfectly well without it, don't I?
> No, I wouldn't say that you do.

The mother lectures the daughter—"your attitude will make you miserable. . . . One man after another"—concluding with the declaration that Jason "lost respect" for the daughter when the two cohabited at college. The daughter screams back with an obscenity, for Jason eventually suffered some kind of mental breakdown—what he "lost" was his mind.

Refusing to talk about it anymore, the mother retires to the bathroom for "hydrotherapy," a relaxing bath. When she has to ask the daughter for a towel, the two make up. The mother is apologetic, and the daughter is shocked to see her mother naked and scarred: "She has two long scars on her belly, operations of the womb, and one breast is misshapen, sunken, indented near the nipple" where a lump was removed.

Insult is soon added to the mother's injuries, however, when, in the story's climax, the daughter puts her sexual theories into practice. The daughter gets a phone call from Daniel, an old California boyfriend who has come east. When they lived together, both had their problems. He smashed dishes, "ran out of the house with his hands across his eyes," and was touchy about his Vietnam war wounds, while she finally developed total frigidity. Still, the daughter, who has been considering a trip to the university to find "an old lover," invites him for a visit. On his best behavior, Daniel at first delights the mother, but her impression of him changes when, on Sunday morning, she hears him and her daughter making love in the bedroom directly above her head. The mother slams the door angrily as she leaves for church.

When she returns, Daniel has left, but her anger remains. Seeing the daughter, the mother goes to the sink and starts washing the clean dishes again. Fearfully, the daughter embraces her, and the mother complains bitterly that "I heard you.... Here, in my own house." Then she hushes and stares into the water while the daughter continues holding her.

Themes and Meanings

At its most obvious level, "Home" is a simple story about a classic subject, the generation gap. The gap is well documented by the differences between mother and daughter in life-styles, tastes (for television, books, magazines, politics), and attitudes toward sex. On this level, the story is almost comic. As youth must, the daughter returns, confronts the beast in its den (that is, her mother and her mother's attitude toward sex), and triumphs.

There are complicating factors in the story, however, some with tragic overtones. One such factor is American history, ever-present in the "sorrowful" countenance of Walter Cronkite, who helped television introduce history into the American home and who "understood that here at home, as well as in starving India, we would pass our next lives as meager cows." In the context of American history, which the author skillfully evokes, the mother represents the World War II generation while the daughter represents the Vietnam generation—and it is no accident that these two generations are named here after wars. Both generations were scarred, in different ways.

Another complicating factor is that mother and daughter are as much alike as different—two sides of the same coin. The mother handed on her antisexual attitudes to the daughter, in whom they appear either as inhibition or a theory of liberation. In actual practice, both women have difficulty in bed, though the mother appears to have enjoyed sex more than the daughter, despite limited opportunity. The mother is not so much against sex for puritanical reasons as she is against further involvement with men. Although much involved with men, the daughter has not escaped the mother's pattern. Both women callously use men, either as financial support or as sexual partners, and each has apparently helped send a good man, the father and Jason, respectively, to his doom (Daniel moves on quickly). Finally, the two women treat each other with a similar mixture of love and hidden resentment.

Style and Technique

The symbolism in "Home" is worthy of a latter-day Nathaniel Hawthorne. Images of masculine sexuality suggest the two women's warped views: The grizzly bear in the *Reader's Digest* story resurfaces as the father in the daughter's dream, and Jason the football star plays "a threatening Nazi colonel"; wounded Daniel, with "his white and feminine hands," seems more to the daughter's taste. Physical scarring represents deeper psychic states: There are Daniel's war wounds and the mother's "operations of the womb," while the girl carried off by a grizzly reappears with "a long thin scar near her mouth." Home is where people go to die, like the submarine crew in an old movie on television (recognizable as Stanley Kramer's *On the Beach*, 1959). Home is where the mother's young aspirations died when she returned to care for her sick mother and to marry an older man, where the family died, and where the mother now lives her hermetic existence and sings out "cancer" at the images on television.

Enter the daughter, who is as obsessed with sex as the mother is with cancer—it is a case of life against death, in the best manner of D. H. Lawrence. Since the story is told from the daughter's point of view, life wins: The daughter overcomes her instilled sexual fears by violating the taboos of her mother's house. The main trouble with the story, however, is the point of view, which appears too short on irony: The daughter is so smug and superior that some readers might find themselves rooting for the mother.

Harold Branam

A HORSE AND TWO GOATS

Author: R. K. Narayan (1906-   )
Type of plot: Comic realism
Time of plot: The twentieth century
Locale: In and around Kritam, a South Indian village
First published: 1965

Principal characters:

MUNI, an old, poor Indian villager
HIS WIFE, who is equally ancient but sharp-tongued
THE SHOPMAN, the owner of the village store
THE FOREIGNER, an American tourist from suburban
    Connecticut

The Story

After setting the scene in Kritam, a tiny South Indian village, the story introduces old Muni and his wife, a poor, childless couple: "She was old, but he was older and needed all the attention she could give him in order to be kept alive." The two have been married since he was ten and she eight: "He had thrashed her only a few times in their career, and later she had the upper hand." At one time Muni was a relatively prosperous herdsman, with "a flock of forty sheep and goats." He sold the sheep's wool and sold the animals for slaughter to a town butcher, who brought him "betel leaves, tobacco, and often enough some bhang." Yet those high old times are past. Now Muni's flock, struck by "some pestilence" (though Muni suspects a neighbor's curse), has dwindled to two goats. Still, Muni follows his daily routine of taking the animals to graze near the highway two miles away, where he sits on the base of an old clay statue and watches the world go by.

Normally Muni's wife starts the day by boiling him some millet for breakfast, then sending him on his way with a ball of leftover millet and a raw onion for lunch. This morning, however, there is no food, so Muni goes out of the hut, shakes the drumstick tree, and gets six drumsticks. His wife offers to boil them with salt, but Muni hankers for something richer—a drumstick curry. His wife agrees to satisfy his "unholy craving" for "big things," provided that Muni can gather the ingredients: "a measure of rice or millet.... Dhall, chili, curry leaves, mustard, coriander, gingelley oil, and one large potato." When Muni goes to the village store, however, the shopman refuses him further credit (he already owes the store "five rupees and a quarter") and belittles the old man in front of other villagers. Muni returns home defeated, and his wife sends him off to graze the goats and to fast for the day. His hope is that she will earn enough money somewhere for an evening meal.

As he passes through the village each day with his two goats, people talk about his diminished status, and Muni quietly hangs his head. Only when he reaches the statue near the highway can he relax and enjoy a little peace. Here Muni sits all day in the shade of the statue—a horse rearing next to a fierce warrior—and watches his goats and an occasional passing vehicle. The vehicles are something to tell his wife about when he goes home at night.

Today Muni will have much to tell, for as he sits enjoying his somnolence, the big world abruptly intrudes. A strange vehicle—a van or station wagon—suddenly runs out of gas and coasts to a stop in front of Muni. Out steps "a red-faced foreigner" dressed in khaki. He asks Muni about gas stations, then sees the statue. He is transfixed by the clay horse, which he immediately desires to own. Muni, meanwhile, is terrified by the official-looking foreigner, who he thinks has come to arrest him. Thus begins one of the most hilarious negotiations in literature, the foreigner speaking only English; Muni, only Tamil.

Muni asserts his ownership of the two goats, despite what his slanderous neighbors might say. In turn, the foreigner smiles, takes out his silver cigarette case, and offers Muni a smoke. Surprised, Muni happily accepts: "Muni drew a deep puff and started coughing; it was racking, no doubt, but extremely pleasant. . . . No need to run away from a man who gave him such a potent smoke." Still cautious, however, Muni shuns the foreigner's business card, thinking that it is a warrant. He disavows any connection with a recent murder, blames it on Kritam's neighboring village, and promises to apprehend any suspicious character and "bury him up to his neck in a coconut pit if he tries to escape."

Observing that the deal must be conducted at a leisurely pace, the foreigner sits beside Muni and relates how he was working last summer "on the fortieth floor of the Empire State Building" when a power failure precipitated a personal decision: "All the way in the train I kept thinking, and the minute I reached home in Connecticut, I told my wife, Ruth, 'We will visit India this winter, it's time to look at other civilizations.'" Muni tells how his village turns thieves from the neighboring village into mincemeat, and the suburban New Yorker says that he also enjoys chopping wood. Noting the stranger's gestures toward the horse, Muni launches into its history and meaning: "This is our guardian, it means death to our adversaries." An embodiment of "the Redeemer" (apparently Vishnu), the horse will come alive at "the end of the world," save the good people, and trample the evil ones. The American promises to install the statue in the middle of the living room: At cocktail parties, "we'll stand around him and have our drinks." Muni then runs over a list of other avatars, tells how he used to enact their stories in village dramas, and concludes by asking the American if he knows the *Ramayana* and the *Mahabharata*.

Seeing a chance to clinch the deal, the American pulls out a hundred rupees and offers them for the horse. Muni, thinking that the American is buying the two goats, is ecstatic: "His dream of a lifetime was about to be realized . . . opening a small shop on this very spot." Leaving the two goats with the American, Muni rushes home to show the money to his wife. Meanwhile, the American flags down another car, buys some siphoned gas, gets help in loading the clay horse, and drives off with it. At home, Muni's wife suspects Muni of stealing the money, which seems to be confirmed when the two goats come trailing in. "If you have thieved," she declares hysterically, "the police will come tonight and break your bones. Don't involve me. I will go away to my parents. . . ."

Themes and Meanings

This comic masterpiece, which first appeared in *The New Yorker*, has the dimensions of an updated fairy tale: A childless old couple find their cupboard empty, but the old man goes out and meets a stranger who buys his last two goats for a small fortune. The tale is updated in that the poverty shown, with each day a new search for food, is only too real. Also real are the related conditions of village life in South India—the close-knit community with its malicious gossip and concern for status, the credit system exemplified by the village store, the bickering of husband and wife, the occasional violence and rough justice, the pervasive influence of religion.

Yet the story's main updating is the clash of this village culture with American culture, represented by the American tourist. The stereotyped American tourist with his monoglot outlook and moneybags is perhaps less real than the story's other characters, but he is individualized somewhat by his New York background: Here the typical suburbanite of *The New Yorker* goes east. As usual, he is an object of gentle satire. He moves about on the floating world with ease thanks to his financial means, but otherwise he is a total nincompoop. He reduces existence to getting and spending, buying an avatar of the just god to install in his living room. His cocktail guests had better stay on their best behavior.

Yet even the American tourist is not entirely oblivious to the existential void: His experience of a New York City power failure—a technological version of the Caves of Malabar—moves him to visit other civilizations. Although dimly understood, his basic instinct to bring the god back home is correct. The clash of cultures is symbolized by the different languages which the tourist and Muni speak, but, amazingly, in the long run they do communicate. Their misunderstandings are hilarious, but they share an understanding beyond language—that is, the human condition. In their little drama of the Absurd, they serve as each other's sympathetic listener, and their cooperation enables each man to cope with his particular need. The two men, like their two cultures, complement each other, but they are more alike than different: Muni is simply a village counterpart of the New York commuter. As they face the universe, society, and their wives, each man no doubt wants to resemble the fierce warrior standing beside the horse, but in actuality they are more like the two goats.

Style and Technique

Part of the fairy-tale element in this story is the result of the author's use of coincidence. From a Western point of view, the story's big coincidence—Muni's opportune meeting with a rich American—may seem a fault: It undercuts the Western sense of probability, of order. Yet that is apparently Narayan's purpose. From a Hindu point of view, which sees the universe in flux, the coincidence is quite logical. In the Hindu view, anything can happen, though contingencies (or actions of the gods) usually balance out over time: Muni is wiped out by the pestilence but reinstated by the American. Just as Muni sells the American an avatar of a Hindu god, so Narayan slyly introduces the Hindu context into this story, complete with a lesson in theology, a reference to the great Hindu epics, and a wild conversation that mirrors the Hindu universe.

Narayan's ability to present Hindu culture to the West is aided by one of the smoothest English styles in the world. Narayan has developed his style over a long career, and "A Horse and Two Goats" shows the style at its best—simple, supple, subtle, able to encompass the Hindu worldview and the demands of *The New Yorker* at the same time. The style entertains without calling attention to itself. It is only one of the reasons that Narayan has often been mentioned for a Nobel Prize.

Harold Branam

THE HORSE DEALER'S DAUGHTER

Author: D. H. Lawrence (1885-1930)
Type of plot: Domestic and psychological realism
Time of plot: The 1920's
Locale: A small town in rural England
First published: 1922

Principal characters:
JACK FERGUSSON, a doctor
MABEL PERVIN, the horse dealer's daughter, twenty-seven years old
JOE PERVIN, her oldest brother, thirty-three years old
FRED HENRY PERVIN, her middle brother
MALCOLM PERVIN, her youngest brother, twenty-two years old

The Story

The three Pervin brothers, left destitute by their late father, sit smoking and talking around the breakfast table in the family ranch house. They badger their sister, Mabel, whom they call "bull-dog," asking what she intends to do with her life now that they all must leave the ranch; she answers them as always, with stony silence. Dr. Jack Fergusson, a physician and friend of the brothers, calls. As he sits talking with them, he becomes intrigued by the gloomy, proud, and strangely detached sister.

Later, while walking about making his rounds, Fergusson sees Mabel in the cemetery, where, clad in black, she is tending her mother's grave. He follows her to a pond and, with continuing fascination, watches her walk into and finally disappear under the murky water. He runs after her, drags her out of the pond, and takes her home. There, he undresses her, rubs her skin dry, and warms her next to the hearth fire.

Mabel awakens in a daze, recognizes the doctor, and asks him what she has done. Realizing her nakedness beneath the swaddling blankets, she asks him, "Do you love me, then?" and becomes certain of the answer herself: "You love me.... I know you love me, I know." The doctor, who "had, really, no intention of loving her," is horrified at her words and her kisses, yet he feels overwhelmed and must embrace her and admit that her words are really true. Mabel's joyful assurance of his love soon passes, however, and she sobs, "I feel I'm horrible to you." "'No, I want you, I want you,' was all he answered, blindly, with that terrible intonation which frightened her almost more than her horror lest he should *not* want her."

The title, "The Horse Dealer's Daughter," suggests that the protagonist is Mabel, but actually she shares the center with Fergusson. At the crucial moment, however, this strange love story, recounting the emergence into passion of both these characters, gives the lead to Mabel. She and Fergusson come to their union from opposite directions, Mabel from the "animal pride" of the Pervins, Fergusson from the logic-dominated repression of science and the conformity of his educated class. The story itself chronicles how they make the journey, and for what conscious and unconscious motives.

The story's opening scene in the dining room emphasizes the family dynamics of the four children still present in the dead horse dealer's home; there is a Cinderella-like quality to Mabel's life—true poverty now, and the solitude of a decade of scrubwork, of holding things together, of living with a stepmother's indifference and without a mother's love. Her brothers, too, have ignored her, except to tease or criticize. That crude life has written its message as an "impassive fixity" on Mabel's face. Yet her "steady, dangerous eyes" have an unsettling effect upon Fergusson, and there are abundant hints of strong emotion under her façade. She manages by means of a dumb endurance: "She thought of nobody, not even of herself." Emotionally, she is already dead, and thus feels herself coming closer to her mother.

Fergusson, with his active mental role, dominates the crucial, central part of the story. In the strictest sense, however, his intellect is largely misleading: He tells himself that he hates the "hellish hole" he lives in, but the people there, "rough, inarticulate, powerfully emotional," excite him. The intense emotion of his witnessing Mabel's suicide attempt, and of his saving her from the pond, forces him out of the comfort of allowing thinking to dominate.

His entering the pond, in fact, is a kind of baptism: In his desperate grab to reach her, "he lost his balance and went under. . . . After what seemed an eternity" he reenters the world, and faces, though reluctantly, the passion that a revived Mabel intuits in him and reveals in herself. She reads events symbolically, from the primitive, unconscious wisdom to which fairy tales speak: On a logical level, her seeing love in the fact that he undressed her is preposterous, but Fergusson's "soul seemed to melt" when she speaks the thought. He fights the realization of his love, his intellect throwing obstacles before it: "his whole will was against his yielding"; to love her would be "a violation of his professional honour" as a doctor. This voice of a conformist society cannot withstand the force of passion; his decision to love seems to be the first nonrational choice of his life.

Finally, Mabel's and Fergusson's awareness of what they have promised each other inspires the confusion and shyness of the last pages, and the adjustment of roles: Fergusson takes the lead by ridiculing Mabel's self-reproaches and by reassuring her of his desire ("We're going to be married, quickly"), and she takes on a subtle and manipulative manner ("'Kiss me,' she said wistfully," and "I don't like you in those [her brothers'] clothes"). Passion might be blind, and is so described even in the final paragraph, but they must live with a knowledge of love, and that will not be simple.

Themes and Meanings

The story occupies itself with D. H. Lawrence's major theme, the difference between what he called "mental consciousness" and "blood consciousness." The characters are first introduced with this theme in mind. The brothers, "callous" but cowed by failure, are revealed as lacking that crucial tension: Joe is in a "stupor of downfall," "a subject animal now"; Fred Henry is "not master of the situations of life" despite his mastery of horses; Malcolm is "the baby of the family," "looking aimlessly." All have a "sullen, animal pride," and after years of living a brutal and coarse life, fathering illegitimate children with women of "bad reputations," they lack Mabel's "blood consciousness," her ability to see the situation and respond deeply to it. Fergusson, whose "slight Scotch accent" foreshadows the severe repression he later reveals, represents "mental consciousness," which has all the power of logic and science, but which cannot by itself do more than deny the instinctive forces of life. Their confrontation combines the wisdom of instinct and the wisdom of logic, but does not suggest that the forces will coexist quietly.

Another important theme is the repressive role of society. It shows itself in Mabel's life after poverty strikes down her pride and forces her to buy cheap food and avert her gaze on the town streets. For Fergusson, on the other hand, success increases the social repression he feels; his sense of class, of professional status, makes him claim to hate the town and feel ashamed of his attraction to its people. Even after his confession of love to Mabel, the shame haunts him: "That he should love her? That this was love.... Him, a doctor! How they would all jeer if they knew!" Though Lawrence keeps society in the distance, its power is clearly in evidence, and the actions of his characters show his eagerness to strike against the still dominant Victorian sense of propriety he believed to be very destructive.

Style and Technique

"The Horse Dealer's Daughter," as is typical of Lawrence's short fiction, has a strong sense of plot, and because the two characters are of almost equal importance to his antibourgeois theme, he adopts the technique of convergence, alternating his focus from Mabel to Fergusson and causing them to meet three times: at the Pervins', at the graveyard, and finally at the pond, where the narrative brings them together and forces them for the first time to communicate. Lawrence accentuates the tension and feeling of inevitability by increasing the pace of the story: The first scene is leisurely, with a large cast, while the scenes following center on Mabel or Fergusson, sometimes both, and are briefer and given more to internal than to external description. They give way to the longest but most dramatically intense scene, that taking place at the pond and continuing beside the Pervin hearth.

Lawrence also illustrates here his pioneering attempts to use language, especially by means of metaphor, to communicate passionate inner states. In the beginning, the story is dominated by dimness and numbness: All the Pervins are "sullen"; the brothers' glances are "glazed" and "callous"; they refer to Mabel as "bull-dog"; her emotions only "darken" her face, and she passes "darkly" through the town and goes "darkly" through the "saddened" fields and the "falling" afternoon to the shadow of the churchyard to her mother's grave. It continues to fall while Fergusson watches Mabel move "in the hollow of the day" to the pond; as the water closes over her, the afternoon is "dead."

Lawrence then makes metaphors of hope (with a suggestion of religious passion) dominate the rescue scene. Fergusson finds, after his own full descent into the pond water that "clasped dead cold round his legs," that Mabel's body has "risen" from the pond, and he himself "rose higher" carrying her out of it. Once by the fire, he drinks "spirits" and revives her instantly by pouring some into her mouth. His watch has stopped; his old spiritless life, dominated by schedule and exactitude, is over.

From numbness to this revival of awareness, Lawrence moves in the final scene to metaphors of heat as the true physical passion of his characters comes to life, from the warmth of the fire and the friction of Fergusson's rubbing Mabel dry to the agony of his "burning" and "melting" heart. Throughout, the narrative conveys by means of its imagery the violent and contradictory nature of passionate love. Among all of Lawrence's quests in his fiction, this was the most significant.

Kerry Ahearn

THE HOUSE IN TURK STREET

Author: Dashiell Hammett (1894-1961)
Type of plot: Mystery and suspense
Time of plot: The 1920's
Locale: San Francisco
First published: 1924

Principal characters:
THE CONTINENTAL OP, the narrator, a private detective
MR. and MRS. QUARRE, an affectionate elderly couple
HOOK, a rough-mannered hood
ELVIRA, a greedy, seductive hood
TAI CHOON TAU, a clever, well-mannered hood

The Story

The Continental Op, a private detective who works for the Continental Detective Agency, has learned that a man whom he is hunting is living in a certain block of Turk Street in San Francisco. After canvassing all the houses on one side of the block and four on the other, he knocks on the door of the fifth house. At first no one answers. As the Op is about to leave, the door is opened by a friendly, fragile-looking old woman who insists that he enter. The Op, after a mild protest, enters the house and is taken into a sitting room, where an equally friendly old man, the woman's husband, is seated comfortably, smoking a cigar. With a twinge of conscience, the Op gives a phony name and tells a phony story in order to obtain information about the man whom he is seeking. As the old couple, Mr. and Mrs. Quarre by name, do their best to provide something helpful, the Op is served a cup of tea and given a cigar. He sits back, entranced by the relaxed atmosphere, and lets his mind wander from the sordid world of private investigation. He longs for the fast-approaching evening so that he can be finished with his work for the day and go home.

Suddenly the Op feels an object against the back of his neck and hears a gruff voice behind him demanding that he stand up. At first he thinks that he must be dreaming, but he feels the object and hears the voice again. He is frisked by the old man, then made to turn around. He faces an unpleasant-looking man holding a gun. Before he can interrogate the Op thoroughly, "Hook" is called into another room by a young woman, named Elvira. The old man covers the Op with a gun, and the old woman cordially invites the Op to be seated again. The Op hears Hook, the young woman, and a third gang member discussing his fate. Hook is in favor of killing the Op, but he is overruled by the calm, British voice of the third gang member, Tai Choon Tau. The Op is thankful.

The Op is tied up and gagged by the old couple, who then leave the house for a prearranged rendezvous. Elvira comes into the sitting room with Hook, goading and seducing him into getting rid of Tai. Carrying a traveling bag, Tai enters the room. After subtle encouragement from Elvira, Hook strikes the much smaller Tai. Tai, however, draws his gun even as he is falling and gets the drop on Hook. He takes Hook's gun, lectures the other two on unity, and matter-of-factly announces that the three of them will double-cross the old couple. Magnanimously, Tai gives Hook back his gun. As the dispute settles down, the Op notes a change in the room. Thinking back quickly, he discovers that Elvira has used the fight as a diversion, replacing the contents of the traveling bag with some of the room's books and magazines. He figures that the original contents of the bag are now hidden in the couch.

The three gang members depart. Tai, the last one to leave, places a gun within the Op's reach and loosens his bonds. The Op manages to get loose and reach the gun just as Hook returns to the house, entering the sitting room with his gun drawn; the Op fires first, and Hook falls dead. The Op quickly examines the couch, finding a cache of bonds. He examines his gun as well as Hook's: Both are without ammunition. Tai was taking no chances when he returned Hook's gun and set up the confrontation between Hook and the Op. The Op takes the bonds upstairs, hides them, and waits for Tai and Elvira to return. Tai and Elvira do, indeed, return, and the Op tries to turn the two against each other. Tai offers to trade the girl for the bonds. Just then, the Quarres return, convinced that they are being double-crossed by Tai, Elvira, and the Op. The old woman covers Tai as the old man takes away his gun, but Tai has two more guns hidden. He shoots the old couple dead. The Op is able to subdue Tai in the resulting confusion. Elvira escapes, reappearing in a later Hammett story.

It turns out that the gang worked a scam in which Elvira would seduce bank employees and get them to embezzle funds. Hook would then play the jealous husband, scaring the victim off minus Elvira and the loot. Tai was the mastermind. The old couple provided a hideout. On the gang's last job, the victim refused to be scared off and was killed in a fight with Hook. Thus the gang thought that the heat was on and that the Op had tracked them down.

The story's twist lies in the Op's ignorance of all this. The Op was unaware of the gang or their crimes. In fact, he was not working on a criminal case at all. Tai refuses to believe the Op. He goes to the gas chamber convinced that the Op is lying to him.

Themes and Meanings

Dashiell Hammett's Continental Op stories were derived from "pulp" fiction, a popular form of reading material in the United States during the first half of the twentieth century. The pulp magazines, so called for the cheap paper on which they were printed, fed the country's growing literacy by providing easy-to-read, sensational stories of adventure, the Western frontier, the supernatural, science fiction, sex (steamy, though not very explicit by modern standards), and crime. The pulps provided what seemed to many to be low-grade entertainment for the masses. On the other hand, some authors who began by writing for the pulps managed to transform the genre into a vehicle for serious commentary on the human condition and on contemporary society. Hammett's work, for example, treats a number of profound themes.

"The House in Turk Street" well illustrates this point. It is, first and foremost, a story about the deceptiveness of appearances. Almost nothing in the story is as it seems. The kindly old couple turn out to be accomplices to murder. Their house, which at first appears to be a haven in a heartless world, is a den of thieves. Hook appears to be tough, but the more gentle and cultivated Tai is tougher. The gang is in the business of deception, using Elvira's appeal to lure young men in search of romance to their ruin instead. Even the Op is not what he seems. He deceives people intentionally in order to gain information, and the entire story is based on the misleading appearance that he is hot on the gang's trail when nothing could be further from the truth.

In Hammett's stories, most of the characters are driven by greed or lust of some sort, social institutions are corrupt, and attempts at social reform are costly and possibly futile. Even Hammett's heroes are anything but saintly. On the other hand, the Op and other Hammett heroes also have a firm sense of duty. Thus, Hammett's skepticism (regarding appearances) and realism (regarding human motives and institutions) do not translate into nihilism, the absence of moral values. Instead, the Op does his duty in Turk Street, helping to uncover truth and bring a criminal to justice.

Style and Technique

Hammett's writing style also elevates his work beyond its start in the pulp magazines. A model of leanness and economy, Hammett's prose has served as a guide for many later writers. These include Raymond Chandler and Ross Macdonald, who went on to continue successfully the tradition of "hardboiled" detective stories. Hammett's style remains a fine model for young writers, particularly those who strive for clarity and who wish to produce a compelling narrative.

Indeed, Hammett's prose lent itself well to the conventions of the detective story, always keeping the reader interested and in suspense, yet moving along quickly enough so that readers would not become impatient. One of Hammett's techniques for accomplishing this was his masterful use of dialogue. Hammett's story lines are often advanced efficiently by conversation between characters, and Hammett's detectives most often seek truth by asking people questions. "The House in Turk Street" is no exception in this regard, though for much of this particular story, the Op is reduced to being a spectator.

Ira Smolensky

THE HOUSE WITH THE GRAPE-VINE

Author: H. E. Bates (1905-1974)
Type of plot: Domestic realism
Time of plot: The 1950's
Locale: England
First published: 1959

Principal characters:
THE SMALL BOY, a lover of the natural splendor of England's past
THE FATHER, the parent who instills this love in the boy
THE OLD WOMAN, the resident of the house with the grapevine

The Story

A small boy growing up in a factory town in England enjoys hearing his father describe what the place was like before it became industrialized. The boy is fascinated to learn that most of the older houses were once covered by grapevines, on which small, dark grapes grew. That his father, when he was eight, worked in a grapevine-covered farmhouse half the day while going to school only part-time is especially appealing. The boy imagines such a life as ideal, but his father reveals that he hated working there, although he will not explain why. The romantic aspects of such a life, however, obscure any possible deficiencies for the boy: "How marvellous it must have been . . . to have stables and a pigeon-cote in the yard instead of only a water-barrel and a slat fence where people beat their mats. What days they must have been—he simply couldn't believe his father hadn't liked them."

The boy waits eagerly for three months before he can go to the farmhouse to see and taste the ripened grapes. When he arrives, an old woman with "a long face like a parsnip that had a few suspended hairy roots hanging from the chin" grabs him and accuses him of coming to steal apples. When he says he is after grapes, she denies ever having any and threatens to have him arrested. She says she once locked in the stable someone who had been "nickin' folkses things." The boy breaks away and runs home.

He never tells his father about going to the farmhouse or asks him again why he had been unhappy working there. He continues, however, to believe in the story of the grapevine.

Themes and Meanings

In the approximately six hundred short stories by H. E. Bates, one of the most frequent subjects is the glories of rural England. Bates dealt with this subject not only in his stories and novels but also in several nonfiction works and a column in *The Spectator* entitled "Country Life." He recognized throughout his career that what he considered an idyllic way of life was undergoing drastic changes, and his writing celebrates what had been and what remained of this peaceful splendor. Bates describes what has been lost in *The Vanished World* (1969), the first volume of his autobiography: "The world of television, jets and space craft dazzles our generation with new if sometimes near useless wonders, but for myself I would cheerfully exchange it for. . . the smell of wood-smoke, the scent of bluebells, cowslips, primroses and the Maiden's Blush, the Turk's Cap lily and the voice of nightingales."

A nostalgic longing for the natural magnificence of the English past dominates "The House with the Grape-vine." Both father and son would prefer their town to be "a place of green fields, with oats and barley and meadows where there were now factory yards, and little spinneys of violets and a farmhouse with apple-trees and a brook at the foot of the hill where sticklebacks swam among the cresses." The boy wants "to make a link with the past," wants to discover "what it was like before the brick boxes and the factories with the gallows-cranes came to smother and obliterate it all." The impossibility of recapturing the past is emphasized when the old woman drags the boy to the wall his father has so lovingly described: "That was the wall all right, but there were no grapes on it. It was empty; there was nothing there."

Yet something positive comes out of the boy's frightening experience. Loneliness and the need for companionship and compassion are other frequent Bates concerns. The boy's father associates the grapevines with the grandmother with whom he lived when he worked at the farmhouse. His mother had died, the grandmother did not live long after that, and there is no mention of his wife. He and the boy seem to have no one but each other. In refusing to explain what happened to him at the farmhouse, the father says, "Perhaps some day there will be something that will make you unhappy and you won't know why it is. I hope not. But you can't always explain things." Finding out about such unhappy things in much the same way that his father did and deciding not to say anything about it help the boy to understand his father better: "When he passed the gates of that house, he remembered the grape-vine. . . . [H]e too hated that house, and, because of it, loved his father so much more."

Style and Technique

Bates uses the grapevine to unify the elements of the story. It is no longer on the farmhouse wall because the old woman has either neglected or destroyed it since she is incapable of appreciating its beauty. She does not remember it because she cannot understand its possible significance. For Bates, the boy, and the father, the grapevine represents the past, the English countryside, childhood, innocence, and optimism. The grapevine can survive only as people and ways of life do: through care and love.

"The House with the Grape-vine" also gives evidence of Bates's descriptive powers. The boy will always remember the day he went to the farm-house: "It might have been chosen specially from all the days of the autumn because the air was so yellow with sunshine that the stone of the house seemed almost the colour of a piece of plain Madeira cake, and because even the small white clouds seemed warm." Such affectionate evocations of time, place, and nature seem Bates's most lasting achievement in his short stories.

Michael Adams

THE HOUSEBREAKER OF SHADY HILL

Author: John Cheever (1912-1982)
Type of plot: Domestic realism
Time of plot: The 1950's
Locale: Shady Hill, a fictional suburb of New York City
First published: 1954

> *Principal characters:*
> JOHNNY HAKE, the narrator and protagonist, a thirty-six-year-old businessman
> CHRISTINA, his wife

The Story

"The Housebreaker of Shady Hill" recounts the process by which Johnny Hake, a stable citizen of a quiet New York suburb, briefly becomes a thief, suffers remorse, and reforms. In the process, it comments satirically upon the mores of modern suburbanites. Johnny's career in theft begins shortly after he resigns his job with a company that makes parablendeum—a kind of plastic wrap. Fed up with office politics, Johnny strikes out on his own, only to discover that he cannot earn a living comparable to his old salary. Unwilling to burden his wife with his financial worries, reluctant to borrow from friends or relatives, Johnny one night enters a neighbor's house and steals a wallet containing nine hundred dollars.

Immediately appalled by what he has done, Johnny finds that his crime preys on his mind all the next day. Everywhere he looks he seems to encounter crime, from the stranger in the restaurant who pockets a tip left by a previous customer, to his old friend who tries to cut him in on a business deal that is "just like stealing." The very word "steal" seems to have a powerful effect upon him; he suddenly feels he is a part of the force destroying the peace and order of the world. At church the next Sunday he imagines that he hears a rat gnawing away at the floorboards, and he is so distracted that he misses the opportunity to take Communion. He comes to a further crisis when his children surprise him for his birthday with the gift of an aluminum extension ladder. In his new paranoia, Johnny imagines the gift to be an indirect comment on his career as a thief. He becomes sharp with the children, fights with his wife, and has packed a suitcase and left the house before the two reconcile.

A few nights later, Johnny attempts another theft. He enters the house of Tom and Grace Maitland, a wealthy but melancholy couple. Creeping into the Maitlands' bedroom in quest of Tom's wallet, Johnny discovers that Grace is in bed with the boy who cuts the Maitlands' grass. Shocked, he hurries home and reflects on the altered picture Shady Hill presents by night.

The next night, on his way to attempt another theft, Johnny has a revelation which turns him away from his life of crime. As he heads for the home of yet another neighbor, the wind begins to stir and suddenly rain is falling, reconnecting Johnny with his sense of the pleasures afforded by mere existence, and reminding him of his love for Christina and the children. His obsession with money seems to fall away, and he is able to go home and sleep peacefully. He even has a restorative dream of sailing a boat on the Mediterranean. The next day, he is offered his old job in parablendeum, and he accepts. Taking an advance on his salary, he returns nine hundred dollars to his neighbors, the Warburtons, and is finally at ease with himself.

Themes and Meanings

"The Housebreaker of Shady Hill" offers two themes which, although seemingly contradictory, in fact are complementary. On the one hand, the story satirizes the values and manners of a certain class of well-to-do suburbanites, suggesting the shallowness of their morality and the limits of their dreams. On the other hand, the story's resolution affirms the worthiness of life's simple pleasures and asserts man's freedom to direct his own life. In some measure, the story's strength comes from the tension between these themes. The overall tone is ironic, and yet there is ultimately an endorsement of certain facets of suburban existence—a nice house and garden, cooking on an outdoor grill, playing softball with the neighbors.

Throughout the story, Cheever introduces characters whose affluence is emphasized, as is their unhappiness. The protagonist is established on the story's first page as a product of an upper-class New York upbringing: He was reared on Sutton Place, an exclusive address, and attended St. Bartholomew's, a fashionable Episcopal church. Yet his parents, long divorced, are depicted as lost souls. His mother lives alone in a Cleveland hotel, refusing to forgive him for getting married. His father, whom he rarely saw, once took him to the theater and offered to buy him the services of any chorus girl whose looks he liked. Johnny fled after plucking fifty dollars from his father's wallet. In his current crisis, he broods on what he perceives as the unlucky origins that have led to his present "sordid destiny."

The wealthy residents of Shady Hill are also satirized. The Warburtons, husband and wife, are described respectively as "the kind of man that you wouldn't have liked at school" and "an aging mouse." Of the very rich Tom Maitland the narrator remarks, "His wife is the fattest woman in Shady Hill, and nobody much likes his children." Other potential robbery targets are the Pewters, "who were not only rich but booze fighters, and who drank so much that I didn't see how they could hear thunder after the lights were turned out." Amid this sea of moneyed unhappiness, Johnny Hake's yearning for affluence seems a misguided quest.

During his brief career as a thief, Johnny is haunted by images of his parents and his neighbors. Their depressing lives, as well as the dark events of the world at large, come to dominate his thoughts. Yet suddenly, in one clear moment, his sense of balance is restored. He stops lamenting his life and returns to a celebration of possibilities. A brisk rain shower awakens his senses, and he realizes that neither his parents nor his recent misdeeds will trap him forever. He thinks with pleasure of his wife and children. The next day, New York City again seems sweet and exciting rather than dark and criminal. Overall, the story affirms the individual's right to choose his way of life and underscores his responsibility to do so honestly. Johnny may have been the accidental offspring of unpleasant parents, he may live in a world riddled with crime, but he has many blessings to contemplate as well.

Style and Technique

Despite its serious topic—the quest for an honest existence in a fallen world—"The Housebreaker of Shady Hill" is often humorous in tone. By interjecting humor, Cheever escapes the risk that his story might seem sermonlike, a cautionary tale warning modern-day sinners not to fall into the trap of worshiping money. This humor emerges principally in the melodramatic imagination of the narrator. Although Johnny can see the humor in the concerns of others, his own problems assume the status of major trauma. Having a cigarette late one night, he feels a twinge in his lungs and becomes suddenly convinced that he is dying of bronchial cancer, fated to leave his wife and children penniless. After his act of theft, he imagines himself as a "child of darkness" and "a miserable creature whose footsteps had been mistaken for the noise of the wind." Raking leaves while his neighbors play softball, Johnny complains, "Why should I be left alone with my dead leaves in the twilight—as I was—feeling so forsaken, lonely and forlorn that I was chilled?" Conscious of his slide into self-pity, Johnny nevertheless commits the ultimate in silly self-absorption when he sees a dogwood tree that has lost its leaves and reflects, "How sad everything is!"

Other poignant humor emerges from the degree to which Johnny's theft has changed his perception of things. The stained glass at church "seemed to be made from the butts of vermouth and Burgundy bottles." His fight with Christina is a lesson in domestic banality. When he discovers his suitcase is torn, he exclaims, "Even the cat has a nice traveling bag." It is a particular indignity to him that he cannot find enough clean shirts to last a week. At the height of his self-dramatization, he hammers a "For Sale" sign onto a tree in the front yard. He marches off to the train station only to discover, anticlimactically, that he cannot get a train until four o'clock in the morning. So, he goes back to Christina, and all thought of divorce is forgotten.

By persistently introducing a humorous tone into the scenes of Johnny's despair, Cheever indirectly reassures the reader that Johnny's fall into sin will not be permanent. A story with this kind of tone will surely end happily, as this one does.

Diane M. Ross

HOW CLAEYS DIED

Author: William Sansom (1912-1976)
Type of plot: Philosophical realism
Time of plot: Shortly after the end of World War II
Locale: German countryside
First published: 1947

> *Principal characters:*
> CLAEYS, the protagonist, a teacher from Belgium
> TWO ENGLISH OFFICERS AND A DRIVER, his companions in a car
> EXPATRIATES FROM EASTERN EUROPE, former prisoners of a
> Nazi labor camp

The Story

A Belgian named Claeys, temporarily attached to the English Army on a civilian mission, is riding in Germany with two officers and a driver two months after the end of World War II. He is a teacher who has volunteered to assist in the rehabilitation of the enemy. He is traveling to one of the camps of displaced persons, mostly Slavs, from a German forced-labor camp.

The car drives through a verdant landscape, where vegetation is already camouflaging the evidence of war, burying the carcasses of abandoned war machines in grass and vines. Yet there is also a bombed-out town which is quite dead, grim evidence of man's power to bring a total disorder that at least temporarily defeats every effort of nature to restore life.

As the car approaches the area of the labor camp, the riders hear a chorus of men singing Slavic songs and a large group preparing, apparently, to march home. The driver advances cautiously with a hand on his gun; there has been trouble recently between the former inmates and a former German soldier returning to his farm. Yet expatriates generally respect the English military. Claeys says that he wants to speak to these men and asks the driver to leave him there alone, drive out of sight around the bend, and wait.

The expatriates approach Claeys, uncertain about who he is and what he wants. Claeys smiles and speaks to them in English, but they obviously do not understand. Then he tries French—again no response. He breaks into Dutch, which comes more naturally—this time there is some interest and arguing among the men, even some menacing gestures. Then he thinks that perhaps some of them might have learned German and reiterates his friendly overtures in that language. Now, the ranks close around him, the looks grow darker. Though they evidently recognize the language, they still do not seem to understand his now desperate "Bitte ein Moment . . . ich bin Freund, Freund. . . ." Slowly he raises his hand in a plea for order and understanding. A man steps forward and swings a scythe, cutting him down. The others close in, shouting and kicking.

Shots from the two officers bring a halt to the mob action, bringing down two of the attackers. Claeys, now dying, tries to speak to the officer who kneels by him, but can only gasp out "mistake!" Claeys lifts his right arm to shake hands with the officer, then gestures to his attackers. The officer, believing that he understands the dying man, walks toward the group of watchers extending his hand. Since it is now bloody, however, he first wipes it, then shakes hands with the Slavs as a sign of peace. The displaced persons do not know if he is vicariously offering the hand of the dying man in friendship or, by wiping his hand first, expressing a repudiation of the man they killed.

Themes and Meanings

The expatriates in this story are obviously confused about the identity and intentions of this stranger in civilian clothes, and when he speaks German, they attack him with the hatred built up for their longtime oppressors. Strangely enough, the reader may also be somewhat puzzled by him. He is apparently willing to forgive his killers in a magnanimous gesture of friendship even as he dies. Yet there is something ambiguous about his character, what little the reader knows of it.

Perhaps the most puzzling statement about him comes early in the story: "Claeys was a teacher, engaged then on relief measures, a volunteer for this work of rehabilitation of the enemy, perhaps a sort of half-brother-of-mercy as during the occupation he had been a sort of half-killer." Does this mean, he was a "half-brother" to Germans? A collaborator, perhaps, or simply one who did nothing while others were killed and who thus feels half-guilty? Was he one whose resistance to the Germans was only theoretical, not actual? "Now he wanted to construct quickly the world of which he had dreamed during the shadow years; now he was often as impatient of inaction as he had learned to be patient before."

The only clues that the reader is given to comprehend his nature come from the burden of his thoughts as he rides through the countryside. He seems to be philosophically inclined, more a man of thought than a man of action. He meditates much of the time on the evidence of both chaos and order in nature, and he wonders about the impact of man on that larger framework of nature. Much of what he sees suggests that even the devastation of war does not seriously unbalance the natural order. Some of the wreckage even seems to suggest organic forms; an abandoned tank nosing up from a cornfield, for example, looks like a large gray toad. Claeys is disturbed, however, by the barren, bombed-out town, which seems beyond reclamation. Its sheer vacuity contrasts forebodingly with the unconcerned fecundity of the fields outside of town.

Perhaps Claeys's tragic flaw is his unrelieved propensity to theorize with little actual experience of what wartime has meant to those in the midst of action. He overestimates his own ability to communicate and help his fellow-men, or perhaps he underestimates the psychological effect of accumulated resentment in the former prisoners. Some of his philosophical phrases, such as "the time for compensation," make an ironic background to the brutality of his death.

At the point of death, he is still racked by confused questions, though he cannot express them: "Broadly, if they could have been straightened out, these questions would have been: 'Order or Disorder? Those fellows were the victims of an attempt to rule men into an impeccable order, my killing was the result of the worst, that is, the most stupid disorder. . . .'" Absolute control over men's lives apparently brings on such outbreaks of irrational chaos.

Style and Technique

Sansom's sure command of visual images is vital to this story—the sense impressions both of vigorous vegetation and of the residue of war. The unique method of the story is the apparent demonstration in concrete terms of its philosophical burden. The protagonist (if not the author himself) is extending what he calls at one point "the intricate anarchy" of nature, which at the human level seems successful and orderly but which involves the continual, indifferent destruction of individual plants and animals, to include the effects of war on individuals and groups. The victims of warfare are like seeds that fall upon stony ground.

The author illustrates this intricate, but random principle of nature in a vivid image of the wind-borne seed, such as that of a dandelion:

> Look at the parachute seed—this amazing seed actually flies off the insensate plant-mother! It sails on to the wind! The seed itself hangs beneath such an intricate parasol, it is carried from the roots of its mother to land on fertile ground far away and set up there an emissary generation! And more—when it lands, this engine is so constructed that draughts inch-close to the soil drag, drag at the little parachute, so that the seed beneath actually erodes the earth, digs for itself a little trench of shelter, buries itself! Amazing! And what if the clever little seed is borne on the wrong wind to a basin of basalt?

In the completely bombed-out town, the protagonist apparently senses, but does not verbalize even in his thoughts, the obvious analogy to "stony ground." He does, however, meditate at length on the frustrated displaced persons, men from Bulgaria, Poland, and Russia, as analogous to seeds which have no chance to develop. The men, even when released from servitude, are far from home and have no means of support in an alien land: "ten thousand displaced souls, newly freed but imprisoned still by their strange environment and by their great expectations born and then as instantly barred."

Perhaps this somewhat fatalistic perception allows the protagonist to accept even his own death as a natural accident, a "mistake," for which blame need not be assigned. The protagonist has been accustomed to thinking in somewhat impersonal, general terms, what a philosopher might call the "view from eternity," wherein local disasters may be, if not rationalized, at least unemotionally accepted.

The error, or perhaps merely the impracticality, of living thus removed from the gritty, concrete experience of human misery is also suggested through natural imagery. The car has been driving on a straight, endless road lined by great beech trees at regular intervals—a seemingly endless order. Ironically, when the beech rows stop and the protective arch of leaves is broken, the effect is a greater confinement, wherein the sky, traditionally called "infinite," is likened instead to a lid over a plate. This image also suggests the freed, yet imprisoned situation of the displaced persons.

> Those who deny the flatlands forget the sky—over flat country the sky approaches closer than anywhere else, it takes shape, it becomes the blue-domed lid on a flat plate of earth. Here is a greater intimacy between the elements; and for once, for a little, the world appears finite.

This revelation of the accordionlike qualities of human perception of time and space is one of the most striking characteristics of Sansom's writing. The open sky as finite reflects the existential reality of each person's individual life, which cannot experience the broad sweep of history in which short-term disaster is comfortably lost in long-term survival of the species. At least one interpretation of this story, therefore, may be as the journey of an abstract thinker into the concrete, existential reality of the "stony ground" created by modern warfare.

Katherine Snipes

HOW I CONTEMPLATED THE WORLD FROM THE DETROIT HOUSE OF CORRECTION AND BEGAN MY LIFE OVER AGAIN

Author: Joyce Carol Oates (1938-   )
Type of plot: Psychological realism
Time of plot: 1968
Locale: Detroit suburbs
First published: 1969

> *Principal characters:*
> "THE GIRL," the sixteen-year-old narrator and protagonist
> THE NARRATOR'S FATHER, a physician
> THE NARRATOR'S MOTHER
> CLARITA, the narrator's female companion
> SIMON, the narrator's thirty-five-year-old boyfriend and pimp

The Story

"How I contemplated the world from the Detroit House of Correction and began my life over again" probes the case of a young girl from a "good" family who turns to crime. The opening lines of the story perfectly identify its content: "Notes for an essay for an English class at Baldwin County Day School; poking around in debris; disgust and curiosity; a revelation of the meaning of life; a happy ending. . . ." The narrator uses the occasion of a school essay to examine the psychological "debris" of her recent life—the emotional turbulence and confusion that led to a stay in the Detroit House of Correction.

The narrator's search for the meaning of her delinquency begins as she mentally revisits Branden's, the large and luxurious department store where she was arrested for shoplifting. The store's plushness and material glitter serve as an immediate symbol of the comfortable, insulated, middle-class existence of her parents against which the narrator rebels. With no logical transition, the girl's notes move readers from the store's interior to the parents' sumptuous home (with "a small library"), where the astounded parents confront her for stealing a pair of gloves. The narrator knows that "there is a connection" between her bridge-playing mother and her physician father (doctor of the slightly ill), and between them and the manager of the store, his doctor, her brother, and the family's maid. She knows that her "salvation" is bound up in these relationships, but their meaning is a painful blur.

The narrator's next notes highlight the tragic alienation between daughter and family. The mother wonders why her daughter is "so strange"; perpetually in motion, she has no clue to the girl's inner life, her secret obsession: "I wanted to steal but not to buy." A status seeker like the mother, the father is equally oblivious to the girl's needs. He is off reading a paper at a medical convention in Los Angeles at the moment the daughter is arrested for shoplifting. The father would agree with the ironic, impersonal note sent home from school, that though the girl made off with a copy of *Pageant Magazine* for no reason and swiped a roll of Lifesavers, she was "in no need of saving her life." The parents' evasion of responsibility leads them to conclude that their daughter's problems are attributable solely to "a slight physiological modification known only to a gynecologist. . . ." The girl hardly remembers her brother, who has been sent to a preparatory school in Maine.

Further notes establish that the atmosphere of affluence that intoxicates her parents nauseates and suffocates the girl. The neighborhood is heavy with conspicuous symbols of upper-middle-class success, yet its rigidly conformist social patterns leave no room for individuality or spontaneous emotional expression. Things appear to matter more than people; the people are mere adornments, attachments like pools, garages, or automatic sprinklers. It is her unarticulated desire to escape this "airproof, breathproof" environment that leads the girl to become a truant from school and to become involved in a social milieu diametrically opposed to her own: a Detroit ghetto where, in a sense, she is befriended by a street-hardened girl named Clarita. There, she meets Simon, a desperate, exploitative man who becomes her lover and pimp. Simon prefers a needle in the arm to the girl's embrace, and he turns her into a prostitute. If Sioux Drive was heavy with material possessions, this environment is heavy with fear and pain, climaxing in the girl's prostitution and then a brutal beating by female inmates of the house of correction. The girl perceives her attackers to be avenging themselves for the cumulative social injustices in their lives.

Out of the hospital, the girl, in her final notes, tells of her return to her safe and comfortable home. Her vow never to leave home again, her declaration that "I love everything here," has a desperately false ring to it. Despite the temporary capitulation to a world that is unreal and plastic as ever to her, she weeps in her living room over the falseness and emptiness of lives that seek salvation through material acquisitions, that look "for God in gold and beige carpeting" or in "the beauty of chandeliers and the miracle of a clean polished gleaming toaster and faucets that run both hot and cold water. . . ."

Themes and Meanings

On the one hand, the girl's notes are an indictment of the soulless materialism of her parents, which stifles the girl's emotional and artistic growth. On the other hand, the notes are, like the art of fiction itself, a gesture of liberation, of purgation and self-discovery. Clearly, this is a portrait of the artist as a young woman, albeit a girl who must take to the streets to search for life-affirming experience to fill the void she feels. So uncertain is the girl's sense of personal identity that she is "a secret" to herself—one more stranger in the sea of bewildering events and faces whose connections and meanings she records and hopes to understand.

In the sterile, suburban utopia of the parents, people are viewed as possessions, adornments, or attachments, valued not for their human qualities but for their ability to function harmoniously in the community's regulated social machinery. The door to the girl's home has a brass knocker "never knocked," and even the weather is described as "planted and performing." In this plasticized environment, people experience "ecstasy" not in relation to one another but in response to a smooth bathtub of bubbly pink water, a man's trouser pockets filled with coins, keys, dust, and peanuts, or income tax returns.

It is her quest for a more honest and spontaneous way of being that takes the narrator into the violent world of Simon and Clarita. The narrator must make herself vulnerable to life, exposing herself to its ravages, to test her own nature in a world not protected from suffering or true ecstasy. If the emotional weather here is erratic and stormy, its turbulence is preferable to the superficial well-being of her previous life—to no weather at all. Desperate love is better than no love, and despite the filth, injustice, and brutality, the day-to-day struggle for street survival is life-affirming. In short, this is an atmosphere in which the girl can breathe (Simon, she says, "breathes gravity into me"), in which people are ready for laughter or tears, and in which, however accompanied by pain, compassion and creativity have a chance to grow.

Still, salvation for this incipient artist is no more likely to come in Simon's anguished, self-destructive world than in the uniform anonymity of her parents' life. While her emotional confusion drives her once more back into the protected world of wealth and privilege, her reference to the "movieland sun" that breaks over her doll's house of a home and to the unfamiliar face that peers back at her from the shiny toaster shows that her crisis is far from resolved, that the role she is trying to assume is incompatible with her future artistic destiny. Suggestive of the final image and words of Dorothy in the film *The Wizard of Oz* (1939), the girl figuratively draws up her legs into a fetal position and vows never to leave home again. Yet a healthier, more positive ending is in store. These notes are her promise to herself that, like James Joyce's Stephen Dedalus, she has an artist's awareness, honesty, creativity, and active social conscience which will allow her entrance into a world of her own artistic creation.

Style and Technique

Rather than presenting her story by means of a smoothly unfolding plot in which actions mount spirally to a climax and then unwind to a denouement, Oates here juxtaposes a series of emotionally charged vignettes, impressions reminiscent of picture slides.

These vignettes are filtered through the narrator's confused, half-formed artistic consciousness; she does not yet comprehend the logical connections, the cause-and-effect relationships, of the events she relates. That she writes "Nothing" under the heading "People and Circumstances Contributing to this Delinquency" suggests her present inability to digest and interpret the painful flux of experience. The key to the story's style, then, is the fact that the girl's fragmentary notes are a rough draft. The finished product should give coherence to her jumbled experiences and lead to understanding of her predicament. Ultimately, with emotional distance and greater artistic awareness, she will see what the careful reader sees—that these impressions are an indictment of the obsessive materialism of her parents. She will gain greater control over her art, but her artistic perception of experience is already evident here, in such unconscious devices as the repeated association of the color pink with her plush but corrupt surroundings, in the metaphorical use of weather to suggest emotional states, and in references to sexual abuse and incest that symbolically link her father to Simon.

For now, it is enough to get these hostile impressions on paper as a purging of fears and uncertainties. The glut of uninterpreted physical detail, the detached, impersonal, third-person point of view (she refers to herself always as "the girl"), the choppy sentences and objective observations, all combine to convey the narrator's numbness of spirit, the aftermath of trauma. Conveyed, too, is the isolation of the girl's inner self—separated for a while from the outside world and from that battered external self who appears to her as a stranger. To heal this split between the perceiving self and the self perceived is an essential quest of the story.

Lawrence Broer

HOW I FINALLY LOST MY HEART

Author: Doris Lessing (1919-   )
Type of plot: Psychological realism
Time of plot: A week in the mid-twentieth century
Locale: London
First published: 1963

Principal character:
THE PROTAGONIST, an anonymous English woman in her
    forties

The Story

In this first-person narrative, an anonymous woman in mid-life reflects on her life and loves and recounts an experience that she has recently had, the experience of losing her heart. She loses her heart neither in the romantic metaphorical sense of being powerless before desire for another nor in the literal sense of cutting her heart out of her body and throwing it away, not that she has not wished to do both in her life. She loses her heart in a transfiguring, dreamlike encounter with her own inner being.

In the narrator's ruminations on her past loves, she distinguishes between the affairs and entanglements and even marriages, however numerous, that "don't really count," and "serious loves." She points out that not only she, but also most people today, fly from lover to lover, ever seeking "serious" love. Acerbically, she observes, "We are all entirely in agreement that we are in the right to taste, test, sip and sample a thousand people on our way to the 'real' one." Although she carries the scars of many loves, she has never lost her heart.

The occasion which precipitates her finally losing her heart takes place on a day on which she lunches with her first "real" love, a man she terms "serious love A." By chance that same afternoon she has tea with another past love, serious love B. Meeting these two loves "that count" and anticipating a meeting with a new man that evening engender in her a startling insight into the nature of her affairs of heart. Standing at a window looking out on Great Portland Street, ready for an evening with the man who might be serious love C, she has a vision of the dynamics of her romantic life. She imagines C, too, standing in his window, anticipating their meeting, hoping like her to be able to give his wounded heart to another. She imagines calling C and asking him to agree that they should keep their wounded hearts to themselves, not hurl them at one another. Her fancied appeal to C is interrupted by an awareness that a large, unknown object has appeared in her left hand. She recognizes this unknown object as her own heart.

She is in turn irritated, appalled, and a bit disgusted by the heart in her hand, but soon enough the problem it presents is clear. How will she get rid of it? Unable to pull the heart off and throw it away, she cancels her date with the man who might be serious love C and sits for four days examining the layers of memory in her forty-year-old heart. She is struck by the realization that examining her heart and its memories will affix her heart to her hand permanently. Freeing herself of her heart will require more than introspection.

Concealing her heart on her hand first in tinfoil, then in a scarf, she moves out on the street and into the London subway system. Sitting unnoticed in a crowded train, she observes a young, rather shabby woman. The woman sits in a twisted posture, stares at nothing, talks to herself in a "private drama of misery" over some betrayal of love. The narrator describes her as absorbed in a "frozen misery," a "passionless passion."

As she stares at this stricken shell of a woman, the narrator suddenly feels the heart in her hand roll loose. She stands and places the heart wrapped in its tinfoil on the seat next to the woman, like a poignant valentine. The grieving woman clutches it to herself as if it were a precious gift, a gift which compensated for all of her pain. The narrator rises and leaves the underground, laughing. Heartless, she is free.

Themes and Meanings

This story portrays a contemporary woman's consciousness surveying the ruins of the myth of romantic love. It is an ironic rumination on the emptiness of the cliché of losing one's heart in love. At the center of the story is the drama of a psychic crisis and its resolution, staged in the chamber of a middle-aged woman's mind. She metaphorically moves into the room of her own being and then into the underground world of her own unconscious. The tale is both the story of a woman's crack-up, her intense experience of her divided self, and the story of her development and new wholeness. The narrator's cool detachment has long covered her submerged torment of disappointment and failure to connect in love. Captive to the myth of losing her heart in love, desiring another to claim responsibility for her and absolve her of her pain, Lessing's contemporary woman explores her own disillusionment and moves toward becoming a "free woman."

The pale, thin, self-absorbed woman on the train is a projection of the narrator's dissociated and long-denied mourning, her inner being gripped by pain. To her tormented doppelgänger, her own living ghost, she gives her heart, at once symbolically freeing herself of the myth of romantic love and confronting and uniting with her own despair. No lover can redeem one from pain. Freedom is found in acknowledging and claiming the pain of love as one's own, thus becoming whole.

Style and Technique

The unifying force of this story is the narrator's voice. Her personal voice, however, is not the language of the heart but of the head. Her style, sophisticated, coolly analytical, even cynical, is the manifestation of her conscious denial of the pain of disappointed love. Lessing uses the device of this voice as a controlling metaphor for her character's detachment from her own grief. The intensely preoccupied tone of the narrator's self-scrutiny reveals her lack of connection, the emptiness of a quest unfulfilled and unfulfillable, the pain of repeated loss and the undiminished hope that "He might turn out to be the one." She long has been victim of such women's magazine phrases, and, like Anna Wulf in *The Golden Notebook* (1962), the narrator has been a woman "who cannot feel deeply about anything." After encountering her two serious loves on the same day, her conventional behavior patterns, including her habitual return to the search for serious love represented by the date with C, crumble under a torrent of new self-awareness.

The appearance of her heart in her hand is a symbol with many valences. It is an ironic literalization of the cliché of losing one's heart or approaching another with one's heart in one's hand. The exteriorization of her heart is also a surreal representation of her moment of psychic upheaval, her revolution in attitude toward love, which leads to a new state of freedom. Her conscious self, embodied in her narrative voice, confronts her unconscious, suppressed pain in the depths of the London underground. Her live, clinging heart wrapped in silver becomes a stylized gift of love to herself. Offered and accepted, it represents an integration of her conscious and unconscious selves and her entry into a new personal realm of freedom.

Like so many of Lessing's characters, this narrator is absorbed in reflection on her aloneness in a journey where loves are not ends but rather way stations. She recounts an experience in which she makes herself, her actions, and her feelings visible to herself. In giving her heart away, she does not die but is reborn in acceptance of and freedom from her own disappointments in romantic love.

Virginia Crane

HOW IT WAS DONE IN ODESSA

Author: Isaac Babel (1894-1941)
Type of plot: Dramatized narrative
Time of plot: Early twentieth century
Locale: Odessa
First published: "Kak eto delalos v Odesse," 1923 (English translation, 1955)

> *Principal characters:*
> THE NARRATOR, who listens to the story
> REB ARYE-LEIB, the storyteller
> BENYA KRIK, a Jewish gangster
> SAVKA BUTSIS, a member of the gang
> RUVIM TARTAKOVSKY, "JEW-AND-A-HALF," a wealthy Jewish merchant
> JOSEPH MUGINSTEIN, a clerk
> AUNT PESYA, Joseph's mother

The Story

"How It Was Done in Odessa" belongs to a cycle of four stories known as the Odessa tales, which were written by Isaac Babel between 1921 and 1923 and published as *Odessa Tales* in 1927. All these tales concern the adventures of a Jewish gangster, Benya Krik. "How It Was Done in Odessa" is begun by a first-person narrator, who asks Reb Arye-Leib how Benya came to be known as "the King." The story that follows is told by Reb Arye-Leib in response to that question.

Reb Arye-Leib's story begins when Benya is twenty-five years old. Benya appeals to the then leading gangster for permission to join the gang, and the gangsters decide to test him by asking him to rob Ruvim Tartakovsky, one of the wealthiest and most influential Jews in Odessa, who has already been robbed nine times before.

Benya accepts the gangsters' challenge and sends an extremely polite letter to Tartakovsky requesting his cooperation. Tartakovsky actually replies to Benya's letter, but the reply is never received, and Benya and his companions proceed to Tartakovsky's office as threatened. When they arrive, the office is occupied only by the frightened clerk, Joseph Muginstein. The robbery proceeds without incident, but as they are emptying the safe, another member of the gang, Savka Butsis, arrives late and drunk. The drunken Savka accidentally shoots Muginstein in the stomach, and the gang runs away.

The shooting of Joseph Muginstein is an accident. It is the way in which Benya behaves after the shooting that earns for him the title "King." As the gang leaves, Benya threatens that if Muginstein dies, he will bury Savka alongside of him. Later, Benya visits the hospital and tells the doctors to spare no expense. If Joseph dies, Benya threatens, each doctor, "even if he's a doctor of philosophy," will receive six feet of earth for his pains. Joseph does die, however, and Benya next drives his red automobile, the horn of which plays the first march from the opera *Pagliacci*, to visit Aunt Pesya, Joseph's mother. There he meets Tartakovsky, who accuses him of "killing live people," but Benya in turn reproaches Tartakovsky for having sent Aunt Pesya a mere hundred rubles in compensation for her son's life. The two men argue and finally agree on five thousand rubles in cash and a pension of fifty rubles a month for the remainder of Aunt Pesya's life.

In the final scenes of the story, Reb Arye-Leib describes the magnificent funeral that Benya arranged for Joseph. Benya himself delivered a funeral oration, at the end of which he invited the crowd to pay their respects to the late Savka Butsis as well. It was at this funeral that the epithet "King" was first applied to Benya.

Themes and Meanings

All the Odessa tales have as their background the Jewish way of life in Odessa at the beginning of the twentieth century. Conventional images of the Jews do not generally include gangsters who tear around in opera-playing red automobiles, however, and "How It Was Done in Odessa" should not be read as a documentary account of the life of the Jews but rather as a burlesque of that life.

This burlesque, although comic, refers to a serious reality. In "How It Was Done in Odessa," casual references to a pogrom remind the reader of the precarious position of the Jews within Russian society. Benya himself addresses this theme when he asks Aunt Pesya, "But wasn't it a mistake on the part of God to settle Jews in Russia, for them to be tormented worse than in Hell?" It is significant, however, that the only violence that occurs within the story itself is perpetrated by the Jews, and great stress is placed on the fact that both Benya and Tartakovsky, who is generally referred to by his nickname "Jew-and-a-Half," belong to the same people.

The narrator, who plays no role in the action of the story, plays a crucial role in developing its theme of appropriate attitudes toward violence in modern society. He has obviously asked Reb Arye-Leib to tell the story because of his admiration for Benya, but Reb Arye-Leib compares the narrator unfavorably with Benya throughout the story and describes him both at the beginning and the end of the story as having "spectacles on [his] nose and autumn in [his] heart." In other words, Reb Arye-Leib represents him as a stereotypical ineffectual intellectual, who is incapable of action although he finds it attractive. The narrator's ambivalence, although not central to the action of the story, nevertheless occupies a central place in any understanding of it.

Style and Technique

Babel was a noted practitioner of what is known in Russian as *skaz*, a dramatic first-person narrative technique which duplicates as closely as possible the natural idiom of the speaker. In "How It Was Done in Odessa," the primary speaker is Reb Arye-Leib, and his language is rich in the rhythms and idioms of his milieu. Yet "How It Was Done in Odessa" is not written in a single uniform style. At the beginning of the story the narrator's manner is reminiscent of medieval Russian epics. Later, Reb Arye-Leib embeds long speeches by the other characters (which he could not possibly have known from his own experience) into his narrative. Benya's excessively genteel letter to Tartakovsky and his address to the doctors fall into this category, and their humor derives from his misuse of the language and ignorance of the conventions generally associated with such occasions.

The effectiveness of "How It Was Done in Odessa" depends on a discrepancy between the manner of speaking and what is actually said. Despite the very funny way in which the story is told, it is actually concerned with robbery and murder, and it is the narrator's ambivalent attitude toward these acts of violence that creates much of the story's interest. The narrator's excessively literary style stands in sharp contrast to Benya's colorful abuse of the language and heightens the reader's awareness of the differences between the two men. Reb Arye-Leib's constant hectoring of the narrator and his frequent suggestions that the narrator emulate Benya and become a man of action himself keep this conflict present in the reader's mind, but such acts of violence are clearly alien to the intellectual narrator. The tension that exists between the light manner of narration and the brutal events depicted reinforces the atmosphere of ambivalence by producing a similar reaction in the reader, who finds the story appealing while at the same time being unable to accept the values of its attractive hero.

Sandra Rosengrant

HOW MUCH LAND DOES A MAN NEED?

Author: Leo Tolstoy (1828-1910)
Type of plot: Parable
Time of plot: The late 1800's
Locale: Russia
First published: "Mnogo li cheloveku zemli nuzhno?," 1886 (English translation, 1887)

> *Principal characters:*
> PAHOM, a landowner who strives for security in owning more and more land
> THE CHIEF OF THE BASHKIRS, who offers Pahom as much land as he can walk around in a day
> THE DEVIL, the tempter who arranges Pahom's land deals

The Story

An elder sister from the city visits her younger sister, the wife of a peasant farmer in the village. In the midst of their visit, the two of them get into an argument about whether the city or the peasant life-style is preferable. The elder sister suggests that city life boasts better clothes, good things to eat and drink, and various entertainments, such as the theater. The younger sister replies that though peasant life may be rough, she and her husband are free, will always have enough to eat, and are not tempted by the Devil to indulge in such worldly pursuits.

Pahom, the husband of the younger sister, enters the debate and suggests that the charm of the peasant life is that the peasant has no time to let nonsense settle in his head. The one drawback of peasant life, he declares, is that the peasant does not have enough land: "If I had plenty of land, I shouldn't fear the Devil himself!" The Devil, overhearing this boast, decides to give Pahom his wish, seducing him with the extra land that Pahom thinks will give him security.

Pahom's first opportunity to gain extra land comes when a lady in the village decides to sell her three hundred acres. His fellow peasants try to arrange the purchase for themselves as part of a commune, but the Devil sows discord among them and individual peasants begin to buy land. Pahom obtains forty acres of his own. This pleases him initially, but soon neighboring peasants allow their cows to stray into his meadows and their horses among his corn, and he must seek justice from the district court. Not only does he fail to receive recompense for the damages, but also he ruins his reputation among his former friends and neighbors; his extra land does not bring him security.

Hearing a rumor about more and better farmland elsewhere, he decides to sell his land and move his family to a new location. There he obtains 125 acres and is ten times better off than he was before, and he is very pleased. Yet he soon realizes that he could make a better profit with more land on which to sow wheat. He makes a deal to obtain thirteen hundred acres from a peasant in financial difficulty for one thousand rubles and has all but clinched it when he hears a rumor about the land of the Bashkirs. There, a tradesman tells him, a man can obtain land for less than a penny an acre, simply by making friends with the chiefs.

Fueled by the desire for more, cheaper, and better land, Pahom seeks directions for the land of the Bashkirs and leaves on a journey to obtain the land that he thinks he needs. Upon arrival, he distributes gifts to the Bashkir leaders and finds them courteous and friendly. He explains his reasons for being there and, after some deliberation, they offer him whatever land he wants for one thousand rubles. Pahom is pleased, but concerned; he wants boundaries, deeds, and "official sanction" to give him the assurance he needs that they or their children will never reverse their decision.

The Bashkirs agree to this arrangement, and a deal is struck. Pahom can have all the land that he can walk around in a day for one thousand rubles. The one condition is that if he does not return on the same day to the spot at which he began, the money will be lost. The night before his fateful walk, Pahom plans his strategy; he will try to encircle thirty-five miles of land and then sell the poorer land to peasants at a profit. When he awakes the next day, he is met by the man whom he thought was the chief of the Bashkirs, but whom he recognizes as the peasant who had come to his old home to tell him of lucrative land deals available elsewhere. He looks again, and realizes that he is speaking with the Devil himself. He dismisses this meeting as merely a dream and goes about his walk.

Pahom starts well, but he tries to encircle too much land, and by midday he realizes that he has tried to create too big a circuit. Though afraid of death, he knows that his only chance is to complete the circuit. "There is plenty of land," he says to himself, "but will God let me live on it?" As the sun comes down, Pahom runs with all his remaining strength to the spot where he began. Reaching it, he sees the chief laughing and holding his sides; he remembers his dream and breathes his last breath. Pahom's servant picks up the spade with which Pahom had been marking his land and digs a grave in which to bury him: "Six feet from his head to his heels was all he needed."

Themes and Meanings

"How Much Land Does a Man Need?" is a classic Tolstoy tale of a man's grasp exceeding his reach. Seeking security in the acquisition of wealth or land instead of seeking it in the humble family life of the peasant, Pahom mocks God and falls into the clutches of the Devil. Tolstoy's story greatly resembles the parable of the rich fool told by Jesus in Luke 12:16-20, in which a wealthy farmer tears down his barns and builds bigger ones to store his wheat, thinking to himself that he has achieved security for the rest of his life. Instead, at the very moment when he surveys his domain with complacent satisfaction, God rebukes him: "Thou fool, this night thy soul shall be required of thee."

Tolstoy's Pahom is thus a man discontented with his lot in life who fails to seek his contentment from the proper source. His boast that with enough land he would not fear the Devil himself is actually a rejection of God as his protector and benefactor. Yet unlike Faust, who openly bargains with an agent of the Devil, Pahom is a victim of his own greed, which obscures his judgment; so obsessed is he with more land, he is unable to recognize the hand of the Devil behind his opportunities. This, clearly, is the moral fault which Tolstoy seeks to underscore in the tale: The sacrificing of a basic trust in God and the surrender of basic human kindness and responsibility for the acquisition of possessions brings a man earthly ruin and eternal damnation.

Style and Technique

Tolstoy regarded the telling force of a moral and the power to reach a wide audience as the key elements in a story. These two elements are bountifully present in "How Much Land Does a Man Need?" In referring to the tale as a parable, critics draw attention to its didactic function. In a parable, the focus is entirely on one or, at most, two characters and a specific circumstance which provides the conflict or challenge that the protagonists must face.

The only fully developed character in Tolstoy's tale is Pahom; neither his wife nor her elder sister nor any of his fellow peasants is given a distinct identity. Tolstoy intends his readers to focus entirely on the plight of Pahom as he seeks his fortune. This, like his other parables, is meant to transmit feelings of God's love and the importance of love of one's neighbor.

The parable form is meant to convey a deliberate sense of "artlessness"—that is, a simplicity of narrative style and content in which a story seems inevitable, or self-telling. In fact, the parable form requires careful attention to achieve this "artless" effect, and Tolstoy has no equal among such storytellers.

Bruce L. Edwards, Jr.

HOW THE DEVIL CAME DOWN DIVISION STREET

Author: Nelson Algren (1909-1981)
Type of plot: Comic ghost story
Time of plot: The 1930's
Locale: Chicago
First published: 1945

Principal characters:
ROMAN ORLOV, the protagonist, who recounts how he became the "biggest drunk on Division Street"
PAPA ORLOV, an accordionist and janitor
MAMA ORLOV, who has second thoughts about the "miracle"
TERESA, Roman's sister

The Story

The "story" in "How the Devil Came Down Division Street" is narrated by a person who heard the tale from Roman Orlov, the "biggest drunk on Division Street." As the story begins, several drunks in the Polonia Bar argue about who the biggest drunk is, but the discussion is decided by the appearance of Roman, who is unanimously accorded that title. Pressed for an explanation about his life and the reason for his drinking, Roman tells the narrator his story in exchange for a series of double shots of whiskey. Roman claims that he has a "great worm inside" that "gnaws and gnaws"; the whiskey helps him "drown the worm." Roman also "obscurely" (as the narrator puts it) states that "the devil lives in a double-shot," but not until the end of the story does the reader learn what Roman may mean. In effect, then, the story is filtered through the personality of the narrator, who treats his subject and subjects with light irony.

Roman's story, as told to the narrator, takes him years back to his early adolescence. It seems that the Orlov family lives in a small tenement apartment that is too small for the six Orlovs and their dog. There are only two beds: Mama and eleven-year-old Teresa sleep in one of them; thirteen-year-old Roman sleeps between the squabbling younger twins to prevent them from fighting. As a result, there is no bed for Papa, who spends his nights playing his accordion for pennies and drinks in bars. When he comes in late, he sleeps under Roman's bed, unless the dog is already sleeping there, in which case Papa sleeps under Mama's bed. Papa never crawls, "even with daylight, to Mama O.'s bed," because he does not feel "worthy" to sleep there. The narrator adds that Papa apparently wants to remain "true" to his accordion, which replaces Mama. At this point in the story "strange things go on in Papa O.'s head," and Teresa is a slow learner at school, but Roman is fine.

Things change with a mysterious knocking at the Orlov apartment. Soon afterward, Mama dreams of "a young man, drunken . . . with blood down the front of his shirt and drying on his hands." Knowing this for a sign that the "unhappy dead return to warn or comfort . . . to gain peace or to avenge," she consults Mrs. Zolewitz, who confirms her fears by telling her about the previous tenants of the Orlov apartment. It seems that the young man who lived there was "sick in the head from drink"; more important to the conservative Mrs. Zolewitz, he lived there "with his lady without being wed." On New Year's Eve, he came home drunk and beat his woman until her whimperings stopped completely, and there was no sound at all until noon the next day, when the police arrived: The woman was dead and the man had hanged himself in the closet. According to Mrs. Zolewitz, the couple was buried together in "unsanctified ground." Mrs. Zolewitz reassures the frightened Mama by telling her that the young man does not intend them any harm but searches, instead, for peace. The Orlovs' prayers, she suggests, will bring that peace.

Meanwhile, Papa has lost, sold, or loaned his accordion, and the lost accordion and Mama's dream coincide, leading her to believe that a change is coming. The change occurs when the prayers begin and when Papa stays home because he lacks the accordion. After Papa prays, he goes to bed with Mama "like a good husband," and she informs the priest that she knows now the knocking was a good omen. He declares that it is the will of God that "the Orlovs should redeem the young man by prayer and that Papa O. should have a wife instead of an accordion."

The results of the changes are immediate and salutary: "For lack of music," Papa becomes the best janitor on Noble Street; the priest blesses Mrs. Zolewitz for her part in the miracle; the landlord, who now has an unhaunted house, frees the Orlovs from their rental payments; the "slow" Teresa "goes to the head of the class"; even the squabbling twins make their peace. In effect, the entire Orlov family, with the notable exception of Roman, benefits from the knocking, the prayers, and the new sleeping arrangements. Because Papa is sleeping with Mama, Teresa replaces Roman between the twins. For four years Roman replaces his father under one of the two beds, and his parents' bed has springs that squeak "half the night as likely as not." Finally, Roman begins sleeping during the day so that he will not have to sleep at night, "and at night, as everyone knows, there is no place to go but the taverns." The narrator notes that Roman consequently took his father's place not only as a person without a bed, but as a drinker.

At the conclusion of his tale, the narrator pauses to reflect about Roman's story. Is it, he asks, "a drunkard's tale or sober truth?" Complicating that answer is the passage of years since the changes: Mama now believes that the knocking young man was the Devil because she believes she gave the Devil a good son, Roman, "in return for a worthless husband." This development causes the narrator to ask if the Devil lives in a double shot, if he gnaws "like the worm," or if he knocks, "with blood drying on his knuckles, in the gaslight passages of our dreams?"

Themes and Meanings

Although the story begins in a bar and contains a humorous turn of events, it explores the nature of guilt, the need to justify one's behavior and one's weaknesses, and the nature of evil. On the superficial and superstitious level, the bloody young man seeks atonement and peace, both of which he apparently receives through the Orlovs' prayers, but the narrator mocks the "miracle" through Mrs. Zolewitz's morality (unwed sex leads to death) and the priest's liberally bestowed "blessings." Mama also suffers guilt for her neglect of Roman, but her guilt is "after the fact" of her renewed sex life with her husband and his eventual death. Hers is the comic guilt of one who repents only after the opportunity for sin no longer exists. Roman's guilt, however, is real, for that "worm" that "gnaws" within him is his own awareness of his wasted life. It is that awareness that prompts his explanation and justification of becoming the "biggest drunk on Division Street." His "lack of a bed" is his "excuse" for his behavior, but the narrator notes that his father's "excuse" at least involved an accordion. Because he still does not have a "home," Roman expects sympathy and understanding, but clearly his psychological wounds have been self-inflicted. While it may help Roman to believe in the Devil as an active presence in the world, the Devil is "within." On the other hand, Algren also suggests that Roman's environment contributes to his fate. Brought up in a community that confuses superstition with religion, that restricts morality to sexual matters, and that regards drinking as a means of achieving status, Roman does not have much chance to escape the confines of the Polish ghetto in Chicago. Like other Algren characters, Roman is trapped, paralyzed, and incapable of action.

Style and Technique

The narration in "How the Devil Came Down Division Street" is atypical of Algren, whose style tends to be figurative and naturalistic in its use of animal imagery, rather than literal and matter-of-fact. In addition, Algren generally relies on omniscient, third-person, rather than first-person, narration. The narrator in this story recounts Roman's story, but he embellishes it, filters it through his own values and attitudes, and then poses questions about the story itself. There are two narrative "voices" or styles in the story. The first is the narrator's retelling of Roman's story "as closely to what he told as I can," without the "sobs" and the "cursing," but with a touch of mocking irony. For the most part, the narrator offers a straightforward account with almost mathematical exactitude. Given the number of people and the number of sleepers, there is domestic trouble; when Papa is added to the equation, someone else will be in trouble. In fact, the narrator begins the paragraphs at the end of Roman's story with the phrases "Thus it came about," "So it was," and "This is why," thereby lending the story an air of logical precision. The other narrative voice occurs at the end of Roman's story, from which it is separated by a break in the text. The second voice is more abstract, philosophical, and questioning, and the language is much more figurative: The narrator asks if the Devil is "the one who knocks, on winter nights, with blood drying on his knuckles, in the gaslit passages of our dreams?" Since the short story concludes with this pessimistic speculation about evil, despair, and the unconscious, Algren apparently intends Roman's story, amusing and touching as it is, as the springboard for some searching questions about the nature of evil.

Thomas L. Erskine

A HUNGER ARTIST

Author: Franz Kafka (1883-1924)
Type of plot: Parable
Time of plot: Unspecified
Locale: Unspecified
First published: "Ein Hungerkünstler," 1922 (English translation, 1938)

Principal characters:
THE HUNGER ARTIST, the protagonist, a tormented performer
of the macabre art of fasting
THE IMPRESARIO, the hunger artist's manager during the years
when spectacles of fasting are popular
THE SPECTATORS, insensitive, skeptical amusement seekers
THE OVERSEER, the circus attendant who hears without
understanding the artist's dying confession

The Story

Kafka's dark parable describes the hunger artist's ritual of self-annihilation and shows the ironic use of dissatisfaction as a stimulus for art. The narrator describes two periods of the artist's life—that of the past, when people took a "lively interest" in spectacles of fasting, and that of recent times, when fasting has lost its popularity. Even in the early days of his career, the hunger artist feels the ingratitude of his audience, which continually questions his honesty. To demonstrate that no trickery is used, the artist sings during his fast. The watchers only consider him more clever for being able to sing while eating. No matter how much he craves respect for his achievement, the artist cannot gain his audience's trust. More important, the hunger artist cannot even please himself, for he knows that he is indeed dishonest, not because he breaks the fast—he never does this—but because he alone knows how easy it is to fast. The fast, then, is not an act of self-fortitude and spiritual purification but rather an expression of the artist's disdain for life.

The impresario reveals himself to be as uncaring as the public toward the hunger artist. The impresario sets a forty-day limit to the fast, not out of concern for the weakened artist but because public interest cannot be sustained beyond forty days. The impresario is concerned only with promoting the performance just as the watchers are interested only in their own amusement.

Epitomizing the isolation of the hunger artist is the description of the artist's defeated reaction to the impresario's display of photographs. When the hunger artist reacts violently to a comforter's advice that the artist's melancholy springs from fasting, the impresario apologizes for the hunger artist, explaining that his moodiness and irritability indeed result from fasting. Photographs are then shown of the artist, who on the fortieth day appears almost dead from malnutrition. The hunger artist watches the audience accept the lie that his depression is caused by fasting. He alone knows that the opposite is true, that his depression comes from knowing that he will soon be forced to eat. As the photographs support the impresario's lie and reinforce the public's misconceptions, the hunger artist feels more frustrated in his desire for understanding: ". . . as soon as the photographs appeared he always let go and sank with a groan back on to his straw, and the reassured public could once more come close and gaze at him." The words "come close" point to the physical nearness and the psychological distance of the audience, while the word "gaze" emphasizes the superficiality of the public's way of seeing.

The second part of the story describes the hunger artist's life after the spectacle of fasting has lost its appeal. The hunger artist is now forced to dismiss the impresario and join a circus. Since he has no manager now to limit his fast, the artist hopes to achieve a record that will astonish the world. The other professionals smile at this boast, for they know that no one really cares about fasting anymore. The emaciated artist's cage is ironically placed near the menagerie, where the artist must suffer the odors of the animals and of the raw meat that is served them. While, in former days, the skeptical public at least displayed curiosity, the public now pays little attention to the hunger artist. The occasional visitors who wish to stand and watch him are jeered by those who believe that their journey to the animal exhibit is being impeded. The circus attendants also neglect the hunger artist. They forget to replace his straw and to change the placard indicating the length of his fast. Finally the hunger artist is forgotten altogether.

The discovery, the confession, and the death of the hunger artist provide the climax of the story. Curious about the seemingly empty cage, an overseer pokes the straw with a stick and finds the hunger artist. When asked if he is still fasting, the hunger artist whispers, "Forgive me, everybody" and explains that no one should admire his fasting because he could not help but fast. When asked why he cannot help it, the artist says, "because I couldn't find the food I liked. If I had found it, believe me, I should have made no fuss and stuffed myself like you or anyone else." With this confession that there is nothing nourishing in life, the hunger artist dies. The nourishment that the hunger artist has craved has been the food of human compassion.

The story ends with the image of the wild panther that now occupies the hunger artist's cage. The contrast between the defeated, malnourished, and spiritually imprisoned artist and the young, vital animal that seems "to carry freedom around with it" is striking. The animal that cares nothing for audience support ironically achieves the understanding and admiration never attained by the starving artist.

Themes and Meanings

The lack of specific names for the hunger artist, the impresario, and the members of the audience suggests the symbolic nature of the story. The hunger artist may represent any artist or any person whose art or existence is grounded on a conviction of life's meaninglessness. The hunger artist, as his name implies, craves nourishment. As the story progresses, it becomes clear that the food desired is spiritual and that physical starvation is merely a metaphor of the soul's malnourishment. The artist's devotion to the art of starvation ironically demands that while consciously attempting to win understanding, he unconsciously must discourage human sympathy. He thus encages himself, turns himself into a grotesque, appeals to the sympathy of people who relish freak shows, refuses to verbalize his feelings, and in the end buries himself under straw. Reflecting a tasteless, monotonous world, the performance proceeds by an absence of action. This passive art ensures the slow deterioration of an already fragile bond between the performer and his viewers. The many allusions to Christ emphasize the parodic nature of the hunger artist's martyrdom. When the hunger artist at the end of a forty-day fast is helped from his cage by two frightened women, his outstretched arms form a cross. The hunger artist, however, unlike Christ, suffers not to affirm spiritual life but to reveal the absence of hope. The hunger artist's consummate performance, the perfection of the art of negation, is death.

The alternatives offered by the story are bleak. The hunger artist with his heightened sensitivity and unhealthy narcissism stands for one way of experiencing life, while the impresario, the public, and the overseer, complacent and uncaring, reveal an alternative way of seeing and feeling. The panther that captivates the interest of the public is placed against these human extremes. Unlike the hunger artist, the panther will devour anything. The animal possesses the joy of life and the sense of freedom that is beyond human reach: "Somewhere freedom seemed to lurk; and the joy of life streamed with such ardent passion from his throat that for the onlookers it was not easy to stand the shock of it." The cat displays a vibrant, wild beauty, for its predatory nature is fitting to its species. The crowd and the impresario, however, while possessing a similar voracious appetite and hardness, are despicable caricatures of human beings. Yet their lack of insight makes them, like the panther, survivors.

Style and Technique

The narrator poses as an objective, unemotional chronicler of a dying social phenomenon. He records the early years of the profession of fasting with cold detachment and with more than a modicum of irony. For example, he exaggerates and then undercuts the moral claim of the hunger artist, describing him as "this suffering martyr, which indeed he was, although in quite another sense." When the public loses interest in fasting, the narrator seems to smile, "at any rate the pampered hunger artist suddenly found himself deserted one fine day by the amusement seekers. . . ." The amused tone of this cosmic chronicler adds to the reader's sense of the artist's growing isolation. As the historian describes the hunger artist's experience in the circus, the tension of the narrative increases. In this section, the narrator often expresses the yearnings and frustrations of the hunger artist: "Just try to explain to anyone the art of fasting! Anyone who has no feeling for it cannot be made to understand it." The narrator's voice again merges with the feelings of the artist when the viewers question the accuracy of the numbers posted on the placard: "that was in its way the stupidist lie ever invented, by indifference and inborn malice. . . ." By shifting from an objective to a subjective perspective, the narrator emphasizes the unbridgeable gulf between the longing artist and the world. The final shift in perspective and tone comes in the description of the hunger artist's death. The narrator now returns to the earlier, uninflected style. The rapid pace of the prose and the cold, impersonal tone emphasize the total insignificance of the artist: "'Well, clear this out now!' said the overseer, and they buried the hunger artist, straw and all. Into the cage they put a young panther." The closing image of the public's admiration of the panther is a disturbing reminder that even a person's death by slow starvation is not sufficient to disturb the placidity of the self-indulgent world.

Catherine Cox

THE HUNTER GRACCHUS

Author: Franz Kafka (1883-1924)
Type of plot: Parable
Time of plot: Unspecified
Locale: Riva, Austria
First published: "Der Jäger Gracchus," 1931 (English translation, 1946)

Principal characters:
SALVATORE, the burgomaster of Riva
GRACCHUS, a hunter from the Black Forest, long since dead

The Story

As various inhabitants of the town of Riva, situated on Lake Garda, go about their apparently customary activities—shopkeeping, reading the paper, drawing water at the well, or simply idling away the time—a boat enters the harbor and ties up at the quay. Two men in dark coats with silver buttons debark, carrying what seems to be a person's body on a cloth-draped bier. The townspeople pay them no particular attention. The boatman, who seems to be their guide, directs the two men to a nearby house. All three enter it with the bier, noticed as they go in by a boy at an upstairs window. A flock of doves arrives and alights in front of the house.

A man in mourning dress, looking somewhat troubled by the appearance of the neighborhood, approaches the house from one of the streets, knocks at the door, and is admitted at once. Some fifty little boys standing in two rows the length of the entry hall bow to him, and the boatman descends the stair and leads the visitor upstairs to a large room at the back of the house, in which the two bearers are busy placing and lighting candles at the head of the bier. The cloth has been drawn back, and on the bier lies a man with tangled hair and beard and tanned skin, looking rather like a hunter. Although his eyes are closed, and he is motionless and seems not to breathe, it is really only his surroundings which suggest that he may be dead.

The man in mourning approaches, touches the forehead of the one lying there, and kneels to pray beside him. The two bearers withdraw, and at a sign from the visitor so does the boatman. At once the man on the bier opens his eyes, turns his face to the mourner, and asks: "Who are you?" "The Burgomaster of Riva," the other replies, getting to his feet. In fact, both know already who the other is, since a dove came to the burgomaster's window during the night and announced to him, "Tomorrow the dead Hunter Gracchus is coming; receive him in the name of the city." Gracchus explains that the doves precede him wherever he goes. He asks the burgomaster if he believes that Gracchus is to remain in Riva. The answer seems to depend on whether Gracchus is truly dead.

He tells the burgomaster that a great many years ago, while hunting a chamois in the Black Forest in Germany, he fell from a precipice and died. The burgomaster observes that he is nevertheless still alive. "In a certain sense," Gracchus answers. His death ship lost its way, he explains, so that ever since that time he who yearns only for the mountains of his homeland has been ceaselessly traveling the waters of the earth, a hunter transformed into a butterfly, as he says. He spends his days on a wooden pallet in the boat's cabin, dirty and unkempt, with a candle at his head, and on the wall of the cabin a small picture, evidently of a bushman, who is aiming his spear at Gracchus and taking cover behind a lavishly painted shield.

Gracchus' great misfortune, as he tells it, was not his death, but the wrong turn, the brief inattention of the pilot, the distraction of his native land— whatever it was that caused the ship to stray from its course. Gracchus had lived and hunted happily, and he welcomed his death as the most natural thing in the world. He believes that he was faithful to his calling and to his fate; the mishap was the boatman's fault, not his. Gracchus says that there is no help for him. None will come to his aid; even if they were asked, people would hide in their houses, under their bedcovers. No one knows of him, and if someone did, that person would not know his whereabouts; even if someone did know it, that person could not halt the boat's voyage and could do nothing for the voyager. "The thought of helping me," Gracchus says, "is an illness that has to be cured by taking to one's bed." So, wish as he might, he resigns himself to his fate and does not call out for help. He needs only to look around him and remember where he is, and any thought of calling out vanishes. The burgomaster asks him if he intends to stay in Riva. Gracchus replies that he intends nothing, that he can know only where he is at present; his ship rides with the wind that blows in the undermost regions of death.

Themes and Meanings

The parable of the hunter Gracchus, with its overtones of both classical mythology and Germanic legend, is perhaps most reminiscent of the folk saga of the Flying Dutchman, the man whose blasphemous boasting condemned him to sail the seas on his ghostly ship forever unless released from his punishment by the faithfulness of a woman. He too, like Gracchus, sought death as a liberation from his endless wanderings, but he found himself powerless to end his own life. Like Gracchus, the voyager of the legend was accorded the chance to come ashore from his ship periodically to seek that which might free him from the curse. Yet Gracchus is condemned to sail wherever the winds may drive his boat without the benefit of knowing the offense of which he is guilty, and this is where his story differs so significantly from the legend of the Flying Dutchman and what makes his plight so characteristic of the human condition as Kafka confronts it. Indeed, as he says, Gracchus lived his life as he had been meant to live it: joyously, proudly, and with distinction. His labors were blessed. He was known as the Great Hunter of the Black Forest. The death that he thought was his, and for which he still wishes, is not a desperate wish, but rather the natural consequence and fitting reward for the life that went before it. He met death gladly and expectantly, donning his shroud as a bride would her wedding gown. "Then came the mishap."

It was the fault of the boatman, Gracchus claims, and if anyone could explain what went wrong in his crossing from life into death, it would be this enigmatic figure. A number of Kafka's novels and stories include such persons. It is sometimes unclear whether they are the guides who show the way or the guards who bar it. Often they appear to be both, seemingly helpful but then again frustratingly ineffectual or even perversely obstructive. The boatman in this story does not speak a word and is no longer present when Gracchus tells his story to the burgomaster, yet he seems to control the course of events. His actions, even if arbitrary and inexplicable, are not subject to question, and the passenger, whatever his station and distinctions otherwise in life, is at his mercy. The boatman calls to mind the mythical ferryman Charon, but he is a Charon in reverse: not the guide who makes entry into the realm of the dead possible, but the one who presumably committed the fatal error and now keeps Gracchus a wanderer while maintaining silence about the reason for it and about the eventual fate of his passenger.

Gracchus (still a hunter, even though he once believed his hunting days were happily over) hovers between two worlds. He tells the burgomaster that he is dead, but also still alive. One might also say that he is neither and that the "no man's land" he now inhabits may help to explain the open end of the story. It has been said of Kafka himself that, occupying a kind of border territory between sociability and solitude, he could not live; but that condition enabled him to observe how life was lived. So it is with Gracchus. He cannot intend to stay in Riva or to leave again, because intending is not within his power now. He can say only, "I am here, more than that I do not know, further than that I cannot go."

Style and Technique

While parables in the traditional sense are thought of as didactic stories with a moral truth or insight to convey, Kafka's tales do not purport to have arrived at such truths. Instead they record observations on the human experience. Since the human condition, at least to Kafka's eye, is experienced as a fragmented, incoherent, sometimes mystifying, and frightening existence, stories such as "The Hunter Gracchus" do not proceed from a clear beginning through a logical series of developments to a conclusive ending. They are marked by apparent disjunctions of thought and seemingly arbitrary, extraneous elements. Told—like parables—in analogous, not literal terms, they nevertheless embody a realism of their own. Yet it is not Gracchus' fantastic story that is realistic; it is rather the sense of unending limbo, a twilight existence between life and death, and the helplessness that he feels which constitute Kafka's realism.

Certain elements of "The Hunter Gracchus" are palpably symbolic—the doves which announce the hunter's arrival, the fifty or so little boys who form the receiving line for the burgomaster, and the picture of the spear-wielding bushman in Gracchus' cabin. Exactly what the symbolism means is difficult to say; this is the sort of device which gives rise to interpretive disputes over Kafka's writings.

There is also a familiar, superficial realism about the story. The waterfront setting in which it begins, with boys playing at dice, a man reading his newspaper, the denizens of the café, a monument to some military hero, the fruit peels littering the street, the exterior and interior details of the house where the bier is taken; these lend the story a "realistic" overlay. Yet in fact they parody traditional realism because they distract from, rather than explicate or complement, the main idea of the parable. This level of realism, especially as it focuses on the ordinary and unswept corners of life, may establish an initial credibility for the narrative, but there is humor in its dull ordinariness, and because of that, it contrasts all the more starkly with the grave existential "illness" that Gracchus' fate engenders in the rest of humanity.

Michael Ritterson

HUNTING SEASON

Author: Joanne Greenberg (1932-   )
Type of plot: Realistic domestic idyll
Time of plot: The early 1970's
Locale: The western American mountains
First published: 1972

Principal characters:
JOSEPH, a young boy who suffers from epilepsy
JOSEPH'S MOTHER, who is extremely concerned about her son's well-being

The Story

On a winter day, Joseph, a youngster of four, nonchalantly mentions to his mother that he wants to go down to the creek near the house. The family lives in a mountainous area, where, during the winter, hunters abound, making it somewhat dangerous for young children to play in the woods. The mother, busy at household tasks, puts off her son briefly before acknowledging his request. She gives in, but only grudgingly, making sure that he is dressed warmly in a jacket that marks him out for hunters so that he will not be mistaken for a target. Additionally, she recites a litany of "dos" and "don'ts" for the boy, which he bears patiently.

When her son is gone, the mother reflects on her behavior toward him. Sorry that her son does not realize that she, too, was once young, the mother begins to realize how little time she has given to communicating with Joseph. In her fussing over details, she has "missed the important things." Yet suddenly, she realizes that this day marks a week since the boy had been put on new medicine for his epilepsy. Though the doctor had assured her that there would be no ill effects, the mother nevertheless has spent the past seven days waiting for the moment when a seizure would strike. Now, her son gone off to wander in a dangerous environment, she fantasizes how he might fall into the creek and suffer a sudden seizure and drown. The mental anguish becomes too much, and she rushes out of the house to find him.

Outside, she searches for the trail that her son has taken. Carefully she picks her way over the mountain, trying to go quietly so as not to let her son know that she is after him. Finally, she spots his turquoise jacket. Trying to remain unobserved, she stalks after him, noting with indignation that he is wandering from the route that he told her he would take. In the distance, the sounds of the hunters are discernible. For a moment, the boy disappears from view, and the mother is again seized with vision of horror. Then she spies him beside the creek. Suddenly, she realizes that she is intruding on his privacy, spying on him. For his part, the boy remains oblivious to his mother's presence. He begins to talk to the rocks across the creek, challenging them as if they were animate creatures. "You're not so tough," he shouts; he tells them that he will learn all about them, and therefore be master of them when he is old enough for school, but that they will never know about him. The outburst, delivered in a tone that the mother recognizes as one she herself uses, makes her retreat quietly to let her son engage this "world of rape and murder" alone, as he must in order to grow up.

Themes and Meanings

It is not surprising that Greenberg included "Hunting Season" in her 1972 collection entitled *Rites of Passage*. This is a story about a passage from innocence to experience. One might expect the story to focus on the young boy's experiences in the forest. Ironically, however, the central interest in "Hunting Season" is the effect that a boy's growing up has on his mother, who must make the hard decision to let her offspring make his way, in whatever small way he can, into the world of adulthood.

Though adults have all been through the process themselves, it nevertheless appears to be a terrifying trial when their children are the ones who are trying to break away from parental control. The mother in "Hunting Season" is not unaware of what is happening. She is disappointed that her son cannot see that she was once a carefree girl who enjoyed many of the same things that he does now. Nevertheless, she is caught up in her role as homemaker, wife, and mother to such an extent that she has little time to share her life with her son. To her, he is simply a child, something to be cared for but not given serious attention.

The mother's world is clearly defined by the limits of her house. She is no longer a part of the outside world; her domain is inside the home, where she brings order and provides for all of her family's needs. As a consequence, she has lost something of herself; the days when she would "stamp windowpanes out of frozen puddles" are gone, and though she is "a little ashamed," she cannot find the time to treat her young son's emotional problems with the same degree of seriousness that she gives to his physical disability: The boy does not know the suffering that epilepsy brings, but he has felt the pain of losing his best friend, who has moved away.

The world outside appears to be a harsh one, and the contrast between "inside" and "outside" is magnified by the presence of the hunters and the physical dangers of the landscape. Psychologically, Greenberg suggests that the comforts of the womb stand in sharp contrast to the world outside. Yet the child must leave that womb, both physically and psychologically, if he is to grow in the world. At the same time, the mother must be willing to set the child free from her body and from her influence if his growth is to be successful. The "passage" in "Hunting Season" occurs primarily on this psychological level.

Style and Technique

The most noticeable feature of "Hunting Season" is its imagery. Virtually every detail in the story focuses the reader's attention on the hunt, which Greenberg uses as an ironic symbol of the mother's pursuit of the child whom she must release. The literal presence of hunters in the woods near the home provides the most significant sign of the dangerous environment outside the warmth and security of the home, which is clearly the domain in which the mother is supreme. The "world of rape and murder" which the mother sees when she ventures out after her son is really there: The land has been ravaged by miners, and the hunters seek to destroy the living creatures that inhabit the mountainous region.

When she dashes out to follow her son, the mother herself becomes a hunter, her son the prey. Searching for him, she "nosed the wind like an animal." A noise prompts her to ask herself "Was that his cry?" When she spots his jacket, she begins "tracking" him "warily," until she finally realizes that she is simply "a middle-aged huntress." Her action—backtracking to avoid his seeing her, trodding carefully so as not to make noise, reinforce this portrait. Greenberg also suggests the nature of this pursuit in her description of the boy, who appears with the characteristics of the wary animal: "He put his head up," when stopping on his trek toward the creek, "reading the air for something."

More subtle is Greenberg's handling of point of view. The opening paragraphs give the reader a glimpse into the minds of both characters: the mother realizing that she is being a bit overprotective, the son patiently enduring the preparations that his mother makes him undergo before venturing into the forest. When the boy leaves the house, however, the reader is forced to follow the story only from within the consciousness of the mother. This technique heightens the sense of suspense that characterizes the mother's pursuit of her son: Will he be safe? Will he be killed by hunters? Will he fall into the creek and drown? The realization that the mother is actually intruding on the boy's privacy and may actually hinder his maturation is made particularly poignant by Greenberg's decision to have the story seen through the eyes of the woman who must make a crucial decision not to interfere if her son is to grow to manhood.

Laurence W. Mazzeno

I LOOK OUT FOR ED WOLFE

Author: Stanley Elkin (1930-   )
Type of plot: Comic realism
Time of plot: The early 1960's
Locale: Urban America
First published: 1962

> *Principal characters:*
> ED WOLFE, the protagonist, a ruthless bill collector
> LA MECK, his boss at the loan company
> OLIVER, a black stranger who agreed to take Wolfe to a party
> MARY ROBERTA, a young black woman who keeps Wolfe
>   company at the party

The Story

Ed Wolfe is a loan officer whose aggressiveness in collecting bills for Cornucopia Finance Company ("Can you cope?" is Wolfe's sardonic rechristening) verges on the maniacal. On the day the story opens, he is fired for doing his job too well: His zeal has transformed into a practice of vicious harassment of delinquent clients, and he is accused by his boss, La Meck, of having degenerated into a gangster. As the story's title suggests, Ed Wolfe is exclusively self-absorbed, a champion of detachment and a heartlessly efficient operator.

Receiving his severance pay initiates a bizarre ritual of dispossession, as though Ed Wolfe, a man obsessed by his orphanhood, has chosen to quit the world rather than accept its dismissal of him. So begins a wildly comic personal liquidation sale: He sells his car and his furniture; he closes his savings account and cancels his insurance policy; he pawns his clothes and disconnects his telephone. He sells himself off with single-minded fervor, melting himself down into dollars, orphaning himself as completely as possible. When he has nothing left to sell—he imagines that his senses, his very skin, have been exchanged—he inventories his worth: $2,479.03. This is the sum total of his accumulated past and his ransomed future, as translated into cash flow.

It is also the measure of his distance from death. The exhilaration of freedom sours quickly as Ed Wolfe realizes that he cannot stave off the inexorable leakage of his assets into the few necessities he has managed to pare his life down to. Ironically, this Thoreau-run-amok, who carries the famous dictum to "simplify, simplify, simplify" to absurd extremes, has not reached his essential being so much as abraded himself into anonymity. Freedom is irresponsibility.

The lone Wolfe becomes an urban nomad, a contemporary Wandering

Jew. He aimlessly makes his way into a hotel bar, where he gets drunk and accosts a black man. Apparently, even Ed Wolfe craves human contact after all; beyond inhibition, he awkwardly forces himself upon the stranger, all the while stressing their camaraderie as social pariahs. Oliver, the black man, invites him to a party. Although Wolfe momentarily hesitates—the reflex anxiety of being at the mercy of murderous blacks—a few more drinks and an ever-deepening sense of fatality finally combine to rid him of all restraint. He is introduced to and dances with Mary Roberta, a young black woman (a prostitute?), to whom he confesses his despair. He then makes some vaguely racist remarks that culminate in a boozy effort to sell her to the increasingly angry onlookers. The story concludes with Ed Wolfe casting his remaining money to the crowd at the party, until the black woman he has witlessly abused silently squeezes his pallid hand.

Themes and Meanings

Stanley Elkin's stories are populated by chronic complainers, whose energies are devoted to lamentation over failures of health, business, love, or aspiration, and by glib finaglers, who ooze oily confidence and dispense inside dope. These are the residents of Elkin's short-story collection, *Criers and Kibitzers, Kibitzers and Criers: Nine Stories* (1965); each has a code, myth, or obsession to sum up society and his place in it. Testifying to the precept that the limits of one's language are the limits of one's world, they share a faith in verbal extravagance as a means of staking out claims for the self. Whether he is after influence, sympathy, or simply an audience, every character is an ear-bender, a salesman, a cajoler, a philosopher. Talk is the common currency of the anxious and the fanatical alike.

Ed Wolfe is a particularly proficient negotiator in an environment that highlights the intimate relationship between identity and expression. The exploitative way he handles people over the telephone, however, dehumanizes the bill collector as well as those he duns. It intensifies the orphan's divorce from the human community. Wolfe's subsequent selling off of everything he owns looks like the programmatic suicide of a man at loose ends; moreover, it may be interpreted either as the bullying method of the bill collector turned inward or as an upgrading of what for him has been a prolonged search for authenticity. At the end of the story, Ed Wolfe, shaved to the bone, has reached bottom; yet even though he is dislocated and desperate among strangers, the closing image of Mary Roberta's brief act of compassion may be a foundation upon which to begin rebuilding his life.

In other words, Ed Wolfe's humiliation may be prefatory to a return to life. The vitality of a strange black woman may serve as an energy transfusion for a man who has been riven by guilt and spiritual isolation. However indifferently he observes the climactic event of the story (and even if he is still not ready to be groomed for virtue), there exists the possibility of a reversal of his depletion. Perhaps he has been purged, in which case he may now be prepared to discover the self for which he has been searching.

Style and Technique

Unlike his novels, which are generally categorized with those by such linguistically venturesome, self-referential writers as Robert Coover, William Gass, and John Hawkes, Stanley Elkin's short stories resemble the more conventionally realistic style of so-called Jewish Renaissance fiction of the 1950's and 1960's—the literary territory carved out by Saul Bellow, Philip Roth, and Bernard Malamud. Nevertheless, what has become the Elkin trademark does occasionally appear in "I Look Out for Ed Wolfe": the establishment of outrageously comic circumstances that spur what might best be called lyrical exhibitionism. Stanley Elkin is responsible for some of the most richly imaged verbal flourishes in American fiction.

Ed Wolfe is a vocation vocalized, for Elkin has mastered the jargon, pace, and patter of the salesman and granted it poetic status. Verbal rhythm and drive: They lend even Ed Wolfe's willful deterioration an optimistic charge— and a plenitude. Rejoicing in voice, the beleaguered ego perseveres.

Arthur M. Saltzman

I STAND HERE IRONING

Author: Tillie Olsen (1913-   )
Type of plot: Interior monologue
Time of plot: c. 1950
Locale: A city in the United States
First published: 1956

Principal characters:
THE MOTHER, the narrator of the story
EMILY, her daughter

The Story

The title of the story reveals that the narrator is engaged in a simple, routine household task. While she is ironing, she meditates about a note she has received from a teacher or adviser where her daughter, Emily, attends school. She feels tormented by the request to come in and talk about Emily, who the writer of the note believes needs help. Yet the mother has no intention of going to see the person who wrote the note. "Even if I came, what good would it do?" she asks.

The rest of the story is an interior monologue, reviewing the lives and relationships of the mother and daughter, followed by a brief exchange of dialogue between the mother and Emily, and a final paragraph of summary of the circumstances in which Emily grew up. At the end, the mother is still standing there ironing.

There is no action and no apparent plot in this story. The interior monologue rehearses the things that the mother might say to the teacher or adviser who wrote the note. Her memories of the daughter's infancy and childhood serve to explain much about the personality and the difficulties of the girl. Her love and tenderness for the girl, and the barriers which separated them physically at first and then emotionally later, are revealed.

Emily was the first child of the mother, who was only nineteen at the time she was born. The mother adored her beautiful baby but was forced to leave her with an indifferent sitter when the child was only eight months old because the mother had to earn money to support them. The father had abandoned his wife and child, and in those days of the Depression and no welfare help, the mother had no choice but to leave the child and find a job. Emily greeted her with a cry each time she rushed anxiously home to gather up her precious infant, and the pain she felt is clear when she notes that the crying was "a weeping I can hear yet."

The child was still an infant when the young mother had to take her to the father's family to keep her for a while. When she finally raised the money to pay for Emily's return, the infant got chicken pox and could not return for yet another period of time. When she came back, the child was thin and so changed that the mother scarcely knew her. The mother was advised to put the two-year-old in nursery school, and it was indeed the only way that they were able to be together at all, because the mother had to spend long hours at work. She recalls that she did not know at the time how fatiguing and cruel the nursery school was. It was only a parking place for children, and she came to realize how Emily and the other children hated it, but there was no other recourse. Emily did not clutch her and beg her not to go as some of the children did, but she would have reasons for staying home. The mother wistfully remembers the child's goodness in never protesting or rebelling.

The young mother married again and was able to be with the child more for a brief time, but even then she and her new husband would go out in the evenings and leave the child alone. Emily was frightened and had to face her terrors alone. Then another daughter was born, and the mother was away at the hospital for a week. When she returned, Emily was ill with measles and so could not come near her mother or the new baby. Even after the disease was over, Emily remained thin and subject to nightmares, so finally the mother was advised to send her to a convalescent home for poor children. The place turned out to be little more than a prison, where the children were denied almost all contact with their parents, not allowed to have any personal possessions, and discouraged from forming any friendships with other inmates.

After eight months of effort, the mother was finally able to get her child released, but when she tried to hold or comfort her after that, the child would stiffen and finally push away. The new baby, her half sister Susan, was a beautiful, plump blonde, which aroused fierce jealousy and a painful sense of inadequacy and plainness in Emily. Although the worst of the poverty and deprivation were over, Emily was needed to take the part of an adult during her growing years; her stepfather was away at war, and her mother needed Emily's help in caring for the four younger children. Emily's schoolwork suffered, and she had little chance to be a carefree child during these school years. She did, however, occasionally try to cheer up her mother by imitating happenings or types of people at school.

The mother once casually suggested that she might do some comic routine in the school amateur show, and Emily entered and won first place. After that she began receiving invitations to perform and displayed a genuine gift for comedy. Yet the mother says that they were not able to help her to develop her talent and the gift has not grown as fully as it might have.

At this point the girl comes in, and the mother senses by her light step and bantering comments about the perpetual ironing that Emily is feeling happy. The daughter chatters as she fixes herself some food, and her mother dismisses the idea that her daughter has any unmanageable problems. She feels confident that the girl will find her way. Then the girl asks her mother not to rouse her in the morning even though it is the day that her midterm exams are scheduled, explaining that the exams do not matter because everyone will be dead from an atom bomb in a few years anyway. The mother knows that Emily believes it, but she has just been reliving the tenderness and the agony of the making of this human being, and she cannot bear to dismiss the life of this girl so lightly.

At this point she makes her statement. She will not try to explain to anyone the events and the anguish that shaped the girl's life. She tells the note-writer (in her mind) to let Emily be. She is not worried that the girl will not achieve her full potential: Not many people do. Emily will still have enough to make a life for herself. Yet she does want Emily to know and believe that she is not a helpless, passive victim of circumstances, or fate, or an atom bomb.

Themes and Meanings

The mother-child relationship is the focus of "I Stand Here Ironing." The close bond created in the days of infancy is threatened as soon as the mother must consign the child to a sitter. Both the mother and the child regret and resist the absences that weaken the bond and make it difficult for the mother to express her love for the little girl, but poverty and the demands of other family members prevail, so that by the time the story takes place, the mother believes that she can be of no help to the girl's further development.

The daughter's view of the relationship is expressed only as it is perceived by the mother. Yet the mother's memories of the infant crying, the small child finding reasons not to be separated from the mother, but never rebelling or begging, the stiffness and silence of the bigger child when her mother tried to hold or comfort her, the help in mothering and in cheering up her mother when the stepfather was away all suggest that the complexity of the relationship has been developing for a long time. Hurt and deprivation and anger have not severed the bond of love, but they have created barriers so that the mother and daughter are very separate people now.

The mother's confidence that the daughter's common sense will prevail if only she can be persuaded that life is not futile is an acknowledgment of the daughter's maturity. The mother was persuaded against her own common sense to feed the child only at set intervals, to send the child to nursery school, and finally to place her in the convalescent home. In acquiescing to the advice of others instead of following her own instincts, she realizes now, she hurt the child emotionally; she will not make the same mistake again.

Style and Technique

The first-person narrative technique permits the development of a very personal interior monologue and the examination of an entire lifetime of events. These reveal the development of the child Emily and her relationship to her mother in a way that exposes the mother's anguish and sadness. The language of the mother in describing the daughter is always loving and tender. She speaks of her as a miracle, beautiful and happy. The simple, direct sentences are appropriate to the interior monologue and reinforce the sincerity and seriousness of the thoughts expressed.

The calm, reflective tone serves to emphasize the resignation of the mother to her ineffectiveness in influencing the course of her daughter's future. It also provides a fitting contrast to the intensity of the final lines of the story, in which the mother admonishes the notewriter to let the girl be, but still urges this unnamed figure of authority to convince the girl that life is not futile.

Betty G. Gawthrop

I WANT TO KNOW WHY

Author: Sherwood Anderson (1876-1941)
Type of plot: Psychological realism
Time of plot: Probably the early twentieth century
Locale: Beckersville, Kentucky, and Saratoga, New York
First published: 1921

> *Principal characters:*
> THE UNNAMED NARRATOR, a fifteen-year-old boy who loves
> horses
> THE BOY'S FATHER, a small-town lawyer
> JERRY TILLFORD, a horse trainer
> BILDAD JOHNSON, a black cook at the racetracks
> SUNSTREAK, a thoroughbred racehorse

The Story

The protagonist of "I Want to Know Why" is an unnamed boy nearing his sixteenth birthday. The events that he relates have occurred almost a year previously, just as he turned fifteen. The boy recalls these events in a mixture of confusion and desperation: He needs to understand exactly what happened and how it has affected him so that he can get on with his life.

The boy lives in Beckersville, a small Kentucky town, and he is fascinated with horses and horse racing. His father is the town lawyer, but the boy wants more than anything else to be a part of the racetrack environment. He remembers that when he was ten, he tried to stunt his growth by eating a cigar stolen from his father so that he might remain small enough to be a rider. "It made me awful sick and the doctor had to be sent for, and then it did no good," he recalls. "It was a joke. When I told what I had done and why, most fathers would have whipped me, but mine didn't." Thus, even in this early action, the boy expresses the sense of disappointment that marks the whole story.

With the realization that he can never be a jockey, the boy turns to other aspects of the racing scene. He hangs around the stables, listening to the touts and stable hands and trainers talk. He learns the lore of horses, absorbs the knowledge and hones the instinct that goes with a true appreciation of the animals. His foremost teacher at this time is Bildad Johnson, a black man who works as cook around the track each spring. The boy appreciates Bildad's honesty and trust. He also gathers from the old man an awareness of the beauty of horses that goes beyond simple admiration—that, in fact, approaches the spiritual: "It brings a lump up into my throat when a horse runs. . . . It's in my blood like in the blood of . . . trainers," he says.

The central event in the story occurs when the boy and three of his friends sneak away and hitch a freight train to Saratoga, New York, to watch a first-class horse race. When they arrive, they look up Bildad and some of the other Beckersville racetrack men who have arrived earlier. The race is the Mullford Handicap, in which Sunstreak, a stallion, will run against the gelding Middlestride. Both horses are from near Beckersville, but the boy pulls for Sunstreak because the horse is special:

> Sunstreak is like a girl you think about sometimes but never see. He is hard all over and lovely too. When you look at his head you want to kiss him. . . . He stands at the post quiet and not letting on, but he is just burning up inside. Then when the barrier goes up he is off like his name, Sunstreak. It makes you ache to see him. It hurts you.

Before the race, the boy visits Sunstreak's stall, where the horse is being groomed. Jerry Tillford, Sunstreak's trainer, notices the boy, and when they share a glance, the boy knows that Jerry is as moved by the horse—by its courage, strength, grace, and vitality—as he is. "Something happened to me," the boy remembers. "I guess I loved the man as much as I did the horse because he knew what I knew. Seemed to me there wasn't anything in the world but that man and the horse and me."

The race between the two horses is barely described by the boy: Sunstreak's victory is a foregone conclusion. Nevertheless, the boy is moved by what he has seen, and that night he parts company with the other boys so that he can be alone to consider the events that he has witnessed. He also wants to be near Jerry Tillford, the one person who most shares his feelings. He has watched Jerry leave in a car with a group of men after the race. With little hope of finding them, he strikes out on the road they took and soon sees the car turning into the driveway of an old farmhouse. The boy creeps up to a window to find out what is going on inside:

> It's what give me the fantods. I can't make it out. The women in the house were all ugly mean-looking women, not nice to look at or be near. . . . I saw everything plain. . . . The women had on loose dresses and sat around in chairs. The men came in and some sat on the women's laps. The place smelled rotten and there was rotten talk, the kind a kid hears around a livery stable in a town like Beckersville in the winter but don't ever expect to hear talked when there are women around. It was rotten.

As the boy watches and listens, Jerry Tillford begins to brag about the race. He takes credit for Sunstreak's win, which the boy knows is foolish. Then the trainer begins to look at one of the women, and the shine in his eyes is the same as the shine that the boy noticed when Jerry looked at Sunstreak before the race. It is this realization that so angers and confuses the boy. When Jerry then kisses the prostitute, the boy is racked by disgust:

"I wanted to scream and rush in the room and kill him. I never had such a feeling before," he says. Instead, he retreats into the darkness and, after a sleepless night, heads for home the next day.

In the time that has passed between this event and the present time of the story, the boy has continued to mull over the adventure. His life has changed: "At the tracks the air don't taste as good or smell as good," he says. "It's because a man like Jerry Tillford, who knows what he does, could see a horse like Sunstreak run, and kiss a woman like that the same day. I can't make it out." Thus the story ends, with the narrator still puzzled, trying to understand the adult world into which he has been so abruptly initiated.

Themes and Meanings

The boy-narrator is a young man growing into the adult world, although he would rather, in a sense, remain a child. This idea is suggested by his wish to stunt his growth by eating a cigar. Although he is thinking in terms of staying small enough to be a jockey, in the larger context of the story it is clear that he is unwilling to face the realities of adulthood. The racetrack, with its magical allure, is a perfect fantasy world for the boy.

The boy's father, the town lawyer, is something of a disappointment to his son. "He's all right, but don't make much money and can't buy me things, and anyway I'm getting so old now I don't expect it," the boy says. In comparison to his friends' fathers—one is a professional gambler—the narrator's father seems rather bland, although the boy appreciates his understanding nature. The reader can recognize that the father is, indeed, a good and wise man, but the narrator, at this age, prefers Jerry Tillford. In fact, he substitutes Jerry for his father on the day of the race. Thus, his shock and his disappointment at Jerry's transgressions are profound: They are a betrayal of the highest order.

The boy's horror takes on an even greater significance when the reader reconsiders the boy's attitude toward horses. As an adolescent, unable to sort out his powerfully confused feelings, the boy has sublimated his sexual urges into the beauty and excitement of racing. Sunstreak is described as a girl whom the boy wants to kiss. The ache, the pain he feels at the horse's running is also vaguely sexual but made acceptable and understandable to the boy because it is pictured in the terms of his childhood world. When Jerry bridges the gap between the spiritual appreciation of the horse and the sexual lust for the woman, he is unknowingly forcing the boy to face the truth about his own feelings and needs. Since the boy has vested Jerry with the role of father, Jerry's act precipitates a distinctly Oedipal crisis. The boy at first wants to kill his "father," whose overt sexual needs reflect the boy's hidden, confused ones. Thereafter, the world is no longer simple; there are no easy, clean answers.

Style and Technique

The most obvious stylistic device in this story is Sherwood Anderson's use of the first-person narrative voice. The naïve speaker finds it difficult to tell his story; he fumbles for the right word, the accurate description. He hesitates to get to the central event. In fact, he circles the event for several pages, nearing it only to withdraw until he can better face it. When he does describe the scene, he can do so only in vague, almost childish language. The house is "rummy-looking"; the women are "ugly" and "mean-looking"; and the place "smelled rotten." How much does the boy actually see? "I saw everything plain," he says. The loose dresses reveal the women's bodies. The men, some of whom "sat on the women's laps," apparently participate in sexual activities before the boy's eyes. He is obviously fascinated and appalled by what occurs and by the reactions he feels within his own body.

"I Want to Know Why" can be compared to "Death in the Woods" (and numerous other Anderson stories) in its rendering of sexual awakening and confusion. In "Death in the Woods," the narrator is a grown man looking back on his childhood. The boy in "I Want to Know Why" does not have that sort of perspective; less than a year has passed since his experience. Still, he does understand that his childhood is over and he no longer has the luxury of innocence. "That's what I'm writing this story about," he says. "I'm puzzled. I'm getting to be a man and want to think straight and be O.K." At the end of the story he still cannot understand—or cannot make himself admit that he understands—but his desire to "be a man" and "think straight and be O.K." indicates that he is beginning to face the obligations and realities of growing up.

Edwin T. Arnold

THE ICE HOUSE

Author: Caroline Gordon (1895-1981)
Type of plot: Social realism
Time of plot: 1866
Locale: The South
First published: 1931

Principal characters:
DOUG, a fifteen-year-old Southern youth
RAEBURN, his friend, also fifteen
A YANKEE CONTRACTOR, unnamed, who hires the boys

The Story

Doug, an enterprising Southern lad, has found a few days' employment with a Yankee contractor. He has been hired to remove from a pit in an ice house the skeletons of Union soldiers who were killed in a battle about four years earlier, in 1862. At that time, the frozen December ground precluded digging graves, and the bodies were placed in the ice house to await a future burial.

After enlisting the aid of his close friend Raeburn, Doug waits for him early on an April morning. When Raeburn is late, he becomes irritated, fearing that the contractor might not pay the agreed-upon sum. Arriving at about six, Raeburn explains his tardiness, saying, "I ain't going to work for nobody on an empty stomach," but Doug argues that they should earn their pay and provide a full day's labor.

The two youths meet the Yankee contractor at the ice house and begin the task of separating the tangle of bones. Working inside, Doug passes armfuls of bones to Raeburn, who places them in a wheelbarrow. The contractor then deposits the bones in the waiting pine boxes. Since the skeletons are not intact and are often without skulls, however, the boys question whether the contractor knows when he has a complete body in any one of the coffins.

At noon the three rest and have their dinner. Raeburn, more sensitive to handling the skeletons than the other two, drinks some coffee but is unable to eat the biscuit and cold meat that he has brought. Doug and the contractor have no such trouble, for to Doug, "handlin' a dead Yankee ain't no more to *me* than handlin' a dead hawg. . . ." Even so, Raeburn offers to exchange places with him, since Doug's job of untangling the bones is the more difficult of the two. On their return to the ice house, however, Doug resumes the same position because, as he points out, "I'm used to it now. You have to kind of get the hang of it. It'd just be wasting time now if we changed places." Since the bodies are lower in the pit, he requests a ladder. In search of one, the contractor inquires at the nearest house, but Mrs. Porter, having lost three sons in the war, is unwilling to help a Yankee, and she directs the contractor to a distant house which he discovers to be abandoned. Unable to obtain a ladder, he returns, but since it is dusk, the boys are finishing up for the day.

As the contractor pays the lads for the day's work, he mentions that he no longer needs them. Doug is surprised; originally he was hired for three or perhaps four days. Furthermore, skeletons of Union soldiers still remain in the ice house. As the boys leave, Doug turns into the woods, and Raeburn soon follows, discovering Doug peering through the undergrowth at the contractor in the distance. The contractor is rearranging the bones, taking some out of the full coffins and placing them into the empty ones, thus making it appear that all the bodies have been removed from the ice house. Doug quickly figures it out: "He's dividing up them skeletons so he can git paid double." The thought amuses him, and he laughs, "There ain't a whole man in ary one of them boxes."

Themes and Meanings

Caroline Gordon is often associated with the Agrarian movement of the 1920's and 1930's, which advocated a return to an economy tied to the land and opposed an industrialized society. Indeed, "The Ice House" can be read as a criticism of the North and its commercialism. The contractor is a Yankee who has come south for the opportunity it provides, a character-type often found in Agrarian literature. He is preoccupied with attaining success. He advises Doug, "Farm work's all right if you can't get nothing else to do, but a smart young feller like you wants to be looking out fer oppertunity. . . ." At the conclusion of the story, the contractor is more eager to make a profit than to fulfill an obligation. In addition to swindling the government, he deceives the families of the men who died in battle. They will assume that their sons have been buried while, in fact, some of them remain in the pit in the ice house. The contractor does not consider the implications of his action, however, only his profit. In Gordon's fictional world, a character who is concerned solely with money is morally bankrupt.

Gordon, a Southerner, is not limiting her criticism to the North. Rather, "The Ice House" is a comment about commercialism everywhere. The contractor is materialistic, but so is Doug. He is prepared to go to work before six in the morning; he worries about not getting paid the full amount; he is preoccupied with getting ahead. Engaging the contractor in conversation, Doug inquires, "Had he ever worked for the government before? And how was he paid? By the day or so much for the job?" Doug's concern with the skeletons is all business. He even appreciates and almost seems to admire the contractor's solution to the remaining empty pine coffins. Doug's attitude suggests that materialism is not specifically a Northern trait but one that seems to have replaced or is replacing the old order.

Although initially the tension appears to be between the North and the South or between the contractor and the two friends as representative figures, actually the contractor and Doug, both of whom are materialistic, occupy one side of the spectrum while Raeburn occupies the other. Raeburn insits on eating breakfast before working. He notices the dogwoods and the sprouting new growth on the pokeberry and the sassafras. He understands the channel catfish and has devised a successful method for catching it. Raeburn's appreciation of nature provides him with a sense of the meaning of life that the other two lack. In Gordon's fiction, nature is important because it represents order in a world threatened by chaos. The characters who are close to nature are laudable figures with a strong moral sense. Furthermore, Raeburn's interest in fishing is a positive action that is seen in some of Gordon's other fiction, including *Aleck Maury, Sportsman* (1934), her most acclaimed novel, in which the protagonist resorts to hunting and fishing as a means of withstanding the pressures of contemporary life.

In addition to his awareness of nature, Raeburn is sensitive to the emotions of others. He realizes that Mrs. Porter would not lend a ladder to a Yankee. In contrast, Doug, who sees only the practical side, comments, "Tain't nothin' to lend anybody a ladder." Doug, as a Southerner, should anticipate Mrs. Porter's hatred, but he does not. Raeburn is more in tune with the natural rhythms of life, with the budding trees, the catfish, and with the emotions of others. Unfortunately, the contractor and Doug represent the future.

"The Ice House" is a lament for the traditional ways of an agrarian society that bespoke an ordered existence and a criticism of the new values of a technological one that seem to encourage chaos. Although opposed to romanticizing the past, Gordon longed for the stability and order found in the pre–Civil War South, a stability that was based on a hierarchial arrangement of classes and a close relationship to the land. She was convinced that twentieth century life bordered on anarchy. Later, after converting to Catholicism, she found, in her religion, the order that she was seeking, but at the time she wrote "The Ice House," she saw nature as the only counterbalance to the confusion and disorder that accompanied the industrial society.

Style and Technique

The spare, economical style and the objective point of view that distinguish "The Ice House" are also found in many of Ernest Hemingway's stories. Like Hemingway, Gordon presents her tale in a straightforward fashion: The author is unobtrusive and the story appears to evolve and develop by itself. In *How to Read a Novel* (1957), Gordon labels this approach dramatic; she suggests that characters should be revealed by their actions as they respond to others and to the environment.

Therefore, since it exposes or displays characters, the environment assumes an enhanced position. Although the details and events in Gordon's fiction are realistic, she invests objects with more than a literal significance because of their role in determining character. For example, in "The Ice House" the manner in which the characters view the bones of the dead soldiers is indicative of their moral stance.

In "The Ice House," the details of the landscape and the use of dialect serve to re-create the atmosphere of the Southern countryside, closely based on the Kentucky tobacco region of Gordon's childhood. Because she evokes the South in her fiction, Gordon has been labeled a regional writer, implying a limited appeal, but while her setting is often the South, her themes are universal.

Barbara Wiedemann

THE ICE WAGON GOING DOWN THE STREET

Author: Mavis Gallant (1922-   )
Type of plot: Psychological realism
Time of plot: 1950-1960
Locale: Toronto, with extensive flashbacks to Paris and Geneva
First published: 1963

Principal characters:

PETER FRAZIER, a middle-aged Canadian, home after ten
    unsuccessful years abroad
SHEILAH, his wife
AGNES BRUSEN, a former colleague in Geneva

The Story

Peter and Sheilah Frazier console themselves on Sunday mornings by re-membering the people they met during the decade they spent trying to live a charmed life abroad. Now they are "back where they started," in Toronto, living with Lucille, Peter's down-to-earth sister. They do not have plans for the future, and they have become soured by "the international thing"; unlike other expatriates, Peter was neither "crooked" nor "smart" enough to find shady business opportunities in postwar Europe. Now as in the past, they try to believe that "hazy and marvellous" experiences lie ahead of them. In order to believe in this wonderful future, they must avoid the dreary present, so they spend their Sunday morning recalling the years that they spent in Europe, carrying the reader back with them to the Paris and Geneva of their past.

In their decade of genteel drifting, only four months in Paris are charmed. Peter does not need to work, for his comfortably endowed childhood has been extended by an inheritance, and Sheilah loves him. They live "in the future" until the money runs out, and then they are "never as happy again." When Lucille finds Peter a lowly job as a filing clerk in Geneva, Peter keeps his self-esteem by convincing himself that a position befitting his social status and family connections will come his way. He rationalizes his situation by deciding that there is a conspiracy among Canadian diplomats and busi-nessmen to punish him, and he becomes secretive about his job. He tries to cultivate connections so that he and Sheilah can move in the proper social circles. Peter behaves as if he "had been sent by a universal inspector to see how things in Geneva were being run," and as if "his real life [were] a secret so splendid he could share it with no one but himself."

His image and his secretiveness are put to the test when a young Canadian woman, Agnes Brusen, becomes his boss. His first assumption, that she is there to spy on him, soon evaporates when he sees her transparent character and is able to recognize her origins. He categorizes her as a provincial person, the product of simple immigrant ambitions; she is devout, purposeful, hardworking, unsophisticated, and direct. She does not seem to have anything that she wants to conceal or of which she is ashamed, and this makes Peter even more defensive and secretive. At a fancy dress party, where Sheilah is in her element and seems to find a lover, Peter recognizes that this social scene has unnerved Agnes and left her "gasping for life." When he helps her home, she tells him of her childhood in Saskatchewan: "I'm not from any other place." Now and two days later, she emphasizes a memory of early morning in her childhood home when she got up alone before her large family crowded the house. Unlike the freezing winter scene in Geneva, this is a picture of summertime, when she looked through the window and saw the ice wagon going down the street: "It's you, you, once in your life alone in the universe. You think you know everything that can happen. . . . Nothing is ever like that again." Agnes' disillusionment with the world of educated people strikes a chord in Peter; he feels that if it were not for Sheilah, he would be like Agnes.

The story ends rather suddenly when Peter shifts back from his memory of Agnes to the present in Toronto. It is implied that not much has changed in the years after Geneva. Nothing has been as important for Peter as that moment of self-disclosure with Agnes, the one secret he has kept from Sheilah. Yet whatever the private importance, it is clear that nothing has changed in Peter's attitude toward himself, toward Sheilah, or toward other people.

Themes and Meanings

This is a story of evasiveness, the portrait of a man who wants to avoid the judgment of his own character and of his accomplishments in life. It is a story without a real climax because the Fraziers have settled into a flat, self-protective life-style, without significant action, purpose, or emotion. As the narrative moves forward, their present is replaced by recollected incidents, but these incidents are remarkable for their insignificance and inconclusiveness, and the Fraziers' memory game is designed to free them from the emptiness of the present so that they can daydream of a glorious future.

In a sense, Peter breaks the rules of the memory game on this particular Sunday morning. He remembers Agnes Brusen, with whom he almost had an intimate relationship: "It is almost as if they had run away together, silly as children, irresponsible as lovers." It is appropriate that they do not become lovers and do not "run away"; Peter does not even fantasize about what might have been. The emotional flatness of his temperament leads him to conclude with relief, "Anyway, nothing happened."

Yet the image of Agnes Brusen has become embedded in his memory. His half-conscious recognition of her significance to him is, perhaps, the climax of the story, although that recognition has such low voltage that Peter finds it easy to remind himself, "Sheilah is here, it is a true Sunday morning, with its dimness and headache and remorse and regrets, and this is life." It is evident that Peter does not want to face the fact that his life might have been more true or more real, and that Agnes Brusen is an image of the narrow but authentic life that he has missed.

The contrast between Peter and Agnes is more striking than the similarity that Peter wishes to recognize. It is true that they are both "lost" in "the international thing," but he only partly realizes that she has a strength of character which he lacks. The image which she recaptures from memory reflects, as he knows, Agnes' integrity as a person and the self-confidence to lead a more purposeful life. While the content of Agnes' childhood vision is so ordinary that it hardly excites interest, what is important is the depth of feeling and wonder with which she invests the scene. Peter's own children are cheered by the return to Toronto, which they want to call home; Agnes has a sense of continuity and rootedness in her identity, whereas Peter realizes that he does not and that the best for which he can hope is that "everything works out, somehow or other."

Style and Technique

This is a psychological sketch of a man who fails to develop and who has replaced action in the world with a compensatory world of recollection and wishes. The form of the story mirrors his state of being. It is a narrative in which nothing happens; there is no climax, and what almost happened has become the object of circular recollection. Apart from the framing scenes in the present, the story is made up of scenes arranged chronologically, but the movement forward which occupies the reader leads to new images and situations which only confirm the initial psychological insights. Peter does not change, nor is he really revealed to the reader more fully. Temporal and spatial displacement are emphasized to heighten the sense of a lost character without any sense of direction.

The story is not an intensive dramatization of this state of being, however, for the narrative voice is a prominent part of the texture of the story. This sardonic voice is counterpointed with the material of Peter's experience, and the satiric and ironic commentary becomes more engaging than the lives and situations presented to the reader. This commentary joins with key images, such as the ice wagon going down the street, to entertain and challenge the reader intellectually while the realistic detail of Peter's experience loses dramatic impact. As the character becomes less coherent, the authority of the omniscient narrator becomes more reliable. In this way, the strong voice which might have seemed intrusive establishes itself as the only stable center in a story that lacks the order that has been traditionally guaranteed by plot and character.

Denis Sampson

THE ICICLE

Author: Abram Tertz (Andrei Sinyavsky, 1925-   )
Type of plot: Fantasy
Time of plot: The 1950's
Locale: Soviet Union
First published: "Gololeditsa," 1961 (English translation, 1963)

> *Principal characters:*
> VASILY, the narrator of the story and its intended reader
> NATASHA, his girlfriend
> BORIS, her estranged husband, who is still in love with her
> COLONEL TARASOV, the officer in charge of Vasily's case

The Story

"The Icicle" is a structurally complex story. It is told by a first-person narrator to "Vasily," who, the reader later learns, is a future incarnation of the narrator himself. In the story's preface, the narrator urges Vasily to find and marry Natasha "before it is too late." The narration that follows will explain this advice.

Shortly before New Year's Eve, the narrator, who has yet to be identified, and Natasha are sitting outside discussing the unseasonably icy weather. During their conversation, the narrator attempts to push his memory as far as it will go and suddenly finds himself projected into what is apparently an Ice Age landscape. The unnerving experience lasts only a moment, but as the couple begins to walk home, they are approached by a large woman walking on the ice. The narrator fancies that he knows her life's story and that in the near future she will slip and fall on the ice. His prediction comes true, and in the conversation that follows, his surmises about her past are confirmed as well.

Against his better judgment, the narrator is persuaded by Natasha to attend a New Year's party at which her former husband, Boris, is also expected to be present. As the New Year approaches, the narrator compares the candles burning on the tree to a man's life. He identifies with one particular candle, and as he whimsically attempts to guess how long he will live, he has a compelling vision of himself approaching death at age eighty-nine. In an effort to dispel the mood of his vision, he offers to read the minds of the party guests. His performance is entirely convincing, but in the course of it he begins to perceive more than one individual in each of the people present. In particular, he realizes that one young man has in previous existences been primarily either prostitutes or priests. He tries to avoid subjecting Natasha to this kind of scrutiny, but as they leave, he realizes that she is missing part of her head.

During the days that follow, the narrator becomes acquainted with his own various pasts and futures. At one point in the twenty-fourth century, he is addressed as Vasily by his wife, who asks him about Russian literature. On another occasion, he realizes that the incarnation that he is watching is aware of him as well. The threat to Natasha that was suggested by his vision of her at the New Year's party is finally articulated: She will be killed by a falling icicle on the nineteenth of January. In a vain attempt to avoid fate, the narrator extorts fifteen hundred rubles from Boris in order to take her out of town. Boris, however, denounces him to the police, and they are arrested before they reach their destination. The narrator attempts to warn Natasha, but as he does so, he realizes that by articulating the threat he has made it inevitable. The narrator's considerable gifts are put to the service of the state, and Natasha, at his request, is put under surveillance, but at the appointed hour on the appointed day she does walk under the icicle and loses her life at the same moment that the narrator loses his gift. In one of his last visions, the narrator sees himself as Vasily standing outside a lighted window trying to attract the attention of Natasha, who sits inside reading. His story is addressed to that Vasily of the future whose happiness with Natasha is still possible.

Themes and Meanings

In one sense, "The Icicle" is about writers and writing. The narrator's reasons for undertaking the story are certainly compelling, but readers can assume that all writers have equally compelling reasons for their work. Practical aspects of the trade are addressed: The narrator hopes that his story will come out in a large edition not for money or glory but because he hopes to increase his chances of reaching Vasily, his future reader. The question of who this future reader will be is central to the story. In an epilogue, the narrator observes that since, like any other writer, he must reread his work, he already has at least one reader. The idea of writing only for himself does not present a difficulty for him, because he realizes that he is writing for a future self. Writing to this future self is his way of combating the inevitability and senselessness of death. Indeed, he observes that "most books are letters to the future with a reminder of what happened."

Another central theme of "The Icicle" is the continuity of life. As the narrator watches the parade of past existences at the New Year's party, he realizes that anyone who examines himself closely will find simultaneously existing within himself thieves, liars, and cheats as well as perhaps great creative artists. Following Natasha's senseless death, it is also important to him to realize that none of these multiple existences is lost, although they may be forgotten. "The Icicle" is his letter to the future, his attempt to remind a future incarnation of his present existence during the Soviet 1950's.

Style and Technique

"The Icicle" is unified by the image of ice that runs through the entire story. The Russian title of the story, "Gololeditsa," refers not to the icicle that killed Natasha but to the icy conditions that produced it. The narrator's first vision of the past takes him to the Ice Age, and he first feels alarm for Natasha after helping the woman who has fallen on the ice. Following that experience, the narrator feels that he must treat Natasha as he would a bag of eggs, and he decides to take her home by trolley because "it really was very slippery." Later, after he knows precisely what will happen to Natasha, he is depressed by the sight of icicles which grow "like mushrooms" on the neighboring roofs.

There is, however, another "icicle" in the story that contributes as much to Natasha's death as does the one that strikes her. Following the narrator's arrest, he is asked to predict the future of Colonel Tarasov, who is handling his case. As he absently answers the question, he has a vision of the entire world covered with ice, and the colonel, who in every incarnation has achieved one rank higher than he did in the previous one, has become a gigantic gleaming icicle in control of everything around him. Specific references to the political climate of the Soviet Union in the early 1950's are infrequent in "The Icicle," but in the epilogue, where the fates of the various characters are summarized, the narrator states very clearly that people such as Colonel Tarasov were not needed following 1953 (the year of Joseph Stalin's death). When one recalls that the period of general relaxation that followed Stalin's death is referred to as the "Thaw," it becomes possible to see Natasha's arbitrary death as produced by the political climate of the period rather than by specific meteorological conditions. "The Icicle," however, is more than mere allegory. Its fantastic hypothesis (the possibility that each of us contains multiple past and future existences) raises it above the concrete reality of the Soviet 1950's and gives it universal significance.

Sandra Rosengrant

IDIOTS FIRST

Author: Bernard Malamud (1914-1986)
Type of plot: Modern fable
Time of plot: The mid-twentieth century
Locale: New York
First published: 1961

> *Principal characters:*
> MENDEL, the protagonist, a poor man
> ISAAC, his retarded son
> A PAWNBROKER
> MR. FISHBEIN, a wealthy man
> YASCHA, an old rabbi
> GINZBURG, a mysterious figure

The Story

"Idiots First" begins with the stopping of Mendel's clock as the old man awakens in fright. The importance of time in the story is foreshadowed in the opening paragraph when the reader is told that Mendel "wasted minutes sitting at the edge of the bed." Once moving, he dresses, summons his son Isaac, and, pocketing a paper bag containing his modest savings, leads his son into the night. The old man seems very fearful, and he warns Isaac to avoid Ginzburg, who came to see Mendel the day before. "Don't talk to him or go with him if he asks you," Mendel cautions. Then as an afterthought he adds, "Young people he don't bother so much."

Though Mendel always refers to him as a boy, Isaac, who has "thick hair greying the sides of his head," is not the child his father perceives him to be. Rather, he is the "idiot" of the title, a thirty-nine-year-old man with the mind of a child. Facing his own death, Mendel attempts in the course of the story to provide for Isaac in the only way he can, sending him by train to California, where he will live with his Uncle Leo. The story traces Mendel's efforts to raise train fare to secure Isaac's safety before his own time runs out.

Their first stop is the pawnbroker's shop, where Mendel tries to get the thirty-five dollars he needs to make up the difference between his savings and Isaac's ticket to California by pawning his watch. Despite Mendel's protestations that it cost him sixty dollars, the pawnbroker will allow him only eight dollars for the old watch. Though Mendel's desperation is obvious as he despairs of finding the money he needs, the money-lender ignores his pleas.

Next Mendel and Isaac visit Mr. Fishbein, a wealthy philanthropist. He proves no less hard-hearted than the pawnbroker as he, too, turns down Mendel's entreaties. Insisting that his "fixed policy" is to give money only to organized charities, Fishbein shows scorn for Mendel's plight and contempt for Isaac's condition. Though he does offer to feed them in his kitchen, the philanthropist throws the pair out of his house with the advice that Mendel should put Isaac in an institution.

As they approach a park bench to rest, a shadowy, bearded figure arises before them. Mendel pales and waves his arms, Isaac yowls, and the stranger disappears into the bushes. The clock strikes ten. From earlier hints, the reader suspects this figure to be the mysterious Ginzburg. He is encountered again when Mendel takes Isaac to a cafeteria for food and they flee from a "heavyset" man eating soup.

His other options exhausted, Mendel now goes to see an old rabbi, to whom he appeals for charity. While his wife insists that they cannot help, the old rabbi, though he has no money, gives Mendel his new fur-lined coat. The wife tries to snatch it back, but Mendel tears it from her. As Mendel and Isaac run into the street, the wife chasing them, the old rabbi diverts her attention by falling to the floor in an apparent heart attack. As they "ran through the streets with the rabbi's new fur-lined caftan," after them "noiselessly ran Ginzburg."

It is very late when Mendel buys a ticket for Isaac and they hurry to the train. The train is still standing in the station, but the gate to the platform is shut; a heavy, bearded man in uniform guards the entrance and refuses to allow them to pass. "Too late," he tells Mendel, "Already past twelve." Mendel begs for a favor, but the guard callously refuses. "Favors you had enough already. For you the train is gone. You shoulda been dead already at midnight. I told you that yesterday. This is the best I can do."

Recognizing his antagonist for the first time as the mysterious Ginzburg, Mendel begs again: "For myself . . . I don't ask a thing. But what will happen to my boy?" Isaac is not his responsibility, Ginzburg tells Mendel, and when the old man asks him what his responsibility is, he says, "To create conditions. To make happen what happens." Later he claims that he serves the "law," and when Mendel asks which law, he says, "the cosmic universal law."

His pleas unsuccessful, Mendel attacks Ginzburg, who responds by threatening to freeze him to death. As Mendel's life fades, he thinks only of dying without helping Isaac. Mendel sees his own terror reflected in Ginzburg's eyes, while Ginzburg sees his terrible wrath mirrored in Mendel's eyes. Suddenly, Ginzburg "beheld a shimmering, starry, blinding light that produced darkness." In the grip of some greater power, Ginzburg allows Mendel to put Isaac on the train. After he is settled and the train is moving, Mendel returns to the platform to see what has become of Ginzburg.

Themes and Meanings

In this simple story, Malamud explores the power of love to change the universe. Throughout the story, the world appears bleak, cold, and dark, while the mood of the tale is one of despair. In a world characterized by the mercenary pawnbroker, the heartless philanthropist, and the greedy wife of the old rabbi, Mendel seems foolish even to hope he might save Isaac, but it is finally his hope in the face of desperate odds that turns the events at the end of the story. Though Mendel's time has run out, some power greater than death stays Ginzburg's cold stare for the final minutes Mendel needs to complete the task for which he lives.

When, in the final scene of the story, Ginzburg identifies himself with a mechanical cosmic law that binds him as well as everyone else, the reader recognizes in him more than a symbol of death, though he is that as well. He is the representative of a meaningless universe in which man can only play out his destiny against a background of impersonal forces or "laws." Cold and heartless, Ginzburg, as Mendel tells him, does not "understand what it means" to be human. His world, like that of the other selfish, unfeeling, and greedy characters in the story, is a world without love.

Ginzburg's opposite is the old rabbi; he says to Mendel, "God will give you," and offers his own new coat to help Isaac. The rabbi has faith in God, but he also acts himself with charity and love, proving that these qualities are not so dead as other characters make them seem. It is through men such as the old rabbi that God works and by their faith that He lives.

Mendel, a long-suffering old man, might be expected to welcome death as an end to a painful life. His love for Isaac has been the meaning of his life, however, and his determination to see his son safe gives him strength to go on even in the face of the inevitable. He sacrifices his last strength in a final attempt to get Isaac to the train, and in that moment the power of love in the universe is revealed. As Ginzburg's power over Mendel fails before a "starry, blinding light that produced darkness," love, faith, and hope triumph over the meaningless universe.

Style and Technique

Superficially, this story is typical of the dark mood of literary naturalism. Its realistic setting and effective Yiddish dialect heighten these effects. Beginning with his first hints that the mysterious Ginzburg might be more than simply another character, though, Malamud gradually builds toward the mystical vision at the end, which totally changes the meaning of the piece. With the exception of the role of Ginzburg, symbols are used sparingly and seem an uncontrived aspect of the narrative. This is true of the various characters who represent the failure of human values, and even more true of the several references to the sky and stars. Only at the end of the story, when Ginzburg beholds the "shimmering, starry, blinding light that produced darkness," does the reader connect the heavens and the stars, points of light in a dark universe, with God. Malamud's ability to combine realism and mysticism in a style that does justice to both in large measure accounts for the powerful impact of "Idiots First."

William E. Grant

IDLE DAYS ON THE YANN

Author: Lord Dunsany (Edward John Moreton Drax Plunkett, 1878-1957)
Type of plot: Fantasy
Time of plot: Early twentieth century
Locale: The River Yann, in Dunsany's imaginary Lands of Dream
First published: 1910

> *Principal characters:*
> THE UNNAMED NARRATOR, a traveler
> THE CAPTAIN, whose ship is the *Bird of the River*

The Story

The narrator arrives at the Yann, where, as prophesied, he finds the *Bird of the River*. Singing sailors swing the ship out into the central stream, while the narrator is interviewed by the captain about his homeland and destination. The ship sails from Fair Belzoond, whose gods are "least and humblest," not very threatening, and easily appeased. The narrator discloses that he hails from Ireland, in Europe, but is mocked, for captain and crew deny the existence of any such places. When he reveals the lands where his fancy dwells, they compliment him, for these places are at least imaginable, if unknown. He bargains for passage to the Gates of Yann.

As the sun sets and the darkness of the adjoining jungle deepens, the sailors hoist lanterns and then kneel to propitiate their gods, five or six at a time, so that no god will be addressed by more than one man at any moment. Meanwhile, the helmsman, holding the ship in midstream, sings the helmsman's prayer, common to all helmsmen of whatever faith. Not to be alone, the narrator also prays, but to a god long ago deserted by men. Night descends as the prayers die out, yet the sailors feel comforted in the face of the Great Night to come.

During the night, under the guidance of the ever-singing helmsman, they pass a number of cities and tributaries with exotic names. Finally, shortly after daybreak, they harbor at Mandaroon. While the sailors gather fruit, the narrator visits the city, silent, moss-covered, and apparently deserted. A sentinel at the gate informs him that questions are forbidden, because when the people awake the gods will die. When the narrator inquires further about these gods, he is driven off.

The ship sets forth again under the full sun, accompanied now by choirs of insects, including the butterflies, whose hymns are beyond human ears, rising to pay homage in flight and song to the vivifying sun. The sun works otherwise with men and beasts: It puts them to sleep. The narrator himself is lulled into dreams of a triumphant but mysterious return.

He awakes to find the captain buckling on his scimitar; they have arrived at Astahahn, where an open court surrounded by colonnades fronts the river and where the people follow ancient rites of dignity and solemnity; antiquity is the rule. The people ignore the passing ship, intent on their ancient rituals, but one bystander states that the occupation of the city is to preserve Time, in order to preserve the gods. These gods, moreover, are "all those . . . whom Time has not yet slain."

Beyond Astahahn the river widens, and a second evening descends. The sailors pray, as before, and the helmsman's prayer guides the ship onward into the dark. In the morning they have arrived at Perdóndaris, a fine and celebrated place, welcome after the jungle. The captain is haggling with a fat merchant. The contest proceeds as if by script, with extravagant rhetorical gestures, the captain at one point threatening suicide because the price offered would disgrace him. Finally he entreats his lesser gods of Belzoond—whom he had previously threatened to loose on the city—and the merchant yields. The watching sailors applaud. The captain breaks out a cask of wine, and their thoughts are soon back home.

In the evening, the narrator visits the city, a formidable place with a massive, tower-surmounted wall bearing plaques advertising the fate of an army which once besieged it. Yet the people are dancing in honor of "the god they know not," because a thunderstorm has terrified them with images of the fires of death. The narrator admires the wealth and prosperity of the city until he comes to the outer wall, where he finds a gate of ivory, carved out of one solid piece. He flees to the ship, fearing the wrath of the animal from which the tusk was taken but revealing his secret to no one.

Finally he tells the captain, who agrees that the gate is recent and that such a gigantic beast could not have been killed by man. The captain decides to escape immediately. Later the narrator learns that some force has indeed wrecked the once mighty city in a single day.

Again they pass a night on the river. As before, the helmsman prays the helmsman's prayer, to whatever god is listening, beseeching safe return to all sailors. His voice rises above the silent river in the songs of Durl and Duz, and fair Belzoond. The narrator awakes to lifting mists and a broadened river tumbling as it mingles with the brawling Irillion from the crags of Glorm. Freshened, the river shrugs off the torpor of the jungle and sweeps through cliffs. It broadens again to wind through marshes, then reaches further mountains with a number of villages, passed by night to the helmsman's songs.

They pass more cities before arriving at Nen, the last great city, where they anchor. The Wanderers, a weird, dark tribe, are also in the town for their once-in-every-seven-years visit. These savages have taken over the city, dancing like dervishes, playing strange music, and performing feats of desert magic, to the consternation of the people of Nen.

The narrator must leave before he can hear the Wanderers' night-hymn, echoed by wolves on the heights surrounding the city. They sail on in silence under the setting sun, until they reach the Gate of Yann, formed by two barrier-cliffs at the mouth of the river, before the sea. Anchoring at the foot of the cliffs, they take a lingering farewell, for they sense that they will not meet again. The captain commends the soul of the narrator to his humble gods of Belzoond.

Themes and Meanings

The story offers little overt material for analysis, for the plot is slight and lacks the conventional conflict and resolution of narrative. In fact, Dunsany stated repeatedly that his material was the stuff of dreams and spontaneous storytelling, that he was not aware of promoting any themes, even by symbol or allegory, and that the only meanings in his stories were those that emerged subconsciously. That does not seem to leave much with which to work.

Yet a little examination reveals subtle patterns. The gods are repeatedly alluded to, and the helmsman's prayer stitches the story together. Peoples are distinguished and identified by their god or gods; yet these tribal, or at best, regional, gods are not in conflict with one another. Furthermore, there seems to be no rivalry among them: The helmsmen along the river pray indiscriminately to "whatever god may hear." This is a continent of mutual toleration.

Yet if the function of the gods is protection and there is no antagonism among them, from what, then, do the gods protect? The story itself gives some clues. Although there is little conventional plot, the structure reflects the action depicted: It is a journey interrupted with stops, and each stop provides a climax of a certain intensity. On the first day, the ship passes the preserved city of Mandaroon, where life is spent in sleep that the gods may not die; that afternoon brings the wordless choral dance of insects and butterflies in praise of the sun, in whom they find life for the moment, regardless of the future. That afternoon they come to Astahahn, where stately rites charm Time into immobility, for otherwise he will destroy the gods. The second day records the bargain at Perdóndaris, mediated by the gods, and the discovery of an impending doom that cannot be deflected by prayers to the god they know not; it ends with the helmsman's prayer to all gods. On the next day, the ship reaches Nen, where the strange gods of the Wanderers have intimidated the people, and finally there is journey's end, which closes with celebrating the little gods of Belzoond who have guided the expedition. Threaded throughout is the chant of the helmsman to all gods.

This sequence does not add up to a definitive statement, and is not intended to. Yet the story consistently suggests that although the gods may be powerless, man needs to defer to and respect them in order to survive his voyage—as, on the first night, the narrator finds himself impelled to pray by the example of the sailors.

Style and Technique

The term most often associated with Lord Dunsany, also appearing frequently in his writing, is "dream," with its relatives "dreamy" and "dreamlike." Some of this derives from his subject matter, for in much of his writing he gives substance to the beasts, men, and gods of his Lands of Dream, a fantasy world distinct from the waking here and now, one endowed with the power of myth. Yet much of it can be attributed to the peculiarities of his style. This story is a good example.

"Idle Days on the Yann" resembles dreams first in its narrative inconsequence. Instead of following an action with a clearly defined beginning, middle, and end, it merely floats along the surface of the river; what happens does not seem to connect with what preceded or follows, except as marking stages of passage. There is no apparent reason why Astahahn should appear on the first day or Nen on the last. There is danger, as there is danger in dreams, but it all seems to come from beyond. Danger is something which happens, not something caused.

The themes are also as evanescent as the meanings of dreams. The reader senses connections in the way that a dreamer gropes for significance; yet the links fragment and the strands part. Meaning drifts off, dangling somewhere just beyond reach, to be replaced by wonder and vague foreboding.

Beyond all else, however, Dunsany accomplishes this creation of a dreamworld by his use of language. This is most apparent in the place-names and the regions that he creates—Belzoond, Darl, Duz, Yann, Irillion. Yet more subtle and more telling are three other qualities. First is the flat, deliberate narrative style, in which events are sketched as if they were taking place on a screen in front of the narrator; he records them, rather than taking part in them. This trance-narration has elements of both children's literature and biblical apocalyptic literature. Second is a use of adjectives and adverbs as modifiers at the expense of more graphic metaphors and images; this lack of definition blurs the events and forces the reader to complete the outline. The third is a habit of compound construction: Long series of clauses are buttjoined by "ands," as in stories told by children. These combine to create a unique representation of pseudodreams in words.

James L. Livingston

I'M A FOOL

Author: Sherwood Anderson (1876-1941)
Type of plot: Psychological realism
Time of plot: c. 1919
Locale: Rural Ohio
First published: 1922

> *Principal characters:*
> THE NARRATOR, the protagonist, a nineteen-year-old boy
> LUCY WESSEN, his "girl"
> WILBUR WESSEN, her brother
> BURT, the black stableboy

The Story

The narrator is a nineteen-year-old boy whose life revolves around his job as a swipe at a local racetrack. Though it is a menial job with no future, the young man brags to the reader about it, describing it in a sort of homespun lyricism which purportedly shows his genuine feelings about his career among horses, jockeys, and trainers. Significantly, his best friend and fellow worker is a black man, Burt, and the young man boasts of the good life that they lead, traveling from track to track tending the horses. What the reader infers from all this is that the swipe's protestations are clearly part of a deep-seated dissatisfaction with his life. In narrating his "adventures" at the track, for example, the swipe remarks on the college men in the grandstand, who "put on airs" and think that they are superior because of their education. Yet the narrator himself does precisely the same thing. One payday, he walks into a bar, orders a drink and expensive cigars, and spurns a well-dressed man with a Windsor tie and a cane who is standing near him and whom he accuses of "putting on airs."

It is the narrator's detestation of the false front and his own use of it that is at the heart of the story. Sitting in the grandstand, the narrator meets Wilbur Wessen and his sister, Lucy. The Wessens take a liking to the swipe, and he in turn becomes attracted to Lucy. He is impressed with her breeding, her charm, and her gentleness, and in an impetuous moment he introduces himself as Walter Mathers, the son of the owner of a noted racehorse.

Later that evening the narrator and Miss Lucy go off to a quiet spot by the lake, and the young man describes his feelings, revealing a sensitivity and gentleness that belie the demeaning crudity of his life as a swipe. He learns that she and her brother are leaving soon by train, and he realizes then that he has lost her. By lying to her, giving her a false identity, he has cut off any possibility of her writing to him and of his being honest with her. He is hurt all the more by his realization also that she genuinely cares for him, not because of his name or supposed wealth, but for himself.

At the end, Miss Lucy leaves, and the swipe has tears in his eyes, hating himself, convinced that he will never see her again and that he has been a fool.

Themes and Meanings

"I'm a Fool" is a poignant treatment of an adolescent's inferiority complex and of his painful journey to maturity and self-knowledge. The narrator is not conscious of his feelings of inferiority, but his constant comparing of his honest, good life at the track with the false, hypocritical life of the rich and cultured clearly gives the reader insight into the young man's problem.

In many of Sherwood Anderson's stories, young people struggle with unconscious desires and with an inability to explain or understand their feelings. The swipe does not understand why he lies to Miss Lucy, for example; he senses only that he was foolish to do so. When he declares that he wishes he could die or at least break a bone so that he could hurt, the young man expresses his feelings but does not understand that their source is not in his "love" for Miss Lucy but in his unconscious dislike for himself, his position in life, and his lack of security about a future—a security symbolized by the man with the Windsor tie and cane, who reappears as an image of contempt in the narrator's thoughts at the close of the story.

On another level, the young man's companionship with Burt is an example of his naïveté about the implications of his social status. As a black man with no education, Burt occupies the lowest rung of the social ladder. As his friend, therefore, the swipe puts himself in the same position, though he invests it with the glories of romance and adventure, oblivious to his low-class family origins. He is, in effect, a fool, not because he lies but because he deludes himself about his background, his present, and his future.

Style and Technique

Anderson's use of the first-person narrator is crucial in creating the subtlety of "I'm a Fool" and illustrates the instinctive quality of Anderson's best work. A third-person narrator, for example, not only would have robbed the character of his emotional intensity but also would have revealed the fragility of a commonplace plot. Instead, the narrator's voice gives the almost banal situation an earnestness, an honesty, that is both powerful and moving.

Though the use of the first-person narrator was certainly not new, Anderson's adaptation of it for this kind of story is significant. Mark Twain had already created the character of Huck Finn in 1884 by allowing Huck himself to record his adventures in his Missouri vernacular. There is, in fact, even an echo of *The Adventures of Huckleberry Finn* in "I'm a Fool" in the relationship between the narrator and the black man, Burt.

Yet the relationship is suggestive more of the narrator's frustration than of his freedom and moral superiority, as is the case with Huck's relationship with Jim. Besides, Huck's narration is often of stirring action, satiric comedy, and shrewd character portrayal. By contrast, the narrator of "I'm a Fool" speaks more about his feelings; he records in his ungrammatical English, not the external action, but the internal, the private, the quiet experience of his emotions.

The indebtedness of "I'm a Fool" to Twain's *The Adventures of Huckleberry Finn* is further evident in the skillful use of irony; like Huck, the swipe communicates deeper meanings than he intends. When, for example, the narrator describes the lakeside setting of his tryst with Miss Lucy, he uses the simplest analogies, comparing the evening to the sweetness of an orange. In so doing, the swipe reveals not only his simplicity but also his sensitivity, his almost poetic "soul."

Furthermore, when the narrator seems to stumble and digress from his "story," he is inadvertently giving clues to the reader about his feelings of inferiority, as when he discusses his family background and begins to mention his proud grandfather in Wales; "but never mind that," he concludes.

Thus, the use of the first-person narrator not only establishes a sensitive personality but also makes the story a collaboration between that personality and the reader, forcing the reader to draw inferences from the narrator's offhanded remarks. Collaboration such as this is a characteristic technique of twentieth century literature.

Finally, if "I'm a Fool" is indebted to *The Adventures of Huckleberry Finn*, it is also in its own right a literary ancestor of such modern works as J. D. Salinger's *The Catcher in the Rye* (1951). Anderson's handling of the sensitive young narrator was emulated by Salinger in the characterization of Holden Caulfield, highlighting the conflict between the compromised world of the adult and the idealistic world of the adolescent. Though Holden is not uneducated in the same way as the swipe, he is as confused and frustrated as his predecessor.

"I'm a Fool" is a modern classic whose deceptively simple style is the chief method by which the emotions and personality of the central character are portrayed.

Edward Fiorelli

IMAGINATION DEAD IMAGINE

Author: Samuel Beckett (1906-   )
Type of plot: Modern fable
Time of plot: Possibly after a nuclear holocaust
Locale: Unspecified
First published: "Imagination morte imaginez," 1965 (English translation, 1965)

> *Principal characters:*
> AN UNNAMED NARRATOR, who discovers the rotunda
> TWO UNNAMED HUMANS, one female, one male

The Story

The terse, ambiguous title of this story is consistent with the tale itself, in which a narrator describes flatly the real (or imaginary) discovery of a small rotunda in a white wasteland, the investigation of the same with some scientific care, and the final withdrawal from it after its dimensions, shape, and occupants have been systematically examined. The narrator leaves, convinced that there will be no chance of ever finding the building again.

The obvious thinness of such an overview may sufficiently convince a reader that something more is going on, and that a more detailed account must be given to make sense of the story. Detail is important in Beckett's world, and this tale is full of it.

The story begins in mid-conversation, in which the oral shorthand must be deciphered by the reader. The speaker seems to be rejecting with abrupt arrogance a comment that there is no sign of life. Unconcerned, the speaker suggests that it is irrelevant so long as imagination exists, but he immediately accepts the possibility that even imagination is dead. Good riddance to it and its inclination to describe the world in terms of the old nature as mankind knew it. The narrator posits a world of unrelieved whiteness, one in which a small building appears. He gets inside the building and measures the interior, a circle divided into two semicircles. Without evidencing any surprise, he records the presence of two human bodies, one in each semicircle. He checks the structure inside and out, testing its solidity, commenting on its bonelike quality. Inside, it is intensely bright and hot. The bodies are sweating.

The narrator goes out, moves away, and ascends. One must presume that there is some kind of vehicle, although it is not mentioned. As he ascends, the building disappears in the landscape and then reappears as he returns. This time, inside the building, the lights start to dim. Over a twenty-second period the room goes black, and the temperature drops to freezing. Then the light and heat come on again. These changes begin to happen irregularly, and the passage back and forth is sometimes interrupted, at which time everything, including the ground, shakes. There is some comfort in the stillness at the extremes of light and dark, and, significantly, a comment is made that such calmness is not to be found in the outside world.

At this point, then, some connection with a past world is established, and some modest feeling is expressed. The building is commented on as a miraculous discovery, and the further point is made that there is no other like it. After what seems to have been a long space voyage through perfect emptiness, a place of peace, albeit a limited peace, has been found.

The story starts to make some sense as a record of the discovery of the last remnant of the world, but at almost the same time, the light and heat patterns become erratic. Attention turns to a precise description of the humans, lying in their jackknife positions back to back. There is now little calm in the room, and the bodies are difficult to observe closely because of the increasing agitation of their surroundings. They are alive, sweating, breathing, and occasionally opening an eye.

There is a very muted suggestion that a sigh might barely raise some reaction in the form of a quickly repressed shudder from the figures, but the narrator does not pursue it. The narrator leaves, suggesting and immediately denying the possibility of a better example of this sort of thing somewhere else. There is no expectation that the rotunda could ever be found again.

Themes and Meanings

Beckett, as an Absurdist, avoids meaning if he can, although the very avoidance is caused by a belief that the world and human life are meaningless. Beckett's stories are aesthetic structures proving that simple idea. It is, however, true that he often illustrates that idea in works which use the landscape and the characters which might be imagined as existing after a nuclear holocaust. This story may (with the stress on "may") be read as an example, a comment on humanity's disastrous possibilities. The narrator can be seen as a survivor, possessed of some technological capacity to travel, coming upon this isolated haven. It is, significantly, a shelter in which the male and female, turned away from each other, simply survive in a fetal position.

That, however, is too easy. The title and the first lines suggest that it may be an exploration of the last vestige of mental life. The rotunda could be a skull, the interior a brain close to death, the two pallid figures representing the weakened capacity of the mind to create and the mind's inability to project creation further since, as the narrator suggests, the imagination is dead. Imagine what it would be like if the imagination were dead, and still try to imagine.

Both these readings lead to the idea that life in general is absurd, without meaning, without hope. Sometimes in Beckett that proposition can be relieved by saucy humor. Here it is relentlessly morbid.

Style and Technique

Beckett often uses solitary characters—nameless, wandering, talkative; they are often tramps. In this story, however, the man has a touch of the professional, the specialist, about him. He seems to be recording his comments, making a detailed report on this unusual discovery of isolated life. The determination to get the details right has a psuedoscientific fastidiousness about it. If the story is read carefully, it will make sense physically; there is a clear picture of when and where everything happens. It is stylistically impersonal, often pedantically so. It is, in a way, simply a more artistically successful form of the overview of the story in this article. It is really a précis of a story— compressed, sticking doggedly to the facts.

It should be no surprise that it is a fragment of what was supposed to be, originally, a longer work. Beckett calls it, outrageously, a novel, and some critics see it as a plot for a novel. It does contain the structure of a short story. Framed by the elusive idea of the imagination fore and aft, it has a beginning, a middle, a slight touch of last-minute reversal, and a conclusion.

The remark about the imagination starts the whole sequence with the discovery of the rotunda (beginning). The narrator stays long enough to record the peculiar situation and the change from pattern to chaos (middle). At the last moment, he notices, possibly, a touch of feeling in the shudder caused by the human sigh, which is quickly suppressed (reversal). The narrator leaves, certain that in the great meaningless cosmos, it will be impossible to find that place ever again (end). It is all very cool, tonally indifferent.

Charles H. Pullen

IMAGINED SCENES

Author: Ann Beattie (1947-   )
Type of plot: Psychological realism
Time of plot: A winter during the 1970's
Locale: Evidently the Northeast United States
First published: 1974

>   *Principal characters:*
>   AN UNNAMED YOUNG WOMAN, the protagonist
>   DAVID, her husband
>   AN OLD MAN, for whom she provides night care
>   HIS SISTER
>   KATHERINE and LARRY DUANE, new neighbors, who never
>   actually appear in the story

The Story

Like much of Ann Beattie's fiction, "Imagined Scenes" is more evocation of a situation than plotted tale. The seven sections of the story cover three days in the life of the female protagonist, who sits nights with an old man while his daughter and son-in-law take a midwinter vacation in Florida. The garrulous old man reminisces about the terrible winter he spent in Berlin and produces photograph albums and postcards, one of which, a silver-spangled picture of Rip Van Winkle walking through a moonlit forest, provides one of the story's many ambiguous echoes. The old man's chatter provides contrast with the scenes between the protagonist and her husband, David. Their marriage seems a wary one, dominated by silences, clichéd expressions of concern, and David's ambiguous disappearances and his relationship with the new neighbors, the Duanes.

The opening section establishes the protagonist's dependence on her husband, who seems to her energetic and supremely competent, able to anticipate her needs and alleviate her fears. Yet their relationship seems very much like that which a brother and sister might have; there is no hint of passion or even deep caring on David's part. There is a smugness about him, communicated in the first section by mention of his "surprise" decision the previous summer to quit work and return to graduate school, and by his guessing that she has dreamed of Greece and then insisting, without asking her opinion, that they will go there. Though the protagonist would rather go to Spain, she silences her objection with the significant line, "she should let him sleep."

The subjects of wandering and sleeping dominate the story. During the three nights she spends watching the old man (the third, fifth, and seventh sections of the narrative), she is increasingly cut off—by the ever-falling snow and by David's absences and ambiguity about the new neighbors—from the comfortable reality of her marriage. She is forced to imagine his whereabouts, and in the fourth, sixth, and seventh sections, to question him without seeming to intrude into his privacy. Appearances suggest that he no longer studies for his Ph.D. orals, and his having given their houseplant to the Duanes puzzles her, as does his reluctance to take her to the Duane home. His failure to answer the telephone late the second night causes her to imagine once again the dream scene of ocean and mountains, and to name it this time, as if in obedience, Greece. His apparent absence the third night when she calls at four in the morning visibly depresses her and reminds her of his previous excuses, that he was walking the dog through the forest at night and that he "could have been anywhere." His surprising appearance the next day to help the old man up from the snow and his excuse for the night before ("I was sleeping") reinforce the connections between him and the Rip Van Winkle figure, and at the same time seem to reinforce his image as an eccentric but caring man, magically able, as in the opening section of the story, to anticipate her needs.

Most important, the scene leaves the protagonist in a true dilemma: The old man has told her that the aged, lacking power to "improve things," learn to make up stories, "to lie all the time," and this young woman, finding her reality to be an indeterminate mixture of speculation and apparent fact, does not know what to make of it. She distrusts David without wanting to, yet she sleeps through the ringing of their telephone even as her subconscious mind registers the sound—just as David claims to have done. "You don't know what it's like to be caught," the old man's sister tells her, but clearly that is not true.

Themes and Meanings

Collected in *Distortions* (1976), this story offers an angle of that theme, presenting a young woman about whom the reader actually knows very little except that she feels as trapped in her life as the old man for whom she cares. Yet whereas he can name some of the distortions to which he has resorted in an effort to manipulate those around him, the protagonist cannot even define the conditions that cause her malaise. Like many of Beattie's characters, she seems to have no interests that define her; she comes to the reader as a collection of perceptions and impressions, so uncertain as to be incapable of anger or of confronting the possibility of getting angry. Her inability to admit her emotions even to herself also means an inability to communicate them to anyone else.

The progression of events in the story, however, implies change. The mystery of David's whereabouts preoccupies her more and more, and as the tension builds, the reader is encouraged by the story's recurrences to wonder if confrontation and/or resolution will result. During the story, the protagonist has come to recognize what tentative knowledge she possesses about her husband. From what she hears about loneliness and powerlessness from the old man, she is invited to see the possibilities of loneliness and powerlessness in her own life. The old man's postcards and photograph album provide him with a refuge of sorts, but the image of Rip Van Winkle takes on a cruelly ironic quality when the old man is knocked down by children in the street. The images of David's walking at night connect him with the postcard Rip Van Winkle and bring to mind that old sleeper's urge to escape his wife. In addition, the old man in Beattie's story has established a kind of truce with his sister, who serves him diligently but not without bitterness, and who, though claiming that she is trapped, insists on maintaining the unpleasant conditions, partly out of a kind of love for her brother, and partly perhaps because she has nothing else. All this hints to the young woman something about the possibilities of life, but the story does not lead to a sudden awakening or epiphany for her. She is at present too timid to look hard at her situation. The story communicates this theme of limited possibilities, as it were, over her head.

In this regard, the crucial set of imagined scenes comes near the end of the story, when the narrative implies that she does not wish to confront directly the essence of her relationship with David. On the way home, with David angry because she allowed the old man to go outside, she hints at her suspicions, but, faced with his simple denial of what seems obvious to her, she takes refuge in a series of four dream images: She imagines him sleeping, as he claims to have done, then walking with the dog in snow "too deep to jump out of," then "asleep, under the covers," then walking up the hill. Something ominous about this willed dreaming—perhaps in the sequence of deep snow and David asleep under covers, or perhaps the alternate acceptance and rejection of his excuse for not having answered the telephone— prompts her to stop. Yet she remains suspicious.

To measure distortion, one must be able to fix an image to serve as a standard, and this is precisely what this young woman cannot do. Her suspicions cannot be escaped or glossed over by her dreams; she has neither illusions nor truths, and that is the worst condition of all.

Style and Technique

Beattie's manipulation of narrative techniques made her one of the 1970's most recognized and original writers, and "Imagined Scenes" gains much of its force from her preoccupation with narrative objectivity and the fragmentation of time's flow.

There is a reportorial quality about the narrative voice that gives the story a very cool ambience. Events are related, but the internal world of emotions remains outside the narrative's view except for what the old man and his sister tell about their feelings of anger, rejection, and powerlessness. With this as counterpoint, the narrator, with the objectivity of a camera's eye, examines the interactions of the younger couple, who do not speak of their inner feelings. This technique effectively creates great emotion by making emotion's absence so obvious. For example, when first describing the new neighbors, David tells her, "He's very nice. Katherine and Larry Duane," and never again does he refer to the woman. That the protagonist does not react to this omission makes her inner torment all the more clear. David touches his young wife only twice during the story: once "on his way out" to the Duanes' house, and once (his cold cheeks sting her) coming back from the same place. Without consulting her, he gives their plant to the Duanes. He takes to making his own coffee and abandons other of their private rituals. When upset, he refuses to speak to her. The narrative records these details with noncommittal economy; in fact, nothing in David's behavior assures a reader that he is anything more than mildly dislocated by having his spouse away every night for a week.

Yet the technique only makes the emotions and judgments more forceful because they remain unstated: finally, during the last telephone conversation with the old man's sister, the young woman seems overwhelmed by the images and emotions she has suppressed, and she mixes them together into a fearful vision of a deserted, snow-covered earth to match the table that David cleared of, perhaps, suspicious evidence?

The fragmentation of the story into seven vignettes nicely complements the apparent disintegration of the young protagonist's marriage, or at least of her naïve confidence in her husband. The first vignette gives the impression of what for her was an ideal past, one of shared instincts: "she expects him to wake up when she does"; "by unspoken agreement, he has learned to like Roquefort dressing." That this situation evolved without apparent effort makes plausible her silence in the subsequent chronological sequence when he seems to drift away; her passivity before life makes it impossible for her to impose a coherence upon its events. The last and longest of the narrative sections shows her feeble attempt at inquiry, the continued suspicion, and the vertigo that results. In this marriage of a passive-aggressive pair, the lack of unity which the story objectively sets out in fragmented sections seems inevitable.

Kerry Ahearn

IMPULSE

Author: Conrad Aiken (1889-1973)
Type of plot: Psychological realism
Time of plot: c. 1920
Locale: Boston
First published: 1932

> *Principal characters:*
> MICHAEL LOWES, the protagonist, who yields to an "impulse"
>   to steal
> DORA LOWES, his wife
> SMITH,
> BRYANT, and
> HURWITZ, Michael's card-playing acquaintances
> A STORE DETECTIVE

The Story

While Aiken's title might suggest that "Impulse" concerns a whimsical, unpremeditated action, the story actually examines an ostensibly "impulsive" action and finds, instead, that the "impulse" is really the logical culmination of a series of actions in the life of Michael Lowes, the protagonist. If fact, the story is a fictionalized psychological study of a paranoid "loser," whose attempts to escape from reality are self-destructive acts which lead to his arrest and conviction for theft and to an impending divorce from his wife.

Just as he is left alone in his cell at the end of the story, Michael is significantly alone when the story begins, and, since he is shaving, he is also characteristically narcissistic. As he shaves, his thoughts reveal a gamut of psychological problems: Ready "to do a new jump," he projects his "restless" feelings on his wife, Dora; "fate is always against you"; his "friends" are inferior, "cheap fellows, really"; and he twice mentions his need for "escape." Michael uses his "friends" to enhance his own self-image, while he maintains a distance from them (he denies that he "likes" them), and he also seems threatened by Dora and the family relationships and responsibilities that the marriage represents. Those responsibilities are represented by the "bills," which he procrastinates paying and which are the result of the "bad luck" that hounds him.

To gain needed respite from his responsibilities, he schemes to meet Smith, Bryant, and Hurwitz for dinner, drinks, and an evening of bridge and conversation. During an intermission from bridge, the four men begin to discuss the nature of impulses and the civilizing social forces, particularly the fear of the law, that prevent people from yielding to those sudden, irrational, and subconscious desires. Michael feels "relief" when he learns that he has not been alone in having "both these impulses," theft and sex, and while his friends turn to other topics of conversation, he recalls the "thrills" he experienced earlier in his life when he stole a conch shell.

When the game ends, Michael leaves for the subway station but stops at the nearby drugstore to get some hot chocolate. Once in the store, he realizes that his real motive for stopping at the drugstore was "to steal something," "to put the impulse to the test." After viewing the "wares," he steals a safety-razor set, but despite his dexterity he is apprehended by the store detective and taken to a back room, where he unsuccessfully attempts to explain the theft as a "joke," the result of a "bet." He is equally unsuccessful at the police station, where a sergeant calls Hurwitz and Bryant to check on his story about the bet; both deny the existence of the bet, and Hurwitz adds that Michael is "hard up."

Dora adds to Michael's predicament because, while she is willing to get him a lawyer and to contact Hurwitz, Bryant, and Smith, her "cold, detached, deliberate behavior" indicates that she does not believe in his innocence. Moreover, she is unwilling to use her own savings in his defense. When his lawyer reports that his friends are unwilling to be involved, his fate is sealed, and he receives a three-month sentence. After his first week in prison, he receives his first posttrial communication from Dora: It is a note informing him that she is instituting divorce proceedings and requesting that he not contest the divorce. Realizing that opposing the divorce would be futile, he resolves that upon his release he will "go west, . . . get rich, clear his name somehow," but he does not know how to accomplish his immature, unrealistic goals and retreats into his memories of his childhood in Chicago. At the end of the story, he concludes that his "whole life . . . had all come foolishly to an end."

Themes and Meanings

In "Impulse," Aiken depicts the psychological problems of a repressed, insecure "loner" who attempts to escape from his problems and whose immature concern for self prevents him from seeing things as they are. His "impulsive" theft is clearly premeditated, the act of an adult who has never "grown up" and who has never had to accept the consequences of his actions. Though he is directly responsible for the theft, the paranoid Michael Lowes sees his predicament as the result of betrayal and "bad luck."

Michael's bridge game is twice associated with "escape" from what he sees as a dreary routine naturally repugnant to a man of his education and cultivation. He seeks a diversion, significantly a "game," which is how he persists in seeing shoplifting, a crime usually associated with youngsters. Alcohol is one method of escape, and while Aiken stresses its importance to Michael, it is not the alcohol which prompts the theft. If Michael is a "trifle tight," he is not unsteady on his feet, and his behavior is extremely methodical. He "examines" the "wares" with a "critical and appraising eye" and carefully considers what to steal. Since Aiken has associated "impulses" with sex and theft, it is significant that Michael's reaction to the safety-razor set is "love at first sight" and that the set is twice described as a "victim." The theft of the set becomes a hostile act for the repressed Michael, who bitterly resents the nagging of his wife, who reminds him of his "non-success." The safety-razor set suggests both hostility and caution, and while Michael is drawn to the "heavy gold," the box is made of "snakeskin," with its association with archetypal evil. (The detective who apprehends Michael has a voice which conveys "venom.") Thus, the literal theft is also quite symbolic.

Michael simply does not regard an "impulsive" theft as a crime, but instead sees it as an adventure, even a "discovery": "Why not be a Columbus of the moral world and really do it?" When he is apprehended, he sees himself as a "thief by accident" (perhaps a reference to the bad luck that "hounds" him). When Dora and his friends tell the truth and will not reshape their accounts to square with the "facts" that Michael has created and now believes to be true, Michael sees himself as persecuted martyr: "It wasn't possible that he was going to be betrayed?" What Michael sees as a "monstrous joke; a huge injustice" is really the impartial functioning of the legal system: The judge decides that it is "a perfectly clear case of theft, and a perfectly clear motive."

Michael cannot impose his vision of truth upon others, but he nevertheless attempts to create a future with which he can live psychologically. That future is expressed in immature terms more appropriate to a child with a temper tantrum: "He would show them. He would go west, when he came out—get rich, clear his name somehow. . . . But how?" Horace Greeley's advice about "going west" is no longer appropriate, and riches and reputation necessitate hard work, behavior that is not consistent with Michael's past. Rather than vowing to change his life—such a vow would be an admission of his faults—Michael regresses to thoughts of his childhood.

Style and Technique

Aiken's "Impulse" relies heavily on psychological terms and concepts, and his language is a blend of literary symbolism and the psychological case study. In order to understand Michael, the reader must know what Michael thinks, but there must concurrently be some distance between Michael and the reader. Aiken's choice of point of view is particularly fitting, because it creates distance—as a first-person account would not—while it allows the reader to see events as they are screened through Michael's distorted perspective. At times, the third-person limited point of view becomes so intimate that it approaches the stream-of-consciousness technique, with its series of impressions that only seem to be unrelated.

As he sits on the bed in his cell, Michael thinks of the past, and Aiken offers a series of memories that account for the "impulsive" decision to steal. Michael's Chicago memories involve his mother (the missing father is important psychologically), who nags him, as Dora does, about being responsible; Michael's theft is perhaps a rebellious act against domineering women. (He is both attracted to Smith's "Squiggles," whose name suggests irresponsibility, and disgusted with her, for he blames her for the police's failure to contact Smith.) The other memories suggest, without being explicit (Michael cannot bring himself to admit weakness), failures and past crimes: The "crowded examination room at college" may well involve an "impulsive" decision to cheat; the lost stamp collection seems innocuous, but the reader knows that Michael had been tempted to steal Parker's stamp collection; and the broken conch shell refers to a stolen conch shell.

The references to the boat ride and the dead boy next door are enigmatic, but given the context of failure and guilt, they doubtless are allusions to other "impulsive" acts that Michael subconsciously remembers but cannot consciously admit as failures. In fact, the reminiscences constitute, for Michael, only a series of "trivial and infinitely charming little episodes." When he again assures himself that "he had really been a good man," Michael indicates that he cannot admit past errors and learn from them; instead, he deludes himself again and remains in a state of arrested emotional development. Michael's "end" does not come, as he believes, "foolishly," but logically, as the inevitable outcome of the rest of his life.

Thomas L. Erskine

IN ANOTHER COUNTRY

Author: Ernest Hemingway (1899-1961)
Type of plot: Psychological symbolism
Time of plot: The late 1920's
Locale: Milan during World War I
First published: 1927

> *Principal characters:*
> AN AMERICAN OFFICER, a young man being rehabilitated after
> having been wounded
> THREE ITALIAN OFFICERS, young men of the same age who
> have received medals for their bravery
> A FOURTH ITALIAN SOLDIER, whose nose was blown off within
> an hour after arriving at the front
> AN ITALIAN MAJOR, formerly a great fencer, who is now
> disabled with a withered hand

The Story

Hemingway's short story "In Another Country" describes the relationships which develop in Milan among an American and five Italian soldiers who have been wounded and are receiving physical therapy. The story is told from the perspective of the American. The townspeople, with the exception of the café girls, resent the young men because they are officers; this resentment, in addition to the young soldiers' war experiences, sets them apart from the street life in Milan.

Within their group, however, there are also differences. The American has received a medal for his accidental war injury. Three young Italians from near Milan, in contrast to the American, have received wounds and medals because of bravery in battle. Another young Italian from a good family was wounded after only one hour on the front line. The American feels close to this young man because his bravery could not be tested. Although, after cocktails, the American thinks that he might have done all the things that the Italians did to receive their citations, he knows that he "would never have done such things," and acknowledges that he is "very much afraid to die."

All the wounded men go to the hospital every afternoon to use machines for physical therapy. The doctor assures the American that he will again play football even though his knee does not bend. An Italian major, who used to be the greatest fencer in Italy before he was wounded, befriends the American, assisting him in learning to speak Italian grammatically. While the youth of the American and the Italians is emphasized, the major seems to be more mature. Unlike the three young "hunting-hawks," the major does not "believe in bravery."

Near the conclusion of the story, the major's young wife suddenly dies. He is distraught and lashes out at the American, but then apologizes and tells him of his loss. After three days of mourning, the major returns to the hospital wearing a black band on his sleeve.

Themes and Meanings

Still significant in the consciousness of the wounded men is the war, which represents both a challenge and a threat. Because of the war, the three young Italians with medals know that they are brave. In addition to representing a test, the war also heightens the soldiers' awareness of death. The story opens with the line: "In the fall the war was always there, but we did not go to it any more." The tall, pale Italian who has three medals is described as having "lived a very long time with death." As a result, their experiences in the war have left them all "detached."

The nature of courage is one of the central themes of "In Another Country." The American officer is afraid of dying and lies awake wondering how he will behave when he goes back to the front. His fear is contrasted with the bravery of the three young Italians who earned their medals: "The three with the medals were like hunting-hawks; and I was not a hawk." The bravery of the three "hunting-hawks," however, is also contrasted with the courage of the major, who is not a hunting-hawk. The American does not understand the major, but he does recognize that he "had been a great fencer" and that he does not "believe in bravery." The major's self-discipline and courage prompt him to befriend the young American. He insists that the American learn to speak Italian grammatically. The major's concern about speaking Italian grammatically illustrates the importance he gives to "form," to living in terms of a strict code of behavior.

The major's courage does not spring from the heedless self-confidence that often passes for bravery; he is willing to continue to try in spite of the likelihood of failure or defeat. Even though the major comes regularly to work with the therapy machines, he tells the doctor that he has no confidence in them.

The major's courage in the face of his wife's death equals his courage in accepting his disability. The death of his wife is particularly tragic as she was very young and as the major had postponed their marriage until after he had been permanently disabled from his war wounds. The major's courage in coping with his young wife's death is contrasted with the bravery of the three "hunting-hawks" in facing danger. In addition, the major's compassion (for the American) sets him apart from the others.

While war offers the challenge of living with death, those who do battle are not the only ones vulnerable to it: The death of the major's young wife from pneumonia underlines the fact of human mortality. The major's courage thus becomes a model of the heroism required to live.

The source for the title "In Another Country" is Christopher Marlowe's *The Jew of Malta* (1589), in which Friar Barnardine says to Barabas: "Thou hast committed—"; the sentence is finished ironically by Barabas, who says, "Fornication—but that was in another country/ And besides, the wench is dead."

The title thus suggests the detachment which the young men feel after living with death during the war. The conclusion of Barabas' speech, "the wench is dead," brutally reinforces the tragedy of the death of the major's young wife. The irony of her death suggests the difficulty of living with courage.

Style and Technique

Hemingway tells the story from the point of view of the young American, but in the objective or pseudo–third person. By telling the story from the American's point of view yet not making him the narrator, Hemingway manages to objectify and distance the surface of the narrative without affecting the intimacy established between the reader and the American.

The restraint with which the characters experience and voice their emotions is reinforced by the stylistic restraints which Hemingway imposes on his narrative. The central issue of the story, that courage is necessary for life as well as death, is not revealed until the end, when the doctor explains the tragedy of the death of the major's young wife. The major's intense grief at his wife's death is conveyed by language which avoids labeling the emotion he feels: "The photographs did not make much difference to the major because he only looked out of the window." The American may or may not understand the major's bitter loss, but the reader inevitably perceives the major's emotional wound and his courage in not giving up.

Hemingway uses images to suggest the feelings of his characters; the emotions of the characters are conveyed indirectly by what they see. The mood or tone of the story is established in the first paragraph, in which the dead game outside the shops is described as "stiff," "heavy," and "empty." The American's awareness of death controls the way he experiences the streets of Milan. Death is a haunting refrain playing quietly under the surface of the narrative. Though the hospital is "very old and very beautiful," the American observes: "There were usually funerals starting from the courtyard."

Irony is used quietly, but with force. The American comments that the wounded men are all very polite when they go to sit in "the machines that were to make so much difference." Since these men are the first to use the machines, the photographs of restored limbs which the doctor first shows the men and then puts on the wall do not inspire great confidence. The machines are not likely to restore their limbs; in any case, nothing can ease the internal wounds epitomized by the suffering of the major.

In spite of his lack of confidence in the machines, the major continues to come to sit in them, even after his wife's death. His regular attendance is like his interest in having the young American learn grammar. The major's discipline and courage in the face of almost certain defeat are powerfully underscored because they are never overtly mentioned.

Jeanie R. Brink

IN DREAMS BEGIN RESPONSIBILITIES

Author: Delmore Schwartz (1913-1966)
Type of plot: Dream narrative
Time of plot: 1909
Locale: Brooklyn
First published: 1937

> *Principal characters:*
> THE NARRATOR, the dreamer of the story
> THE NARRATOR'S FATHER
> THE NARRATOR'S MOTHER
> THE USHER, who works in the theater where the narrator "views" the silent film
> THE OLD LADY, who is one of the theater audience
> THE PHOTOGRAPHER, who poses the parents at Coney Island
> THE FORTUNE-TELLER, who provokes a quarrel between the parents

The Story

The first-person narrator sets a tentative tone at the beginning with his uncertainty: "I think it is the year 1909." The reader then learns that the narrator is dreaming that he is in a motion-picture theater, viewing a Sunday afternoon in 1909. He sees the man who is to become his father walking the streets of Brooklyn on the way to visit the woman whom he is courting. As the narrator dreams and casts the characters, he can know their thoughts and feelings: his father's awkward impressiveness, for example, his hesitancy about marriage. The couple—the narrator's "prospective parents"—go to Coney Island, where they stroll the boardwalk, watch the bathers, and stare at the ocean. Throughout this section, the narrator reacts to their movements and is shocked by the seeming shallowness of his father and mother. He knows that the father is hesitant about marriage, exaggerates his earnings, and has always believed that "actualities somehow fall short." The narrator begins to weep but is consoled by an old lady in the theater of his dream. Unable to control his tears, he leaves the theater momentarily but returns to view his parents riding on a merry-go-round, after which they walk at dusk to a fashionable restaurant "so that they can look out on the boardwalk and the mobile ocean." As they eat, the father talks about his plans for the future, about his achievements, about his independence since he was thirteen, until, moved by the music of the waltz being played, he almost accidentally proposes to the mother.

The narrator stands up in the dream theater and shouts, "Don't do it," but when the audience, the old lady, and the usher urge him to be quiet, he resigns himself. The next scene shows his father and mother having their picture taken, although the photographer has difficulty posing the two and is certain that "somehow there is something wrong in their pose." The father impatiently goads the photographer, who takes the picture, and as the parents wait for it to be developed, "they become quite depressed."

The final dream sequence features a fortune-teller, whose booth the mother wants to enter, while the father does not. Although the father momentarily concedes, inside the booth he again becomes impatient and in anger strides out. The narrator at this point once more shouts to them to consider what they are doing. The usher drags him out of the theater, telling the young man that he cannot do whatever he wants, that he cannot behave so emotionally. The narrator wakes then, to the "bleak winter morning of his 21st birthday, the windowsill shining with its lip of snow, and the morning already begun."

Themes and Meanings

The young man, through his dreams, is able to expose his ambivalence toward himself and his parents, and toward the imminence of manhood and responsibility. As he re-creates his parents' lives before his birth, he judges and evaluates their personalities, their shortcomings, and their incompatibility. In that dreamworld, the youth can also become aware of his own consciously repressed sense of terror and anguish. Although he feels detached and anonymous as the film begins, the succeeding images force him to confront his own fate—his birth and his impending responsibilities as he enters manhood on his twenty-first birthday. The ambivalence of youth toward parents is clearly revealed as he deplores his father's materialism and smugness, his mother's stubbornness. The sensitivity of the narrator is paralleled by the seeming stolidity of his parents, who sense nothing of the menace in the power of the ocean or in their awesome responsibilities as prospective parents.

Throughout the dream, the narrator's place in society is also explored, when, for example, the old lady in the theater admonishes him or when the usher establishes the conventions of proper behavior. Fluctuating between his need to stay in the theater (society) and his ambivalence toward the incompatibility that he senses in his parents, he is yet caught with the desire to be born—to live. What could have been a banal story of the generation gap, of youthful sensitivity versus parental callousness, of coming of age and the acceptance of responsibilities, is transformed by means of Delmore Schwartz's technique.

Style and Technique

Schwartz combines two imagistic devices—the whole a dream structure within which the narrator is watching a film. The dream device permits quick switches of time and place, distorted focus, and shifting images. The narrator, though unable to control or choose his parents in real life, has control in the sense that he is able to know their thoughts in the past of the film and contrast them with his emotional reactions in his own present. The narrator, once the silent-film atmosphere is set, can then posit a surrounding audience, which serves also to reinforce the theme of the young man's growing awareness of the restraints and judgments in society. The film device combined with the dream permits abrupt shifts in scenes, time telescoping, and sharp, telling visual images. The narrator thus can both view and feel because of the interaction between the internal dream and the seemingly external film.

With the swings between the narrator's understanding and rejection, the paradox of denying his parents' fitness and yet desiring his own existence, Schwartz uses the dream device to suggest the youth's ambivalence and to compress the whole family life into a few pages. The focus is on the narrator's reactions, but without the overt self-pity that a direct first-person "realistic" narration might have engendered. The narrator's level of perception suggests his sensitivity without explicit statement. His perceptions provide insight into his capacity to feel. The narrator does not need to "tell" the reader. His growing awareness is set with sharp images, bleakness contrasted with shining, the reiteration of the paradox of rejection and acceptance, and the suggestion that he realizes through the dream that after all, for everyone, what one does matters very much.

Eileen Lothamer

IN GREENWICH THERE ARE MANY GRAVELLED WALKS

Author: Hortense Calisher (1911-   )
Type of plot: Social realism
Time of plot: c. 1950
Locale: New York City
First published: 1951

Principal characters:
PETER BIRGE, the protagonist, a twenty-three-year-old
  journalism student
ANNE, his mother
ROBERT VIELUM, Peter's older friend, a "perennial taker of
  courses"
SUSAN, Robert's twenty-year-old daughter
VINCE, Robert's current young roomer
MARIO OSTI, Robert's new young friend, an Italian painter

The Story

As the story opens, Peter Birge has just returned from Greenwich, where he left his mother, Anne, at a sanatorium. Peter's father, a Swedish engineer, died when Peter was eight, but his patents have provided income for Peter and Anne ever since. When not in sanatoriums, Anne has maintained an apartment for herself and her son in Greenwich Village, to the consternation of their more conservative, suburbanite relatives. This unconventional upbringing taught Peter early the limitations of life's promises for many and inevitably alienated him from the optimism common to his age group. Not surprisingly, therefore, the friend he seeks out on his return to town is an older man, Robert Vielum.

Robert, who in many ways is a mystery to Peter but in whose apartment Peter and other young students have found "a heartening jangle of conversation and music," takes courses but avoids degrees and has no known source of income beyond the money that he earns renting the extra bedroom in his apartment to a series of young male students. Peter's arrival discovers Robert entertaining a new young man, an Italian painter named Mario Osti, much to the dismay of his current renter, Vince. Vince is further upset, Peter learns, because Robert is expecting a visit from his daughter Susan and has offered her Vince's room for the remainder of the summer while Robert and Mario vacation in Rome. Robert had been planning a trip to Morocco with Vince before Mario and Susan entered the picture.

Vince's dismay threatens to become violence just as the doorbell rings. As Vince retreats to his bedroom, Robert ushers in Susan, who is caught between camp and home while her mother and stepfather are finishing divorce arrangements. Susan's mother apparently "marries" for a living; the current stepfather is Susan's third. "'I wouldn't want to be an inconvenience,'" she assures her father, "with a polite terror which suggested she might often have been one."

With the cast now complete, the real action begins: Vince leaps from the bedroom window to his death. After the confusion of police and ambulances, Robert exits to the police station, and Peter escorts Susan to a restaurant before inviting her to use his mother's room if she has nowhere else to stay. After checking her stepfather's home and finding it bolted against her, she accepts his offer. "It was a nice room I had there. Nicest one I ever did have, really," she remembers. Then she admits that she really does not care about "my parents, or any of the people they tangle with," although she wishes that she could. As they drive to his apartment, Peter thinks about taking her for a drive the next day: to Greenwich.

Themes and Meanings

In her preface to *The Best American Short Stories of 1951*, Martha Foley describes the reaction to this story in a classroom of Columbia University: "The younger generation in the room considered it a heartbreakingly beautiful story of two young people, lost like themselves, in a world they never made." Susan and Peter, much like the eponymous characters Franny and Zooey in J. D. Salinger's novel, were more familiar to the youth of the 1950's than were, perhaps, the television role models promising the happy days of ideal American families such as the Nelsons. Ozzie did not divorce Harriet, nor did Harriet become an alcoholic. How could David and Ricky represent the generation growing up in the aftermath of World War II? Susan and Peter, on the other hand, respond to the sensitivity in each other and passively resign themselves to the insensitivity and sordidness of the world around them.

Hortense Calisher chose to open the 1975 edition of her collected stories with "In Greenwich There Are Many Gravelled Walks," so that the book would follow what she explains in its introduction as the "natural rhythms" in her work. One of these, she explains further, is going "from an untrustworthy reality to a joyously recognizable fantasy." Her later works include, in fact, two novels that can loosely be described as science fiction in that search for the fantasy. This story, as part of her first published collection, best represents the "untrustworthy reality" of which she speaks.

What is "untrustworthy" in the world of Peter and Susan is not the sordid surface of broken homes and children assuming responsibilities while parents pursue pleasure or escape. Rather, it is the greater society, which offers an American Dream and ignores individual nightmares. Peter cannot communicate with his cousins, whose "undamaged eyes were still starry with expectancy"; Susan admires even the neurotic Vince, who can care enough to commit suicide. In finding each other, each has finally discovered the company that misery loves. It took Calisher another twenty years to discover the "joyously recognizable fantasy" that perhaps first emerges in the two works that she published in the mid-1960's: *Journal from Ellipsia* (1965) and *The Railway Police and The Last Trolley Ride* (1966).

Style and Technique

Not surprisingly, the "untrustworthy reality" of this story is captured in a style rich in social realism. With almost classical restraint, Calisher limits the time to one afternoon and evening in early August, the primary action to the meeting of Peter and Susan, and the primary place to Robert's apartment. The action that would seem to demand center stage, the suicide, is presented only after the fact, as first Mario and then the young couple look out the window to see the body lying below.

The story is offered from Peter's perspective; the reader learns of the others only what Peter knows about them or what they reveal about themselves in the course of the story. The homosexuality implied by Robert's relationships with "young male students" is never stated; neither Peter's nor Susan's parents actually enter the story, although the reader learns much about Anne because the experience which drives her back to the sanatorium is fresh in Peter's mind.

Most notably, as the title intimates, the story is conveyed by setting. Peter and Susan are products of urban America; even the suburbs seem to be out of their reach. Peter's cousins at Rye can claim "the hot blue day, the sand, and the water, as if these were all extensions of themselves," while Peter's escapes from his mother's Village reality have only been brief respites in boarding school, an abortive attempt to move uptown to Central Park West, and a stint in the army. Her latest trip to the sanatorium will cost him his latest hope for a summer abroad.

Susan does have one setting which frees her from her mother's residences in Reno, her stepfather's brownstone, and the hotels at which she and her mother have stayed "in between." She counsels at a children's camp and can at least say that "I like helping children. They can use it." Yet even this setting is prematurely denied her as a polio scare closes it down early and sends her to stay with Robert.

Robert, too, is defined by his "old-fashioned apartment, on Claremont Avenue," and by the places to which he has traveled, which he seems to share with his guests by assuming that they, too, are familiar with both the places and the languages. Even Mario and Vince can be seen in the temporary status of the room for rent and the vacation companion.

Finally, it is the mother's place which closes the circle of Peter's world and provides the symbolic title. The "gravelled walks" of the sanatorium in

Greenwich, lined with nurses rather than trees, are the only "country" reality that Peter has to offer Susan, as she agrees to fill his mother's room at least temporarily. Theirs is the reality that Calisher, a New Yorker herself, knows most intimately and can best convey to the reader.

Thelma J. Shinn

IN THE CAGE

Author: Henry James (1843-1916)
Type of plot: Psychological realism
Time of plot: The late 1890's
Locale: The Mayfair section of West London
First published: 1898

> *Principal characters:*
> THE PROTAGONIST, an unidentified female telegraph operator
> MR. MUDGE, her fiancé, a grocer
> CAPTAIN COUNT PHILIP EVERARD, a roué and the primary
>   object of the protagonist's attention
> LADY BRADEEN, who is destined to be Everard's wife
> MRS. JORDAN, a florist and occasional confidante of the
>   protagonist
> COCKER, the man who owns the store that houses the post-
>   and-telegraph cage

The Story

The protagonist of "In the Cage" is a young woman whose identity is never revealed by James, thus reinforcing the very anonymity of her status in life: She works in the post-and-telegraph cage of Cocker's store in the Mayfair section of West London. From the outset, James makes clear two facts about her personal life. First, she has grown up and still lives in relative poverty. As a consequence, she does not look kindly upon the many idle rich who come to Cocker's day after day to send telegrams.

Second, she is engaged to a grocer named Mr. Mudge. He is a most caring, decent man; he is, however, also dull and pedestrian. She does not encourage him as he sets forth tentative wedding plans. The principal reason for her reluctance to marry has to do with her fascination with the upper-class patrons of Cocker's. For some time she has carried on a love/hate affair with them—in her mind. She knows that these privileged people are boring, profligate, and often engage in illicit liaisons. Although she has confided to a friend that she sees them as "selfish brutes," she is driven by a genuine fascination with them. Like many of James's characters, she is an inquisitive person: She has to *know* what is going on in their lives. When she waits on them, she sharply scrutinizes them; she carefully listens to their conversations; and she quickly memorizes their telegrams. From these gleanings, her hyperactive imagination is quite capable of rendering for her in most dramatic fashion their current anxieties, intrigues, and crises.

When she encounters at Cocker's a Captain Count Philip Everard, a smiling, handsome aristocrat, she makes a quantum leap from simply immersing her acute imagination in the affairs of her wealthy clientele to becoming a part of their lives. From the beginning, she understands that he is what she has been waiting for. (In an ancillary way she is also caught up in the life of a patron named Lady Bradeen, who has some kind of shadowy connection with Everard, although her eventual single focus will be on him.) Not only can she re-create Everard's romantic life with all of its selfishness and immoral behavior, but now—from her modest position as telegraphist—she also will be able to do him eager service in whatever humble way she can. Her imagination wills her to believe that Everard needs her, depends upon her advice, and is singularly attracted to her.

"In the Cage" moves toward its climax when the protagonist wants to expand her connection with the captain beyond the confines of Cocker's. To that end, she begins to haunt his residence, the exclusive Park Chambers, during her off-hours. They meet early one evening, and he invites her to sit on a nearby park bench. In vintage Jamesian dialogue, her speeches to him assume all that she has assumed these many months: to inform him that theirs is a passionate and reciprocal relationship. Everard, in his turn, apparently has only one purpose in asking her to sit with him in the August twilight: to tell her that as a public servant she is greatly appreciated for all of her favors to him as a patron of Cocker's.

He is perplexed when she announces that she may be induced to move on (this is a reference to Mudge and the wedding plans). Startled by the news, Everard selfishly cries out that he will be upset if she goes: "I shall miss you too horribly." Taking his hyperbolic rhetoric at face value, she leaves Everard with a stern warning that she will not give him up. Later that summer, while on vacation at Bournemouth with Mudge and her mother, she advises Mudge that her duty now is to stay at Cocker's, to go on assisting her captain in his dalliances.

Weeks later, a troubled Everard comes to Mudge's betrothed and asks about a particular telegram that Lady Bradeen had sent earlier in the year. James does not explain why Everard is upset, but when the telegraphist is able to recite the contents from memory, Everard is relieved inasmuch as Lady Bradeen has sent the wrong message. The crisis is over. Everard departs without a gesture or word of thanks or good-bye. She never sees him again.

Once more, weeks go by and the telegraphist is chatting with a friend of hers, a Mrs. Jordan, who is a widow but is soon to be married to a Mr. Drake. He is a servant of Lady Bradeen, and Drake tells Mrs. Jordan that Everard and Lady Bradeen will also be marrying soon. Mrs. Jordan is unable to supply pertinent details, but several facts emerge from her conversation with the telegraphist: Everard is not wealthy; he is a philanderer and a fortune hunter; Lady Bradeen once went so far as to steal something in order to protect him; and, finally, Mrs. Jordan concludes that Everard is wedding

Lady Bradeen because she has the power to coerce him into marriage.

"In the Cage" ends with the disillusioned telegraphist ready to take Mudge up on his offer of marriage—as soon as possible. Further, she is perturbed at having to hear all of this scandalous news from Drake through Mrs. Jordan. The protagonist has long seen herself as being a principal source of reliable information on the doings of the Everard-Bradeen set. Mudge's betrothed thinks of the disturbing description of Everard by the future Mrs. Drake. It reinforces in a most succinct way what the telegraphist has known all along. No longer can she idealize him; she can see him now with merciless clarity for what he is: unscrupulous, selfish, and materialistic. There is no shatteringly powerful scene as the protagonist comes to terms with Everard and her association with him—both the imagined and the real. After she bids good-bye to Mrs. Jordan, she walks alone along the Paddington canal. James writes that her mind is jumbled with thoughts. Knowing, however, that her obsession with Everard is over and that marriage to Mudge is inevitable, the telegraphist curiously muses on one aspect of all that has happened: "It was strange that such a matter should be settled for her by Mr. Drake."

Themes and Meanings

James's life, both private and professional, was rather limited in its own way. He had little to do with the lower strata of society. On occasion, however, he could do dramatic justice to a woman such as the telegraphist, whose position in London life is both lowly and uneventful. To that end, two of James's standard themes surface in this tale: the need to take advantage of life, or, to use different words, to live all that one can; and the reductive power of leading a life of renunciation. At first these themes might seem to be antithetical, at odds with each other. They are—but they are both present within the life of the protagonist. She is the embodiment of both themes as she embraces Everard figuratively and pursues him literally. Indeed, the telegraphist is one of those well-known James characters who is eager to live pleasurably in an imagined world, while at the same time, and without regret, she is happy to set aside her life in the real world.

More specifically, these themes coalesce in the life of the protagonist as she lives all she can in her fantasized relationship with Everard; unfortunately, she is at the same time forfeiting the potential in her own young life by giving Everard many months of selfless servitude at Cocker's. In time, her imagination becomes the controlling factor in the calculus of her life: For her, nothing is more genuine and central in her day-to-day existence than the Everard interlude. In fact, there is every reason to assume that she would have gone on for months—perhaps years—in her persistent attraction to Everard had he not so abruptly ceased to do his business at Cocker's. Oddly enough, she knows from the beginning the sordid nature of his dalliances.

She is not blind to his vices. When they have their one meeting away from Cocker's, she bluntly reveals to him that she is aware of his adulterous activities. Yet she continues to live her life through his until the Lady Bradeen-Everard marriage is arranged.

So far as renunciation is concerned, the telegraphist is fully conscious of the double life that she is leading as she preoccupies herself with Everard's activities. James unambiguously describes that consciousness: "She was perfectly aware that her imaginative life was the life in which she spent most of her time." Yet the lady telegraphist considers it time very well spent.

Style and Technique

"In the Cage" provides James with the requisite length (about forty-five thousand words) for him to explore as fully as he wants the whole range of emotions which his telegraphist experiences as her life becomes entangled with that of Everard. In the hands of another writer, "In the Cage" might have been a much shorter tale: relatively taut, compact, and efficient. James, however, had a passion for telling it all, and his principal narrative technique was to explore the mind of the protagonist until all—or almost all—had been said.

James's saturation technique is seen most directly in his presentation of the telegraphist vis-à-vis Everard. That is, she is always the protagonist, but different moments with Everard call for a different persona. Like a chameleon, she manages to become a variety of women while still remaining a telegraphist. In a sense, then, she is an actress who writes her own script—and chooses her own parts.

When Everard first comes to her attention, she is the dazzled, awestruck clerk. Shortly thereafter, once she has recognized his value to her and to her imagination, she becomes the enamored young woman, one of her favored roles. From time to time, while waiting on him, she sees herself as the dreamy, soulful paramour. On occasion, when she fears that her admiration for Everard may be showing on her face, she assumes the role of the poker-faced minion who singles out no patron for special attention. When she strolls by his residence of an evening, she is the lover hungry for even a fleeting glimpse of her beloved. Everard, so taken with himself and his ongoing intrigues, is conscious only of her presence as a helpful clerk at Cocker's.

Most of her various roles are enacted briefly and then only in response to a given situation. Even after their evening meeting at the park near his home proves conclusively that he has no romantic interest in her, she persists in the old myths. Strangely enough, in their last meeting, as he anxiously asks her to recall a telegram sent by Lady Bradeen some months earlier, the protagonist presents a new face to Everard, a smug, knowledgeable face. She knows that she is easily able to quote the telegram from memory, but as playful teaser she holds off doing so until she deems it to be the right moment.

Again, Everard does not recognize that his telegraphist is a competent and self-assured actress in the little theater of her own mind. Everard is a constant in the tale: He is always merely the adulterous roué.

Gerald R. Griffin

IN THE GARDEN OF THE NORTH
AMERICAN MARTYRS

Author: Tobias Wolff (1945-)
Type of plot: Satirical realism
Time of plot: Unspecified
Locale: Colleges in Oregon and upstate New York
First published: 1980

Principal characters:
 MARY, the protagonist, a history teacher at an Oregon college
 LOUISE, Mary's former colleague, a professor at an upstate
  New York college
 TED, Louise's husband
 JONATHAN, Louise's lover
 ROGER, a student campus guide at Louise's college
 DR. HOWELLS, the history department chairman at Louise's
  college

The Story
 "In the Garden of the North American Martyrs" begins with a summary of Mary's career, a sort of *curriculum vitae* establishing her credentials as an uninvolved person: a college history teacher who "watched herself." Early in her career, she witnessed the firing of "a brilliant and original" professor whose ideas upset the college's trustees. To diminish the chances of similarly offending, Mary carefully wrote her lectures "out in full" beforehand, "using the arguments and often the words of other, approved writers." She just as carefully avoided entanglement in departmental politics, the cliques and ongoing quarrels of her colleagues. Instead, Mary adopted the role of a campus character, cultivating little eccentricities and making people groan with her corny jokes, culled from books and records. She was also such a good listener that eventually she had to get a hearing aid.
 Thus, Mary's innocuous career of playing it safe coasted along for fifteen years at Brandon College. Then, suddenly, Brandon College went bankrupt (the result of the business manager's speculations) and closed. Shocked, Mary was forced into a tight job market. She did get another job, but in a miserable Oregon college housed in one building (apparently a former high school or junior high). Mary found the weather in Oregon equally miserable: The incessant rain troubled her lungs and hearing aid, flooded her basement, and encouraged "toadstools growing behind the refrigerator." Mary kept applying for jobs elsewhere but received no further offer.
 When the story's main action begins, Mary is in her third year at the Oregon college. One day she receives a surprise letter from Louise, a former Brandon colleague who "had scored a great success with a book on Benedict

Arnold and was now on the faculty of a famous college in upstate New York." Louise says there is an opening in her department and invites Mary to apply for it. Although Mary has never considered Louise to have much "enthusiasm for other people's causes," she sends in her application. In rather short order, Louise, chairwoman of the search committee, calls to schedule an on-campus interview for Mary. Mary thinks things are looking good, but as she flies east she cannot get over a strange feeling of *déjà vu*.

Mary's feeling intensifies in Syracuse, where Louise meets her at the airport. She even mentions the feeling to Louise, but Louise brushes it aside: "Don't get serious on me. . . . That's not your long suit. Just be your funny, wisecracking old self. Tell me now—honestly—how do I look?" Obviously Louise is still her egotistical old self, just as she expects Mary to assume her old roles, particularly the role of good listener. Seeking Mary's approval and occasional flattery, Louise talks almost nonstop about herself during the hour's drive to the college. The most interesting news is that Louise has a lover, Jonathan, and that Ted (her husband) and the children are not at all understanding about him. Finally, Louise turns the talk to Mary, telling her not to worry about the interview and lecture. Mary is shocked to learn that she has to deliver a lecture, unprepared as she is, but Louise offers her unpublished article on the Marshall Plan for Mary to read. Mary hesitantly accepts, concerned that "reading Louise's work as her own . . . would be her first complete act of plagiarism."

After dropping Mary off at a college guest cabin, Louise returns later in the night, distraught and in need of further sympathy. That scoundrel Jonathan, whom she has been with, had the nerve to tell her that she was not "womanly" and had "no sense of humor." Eventually Louise calms down and stretches out on the couch, but for the rest of the night before the big interview, neither woman gets any sleep. The next day during Mary's private campus tour, Roger the student guide informs her that, even though the school is a replica of an old English college, it is up-to-date: "They let girls come here now, and some of the teachers are women. In fact, there's a statute that says they have to interview at least one woman for each opening."

Mary's interview is one of the most perfunctory on record. The interviewing committee is twenty minutes late, giving Mary an opportunity to discover that no one has read her two books lying on the table. When the committee members arrive, they are all men except for Louise. After a preliminary remark or two, Mary and Dr. Howells, the department chairman, briefly discuss the Oregon rain. Dr. Howells, a native of Utah, likes a dry climate: "Of course it snows here, and you have your rain now and then, but it's a *dry* rain." Then the interview is over, and Mary realizes that she has been the token woman candidate. Questioned afterward, Louise confirms that Mary has been interviewed only to satisfy the statute. Louise thought Mary would not mind the free trip, and, anyway, Louise needed to see her old friend: "I've been unhappy and I thought you might cheer me up."

Mary decides not to give the lecture, but Louise tells her that she must, after all of their expense. Mary goes into the lecture room, looks over the crowd of students and professors, and dispenses with her prepared text on the Marshall Plan. Instead, she speaks extemporaneously: "I wonder how many of you know. . . that we are in the Long House, the ancient domain of the Five Nations of the Iroquois." Her new subject is the cruelty of the Iroquois, who slaughtered people mercilessly and tortured prisoners fiendishly. She presents the example of the two martyrs Jean de Brébeuf and Gabriel Lalement, Jesuit priests who went on preaching even as the Iroquois tortured them. Mary describes, in detail, the tortures inflicted on the priests. She pretends to report Brébeuf's sermon, telling her audience, "Mend your lives. . . ." The professors are aghast. Dr. Howells and Louise leap up and wave, shouting at Mary to stop, but Mary turns off her hearing aid and goes on speaking: "Mary had more to say, much more. . . ."

Themes and Meanings

This story is a wicked satire of American academia, shown here in three of its guises: a college going bankrupt, "a new experimental college in Oregon," and a pretentious Eastern college that is "an exact copy of a college in England, right down to the gargoyles and stained-glass windows." None of these colleges inspires confidence in American higher education, nor do the faculty members shown: mousy Mary, tediously copying out her lectures; egotistical Louise, expert on Benedict Arnold; Dr. Howells, native son of Utah, with his "porous blue nose and terrible teeth"; the young professor who talks around the pipe in his mouth; and assorted other members of the faculty menagerie. They are shallow, conventional, and phony, like bad actors in an academic *commedia dell'arte*, with Louise as stage manager. The only exception is the "brilliant and original" professor who is fired.

If the trustees make an example of the outspoken professor, the author makes an example of Mary, but of the opposite sort: She illustrates what can happen to people who sell themselves out for security. From the professor's firing, Mary takes warning: "She shared his views, but did not sign the protest petition. She was, after all, on trial herself—as a teacher, as a woman, as an interpreter of history." The irony of these words reverberates through the story, since Mary is a failure in all three respects because of her career of self-censorship. She stifles her own ideas until "without quite disappearing they shrank to remote, nervous points, like birds flying away." She deliberately molds herself into a faintly ridiculous role until her eccentricities, jokes, and hearing aid qualify her for the ranks of the collegiate grotesques. Yet, ultimately, Mary's self-betrayal does not prevent her from being betrayed by her college and by her colleagues, who tend to accept her at face value.

Mary's betrayal by the system, however, might also be what saves her from it. As a college history teacher, she has denied not only her own authenticity but, ironically, her involvement in history. Her hard knocks, along with the Oregon rain, begin to cleanse her soul, to make her see that even a college campus is not a safe refuge from life. In the story's remarkable ending, Mary at last finds her own voice via a "brilliant and original" interpretation of history that encompasses herself and the system.

Style and Technique

There are several lines of symbolic imagery in the story—references to birds and "winging it" (in lectures), to rain and dryness—but the most important imagery expands on the story's title by developing parallels between Mary and the two martyrs. The closer Mary gets to Iroquois country, the more she feels a sense of *déjà vu*. The strained appearance of Louise the hatchet woman reminds Mary of "a description in the book she'd been reading, of how Iroquois warriors gave themselves visions by fasting." In the lecture room which Mary calls "the Long House," sunlight streams through windows of "stained glass onto the people around her, painting their faces." Mary is, in effect, being roasted at the stake: "Thick streams of smoke from the young professor's pipe drifted through a circle of red light at Mary's feet, turning crimson and twisting like flames." Like the priest who kept preaching through torture, Mary delivers her lecture; in the words which Mary imagines the priest speaking, time past and time present come together.

Mary herself is perhaps intended as a representative figure of higher education in the United States. In her days of clownish conformity, she became Brandon College's presiding spirit, "something institutional, like a custom, or a mascot—part of the college's idea of itself." Her "martyrdom" is also typical of horror stories about cruel hiring practices in academia. "In the Garden of the North American Martyrs" should be on the required reading list of everyone contemplating a career in higher education.

Harold Branam

IN THE HEART OF THE HEART OF THE COUNTRY

Author: William H. Gass (1924-   )
Type of plot: Antistory
Time of plot: The 1960's
Locale: A small town in Indiana
First published: 1967

> *Principal characters:*
> THE NARRATOR, a self-proclaimed poet and a college teacher
>   who has lost his lover
> MRS. DESMOND, an elderly lady who often visits him
> BILLY HOLSCLAW, an elderly man who lives near him
> UNCLE HALLEY, an elderly man who shares his collection with
>   the narrator
> MR. TICK, the narrator's cat, which the narrator envies

The Story

Following the modernist tradition of elimination of traditional narrative line, this story could be loosely described as a series of thirty-six prose poems, repetitious in subject and title, connected only by two devices—the setting (a small Midwestern town) and the first-person narrator. The shorter titles within the story at first glance seem quite straightforward: abstract, factual, almost guidebook dull. The longer titles tend to emphasize possessions of the narrator: "My House, This Place and Body."

Closer inspection, however, reveals that the content of a given section may have only a tenuous connection with the title. In the "Politics" section, only five lines refer to the Cuban Revolution; the rest of the section attempts an extended and overstrained comparison of love and politics, which veers entirely out of control. At one time, the narrator may have only a sentence or two to say about his ostensible subject of the moment; at another, several paragraphs or pages. Nor do the topics recur in any definite pattern, but in an almost obsessively arbitrary one. In addition, the narrator's implied objectivity often slips away, giving the reader several different versions of a place or a character. In short, if the reader does not fairly quickly grasp that the real story is the self-revelation of the narrator, he will soon be floundering amid seemingly unconnected, repetitious, or even contradictory data. Nothing much actually happens in the present tense of the story.

From the multiple sections, however, a relatively old-fashioned plot line emerges, introduced in the last line of the first paragraph: "And I am in retirement from love." Rearranged in a linear fashion, the action preceding the beginning of this story is fairly simple. The first-person narrator, a forty-one-year-old college teacher and self-proclaimed poet, came to B——, Indiana, full of the hope of establishing a new beginning for himself: a new job, new companions, a new home, and new roots—perhaps, he suggests, even a new youth. He also found a new lover, a young, tomboyish girl with whom he believed that he had escaped from his old routines. Soon, however, it is she who escapes, leaving both him and the Midwest far behind.

As the story begins, he is reminiscing about the failure of all of his hopes, especially his lost love, and occasionally trying to pull himself together, to get back to his poetry, to understand his sense of being trapped in coldness, isolation, and fragmentation. He tries to give an objective examination of the town—its businesses, clubs, politics, churches, schools, some of its inhabitants, the land, and the seasonal cycles of the weather. Yet he reveals much more about himself than he ever understands or intends.

Living totally within himself, looking at nature through windows or from platforms, and running from actual encounters with real people and real problems, this narrator egotistically and sentimentally wallows in self-pity, coloring every piece of data with the despairing, cold grayness of his own mind and heart. Lacking in self-discipline and willpower, he asserts that he "cannot pull himself together." He acknowledges that in B—— he has not been able to find a new youth; he has merely confirmed his advancing age. His poetry, which he considers only a "physical caress," will die as his senses diminish until death.

Themes and Meanings

William Faulkner once said that the basis of all great literature is the human heart in conflict with itself. William H. Gass's intellectual first-person narrator (a college professor and poet) is a perfect example of carrying this conflict to an undesirable end. The title and opening lines of the story identify the most crucial conflict: the heart of the country (a clichéd metaphor for the Midwest) is presented as withered, too long deprived of love and true union with others, with nature, or with any real order beyond the individual's own mind. In turn, the heart of the Midwest is presented through the words and mind of one individual, who both typifies and identifies the conflicts which have crippled his own heart and, by extension, the heart of his vast country.

Although the reader can and must see beyond the narrator's acknowledged narrow point of view, the reader cannot deny the strength of the conflicts that the narrator exposes. The heart cries out with longing for love of and love from others but seldom finds lasting union and harmony, and even then, it knows deeply that they will pass. Man, like the narrator, desires an always blooming spring of youth and a fruitful harvest of fame, always full of new hopes and promises, only to find that, because he has neglected pruning and spraying the fruit trees, there is only rotten fruit to harvest. The heart, then, becomes fearful, depressed, isolated, and cold, retreating before the forces of the other half of the natural cycle—decay and death—leaving only the intellect to cope with these facts.

This isolated mind of man becomes chaotic and disorganized; not united with the heart or the body, it recognizes only partial truths, as reflected in the narrator himself and in the structure of the story. In a world of entropic chaos, he cannot will himself into order. He sees harmony in body, will, and nature existing only in animals—a cat, some birds, flies that are unaware of the implications of time and death. His heart longs for an affirmation of some sort, perhaps any sort, of harmony. Yet neither man's senses nor his intellect, grasping at received data, finds evidence of any order or eternity. Baffled, like this narrator, the intellect may simply give up in despair.

Gass, however, suggests that another avenue to experience and recognition is open to human beings. Because he has an intellect, the narrator may be more isolated from nature than the cat, but he also can have revelations received from literature, most important, from poetry. Poetry may be a sensual caress, as the narrator claims, but it also can enlarge and enrich the intellect. Art, nature, spirit, and cycles of time can be affirmative alternatives to despair. Rules, responsibility, and, most important, the imposition of self-will and the rejection of self-pride are necessary if man is to find patterns of harmony in the universe. It is this type of harmony that the narrator knowingly rejects in his remarks about Rainer Maria Rilke's concerns with poetry helping the spirit of man, and it is to his eternal isolation and death that the narrator does so.

Style and Technique

William H. Gass has used multiple techniques to emphasize the complexity of theme and subject of this story. The story's title and structure, its patterns of imagery, allusions, and brilliant stylistic transformations all add to the reader's ability to understand and respond, both intellectually and emotionally. The fragmented, nonlinear structure suggests the manner in which the mind actually works, as opposed to the rules of logic. The narrator is both lacking in will and obsessed with thoughts of his lost love, with fears of death and age, and with his isolation from his environment and his community. These topics appear again and again; even when he tries to concentrate, his mind moves in circles, and he sees similar patterns wherever he looks. The Ferris wheel, seasons, old records—all these cycles the narrator identifies as deadening ruts. He is unwilling to consider the cycle as an image of natural completion and harmony.

Stylistically, Gass uses sentences that move, almost unnoticeably, from flat, blunt, factual realism to highly evocative, poetically imaginative flights of fancy. He will even alternate the two types of sentences in one section, suggesting the internal conflicts of the narrator. Finally, his use of allusions to other poets illuminates the story and offers the reader standards for judging the narrator's conclusions. The use of Whitmanesque lists, the narrator's rejection of Rilke's spiritual poetry, and, most significant, the opening quotation from William Butler Yeats's "Sailing to Byzantium" hand the reader keys to a poet's ideal belief in something beyond this physical world and beyond his isolated intelligence. The line from Yeats, for example, is a triumphal affirmation of an eternal world of pattern and artistic design achieved by acts of will, a world of the soul and imagination, to replace this natural world, in which time, age, and death make man seem paltry, only a heart fastened to a dying animal. In contrast, the poet-narrator of this story, eloquently but with pity and hate, can only describe the dying animal's longings, for he lacks both the will and the imagination of a Yeats. His heart and that of "his country" remain thin and gray.

Ann E. Reynolds

IN THE PENAL COLONY

Author: Franz Kafka (1883-1924)
Type of plot: Allegorical fantasy
Time of plot: Early twentieth century
Locale: A penal colony on an island in an unspecified, remote region of the world
First published: "In der Strafkolonie," 1919 (English translation, 1941)

Principal characters:
AN EXPLORER, who arrives in the penal colony to investigate its conditions
AN OFFICER, who believes in the organization of the colony as devised by the dead commandant

The Story

An explorer arrives in a penal colony, at the invitation of its new commandant, to investigate its organization and report his findings to a commission created by the commandant. Kafka calls the explorer *Forschungsreisende*, a "research traveler," and in the story's context he is clearly more than an amateur: He is an enlightened modern naturalist and relativist, trained to observe and analyze dispassionately the customs of diverse cultures—such comparative anthropologists as Bronislaw Malinoski (1884-1942) come to mind.

The explorer is introduced to the machine which is the central edifice of the colony's structure by an officer zealously loyal to the former commandant's administration of the colony. The machine is an instrument of torture and execution, the complex operation of which is described in devoted detail by the officer. "It's a remarkable piece of apparatus," he exclaims in the story's opening words, and he proceeds to explain, with the rapture of a totally committed believer, the coldly glamorous intricacy of the coordination of its three main parts: the "Bed," on which the condemned prisoner is strapped; the "Designer," whose cogwheels control the machine; and the "Harrow," which adjusts its needles to the dimensions of the condemned man's body and then engraves his sentence upon it. The prisoner is thus literally forced to feel the pain of his punishment, in a ritual that lasts twelve hours.

The criminal whose execution the explorer is invited to witness is a servant/sentry assigned to a captain. His duties are bizarrely twofold: to serve his master by day and to protect him by night. The previous night the captain had found him derelict in his obligation to rise every hour and salute his master's door. Has he had a trial? No. Does he know his sentence? No: It is "HONOR THY SUPERIORS!" and "He'll learn it on his body." After all, says the officer, he is acting in the spirit of his former commandant's plans for the colony, and his "guiding principle is this: Guilt is never to be doubted."

Such monolithic simplicity in applying an ethic of unrelenting vindictiveness and cruelty appalls the explorer, whose temperament has been shaped by Western concepts of due process, tolerance, and humaneness. He therefore refuses the officer-judge's plea that he intercede on behalf of the Old Order's judicial system when appearing before the liberal new commandant. Since he is "fundamentally honorable and unafraid," he tells the officer, "I do not approve of your procedure." Yet he adds, "your sincere conviction has touched me, even though it cannot influence my judgment."

The officer's response is cryptic: "Then the time has come." He frees the condemned prisoner, adjusts the Harrow's legend to read "BE JUST!" and submits his own body to the machine. Yet instead of redeeming him, as the officer insisted that it would, the machine kills him and in the process disintegrates, ending the Old Order's execution of "justice."

Shaken by this strange martyrdom, the explorer decides to issue no report to the new commandant. Instead he seeks out the grave of the old commandant, reads the inscription on the tombstone, which prophesies his return, and then leaves the penal colony by boat, refusing to take with him the liberated former prisoner and a fellow soldier.

Themes and Meanings

The story is a fantasy-allegory portraying the critical condition of religion in the modern world. The explorer, representing the humanitarian outlook of a secularist culture, visits an earth which is in a state of sin. The old commandant created and organized the penal colony and invented its dreadful machinery of justice/injustice—call him the god of an authoritarian faith. Somehow he lost his hold over the colony, but one day he may return and reclaim it. Meanwhile his fanatic disciple, the officer, serves the colony as its policeman, judge, and executioner.

What the explorer must choose on this island is either morality or spirituality, for Kafka regards the two as having suffered schism. The Old Order is revoltingly sadistic, but, according to the officer's testimony, it does offer mankind redemption through an agonizing ritual of pain. "How we all absorbed the look of transfiguration on the face of the sufferer," exults the officer. "What times these were, my comrade!" Nevertheless, the explorer has no difficulty condemning the Old Order's inquisitorial severity: "The injustice of the procedure and the inhumanity of the execution were undeniable."

The New Order is humane, sentimental, and concerned with the colony's economic and political recovery. It allows the machine to fall into disrepair while improving the island's harbor installations. The New Order, however, lacks the strength of conviction to confront the practices of the Old Order directly and abolish them outright. It is slack, shallow, and worldly, unable to offer man more than palliatives and fleshly indulgences. The new commandant immerses himself in a sea of admiring women, who weaken the law's rigor through erotic enticements.

The victory that the New Order achieves over the Old Order is therefore unredemptive and pyrrhic. The explorer, while convinced of the Old Order's injustice, is also careful to keep his distance from the new dispensation's slovenly ways. He admires the officer's dedication to his faith and willingness to martyr himself to the machine. "If the judicial procedure which the officer cherished were really so near its end . . . then the officer was doing the right thing; in his place the explorer would not have acted otherwise." Unlike the officer, the explorer is adrift in a sea of aimless, situational ethics, anchored to no absolute standard, trained only in rational positivism.

Why does the machine execute the officer and in the process commit suicide? Possibly because the injunction it is asked to write—"BE JUST!" contradicts the despotic nature of the Old Order and therefore violates the nature of the machine's tyranny. In the hour of its self-destruction, the machine becomes animated as a horrifying monster that shows its teeth as it jabs the officer's body and drives its iron spike into his forehead, murdering him without granting him absolution or transcendence. Like the hunter Gracchus in Kafka's later sketch by that title, the dead man remains earthbound and unredeemed.

The story's conclusion has puzzled many readers. Since the explorer has denounced the Old Order as inhumane for its cruel treatment of the soldier-prisoner, he might be expected to exhibit his own humaneness by taking the freed man aboard his boat as he leaves the island. Instead, he threatens him with a heavy rope to prevent him "from attempting the leap." Perhaps Kafka means to have the explorer show his contempt for the condemned man's previously demonstrated refusal to extricate the officer from the machine's harrowing needles. In effect, the explorer enacts the adage, "A plague on both your houses!" In allowing the explorer to escape the colony, Kafka also allows him to evade a meaningful choice between a purposeful but blood-drenched religion and a purposeless but humane secularism.

Style and Technique

Kafka's allegory does not establish a strict, point-for-point parallelism between its literal and abstract levels of meaning, as do Edmund Spenser's *The Faerie Queene* (1590, 1599) and John Bunyan's *The Pilgrim's Progress* (1678, 1684). The Old Order does not pointedly correspond to the Hebrews' Old Testament era or the strictures of John Calvin's Christianity. The deadly purpose of the old regime's machine violates the Sixth Commandment: "Thou shalt not kill." Nor does the Old Order's ethic confirm a reciprocal covenant between God and mankind, as the Judeo-Christian Scriptures do.

Still, the Old Order does symbolize all religions that base their authority on transcendent rites and absolute decrees. The machine's Bed is an altar on which humans are sacrificed to appease the wrathful majesty of a Moloch-like Law. Its creator clearly corresponds to a Lord of Hosts, and the labyrinthine script that guides the machine's operation stands, not necessarily for the Hebrew Torah recording Judaism's laws and learning, but for Scripture in general. When the explorer, unable to read the script, describes it as *sehr kunstroll*—that is, "highly artistic"—he defines himself as a representative modern man who can admire the Bible as literature but refuses to accept it as dogma.

Kafka's style is realistic in its Swiftian accumulation of plausible detail, stressing a sober sense of documentary verisimilitude. After all, the explorer is an empirically trained social scientist, conditioned to observe cultural patterns dispassionately and maintain an attitude of suspended judgment. As the onlooker through whose perspective Kafka chooses to filter the action, he validates what might otherwise be an incredible fantasy by convincing the reader that a fable which violates ordinary notions of probability is nevertheless credible: "I, an accredited anthropologist, saw and heard all this."

Kafka was never wholly satisfied with the ending of this story. He wrote an acquaintance that "two or three pages shortly before the end of the story are contrived." In these pages, the explorer kneels before the tombstone over the old commandant's grave so that he can read the "very small letters" on it, which promise that the commandant "will rise again and lead his adherents . . . to recover the colony. Have faith and wait!" Does the explorer's physical gesture of obeisance signify his subconscious respect for the Old Order? Does Kafka want the reader to accept the Old Order's relentless religion of victimization and painful punishment as morally superior to a sentimental, mild materialism? His conclusion is inconclusive.

Gerhard Brand

IN THE WHITE NIGHT

Author: Ann Beattie (1947-   )
Type of plot: Domestic and psychological realism
Time of plot: A winter night, evidently in the 1980's
Locale: A suburb or town
First published: 1984

> *Principal characters:*
> CAROL and VERNON, who have been married twenty-two
>   years
> MATT and GAYE BRINKLEY, their longtime friends
> SHARON, Carol and Vernon's daughter, who is dead
> BECKY BRINKLEY, Matt and Gaye's daughter

The Story

Ann Beattie's story narrates the events of scarcely more than half an hour, the time that it takes Carol and Vernon to leave a party at the home of their friends Matt and Gaye Brinkley, drive home through the snow, and lie down to sleep. The story takes on greater spaciousness, however, because of its focus on the consciousness of Carol, whose thoughts range through time and among a number of persons and events. She thinks first of the party and of a childish game that Matt Brinkley had played (significantly, the game is called "Don't think about . . ."), and by association moves to thoughts about her daughter, Sharon, and Becky Brinkley when they were very young together, and from that to an account of Becky at present, and then to a reminiscence of Sharon's death from leukemia and that trauma's continued effect on Vernon despite his dedication to optimism. After all this, Carol returns to the present to ask Vernon if Matt had mentioned Becky; he answers that nothing was said of that "sore subject."

The narrative breaks and then takes up a comparison between the two married couples: Vernon claims with some seriousness that the Brinkleys are their alter egos, suffering crises in their stead. Clearly, he refers to the many difficulties Becky Brinkley has brought into their lives, and thus obliquely refers to the death of Sharon and the absence of children in his and Carol's lives. This thought makes Carol consider the randomness of events and the impossibility of finding sanctuary. At home, she disguises the fact that she is crying, hides for a few moments in a bathroom to compose herself, and emerges to find Vernon asleep on a sofa, her coat "spread like a tent over his head and shoulders." Carol lies down on the floor under his coat, and her last waking thought is of Sharon as an angelic witness who could understand the significance of this tableau of sleepers.

Themes and Meanings

Children and parents, a frequent theme in Beattie's earlier fiction, appear in this story as the dramatic center, but it is the parents' isolation and loneliness that preoccupies her here, not the children's. Similarly, the parents are not characterized as the irresponsible, never-to-grow-up breed Beattie presented so deftly in her fiction of the 1970's. This story is a subtle evocation of the pains of adulthood and points to the larger theme of sanctuary, summarized by Carol's thinking, "Who could really believe that there was some way to find protection in this world—or someone who could offer it?"

The theme develops from the paired situations of the two couples, analogous to Carol's memory of the range finder camera that superimposed two images of the subject to make it leap into clearest focus. Both have had a child, thus making themselves more vulnerable to fate, and both have suffered thereby: Becky Brinkley's teenage troubles—her having had an abortion at age fifteen and her lack of direction even at the present—alter her parents' lives in ways Vernon and Carol cannot truly know. Yet Vernon's notion that he and Carol have been spared misfortune and "chaos" because of their Sharon's early death is to Carol's mind a piece of sophistry—his optimism seems to her a frightening thing, based as it is upon the twisted assumption that the great misfortune of Sharon's death, having struck them early, has somehow insulated them against further shocks. Carol remembers the small traumas since: Vernon's mononucleosis (what an "unbearable irony," the hospital attendant had said, "if Vernon had also had leukemia"), the exploding Christmas tree, the pet put to sleep—all had hinted that life might again exact a great price from them.

The alternative is to play Brinkley's game of "Don't think about . . . ," and the early image in Carol's mind of Matt and Vernon's acting like children at the party invites the interpretation that only the women are serious. Gaye must, after all, pull Matt into the house at the end, and Carol suspects that it had been Matt's idea to have the party so soon after the death of Gaye's father. Toward the end of the story, however, Beattie reveals that the perceptions of husband and wife, as represented by Vernon and Carol, provide another double image, and when they are superimposed, another theme emerges clear. Their responses, his optimism and her supposedly clear-eyed realism, are belied by other gestures, such as her foggy-eyed crying and his habit of reacting physically to that; something about Vernon's unexpected bedding down on the couch under Carol's jacket causes her to revise her opinions and reminds the reader of Vernon's continued self-accusations over Sharon's death. His optimism is simply a cover, as was Matt's game. Whereas Carol had hidden in the bathroom, fearing that he would want to rid her of sadness by making love, she is now reminded that they "had learned to stop passing judgment on how they coped with the inevitable sadness that set in, always unexpectedly." Carol's last thought is nothing if not escapist and optimistic: "In the white night world outside, their daughter might be drifting past like an angel. . . ."

The inevitability of sadness and pain, this story suggests, can hardly be coped with by a single response. Nor can any single response be judged better than another. Among the adults described, all do their share of compensating, pretending, escaping, and standing firm one way or another. Yet in the juxtaposition of two responses, Vernon and Carol seem able to find perspective and avoid pessimism and cynicism.

Style and Technique

Irving Howe, introducing an anthology entitled *Short Shorts* (1982), claimed that in very brief stories ("In the White Night" is little more than two thousand words long) "situation tends to replace character, representative condition to replace individuality." Indeed, the reader knows very little about Carol and Vernon and much less about anyone else in the story. The reader knows, for example, how many bedrooms the house has, but not what Carol and Vernon do for a living or what color their eyes are or what political views they hold, if any. Beattie has presented Vernon and Carol as individuals who think of themselves as parents though they do not seem to have any children, and thus the spaciousness of their house, a seemingly insignificant detail, conveys a powerful emotion. Their relationship with the Brinkleys is to a large extent controlled by the contrasting fates of two daughters: What can or cannot be talked about, as well as what is talked about, inevitably finds a referent there. In the context of the evening portrayed, the same might be said of Vernon and Carol's relationship with each other. The vacuum left by Sharon's death is the center of these lives. In this way, the story deals with types rather than individuals (Vernon's mental gymnastics to promote optimism and Carol's emphasis upon visual and emotional connections remind one of male and female stereotyping), but its use of ambiguous characterization instills a mystery about the characters that saves them from becoming clichés.

The narrative moves, as is suggested by the progression of events summarized above, by association, which helps characterize Carol's mental processes. Superimposed on that is a habitual pairing whose real purpose is contrast: Matt's loud garrulousness against Vernon's quietness (he speaks directly only three words), the death of Gaye's father (in the normal progression of generations) against Sharon's death, Sharon's bed as a "battlefield of pastel animals" against Vernon's refusal this night to use a bed, Sharon's leukemia versus Vernon's mononucleosis, Sharon versus Becky, the implications of Carol's hiding in the bathroom to avoid sex (the situation of the stereotyped bride) versus Becky's abortion at fifteen, the idea of inevitable sadness versus the recognition that "very few days were like the ones before." Such definition by contrast means that much is implied about the complex relationships among all the events of these ostensibly peaceful lives, and little is categorically excluded.

Beattie has moved away here from the laconic, cool voice of much of her early fiction, which often communicated her condescension toward the characters portrayed. In allowing the story to move in the patterns of Carol's associations, Beattie has relinquished the satirist's hold upon narrative and has made possible the communication of Carol's complex responses, both willed and unconscious. As a result, "In the White Night" shows the sympathy which, in replacing satire, has allowed Beattie to portray mature adults and their existential problems. Like Carol and Vernon, Beattie has found that sometimes it is best "to stop passing judgments."

Kerry Ahearn

INDIAN CAMP

Author: Ernest Hemingway (1899-1961)
Type of plot: Realism
Time of plot: c. 1910
Locale: Michigan's upper peninsula
First published: 1924

> *Principal characters:*
> NICK ADAMS, a young boy, the protagonist
> DOCTOR ADAMS, his father, a physician
> UNCLE GEORGE, Nick's uncle
> AN UNNAMED INDIAN, who commits suicide
> HIS PREGNANT WIFE, who endures a difficult labor

The Story

"Indian Camp" is a story of initiation in which young Nick Adams accompanies his father, a physician, on a call to an Indian camp, where the father delivers a baby by cesarean section using only his jackknife. The violence and pain of the birth contrast sharply with the ease of the suicide of the pregnant woman's husband, brought on by her screams, and introduce Nick to the realities of birth and death.

The story begins in the dark, before sunrise, as Nick, his father, and Uncle George are rowed across the lake by some Indian men. Nick's father explains that they are going to the camp to treat an "Indian lady who is very sick." The trio follow an Indian with a lantern through the dewy grass. Their way becomes easier and lighter when they are able to walk on the logging road that cuts through the woods, and eventually they are greeted by the dogs that live at the edge of the shantytown occupied by the native bark-peelers. The lighted window and the woman holding a light at the doorway of the nearest hut direct the two men and the boy to the woman in labor.

Inside on a wooden bunk lies the pregnant woman, who has been in labor for two days and who cannot deliver despite the help of the other women in the camp. The woman screams as the men enter. The interior of the hut is sketchily described, except for the bunk beds, the lower berth of which is filled by the woman and the upper berth of which holds her husband, who hurt his foot with an ax three days before. The room smells very bad.

Nick's father goes into action, demanding hot water and trying to tell Nick that the woman is going to have a baby. His condensed but rather technical explanation is interrupted by the woman's scream and by Nick's asking if his father can give her something for the pain. His father explains that the screams are not important and that he does not hear them. The husband in the top bunk turns over to face the wall. While scrubbing up, Nick's father explains to Nick that he will have to operate. With Uncle George and three of the Indian men holding her down, Doctor Adams performs a cesarean section, without an anesthetic, using his sterilized pocket knife. The woman bites Uncle George, who calls her a "damn squaw bitch." Nick holds the basin for his father during the operation, which takes a long time.

The arrival of the baby breaks the tension, and Doctor Adams asks Nick how he likes being an intern. Nick turns away so as not to see his father removing the cord or sewing up the incision. The doctor assures the woman, now quiet and pale, that the nurse will drop by the next day and bring all that she needs. Exhilarated after the operation, like a football player in the locker room after the game, Doctor Adams brags that this has been one for the medical journals, using a jackknife and tapered gut leaders.

Brought back to his duties, the doctor looks at the father in the top bunk only to find that in the quietness he has cut his own throat with a razor. Although Nick's father orders George to take Nick out of the hut, it is too late, since Nick has already seen the man and the pool of blood.

On their way back to the lake, his postoperative exhilaration gone, Nick's father apologizes for bringing him along. Nick, however, is full of questions, about childbirth, about the woman's husband, about death. Back on the lake, Nick's father rows in the early morning chill. Nick, sitting now in the bow of the boat, trails his hand in the water, which feels warm in the cool of the air. A bass jumps and makes a circle in the water. In the early morning on the lake sitting in the boat while his father rows, Nick feels quite sure that he will never die.

Themes and Meanings

"Indian Camp" is first and foremost a tale of initiation. During the course of the story, Nick witnesses birth and death, the difficulty of the first and the ease of the latter. In the beginning, as Nick and his father are rowed across the lake, Nick nestles, protected and warmed, in his father's arms. On the return trip, with his father in the bow, Nick sits by himself in the stern, now separated forever from his innocence and from the protection of his father by the experiences of the night at the Indian camp, even though it is obvious from the ending that Nick does not fully grasp, or perhaps cannot absorb, the harshness of what he has witnessed.

The story, on a larger plane, also deals with such themes as the conflict between the civilized and the savage. The doctor, as a man of reason and science, is plunged into a dark region of the primordial as he and his son are transported into the heart of the dark forest. Both as a man of science and as a father, the doctor fails to cope adequately with the primitive forces of death and life.

Nick Adams by his very name calls forth the tension between Adam, the first man, and "old Nick," or Satan, suggesting a combination of good and evil inherent in all humankind. "Indian Camp" is the first of a series of stories about Nick Adams, and it reflects the recurring themes of the sequence: discovery and loss, innocence and experience, good and evil.

Style and Technique

Hemingway once said that when he wrote he was trying to make a picture of the whole world but was always boiling it down. "Indian Camp" is one of his most boiled-down stories, and it occupies an important place in the Hemingway canon. It is, as noted above, the first Nick Adams story, and it was the opening story in Hemingway's first book, *In Our Time* (1924). It introduced his early readers to the "Hemingway style," clipped, pared-down, exact, a style which would make the writer famous and much, too much, imitated.

The plot of the story is minimal (a simple night's experience), the images are few, and the modifiers scarcely in evidence. Yet each word has been chosen with a poet's care. In 1924, it was a new kind of writing in prose; each word carried weight and seemed endowed with a meaning beyond itself. What Hemingway left out was as important for his style as what he retained. The ending of "Indian Camp" offers a good example of Hemingway's working method.

Initially the story was to end with Nick experiencing the dawn, his hand trailing in the warm water of the lake as the bass jumped making a circle. Now, however, the story concludes with a modifying series of prepositional phrases, each of which introduces both the irony and the innocence of the moment on the lake, suggesting the motif of therapeutic forgetfulness which later formed a central part of all the other Hemingway characters. The tightness of the rolling phrases, their flow, and their association provide a useful example of how Hemingway layers so much onto his prose without the excesses of authorial intrusion or literary hyperbole.

Charles L. P. Silet

THE INDIAN UPRISING

Author: Donald Barthelme (1931-   )
Type of plot: Parody
Time of plot: Early twentieth century
Locale: "The city"
First published: 1968

> *Principal characters:*
> THE UNNAMED FIRST-PERSON NARRATOR, the protagonist
> SYLVIA, his sometime companion
> MISS R., an "unorthodox" teacher
> A COMANCHE BRAVE, a torture victim

The Story

Donald Barthelme constructs "The Indian Uprising" as a battle-scene progress report. Yet the narrator, clearly one of the leaders of the city forces, shows none of the tactical or organizational skills of a military officer, and his fragmented account mixes very detailed frontline news, sentimental love talk, asides directed at persons about whom the reader knows nothing, information on torture methods, and so forth. There is no story here in the conventional sense, but rather a collage of smug observations leading to a surprising reversal in the final paragraph.

The title suggests that the subject at hand is the familiar material of countless American stories: Narratives of Indian uprisings have been best-sellers in the New World since the last part of the seventeenth century, and Hollywood has made countless cinematic versions by adding the complications of romantic love to the dangers of the fight. In the first paragraph, Barthelme echoes much of that mythology by implying that the city is a kind of El Dorado, with yellow-brick streets, that its main thoroughfares are named after military heroes, and that an anguished, morally aware couple will add a sophisticated philosophical inquiry on what makes "a good life."

The coherence is soon upset. Sylvia proves at least part of the time to be fighting on the Indians' side, and the narrator himself takes part in the torture session. Yet through the accumulation of detail the story creates a collage of images, and through this collage the reader comes to know not so much the individuals' motivations and fates as the general social reality.

First, there is city life itself. The scene could be any American metropolis, with its ghetto, heterogeneous population, and incredible accumulation of material goods. The list of objects piled in the barricade does much to describe an entire culture. The narrator, clearly well-off financially, defends the status quo in every sense and conveys the smugness of his urban class by his surprise that the ghetto dwellers join the insurgents, by his long list of live-in girlfriends (each of whom he has given a table made from a hollow-core door), by his preoccupation during the Uprising with his latest door project, his latest girlfriend (presumably a film star), and his personal development under the teacher Miss R. He is culturally sophisticated yet blind to the implications of the chaos around him and within him.

Second, the narrative plays with the conventional idea of the "initiation story." The narrator admits early (echoing the dying words of Montaigne), "I decided I knew nothing." His friends direct him to Miss R., who sets out to teach him the truth, "the litany," "the hard, brown, nutlike word." He fails to recognize the danger of her dress "containing a red figure," and she makes his initiation an ironic one when at the end she represents the Indians' Clemency Committee, which arrests him and presumably will torture him in turn.

Finally, the promise of a love story is withdrawn during the chaos of the narrative. Sylvia turns out to be the narrator's enemy (many of the city "girls" find the Comanches attractive, it seems), no hint is ever given about his relationship with Jane, nor is much revealed about the female "you" of whom he speaks longingly several times. The most humorous mislead is the narrator's connection with Miss R., who at times seems madly romantic, calling him "my boy, *mon cher*, my heart." In this regard, her final demand that he strip makes wonderful irony of the whole theme of romance.

Themes and Meanings

Barthelme's improvisation in this instance creates a typically divided piece: It is as much about the conventions of narrative fiction as it is about life, and thus it balances the ordered and chaotic, the recognizable and confusing, and the tragic and comic in an attempt both to attract and to repel the reader. The story appeared during the height of the antiwar turmoil surrounding the Vietnam War (late in the story the helicopters kill "a great many in the south," though that is the section still held by the city's forces); guerrilla warfare and memories of ghetto riots in Newark, Harlem, and Watts were fresh in the minds of everyone.

The primary issue in "The Indian Uprising" is cultural crisis both as a fact and as a literary problem. If art grows from culture, what in American culture seems to value and foster art? The first-person narrator could not say, for he seems untouched by his own sophistication—he is vicious, complacent, amoral, and self-deluded. Here Barthelme seems to offer a genuine prophetic impulse, a desire to give a warning about the chaos of this life of replaceable partners and disposable, "merely personal emotions," and the dangers of a culture that worships cold pragmatism, chooses its heroes from among its generals and admirals, and uses its technology to make war on peasants and children. Moreover, questions about what, in a social context, is "a good life," of what use knowledge is in finding such a life, and what effect art has in modifying mankind's savage instincts cast a strong shadow over the narrative.

Barthelme's humor, however, especially his mocking echoes of heavily shadowed works by Thomas Mann, T. S. Eliot, and even William Shakespeare, should make any interpreter beware. The narrator, after all, cannot with complete fairness be thought of as a "person." The same might be said of the other characters, so fragmented and chameleonlike do they come to one. Above all, Barthelme is a comic writer; the first-person narrator does not control the arrangement or sequence of details, but is rather controlled throughout by Barthelme's virtuosity.

Thus any discussion of ideas in Barthelme's fiction runs into the issue of his skepticism about ideas and systems. There is no commitment in his fiction, no affirmation of particular truths, and for some readers this makes Barthelme a less than major writer. His portrayal of a confused world of insatiable egos, each pursuing material goals that look unmistakably like junk when realized, suggests a pessimism that the comic impulse does not hide. Yet there is also a sense of the paradoxical in this story, that the imagination (not the narrator's, but the author's, and presumably the readers' in turn) continues to supply wonderful responses to experience. "The Indian Uprising" shows such a response and hints at morality even if the argument cannot be logically and systematically presented.

Style and Technique

The coherence of the narrative comes not from plot, for that would suggest a coherence of human events, but from a repetition of images, gestures, actions, and phrases. In general, the story illustrates that from beginning to end, the situation of civilization is getting worse, but the details of the narrative are not organized to demonstrate that. Two motifs, however, run through the entire story: the torture of a Comanche brave, and the narrator's preoccupation with women, including an unidentified "you" of whom he speaks yearningly. This combination of love and war in one narrative and in one person is itself a cliché, and through it Barthelme mocks popular literary tradition and also the American culture's eagerness to romanticize war.

Barthelme's methods can be summed up in two words: irony and parody. Both are forms of mimicry, commencing with someone else's prior form and statement, and both are essentially negative responses to that original statement.

Barthelme takes the forms of conventional short fiction, but not for conventional purposes. The modern short story has developed a heightened sense of the significance of repetition: events, colors, gestures, and so forth. These correspondences are usually associated with meaning. "The Indian Uprising" illustrates the patterning, and follows the forms, but denies the link with meaning. The Wild West fiction that Barthelme mimics would depend on a suspenseful plot and a confrontation at the end between representatives of good and evil. Sylvia's apparent betrayal, the female schoolteacher, and the love story mimic the traditional elements: In the classic manner, all three help lead to the obligatory showdown, but not in the traditional way. That the schoolmistress should be the turncoat denies conventional expectations and mocks the idea of education as a cohesive force in a culture.

There are many examples of the use of patterns of images and repetition of gestures, but the question of meaning is made problematical very early, as when the narrator lists (he uses the term "analyze") the contents of the barricade in front of him and can conclude only that he knows nothing. A similar fate awaits anyone trying to analyze the details of the narrative. On the map, for example, the Indian-held territory is green, and the narrator's side holds the blue; the city girls, including Sylvia, wear blue mufflers which collectively seem like a blue fog; Miss R. wears a blue dress; blue ends her litany list. None of this comes to mean anything. Similarly, the narrator several times repeats the line, "See the table?" which might be a secret joke on Platonic essences, but it means nothing in the context of the narrator's intentions. The narrator notes near the end that "strings of language extend in every direction to bind the world into a rushing, ribald whole," a sentence so neatly balancing confinement and free impulse that it can stand for Barthelme's methods of irony and parody: In fact, there is no ribaldry in that world (except perhaps from the Indians' "short, ugly lances with fur at the throat"), and no unity, but the narrator unwittingly communicates Barthelme's intention to create the illusion of a whole world of fragments. To make that illusion, Barthelme beguiles his readers with sheer wackiness. The paragraph as a logical or narrative unit does not exist in this story; each is a collage of ironic and sometimes shocking juxtapositions. The details accumulate like debris and, like the objects in the barricade, might reveal much ironically by their disordered presence, but not by logic or system.

Kerry Ahearn

INDISSOLUBLE MATRIMONY

Author: Rebecca West (Cicily Fairfield, 1892-1983)
Type of plot: Psychological realism
Time of plot: Early twentieth century
Locale: An industrial city and the surrounding moorlands in Great Britain
First published: 1914

Principal characters:
GEORGE SILVERTON, a solicitor's clerk
EVADNE SILVERTON, his wife

The Story

As the story opens, with George Silverton, a solicitor's clerk, entering his darkened house after a day's work, there is an immediate sense of unease. George is evidently a sour, dry, secretive man, who resents everything about his wife Evadne—her exotic beauty, which can sometimes change to ugliness; her quick, emotional response to things which he regards as trivial; her small, sensual pleasures; and above all her apparent refusal to respond to or even, perhaps, notice his growing irritation.

All this might seem to be typical of the situation between an ill-matched husband and wife. As the author describes George's life before marriage, however, George emerges as a misogynist with a neurotic fear and hatred of sex. He had cherished the idea of wife-desertion as a justifiable way for a man to cleanse himself of what he called "the secret obscenity of women." He married Evadne in the belief that they shared a bond of spiritual purity but quickly came to the conclusion that her interest in the marriage was purely physical. This disgusted him.

Ten years later, he feels cheated and physically defiled. The crisis point is reached when a letter arrives enclosing a handbill announcing that Mrs. Evadne Silverton is to speak at a public meeting in support of Stephen Langton, a Socialist candidate for the town council. Although George is a radical, in the mild reformist meaning of the term, the word "socialism" and the sight of Evadne's name—his surname—on the handbill appall him. His evaluation of his wife as a woman of emotional and intellectual triviality is underlined by his refusal to acknowledge even to himself that she has become a popular and respected political speaker and writer.

Political bigotry becomes mixed up with sexual bigotry. He tells her that Langton is a man of low morals, and when Evadne tries to defend him, he accuses her of being a "slut" and threatens to throw her out of the house if she speaks at the meeting. She hides her hurt by going into the kitchen and noisily washing up. George follows her and picks up a knife, as if to throw it at her—a presage of the murderous confrontation at the climax of the story. Evadne's "weapon"—a soggy dishcloth which she decides not to use—is considerably less lethal. George repeats his threat.

When Evadne gathers her outdoor clothes and dashes out of the house, crying for the first time in their married life, he totally misreads her intention. He is convinced that she is going to meet Langton and that Langton is her lover.

As George, in slippered feet, painfully follows Evadne up a hill and into the green fields and the moors beyond, the wild thoughts of secret assignations and sexual betrayal which clutter his mind match the wildness of the countryside. The idea, expressed earlier, of purification through desertion, takes on urgent force. He is determined to witness his wife's adultery so he can divorce her and be released forever from sexual contact with her.

His humiliation on discovering that Evadne has simply come out for a swim in the lake to cool herself down after the argument leads to the most blistering thought of all: There is no adultery—and therefore no divorce and no escape. Evadne is infected by the intensity of George's emotions: The two people confront each other with murderous intent. All of their past petty misunderstandings are stripped away to reveal a profound underlying hatred. Evadne, stronger than George, seems ready to kill him, but the weaker side of her nature prevails and he strikes her first. As she falls, she drags him down with her into a raging river.

A long, agonizing description of George's struggle in the water, crashing painfully against the rocky banks, ends when he manages to grasp hold of a mooring ring. Having hauled himself out, he puts his feet into the water again and strikes a soft surface, which he identifies as the curve of Evadne's back. He pushes her under the water and holds her down.

Making his painful way home, he has several changes of mood. He is buoyed up with pride in his own strength and masterfulness; then chastened by the thought that he will be hanged for murder; then elated again as he visualizes the ultimate solution—suicide, by gas, in his bedroom. He will thus demonstrate his own strength of purpose and achieve the dignity of purification by death.

The discovery that Evadne, having escaped from what he had imagined to be his deathblow, is now sprawled asleep, wet and muddy, on the bed which he had planned for his own noble death scene, is his final humiliation. He cannot even gas himself, for Evadne has, with her customary thrift, turned off the gas at the mains. Resignedly, he gets into the bed beside her. Her arms slip around him—a warm, unaffected gesture indicating that life will go on as before. This symbol of Evadne's resilience is perceived by George as total defeat.

Themes and Meanings

At the time of publication, Rebecca West, although only twenty-one, had already won considerable recognition in British avant-garde circles for her incisive contributions to feminist and socialist journals. The story reflects not only her political and feminist preoccupations but also the emotional turbulence of her private life.

The heightened melodrama of the plot overlays a profound and biting criticism of institutionalized marriage, with particular concern for the role that women are expected to perform. Until the moment of murderous confrontation, when the pure loathing which underlay their previous petty disagreements is laid bare, neither partner knows anything of the other's true characteristics or inner thoughts. To Evadne, George is a weak but attractive man with a pleasing, albeit indecisive, intellect. She ascribes his frequent moods of irritability to pressures at work and has no inkling of the sexual disgust with which he regards her. To her, the marriage is dull, but tolerable, and gratifying to her physical needs.

George sees Evadne as a trivial, sensual creature with no inner depth or spirituality. His deliberate blindness to her public achievements demonstrates his fear of not being able to master her—an indication that his disgust with her sexuality may also be based on fear of inadequate manhood.

In a very complex and illuminating passage analyzing Evadne's hesitation at the point of murder, the author describes the contradiction which she perceives as central for most married women—on the one hand, her need to maintain confidence in her own powers and capabilities, and, on the other, the "unnatural docilities" which are dictated by custom, upbringing, and habit—"a squaw, she dared not strike her lord." It is this acquired docility which prevents Evadne from striking the first blow. Her expression of utter contempt, which George observes as she falls into the river, is a humiliation which he will have to live with; paradoxically, her submission becomes part of her strength.

Rebecca West's conception of Evadne as a woman with "black blood in her," although expressed variously in a vocabulary that would not be acceptable to later generations, is vital to the sharp contrast which she seeks to make between husband and wife—a physically weak white man brought up with and espousing some of the narrower and more puritanical aspects of Christianity, and a strong woman of mixed ethnic origin whose diverse cultural background has endowed her with greater freedom and flexibility. By centering her story on absolute opposites, the author is able to create a flash point explosive enough to unleash the fierce sexual antagonisms which, she implies, lie beneath the petty squabbles of most marriages but rarely come to the surface.

Style and Technique

Rebecca West's rich, reverberating prose crescendos to a tumultuous pitch in the scene on the moors—a powerful evocation of elemental passions in an elemental landscape. Her style echoes some of the qualities of Charlotte

Brontë's writing but without the Brontë Romanticism. Rebecca West reveals herself to be emphatically antiromantic; her story tears away at the myths of conventional marriage and exposes its raw interior nerve.

Her narrative technique is, in fact, modernist, and it is significant that the story was published in the first issue of *Blast*, which rapidly became the main organ of the vorticist movement, bringing together writers and artists who embraced the concept that its editor, Wyndham Lewis, described as "the hard, unromantic external presentation of kinetic forces."

Most of the narrative is expressed from George's viewpoint, and for much of the time Evadne's character is presented in his subjective terms. The positive quality of her actual nature is defined by occasional, definitive interventions in the writer's own voice. This duality of voice—subjective and objective—heightens the contrast between the two people. It emphasizes George's physical and intellectual weakness and his self-delusions, and it gives authority and power to the characterization of Evadne and to her function in the story as the indissoluble element in the marriage.

The story, with its passionate overtones and intricate underlying analytical structure, was acclaimed as a brilliant achievement—particularly impressive in that so young a writer was able to handle profound and difficult emotions with so much confidence and power. The story was an early indication of the qualities of Rebecca West's more mature works, many of which pursue and develop this story's themes with similar stylistic intensity.

Nina Hibbin

THE INFANT PRODIGY

Author: Thomas Mann (1875-1955)
Type of plot: Sketch
Time of plot: Late nineteenth or early twentieth century
Locale: A European city
First published: "Das Wunderkind," 1903 (English translation, 1936)

Principal characters:
BIBI SACCELLAPHYLACCAS, a Greek child pianist, the prodigy
THE IMPRESARIO, who manages Bibi and produces the concert
VARIOUS MEMBERS OF THE AUDIENCE

The Story

Bibi Saccellaphylaccas, the child prodigy, enters the packed concert hall to the applause of an audience already favorably disposed because of advance publicity. Dressed all in white silk, the eight-year-old boy, whose age is advertised as seven, sits at his piano and prepares to play a concert of his own compositions. The hall's expensive front seats are occupied by the upper class, including an aging princess, as well as by the impresario and Bibi's mother. Bibi knows that he must entertain his audience, but he also anticipates losing himself in his music.

As Bibi plays, it is clear that he knows how to work his audience. He flings his body with the music and bows slowly to prolong the applause. Recognizing that the members of the audience respond more to a show than to the aesthetics of the music, he thinks of them as idiots.

In fact, his listeners react to the performance in the context of their individual interests and experiences. An old gentleman regrets his own musical inability but views Bibi's talent as a gift from God to which the average person could not aspire. There is no more shame in falling short of Bibi's accomplishment than in bowing before the Christ Child.

A businessman, believing art to be merely a pleasant diversion, calculates the profit from the concert. A piano teacher rehearses the critical comments that she will make after the concert concerning Bibi's lack of originality and his hand position. A young girl responds to the passion of the music but is confused that such passion is expressed by a child. A military officer equates Bibi's success with his own and applauds in smug self-satisfaction.

An elderly music critic reacts disdainfully, seeing in Bibi both the falseness and the rapture of the artist. Contemptuous of his own audience, the critic believes that he cannot write the truth because it would be beyond his readers. He thinks that he would have been an artist had he "not seen through the whole business so clearly."

As the concert nears its end, laurel wreaths are brought to Bibi. The impresario places one around his neck and then kisses him on the mouth, sending a shock through the audience and leading to wild applause. The critic sees this as a ploy to milk the audience and seems almost sorry that he can so easily see through it.

Bibi's final number, a rhapsody, merges into the Greek national hymn, exciting the Greeks in the audience to shouts and applause. Again the critic deplores this exploitation and plans to criticize it but then wonders if it is perhaps "the most artistic thing of all." After all, an artist is "a jack-in-the-box." He leaves, reflecting that criticism is on a higher level than art.

When the concert ends, the audience forms two groups, one around Bibi and the other around the aging princess. The princess meets Bibi and asks if music simply comes to him when he sits down. He responds that it does but thinks to himself that she is stupid.

As the audience leaves, the piano teacher is heard remarking on Bibi's lack of originality. An elegant and beautiful young woman and her two officer brothers go out into the street. An unkempt girl says to her sullen companion that "we artists" are all child prodigies. The elderly gentleman who had been impressed with Bibi hears the comment and wonders what it means, but the girl's companion nods his head in agreement. The final paragraph shows the girl watching the beautiful young woman and her brothers; she despises them but gazes after them until they are out of sight.

Themes and Meanings

Mann has spoken of this sketch, along with several others written at about the same time, as wearing "the impress of much melancholy and ironic reflection on the subject of art and the artist." Clearly, there is cynicism on the part of both artist and audience. The performance is not staged as an aesthetic experience but is designed to draw the greatest possible reaction from an audience composed of those whom Bibi views as idiots. Everything is calculated to appeal to emotionalism, from Bibi's dress and the misrepresentation of his age to the timing of bows and the selection of compositions. There seems to be more gimmickry than art, and the story hints that the impresario, who manages the show, may be more responsible than Bibi for its final effect. Even the title of the story calls attention to the age of the performer rather than to the artistry of the event.

Those in the audience respond in terms of their own preoccupations and needs and, thus, cannot give themselves over to the music. The piano teacher is unable to relinquish her claim to expertise, and the young girl relates all to her feelings of sexual passion. The music critic is determined to demonstrate his intellectual superiority, although at times he seems to regret his inability to participate emotionally in the concert. The performance is a social occasion, with even the seating divided by class and with the audience responding similarly to Bibi and to the aging princess. The unkempt girl sees herself, like

Bibi, as an artist, but clearly she envies the beautiful socialite.

Although the sketch questions the motives of artist and audience, it leaves open the possibility that the illusion created is, as the music critic suggests, "the most artistic thing of all." Art, by definition, is contrived; it is artifice.

Style and Technique

Much of the effect of the sketch comes from the omniscient perspective of a narrator who can recount the thoughts of all characters, thus allowing the reader to see beneath the surface of the concert. This permits the ironic contrast between, for example, Bibi's condescending view toward the audience and the equally condescending view of the piano teacher and the critic toward Bibi. Nearly all the characters are subject to this ironic vision. At times, the irony is quite straightforward, as when the best seats are described as belonging to the upper class because they "of course" feel the most enthusiasm for art. At other times, the position of the narrator is more difficult to determine. When one of Bibi's pieces is called "an effective childhood fantasy, remarkably well envisaged," is that description an objective assessment by the narrator or a mocking of the rhetoric of the concert's program?

The irony is supported by Mann's precise observation and imagery. When the princess applauds, she does so "daintily and noiselessly pressing her palms together." Her companion, "being only a lady-in-waiting," must "sit up very straight in her chair." Images of water are used to contrast Bibi the performer and Bibi the artist. As a performer, he is described as "diving into the applause as into a bath." As an artist, he regards the "realm of music" as "an inviting ocean, where he might plunge in and blissfully swim."

Larry L. Stewart

INNOCENCE

Author: Seán O'Faoláin (John Whelan, 1900-   )
Type of plot: Comic pathos
Time of plot: c. 1915
Locale: Dublin, Ireland
First published: 1946

Principal characters:
THE NARRATOR, the father of a seven-year-old boy about to
  have his first confession
THE OLD AUGUSTINIAN PRIEST

The Story
  A father reminisces about what happened to him forty years earlier when, after confession, for "the first time I knew that I had committed sin." The occasion for this recollection is the sight of his seven-year-old son being prepared by nuns for his first confession: The father knows that his son does not really believe in the practice—it is "a kind of game" between the nuns and the priest. The father recognizes that his boy, who often calls his father "A Pig," is "a terrible liar," given to tantrums. Yet the father's love allows him to understand and value the son's childishness.
  Given hindsight, the father knows that someday his boy "will really do something wicked" and will be overcome with fear. He recalls how he experienced terror when, as a boy, he falsely confessed to an old and feeble priest that he had committed adultery. It was the priest's reaction to this confession which generated the terror that the narrator knows his son will one day feel: "Then horrible shapes of understanding came creeping toward me along the dark road of my ignorance"—the priest had mistaken him for a girl. To escape, he was ready to tell any lie: "I was like a pup caught in a bramble bush, recanting and retracting," desperately seeking the words of absolution and penance.
  The father recollects vividly his fear and guilt, his sense of being polluted: "I knew that from then on I would always be deceiving everybody because I had something inside me that nobody must ever know. I was afraid of the dark night before me." He realizes now how the innocence of his son resembles "that indescribably remote and tender star" that he glimpsed in his isolation. This insight converts his son's mischief into a precious sign of a necessary but now past and irretrievable stage of spiritual development.

Themes and Meanings
  As the title indicates, the story concerns the nature of innocence, sin, and forgiveness. The narrator reflects on how the Church's practice of preparing

children for confession does not introduce them to the real world, especially the fear of knowing that one has done something "wicked." Confession is a game for most children, a ritual which marks the boundary between childhood and maturity.

As the narrator-father muses on his son's transparent and innocent lying, he recalls "the first time that I had committed sin." The emphasis is on knowledge, one's coming to awareness. Because the occasion is pivotal to his growth, the narrator provides a meticulous description of the setting and cultural context: The Church connotes Saint Augustine's view of the inherent sinfulness of man; the gloomy and battered surroundings evoke neglect, exhaustion, and fragility. Opposed to this bleak atmosphere is the narrator's love for the bright candles surrounding Saint Monica, the mother of Saint Augustine, and his adolescent fascination with dark nooks and "the stuffy confessional boxes with their heavy purple curtains."

If one scrutinizes the motive which made the narrator (as an adolescent) decide to play the game and confess having committed adultery, one perceives that it was the experience of "terror that crept into me like a snake," a dread like that of a criminal suddenly apprehended by a policeman, that compelled him to deviate from his usual practice of confession.

More revealing is the process of his shock at the insistent questioning by the old priest into the details of his sin, his panic at the thought of "harm" done to him. What shocks him more, spawning "horrible shapes of understanding," is the priest's mistaking him for a girl. At this point, the boy becomes desperate in wanting to escape, ready to fake anything so that the priest will desist. Yet what "utterly" breaks him is when the priest, finally convinced that the narrator is a man, asks whether the woman he victimized "was married or unmarried." With this mapping of the possibilities of evil, the child is initiated into adult knowledge and practices, into the perverse delight that adults derive from the thought of prohibited or sinful acts.

Although the narrator as child does not fully grasp the nature of his discovery—which is less about himself than about adult behavior (in the person of the old priest whose feebleness blunts the satire)—he sums up the event in a double-visioned comment: First, it was "an absurd misadventure" worthy of laughter among friends; second, he compares himself to "a pup caught in a bramble bush," a deflating image. From a distance of forty years, the incident appears trivial. Yet the last three paragraphs of the story explore the psychological experience of the boy who felt the world become sullen and hostile. With a feeling that "I had done something inside me that nobody must ever know," the secret transforms the adolescent into an adult. His claim, taken seriously, produces an interiority, or a double, the guilty self behind the innocent mask presented to the public; the narrator "cannot laugh" at this because it signifies the end of childhood innocence.

In the last paragraph, the narrator affirms the beneficent "fatherhood" of priests who can compassionately instruct children. Yet he laments the fact that his son, "this small Adam," will grow up, his innocence transposed into an "indescribably remote and tender star." Implicit here are the traditional notions that duplicity characterizes adult experience, that because sin pervades the world, the need for confession and penance will always be felt.

Even though the narrator as father glories in his son's childish conduct, the narrative centers on the loss of his own youthful innocence as he is caught in the calculus of sins in the penny prayer book. While the narrative alludes to the institutional or cultural framework within which innocence is lost, the narrator persists in purveying a dualistic metaphysics of innocence/guilt, of sin/childhood fantasies. The ideology of Augustinian moralizing is subtly reinforced by the attractiveness of a seemingly unpremeditated game, a spontaneous act of freedom. Yet the penny prayer book and the act of confession entail a total worldview that contradicts the sentimental if dubious idealization of childhood innocence.

Style and Technique

In an anthology of short stories which he edited, O'Faoláin describes one of the most intense, strange, and painful pleasures of good fiction, an experience which he calls "Moral Shock": "the excitement and challenge of being brought face to face with some way of life, apparently coherent, seemingly practical, yet disturbingly different from our own."

The central incident in this story may not be strange to a Christian audience, but what may perhaps disturb the common reader and trigger "moral shock" is the idea that the sense of guilt associated with maturity can only materialize in a discourse polarized around the categories of good and evil. The text itself is polarized between the world of childhood with its make-believe creatures (such as the Robin in the Cow's Ear) and the domain of religion.

Except for tidbits about his son's prankish temper and fits, his calling his father "A Pig" (the capitalization hints at the totemic stature of the father), the narrative elaborates on the occasion when the narrator was "primed" for his act: The "dim, wintry afternoon" inside the "old, dark, windy church" is described in full, including such seemingly insignificant details as "the heels of the penitents stuck out when they knelt to the grille." The connotative texture combines an abundant use both of adjectives and the evocation of a self-conscious, ascetic discipline: "The priests dressed in the usual black Augustinian garment with a cowl and a leather cincture." The visual imagery of light and dark; the juxtaposition of Saint Monica and Saint Augustine, of the penny prayer book and the sin of adultery; the old and feeble priest confronting the child attracted to the bright candles and the sensuous surface of the world—all these generate an allegory of two opposing but interpenetrating realms: adult sinfulness and the natural virtue of youth.

After the exposition on the father-son relationship and the impressionistic rendering of setting and atmosphere, the text begins to dramatize the exchange between the priest and the boy. This is the heart of the story, where the process of discovery occurs. O'Faoláin's technique is orthodox: He describes the boy's reactions and sensations. After capturing the priest's tired, ambiguous tone, he intrudes a distant perspective in order to comment on the whole affair, after which he resumes the effort to transcribe the boy's mood following the harrowing ordeal. The conclusion seeks to formulate a lesson to the effect that playing fables can precipitate one's passage to the real world, but the quoting of his son's monotonous litany of misdeeds tends to dissipate the serious didactic aim with a humorous note.

O'Faoláin's technique may be defined as seriocomic when it mixes the boy's fantasy world and natural outbursts of rebellion against the father's authority (lumping humans with animals) with the reflective and somewhat disabused stance of a moral observer far removed from the scene. The narrator's voice tries to convince the reader of its sincerity and authority, but it also wants to entertain and distract through the deliberately adopted tone of the solicitous and loving father who himself was once an erring adolescent. The first-person point of view is meant to convey the authenticity of the event, but it also produces an ironic undercutting of itself when the reader realizes that he is also the target of the narrator's deception: "I knew that from then on I had something inside me that nobody must ever know." In effect, the story is the narrator's act of confession to the reader, who cannot help now but share the secret that he has been trying to hide all these years.

E. San Juan, Jr.

INSTRUCTIONS FOR JOHN HOWELL

Author: Julio Cortázar (1914-1984)
Type of plot: Fantastic tale
Time of plot: The late 1960's
Locale: London, England
First published: "Instrucciones para John Howell," 1966 (English translation, 1973)

Principal characters:
RICE, a spectator at a play
AN ACTOR, the man who plays the role of John Howell
AN ACTRESS, the woman who plays the role of Eva
FLORA, an actress who plays the role of the woman in red
AN ACTOR, the man who plays the role of Michael
THE TALL MAN, who gives Rice the instructions for John Howell

The Story

The title of the story, "Instructions for John Howell," is ambiguous, for the identity of John Howell is only tentative. John Howell is a fictional character in a play that Rice attends. John Howell is also the actor who appears in the role, and, during the second and third acts of the four-act play, John Howell is Rice himself.

During the first intermission of the play that Rice is attending at the Aldwych Theater, a man in gray invites him backstage, gives him a costume and wig, and instructs him to act the part of John Howell. When Rice protests that he is not an actor, the man agrees, saying that he is John Howell. Onstage during the second act, Rice finds that his lines are entirely predetermined by the words of the other characters. He has no freedom to do what he wants to do or say what he wants to say. As the act progresses, it becomes clear that the character Eva is deceiving her husband, Howell, by having an affair with another character in the play, Michael, and that the mysterious woman in red seems to be implicated in the infidelity in some way. At one point during the action, the actress who plays Eva whispers to Rice in her offstage voice, "Don't let them kill me."

During the second intermission, the man in gray and a tall man congratulate Rice on his performance and serve him several glasses of whiskey. The tall man gives Rice extensive instructions on what he is to do during the third act, and it becomes apparent that the decisive moment of the play comes at the end of this act, when the woman in red speaks a line that determines the denouement of the play in the last act.

In the third act, under the influence of the alcohol and resisting confinement to the predetermined plot, Rice begins to improvise. By the lines that he delivers, he creates problems for the actor playing the role of Michael. He is amused by the display of anger that he sees in the wings as the tall man protests what he is doing. He is disturbed by Eva's plea—again in her off-stage voice—that he stay with her until the end. Rice tries to delete the last line of the third act by leading Eva offstage, but she turns around to receive from the woman in red the inevitable words that will determine the outcome of the play.

In the third intermission, the tall man and his accomplices throw Rice out of the theater. When he returns to his seat to watch the last act, he is surprised that the theatrical illusion takes over immediately, so that the audience does not protest the change of actors. The actor who played Howell in the first act is again in the role. At the crucial moment, as Eva is about to drink the tea poisoned by the woman in red, Howell startles her so that she spills the tea. In the confusion that follows, there is a sharp cracking sound. Eva slowly slips into a reclining position on the sofa and Howell runs offstage.

Rice runs out of the theater and through the streets of London. He realizes that someone is following him and turns to find that it is the actor who played the role of Howell. When Rice states that he tried to stop the irrevocable action of the play, the actor responds that amateurs always think that they can change things, but that it never works. It always turns out the same way. When Rice asks why they are both fleeing, if it always happens this way, the actor begs Rice not to leave him in his predicament of forever running away, then disappears in flight down the street. As he hears the sound of whistles in the streets, Rice runs in the opposite direction, reminding himself that there will always be streets and bridges on which to run.

Themes and Meanings

"Instructions for John Howell" is representative of the artistic and political concerns that are evident in all of the fiction of Julio Cortázar. As in many of his stories, Cortázar here elaborates on a familiar theme: the juxtaposition of art and life through the device of a play viewed by a spectator who cannot distinguish the theatrical illusion from the world of real experience. The theme is primarily an artistic one, for it questions the relative authenticity of reality and art, but it becomes in Cortázar's story a symbolic representation of the conflict of individual liberty and the restrictiveness of organized social and political forces. Rice is forced into the role that he must play, is given specific instructions on how to play it, and is ostracized and then pursued by unseen oppressive forces when he exerts his individual will in an effort to change the inevitable outcome of the events.

Although Cortázar always declared himself in sympathy with socialist societies such as Salvador Allende's Chile and Fidel Castro's Cuba, he did not align himself with any particular political ideology; rather, he was committed to the principle that the exploitation of human beings is evil. It is possible to view Cortázar's political commitment as naïve, but in fact that naïveté is one of the themes of his fiction. The story of Rice is a narrative of a loss of innocence, as the character—bored with the weekend in London and then impatient with the mediocrity of the first act of the play—is confronted with the terror of the infringement of his personal liberty and the persecution that follows his rebellion against the authoritarian directorial staff of the play. The actor, who has experienced this conflict night after night with each performance, is less naïve than Rice, for he understands the system and the impossibility of escaping the oppression.

The theme of the loss of innocence in any of the many forms that it may take dominates the stories of Cortázar, particularly those published in the 1950's, in English in 1963 with the title *End of the Game and Other Stories*, then again in 1967 as *Blow-Up and Other Stories* after the success of the Michelangelo Antonioni film (*Blow-Up*, 1966), based on the lead story. The innocence is sexual in "Final del juego" ("End of the Game"), artistic in "Las babas del diablo" ("Blow-Up"), and overtly political in "Las armas secretas" ("Secret Weapons") and "El perseguidor" ("The Pursuer").

Style and Technique

Through the device of the theatrical illusion in "Instructions for John Howell," Cortázar develops one of the more terrifying aspects of the loss of political innocence. The actor who portrays John Howell *becomes* John Howell. In like manner, the tall man who gives the instructions points out that Rice is no longer Rice, nor is he an actor. Rather, he is John Howell. The transformation of the "real" person into the character that he is portraying occurs in the text through the language of the narrator, who frequently refers to the actor as Howell and, in the last moment of the story, uses pronouns ambiguously to confuse the identities of the two men: the two John Howells crouched in the alleyway to elude their unseen pursuers. Thus, the narrator's linguistic structures reinforce the theme of the effect of oppression on the freedom of the individual.

The transformation of the character into another person, or the mutation of the individual into an object with which the individual is obsessed, occurs frequently in Cortázar's stories, and it always is effected through the narrative voice. It is evident that Rice becomes John Howell onstage not so much because of what he does but because of what he says, and because of his conviction that he can alter the reality of the play by his words. The illusion of the play becomes for Rice/Howell an inevitable reality that can be changed only by the force of his linguistic resources.

The narrator begins the story with words that provide an explanation for the seemingly impossible events: "Thinking about it afterwards—on the street, in a train, crossing fields—all that would have seemed absurd, but what is theater but a compromise with the absurd and its most efficient, lavish practice?" These words not only justify the denouement of the plot but also create a symmetry in the narrative, for the reference to street, train, and fields anticipates the aftermath of the events: Rice (or Howell) fleeing his pursuers by way of streets, trains, and fields.

Gilbert Smith

AN INTEREST IN LIFE

Author: Grace Paley (1922-   )
Type of plot: Ironic realism
Time of plot: The 1950's
Locale: New York City
First published: 1959

> *Principal characters:*
> VIRGINIA, the female protagonist, the abandoned mother of
> four children
> MRS. RAFTERY, her downstairs neighbor, a busybody
> JOHN RAFTERY, Mrs. Raftery's son, who visits both his mother
> and Virginia every Thursday

The Story

The plot is quite simple: "An Interest in Life" offers a first-person account of a young woman, Virginia, who is deserted by her husband shortly before Christmas. Thanks to the advice of her downstairs neighbor, Mrs. Raftery, rent and food money from the Welfare Department, the amorous attentions of Mrs. Raftery's son, John, and her own sense of humor, Virginia and her four children manage quite well without her husband.

The husband's parting gifts are a new broom and a passionate, mean kiss intended to let her know what she will be missing. With only fourteen dollars and the rent unpaid, Virginia turns for help to her downstairs neighbor. Mrs. Raftery's advice: Tell Welfare, the grocer, and the cops, who will provide toys for the kids, and look around for comfort; "With a nervous finger she pointed to the truckers eating lunch on their haunches across the street. . . . She waved her hand to include all the men marching up and down in search of a decent luncheonette. She didn't leave out the six longshoremen loafing under the fish-market marquee." The tone is set; the story continues in this earthy and ironic vein as Virginia's tough-kid humor and self-mockery protect her against self-pity.

One night, Mrs. Raftery advises her son to visit his old friend, Virginia. Soon he comes regularly, bringing presents for the kids and even offering to do the dishes. He takes a special interest in Girard, Virginia's most difficult child; he gives him an erector set, signs him up for Cub Scouts, and plays the father Girard never really had. Nevertheless, Virginia rejects his first advances, fearing that the world will blame her for corrupting an upstanding member of church and community; then, too, John is not as sexy as her husband, whose "winking eyes" she still misses.

When John questions Virginia about her husband, she makes excuses about his need to do well in the world, while thinking to herself how cruel he was, trying to turn neighbors and friends against her and constantly putting her down. John listens patiently, continues to help with the kids, but finally stops coming, apparently discouraged by her cold responses.

In despair at the loss of this one true friend, Virginia decides to submit a list of her troubles to "Strike It Rich." Soon after the doorbell rings, "two short and two long meaning John." "As always happens," Virginia tells herself, "where you have begun to help yourself with plans, news comes from the opposite direction." She thinks about how easy it would be for John to walk out of their lives forever and decides "not to live without him."

John mocks her dream of being chosen for "Strike It Rich," reducing her troubles to "the little disturbances of man" as Paley, the author, does to the troubles of so many of her would-be victims. Soon after, Virginia and John become lovers; Mrs. Raftery approves because now John comes to visit every Thursday; Virginia maintains her way of life, noting how remarkable it is that "a man who sends out the Ten Commandments every year for a Christmas card can be so easy buttoning and unbuttoning"; and the reader is ready for a happy ending of sorts. Instead Paley throws a curve; Virginia dreams that her husband returns, "raps her backside," and they are right back where the story started. The last line, "The truth is, we were so happy, we forgot the precautions," makes it clear that the future will repeat the perpetual cycle of passion, childbirth, and desertion. Virginia may have the spunk of a survivor, but her dependence on men and her own sexuality condemn her to a life of poverty.

Themes and Meanings

"An Interest in Life" is the central story in Paley's collection *The Little Disturbances of Man: Stories of Men and Women in Love* (1959). As the title suggests, this story demonstrates one of Paley's favorite themes, the way in which a good sense of humor and a healthy appetite for life can reduce apparent tragedies to minor disturbances. Virginia seems a survivor, whose intelligence, honesty, and street smarts mark her kinship with the picaresque heroes of J. D. Salinger and Saul Bellow. There is, however, a darker side to Paley's work—a grim picture of urban poverty, of men who are irresponsible and of women who find them irresistible, of a culture and an economy in which the poor are lulled into dreams of sudden riches rather than encouraged to find realistic ways to better their plight.

Early in the story, Virginia's self-awareness wins the reader's admiration: "I don't have to thank anything but my own foolishness for four children when I'm twenty-six years old, deserted, and poverty-struck. . . . A man can't help it, but I could have behaved better," she tells herself. Yet, at the end of the story, she envisions herself making the same mistake once again. This conclusion seems quite intentional on Paley's part, a warning to the reader not to romanticize the lusty life of the poor, to see Virginia for what she really is: a survivor, yes, but not a heroine.

Style and Technique

There is general critical consensus that what makes Paley so popular is the authenticity of the language which her characters speak and the wonderful irony and wit which underlie her stories. Her characters are brought to life not so much by what they do, but by how they think and talk. This is especially true of her first-person narratives. Whether it is that of an old woman telling her niece the story of her long-term relationship with a second-rate actor ("Goodbye and Good Luck") or a sexually precocious fourteen-year-old explaining how she got herself engaged to her sister's boyfriend ("A Woman, Young and Old"), the first-person voice is used by Paley to reveal the core of naïveté and vulnerability behind the tough façade that her narrators present to the world.

Paley also uses a classic unreliable narrator as a vehicle for dramatic irony. In the process of telling their stories to other people—boyfriends, mothers, aunts, nieces—Paley's narrators acknowledge the temptation to gloss over the uglier parts. They are, in fact, more honest with themselves; for example, Virginia hides some of the truth about her husband from John Raftery, yet tells the reader how cruel he really was. The implied author, whose point of view the reader understands from the structure of the story, suggests that there are deeper truths the narrator will never understand because of her limited perspective on her own life. The typical Paley narrator interprets the ending of her story as a happy one; the implied author provides evidence of a different perspective. Thus, the reader understands that Rosie in "Goodbye and Good Luck" may get her man in the end, but only after thirty years spent without a home of her own. At this point, her lover must be close to seventy and may not have much life left in him. Josephine, the fourteen-year-old in "A Woman, Young and Old," feels proud to be engaged, yet the reality of venereal disease, adultery, and promiscuity surrounding this engagement promises little hope for a happy future.

This darker side to Paley's stories provides tension and depth but does not dampen their surface vitality. The language her characters speak expresses optimism and spunk, never self-pity. Because Paley depicts a world dominated by poverty and infidelity through the eyes of a narrator who accepts her own plight, the reader can applaud the small triumphs and hopes that make daily life possible in the ghettos of New York.

Jane M. Barstow

THE INTERLOPERS

Author: Saki (Hector Hugh Munro, 1870-1916)
Type of plot: Suspense
Time of plot: Late nineteenth century
Locale: The Carpathian Mountains in Eastern Europe
First published: 1919

Principal characters:
> ULRICH VON GRADWITZ, a nobleman and landholder in the
> Carpathians
> GEORG ZNAEYM, a lesser landholder in the same region

The Story

This fablelike story of vendetta and reconciliation begins with a short history of conflict between two families in the Carpathian Mountains of Eastern Europe. Ulrich von Gradwitz, the local nobleman, is patrolling a narrow stretch of scrubby woodland that borders his much larger and more valuable holdings of forestland. The land that he patrols, however, acquires its value in his eyes because it was the subject of a lawsuit between his grandfather and the grandfather of a neighbor, Georg Znaeym, now his archenemy. At the origin of the conflict, each family held that the other claimed the woodland illegally; now, although Ulrich patrols the land as his, Georg regularly hunts its poor woods, simply to indicate his continued claim of rightful possession. What began as a legal battle generations before has become a personal and hate-filled conflict between the two current representatives of the families in the dispute.

On this particular night, both Ulrich and Georg, assisted by their retainers and huntsmen, have come out onto the land. Each comes nominally to defend his claim, but actually to destroy his great enemy by shooting him down in his tracks on the land over which they have disputed for so long. Despite a windstorm that would usually keep the wildlife in secure hiding, many animals are abroad, and Ulrich is sure that this restlessness indicates the presence of his enemy on the slopes.

Straying from his party of retainers and wandering through the woods, Ulrich unexpectedly comes face-to-face with Georg. Each is armed with a rifle, and each intends to use it since no interlopers will interfere, but not without some parting words of vengeance and hatred. Before either can speak, however, a sharp blast of wind tears from the ground the giant beech tree under which they stand, pinning them under the massive trunk and crippling both.

After the impact and first physical shock that leaves them speechless, Ulrich and Georg realize that they are both still alive, and they pick up their conflict in words rather than rifle shots. Each threatens the other with the possibility that his retainers will arrive first, in which case it will be easy for an "accident" to be arranged in which the tree will have apparently crushed the hapless victim, leaving the survivor free of the charge of murder. Their threats made, they relapse into silence and discomfort as they stoically await the arrival of one or the other party of retainers.

After some effort, Ulrich frees an arm and reaches into his pocket for a wine flask that he carries, greatly enjoying the restorative effect of the drink as it warms his body. As he looks across at his enemy, some unaccountable change comes over him. He offers Georg a drink from the flask, which the other is barely able to reach. Under the combined effects of the situation, the shock, and the wine, Ulrich sees the similarity between him and his fellow sufferer, and a sudden transformation alters his old hatred. He tells Georg that, although the other is free to do as he pleases, if Ulrich's men arrive first, they shall be instructed to free Georg; at first surprised, Georg is then caught up in the change of attitude, and makes a similar promise to Ulrich.

Each now awaits his retainers more eagerly than before, but instead of eagerness for vengeance, each feels anxious that he may be the first to demonstrate his magnanimity. Instead of raging at each other, the two now reflect together on the impact that their reconciliation will have on the surrounding countryside—how amazed the other landholders and peasants will be when they see the sworn enemies in the marketplace as friends! The two begin planning the ways in which they will demonstrate their reconciliation by sharing holidays and visits back and forth between their two houses.

During a lull in the wind, Ulrich suggests that they shout together for help. After no response, they call again, and Ulrich thinks that he hears an answering cry. A few minutes pass before Ulrich cries out that he can see figures coming down the hill, and the two shout again to attract the attention of the hunters. In the last few sentences of the story, Georg, anxious to know whose party will arrive first, asks Ulrich if they are his men:

> "No," said Ulrich with a laugh, the idiotic chattering laugh of a man unstrung with a hideous fear.
> "Who are they?" asked Georg quickly, straining his eyes to see what the other would gladly not have seen.
> "*Wolves.*"

Themes and Meanings

Although Saki's design is clearly to draw as much suspense and surprise into as narrow a compass as possible, the story itself nevertheless presents some of the great abstract themes of justice in the human world and of the human relationship to the natural world.

The most obvious of these themes involves the dissection and final denial of the vendetta mentality that motivates these two figures. The early history of the conflict shows how accidental the hatred between these two men actually is. They inherit a conflict that is not rightly theirs, and it distorts their relationship not only to each other but also—as the reference to the surprise in the marketplace shows—to the community in which they live. Furthermore, the parties of huntsmen and retainers (who never actually appear in the story) represent further ramifications of injustice, wherein the dependents are also caught up in the hatred between the principals, much as the Montagues and Capulets are trapped in the conflict that leads to the death of Romeo and Juliet. The physical blow that levels both men thus paradoxically symbolizes the sudden consciousness of the distortions that the vendetta has caused: Their common plight makes Ulrich and Georg recognize, apparently for the first time, how much they have in common, and thus how much more reasonable friendship would be. Having once seen the world from this new perspective, the two are quick to correct the fundamental distortion of their relationship, and the apparent ease with which the former hatred and distrust dissolve indicates how insubstantial their former condition actually was.

The appearance of the wolves, the unexpected "interlopers" of the story's title, points out the fundamental irony of the tale as a whole and thus touches on the second great theme that the story presents. From this perspective, the story may be said to belong to the school of literary naturalism, in which fundamental natural processes are shown working themselves out in the human world, regardless of human designs or wishes. The essential mistake that Ulrich and Georg make is their assumption that this narrow stretch of almost worthless woodland is somehow theirs to possess in any real sense. They, like their fathers and grandfathers before them, have assumed that legal rights, established in human courts and supported by human institutions, actually establish true dominion over the world of nature.

The fablelike elements of this story show how mistaken such an assumption is. At virtually every turn, the plans of the human characters are thwarted or altered by the different design of the natural world: The best opportunity for settling their vendetta, when no interlopers are present, is cut off by the wind and the falling tree; after their reconciliation, their plans for the future are erased by the advent of the unexpected interlopers. Finally, the wolves themselves symbolize the utter indifference of nature to "important" human disputes and resolutions. The surprise conclusion thus reveals and summarizes this primary theme of literary naturalism with sharply dramatic and terrifying indirection, suggesting in its irony that nature may not be indifferent so much as malicious toward the proud designs of humankind.

Style and Technique

This brief masterpiece is an excellent representation of the principal stylistic and technical elements of Saki's achievement. Above all, the economy of the story's construction—the swift drafting of the background, with its elements of local color and drama; the limited cast of characters; the neat, subtle introduction and arrangement of the plot details necessary to the surprise conclusion—is typically masterful, and indeed necessary to the success of the story because the reader must not have time to doubt the realism of the situation, in either its physical or its psychological aspects.

The quiet, calm voice of the omniscient narrator seems initially to comfort the reader with a sense of control over the events that it narrates, yet as the disquieting details accumulate—the restlessness of the forest creatures, the "accident" of the tree's falling at just the right moment, the "success" of the men's calls for help, the alarming hysteria of Ulrich's laughter—the lack of modulation in the tones of the narrator becomes one of the principal devices by which the suspense is developed and sustained. The end of the story reveals Saki's powerful control in the fact that the surprise is held back until the very last word—a word that, in retrospect, explains and justifies all the details and arrangements made in the careful crafting of the story as a whole.

Dale B. Billingsley

THE INVISIBLE MAN

Author: G. K. Chesterton (1874-1936)
Type of plot: Detective fiction
Time of plot: 1910
Locale: England
First published: 1911

> *Principal characters:*
> FATHER BROWN, a detective-priest
> LAURA HOPE, a clerk in a confectionery
> JOHN TURNBULL ANGUS, a suitor of Laura Hope
> ISIDORE SMYTHE, an inventor and competing suitor for Laura
> JAMES WELKIN, a rejected suitor of Laura who threatens
>   Isidore Symthe
> FLAMBEAU, Father Brown's protégé

The Story

The story begins as John Turnbull Angus pines for his reluctant, would-be fiancée, Laura Hope, outside the confectioner's shop where she works. Angus enters the shop and begins his familiar banter about marriage and the particular bliss which Miss Hope would presumably enjoy as his bride. She attempts to discourage the ardor of her young suitor by telling him the history of her past admirers.

Laura's father, she tells Angus, was the owner of an inn in Ludbury, outside London, and she often served tables there. Two of her customers, one a dwarf, the other a man with an appalling and disfiguring squint, sought her hand in marriage. Trying not to hurt their feelings and declining to tell them that the real reason she could not marry them was that they were "impossibly ugly," she told them instead that she could not possibly marry anyone who had not "made his way in the world." This white lie, however, merely encouraged further competition between the two, as both of them left to seek their fortunes and win her love.

After leaving her father's inn, Laura discovered that one of the two, Isidore Smythe, had become a success. Smythe had made a fortune with his Silent Service, providing household robots that performed various custodial chores in the home. The other suitor, Welkin, had disappeared mysteriously, but Laura had the strange experience of hearing his laughter without seeing his physical form. She now lives in fear that one or both of them will appear and that she will be forced to marry one of them.

As she finishes this strange tale, and Angus begins to make light of it, Smythe appears just in time to discover a threatening note written on stamp paper pasted to the window of the confectionery: "If you marry Smythe, he will die." Smythe declares that the note is in Welkin's handwriting, and he and Angus resolve to return to Smythe's apartment and enlist the aid of Flambeau, a local detective. While at the apartment, Angus is struck by the strangeness of Smythe's home, filled as it is with the silent robots that serve Smythe and his guest. As an air of otherworldliness pervades, Smythe shows Angus another note that he has received from Welkin: "If you have been to see her today, I shall kill you." Sensing imminent danger, Angus leaves to find Flambeau and solemnly charges the chestnut seller and the policeman outside Smythe's apartment to watch it carefully and monitor anyone who enters or leaves it.

Angus encounters Father Brown at Flambeau's house, and the three of them hasten back to Smythe's apartment only to find blood on the floor and Smythe missing. On being questioned, the chestnut seller and the policeman testify that no one has entered Smythe's apartment. Angus declares wildly that an "invisible man" is responsible for the crime. As Smythe's body is found in the canal, Father Brown takes charge of the investigation.

The priest surveys the scene and suggests that no preternatural invisible man has committed a crime, but one who has become "invisible" by virtue of his familiarity to the observers. Welkin, dressed as the postman, had previously delivered the threatening notes, and easily entered the apartment without attracting notice, murdering Smythe and carrying his dwarfish body away in his mail sack. The resourceful Father Brown has solved another mystery.

Themes and Meanings

By choosing to entitle this story "The Invisible Man," Chesterton was inviting comparison with the more famous novella of the same title by H. G. Wells. In Wells's tale, the invisible man is literally invisible, a young scientist who discovers the principle of invisibility and goes mad, using his new power to murder and to plunder the environs of London. Chesterton's invisible man is by contrast quite ordinary—a simple postman—but invisible in his own way. Chesterton's biographer, Alzina Stone Dale, suggests that "in Chesterton's story there is no upwardly mobile young scientist exploring the outer limits of the universe for what he can gain, but a social statement that many members of society are 'invisible,' like his murdering postman, who 'has passions like other men.'"

It was Chesterton's intent in his fiction to draw attention to the "invisible" elements in society—the common, ordinary items and persons of everyday life—in order to defamiliarize them. In so doing, he hoped to force the reader to notice what would otherwise be taken for granted: the real moments, relationships, and situations that make up one's life. The selection of a common parish priest to be his detective-hero, one who outfoxes both society's criminals and society's authorities, illustrates this thematic concern.

Father Brown lives in a very concrete world; he takes note of the subtleties and ambiguities of human affairs in ways that the people he encounters do not; as a result, the world is vividly real to him. What may go unnoticed in the daily abstractions that others call "real life," Father Brown regards as the foundation of human existence. This sharpened perception makes him an excellent detective but, more than that, a shrewd observer of human behavior and its ironies. Those who read the Father Brown tales to see how the crafty detective will solve the mystery receive this bonus: an invitation to recover their childhood sense of wonder and a challenge to celebrate the splendor of the ordinary in the course of everyday life.

Style and Technique

Chesterton wrote nearly fifty Father Brown mysteries in five collections during a period of twenty-five years. Each of the Father Brown stories follows a fairly recognizable formula; toward the end of the tale, the priest unravels the chain of events that have led to a seemingly unsolvable crime—astounding the principals in the story as well as Father Brown's protégé-detective, Flambeau. In many ways, Father Brown is the prototype of the modern detective who discovers the "unfamiliar in the familiar." In "The Invisible Man," Father Brown notices what the others in the story do not: the "invisible" postman working anonymously in their midst. His eye for the seemingly insignificant detail sets him apart from his fellows and heightens his deductive powers.

The remarkable Father Brown is less a typical parish priest than a spokesman for Chesterton's own orthodox Christian social views. Consequently, the Father Brown tales often contain wry social commentary on the class structure in Britain and deflate the pomposity and pride that the intellectuals of Chesterton's culture often evinced. Chesterton was nothing if not a defender of the "common folk," and his Father Brown series consistently champions the ordinary and the commonsensical over the flamboyant and the intellectualized. The world of Father Brown is thus the idealized world that Chesterton imagined a truly Christian society would evoke.

Bruce L. Edwards, Jr.

IT MAY NEVER HAPPEN

Author: V. S. Pritchett (1900-   )
Type of plot: Humorous satire
Time of plot: c. 1917
Locale: London
First published: 1945

Principal characters:
VINCENT, the narrator and protagonist, seventeen years old
MR. BELTON, Vincent's uncle, a partner and salesman in a
    furniture factory
MR. PHILLIMORE, Belton's partner
MISS CROFT, the company secretary, slightly older than
    Vincent
MR. SALTER, Belton's former partner, now a competitor

The Story
    At age seventeen, Vincent is sent to work for his Uncle Belton, a dapper, dreamy man who makes Vincent believe that this job is the opportunity of a lifetime. Everyone assures Vincent that he has his foot on the first rung of the ladder, that life is now beginning for him. On his first day, Vincent takes the train to work with his uncle, who along the way gives the boy the impression that Mr. Phillimore, his partner, is the genius of the firm, a man to be feared and respected. He encourages Vincent to remember young Samuel of the Old Testament, who, when he heard the voice of God, replied, "Speak Lord, thy servant heareth." Belton thinks it would not be inappropriate to think the same thoughts when Phillimore calls.
    The Beautifix Furniture Company turns out to be a modest enterprise, precariously supported by the capital Phillimore brought to the firm. In Belton's eyes, however, it was he who saved Phillimore from the clutches of a possessive mother. Phillimore is also something less than the godlike figure Belton had described on the train. Effeminate, clumsy, and dithering, his chief virtue in Belton's view is his high regard for Belton. Vincent soon learns that their partnership is like a marriage, each member of which is sustained by the weaknesses of the other. Belton and Phillimore are temperamental opposites, too. Belton is dreamy, optimistic, and idle, while Phillimore is fretful and pessimistic. One day, Belton returns to the office with a framed needlework piece bearing the motto, "It may never happen." Predictably, the two men differ on its interpretation. For Belton, it is an encouragement not to worry about problems that may never arise; for Phillimore it means precisely the opposite, that life would be futile if one's fears were never realized. "I should die!" he confides to Vincent, who is beginning to think that Phillimore is no fool.

As time passes, Vincent increasingly realizes the uncertain future of the business. Belton's fears (when he can confront them) are focused on the competition from his ex-partner Salter, whom he regards almost as Satan incarnate. One day at lunch, however, Vincent sees this enemy, who turns out to be just as worried and dejected as Phillimore in his worst moments. Rumors circulate through the office that Belton is looking for another partner to provide a new influx of capital, and Phillimore begins behaving more strangely than usual, dropping hints that young Vincent (whom he continually calls Vernon) should be courting Miss Croft. Miss Croft regards young Vincent with the disdain a young woman always has for an adolescent boy, while he regards her as something remote, exotic, and untouchable. He believes that she is in love with Phillimore. All these tensions—commercial and romantic—come to a climax one day when Phillimore comes into the office drunk and insults Miss Croft by emptying a drawer full of papers over her head. Later that day, Phillimore also tries to kiss her, but she rejects his advances. Phillimore walks out of the office and does not return. They learn eventually that he has joined the enemy—Salter.

Eighteen months later, Vincent sees Phillimore in a crowd and overhears his say to someone, "I should die." Phillimore then sees Vincent and gives him a contemptuous look before disappearing forever into the crowd.

Themes and Meanings

"It May Never Happen" is a typical V. S. Pritchett story in dealing not with social or political issues but with character revelation. The story's satire is directed in part at the values and mores of the lower middle classes, but its main concern is with the interactions of the characters, each of whom turns out to be at least slightly ridiculous. The most obviously humorous character is Belton, who dreams of commercial success. His persistent optimism undermines those very dreams, for it prevents him from seeing anything clearly, especially himself. He would rather daydream than work, and he habitually avoids responsibility by spending his money on luxuries when he should be devoting his time to selling the company's products. Young Vincent regards Phillimore's pessimism as more farsighted than Belton's cockeyed optimism, but Phillimore himself is weak and flighty. His clumsy attempt to win Miss Croft is typical of his inability to deal with life. Vincent and Miss Croft are typical young people, naïve and self-centered, struggling to enter the adult world yet fearful of its responsibilities. Vincent, as narrator looking back on these youthful experiences, sees all too clearly his own awkward gropings toward insight and experience while at the same time revealing the absurdities of the elders he once admired and feared.

Thus, Pritchett's humor is directed ultimately at the follies of human beings in general, at their posturings and lack of self-knowledge, their fears and weaknesses, their sexual anxieties, and their general ineffectualness. As always, however, Pritchett's satire is more compassionate than condemnatory. He sees and reveals so that readers may laugh with one another, not at one another. In his world, everyone is slightly ridiculous, and hence, everyone is joined together in common, flawed humanity.

Style and Technique

In this, as in most of Pritchett's stories, there is little emphasis on plot as normally defined. Although there is a chronological order to the events of the story, these events seem almost incidental. Pritchett's focus is on the characters and the surface details of their lives and surroundings. He presents these in a lean, uncluttered prose that deceives by its very simplicity. There are no verbal tricks or fancy literary devices in Pritchett's writing, only direct, clear language which manages, in spite of its surface clarity, to suggest much more than it appears to say. Tone of voice, turn of phrase, and implication of gesture carry the burden of the story's meaning. The reader who fails to pay close attention to these details will conclude that this is no more than an amusing anecdote about eccentric Londoners. The more careful reader, perhaps puzzled by the story's inconclusive ending, will read again, this time relishing the details by which Pritchett reveals his characters. The tone throughout is wry and sardonic, as if the author were glancing out of the corner of his very keen eye at the passing human comedy. Pritchett's art is his artlessness, his refusal to preach, moralize, or oversimplify. His broad and lasting appeal derives not from commentary on abstract issues but from his desire to reveal and understand the ordinary person and the defenses that all people erect to deal with the world and their own failures in it.

Dean Baldwin

IVY DAY IN THE COMMITTEE ROOM

Author: James Joyce (1882-1941)
Type of plot: Social satire
Time of plot: Early nineteenth century
Locale: Dublin
First published: 1914

> *Principal characters:*
> MR. HYNES, a journalist
> MR. HENCHY, a canvasser for the local Nationalist election
>   candidate
> MR. O'CONNOR, another canvasser for the local Nationalist
>   election candidate
> MR. CROFTON, a Conservative canvasser for the local
>   Nationalist election candidate
> JACK, the caretaker of the committee room

The Story

There is much more talk than action in "Ivy Day in the Committee Room." On a rainy autumn afternoon, election canvassers drift in from the Dublin streets to warm themselves around a meager fire in the election committee room. As the story begins, there are only two people in the dimly lit room: Jack, the old caretaker of the committee room, complains to O'Connor, one of the canvassers, about his uncontrollable, ne'er-do-well son. Jack falls silent, however, as other canvassers join them, and the conversation turns to local politics. Their candidate is "Tricky Dicky Tierney," and they discuss him and his cronies, as well as one another, with varying degrees of cynicism. Another topic of keen interest is the likelihood of Tierney's buying them a round of stout.

When the stout does, indeed, arrive, they become more enthusiastic in their support of Tierney. Henchy, one of the canvassers, defends Tierney's willingness to welcome a visit from King Edward VII. This discussion inevitably leads these Dubliners to the subject of Charles Stuart Parnell, the great Irish political leader who led the fight for Home Rule, meaning Irish self-government, until his fall from power and his death shortly thereafter, on October 6, 1891. The story takes place on October 6, some years later. O'Connor wears an ivy leaf in his lapel to commemorate Parnell's death.

Parnell's involvement in a divorce case led to his fall from power, and the men argue briefly about his character, but they are soon praising him with an odd mixture of sincerity and cynicism: "We all respect him now that he's dead and gone—even the Conservatives." Henchy asks the journalist among them, Hynes, to recite his poem "The Death of Parnell." After a long silence, Hynes does so. His poem condemns the politicians and Catholic priests who contributed to Parnell's downfall. The canvassers are greatly moved by this recital, except the Conservative, Crofton, who compliments it carefully as "a very fine piece of writing."

Themes and Meanings

"Ivy Day in the Committee Room" is from James Joyce's celebrated collection of stories, *Dubliners* (1914), and was the eighth of the book's fifteen stories to be written. It is included, however, in the fourth and final informal category of stories into which Joyce retrospectively arranged the collection; with "A Mother" and "Grace" it comes under the heading "stories of mature public life." These stories deal with Irish culture and society in the early twentieth century. Their emphasis is on civic institutions and public mores. Their tone, as "Ivy Day in the Committee Room" bears out, is slyly but relentlessly satiric. Unlike the generally introspective and emotional interests of their companion pieces in *Dubliners*, these stories deal almost exclusively with the external features of their contexts, as befits their public orientation. Concentration on externals enables Joyce to vary and extend his use of epiphany, the method which he originated of endowing characters and their worlds with ostensibly complete autonomy, in order that they reveal their own typical nature.

"Ivy Day in the Committee Room" depicts a condition embodied by a small group of Dubliners but shared by a large number of people throughout the country. Their condition is one of shock, defeat, and social paralysis brought about by the eclipse of the political career of Charles Stewart Parnell, the nearly mythical figure who led the fight for Irish Home Rule. His departure from the political scene, followed by his sudden and untimely death, left Irish political hopes in a traumatized condition for a generation— James Joyce's generation.

Parnell, known at the height of his powers as "the uncrowned king of Ireland," exists in the story as an ironic contrast to the impotence of his bereft adherents and as a far more desirable political option than that offered by the crowned king of Ireland, Edward VII. Yet, in the allusive manner of the story, such an irony has more than merely political resonance. It also points up the emotional poverty of one of the characters: Jack, the caretaker, is unable to enforce "home rule" in his own household. Even such a vehement Parnellite as Henchy is to be viewed satirically, since he is a caricatured embodiment of the vehement moralism which terminated Parnell's political career.

"Ivy Day in the Committee Room" draws attention to the poverty of contemporary political activity in Ireland in a variety of ways. The bland platform of Tricky Dicky Tierney, its apparent ability to satisfy both Nationalist and Conservative voters (who ordinarily would be at opposite ends of the political spectrum), is presented in strong, if implicit, contrast to Parnell's individual integrity. Tierney's nickname further emphasizes this contrast. To underscore the difference still further, Joyce has given his candidate a surname the Gaelic root of which (*tiarna*) means "lord." Clearly, in contrast to the noble Parnell, there is nothing lordly about the latter-day bearer of the electorate's aspirations.

Tierney's henchmen are aware of the contrast, but their inability to make anything of a public nature out of this awareness becomes clear when their criticism of him is washed away with drink. Infidelity to Tierney is replaced by infidelity to themselves, a development which is all the more graphic for being unconscious. Accepting Tierney's drink is a vivid example of the characters' undependable allegiances, lapsed idealism, and self-forgetfulness. It is also the story's clearest illustration of the discontinuity between thought and action which seems typical of the post-Parnell political world in Ireland.

Indeed, the central activity in "Ivy Day in the Committee Room" is inactivity. The characters' devotion to waiting, wondering, and killing time reveals a state of lethargy and vague regret which suffuses the story. Drawing on a general sense of ebb and aftermath, the story gives such deficiencies an authentic reality by conceiving of them as central features of the characters' public presence. Condensed in the story's brief temporal span is the history of a political generation which has lost its way. Time is the medium through which history asserts itself, but Henchy and company seem to be refugees from time. The sodden conditions outside the room, added to Jack the caretaker's difficulty in scraping together an adequate fire, connote the ungenial nature of the environment and the bleak outlook for the petty characters.

Joyce, as though to establish the terms of his own artistic integrity, is unsparing in his exposure of the venality and indifference of these lowest of the political low (foot soldiers in the petty skirmish of a ward election). Even Hynes, who is admittedly a cut above the others in the committee room, comes under the author's satiric lash. Indeed, his poem, for all the sincerity with which Hynes delivers it, is the last word in banality and bathos. A superb parody of derivative rhetoric and outmoded language, it fails literally to merit Crofton's judgment of it as "a very fine piece of writing." Its naïve and outspoken genuineness of sentiment is in brilliant contrast to the tacit, guileful satire of the story whose climax it is.

Style and Technique

If he had written nothing else, Joyce would be assured of a place in literary history because of his innovations in short fiction. His counterdramatic sense of his material, his stylistic resourcefulness, and his celebrated deployment of epiphany enable him to distill aesthetic and cultural validity from superficially unpromising raw material.

Joyce's use of anticlimax as revelation is seen to good advantage in "Ivy

Day in the Committee Room." That aspect of the story's technique may be thought of, in effect, as being synonymous with its subject matter. In addition, the drifting, unpredictable flow of conversation in the story mirrors the characters' rudderless, improvised social existence. At the same time, however, without the characters' knowledge, their conversation creates a structure of thematic relationships, conceived around the issues of loss, impoverishment, and venality.

Speech, and verbal utterance of all kinds, are extremely important in all of Joyce's stories, and "Ivy Day in the Committee Room" is noteworthy for its talkativeness and for the witty and fastidious precision with which it mimics local Dublin usage. This emphasis on talk, its implicit contrast between talk and action, and its mocking and tacit allusion to the cliché that "talk is cheap" confer on the reader the role of eavesdropper. The intimacy thereby created between speaker and auditor, or between character and reader, is a demonstration of one of Joyce's most characteristic artistic strategies, the impersonality of his authorial presence.

This strategy, coupled with (or indeed expressed as) a rejection of omniscience, gives the reader an unmediated, though artfully contrived, experience of the material. As a result, the material achieves a definitive showing forth of itself, ostensibly on its own terms. In Joyce's terms, it attains "epiphany." Economically, unobtrusively, incisively, but above all, inferentially, Joyce lays bare the pathetic stagnation of public life in Dublin as he knew it; that unheroic, degraded present which he could neither forgive nor forget.

George O'Brien

IVY GRIPPED THE STEPS

Author: Elizabeth Bowen (1899-1973)
Type of plot: Psychological realism
Time of plot: 1944, with a flashback spanning the years 1910 to 1912
Locale: An English coastal town across the channel from France
First published: 1945

Principal characters:
> GAVIN DODDINGTON, the protagonist, who is in his early forties, a youth in the flashback
> MRS. LILIAN NICHOLSON, a widowed school friend of Gavin Doddington's mother
> ADMIRAL CONCANNON, a neighbor of Mrs. Nicholson

The Story

"Ivy Gripped the Steps" is divided into three sections: The first and the third act as frames, being short and set in the present, 1944; the second, by far the longest section, contains a flashback to 1910-1912, when the middle-aged protagonist is between eight and ten years old. As the story opens, an external narrator describes the outside of a brick-and-stone house, which once was prominent but which has become abandoned and neglected since the war made Southstone, on the coast of England, part of the front line. Ivy overwhelms the house, leaving a grotesque rather than a stately impression. Gavin Doddington, having a few days of vacation from the Ministry, has come to see the house where as a youth he visited his mother's school friend, Mrs. Lilian Nicholson. During his last visit, which took place more than thirty years ago, he experienced a painful awakening regarding his relationship with Mrs. Nicholson.

In the second section, three visits by young Gavin to the prominent house at the seaside resort of Southstone are presented: the first in June, a second in January, and a third in September. As an eight-year-old boy coming to Southstone to shore up his health against the damp climate of his own inland home, Gavin is impressed with the luxury and ease at Mrs. Nicholson's home. While at Southstone and under the care of the maid, Rockham, Gavin soon becomes enchanted with Mrs. Nicholson, whose life as a beautiful and charming widow of independent means seems constituted of social engagements and leisure. Her life contrasts with his own; his family struggles to make a living from the land. During his first visit, Gavin becomes aware of three important facts that he does not fully understand because of his youth: Mrs. Nicholson does not treat him like a child; he has become infatuated with her; and Admiral Concannon in conversation calls her "my dear."

During his second visit, the intimacy between Gavin and Mrs. Nicholson grows, partially as a result of Rockham's illness and partially because of Mrs. Nicholson's manner. At a dinner party at the admiral's and afterward in her conversation with Gavin, Mrs. Nicholson reveals her social nature to the reader but not to the young Gavin: She is generally self-centered and flirtatious. It is during the third visit to Southstone that Gavin experiences a painful awakening. He has been growing fonder of Mrs. Nicholson and has been treated kindly by her. He, however, overhears a conversation between Admiral Concannon and Mrs. Nicholson that makes him realize the true nature of the unlikely triangle made up of Mrs. Nicholson, Admiral Concannon, and himself. The admiral rebukes Mrs. Nicholson for being flirtatious with him and for mesmerizing Gavin. Mrs. Nicholson, not in control of this social situation, likens Gavin to a pet dog by way of excusing her behavior. When Gavin enters the room, Mrs. Nicholson attempts to retain her social veneer by speaking to Gavin as if nothing unpleasant has happened.

The last section of the story picks up chronologically after section 1: Gavin Doddington, who before the lengthy flashback has been staring at the abandoned house that once belonged to Mrs. Nicholson, notices that he has unconsciously picked a leaf of the ivy. Presumably, the flashback has been running through Doddington's mind as he faced the house. He is surrounded by the devastation of war—an evacuated town, buildings intact yet left neglected, bombed sections of buildings, barbed wire, cement barriers—and the memory of the devastation of his feelings of love. It has only been with Mrs. Nicholson, before her veneer was shattered in that overheard conversation, that he has experienced such strong emotions. Gavin Doddington after his awakening is left with no feelings, "nobody to talk to"—"not a soul." He in vain tries to pick up a young woman but is left alone amid the debris of war and emotional devastation.

Themes and Meanings

"Ivy Gripped the Steps" appears in a volume of war stories written by Bowen during World War II. Gavin Doddington reflects on his shattered life amid the ruin of a deserted and bombed coastal town in England. His specific loss—his inability to love—caused by Mrs. Nicholson is a microcosm for the loss felt by those who experience war. Although the war occurs some thirty years after Doddington's traumatic experience at Southstone, it is the war-torn city that calls him back to relive his experience of devastated love. War is continually alluded to even in the flashback section of the story, which takes place between 1910 and 1912. The admiral forecasts war, warning that England will have to protect herself from Germany, and the Concannons host a meeting to promote the Awaken Britannia League. As an adult, Doddington still considers World War I to be Admiral Concannon's War, the one that the admiral predicted. He remembers the talk of war and Mrs. Nicholson's refusal to believe in it. The admiral, Mrs. Nicholson, and Gavin

Doddington's diverse views on the possibility of war reflect their characters: The admiral reacts with concern; Mrs. Nicholson reacts either with un-concern or with denial; the young Gavin reacts with confusion. Similarly, in the social triangle—including Admiral Concannon, Mrs. Nicholson, and Gavin—which was only a triangle of love to Gavin, the behavior of the three follows the same pattern. Gavin, who is too young to comprehend either the imminence of war or the mere façade of love, suffers as a result of Mrs. Nicholson's ego. She acts with insensitivity and selfishness, while the admiral shows concern for Gavin's feelings. The shallowness of Mrs. Nicholson's world has proved ephemeral. Her society, as well as her character, is only a façade; neither can survive reality. The once carefree community of South-stone—a town now in ruins—is slowly being released from the grip of war; Gavin Doddington, a man emotionally devastated, has not yet been released from the grip of the past. As the town retreats into darkness at the end of the story, Doddington is left alone with his memories.

Style and Technique

An external voice narrates "Ivy Gripped the Steps"; the voice speaks of Gavin Doddington, as well as all the other characters, in the third person. Yet the narrative stance emphasizes Doddington as the protagonist since no information given in the story is foreign to him: The description of the ivy-choked house is given to the reader as Doddington looks at it; the long flash-back section is presumably a memory of Doddington; and the scene outside the Concannons' home centers on Doddington. Although he does not nar-rate the story technically, his experience controls the narration. As an eight- or ten-year-old, he is not sophisticated enough to understand the full reality of his experience with Mrs. Nicholson, but as an adult he is: He knows that he is alone and restive at Southstone with his memory. His feelings of love, devastated at an early age, have never recovered.

Bowen begins early to establish the tone of her story through her diction. Ivy-covered houses, frequently considered stately and prestigious, are shown capable of carrying negative connotations. In the title and in the first three paragraphs of the story, the diction suggests that the ivy is a destructive image: "Gripped," "sucked," "deceptive," "matted," "amassed," "con-sumed," "brutal," "strangulation." The ivy that gripped the house has taken it over and made it grotesque. All other places in the story where the word "gripped" is used also convey negative connotations. The admiral grips his hand behind his back after he confronts Mrs. Nicholson with her flirtatious behavior; Doddington grips a cigarette in his mouth as he is turned down by the young woman and is left alone and desolate. Twice Gavin Doddington's being gripped by his love for Mrs. Nicholson is emphasized. The first situ-ation occurs when Gavin at age eight has an early intuitive feeling that he can never approach Mrs. Nicholson:

Gavin, gripping the handrail [along the cliff], bracing his spine against it, leaned out backwards over the handrail into the void, in the hopes of intercepting her [Mrs. Nicholson's] line of view. . . . Despair, the idea that his doom must be never, never to reach her, not only now but ever, gripped him and gripped his limbs. . . .

Bowen employs the same images in a later scene describing Gavin's relationship with Mrs. Nicholson. He has just been called a child by her, and his reaction is one of anguish: "Overcharged and trembling, he gripped his way, flight by flight, up the polished banister rail, on which his palms left patches of mist; pulling himself away from her up the staircase as he had pulled himself towards her up the face of the cliff." Just as the ivy has taken over the house and turned its image from a positive to a negative one, the feelings that Mrs. Nicholson nurtured in Gavin toward herself not only have caused him pain but also have doomed him to a life without genuine feeling, to a life without love. Both Mrs. Nicholson and the leisurely, irresponsible life she led are shown to be destructive forces.

Marion Boyle

JACKALS AND ARABS

Author: Franz Kafka (1883-1924)
Type of plot: Parable
Time of plot: Unspecified
Locale: An oasis in the North African desert
First published: "Schakale und Araber," 1917 (English translation, 1946)

Principal characters:
THE NARRATOR, a European man
AN OLD JACKAL, the spokesman for the pack
AN ARAB CARAVAN DRIVER

The Story

At night in a desert oasis, the narrator, traveling with an Arab caravan, tries to get to sleep. The distant howling of jackals causes him to sit up again, and in no time the pack is swarming around him. One of them presses close against his body, then stands before him and speaks. It is the oldest in the pack, and it assures the narrator that his arrival here has been awaited for a long time, by countless generations of jackals, in fact. This sounds curious to the man, as he has only come by chance and on a short visit to the African desert.

As if to cast the newcomer in the role of a messiah or liberator, the jackal explains that he and his race are the persecuted enemies of Arabs and place all their hopes in a "Northerner," whose intelligence far exceeds that of an Arab. The blood enmity between jackals and Arabs requires the extinction of one or the other. The narrator at first thinks the jackals mean to attack the Arabs sleeping in the camp, and he warns that they themselves would undoubtedly be shot down in dozens. Meanwhile, two younger beasts have set their teeth into his coat and shirt and are holding him down.

The old jackal corrects the man's misunderstanding and tells him that jackals have only their teeth for weapons and that to attack and kill the Arabs would make the animals unclean forever—a kind of unpardonable sin. To be rid of Arabs is what they desire, to return their territory to the natural order of cleanliness: "Every beast to die a natural death; no interference till we have drained the carcass empty and picked its bones clean. Cleanliness, nothing but cleanliness is what we want." Their wish is for the man to slit the Arabs' throats for them, and to facilitate the deed they now present him with a small, ancient, rusted pair of sewing scissors.

At this point the leader of the caravan appears from downwind, cracks his whip over the jackals, and sends them fleeing. He knows what has been going on and explains to the narrator that the jackals regard every passing European as their chosen savior and entreat him to kill the Arabs for them.

The rusted sewing scissors follow his people like a curse until the end of their days, he says. For the jackals it is a vain, foolish hope, and that is why the Arabs like them. To demonstrate his point, he has a dead camel carried up, and the jackals abandon every thought but that of the carrion. They approach, their fear of the whip forgotten, and soon they are swarming over the carcass. Now the caravan driver begins to lash them with his whip, bringing them to their senses and driving them off in pain and fear. Yet they have tasted the blood and flesh and are drawn irresistibly back. The Arab raises the whip again, but the narrator grasps his arm. It is enough; the demonstration is clear. "Marvelous creatures, aren't they?" smiles the caravan driver, "And how they hate us!"

Themes and Meanings

For Franz Kafka and for his narrator, the world of this story is an alien one, geographically and culturally. The two sides between which he finds himself know their places and their desires, but the outsider is subjected to confusion. As in many of Kafka's narratives, he hears conflicting sides of an issue and is not in the position to know which is correct. In fact, probably both are valid in "Jackals and Arabs." The beasts and the men exist in a dual relationship of enmity and symbiosis, hating each other and needing each other to survive and flourish. Their symbiotic existence may be considered a part of the natural order of life, but not their enmity, for it relies on deception and duplicity, and these are human, not animal, traits. Thus, the jackals appeal to a noble sense of cleanliness in order to have the stranger assume the guilt of murdering their enemies. The Arabs are equally perfidious, if less sophisticated, in their treatment of the beasts. The caravan driver asserts that the jackals make finer dogs than any of the ordinary kind, yet he gives them the food they crave most and then would drive them repeatedly from it with his whip. It is a closed world which functions handsomely and is founded on age-old traditions of coexistence, yet the sum of its parts is paradoxical.

Alongside this commentary on the strange system itself is the portrait Kafka presents of the outsider momentarily caught in it. "Jackals and Arabs" is also about the "Northerner," the European, a satire on the presumed superiority of Western thought and culture. It is given to the cunning old jackal to flatter the storyteller as a savior from the North, clever and possessed of an intelligence not found in the Arabs, and it is possible that he would be taken in by the flattery. Should his European wisdom fail him, in any case, there is great persuasive force in the teeth of the encircling jackals, two of them already locked on his clothing. Luckily, however, the narrator has no time to consider the rightness of what he is asked to do, for the caravan leader's intervention relieves him of making that decision.

Style and Technique

As in many of his other stories, Kafka here employs a simple, matter-of-fact narrative style to recount a plot both realistic and fantastic. As a result of that style, one can easily overlook the logical incongruities of the mixture. Most evidently, Kafka has animals converse with men about matters normally thought to preoccupy only human beings: subjugation and liberation, sin and guilt, the upholding of cultural traditions. He has them act with a cunning and deceit of the sort also generally thought to be humankind's exclusive talent—or weakness. If the conversation at the heart of "Jackals and Arabs" makes exceptional creatures of the jackals, however, it also implies a critique of humanity. The animal chosen for this parable is not a noble one in the popular mind, but one thought of as a scavenger, unclean, ill-tempered, and cowardly.

For most northern Europeans, a desert oasis is not an ordinary and familiar place, but the overlay of Kafka's realistic description nevertheless includes occasional glances into its far-from-exotic corners, as with the references to the unbearably rank smell which the beasts emit and with the account of the jackal which sinks its teeth into the dead camel's throat, working at the artery "like a vehement small pump." Even when his purpose is serious, Kafka's essentially humorous view of events is apparent. The narrator glosses his delicate situation among a pack of unpredictable jackals with dry understatement of the dangers. Both the jackals and the Arab caravan driver are given to sarcastic opinions of each other; at a point of potentially high philosophical seriousness, the jackals resort to comic buffoonery to illustrate the uncleanness of killing.

On the subject of parables, Kafka once said that they reside in and refer to a fabulous realm and have no use in practical, everyday life. The most they can do is tell readers that the incomprehensible is incomprehensible, and they know that in any case. To follow parables one would have to abandon reality and become a parable oneself. As usual, "Jackals and Arabs" will be comprehensible to the jackals and Arabs in the story. To the "Northerner" on his brief stay in their country, and to the reader, it offers no explanation of its paradoxes.

Michael Ritterson

JACKLIGHTING

Author: Ann Beattie (1947-   )
Type of plot: Social realism
Time of plot: The 1970's
Locale: Charlottesville, Virginia
First published: 1982

> *Principal characters:*
> THE ANONYMOUS NARRATOR, a woman
> WYNN, her boyfriend
> SPENCE, their friend, whom they are visiting
> PAMMY, Spence's girlfriend

The Story

Nicholas has died sometime during the past year from injuries incurred while he was taking a midnight ride on his Harley and a drunk, driving a van, hit him head-on. Last year, on his birthday, he was alive but in the hospital, brain-damaged from the accident. This year, on his birthday, he is dead, and the narrator and her boyfriend, Wynn, both of whom used to drive from New York to Virginia to spend Nicholas' birthday with him, have come instead to visit Nicholas' brother, Spence, who now lives alone in the house that the brothers once shared.

The first half of the story takes place on the day before the anniversary of Nicholas' birthday. It is August and hot, but Spence makes jam so the narrator and Wynn can take some back with them to New York. He stays in the kitchen cooking because he does not want to talk with them. Spence's girlfriend, Pammy, sleeps upstairs with a small fan blowing on her. She is a medical student at Georgetown and has just arrived in Virginia after finishing summer school. Wynn stands in the field across from the house, pacing with his head down. At thirty-one, he thinks that he is in love with one of his students and is going through a mid-life crisis. The narrator watches Wynn from the house as he swings a broken branch and bats hickory nuts in the field. When Spence walks through the living room, he comments on Wynn's foolishness and on Wynn's September birthday, of which he wants to be reminded. The narrator tells Spence that last year she gave Wynn a Red Sox cap for his birthday.

When Nicholas was hit by the van, he, presumably, was not wearing his helmet because he had established in it a nest of treasures—dried chrysanthemums, half of a robin's blue shell, a cat's-eye marble, yellow twine, a sprig of grapes, a piece of a broken ruler—while baby-sitting the neighbors' four-year-old daughter. The narrator realizes that the head-on collision could have happened to her or Wynn or Spence because they all had ridden on the back of the Harley without helmets. She also wonders how she and Wynn and Spence are going to feel themselves again, without Nicholas—the Nicholas who saw the world, the Nicholas who taught the narrator to trust herself and not settle for seeing things the same way, the Nicholas who made her a necklace with a lobster claw hanging from it and placed it over her head.

Even though the second half of the story takes place on the anniversary of Nicholas' birthday, no one brings it up. Spence makes bread. Pammy and the narrator sit on the porch: Pammy reading the *Daily Progress* and polishing her nails, and the narrator waiting for Wynn to return from his walk. Pammy mentions that she is older than she looks but that Spence, for a "joke," tells people that she is twenty-one. She also mentions that she was once addicted to speed. During that time, she traveled the subway, watched horror films, and slept with a stockbroker for money. She considers that time of her life actually another life and feels snobbish toward other people (including the narrator, Spence, and Wynn) who have not lived this way. The narrator, in turn, feels snobbish toward Pammy because Pammy's addiction makes the narrator realize that other people are confused too.

Spence and the narrator play catch in the heat to distract her from Wynn's taking a walk. Spence suggests that next year they go to Virginia Beach, rather than smolder at his house, in tribute to Nicholas' birthday. The narrator says that she and Wynn came because they thought it would be a hard time for Spence and they did not know that Pammy would be there. Spence does not know why he failed to mention the person who is supposed to be his lover.

Nicholas' past birthdays were celebrated with mint juleps, croquet games, cake eating, and midnight skinny dips. Yet there is no celebrating on this anniversary of his birthday: Wynn is sure that he is having a crisis, Spence is crying about his overdone bread, and Pammy feels both isolated from the others and unsure about continuing medical school. The narrator, depressed and drinking on the porch, remembers Nicholas as possessing imagination, energy, and a sense of humor. She realizes that she knows nothing. She remembers that the drunk in the van had thought he had hit a deer when he hit Nicholas. She sees the intense stars. She remembers that every year Spence reports people on his property who are jacklighting.

Themes and Meanings

The title suggests the story's preoccupation with hunting. Jacklighting is night hunting done with a light used as a lure. Although no actual hunting occurs in "Jacklighting," the final sentence of the story suggests that hunting has occurred on Spence's land and will occur again. More important, the reference to jacklighting connects Nicholas' death with hunting. The drunk driver, who hit Nicholas, thought that he had hit a deer. The image of a deer, stopped in the middle of the road because it is blinded by oncoming headlights, is the same image of a deer being lured with lights and then killed by hunters. Nicholas, too, being hit head-on, was presumably blinded by the van's headlights or, symbolically, hunted by the drunk driver. The suggestion that the van driver is a hunter—a killer—gives the story social reverberations, albeit subtle ones. There is no mention that the van driver was penalized for his crime, and apparently the only recourse Spence can take for his brother's death is to chase hunters off his land or stalk upstairs with a rolled newspaper to kill the wasp that is bothering Pammy.

The preoccupation with hunting expands to an abundance of animal references in the story. Other animals besides deer are hunted, if not by hunters with jacklights and guns then by death itself, which is continuously pursuing anything living. Whereas Nicholas has already been hunted down, the other characters are in the process of being hunted simply because they are getting older and having birthdays. Beattie concludes the story with the narrator sitting on the porch, in the dark. The stars are shining down with the intensity of flashlights—an image that is chillingly similar to the hunters' jacklights shining from the dark—an image that, symbolically, suggests the narrator being hunted.

Hunting, on another, less malignant level, is simply a sport or game that people play on Spence's land. Other games—croquet, baseball, catch, the descriptive game Nicholas invented—function, like hunting, as a distraction from the enigma of life and death.

Style and Technique

Ann Beattie, like other postmodernists, writes many of her short stories in scenes, rather than in a straight narrative. "Jacklighting" is written in six: the first, third, and last scenes present information from the narrator's point of view; the remaining scenes function more dramatically because of their inclusion of dialogue and action between characters. Quite tellingly, there are dramatic scenes between the narrator and Pammy and the narrator and Spence, but not between the narrator and Wynn—the man to whom she is supposedly closest.

One effect of writing in scenes is fragmentation. Each scene functions as a separate (and on one level complete) piece that, when placed with the other pieces, makes up the whole story. No matter in what order the pieces are placed, the reader must make a transition in time and space between them. Furthermore, simply because the reader must make these transitions, it is inferred that there are other fragments—other unwritten pieces—between the scenes. Ultimately, the fragmentation of the story's form complements the fragmented lives of the story's four characters.

Cassie Kircher

THE JAPANESE QUINCE

Author: John Galsworthy (1867-1933)
Type of plot: Social criticism
Time of plot: Late nineteenth or early twentieth century
Locale: London, England
First published: 1910

> *Principal characters:*
> MR. NILSON, a well-to-do and important London
> businessman
> MR. TANDRAM, another well-to-do and important London
> businessman, Mr. Nilson's next-door neighbor

The Story

Though "The Japanese Quince" has far-reaching ramifications about the main characters' lives (as does its central symbol), the story's events transpire in less than an hour in the compressed length of less than three pages. Upstairs in the midst of his early morning pre-breakfast routine, Mr. Nilson becomes aware of a disturbing sensation that he cannot identify. Downstairs, when the sensation recurs, he decides to take a stroll in the garden square surrounded by the exclusive row houses of his neighborhood. Once outside, he is charmed by an ornamental tree and a blackbird singing in it. Suddenly, he becomes aware that his next-door neighbor is nearby, also admiring the tree, and the two, who have not been formally introduced, exchange a few laudatory remarks about the Japanese quince and the blackbird. Then, both becoming embarrassed, the pair bid each other good morning and return to their houses. About to reenter his house, Nilson again gazes at the tree and the blackbird, experiences the disturbing sensation, notices his neighbor (also about to reenter his house) gazing at the tree and bird, and then, "unaccountably upset," turns "abruptly" into the house and opens his morning newspaper.

Themes and Meanings

The primary themes of the story can be formulated as a series of conflicts: emotion or spirit versus convention or habit; the aesthetic versus the pragmatic, communion versus loneliness or self-centeredness; and self-knowledge versus willful ignorance. Each of the businessmen is jarred out of his dull, self-centered routine by the intrusion of nature and by a sudden, piercing awareness of beauty. When each businessman becomes slightly uneasy about appearing to be romantic—an impractical admirer of beauty—in his neighbor's eyes, however, the brief communion of the pair is broken off, and each one returns to the world of practical events and financial matters reported in and symbolized by the morning newspaper each one carries. Each man resumes living within the restrictive confines of his row house, his daily routine, and his society's conventions (so restrictive that because the neighbors' wives have not met, they have not met socially, either, though they have lived next door to each other for five years). The flight from self-knowledge to willful ignorance is suggested in the story's last sentence: Nilson refuses to analyze the unaccustomed emotions which have disturbed him, instead deflecting his attention to his morning newspaper. Failing to acknowledge that he is bothered by the thought of communing with another human being and by the recognition of an aesthetic or romantic side of himself that is mirrored in Tandram, Nilson escapes to the pragmatic world of quantification and measurement. Nilson quantifies not only in meditating on stock prices such as those of Tintos (in the story's beginning) but also in pondering the disturbing sensation, of which he seeks the exact physical location (just under his fifth rib) and physical cause (wondering whether it could be something that he ate the night before). Thus, he does not realize that what bothers him are nonmaterialistic things missing from his life: beauty, friendship, and emotion.

Style and Technique

Besides the tree and its blackbird occupant, "The Japanese Quince" has a number of other symbols. Both Nilson's mirror, at which he gazes in the story's second paragraph, and the scrolled stairs leading up to his house suggest the themes of self-knowledge and the aesthetic versus the pragmatic. When Nilson searches in his mirror to find the cause of the disturbing sensation, he mistakenly looks for the physical or superficial rather than within himself. At the story's conclusion he remains a mystery to himself, like a scroll (the shape of his stairs) that has remained wound up rather than being unrolled and read. Conversely, what he is missing from life is, at the same time, suggested by the mirror and stairs. Though his hand glass has its practical side (literally), its back is made of ivory, which is there for its aesthetic appeal. Though his stairs are eminently usable, their scrolled design is beautiful rather than utilitarian.

That the Japanese quince is enclosed in the "Square Gardens" suggests a social and man-made confinement of nature, paralleling the main characters' repression or walling off of things natural. The tree and blackbird themselves have manifold symbolic aspects. The blackbird resembles in some respects both Nilson and Tandram. They are both dressed in their business "uniforms" of formal black frock coat; they, like the blackbird singing in the tree, have been emotionally stirred by spring and the Japanese quince. Moreover, the bird is described not only as "chanting out his heart" but also as perched in the "heart" of the tree, the repetition of the word "heart" reinforcing the ideas of emotion, passion, or romance. Lastly, the bird is in a kind of communion with the tree, each one contributing to the other: The bird gives the tree an added musical beauty and vitality, while the tree shares its fragrance and shelter with the bird. For a brief moment, Nilson and Tandram also commune and communicate with each other, though all too soon their practicality intervenes and interdicts. Their black frock coats, after all, though resembling the blackbird's plumage, are the sober, colorless badges of the sedate and matter-of-fact business world.

The tree is an exotic rather than a fruit-bearing one, a feature implying the theme of the contrast between the aesthetic and the pragmatic: It is simply beautiful to look at, though it will not provide a crop to be eaten or sold. In this respect, it resembles a work of art. While various edifying concepts can be derived from books of sociology, psychology, history, critical essays, and the like, what will be missing are the beauty, emotion, and pleasure to be gained from seeing a beautiful tree, listening to a blackbird's song, or reading a story such as "The Japanese Quince."

Norman Prinsky

JEAN-AH POQUELIN

Author: George Washington Cable (1844-1925)
Type of plot: Local color
Time of plot: c. 1805
Locale: New Orleans
First published: 1875

Principal characters:
JEAN MARIE POQUELIN, the protagonist, a Creole
JACQUES POQUELIN, Jean Marie's younger brother
MR. WHITE, Poquelin's American neighbor, the secretary of
the Building and Improvement Committee

The Story

People wonder about the transformation of Jean Marie Poquelin. He had been a gregarious, successful indigo planter, but his gambling led to the loss of his fortune and all but one slave, and indigo ceased to be a profitable crop. In an effort to recoup his fortune, Poquelin turned to smuggling and the slave trade. Yet there, too, success eluded him: His last voyage to Africa ended in disaster, and he came home one night without his ship or his cargo.

He also returned without his younger brother, Jacques, who had insisted on going along, and people wonder about this circumstance, too. Poquelin was devoted to Jacques, always praising his bookish brother's learning and intelligence, but Poquelin also is known for his bad temper. Did he murder Jacques in a fit of rage?

No one knows, and no one asks. The once proud estate decays, its fields reverting to marsh. Dwarf palmettos grow up as a fence around the property; in the canal alligators crawl, and in the brackish ponds snakes lurk beneath the carpet of water plants. Strange stories, like the strange flora, grow up about the house: At sunset all the windows are reputed to turn blood red; beneath the front door there is rumored to be a bottomless well to receive unwelcome visitors—and no visitor is welcome. Only an occasional hardy schoolboy ventures near to watch Jean Poquelin being rowed by his one remaining slave, an old mute.

With time, though, developers come. They want to drain the marsh, fill in the canal, and run streets through Poquelin's property. The new American government will pay Poquelin for this land, which it wants in order to provide housing for the influx of Yankee immigrants.

Poquelin, however, does not want anyone encroaching on his property. He goes first to the governor and then to the municipal authorities, where, with growing irritation, he insists on his right to keep his land, but the official is adamant. Finally Poquelin departs, bestowing a shower of French curses on the Americans and their government.

After Poquelin leaves, the official wonders aloud why Poquelin objects to having the value of his property increased through drainage and development. His interpreter tells him that Poquelin does not want neighbors because he is a witch. One evening, the interpreter had been hunting in the swamps and had returned after dark. As he passed Poquelin's house he saw the old man walking, but Jean was not alone. Beside him was something that resembled a man but could not have been because it was too white.

Despite Poquelin's objections, the street is opened, the marsh drained, the canal filled. Snakes and alligators retreat, and in their place come new buildings, new settlers. Amid these changes, Poquelin clings to his old house and old ways, thereby increasing his reputation as a witch. If a woman dies, a child is lost, or a crop fails, Poquelin is blamed. Children taunt him in the street. A Building and Improvement Committee organizes to buy Poquelin's house.

Among the committee's members is the city official who heard the interpreter's ghost story. He suspects that the white figure is Poquelin's brother, who is being held in seclusion against his will. If the committee can prove that this is so, they can proceed against Poquelin and thereby get his property. White, the committee's secretary, is sent to spy.

The next day, shortly before dark, White steals onto the Poquelin property. He sees Jean and, shortly afterward, the white figure, from which comes the odor of death and decay. As soon as the two go inside, White prepares to leave. Then he hears voices, one belonging to Jean, the other hollow, unearthly. White flees.

Henceforth, the secretary becomes Poquelin's defender. He orders the children to leave Poquelin alone. He squelches every rumor about the old man and stands up for him at the committee's meetings. When a group of Creoles comes to taunt Poquelin with a noisy charivari, White confronts the mob and turns it away.

Hours later, toward morning, the noisemakers return, and this time White cannot stop them. Yet Poquelin has escaped their jeers; when they invade Poquelin's property, they find him dead beneath a tree, attended by his African mute. Chastened, the mob wants to leave, but White insists that its members attend the funeral to discover Poquelin's secret. As they watch, the slave leads a brown bull pulling a cart with the coffin, and behind walks Jacques Poquelin, a leper. As they go off into the swamp, everyone realizes how much Poquelin suffered and sacrificed to guard his brother's secret, the discovery of which would have led to their separation.

Themes and Meanings

In the first sentence of this story, Cable establishes the time and place of his story: "In the first decade of the present century, when the newly established American Government was the most hateful thing in Louisiana ... there stood, a short distance above what is now Canal Street ... an old colonial plantation-house half in ruin." In addition to giving the setting, Cable here establishes his theme, which is the clash of two cultures.

Representing the old world is Jean Poquelin, the aristocratic Creole. He lives in an old house that he refuses to tear down or modernize, despite the urging of his neighbors. He can speak some English but prefers to use French, even when he confronts American officials. Believing in a government by aristocracy rather than by bureaucracy, he goes directly to the governor with his problem: "I know not the new laws. I ham a Fr-r-rench-a-man! Fr-r-rench-a-man have something *aller au contraire*—he come at his *Gouverneur.*" A Creole goes to his governor because he believes in personal loyalty, in ties of community and kinship. Poquelin visits the graves of his parents every day, and this same impulse drives him to shield his brother so that no one will learn of his disease and force him to go to the leper colony.

Cable sympathizes with the plight of the Creole represented by Poquelin. He has White say that Poquelin was "a better man" than his persecutors. At the same time, though, Cable realizes that Poquelin's world is doomed. His house is decaying, and, so, too, is his brother. The aggressive, industrious Americans are physically transforming the city, bringing new values with them. They cannot understand why Poquelin should resist improvements to his property, since these will make money for him. Cash, not community or tradition, concerns them, and they corrupt the natives with their outlook. The lower-class Creoles stage the charivari, but only at the prompting of the Americans.

In the clash of cultures, the old falls before the new. Poquelin dies; the mute slave and Jacques retreat into the swamp, which is itself retreating before the onslaught of outsiders. The Poquelins have yielded to a more successful but less humane world.

Style and Technique

After the Civil War, local colorists across the country sought to preserve the landscape and habits of their section before progress erased their memory. Joel Chandler Harris, for example, recorded his "Uncle Remus" stories because he feared that black folklore would soon disappear. What Harris sought to do for black folklore, Cable did for French New Orleans. His goal was to preserve a sense of *jadis*, the world as it was in an earlier time. He paints a small, intimate city limited to "the few streets named for the Bourbon princes." Beyond are the marshes navigated by canoes paddled by slaves owned by French-speaking aristocrats.

Cable evokes a sense of nostalgia for this vanished era. Yet he looks at it realistically, recording it with the accuracy of a social scientist. When the Boston *Literary World* objected to Cable's use of dialect in "Jean-ah Poquelin" as unrealistic, Cable replied that he heard that patois every day. He notes the Creoles' clothes, mannerisms, customs (including the charivari), and landscape with careful detail. The conflict between Creole and American is also precisely rendered, as Cable shows the innovations so hateful to the older inhabitants: "trial by jury, American dances, anti-smuggling laws, . . . the printing of the Governor's proclamation in English."

Living in a period of rapid social and economic changes brought about by the Civil War, Cable looks back to an earlier yet similar time shortly after the Louisiana Purchase turned New Orleans from a French colony into an American outpost. "Jean-ah Poquelin" stands like a wrought-iron gate that grants one admission from the busy street into a quiet courtyard of the past.

Joseph Rosenblum

THE JEWBIRD

Author: Bernard Malamud (1914-1986)
Type of plot: Fable
Time of plot: c. 1961
Locale: New York City
First published: 1963

> *Principal characters:*
> HARRY COHEN, a Jewish frozen-foods salesman
> EDIE, his wife
> MORRIS (MAURIE), their ten-year-old son
> SCHWARTZ (THE JEWBIRD), a talking blackbird who comes to
> live with them

The Story

Harry and Edie Cohen, a lower-middle-class Jewish couple, live with their ten-year-old son, Morris (Maurie), in a small top-floor apartment on the Lower East Side of New York City. Cohen, a frozen-foods salesman, is angry and frustrated by his relative poverty, by his dying mother in the Bronx, and by the general mediocrity of his family and his life.

When the story opens, the Cohen family is sitting down to dinner on a hot August night, their recent attempt at a vacation cut short because Harry's mother had suddenly become ill, forcing them to return to the city. While this less-than-happy family is eating, a ruffled blackbird comes flying through the open window and plops down on their table in the middle of their food. Harry curses and swats at the bird, which flutters to the top of the kitchen door and amazes them by speaking in Yiddish and English. The bird explains that he is hungry and is running (and flying) from what he calls "Anti-Semeets" (anti-Semites). He says that he is not a crow but a "Jewbird," and he demonstrates this by immediately beginning to pray passionately, a prayer Edie and Maurie join, but not Harry.

The Jewbird says that his name is Schwartz, and he asks for a piece of herring and some rye bread rather than the lamb chop the family is eating. Harry insists that the bird eat out on the balcony, so Maurie takes Schwartz there to feed him and asks his father if the bird can stay. Harry says that Schwartz can remain only for the night, but he relents the next morning after Maurie cries at the prospect of losing his new friend.

The uneasy truce between Schwartz and Harry is threatened by Schwartz's requests for Jewish food and a Jewish newspaper as well as by his general garrulousness. Harry resents the bird and the fact that Schwartz calls himself Jewish. Harry makes Schwartz stay on the balcony in a wooden birdhouse even though the bird much prefers being inside with the family, where he can be warm and smell the cooking. When Harry brings home a bird feeder full of corn, Schwartz rejects it, explaining later to Edie that his digestive system has deteriorated with his old age; he prefers herring.

In the fall, Maurie returns to school and Schwartz becomes his tutor, helping him with his lessons. He becomes the boy's companion and friend, urging him to do his homework, listening and coaching while Maurie struggles with his violin, playing dominoes with Maurie when his chores are finished. When Maurie is sick, Schwartz even reads comic books to him (although the bird dislikes comics). Maurie's school grades improve (to nothing lower than C-minus) and Edie gives Schwartz credit for the improvement, but the bird denies the suggestion that he really had anything to do with Maurie's rising academic status.

Schwartz's unkempt appearance continues to annoy Harry until one night he picks a quarrel with the bird, complaining about the way it smells and the fact that its snoring keeps him awake. Harry curses the bird and is about to grab it when Maurie appears and the argument ends. From then on, Schwartz avoids Harry when he can, sleeping in his birdhouse on the balcony but longing to spend more time inside with the family. Edie suggests to Schwartz that there might be some reconciliation if he would take baths as Harry wishes, but Schwartz argues that he is "too old for baths." Schwartz claims that he smells the way he does because of what he eats; he asks why Harry smells.

As winter approaches, Schwartz's rheumatism bothers him more and more; he awakens stiff, barely able to move his wings. Harry wants the Jewbird to fly off for the winter, and he begins a secret campaign of harassment. Harry puts cat food in the bird's herring and pops paper bags on the balcony at night to keep Schwartz awake. As a final stroke, he buys a cat, something Maurie has always wanted, but the cat spends its days terrorizing Schwartz. The bird suffers greatly from all this harassment, losing feathers and becoming ever more nervous and unkempt, but somehow he endures.

The end comes on the day after Harry's ailing mother dies in her apartment in the Bronx. While Maurie and Edie are out at Maurie's violin lesson, Harry chases Schwartz with a broom. Harry grabs the bird and begins swinging it around his head; fighting for his life, Schwartz is able to bite Harry on the nose before Harry furiously pitches him out the window into the street below. Harry throws the birdhouse and feeder after him, then sits waiting with the broom, his nose throbbing painfully, for Schwartz's reappearance. The Jewbird does not return, however, and when Edie and Maurie come home Harry lies about what happened, saying that Schwartz bit him on the nose so he threw the bird out and it flew away. Edie and Maurie reluctantly accept Harry's version of the incident.

In the spring, after the snow has melted, Maurie looks for Schwartz and finds the bird's broken body in a vacant lot. "Who did it to you, Mr. Schwartz?" he cries; "Anti-Semeets," his mother tells him later.

Themes and Meanings

Bernard Malamud, like many Jewish writers, frequently examines in his fiction the changing attitudes Jews display about their religion and their heritage. In this story, readers see a Jewish family that is moving away from the orthodox Jewish traditions. Schwartz, who says he is a Jewbird, represents those traditions. His black color resembles the dark clothing traditionally worn by rabbis; he instantly falls into prayer on his arrival. He eats traditional Jewish food and generally scorns the meals the Cohens serve. Schwartz's values reflect the values of orthodox Judaism, values Harry Cohen, at least, has forgotten or is trying to forget. Schwartz becomes the equivalent of an aging Jewish relative: a grandfather or uncle for Maurie, a Jewish father for Harry. Ironically, Harry's real mother (Maurie's grandmother) is slowly dying in her own apartment, ignored except when her illness interrupts Harry's life. If she were brought into their household and cared for, she would probably help Maurie in the way that Schwartz does; presumably she would also irritate Harry in the way that the Jewbird does. Schwartz tells the Cohens that he is fleeing from anti-Semites, people who persecute Jews because of their religion and traditions. Edie Cohen's remark that anti-Semites killed Schwartz points out that Harry Cohen is a kind of anti-Semite himself, although he is probably not aware of it. He has turned his back on his religion and his heritage and has become in turn a bitter and frustrated human being.

Style and Technique

Malamud subtly builds his story toward the climax found in the final paragraphs. The fact that Harry Cohen's mother is ill, yet living alone nearby, is mentioned in the first paragraph but allowed to remain in the background until the end of the story, when Harry attacks the bird the day after the death of his mother. Presumably Schwartz is at that point a symbol of the Jewish parent Harry has essentially ignored and allowed to die alone. By throwing the bird out the window, Harry is able to exorcise the guilt he may be feeling about his treatment of his mother.

Malamud uses dialogue to establish Schwartz's Jewishness ("If you haven't got matjes, I'll take schmaltz") and to make this talking bird seem perfectly human. The fact that Schwartz can read comic books, play dominoes, or coach Maurie on the violin seems quite plausible because of the bird's conversational abilities. By the point in the story that Schwartz is being urged to take a bath, he seems simply to be one of the family, an elderly relative, and not a bird at all. His politeness ("Mr. Cohen, if you'll pardon me") only accentuates his human qualities. Conversely, Harry's language, his profanity and his basic rudeness ("One false move and he's out on his drumsticks"), underscores his own lack of humanity. There is no logical reason for his intense hatred of Schwartz, as there is no reason to call the bird names and swear at it the way he does. Schwartz, after all, brings much to Maurie's life and asks for only a little food and warmth in return. It is through Harry's anger and his begrudging attitude toward Schwartz that Malamud displays the real character of this Jewish frozen-foods salesman, a man who has lost his heritage and ignored the cries for help of his own people.

In the final paragraphs of the story, the hints Malamud has been dropping fall into place. Edie Cohen realizes that although Schwartz told them he was fleeing from "Anti-Semeets," his death was the result of an encounter with anti-Semites, the Cohen family itself. Edie and Maurie, the more sensitive members of this family, recognize and regret their failings; Harry Cohen presumably will never again recognize the lessons of his faith, whether they are delivered by humans or by birds with human souls.

Don Richard Cox

JIM BAKER'S BLUEJAY YARN

Author: Mark Twain (Samuel Langhorne Clemens, 1835-1910)
Type of plot: Tall tale
Time of plot: c. 1860
Locale: The California Mother Lode country
First published: 1879

Principal character:
JIM BAKER, a California hermit

The Story

"Jim Baker's Bluejay Yarn" was first published as chapter 3 of Mark Twain's travel narrative, *A Tramp Abroad* (1880). In that version, the actual narrative is preceded by an introduction, which appears at the end of chapter 2, in which the narrator of *A Tramp Abroad* introduces Jim Baker as "a middle-aged, simple-hearted miner who had lived in a lonely corner of California among the woods and mountains a good many years, and had studied the ways of his only neighbors, the beasts and the birds, until he believed he could accurately translate any remark they made." Also in the introductory section, Jim Baker elaborates on his high opinion of jays, offering the opinion that they are "just as much a human as you be," and concluding that "a jay will lie, a jay will steal, a jay will deceive, a jay will betray; and four times out of five, a jay will go back on his solemnest promise." The narrator affirms that he knows this to be true, since Jim Baker told him so himself, thus establishing his own naïveté and gullibility. This beginning establishes a "frame" for the story.

Some editors print the introductory material as part of "Jim Baker's Bluejay Yarn," while others include only the material from chapter 3 of *A Tramp Abroad* which is discussed below. Since the story materially benefits from establishing Jim Baker's character and his views on jays, it is best to read a complete version.

Jim Baker's "yarn" cannot be captured in a simple summary of events, because, as Mark Twain pointed out in an essay entitled "How to Tell a Story," a "humorous story depends for its effect upon the *manner* of the telling," rather than on its contents. Thus, the events of the story are unimpressive unless presented with the droll style of the master storyteller. Even when read aloud, the yarn falls flat unless it is artfully presented. Being such a master raconteur, Jim Baker must be "heard" as he elaborates this tale of an excessively ambitious bluejay whose reach far exceeded his grasp.

Baker begins in a matter-of-fact way by establishing his authority as an expert on bluejay behavior by setting the story at a time in the past "when I first begun to understand jay language correctly." Being the last remaining soul in the region, Baker no doubt gained his knowledge of jays by doing just what he describes in the story: watching bluejays from his front porch. In fact, he seems to have nothing else in particular to occupy his time, so on this Sunday morning, Baker says, "I was sitting out here in front of my cabin, with my cat, taking the sun, and looking at the blue hills, and listening to the leaves rustling so lonely in the trees, and thinking of the home away yonder in the states, that I hadn't heard from in thirteen years, when a bluejay lit on that house, with an acorn in his mouth, and says, 'Hello, I reckon I've struck something.'" In this way, Twain not only establishes the "authenticity" of the story but also subtly characterizes the narrator and his way of life.

As Baker watches, the jay becomes intrigued by a knothole he has discovered in the roof of the abandoned cabin on which he is perched. After an elaborate examination to satisfy himself that it is indeed a hole that he has discovered, the jay drops an acorn into the opening and awaits the sound of it hitting bottom. When he hears nothing after a proper interval, he seems first curious, then surprised, and finally indignant. Baker is able to infer this because, as he told the reader at the outset, he understands jay language. In this context, the elaborate description given of the jay's behavior is Baker's way of describing the bird's language. "He cocked his head to one side, shut one eye and put the other one to the hole, like a 'possum looking down a jug; then he glanced up with his bright eyes, gave a wink or two with his wings—which signifies gratification, you understand—and says, 'It looks like a hole, it's located like a hole—blamed if I don't believe it *is* a hole.'" For the remainder of the yarn, Baker alternates between elaborate descriptions of bluejay behavior and interpretations of the meaning of the activity.

The first acorn having been lost in the recesses of the hole, the jay quickly fetches another, only to drop it in with the same results as the first. He tries to drop acorns, then quickly peep in the hole to see where they fall, but this technique, too, is unsuccessful. After a marvelous bout of cursing, he finally concludes that this is a hole of a kind that is new in his experience, but his frustration only strengthens his resolve. "Well," he says, "you're a long hole, and a deep hole, and a mighty singular hole altogether—but I've started to fill you, and I'm d——d if I *don't* fill you, if it takes a hundred years!"

The jay works himself into a frenzy dropping acorns into the hole, but again with no noticeable results. This time his cursing attracts another jay, and the two hold a noisy conference on the ridgepole. The second jay, unable to make any more sense of the mysterious hole than the first, "called in more jays; then more and more, till pretty soon this whole region 'peared to have a blue flush about it." All the jays offer their opinions, leading to a cacophony of disputation. This continues until one old jay eventually finds his way through the open door of the house and finds all the acorns scattered over the floor.

The other jays' curiosity and interest now turns to derision, and they join in laughing at their silly companion. Baker finishes his story by telling the reader that "they roosted around here on the housetop and the trees for an hour, and guffawed over that thing like human beings," then concludes in defense of these silly creatures, "it ain't no use to tell me a bluejay hasn't got a sense of humor, because I know better. And memory, too. They brought jays here from all over the United States to look down that hole, every summer for three years." Other birds came also, and all saw the humor except an owl from Nova Scotia who had come west to visit "the Yo Semite" and stopped by on his way home. "He said he couldn't see anything funny in it. But then he was a good deal disappointed about Yo Semite, too."

Themes and Meanings

At the beginning of *The Adventures of Huckleberry Finn* (1884), Mark Twain threatens to shoot anyone looking for a moral in his book. He would probably say much the same about a search for themes and meanings in "Jim Baker's Bluejay Yarn." Unlike the animal fables of Aesop, Jean de La Fontaine, or Joel Chandler Harris, Twain's animal tales are not classic fables meant to illustrate some moral point. Though the bluejays are described in very human terms, and though their behavior parallels that of human beings, one should not impose some heavy moral implication on the story. For Twain, this type of narrative was an art form more closely related to performance than to serious literature. Its humor is its point, and that humor lies more in the style of telling the tale than in the material itself.

Style and Technique

In "How to Tell a Story," Twain observes that "the humorous story is strictly a work of art—high and delicate art—and only an artist can tell it; but no art is necessary in telling the comic and witty story; anybody can do it. The art of telling a humorous story—understand, I mean by word of mouth, not print—was created in America, and has remained at home." The distinction Twain makes between comic and witty stories—that is, stories depending on a "punch line" or clever play on words—and the "humorous story" is an important one for appreciating the artistry of "Jim Baker's Bluejay Yarn," as well as for understanding the high value Twain placed on humor as an indigenous American art form.

The humorous story depends for its effect almost entirely on the artistry of a master storyteller. Foremost among the techniques necessary to tell such a story effectively is the characterization of a narrative voice appropriate to the material. Such stories, Twain says, are "told gravely; the teller does his best to conceal the fact that he even dimly suspects that there is anything funny about it." Properly told, the humorous story results in "a performance which is thoroughly charming and delicious. This is art—and fine and beautiful, and only a master can encompass it."

Mark Twain was himself such a master storyteller, as he demonstrated in his career as a comic lecturer. From his work on the stage, as well as from firsthand contact with other storytellers, he mastered not only the art of performing stories but also the art of writing them down as published tales. Few writers have recorded the oral tradition on the page as well as Twain did in such pieces as "Jim Baker's Bluejay Yarn." Reading the story tends to be anticlimactic unless one can, either aloud or in the imagination, read it so that Jim Baker's voice is heard. In the hands of a fine performer, this simple tale of some silly bluejays can still produce the laughter that it did when Twain himself told it to his audiences.

William E. Grant

JOHN NAPPER SAILING THROUGH THE UNIVERSE

Author: John Gardner (1933-1982)
Type of plot: Psychological realism
Time of plot: The late 1960's and early 1970's
Locale: London, Paris, and the United States
First published: 1974

> *Principal characters:*
> JOHN NAPPER, the protagonist, a painter
> THE NARRATOR, a writer
> JOAN, the narrator's wife, a composer
> LUCY, the narrator's eight-year-old daughter

The Story

The narrator, a writer who teaches in a rural American university, is driven home from a party one night by his wife Joan. Feeling old and perceiving death all around him, and goaded by his wife's nostalgia for John Napper, a successful painter they once knew, the narrator tells the story of his and his family's experience of the painter John Napper.

The narrator became acquainted with Napper when the latter served for a time as artist-in-residence at the narrator's university. John Napper had a commanding physical presence despite his old age: bohemian, big, and energetic. His enthusiasm for everything—including Irish music, which he sang with zest, accompanying himself on a guitar—was unflagging. No intellectual debate fazed him: To both sides he would say, "Exactly" or "Marvelous" (his favorite words), impartially, as it were. For example, the narrator believes that Welsh music is better than Irish, and Napper would find his choice "marvelous," while at the same time expressing—too jovially to be gainsaid—his distaste for Welsh music and his admiration for Irish music.

After Napper returns to Paris, the narrator's wife finds herself unable to compose music and wants to visit Napper and his wife Pauline, a mosaic artist. The narrator, who always wears a black hat and has a cynical outlook on the world, and is both repelled and attracted by Napper's optimism, as well as passionately hostile to any kind of fakery, manages to get a grant which finances his family's visit to the Nappers.

They find a young couple staying in the Nappers' Paris studio. The young man is an American, a cartoonist, and he shows the narrator and his wife some of John Napper's old paintings, which he found under the bed. The paintings are violent and gloomy, in surprising contrast to the paintings of Napper's old age, which invariably feature flowers. Learning that the Nappers are staying in London, the narrator and his family visit the Nappers in their apartment there.

When confronted by the information that the narrator has seen his old paintings in Paris, John Napper shows him a selection of similar paintings, mentioning that some of his works have been lost along the way. They are all pessimistic and foreboding. With his typical energy he judges his artistic past "Amazing!"—as though it were something from which he had miraculously escaped. At this point, the narrator's daughter Lucy asks Napper to do her portrait for seven cents, and Napper agrees. The narrator's son Joel is jealous of his sister because of this, so Napper promises to show him the armor in the Wallace Collection in London.

After he does this, Napper sketches Lucy in the courtyard of the building. That night in the pub in the narrator's hotel, Napper and the narrator drink beer and sing for the Irish clientele. The narrator sings gloomy Welsh songs and plays his banjo; Napper plays his guitar and sings sentimental Irish songs, about which the audience is enthusiastic.

The narrator has been writing an epic poem about the Greek mythic hero Jason, and he shows it to Napper in his studio. They discuss epics for a while, with Napper focusing on the destruction often featured in epics. They are interrupted by a girl—a former student of Napper in Paris—and before the narrator can read her any of his epic, the couple staying in Napper's Paris studio appear, thus effectively cutting off the narrator's performance.

The next day, the narrator does manage to read some of his epic to Napper. Napper continues to paint after this and talks about music and painting, which excites the narrator more than the Scotch he has been drinking. (The narrator drinks a considerable amount of Scotch in the story; Napper, hardly anything.) Napper has been working on his painting of Lucy, and the narrator, looking at a large seascape by Napper on the wall, is reminded of its similarity to Joseph Turner's work and of Napper once telling him that Turner led a double life as a sailor and a miserly-seeming philanthropist, with a separate wife for each role. Napper, while he and the narrator are still in the studio that evening, insists that artists are piggish, especially when they are young (that is, that they are unscrupulous in their passions), and that he is glad to be much less so now that he is old. The narrator observes a recent painting of Napper's wife Pauline. Among a profusion of light and flowers, Pauline has a funereal look, and at the edges of the painting the gaiety of its tone is vaguely sinister. Lucy's painting is also gay, but there is a sly look in her eyes, whereas Pauline's face has a hieratic quality. Quite drunk by now, the narrator understands that Napper, in searching for his own vision of light in things as they are, found darkness instead and, rather than yield to it, decided to invent the world itself in his paintings—a world of light and gaiety.

Napper and his wife accompany the narrator to a restaurant where the narrator's wife, Joan, has been waiting for her husband to arrive. She has already eaten by the time they get there, and she is angry. Napper soothes her with flattery and a story, after which the narrator gets into a fistfight with (ironically) a Welshman over Samuel Beckett, a writer famous for his metaphysical gloom. Joan runs out, followed by Pauline, and the narrator and Napper end up in a taxi together. Napper, with his usual paradoxical enthusiasm, praises the narrator's violent stupidity and his own insane optimism.

Themes and Meanings

At the heart of this story is the conflict between optimism and pessimism. How does one face a world that seems to be ruled by chaos in the end? Both John Napper and the narrator see this chaos. Napper had hoped to find a positive meaning in the world when he was young, but all he saw in his search was the destruction in the world and the violence of the search itself, both of which he embodied in his paintings. The narrator, unlike Napper, is still searching, and so far he has not gotten beyond the signs of destruction, his vision of which he expresses through his taste for gloomy things and his destructive behavior—his drinking, for example, and the songs he sings about tragedy, as well as the hostile tricks he plays on the hypocrite who replaces Napper at the university and the fight he gets into at the end of the story. The narrator, in fact, is at the level that Napper was when he was young.

To be sure, the narrator is a pessimist, and John Napper is an optimist. It is more complex than that, however, for the narrator is a pessimist who yearns to be an optimist, while Napper is an optimist who refuses to give in to his essential pessimism. He has decided that if chaos informs the world, he will re-create the world from scratch, as it were, in his art. He will make the world a mask that hides the face of chaos. The irony here, as the narrator sees, is that some of the chaos comes through the mask in innuendos, and it is this which gives his paintings an air of mystery and makes them unique. If there is something unreal, even fake, about Napper's optimism, though, the narrator is still attracted to it. Napper's passionate enthusiasm, including its ragged edges, amounts to an inspiration for the narrator and his wife, who find life boring and depressing without him near. They are able to overcome their blocks and create when they visit Napper in London—the narrator continuing an epic of search and his wife composing music for the flute.

Finally, the story is about vision and how it is acquired. All the adult characters in the story are artists, to whom vision is essential. The artist, the story says, uses art to find a vision of the world's meaning and record what he sees along the way. Napper arrives at a vision that belongs only to him, and it suggests that the artist is like God creating the world to suit his own desires, as well as his knowledge of the conflict between his personal will and the blind and sinister energy governing phenomena. The narrator, on the other hand, creates an art that dramatizes the search for a positive vision—indeed creates the story "John Napper Sailing Through the Universe," which shows his vision of all the phases of the artist's vision itself.

Style and Technique

Since vision is so important to the story, and since the protagonist is a painter, imagery is John Gardner's chief tool in projecting the story's meaning. Light and darkness figure prominently throughout. Both are used to show the two sides of John Napper's vision. Darkness predominates in his early paintings, emphasizing pessimism and the violence of Napper's search for order and the violence in the world, especially the human world. Light predominates in his later paintings, underscoring the willfulness of his optimism and enthusiasm. Light is also embedded in the image of Napper's hair, which is wild and white and often mentioned, and is meant to suggest a light in the darkness, optimism against a background of pessimism. Light is further inferred in the narrator's epic poem, which is about the mythic hero Jason; the golden fleece he searches for corresponds to the light of a happy vision for which the narrator is searching.

There are other images in the story which belong to the contrast between light and dark, such as the bright flowers which are a staple of Napper's paintings, and the black hat which the narrator wears everywhere, the dark house and landscape readers see him in at the beginning, and the tomblike hotel he is staying in at the end.

Besides its use in dramatizing the meaning of the story, imagery is a mainstay of characterization in it. It is often through imagery that the characters are revealed, with Napper's hair, bright eyes, untidy clothes, and gaily sinister paintings pointing to his mind and personality, and the narrator's hat and Scotch pointing to his.

Finally, it should be pointed out that this story is autobiographical to an unusual degree. The narrator is clearly John Gardner himself, at work on the book which eventually became *Jason and Medeia* (1973). Gardner's first wife was named Joan; their children appear in the story as well. The title character, the painter John Napper, illustrated Gardner's novel *The Sunlight Dialogues* (1972). Here, as in other stories in the collection in which "John Napper Sailing Through the Universe" appeared, *The King's Indian* (1974), Gardner is playing with the conventions of fiction, testing them, experimenting with them. Only a reader with an intimate knowledge of Gardner's life— and John Napper's life—could say with authority where the autobiography stops and the "fiction" begins.

Mark McCloskey

THE JOLLY CORNER

Author: Henry James (1843-1916)
Type of plot: Psychological mystery
Time of plot: Late nineteenth or early twentieth century
Locale: New York City
First published: 1908

>   *Principal characters:*
>   SPENCER BRYDON, the protagonist, an owner of property in
>   New York City who has lived abroad for many years
>   ALICE STAVERTON, an old friend of Brydon
>   MRS. MULDOON, the housekeeper for Brydon

The Story

After an absence of thirty-three years, Spencer Brydon returns from abroad to New York City. He makes this dramatic move in order to oversee improvements to his property, which consists of two houses that have been the source of his financial independence throughout his life. One is in the process of being converted into apartments, while the other, the "jolly corner" of the title, is the house in which Brydon grew up and which he therefore is loathe to alter in any way.

In the course of conversations with Miss Staverton, Brydon reflects upon what sort of person he might have become had he not chosen to tramp about the world for most of his adult life and had stayed instead in his native United States. Miss Staverton has her views, which do not entirely coincide with those of Brydon. It transpires that Brydon harbors a desire to confront what he terms his "alter ego," the self he might have been. Miss Staverton reveals that, somewhat incomprehensibly, she has already seen this other self—in her dreams. She, however, declines to disclose what she has seen.

Brydon is in the habit of coming to the jolly corner in the evenings after he has dined out and before retiring to the hotel where he lodges (the house itself remaining empty for the moment). In the course of his nocturnal prowlings about the premises, he hopes to encounter his alter ego, who, in Brydon's view of things, haunts the house as a ghost. While stalking the creature, Brydon one night discovers that he himself has been turned into the prey, that the ghost is following him.

The climax to the tale occurs one evening when Brydon comes once more to the house, wanders about more or less as usual, but discovers in retracing his steps that one door, which he believed he had left open, has been mysteriously closed, and another that had been closed has been opened. As Brydon retreats carefully down the staircase toward the front door and escape from the pursuing specter, he pauses on the final landing, only to become aware of a vague shape in his view. The shape assumes human form, a man with a monocle, dressed in evening clothes, whose face is hidden by white-gloved hands with two of the fingers missing. As the ghost drops his hands revealing his face, Brydon is shocked to recognize someone or something totally other than himself—a ghost who is not, so far as Brydon can discern, his other self at all. As the ghost aggressively advances, Brydon retreats and finally faints away at the bottom of the staircase. He awakes to discover the face of Miss Staverton, who had dreamed of Brydon's confrontation and had been thus prompted to come to the jolly corner to save him. Brydon protests that the ghost was not his other self, a view which Miss Staverton reinforces with "And he isn't—no, he isn't—*you!*" at the tale's close.

Themes and Meanings

As the comparative brevity of the incidents indicates, the interest of "The Jolly Corner" lies primarily elsewhere than in the structure of its plot. As is not uncommon in the later James, both in the novels and in the tales, the amount of incident is severely circumscribed, while the space given to reflection and elaboration on the inner states of the characters (here only one character, Spencer Brydon) is correspondingly expanded to such an extent that the story is virtually consumed by this psychological interest. If one compares "The Jolly Corner" with, for example, the earlier *The Turn of the Screw* (1898), surely James's most famous ghost story, one sees immediately how comparatively slender is the thread of the plot in the later story. All the interest and all the importance in this tale reside in its disclosure of Brydon's thoughts, his fears and anxieties, his inability to confront the ghost of his former, or other, self.

The two major symbolic figures in the story are the house—Brydon's "jolly corner"—and the ghost. Both are described in some detail, and it is in the intricacy of their symbolic resonance that the key to this story lies. The house is of several stories and contains many rooms, each of which possesses a door. The psychoanalytic dimension of this feature is surely not inapposite (regardless of whether James knew about psychoanalysis proper—and there is some evidence to indicate that he did). Entering a closed room, according to psychoanalysis, symbolizes unlocking previously suppressed memories of one's mental life. The fact that James himself, in one of his autobiographical volumes written not long after "The Jolly Corner," recounts a dream in which he recovers the world of his youth by passing through a locked door suggests that he was perfectly aware of the psychic implications of this aspect of his story. Brydon's search for his other self, what he might have been had he remained in America and pursued, as he likely would have done, a career in business, is a search into previously unexplored corners of his own mind and self.

The other major symbol is simply that self which Brydon does finally confront near the end of the tale—despite the fact that he stubbornly refuses to recognize himself in the visage of the ghost. The figure's opulent dress (white gloves, evening clothes, monocle—all indicate his wealth, the fact that, as Brydon observes to Miss Staverton, this figure is a millionaire), along with his damaged extremity, does not at first put Brydon off. He has already observed that by abandoning New York City, he blighted or stunted the proper development of his other self. Yet when the specter lowers his hands to reveal his face, Brydon not only is appalled at the sight (the details of what he sees are never given), but also steadfastly refuses to acknowledge the ghost's identity with himself. It is not he, but, as the story pointedly puts it, "a stranger." This refusal to recognize the other, to admit that what one might have been (or indeed, in strict psychoanalytic terms, what one invariably *is*), constitutes a classic example of repression, a symptomatic defense of the integrity of the self against the threat of its dissolution, the alternative being classic schizophrenia, the splitting of the self into two (and possibly more) warring and irreconcilable parts. James's choice of an ending reasserting the mental health and wholeness of his hero (in contrast to the rather different handling of this motif by his friend Robert Louis Stevenson in *The Strange Case of Dr. Jekyll and Mr. Hyde*, 1886) signifies what has often been noted as characteristic of his writing and his project as a man: the necessity for some level of repression and control over the darker impulses of the psyche if human society is to continue to function, possibly even to prosper. James's faith in the power of the imagination to maintain its balance in the face of threatening influences and disruptive forces is nowhere more apparent than in Brydon's shutting out of the ghost he cannot recognize as himself if he is to remain who he is.

Style and Technique

The other notable feature of this, one of James's last completed stories, is its characteristic density of syntax. "The Jolly Corner" provides an excellent example of that "late style" which has captivated James's admirers and infuriated his critics. Several explanations have been offered for this gradual shift in James's stylistic practice toward greater and greater intricacy and attenuation. (One of the least convincing is Leon Edel's assertion that this shift was caused by James's change from composing in longhand to dictating to a secretary.) Whatever the reasons for the markedly increased difficulty of James's writings from the turn of the century onward, one thing is indisputable: The attenuation of direct statement, the endless qualification and hedging around a point, serves to reinforce one's sense of the tentative and uncertain quality in the thinking of James's characters. The whole point about Spencer Brydon is that by leaving the United States he has abandoned that life of active and vigorous intervention in the world (figured here in the possibility that he would have pursued a career in business) in order to live more or less freely (if narrowly) and unencumbered by the necessity to act directly or decisively. James's stylistic practice thus motivates and effectively realizes a character whose *raison d'être* is precisely not to be decisive, powerful, direct. Brydon's incapacity to decide who he is or might have been, his tentativeness in confronting his alter ego (despite his manifest desire to meet this creature) is in part the result of the very circumlocutions, the syntactic irresolution of James's style. Whatever may have been the motivation of James's later style, it would seem that here at least the fit between thematic focus and linguistic practice is most intimate.

Michael Sprinker

JORDAN'S END

Author: Ellen Glasgow (1873-1945)
Type of plot: Psychological realism
Time of plot: The 1890's
Locale: Virginia
First published: 1923

Principal characters:
THE NARRATOR, a young doctor, called to Jordan's End to examine the master of the house
JUDITH YARDLY JORDAN, the wife of Alan Jordan, mistress of Jordan's End
FATHER PETERKIN, a gnarled old man, who helps his son sharecrop land on Jordan's End

The Story

As the story opens, the narrator, a young doctor beginning practice in an isolated section of Virginia near the turn of the century, is on his way to Jordan's End, a country estate at some remove from a small town. He has been sent for to examine Alan Jordan, the owner of the place. As he goes along in his horse and buggy, he encounters a fork in the road: One branch of its gives indications of having been well traveled; the other, deeply rutted but covered with grass and overhanging leaves, appears to have been little used. As he ponders which road to take, a voice from the bushes by the side of the main trail advises him to take the well-traveled road if he is going to the country store. Emerging from the woods, a stooped old man appears in the road, and when the doctor inquires the way to Jordan's End, the fellow points to the less used trail and says that if the doctor is going in that direction he would like to ride along.

As the two travel the road to Jordan's End, Father Peterkin, in response to the young doctor's questions, provides information about the ill fortune which has beset the master and mistress of the place. It appears that ever since the Civil War the fortunes of the Jordan family have been in severe decline. Now, according to Father Peterkin, young Alan Jordan has been taken ill and the management of the place is in the hands of his wife, Judith, the mother of their nine-year-old boy. Aside from a few black field hands, the only other personages at Jordan's End are three old women related to Alan by blood or marriage.

When the doctor arrives at the Jordan place, he is seized by a kind of foreboding, a feeling that is intensified by the appearance of the house itself—a crumbling Georgian manor house, with rotting eaves and windows without panes. Everywhere there is evidence of deterioration, of decline. His conversation with Father Peterkin provided him with information about the history of insanity among the male members of the Jordan family, but nevertheless he is unprepared for the sight of this relic.

Receiving no answer to his knock upon the main door of the house, he proceeds toward the rear and encounters there Judith Jordan, the mistress of Jordan's End. He is very much taken by her haunting beauty. She welcomes him and acquaints him briefly with the recent illness affecting her husband. Alan Jordan is confined in an upstairs room of the house and is being watched over by two of the few remaining field hands. Implicit in her depiction of the trouble afflicting the master of the house is that he has lost his mind and must be watched constantly. The doctor accompanies her to the room, where Alan Jordan sits aimlessly in a chair, flanked by the two servants, playing listlessly with the fringe of a plaid shawl that has been draped around his shoulders. At a glance, the doctor sees that Jordan is "helplessly lost in the wilderness of the insane."

Informed that a famous alienist, Dr. Carstairs, is coming from Baltimore the next day to examine Jordan, the young doctor provides an opiate for use in sedating the patient should he become violent. He leaves Jordan's End, indicating to Judith Jordan that he will come again after Dr. Carstairs has made his visit.

On the following day, he encounters the doctor in the town as the celebrated alienist is about to board the train. In a brief conversation, he learns that Jordan's situation is hopeless; Jordan will not recover his faculties. Later that day, an old black man from Jordan's End comes to town and asks the doctor to return with him. When he arrives at Jordan's End, one of the old women greets him at the door and sends him upstairs, where he encounters the body of Alan Jordan, attended only by his wife and son, and being prepared for burial by two old women. Still young, handsome, and in his physical prime, the corpse of Alan Jordan moves the doctor emotionally. He realizes that Judith Jordan has administered the sedative in a dose sufficient to end the life of her husband and to end her own suffering.

The young woman who had come to Jordan's End as a bride only ten years ago and who had watched the result of generations of intermarriage destroy her beloved husband, as it had destroyed his father and his father's father and beyond, must now go on alone. The doctor, torn apart inside by the agony he knows the lovely, still young woman must feel, asks her if she wishes him to come back to Jordan's End again. She demurs, and he knows that she will never send for him. As the tale ends, the doctor drives off in his buggy through the gloomy woods.

Themes and Meanings

The title of this story is deliberately ambiguous: Jordan's End is both the name of the house and a declaration about the fate of its owners. As does

Edgar Allan Poe's House of Usher, the condition of the physical place wherein resides the latest in the line of Jordans mirrors the condition of that line, and by extension, the decline of a way of life. (This theme was taken up by William Faulkner a few years after the publication of this story.) Yet Glasgow holds out some hope for the future in the person of Judith Jordan. Judith tells the doctor, "I must go on." The reader believes she will, heartrending though her plight may be.

It was narrow-mindedness born of pride, ethnocentrism born of ignorance, that led families such as the Jordans to the kind of inbreeding that produced insanity in generation after generation. The way of life, the way of thinking, and the refusal to admit that things had changed—all were causes for the decline of Southern aristocracy. These two young people, so much in love, had come to Jordan's End full of hope and had seen that hope dashed by the onset of Alan's mental illness. It is not, however, the house that destroys these young lives; rather, they are destroyed by their unswerving allegiance to a belief system which is false at its very base. In some sense, then, this is really a kind of ghost story. It is the ghost of the past which haunts the corridors of Jordan's End. It is a belief in this ghost that deranges succeeding generations of Jordan males.

Style and Technique

The use of the first-person narrator, a young, impressionable physician who is just starting out in life, provides the author with the opportunity to reveal to her readers a tale which impacts upon the doctor's sensibility. He is both sobered and saddened by what he encounters at Jordan's End, and because he represents a new generation, a kind of new Southerner, his "getting of wisdom" makes a statement about the future as well as the past. Moreover, Glasgow's use of the physical description of the road leading to Jordan's End and of the house and the grounds—and of the dimly lit room in which young Alan Jordan is confined—contribute to the sense of foreboding, and to the picture of decay. Adding to this is the raw autumn weather in which the story takes place. Although the story is a flashback with the narrator in the present recollecting something that happened some thirty years ago, Glasgow trades upon the reader's awareness that there are many old houses at some remove from towns everywhere—houses that would yield, if they could only speak, similar tales of decline and fall.

Dale H. Ross

JORINDA AND JORINDEL

Author: Mavis Gallant (1922-   )
Type of plot: Psychological realism
Time of plot: Early twentieth century, probably the 1920's
Locale: A lake not far from Montreal, Canada
First published: 1959

Principal characters:

> IRMGARD, the protagonist, a seven-year-old girl
> FREDDY (ALFRED MARCEL DUFRESNE), a poor French-Canadian orphan boy
> BRADLEY, Irmgard's cousin from Boston, who is ten years old
> MRS. BLOODWORTH, a drunken wedding guest
> GERMAINE, Irmgard's French-Canadian nursemaid
> MRS. QUEEN, the English cook

The Story

In the course of a summer at the lake, Irmgard, a rather spoiled child of an upper-middle-class Canadian family, loses some of the innocence and charm of early childhood. In doing so she becomes, regrettably, more like her smug parents and her rather unpleasant cousin Bradley.

Like most children, Irmgard is a secret observer of adult life. Her parents have parties that sometimes drag on into the next day. The most curious leftover guest at a recent wedding party was a drunken woman named Mrs. Bloodworth, who spent a noisy night practicing the Charleston and possibly getting incorporated into the little girl's dream as a witch—that is, the witch that in the dream captured Jorinda and reached out to turn Jorindel into a bird.

The child is a bit confused in her folklore, since in the Grimms' fairy tale, it is Jorinda, the girl, who is turned into a bird, while Jorindel, the boy, stands paralyzed as a stone. When her cousin Bradley, who visits all during August, goes back to Boston, he is said to have "fallen out of summer like a stone." At the beginning of the story, it is Bradley whom she identifies with the Jorindel of her dream. By the end of the story, however, she has decided that it was probably her local friend Freddy who was spirited away by the wicked witch of the forest.

Freddy is a poor French-Canadian orphan who works on his uncle's farm for food and shelter. He was reared in an orphanage until age seven, when he was considered old enough to work. He was never taught to read or write or even to eat politely, but he has visions of the Virgin Mary. Freddy is quite entranced with Irmgard, who taught him to swim and knows intuitively what he is thinking.

When Bradley, the ten-year-old cousin, shows up for a visit, all that is changed. The inarticulate Freddy stands on the sidelines waiting for an invitation to join the two children. When Bradley asks who he is, Irmgard disclaims knowing him, not once but three times.

Freddy disappears and Irmgard does not even think about him until Bradley leaves almost a month later. Bradley has proved to be a rather unsatisfactory companion, since he is very self-centered and contemptuous of girls. He is big, healthy, and stubborn, however, quite like Irmgard herself in that regard, and claims officiously that he is going to be a mechanical and electrical engineer when he grows up. Irmgard has only aspired to be a veterinarian or a nun. By comparison to the pair of them, Freddy looks old, undersized, and undernourished.

When Irmgard at last remembers Freddy again and goes to find him, the rapport they once knew is gone. She no longer knows what he is thinking, and he has discovered that he can live without her. He agrees to go swimming with her, not at her place but at the dirty public beach where she has been forbidden to go. Since they have no swimming suits, he swims naked and she with bloomers on.

Mrs. Queen, the cook, says that Freddy will be sent back to the orphan asylum. Irmgard remembers her dream, however, and says that Freddy was sent on an errand into the forest and got lost. After all, there is a witch there who changes children into birds.

Themes and Meanings

On one level, this story reveals the peculiar combination of fact and fancy that constitutes the mental life of children. On another level, it is social criticism of a class society which perpetuates callousness and prejudice. Although Irmgard may project the idea of witch on the outsider, Mrs. Bloodworth, because of her bizarre behavior, the real witches who destroy childhood are the adults who perpetuate pride and prejudice and who condone neglect.

Differences in language conveniently underline the distinctions between British Canadians and French Canadians. Irmgard unconsciously learns this distinction close at hand in the kitchen, where she is more at home, no doubt, than in the drawing room with her parents. Mrs. Queen, the chronically complaining cook who used to serve the upper classes in England and has absorbed some of their snobbishness, disdains to learn French. Germaine, the loving but somewhat simple nursemaid, speaks nothing but French. Though the two servants are necessarily much in each other's company, they do not communicate. Irmgard, as a small child who unconsciously learns to understand French from her nurse, simply accepts this odd situation among grown-ups as a matter of course. Her experience of losing the ability to communicate with her friend Freddy further suggests the consequences of such class divisions.

The relationship between Germaine and Irmgard is also changing, and that link with the "other world" of French Canadians will soon be broken. Irmgard will outgrow the need for a nursemaid and become more like her cousin Bradley, who never sees visions and explains everything with the formula, "Well, this is the way it is." The imaginary world, shared to some extent by Irmgard, Germaine, and Freddy, will fade away into the seemingly factual but severely limited perception of middle-class society.

The implied criticism of the adult generation is not, however, exclusively directed against the middle class. Freddy's uncle appears only once in the story, but surely he must bear some kind of responsibility for the almost barbaric state of little Freddy. He gives him shelter only when the child can work for his keep, and apparently makes no effort at all to educate him. When Irmgard shows up at the uncle's farm to renew her acquaintance with Freddy, the boy's uncle curses her in obscene language. Both children are shocked, Irmgard because she does not understand these words, Freddy because he does. Although Freddy's return to the orphanage in Montreal may have something to do with disapproval of the children's swim at the public beach, that was apparently the pattern of his days, anyway. The uncle obviously does not care to be burdened with a child when his services are not valuable. Freddy, in any case, is the loser, since he has had a glimpse of a gentler life which is denied him.

Nevertheless, this is not an exercise in social realism where all evil derives from social structures. Irmgard's triple denial of her friend, vaguely suggestive of Peter's denial of Christ, is a flaw not directly attributable to social conditioning. To some extent, at least, it is a fall from grace, when the child "advances" from the innocent blend of fact and fancy to deliberate lying and betrays a sacred bond.

Style and Technique

Though the deeper implications of this story are grim and unsentimental, the style is light, sometimes humorous, and perceptive about childhood experience. After all, no one really expects children to be especially angelic. When Irmgard is asked if she still likes Freddy now that Bradley is here, she offers some rationalization which even she suspects is not adequate:

"Oh, I still like Freddy, but Bradley's my cousin and everything." This is a good answer. She has others, such as, "I'm English-Canadian only I can talk French and I'm German descent on one side." (Bradley is not required to think of answers, he is American. . . .) Irmgard's answer—about Freddy—lies on the lawn like an old skipping rope, waiting to catch her up. . . . "I like Freddy," Irmgard said, and was heard, and the statement is there, underfoot. For if she still likes Freddy, why isn't he here?

Nevertheless, at this stage of limited sophistication, Irmgard is only subliminally aware of moral or emotional implications. Although Freddy is forgotten for a while, Irmgard becomes convinced that she has left something behind in Montreal. She goes over her personal belongings to see what is missing, even getting up in the night to see if her paint box is still there. Not until Bradley leaves does she account for this unexplained vacuity as Freddy's absence.

Gallant is especially perceptive about this limited or selective awareness that makes childhood a private place where witches turning children into birds may adequately explain an unpleasant fact for which she and others may share some guilt. Grown-ups make more sophisticated rationalizations.

Irmgard's father and mother do not figure prominently in the story, but close to the end Irmgard, observing their reaction to Mrs. Bloodworth, interprets their expressions in the light of her own experience.

> They weigh and measure and sift everything people say, and Irmgard's father looks cold and bored, and her mother gives a waking tiger's look his way, smiles. They act together, and read each other's thoughts—just as Freddy and Irmgard did. But, large, and old, and powerful, they have greater powers: they see through walls, and hear whispered conversations miles away. Irmgard's father looks cold, and Irmgard, without knowing it, imitates his look.

The last episode returns to the dream which Irmgard remembers at the breakfast table. She remembers that it was Freddy who was sent on an errand. "He went off down the sidewalk, which was heaving, cracked, edged with ribbon grass; and when he came to a certain place he was no longer there. Something was waiting for him there, and when they came looking for him, only Irmgard knew that whatever had been waiting for Freddy was the disaster, the worst thing. . . . But she does not know exactly what it was." Nor is she sure whether it was Freddy, Bradley, or herself who encountered "the worst thing."

In an effective closing, the author suggests how far the parents have come from even the limited insight their daughter demonstrates. Irmgard starts to tell them about her dream, but her father cuts her off impatiently with "Oh, no dreams at breakfast, please." Her mother agrees: "Nothing is as dreary as a dream. . . ." The reader may intuit that the dream is, after all, no drearier than reality.

Katherine Snipes

JOSEPHINE THE SINGER
Or, The Mouse Folk

Author: Franz Kafka (1883-1924)
Type of plot: Animal tale
Time of plot: Unspecified
Locale: Unspecified
First published: "Josephine die Sängerin: Oder, Das Volk der Mäuse," 1924
   (English translation, 1942)

>*Principal characters:*
>JOSEPHINE, a mouse and singer
>THE NARRATOR, an anonymous member of the mouse folk

The Story

The narrator, a philosophizing mouse, reflects on the powerful effect that the singing of his fellow mouse Josephine has on the unmusical community of mice. Among the practical, sly, and care-laden mice, Josephine is an exception. She alone loves music and knows how to supply it. Yet there are some mice who do not find anything extraordinary in Josephine's singing. The narrator partly includes himself in this opposition group that finds nothing artistic in her song, which seems to be nothing more than common mouse squeaking. The narrator adds, however, that one must see her as well as hear her in order to understand her art, which derives its uniqueness from the way she stands before the assembled mice and does with great ceremony what every other mouse does without thinking. The fact that she is somewhat less proficient in squeaking than the average mouse seems only to heighten the effect of her performance.

It is times of trouble that Josephine deems most fitting for her recitals, for at such times the restless and anxious mice are eager to come together for mutual support and comfort. "Quiet peace is our most beloved music," the narrator notes early in the story, and when the mice fall silent in her auditorium, it is as if they were participating in this longed-for peace. Thus, the narrator asks himself: "Is it her song that delights us, or perhaps rather the solemn stillness, with which her weak little voice is surrounded?" In order to gather the scurrying mice, Josephine usually needs only to assume her singing pose, with her head tilted back, mouth half open, and eyes turned to the heights. If the number of listeners is too few, she will stamp her feet, swear, and even bite until a suitable audience is found.

Why do the mice go to such lengths for her? the narrator asks. He suggests that the community sees itself as Josephine's protector, as a father for this fragile, needy child. Josephine, on the other hand, believes that her role is to protect the mice from their daily troubles. Her song supposedly saves them from their serious economic and political situation. Yet it is all too easy, the narrator insists, to pose as the savior of the mouse folk, who are accustomed to suffering and capable of overcoming on their own any challenges to their survival.

Josephine's singing profits from a childlike quality that characterizes the mouse folk. Life is too difficult for the mice, their enemies too many, and the dangers facing them too incalculable for a prolonged, carefree, and playful childhood. In contradiction to their practical intellect, their underdeveloped childish side causes them to behave foolishly for the sake of a little fun. Yet they are also grown-ups for too long, which leads to a certain tiredness, despondency, and lack of musicality. "We are too old for music," the narrator claims.

During Josephine's concerts, only the young mice pay attention to the nuances of her delivery. In these brief moments of rest from their struggles, the older mice withdraw dreamily into themselves: "It is as though the limbs of each individual were loosened, as though the restless one were permitted for once to relax and stretch out pleasureably on the great warm bed of the people." Josephine's staccato squeaking resounds in the dreams of her listeners and liberates them from the fetters of their daily lives: "Something of our poor brief childhood is in it, something of lost, never to be recovered happiness, but also something of the active life of today, of its slight, incomprehensible cheerfulness that lasts in spite of everything and is inextinguishable."

This is not to say, though, that Josephine herself gives new strength to the mice in times of danger, which is what she and her adherents like to believe. Nor does the power of her singing justify the demands for special privileges that she makes, especially the demand to be freed from all daily work, which she claims damages her voice. What she really wants, according to the narrator, is unequivocal and lasting public recognition of her art. This is precisely what eludes her.

Recently Josephine has stepped up her struggle for recognition, threatening to overwhelm her opponents with her singing or, failing that, to cut her coloratura arias. The narrator dismisses these notions as empty rumors circulated by her followers. She is unrelenting, however, claiming to have injured her foot or to be indisposed. Her concerts have turned into theatrical performances. After her adherents flatter and coax her into singing, she still breaks down and eventually leaves, but not without first checking the crowd for the least sign of their understanding of her music.

The latest news is that she has disappeared on an occasion when her singing was expected, and that the search for her has turned up nothing. Although she may go into hiding and destroy the power of her song, the mouse folk are strong and can overcome even her death. They will not have to forgo much, for the memory of her squeaking will live on in future assemblies, perhaps with greater vitality.

As for Josephine herself, she will be delivered from her earthly torment and happily lose herself among the countless heroes of the mouse folk. As the mice do not practice history, she will soon be forgotten "in heightened redemption like all her brothers."

Themes and Meanings

Written only a few months before his death, Kafka's last tale depicts the conflict between an artist seeking proper recognition for her work and a community that has only limited understanding of her artistry. As the title indicates, Josephine, a name that echoes that of Joseph K., protagonist of Kafka's novel *Der Prozess* (1925; *The Trial*, 1937), and the mouse folk exist in a reciprocal relationship, one in which, however, neither side can comprehend the truth of the other. Since Josephine is seen through the eyes of one of her critics, albeit one who tries hard to be as objective as possible, it is hardly surprising that the outcome of the narrator's reflections is the downfall of the artist and the triumph of the superior wisdom of the mouse folk.

The narrator ascribes the powerful effect of Josephine's singing not to any vocal talent—her squeaking is clearly substandard—but to the gestures and style of her performance and, more important, to the receptivity of her audience. The mice appear to be particularly moved by the silence that precedes her singing as well as by the opportunity it provides for a communal respite from their labors and worries. Josephine's insistence on special privileges and recognition of her exceptional status, however, eventually undermines any claims she might have to be a protector of the mouse folk.

At the end of his life, Kafka thus seemed to condemn the artist's claim to autonomy and radical individuality and affirm instead the artist's function within a responsive community. Neither Josephine's personality nor the quality of her art will be remembered by this ahistorical folk, but rather the liberating power of her performances in the midst of danger, worry, and haste. Paradoxically, her redemption will come about only when she as a heroic individual is forgotten, leaving nothing but the collective memory of the dreams and the sense of well-being that her singing induced.

Style and Technique

The mouse-narrator presents his observations, analyses, arguments, and counterarguments with careful precision and in a tone of utmost seriousness that sharply contrast with the quaint world of anxiously scurrying mice. Even when he states that Josephine's auditorium was "still as mice," the pun is not consciously his. Similar incongruities—mention of the dispersion of the mice out of economic considerations (which some commentators take as a veiled reference to the Diaspora of the Jews), their neglect of history and lack of a musical tradition, their serious economic and political circumstances—demonstrate both the breadth and the limitations of the scholarly mouse's vision.

Kafka leaves the boundary between the mouse and human worlds deliberately fuzzy. The mouse writes in an impeccable German, records his observation of Josephine and her effect on the community from a number of
angles, and qualifies his generalizations and judgments for the sake of clarity
and objectivity, yet he is an integral member of the mouse folk and shares
their hopes, desires, cares, and disappointments. The result of this dual
aspect is a sharpening of the contrast between the grand seriousness of the
subject of the narrator's meditations (the relationship of artist and community) and the slightness of their context within the mouse world. This ironic
interplay between human and mouse, great and small, serious and comic,
produces a marvelously rich text that further trivializes Josephine's meager
performances. The true artist is Kafka in the guise of his philosophical
mouse.

Peter West Nutting

JULIA AND THE BAZOOKA

Author: Anna Kavan (Helen Woods Edmonds, 1904-1968)
Type of plot: Psychological realism
Time of plot: 1910-1940
Locale: London, England
First published: 1970

> *Principal characters:*
> JULIA, an adventurous young woman and heroin addict
> HER BRIDEGROOM, "a young man with kinky brown hair"
> THE TENNIS PROFESSIONAL, who first introduces Julia to drugs
> A DOCTOR, who helps Julia get her heroin

The Story

"Julia and the Bazooka" is the story of a young girl who grows up to become a heroin addict, but who dies, not because of her addiction, but as a victim of World War II. The story is narrated in a nonsequential manner and overlaps and doubles back on itself, but even in its convoluted form, it is a simple and powerful narrative.

The story begins directly enough—"Julia is a little girl with long straight hair and big eyes"—but the chronological order is soon abandoned and past and present mix together without temporal value, and readers must piece together the chronology themselves. Rearranging the elements of the story into sequence, the narrative of Julia's life would look roughly like this: She has never known her father, and "her personality has been damaged by no love in childhood so that she can't make contact with people or feel at home in the world." As a child she loves flowers, but she has "sad" eyes and does not share the "enthusiasm for living" of her classmates. "She feels cut off from people. She is afraid of the world."

Drugs change all that. A tennis professional introduces Julia to heroin—or at least, he gives her a syringe to "improve her game"—and with her "bazooka," as the tennis professional jokingly calls the drug apparatus, she wins a tournament and a silver cup. By the time she gets married to "a young man with kinky brown hair" (and there is no way of telling the exact distance between events), the syringe has a permanent place in her purse. "Now Julia's eyes are not at all sad," and "she no longer feels frightened or cut off now that she has the syringe."

Julia lives for twenty years as a heroin addict, and the reader catches glimpses or fragments of her life. She travels "with her bridegroom in the high mountains through fields of flowers." Later she drives "anything, racing cars, heavy lorries. . . . Julia always laughs at danger. Nothing can frighten her while she has the syringe." Still later, she befriends a doctor, "understanding and kind like the father she has imagined but never known," who sees that the syringe "has not done Julia any great harm" and who tells her "'you'd be far worse off without it.'" Indeed, the narrator explains, "Without it she could not lead a normal existence, her life would be a shambles, but with its support she is conscientious and energetic, intelligent, friendly."

It is suddenly wartime. Julia has a rooftop garden—in London? space is as vague here as time—and as the bombs are falling, "Julia leaves the roof and steps on to the staircase, which is not there." She is covered by a blanket and dies alone, although she appears to retain consciousness for some time and to continue to recognize people. At the same time, her bridegroom of years before is killed in a battle at sea, and dies because of the selfishness of another.

The last part of the story is even more dreamlike, as Julia passes through cold and then heat, pursuing the spectre of death. She is cremated; her ashes are put in her silver tennis trophy and placed in a niche in a wall by a winter sea "the colour of pumice." There are no flowers. "There is no more Julia anywhere. Where she was there is only nothing."

Themes and Meanings

"Julia and the Bazooka" is an apologia for heroin addiction, but, beneath this story of drugs, there is a portrayal of the essential isolation and cruelty of twentieth century life.

Anna Kavan was herself a drug addict for thirty years, but she did not fulfill the popular image of the drug addict, for, as she says about Julia, she did not "increase the dosage too much or experiment with new drugs." Much of Kavan's writing is autobiographical, and "Julia and the Bazooka" mirrors Kavan's own immersion in and simultaneous escape from the world, through drugs.

The story is, first, the narrative of a woman and her attachment to her syringe, her "bazooka," and the relief she gets from it. Her syringe helps her to compensate for childhood deficiencies and provides a barrier against the coldness and ugliness of the modern world. "She hardly remembers how sad and lonely she used to feel before she had the syringe." In the end it is not drugs that kill her, but the bombs in wartime London, which are a perfect symbol for human isolation and hatred.

This is the deeper level of the story which, for at least a quarter of its length, describes the cold isolation of Julia's ashes in the wall. The syringe has been a weapon itself against the cold inhumanity of the world, a cold she can no longer feel in death, as in drugs. Certainly Julia plays with death, tempts it, in her drug addiction. Yet drugs also help Julia avoid the death-in-life that Kavan portrays as inherent in modern life.

Style and Technique

"Julia and the Bazooka" is slightly longer than two thousand words, yet much is packed into it—a whole life, in fact, a life of adventure, of addiction, and of death in wartime. It is a short, powerful story whose effect is based, in large part, on Kavan's precise and beautiful prose.

Much of the power of the story comes from Kavan's language and imagery, which are simple and direct. A typical sentence in the story ("Julia is also dead without any flowers. . . .") is simple in structure, spare in language, and present in tense. Within those limits, though, her imagery is rich: "Snow is Julia's bridal veil, icicles are her jewels." The dominant imagery in the story is flowers: Julia is picking red poppies in a field ("the front of her dress is quite red") at the opening, and she dies amid her pots of geraniums (she lies beneath the blanket "in her red-stained dress") at the end. Yet the flower imagery contrasts starkly with the other dominant imagery of military weapons in the story—both the "bazooka" and the "flying bombs" that will kill Julia. The story is also highly symbolic, in the sense of dreams, and the bazooka stands, not only for the syringe, but also for the weapon Julia uses in her fight against the isolation of modern life, as a bomb is a weapon in the wars of that life.

Aside from language and imagery, the most notable element in the story is its structure. The story is told in a continuous, overlapping present, and events are linked, not by clear temporal causation, but by some discontinuous order only the narrator knows. Similarly, characters and events are not described in any great detail in the story (often they are not described at all), and the cumulative effect of this structure is to render accurately the isolation and fragmentation of contemporary life. Certainly, a number of other writers have used Kavan's fictional methods (compare the American writers John Barth and Donald Barthelme), but Kavan put her own spare stamp on this style. Kavan's prose does not call attention to itself, yet it has a powerful sensory effect, from the colors of Julia's flowers through the cold and heat of her death. The story leaves a lasting impression.

David Peck

KEELA, THE OUTCAST INDIAN MAIDEN

Author: Eudora Welty (1909-   )
Type of plot: Modern fable
Time of plot: The 1930's
Locale: Cane Springs, Mississippi
First published: 1940

> *Principal characters:*
> LITTLE LEE ROY, a clubfooted black man who was once in a carnival sideshow
> STEVE, a young man who was Lee Roy's barker for the sideshow
> MAX, the man who takes Steve to see Lee Roy at his home in Cane Springs

The Story

Practically the entire story "Keela, the Outcast Indian Maiden" is presented as a dialogue between Steve, a young man who once was the barker for the sideshow in which Little Lee Roy, a clubfooted black man, was presented as Keela, the Outcast Indian Maiden, and Max, a man who runs a café near Lee Roy's home and who brings Steve to see him. Occasionally, Lee Roy himself enters into the conversation, but primarily the story focuses on Steve trying to explain to Max why he continued in the barker's job. Ostensibly, Steve has come to find Lee Roy and give him some money, or something, and thus expiate his sin against the humanity of the clubfooted black man. Once he finds him, however, he takes little note of him at all, directing his attention primarily to Max, ignoring Max's repeated question about whether this man is the same as Keela. The only thing on Steve's mind is to tell his story.

Steve has come to find Little Lee Roy, the story soon makes clear, not to make any reparation but, like Samuel Taylor Coleridge's Ancient Mariner, to implicate someone else, to force Max to understand the meaning of the situation and to make him care. In horrified accents, Steve tells of Keela/Lee Roy biting chickens' heads off, sucking their blood, and then eating them raw. In his anxious state, Steve says, "I was the one was the cause for it goin' on an' on an' not bein' found out—such an awful thing. It was me, what I said out front through the megaphone."

Steve then tells how one man came to the show and exposed the fraud and freed Lee Roy. He insists, however, that he himself did not know the show was a fraud, that he did not know Keela could tell what people were saying to "it." He says he has been feeling bad ever since and cannot hold on to a job or stay in one place. The fact that he still refers to Keela/Lee Roy as "it," however, and that he does not see that his continuing to work for the show was immoral regardless of whether the so-called freak was an outcast Indian maiden or a clubfooted black man, indicates that Steve still has not faced the nature of his guilt. He seems puzzled that the man who freed Lee Roy could have studied it out and known something was wrong. "But I didn't know," Steve says. "I can't look at nothin' an' be sure what it is. Then afterwards I know. Then I see how it was." He insists that Max would not have known either, that he, too, would have let it go on and on just as he did.

When Max says he bets he could tell a man from a woman and an Indian from a black person, Steve hits him in the jaw and knocks him off the steps. Max makes no attempt to fight back, and Steve explains his action by saying, "First you didn't believe me and then it didn't bother you." Then, without ever admitting that he has actually found Lee Roy, Steve says that he has to catch a ride someplace. The anticlimactic conclusion of the story is reached when Lee Roy's children come home and he tells them that two white men came to the house and talked about "de old times when I use to be wid de circus," to which his children reply, "Hush up, Pappy." The final irony—that what for Steve has been a horrifying experience of his own guilt is for Little Lee Roy a memory of the days with the circus when he was the center of everyone's attention—does not erase the responsibility of the white man for setting up the freak show and exploiting the black man. It is, after all, such moral indifference—Steve's, Max's, and even Lee Roy's—that is at issue here.

Themes and Meanings

The most obvious thematic point of the story depends on the gap between Steve's need to exonerate himself and Lee Roy's seeming incomprehension of the moral crime that the white men have perpetuated on him. The related theme of moral blindness is reflected by Steve's inability to accept the fact that this black man before him is indeed the same as Keela, who was made to act as a freak in a sideshow, and by Max's seeming indifference to the moral crime that has been committed. Welty has said that she got the idea for the story one day on assignment at a fair. A man building a booth told her a story about a little black man in a carnival made to eat live chickens. It is the only real-life story she ever used, she says, for it was too horrible for her to have made it up.

Certainly the actuality of the story is horrible enough, but Welty sees more in the case of Little Lee Roy than one example of man's cruelty to man. Lee Roy also surely catches her imagination as a real-life example of the mythical outcast figure forced to serve as scapegoat for the bestiality of society itself. She transforms the little black man into one of her holy innocents, exploited and elevated into a mythical figure.

Steve's inability to look at things and know how they are and his insistence that this probably had to happen suggest that in some ways the story is a kind of parable of the guilt of the Southern white man about his responsibility for slavery. Just as the white slave owner insisted that he did not know how bad things were for the black man or argued that he was meant to live in servitude, Steve attempts to justify what happened to Little Lee Roy. The fact that the geek, or sideshow freak, in the story is black also allows Welty to suggest the broader and more complex sources of the white man's exploitation of the black man: as a scapegoat figure for his own dark nature.

The black-man-as-scapegoat theme is amplified by the explicit focus of the sideshow freak functioning also as scapegoat. Although man's desire to view a freak can partially be attributed to his curiosity to see abnormality, curiosity alone does not explain the phenomenon. His desire to see the freak is a basic, and perhaps base, cathartic need. That people pay money to see such acts as someone biting the heads off chickens can be explained in typical scapegoat fashion, that seeing such abnormality makes one more comfortable in his own normality. The fact that people frequent such shows, even when they know that the Outcast Indian Maiden or Lost Swamp Woman is actually a destitute local, further indicates that the geek show is a primitive ritual of scapegoat significance, complete with grotesque disguises, audience suspension of disbelief, and communal catharsis.

Style and Technique

The basic technique of "Keela, the Outcast Indian Maiden," typical of Welty, is the imposition of a mythic framework upon a seemingly realistic situation. Welty draws upon her knowledge of ancient myth to create around Little Lee Roy an aura of archetypal significance. The first clue to this is the name Little Lee Roy, which (given the French words for "the king," *le roi*) suggests "little king." Moreover, because Lee Roy is clubfooted, he suggests the maimed king, a variation of the Fisher King of the Holy Grail story. As such, he fulfills the role of scapegoat described in anthropological studies of myth. Steve, as the outsider who comes into his kingdom to do something about the king's injured condition, becomes the Quester of the myth. One primary task of the hero in the ancient myth is to ask the king the important question, "What aileth thee, mine uncle?" Steve's failure to pose the liberating question to Little Lee Roy while he was in the freak show and his further failure to inquire of him now that he is back home in Cane Springs make Steve's guilt the same as that of the Quester in the myth who fails to pity the king.

Welty's creation of such a figure which embodies so many subtle aspects of the social scapegoat implicates the reader in Steve's guilt for letting it go on and on and not being found out. It is not only the concrete image of a disguised little black man biting chickens' heads off in a carnival sideshow that horrifies the reader, but rather his realization that he has always paid his money to see such things and then tried to deny their reality. The story's impact cannot be attributed solely to the physical horror it depicts, although that indeed is shocking enough. Like any good short story, "Keela, the Outcast Indian Maiden" presents a moral dilemma which has the power to involve the reader directly, but which does so through the symbolic power of the language of the story itself.

Charles E. May

THE KEPI

Author: Colette (Sidonie-Gabrielle Colette, 1873-1954)
Type of plot: Psychological realism
Time of plot: c. 1897
Locale: Paris
First published: "Le Képi," 1943 (English translation, 1959)

Principal characters:
  COLETTE, the narrator, a young wife
  PAUL MASSON, her friend
  MARCO, a forty-five-year-old woman who ekes out a living as
    a ghostwriter
  LIEUTENANT TRALLARD, Marco's young lover

The Story

Colette's good friend Paul Masson senses her loneliness and visits her frequently to cheer her up with his "lies." One day he tells her about the lady of the library, who has never had a lover. Once she had a husband, but he mistreated her and she left him; nowadays she makes a living ghostwriting cheap novels for a sou a line. This, however, is not another of Masson's lies—Marco really exists.

Colette is intrigued by the tale of the struggling, middle-aged writer and accompanies Masson to Marco's dilapidated apartment. There she finds a thin, graceful woman with beautiful eyes and elegant manners. Marco's clothing is threadbare, yet she entertains her guests with dignity and tact.

The two women become good friends. Although their friendship is not one of great intimacy, Marco makes a rare confession one day.

> To be perfectly frank with you, I'm convinced that fate has spared me one great trouble, the tiresome thing that's called a temperament. No, no, all that business of blood rushing into the cheeks, upturned eyeballs, palpating nostrils, I admit I've never experienced it and never regretted it.

On her part, the twenty-two-year-old Colette plays the role of fashion mentor, giving her friend hair and makeup tips. Because of Marco's poverty, she cannot afford new clothing and toiletries, yet she suddenly receives a minor windfall: Her husband, apparently prospering in America, sends her fifteen thousand francs. Marco accepts her good fortune with composure and prudently uses the money to move to an apartment only slightly larger and more comfortable; she also allows Colette to help her choose a smart new wardrobe.

One evening, Masson, Marco, and Colette compete to see who can write the best response to a letter in the newspaper's lovelorn column from a "warmhearted, cultured" lieutenant. Marco's letter piques the lieutenant's interest, and a correspondence begins between the two. When Marco shows one of Lieutenant Trallard's letters to Colette, the young woman obliquely criticizes its banality, but Marco is only half listening—her response is to ask Colette for a toothpaste recommendation.

The correspondents eventually meet and quickly become involved in a passionate affair. Marco develops all the symptoms of a "belated, embarrassing puberty": She describes her lover (who is apparently much younger than she) in idealistic terms, blushes easily, and is dreamily absentminded. At the beginning of the affair Marco is nervous and drawn, but as she comes to accept her new sensuality she begins to gain weight, her plumpness reflecting her now sated, even surfeited, appetites. Yet one day eight months later, she announces to Colette that the affair has abruptly ended.

She recounts that while lying in bed with the lieutenant during a rainy afternoon of lovemaking, she playfully placed his hat—the round, flat-topped kepi—upon her head in a waggish move. As she did so, she saw something change in the man's eyes as he viewed his middle-aged lover in her post-coitus dishabille striking the pose of a flirtatious teenager, suddenly setting off her own age in conspicuous relief. She has not seen him since: The affair was terminated as expediently as it was begun.

Colette does not hear news of Marco for some time, until one day Masson mentions that she is back at the library. "So she's taken up her old life again," remarks Colette.

> "Oh no," said Masson. "There's a tremendous change in her existence!"
> "What change? Really, one positively has to drag things out of you!"
> "Nowadays," said Masson, "Marco gets paid two sous a line."

Themes and Meanings

In many of Colette's stories, love, or a semblance thereof, leads to disappointment—not because love is naturally disappointing, but because people mismanage it. In "The Kepi," the innocent Marco pursues love in the wrong way from the beginning when she refuses to see the distressing usualness of the lieutenant's letters that Colette perceives. Colette further hints at the problem when Marco pops in one afternoon shortly after first meeting the lieutenant. Because Marco is in high spirits, Colette believes that she has control of the situation and is keeping the liaison in its correct perspective. This is not the case, though, for Marco's emotions are out of control to the extent that she half-seriously believes her lover has cast a spell upon her. This lack of control is symbolized in her weight gain and in her final imprudence with the kepi. Colette intimates that vigilance, perspective, and a measure of self-control, both physically and emotionally, are necessary to maintain love, even more so when one of the parties can no longer rely on youthful attractiveness to gloss over infractions. If Marco's response to unlooked-for love had been the same gracious equanimity with which she received her financial good fortune, then she may still have lost her love, but not her dignity, Colette seems to say.

Masson's closing comment, that payment of two sous per line constitutes a "tremendous change" in Marco's life, reminds the reader ironically of the other "tremendous" (that is, trite) change that Marco underwent, from poised woman to foolish soubrette. Although the narrator implicitly criticizes Marco's behavior, Colette herself contributes to her friend's downfall. Fashionable details ("the new 'angel' hairstyle," "more nipped-in waistlines," and "a rosier shade of powder") preoccupy both the narrator and the character Colette. Becoming more attractive under Colette's care not only makes Marco more alluring to the opposite sex but also primes the austere and dignified woman to see herself as romantic heroine. The narrator's tone implies that Marco's misadventure is the result only of Marco's poor judgment; Colette never acknowledges her own complicity.

Style and Technique

Colette is not only misleading in suggesting that she had nothing to do with Marco's downfall, but also deceptive in another way. Autobiography does not simply creep into "The Kepi"; it leaps in. The first four paragraphs, for example, could be culled directly from Colette's autobiography. As in many of her stories, the line between fact and fiction is blurred, the distinction between author and first-person persona negligible. Because of this, Colette is at once the most honest writer of fiction and the most deceptive. She is honest in that she does not attempt to disguise herself and speaks candidly about her life and the people she knew, such as Paul Masson. She is deceptive because "The Kepi" remains, nevertheless, a work of fiction. Having introduced herself as Colette, a real person with a real life, her implicit message is that everything she relates must be true, too, which is not the case. Her daring and unashamed mixture of fact and fiction provides her work with a tantalizing realism to some readers, and a measure of frustration to others who like their genres more clear-cut.

In the end, the kepi is a powerful symbol because of the antithesis developed by Colette's scattering of feminine details throughout the story. Even her digressions relate to style; for example, when she moves to a new apartment, Colette relates that she purchased "white goat skins, and a folding shower bath from Chaboche's" to decorate it. More important, Marco and Colette's relationship is founded upon and solely nourished by feminine concerns: hair, clothes, makeup. These details establish the effectiveness of the kepi as the vehicle of Marco's debasement, the irony being appropriately struck by the introduction of the sole item of masculine fashion in the story.

Susan Davis

THE KERCHIEF

Author: Shmuel Yosef Agnon (1888-1970)
Type of plot: Lyric recollection
Time of plot: Probably the early twentieth century
Locale: Galicia (a former province of southern Poland)
First published: "Ha-mitpahat," 1932 (English translation, 1935)

> *Principal characters:*
> THE NARRATOR, a small boy
> THE NARRATOR'S FATHER
> THE NARRATOR'S MOTHER

The Story

"The Kerchief" is a lyric memory of a pious, naïve childhood in a traditional Jewish household in Galicia. In a series of thirteen episodes, or chapters, requiring from one to a very few paragraphs each, the first-person narrator recalls his relationship with his mother and father, the background of the kerchief, which was a gift from his father to his mother, and the time of his Bar Mitzvah at age thirteen, when he gave away the precious kerchief to a beggar.

The first ten sections of the story focus on the emotional effect on the family of the father's yearly weeklong visit to the Lashkowitz fair, where Jewish merchants gathered together from all over the district to sell their wares. The narrator remembers especially the sadness of his mother in his father's absence, during which she refrained from rebuking the children severely and spent much time standing at the window looking out. These absences of the father are likened to the week of the Ninth of Ab, observed in memory of the destruction of the Jerusalem Temple.

While his father was gone, the narrator slept in his father's bed. He used to meditate about the promised Messiah who would reveal himself suddenly in the world and lead them all to the Land of Israel, where his father would not have to go to fairs and he himself would not have to go to school, but would walk all day in the courts of the House of God.

The child would sometimes dream of this fabulous event of the future, when the precious gifts of God would seem like a heaven of many-colored lights. Yet often a great bird would come and peck out the lights. One night the dreamer tied himself to the wings of the bird and commanded it to take him to Father. The bird took him instead to the gates of Rome, where he saw a miserable beggar suffering from many wounds. The dreamer turned his eyes away so as not to see the beggar's suffering, but where he directed his eyes a great mountain arose covered with thorns, thistles, and evil beasts. He was terrified, but he did not scream lest the creeping things on the mountain should enter his mouth. Then Father appeared, wrapped him in his prayer shawl, and returned him to his bed.

The father always brought gifts for everyone when he returned from the fair. The child thought that the Master of Dreams must have informed the father of their most secret desires, for the presents were always something for which each had been longing. One day Father brought for Mother a lovely silken kerchief adorned with flowers. She wore it on her head thereafter on all the most sacred occasions of family ritual and religious festivals. The narrator remembers, "I used to look at Mother on the Day of Atonement, when she wore her kerchief and her eyes were bright with prayer and fasting. She seemed to me like a prayerbook bound in silk and presented to a bride."

The eleventh section concerns an unlucky beggar who arrived in town sick with running sores. Children used to throw stones at him. Even the grown-ups, who were not by nature cruel and who generally were hospitable to the poor and suffering, rejected this particular beggar and drove him away.

The twelfth section recalls the day of the narrator's Bar Mitzvah at age thirteen, "when I entered the age of Commandments and was to be counted a member of the congregation." He was very happy and pleased with himself and dressed "like a bridegroom." Best of all, his mother had tied her precious kerchief around his neck before he went to the House of Study. As he walked home alone, he came suddenly upon the despised beggar sitting on a heap of stones. The boy was terrified, "as a man who sees in waking what has been shown him in dream." Overcome, however, by an unaccountable sweetness he had never experienced before, he untied the kerchief from his neck and gave it to the beggar, who took it and wound it around his sores.

The last section tells of his confrontation with his mother when he had to beg forgiveness for having given away her most precious possession. His mother accepts the deed with love and affection, apparently as evidence of obedience to the Holy Law.

Themes and Meanings

Agnon, who was born in Galicia, then called Austria-Hungary, in this story celebrates some of the most endearing of traditional Jewish values, especially the sacredness of the family and its implied reflection of the love between God and His children. Seeing this idyllic vision through the eyes of a child allows the writer to present it simply and reverently, without any tinge of whatever frustration or disillusionment adult experience might bring. In his later stories, Agnon is just as adept, with a Kafka-like awareness of disorder, doubt, and alienation that seems, perhaps, more typical of modern Jewish experience. The confusion and ambiguity of such stories as "A Whole Loaf" stand in stark contrast to this more transcendent vision of wholeness and spiritual integrity, rooted in family devotion and compassion for those who suffer.

According to Hebrew legend, the Redeemer awaits the time of His coming by sitting among the beggars at the gates of Rome, binding his wounds. In his dream, the child first imagines the deliverance of the Israelites as the receiving of gifts, like the delightful return of his father with toys for all the children. Yet when he gains enough courage to tie himself to the great overshadowing bird which dims that vision, he is taken to the gates of Rome and confronted with the suffering Redeemer as beggar. He is, at that point, unequal to this confrontation and turns away to the ominous mountain, which probably represents the inherited burden of human guilt that makes redemption necessary. His father rescues him in his dream from a situation he is not yet mature enough to bear.

When, on the day of his Bar Mitzvah—an appropriate time to accept moral responsibility—the boy comes face-to-face with the despised beggar, he accepts him as the Redeemer of his dream, and this time he does not turn away. Transfixed with mingled compassion and joy, he offers the most valuable thing he has: his mother's kerchief, a symbol of the sacredness of the home.

Only later, when he must account for its absence to his mother, does he realize that he has incurred some debt of guilt for giving away her property. The fact that the mother accepts his action confirms the idea, demonstrated elsewhere in the story when the father's gifts are broken or wear out, that material things are only temporary, but the spirit of the giving lives on in the heart.

Style and Technique

This story succeeds through a lyrically rhythmic, lucid style that reflects the uncluttered, trusting perception of the naïve boy with just a touch of the older, wiser understanding of the man who looks back nostalgically at his childhood:

When my father, of blessed memory, went to the fair at Lashkowitz for the first time, my mother was once standing at the window when she suddenly cried out, "Oh, they're strangling him!" Folk asked her, "What are you saying?" She answered, "I see a robber taking him by the throat," and before she had finished her words she had fainted. They sent to the fair and found my father injured, for at the very time that my mother had fainted, somebody had attacked my father for his money and had taken him by the throat; and he had been saved by a miracle. In later years, when I found in the Book of Lamentations the words "She is become as a widow," and I read Rashi's explanation, "As a woman whose husband has gone to a distant land and who intends to return to her," it brought to mind my mother, peace be with her, as she used to sit at the window with her tears upon her cheeks.

This episode, with its suggestion of clairvoyant sensitivity in the mother, is one of several which suggest the invisible bond of family love that transcends time and space. At one point, the narrator's little sister puts her ear to the dinner table and listens intently, then announces with joy, "Father is coming! Father is coming!" and it was so. The periodic separation and joyful reunion establish a rhythm in the story, in the boy's childhood, and, by analogy to the Old Testament relationship between God and his chosen people, in the religious understanding of history.

The encounter with the beggar has a speechless, almost surrealistic quality. The presence of the brilliant sun suggests that Heaven alone witnesses and approves the deed. Whether the beggar is literally the Redeemer does not matter in the purity of symbolic action.

> The sun stopped still in the sky, not a creature was to be seen in the street; but He in His mercy sat in Heaven and looked down upon the earth and let His light shine bright on the sores of the beggar. I began loosening my kerchief to breathe more freely, for tears stood in my throat. Before I could loosen it, my heart began racing in strong emotion, and the sweetness, which I had already felt, doubled and redoubled. I took off the kerchief and gave it to the beggar. He took it and wound it around his sores. The sun came and stroked my neck.

The author's use of Hebrew legend and ethnic customs and rituals precludes a judgment of sentimentality which might otherwise arise when childhood experience is somewhat idealized. One realizes that such a story transcends realism, expressing the archetypal dreams of a devout people.

Katherine Snipes

THE KILLERS

Author: Ernest Hemingway (1899-1961)
Type of plot: Social realism
Time of plot: The Prohibition era
Locale: Summit, Illinois
First published: 1927

Principal characters:
NICK ADAMS, a young boy traveling on his own
OLE ANDRESON, a former prizefighter who has incurred the
enmity of the mob
GEORGE, a counterman in a small diner
SAM, a black cook in the diner
AL, a gangster
MAX, another gangster

The Story

The story begins abruptly with two gangsters, Al and Max, entering a small diner in the town of Summit, Illinois, near Chicago. They try to order dinner, but George, the counterman, tells them that the dinner menu will not be available until six o'clock. After asking for eggs with ham and bacon, the two gangsters order the only other customer in the place, Nick Adams, to go behind the counter with George. Next they ask who is in the kitchen, and they are told that the only other person there is Sam, the black cook. They tell George to have him come out. Al takes Nick and Sam into the kitchen, where he ties and gags them; then he props up the slit where dishes are passed through from the kitchen and positions himself with a sawed-off shotgun aimed at the counter, while Max remains at the counter talking to George. He tells George that they are going to kill Ole Andreson, a Swede who usually comes into the diner at six.

They wait until after seven for Ole Andreson, who never comes in, and they finally leave, with Al concealing the shotgun under his coat. George goes into the kitchen and unties the other two. He tells Nick where Andreson lives and advises him to go and warn him. Nick goes to Andreson's boardinghouse, and, after speaking to the woman who looks after the place, he goes to Ole's room, where he finds Ole lying in bed. When Nick asks Ole if he should go and tell the police, Ole tells him not to, that it would not do any good, and he rolls over in the bed toward the wall, saying he "got in wrong," and that there is nothing he can do to save himself.

Nick then returns to the diner, where he tells George and Sam what Ole said. Sam says that he does not want to hear it and shuts the kitchen door. George says that Ole must have double-crossed someone from Chicago, and

Nick says that he "can't stand to think about him waiting in the room and knowing he's going to get it," and that he is going to get out of town. George tells him that that is a good thing to do, and that he had better not think about Ole's dilemma.

Themes and Meanings

Hemingway's style gives the clue to the real meaning of the story. On their first reading, most readers think that the killers and Ole Andreson are the central figures, but the reader never learns what Ole did or what will ultimately happen to him. Instead, the story simply ends with the three bystanders back in the restaurant discussing what has happened. While the tone of the story is objective throughout—indeed, the story consists almost entirely of dialogue, with little interpretation or judgment by the author—the focus is clearly on the three bystanders, especially Nick Adams.

Of the three, Nick Adams is the only one whose last name is given, and he is the one who goes to warn Ole, so the narrative follows him throughout. In addition, one of the few interpretative comments on the action by the author concerns Nick. When Nick is untied by George, Hemingway mentions that Nick has never had a towel in his mouth before and that his reaction is one of "trying to swagger it off." At the end of the story, it is only through simple dialogue that the reader learns the reactions of all three. Yet Nick's reaction is most important, as the other two are from the area and are apparently more accustomed to violence. Their reaction is less out of shock than an attempt to avoid involvement. Nick is more impressed by what he has witnessed and decides that he does not want to have anything to do with the kind of town where such things happen. It is an initiation for Nick into the evil that exists in the big city. This is one of many stories by Hemingway which deal with the experiences of Nick Adams. Most of the Nick Adams stories appear in the collection *In Our Time* (1924, 1925).

That the story is set near Chicago during the Prohibition era, when lawlessness was rampant, further adds to the realization of evil to which Nick comes. The gangsters are described in an almost comic way as stereotypical mobsters; both wear overcoats and derby hats, and gloves which they do not remove when they eat. As they talk with George, they openly discuss their plan to kill Andreson, and they remain in the diner for more than two hours, having George tell the other customers that the cook is not in. They show very little concern about being apprehended. As they leave, with Al only partially concealing the sawed-off shotgun, they further flaunt their disdain for the law. All this to Nick is a rude awakening to the acceptance of violence by those who live in and near the larger cities.

Style and Technique

The typical Hemingway style is evident in this story. Almost entirely narrated in an objective style, with very little interpretation by the author or any but the most rudimentary descriptions, Hemingway's story makes the reader interpret the significance of the action. Those descriptions which are given are sparse and designed only to establish the mood, such as the few details about the gangsters wearing tight overcoats, derby hats, and gloves. The story is developed through dialogue in a series of short dramatic scenes.

In the dialogue, Hemingway uses a spare, terse style, typical of conversation. Much of the dialogue is concerned with trivial things, with the result that the seriousness of the central incident is consistently undercut. For example, the two gangsters order dinners, and George tells them that dinners will not be available until six o'clock. They then haggle over what time it is and haggle more before they decide to order eggs and bacon and eggs and ham. Ultimately, this conflict between the reality of murder and the casual, matter-of-fact attitude toward it which typifies both the killers and the citywise bystanders is central to the story: While the other characters, even the doomed Andreson, accept this state of affairs, Nick struggles against it.

Roger Geimer

KING SOLOMON

Author: Isaac Rosenfeld (1918-1956)
Type of plot: Parody
Time of plot: The twentieth century and the time of the biblical Solomon
Locale: Jerusalem
First published: 1956

> *Principal characters:*
> SOLOMON, at once King of ancient Israel and a successful
>   modern Jewish old man
> THE QUEEN OF SHEBA, a guest
> THE COUNSELORS

The Story

A man of great eminence and amatory prowess is entering old age with powers undiminished. The women still flock to him, and he periodically publishes books of deep thought. Yet there is nothing impressive about him physically, and his aphorisms seem remote from reality and from the life he leads.

The great man's counselors are at once his audience, before whom he disports himself and his achievements, and his severest critics—among themselves. They decry his taste; they are jealous of and voyeuristic about his love life; they try in vain to ascertain the source of his success. As the old dictum has it, no man is a hero to his valet.

The climax of the story is the visit of the Queen of Sheba. She may be merely another woman drawn to this charismatic man, but she stands out by being a queen, by coming from afar, and by injecting herself into Solomon's life as perhaps no other individual, certainly no woman, ever did. The consequences of her visit are no less ambiguous than her personality is. On the one hand, she turns out to be as unromantic and self-absorbed as Solomon. She is middle-aged; she eats too much and is overweight; she is indecorous, exhibitionistic, and vulgar. At last, she virtually throws herself at him and succeeds only in embarrassing him.

On the other hand, she has some insight into Solomon's main defect. Though neither saint nor sage, she presents in her parting speech a keen analysis of Solomon as a man who lives for a love that takes rather than gives, a self-absorbed man who arouses love in others but has little of it himself, who mistakes sexual adventurism for something tender or spiritual.

The climax of their affair or relationship is the climax of the story as well. The affair neither draws Solomon out of himself nor ends with a marriage. The last section of the story is therefore a sorry coda, bringing Solomon into late old age, with all of its attendant indignities. He grows more obsessed with possessing women, strays from God, quarrels with his priests, grows out of touch with the people he governs, and becomes bogged down in bureaucratic procedures.

The story closes poignantly with glimpses of Solomon as a doddering old man. He loses what little hold he has on reality. Approaching death, he, like all human beings, becomes overwhelmed by the mystery of existence, the absence of the meaning of life, the transience of all achievements. Sleep becomes elusive, the body falls apart. Even animal sensual gratification becomes elemental, as a hot water bottle replaces wife or mistress.

Themes and Meanings

The classics of early literature—the Bible, Homer, Greek and Shakespearean tragedy—deal with heroes who are larger than life and who, whether they be good or evil, grapple with important philosophical and moral issues. The heroes of modern literature, by contrast, are swamped by the trivia of daily life. Getting through each day with a modicum of dignity is their task as much as wrestling with God, Fate, or mystery was that of the earlier heroes.

The difference in literary presentation is attributable to a host of cultural factors. Just as writing about Achilles' or Hamlet's laundry lists would have been incomprehensible to Homer or Shakespeare, so too would a story written today which presents a hero in the antique mode be dismissed by the sophisticated reader as hopelessly naïve and one-dimensional. Isaac Rosenfeld's story is an attempt to cross the great divide between the archaic heroic vision and the modern mundane one. How could the romantic, semi-legendary figure of the ancient Israelite king be made comprehensible and relevant to the modern reader? What would result from a juxtaposition of the heroic mode and the quotidian? What would Solomon be like were he alive today or were modern readers transported, with their modern sensibility, to ancient times?

Rosenfeld's Solomon moves in a world of telephones, newspapers, kosher markets, radio, stamp albums, pinochle, overtime pay. The biblical Solomon, or the historical figure on which he is based, must have relaxed with the ancient version of pinochle or stamp collecting, but such activities, not part of the heroic dimension, are excluded from the Bible.

The biblical Solomon is one of the great Israelite heroes. A man who ruled over the ancient Judaic kingdom at its zenith, he was especially renowned for his wisdom and amatory powers. Yet he was human enough to transgress at last, by worshiping false gods at the prompting of his pagan wives. Rosenfeld's Solomon, by contrast, is seen mainly in his declining years. He is a seedy, idiosyncratic old man whose charisma is incongruous. His thoughts on everything, himself included, are inscrutable. His famous sayings are remote from experience, hardly remembered by him, and seem to be part of a pose. The stories he tells children do not amuse them. Even his physical presence does not impress: He is a sloppy, overweight, bespectacled old man often seen in an undershirt, with glasses and cigar. His counselors are not reverential but, as they would be in life and in modern literature, envious, carping, and exasperated. The advent of the Queen of Sheba, a glorious event in the Bible, is here merely the occasion for further signs of his decline. He does a poor job of impressing her, and their relationship is a pathetic and vain attempt by two aging persons to understand each other.

The central vision of the story is the modern one—that a king is merely another human being; that greatness in human affairs is enigmatic and fortuitous; that a man, even if a famous achiever, is reduced by time to the grim animal level; that life, even at its best, is sad and not at all what it is made out to be in idealizing literature and chronicles. God and redemption are—given the biblical material—glaringly absent.

Style and Technique

This is less a conventional short story, with dialogue and dramatic climax, than a chronicle presenting an overview of events and characters. Important are not only the literal events but also the biblical version of them in the back of the reader's mind. The telling, tone, and manner are as much a part of the meaning as is the matter. The biblical version is dismissed as the "official chronicle" commissioned by a king concerned with his "image." Rosenfeld's story presumes to show the reader the way things really were, which in modern times means the unsavory underside. The narrator even irreverently describes the Scriptural version as "a bit thick," evasive, unreliable, and sycophantic. One of its most famous anecdotes is called an "abominable invention."

This approach makes the omniscient narrator one of the main characters of the story. His style is that of a debunker, an investigative reporter or revisionist historian who is getting behind the formal, official, solemn canonical version of events and setting the record straight, no matter how unsavory the results. A biblical passage is even quoted in order to establish the contrast in styles and in visions of reality and in order to subject it to sardonic questions. In fact, Rosenfeld's Solomon is often a comic figure; a biblical epic has become a Jewish anecdote about a *schlemiehl*—a fool.

Manfred Weidhorn

THE KING'S INDIAN

Author: John Gardner (1933-1982)
Type of plot: Modern fable
Time of plot: Early nineteenth century
Locale: Boston, Nantucket, and the Atlantic and Pacific oceans
First published: 1974

> *Principal characters:*
> JONATHAN UPCHURCH, a nineteen-year-old Boston
>   schoolmaster
> DR. LUTHER FLINT, a mesmerist
> MIRANDA FLINT, his daughter
> CAPTAIN DIRGE, the captain of the whaler *Jerusalem*
> AUGUSTA, his daughter
> JEREMIAH, his blind companion
> MR. KNIGHT, his first mate
> BILLY MORE and
> WILKINS (SWAMI HAVANANDA), seamen
> JIM NGUGI, an African harpooner
> KASKIWAH, an American Indian harpooner
> WOLFF, a mutineer

The Story

John Gardner's "The King's Indian" is told by an ancient mariner to his "guest," later revealed to be Gardner himself. The tale is about hoaxes, according to Jonathan Upchurch, its narrator, as well as "devils and angels and the making of man." Upchurch promises to answer the question, "Ain't all men slaves, either physical or metaphysical?"

Upchurch begins with his boyhood infatuation with beautiful seven-year-old Miranda Flint, the stage foil to her mesmerist father, Dr. Luther Flint. Nine-year-old Jonathan experiences visions of birds during one of Flint's exhibitions, and Miranda's sharing his screams makes the boy even more obsessed with her. A decade later, Upchurch, a schoolmaster in Boston, saves his money so that he can fulfill his dream of moving to southern Illinois and starting a farm, but some sailors get him drunk and exchange his savings for a sailboat. Impulsively, he decides that "in landlessness alone lies the highest truth, shoreless, indefinite as God!"—a line borrowed from the greatest of sea narratives, Herman Melville's *Moby Dick* (1851)—and he sets sail, only to be overrun by the Nantucket whaler *Jerusalem* and taken aboard.

Upchurch soon learns that the ship is no ordinary whaler, that—in violation of all New England beliefs—it is carrying slaves, though the crew denies their existence. A second mystery, also denied, is the presence of a woman whose voice "haunted me as once Miranda Flint's eyes had done." The mystery is only intensified when Upchurch finally sees the beautiful girl with the humpbacked Captain Dirge and his constant companion, the blind and mysterious Jeremiah.

Upchurch becomes acquainted with the crew, especially the red-bearded Billy More, who rescues him from falling from the rigging of the mainmast. Upchurch suspects that the entire crew, including the taciturn first mate, Mr. Knight, and the garrulous "multi-breed" Wilkins, are mad, perhaps infected by the brooding Dirge. The captain discovers Upchurch's learning and appoints him tutor to his seventeen-year-old daughter, Augusta. Already in love with her, Upchurch falls even deeper, becoming enraptured by her "unearthly" eyes. Their relationship develops quickly, and soon this "fleshed ideal" kisses her walleyed tutor.

Captain Dirge boards every ship that the *Jerusalem* encounters, and Augusta grows exceedingly distracted each time. Pretending to be one of the slaves after blackening his skin with burnt cork, Upchurch goes along on one of these trips, only to discover Augusta in the same disguise. A sailor on the ship that they are visiting tells Upchurch that Captain Dirge is an impostor, that the real captain is dead, but the sailor is killed before he can say more.

Back on the *Jerusalem*, Kaskiwah, an American Indian harpooner, gives Upchurch two mushrooms to eat, causing him to have a vision of a ship that appears from beneath the sea bearing a white-bearded man issuing cryptic epigrams. After the man returns to the sea, a huge "pigeon-like thing" also delivers a message to Upchurch: "Fool, retreat!"

Billy More then tells Upchurch the secret of Captain Dirge's quest. Four years before, three American ships saw the *Jerusalem* go down near the Vanishing Isles in the Pacific Ocean with only a portrait from the captain's cabin surviving. When Dirge and his ship arrived in Nantucket to learn that they had been reported dead and to see the painting exactly like the captain's own, the captain vowed to solve the mystery. Dirge consulted experts in the "praeternatural," one of whom took special interest because the portrait was of him: Dr. Flint. Dirge's objective is not whales but "a crack in Time." Later, Augusta tells Upchurch that their quest is no less than to "understand . . . *everything.*"

Upchurch begins to complete the puzzle, realizing that Augusta is really Miranda Flint. Wilkins and a seaman named Wolff then lead a mutiny to uncover the rest of the deceit, killing Mr. Knight and Billy More along the way. Jim Ngugi, an African harpooner, saves Upchurch from the same fate, but Miranda is not so lucky, being beaten and raped by Wilkins. Upchurch discovers that Miranda's magnificent beauty is yet another trickster's fraud.

Wilkins takes complete control by killing Wolff and reveals the depth of the knavery. The "ghost ship" story is nothing but a hoax arranged by the *Jerusalem*'s owners with the help of Swami Havananda, Flint's rival and Wilkins' true identity. Flint, unaware of the hoax, killed the real captain and Augusta and replaced Dirge with a ventriloquist's dummy, which he operated in the guise of Jeremiah. Wilkins/Swami Havananda, after revealing his part in all this, kills himself.

Upchurch and Ngugi take charge of the ship and their destiny. After eighteen days of calm near the South Pole, surrounded by icebergs, singing whales, and huge white birds, Flint comes out of hiding. Upchurch sees his antagonist as nothing but "an impotent old goof hardly better than the puppet he scared me with before." Flint challenges Upchurch to a chess match: Should Upchurch lose, he will become the old hoaxer's disciple, and if Flint loses, he will give up Miranda. Upchurch, who has claimed not to know the game, surprises Flint with the King's Indian, an expert's opening, and the mesmerist bursts into flames, the victim of spontaneous combustion and of his own villainy.

Following a debate about truth, innocence, and similar issues, Upchurch and Miranda make love. The wind finally rises, and so does a giant sad man in white from the sea. Ignoring this vision, Upchurch and his crew set sail for "Illinois the Changeable!"

Themes and Meanings

"The King's Indian" is in the tradition of narratives using journey motifs and naïve young protagonists to explore initiations into the worlds of self-discovery and values. Dr. Flint may intend his quest to reveal one kind of truth, but for Jonathan Upchurch, it is a voyage of faith and love. Such themes are fitting for a story by the author of *On Moral Fiction* (1978), who insists that writers should create in their art an affirmation of life.

Mr. Knight, as his name suggests, sees only darkness around him; his faith ended by science, he wonders if the world is merely mechanical. The real Captain Dirge loses his life because he misplaces his faith, believing in the brimstone demon Flint. After saving Upchurch from annihilation, Billy More warns him to "banish all thought of Nowhere by keeping yer mind from belief in it. . . . If ye *must* think, think of Faith itself. . . . Faith, that's the secret! Absolute faith like a seagull's." Upchurch decides that one is the slave either of some purposeless power or of "some meaningful human ideal." He can discover that ideal, and therefore faith, only through love.

"Human consciousness," Upchurch explains, "is the artificial wall we build of perceptions and *conceptions*, a hull of words and accepted opinions that keeps out the vast, consuming sea." Melville's Captain Ahab wants to smash through this wall by conquering a giant whale; Flint plans to do the same by finding the time warp; Upchurch has a simpler solution: "A mushroom or one raw emotion (such as love) can blast that wall to smithereens."

Flint bursts into flames because his only vestige of humanity, his love for his daughter, has been consumed by his own overwhelmingly evil nature.

Upchurch's victory seems ironic, since Miranda has lost her beauty, but such is mere appearance, like the stage magic of her father. Faith must go beyond mere surfaces: "no more illusions, no more grand gestures, just humdrum love." Miranda also recognizes the power of love. "You're so *wall*-eyed!" she exclaims to Upchurch. "Jonathan, I love you. . . . You're grotesque." Armed with love and faith, Upchurch ignores the "solemn white monster" who appears out of the sea, and he implores his crew of ruffians, "We may be the slime of the earth but we've got our affinities!"

Style and Technique

In *On Moral Fiction*, Gardner criticizes writers who create elaborate verbal palaces with no life inside, and he has Billy More issue the same complaint: "Words, whatever their sweetness and juice, turn prunes at last, and eventually ashes." Yet there is still pleasure in an elaborate, self-conscious style when the writer has confidence that he is creating more than the sand castle that Jonathan Upchurch says this story is.

The novella-length "The King's Indian" is full of grandiose, usually comic, celebrations of figurative language. Upchurch experiences "the smell of unlimited futurity stinging" his "nosedrills." He sees a sperm whale with "teeth that would serve as Plato's form for the fall of civilizations." Billy More—all the characters are philosophers and poets—describes Captain Dirge's house as "so crammed with brass and silver and gold it would keep a dead Eskimo sweating for fright of thieves."

More important, "The King's Indian" is a virtual catalog of allusions to past masters, especially the literature of the sea. The story's mariner-guest frame and its albatrosses come from Samuel Taylor Coleridge's *The Rime of the Ancient Mariner* (1798). Miranda is named for the heroine of William Shakespeare's *The Tempest* (1611), her father is Gardner's version of Shakespeare's Prospero, and Wilkins is his Caliban.

Most of the time, Gardner pays homage to American masters. Flint the mesmerist and ventriloquist and his spontaneous combustion come from Charles Brockden Brown's *Wieland* (1798). Gardner reminds the reader of the debt that his moral tale owes to Mark Twain's *The Adventures of Huckleberry Finn* (1884) when Miranda refers to Ngugi as "Nigger Jim." The mad captain's quest for knowing the unknowable is obviously inspired by *Moby Dick*. Gardner's primary homage, however is to Edgar Allan Poe's *The Narrative of Arthur Gordon Pym* (1838). Both Upchurch and Pym make unplanned, nightmarish voyages toward some mystical whiteness near the South Pole, accompanied all the way by screaming white birds. Numerous specific references to Poe's novel appear, including Pym's initials carved on the *Jerusalem*'s bulkhead.

When the guest identifies himself as Gardner, he acknowledges "the help of Poe and Melville and many another man," and he says that his tale is "not a toy but a queer, cranky monument, a collage: a celebration of all literature and life." Most of all, perhaps, it celebrates the storyteller as one who gives shape and meaning to existence while entertaining his audience as well.

Michael Adams

THE KISS

Author: Anton Chekhov (1860-1904)
Type of plot: Psychological realism
Time of plot: The 1880's
Locale: The village of Mestechki and various small towns in Russia
First published: "Potseluy," 1887 (English translation, 1915)

Principal characters:

LIEUTENANT RYABOVICH, a timid artillery officer
LIEUTENANT LOBYTKO, a boastful womanizer
LIEUTENANT MERZLYAKOV, a coldly analytic intellectual
LIEUTENANT GENERAL VON RABBECK, Mestechki's leading
  landowner

The Story

The setting of "The Kiss" is a Russian village on a May evening. The officers of an artillery brigade encamped nearby are invited by a retired lieutenant general, von Rabbeck, who is the leading landowner in the village, to spend an evening dining and dancing in his residence. After describing a panoramic scene of aristocratic society, Chekhov focuses on one of the officers, Ryabovich, who characterizes himself with the diagnosis: "I am the shyest, most modest, and most undistinguished officer in the whole brigade!" He is an inarticulate conversationalist, a graceless dancer, a timid drinker, and an altogether awkward social mixer. During the evening he wanders away from the activities he is unable to enjoy and strays into a semidark room which is soon entered by an unidentifiable woman, who clasps two fragrant arms around his neck, whispers, "At last!" and kisses him. Recognizing her mistake, the woman then shrieks and runs from the room.

Ryabovich also exits quickly, and soon shows himself to be a changed man: "He wanted to dance, to talk, to run into the garden, to laugh aloud." He no longer worries about his round shoulders, plain looks, and general ineptness. He begins to exercise a lively romantic fancy, speculating which of the ladies at the dinner table might have been his companion. Before falling asleep, he indulges in joyful fantasies.

The artillery brigade soon leaves the area for maneuvers. Ryabovich tries to tell himself that the episode of the kiss was accidental and trifling, but to no avail: His psychic needs embrace it as a wondrously radiant event. When he tries to recount it to his coarse fellow officers, he is chagrined that they reduce it to a lewdly womanizing level. He imagines himself loved by and married to *her*, happy and stable; he can hardly wait to return to the village, to reunite with *her*.

In late August, Ryabovich's battery does return. That night he makes his second trip to the general's estate, but this time pauses to ponder in the garden. He can no longer hear the nightingale that sang loudly in May; the poplar and grass no longer exude a scent; he walks a bridge near the general's bathing cabin and touches a towel which feels clammy and cold; ripples of the river rip the moon's reflection into bits. Ryabovich now realizes that his romantic dreams have been absurdly disproportionate to their cause: "And the whole world... seemed to [him] an unintelligible, aimless jest." When the general's invitation comes, he refuses it.

Themes and Meanings

This is a masterful tale, as Chekhov demonstrates his vision of life as a pathetic comedy of errors, with misunderstanding and miscommunication rooted in the psychic substance of human nature. Lieutenant Ryabovich, the least dashing and romantic of men, is transformed by the kiss meant for another into a person with a penchant for an intense inner life that runs its dreamy course virtually separate from the dreariness of external reality. He inflates an insignificant incident into an absurd cluster of fantasies centering on ideal love and beauty. All the more embittering, then, is his plunge from ecstasy to despair as he recognizes, in the story's anticlimactic resolution, the falseness of his hopes, the frustration of his yearnings.

Chekhov dramatizes two of his pervasive themes in "The Kiss." One is the enormous difficulty, often the impossibility, of establishing a communion of feelings between human beings. Ryabovich discovers that he cannot communicate to his fellow officers his happiness "that something extraordinary, foolish, but joyful and delightful, had come into his life." Lieutenant Lobytko regards Ryabovich's experience as an opportunity to parade and exaggerate his own sexual adventures. Lieutenant Merzlyakov dismisses the lady in the dark as "some sort of lunatic." The brigade general assumes that all of his officers have his own preference for stout, tall, middle-aged women.

The other great Chekhovian theme (which he shares with Nikolai Gogol) is the contrast between beauty and sensitivity, and the elusive characteristic best expressed by the Russian word *pošlost'*. The term is untranslatable, but it suggests vulgarity, banality, boredom, seediness, shallowness, suffocation of the spirit. Ryabovich, surrounded by the coarseness of his comrades, depressed by the plodding routine of artillery maneuvers, poignantly tries to rise above this atmosphere of *pošlost'* by caressing an impossible dream.

Style and Technique

The story's structure is contrapuntal, with Chekhov using unobtrusive symbolism and situational irony to contrast the two worlds of romance and drabness. After his kiss, Ryabovich soars on wings of joy, exhilarated by "a strange new feeling which grew stronger and stronger." After dining and dancing, he and the other officers walk through their host's garden on their way back to camp. Chekhov bathes the scene in an atmosphere of lyric romanticism, as stars are reflected in the river's water, sandpipers cry on its banks, and a nightingale trills loudly, "taking no notice of the crowd of officers"; they admire its self-absorption. The nightingale serves to symbolize Ryabovich's state of sensibility. Like the bird, his soul is singing loudly and is indifferent to its surroundings.

The counterpart to the nightingale is the ass, Magar, which paces ploddingly at the end of the dusty procession of the brigade's cannons, horses, and men, with Chekhov describing the dullness of artillery life precisely and minutely.

When Ryabovich returns to Lieutenant General von Rabbeck's garden in late summer, "A crushing uneasiness took possession of him." His exultant mood has disappeared as he confronts the prospect of a nonexisting reunion with a nonexisting beloved. Again, Chekhov symbolizes Ryabovich's feelings of rejection and disillusionment: "there was no sound of the brave nightingale and no scent of poplar and young grass." As Ryabovich touches the general's cold, wet bathing towel and observes the moon's reflection this time torn to bits by the river waters, he has a shattering epiphany of heartbreak: "How stupid, how stupid! . . . How unintelligent it all is!" he exclaims, interpreting the endless, aimless running of the water as equivalent to the endless, aimless running of his life—of all lives. "What for? Why?"

Gerhard Brand

KLEIST IN THUN

Author: Robert Walser (1878-1956)
Type of plot: Biographical sketch
Time of plot: 1802
Locale: Thun, Switzerland
First published: 1907 (English translation, 1957)

Principal characters:
THE NARRATOR, a former clerk in a brewery in Thun
HEINRICH VON KLEIST, a Prussian writer
KLEIST'S SISTER

The Story
   The narrator imagines to himself how the Prussian writer Heinrich von Kleist, then twenty-five, might have lived during the spring and summer of 1802 in a villa on a small island in the Aar River near the town of Thun. Kleist's arrival was probably unspectacular: He walked over a short bridge, rang the bell, and someone lazily answered. It was the charming Bernese girl who would become his housekeeper. He is satisfied with the rooms she shows him, but he feels a little sick and wonders why, especially in the midst of such beautiful natural surroundings.
   He writes—it is the beginning of his writing career—and occasionally reads from his work to friends in nearby Bern. Yet he is dissatisfied with what he produces, among other things, his comedy *Der Zerbrochene Krug* (1808; *The Broken Jug*, 1930). The lazy spring weather is maddeningly distracting: "It is as if radiant red stupefying waves rise up in his head whenever he sits at his table and tries to write." He had intended to become a farmer after arriving in Switzerland.
   He often sits at the window and muses on the stunning yet unsettling landscape of the lake, fragrant fields, and bewitching mountains. Lonely, he longs for a nearby voice, hand, or body. By gazing intently on the beauty around him, he tries to forget himself, but memories of home and his mother disturb him. He runs out into the garden, rows a boat onto the open, sunny lake, swims, and hears the laughter of women on the shore. Nature, he thinks, is "like one vast embrace."
   His enjoyment of the scene is never without pain and longing. Sometimes it feels like the end of the world here, and the Alps seem like the unreachable gates to a high, distant paradise. The light at dusk is spellbinding, yet its beauty is tinged with sickness. Kleist deems himself superfluous and longs for a heroic life. Pursued by a vague uneasiness, he climbs up the castle hill, then races back to his room, resolute on writing, which unfolds once he at last forgets where he is.

Rainy days are intolerably empty, dark, and confining. Sunny Sundays and market days, on the other hand, he likes, for they are full of life, movement, sounds, and aromas. He feels almost as if he were in Italy. Normal workdays, though, seem still and lifeless. On a fragrant summer evening he looks down on the lake, whose fiery, sparkling surface conjures up the image of jewels on the body of a vast, sleeping, unknown woman. He wants to drown in the image of the alluringly beautiful depths, and soon the thought of shimmering breasts and lips chases him down the mountain and into the water, where he laughs and cries.

Insisting on perfection in his work, he tears up several manuscripts, but keeps on writing, only to be defeated again: "The good fortune to be a sensibly balanced man with simple feelings he sees burst into fragments, like crashing and thundering boulders rolling down the landslide of his life." He resolves to accept his self-destructive nature, "to abandon himself to the entire catastrophe of being a poet."

In the fall he becomes ill, and his sister comes to bring him home. His inner suffering is reflected in his haggard face and matted hair. She asks what is wrong, but he is unable to tell her. His manuscripts lie strewn over the floor, and he gives her his hand to stare at.

They leave Thun behind on a bright autumn morning. Dejected, Kleist sees nothing of the landscape passing by the coach. He dreams instead of clouds and images and caressing hands. His undefined pain seems to ease. His sister urges him to take up a practical activity, and he agrees.

"But finally one has to let it go, this stagecoach," the narrator concludes. Last of all, he wishes to mention the marble plaque on the villa indicating that Kleist lived and worked there. Time and interest permitting, anyone can read it. The narrator says he knows the area around Thun a little, for he once worked there as a clerk in a brewery. There was a trade fair there a little while back; he is not exactly sure, but he thinks it was four years ago.

Themes and Meanings

In this early masterpiece of biographical description, Walser clearly identifies with the struggles of the young Kleist to establish a writing career. Writing, the text suggests, was a painfully difficult process for both writers, particularly in their respective foreign environments (the Swiss Walser wrote his Kleist story near the beginning of his eight-year stay in the Prussian capital of Berlin). Bordering on madness, yet seductive in its images, writing was no longer a romantically innocent activity or a matter of simple inspiration. For Kleist, artistic ambition and the drive for expressive perfection were undermined by longing for physical contact, on the one hand, and a vague heroic idealism, on the other. The lush and sensual natural surroundings of the Bernese Oberland stirred up the images of desire that were so detrimental to his writing. Thus, nature, instead of being an idyllic model of creative simplicity, took on a foreboding quality and caused the numerous radical shifts in his mood. His rescue by his sister implied that only a life of mundane routine could save him from the catastrophe of the madness of the solitary writer, but few things could have been more threatening to his creative energy than the example of normalcy held up to him by his sister's life and education. In contrast to the simple marble commemorative marker, Kleist's brief visit to Thun was, at least for Walser, an occasion for the complex manic-depressive turmoil that would later tear Kleist apart.

Style and Technique

The narrator relates the intensity of Kleist's emotional instability with remarkable coolness and ironic detachment. There is a playfulness in the framing of his narrative: He begins by trying to picture in his mind Kleist's visit to Thun and ends with the almost frivolous remarks on tourists and a trade fair that deserves to be forgotten. In between, the grimness of Kleist's agitation is greatly alleviated by the light touch with which the narrator tells his story. By mentioning casually at the end that he is a former clerk in a brewery, he tries to trivialize his role, yet his story is filled with poetic figures and betrays a high degree of literary consciousness.

Although the persistent use of the present tense and the occasional sentence of quoted monologue bring an immediacy to Kleist's perceptions and experiences, the reader is constantly made aware of the narrator's own voice. The vividness of his imagery and poetic language remain in the foreground as a reminder of the narrator's loquacity in contrast to the silence of Kleist's destroyed manuscripts. The narrator's ironic distance from his subject undercuts the temptation to identify Walser with Kleist. Kleist would never have written and published a work of such poetic intensity on an incident so slight and lacking in dramatic conflict. Walser obviously delights in the sound and rhythm of his sentences and the brightness of his imagery. Nevertheless, the tragic consequences of the drive for self-expression are easily discernible beneath the alluring poetic surface of Walser's text.

Peter West Nutting

THE KUGELMASS EPISODE

Author: Woody Allen (1935-   )
Type of plot: Parody
Time of plot: The 1970's
Locale: New York City and Yonville, France
First published: 1977

> *Principal characters:*
> SIDNEY KUGELMASS, a professor of humanities at City College of New York
> DAPHNE KUGELMASS, his unappealing second wife
> DR. MANDEL, his psychoanalyst
> PERSKY, a magician/inventor
> EMMA BOVARY, the heroine of the novel *Madame Bovary*, by Gustave Flaubert

The Story

Psychoanalysis is incapable of curing the civilized discontent of Professor Sidney Kugelmass. He feels frustrated in his second marriage—to a woman whom he regards as an overweight oaf—and pressured by the alimony and child support that he must pay his first wife. He longs to transcend the banality of his existence and fantasizes doing so in an adulterous affair with a glamorous woman.

His opportunity comes with an unexpected phone call from a tinker in Brooklyn who dubs himself "The Great Persky." Persky has constructed a cabinet that can somehow transport its occupant into the world of a literary work. All Persky need do is toss in a book, tap three times, and whoever is inside will find himself within that book's fictional universe.

Kugelmass decides that he wants to pursue a romance with Emma Bovary. He pays Persky twenty dollars and, soon after getting inside the cabinet with a paperback of Gustave Flaubert's novel *Madame Bovary* (1857; English translation, 1886), finds himself in the Bovary house in provincial Yonville. Kugelmass and Emma spend a romantic afternoon alone together in the French countryside, which ends when he must return to meet his wife Daphne at Bloomingdale's. Kugelmass goes back to nineteenth century Yonville many times during the next several months. He and Emma become passionate lovers.

Fascinated by Kugelmass' tales of the world from which he comes, Emma is eager to visit it. Persky manages to transport both of them back to New York City, where they pass a rapturous weekend at the Plaza Hotel. On Monday morning, Kugelmass must return to his wife and his job, and he brings Emma to Persky's house in order to have her dispatched back to

Yonville. This time the cabinet does not work, however, and Emma must spend the week ensconced at the Plaza Hotel, while Persky desperately attempts to repair his invention and Kugelmass, afraid that his liaison will be discovered, begins to panic. By the time Emma is able to return whence she came, her relationship with Kugelmass has disintegrated. He is now reconciled to a banal life with Daphne in twentieth century America.

Nevertheless, three weeks later he returns to Persky to seek another romantic adventure, an affair with one of the beautiful women in Philip Roth's sexually explicit *Portnoy's Complaint* (1969). The cabinet malfunctions, however, killing Persky, and substituting an old Spanish textbook for *Portnoy's Complaint,* so that a terrified Kugelmass finds himself pursued at the end by the irregular verb *tener* ("to have").

Themes and Meanings

Like the Flaubert novel whose main character it appropriates, "The Kugelmass Episode" examines the futility of the quest for personal happiness. Although it is cast in a comic key, Allen's story, like *Madame Bovary*, is organized around a logic of disillusionment. Each stage of transcendence is a disappointment, and the more that Kugelmass, who has already been through two marriages at the outset of the story, reaches for something exotic that is beyond his grasp, the more miserable he becomes. It is appropriate that he is last seen hounded by the verb *tener*, a graphic reminder of the elusiveness of the heart's desire: People cannot have what they want, and do not want what they have.

Woody Allen is best known for his achievements in film—as a prolific director, writer, and performer. Many of his cinematic works explore the complex relationship between art and life by being playfully metafictional; when characters mug to the camera or are themselves artists, the medium becomes aware of itself. "The Kugelmass Episode" is a similar fiction about fiction. Its interaction between "real" and invented characters anticipates the premise of Allen's film *The Purple Rose of Cairo* (1985), in which a film character walks off the screen and into a romance with a woman in the audience.

As a professor of humanities, Kugelmass is a professional reader of literature. Like Flaubert's Emma, whose addiction to extravagant love stories ultimately leads to her depression and suicide, Kugelmass is more stimulated by literary images than by the people and situations he encounters outside books. The simple diagnosis of his skeptical psychotherapist, Dr. Mandel, is that he is "so unrealistic." Kugelmass is unable to reconcile the realities of his ordinary existence with the enchanting plots and persons he has encountered in his reading. Neither Flo, his first wife, nor Daphne, his second, could possibly be more exciting than Sister Carrie, Hester Prynne, Ophelia, or Temple Drake. Literature has spoiled him for life.

Allen assumes that his readers will catch these and other literary allusions, that his readers, like Kugelmass, are intimately acquainted with the most prominent works of Western literature and will pride themselves on their ability to follow the learned references, but, even more so, on their privileged detachment from the pathetic professor in the story. They may share his enthusiasm for books, but they have a redeeming awareness that undercuts the kind of uncritical absorption which undoes both Emma and Kugelmass—at least, such an awareness is assumed by Allen's mocking text.

Even after discarding Emma, Kugelmass has not learned his lesson. He is soon lusting after another literary figure and deprecating his life outside of books. It is a futile, destructive cycle of desire and deceit, one that the story's conclusion suggests must be broken: The eternal quest for happiness yields only eternal dissatisfaction. Persky's extraordinary machine is destroyed, and the wizard himself dies. As the story approaches its final words, abjuring its own rough magic, it seems to be endorsing Dr. Mandel's insistence on confronting the ordinary and coming to terms with it. The story does so, ironically, through Allen's farfetched fictional contrivance.

Style and Technique

"The Kugelmass Episode" is a very amusing story, and its humor is that of a network of incongruities. There is a striking disparity between anxious, balding Kugelmass and the glamorous life that he would lead. The reader laughs at his pretensions and groans for his frailties. Kugelmass is yet another version of the distinctive Woody Allen persona, familiar from other stories and from Allen's film roles. He is a contemporary American reincarnation of the Yiddish schlemiel figure: the hapless man who, according to the Yiddish proverb, falls on his back and breaks his nose. Though Sidney Kugelmass, whose very name ludicrously undercuts his romantic aspirations, has failed at everything, including freshman English, he naïvely keeps returning for more.

After Emma and Kugelmass exchange their first remarks, the reader is told, "She spoke in the same fine English translation as the paperback." By the end of the relationship, Emma is complaining to Kugelmass that "watching TV all day is the pits." Much of the humor in this story results from juxtaposing the florid style of a literary classic—about a woman steeped in literary rhetoric—with the casual vernacular of a modern, irreverent New Yorker. Kugelmass holds a respected social position and is in awe of Emma Bovary, but his speech is laced with outdated proletarian slang: "sock it to me," "scam," and "jitterbug." His streetwise talk is as affected as are provincial Emma's aristocratic airs. Although Emma covets elegant formal clothing, she is fascinated by the marked-down leisure suit that her new lover wears. It is difficult to imagine an odder, and more appropriate, couple than Emma Bovary and Sidney Kugelmass. One is a French heroine and the other an American antihero, but both are in love with a narcissistic idea of love.

As its title suggests, "The Kugelmass Episode" is more a sketch than a fully realized fictional universe of three-dimensional characters. It is an essay in narrative form, an inventive meditation on *Madame Bovary*. Much of its charm derives from its self-mockery and its awareness of its own artifice. One of the more remarkable moments in the piece occurs when a professor at Stanford who is a specialist in Flaubert suddenly discovers a strange character named Kugelmass in his familiar novel. He rationalizes that it is the mark of a classic always to surprise on each reading. In depicting a nineteenth century literary character visiting the urban American culture of television, films, and football, Allen's brief, perceptive fantasy delights on each reading.

Steven G. Kellman

LADY MACBETH OF THE MTSENSK DISTRICT

Author: Nikolai Leskov (1831-1895)
Type of plot: Realism
Time of plot: Mid-nineteenth century
Locale: Mtsensk District, Russia
First published: "Ledi Makbet Mtsenskogo uezda," 1865 (English translation, 1922)

Principal characters:
KATERINA IZMAYLOVA, the protagonist, a merchant's wife
ZINOVY BORISOVICH IZMAYLOV, her husband
SERGEY, her lover
BORIS TIMOFEYEVICH, her father-in-law
FEDYA LYAMIN, her nephew
SONETKA, a convict

The Story

Leskov's storyteller begins his tale with a description of the oppressive boredom of the provincial Russian merchant household, where the men leave to conduct their business and the women are left in a latter-day harem, to look after the children—if there are any—and the larders. Katerina Izmaylova, the young wife of Zinovy Borisovich Izmaylov, is attractive, spirited, and quite unprepared by her poor but free and simple childhood for the stultifying narrowness of her husband's way of life. Her five-year marriage has brought no children, and despite the fact that Zinovy Borisovich's first wife bore no children either, Katerina is reproached for her barrenness, for "ruining her husband's life." Passive, languid, Katerina wanders the silent house, sleeps, watches the servants from her attic window.

It is from that attic window, her bedroom window, that Katerina looks out on the spring garden in the sixth year of her marriage and decides to go for a stroll. She hears laughter near the barns and finds her father-in-law's clerks teasing the fat cook by hoisting her into a flour vat to weigh her. The chief culprit is Sergey—young, handsome, insolent, and more than ready to test Katerina's boast of her strength. In doing so, he embraces her—and a flustered Katerina leaves, but not without finding out that Sergey is a newcomer, fired by his last employer for carrying on with the mistress.

That evening, Sergey appears at Katerina's door, complaining of loneliness and boredom. He has little trouble sweeping Katerina off her feet and into bed, and the two lovers spend every night together for the week thereafter. Then Boris Timofeyevich, Katerina's father-in-law, catches Sergey sliding down a pillar beneath the attic window and takes the unrepentant sinner to the storeroom, flogs him brutally, and locks him in. He sends for his absent son, and in the face of Katerina's pleas and brazen lack of shame, decides to send Sergey to prison.

On the day of his decision, however, Boris Timofeyevich falls ill after eating his porridge and mushrooms, and toward evening dies "just like the rats in his granaries." No one is particularly suspicious, since mushrooms are a tricky thing, and Boris Timofeyevich is an old man—and the mistress' affair is the mistress' business. Zinovy is delayed, Sergey recovers in the master's bed, and all appears to be going well. Katerina and Sergey make love and go through rituals of jealousy and reassurance. One night, however, Katerina dreams twice of a huge cat, and the cat speaks with the voice of her murdered father-in-law. She awakes from the nightmare to hear her husband's key turning in the locked gate outside.

Sergey hides, and Zinovy confronts his wife. She at first denies everything, but then loses her temper and calls Sergey out of hiding to taunt Zinovy. Enraged, he strikes her, and at this point Katerina's vaunted girlhood strength returns. She throws her husband to the floor, and she and Sergey, hands entwined, strangle him. To make sure, Katerina finishes him off with a heavy candlestick and then carefully wipes the cherry-sized drops of blood from the floor. Sergey buries Zinovy in the cellar, and no one is the wiser. Everyone assumes that the master has mysteriously disappeared before reaching home.

Katerina, pregnant, is about to assume control of her husband's properties, but another heir appears on the scene, Zinovy's young nephew Fedya Lyamin. Now it is Sergey who is uneasy, the "unhappiest of men," and he constantly hints, insinuates, and suggests to Katerina that Fedya's continued existence is an obstacle to their happiness. Fedya falls ill and is forced to stay home from an evening holiday church service. With the entire household gone, Katerina sees her chance. She and Sergey smother the child with a pillow. This time, however, there are witnesses. A group of young men returning from the church service, curious about the mistress' "amours," decide to peep through the window to catch the lovers in the act—but the act they catch them in is murder.

The two are tried, flogged, and sentenced to hard labor and exile in Siberia. They begin the long trek together, in the same gang of convicts. Katerina's baby, still the legal heir, is given to Zinovy's relatives to rear, but as long as Katerina can be near Sergey, she has no thought for anything else. Sergey, however, tires of her passion and her devotion now that she is no longer a wealthy merchant's wife, and he takes up first with one female convict, then another. He and Sonetka, his new love, humiliate and taunt Katerina, finally tricking her into giving Sergey her last pair of warm stockings—which end up on the devious Sonetka's feet.

As the gang is herded onto a barge to ferry across a turbulent river, Katerina seems numb to the jibes and laughter of her tormentors, but as the ferry reaches midriver, she acts. She leaps into the water, taking Sonetka with her. Sonetka emerges from the waves to grasp for the boat hook, but Katerina, in her last show of strength, pulls her down, and both disappear for good.

Themes and Meanings

"Come you spirits that tend on mortal thought, unsex me here," says William Shakespeare's Lady Macbeth as she steels herself for Duncan's murder. There are no such words from Leskov's merchant murderess, Katerina Izmaylova, as she dispatches first her father-in-law, then her husband, then her nephew—and finally her rival and herself. She neither reflects, nor rehearses, nor suffers remorse. No abstract notions of power or kingship rule Katerina's actions—her lover Sergey can bring her nothing in the way of authority or status—nor, until the third murder, does she show any trace of greed. When the authorities ask her why she has committed these crimes, she answers simply, nodding at Sergey, "For him." The source of Katerina's newfound strength of will, so murderously directed, is passion itself—purely physical, sexual passion, inseparable from her femaleness.

Leskov had originally intended his Katerina to be one of a series of female types from the area along the Oka and Volga rivers, types to be taken from the peasant, merchant, and gentry estates. His series of sketches never materialized, but "Lady Macbeth" has become one of Leskov's best-known, most powerful tales. This "dark kingdom," the patriarchal, superstitious merchant milieu, was mined by other Russian writers of the mid-nineteenth century, such as Aleksandr Ostrovsky in his plays and Fyodor Dostoevski in *The Idiot* (1868), but Leskov's treatment is unsurpassed—all the more so because, unlike Ostrovsky, he does not set out to draw a genre picture or an exposé of this pious and ignorant but shrewd and pragmatic class, a class whose domestic customs and habits date back to Byzantine books of instruction on the proper conduct of households, wives, and children. That Katerina is unjustly reproached for her childlessness, that her relatives inspect her every move for signs of waywardness or impropriety, that her husband threatens to torture the truth out of her—these things Leskov presents as a matter of course, as givens. What interests him and what interests the reader is not so much sociology or psychology as character—human nature, Katerina's nature.

Leskov does not sentimentally justify Katerina's crimes, but it is clear that she is neither fundamentally evil, nor weakly corrupt, nor cruel. Like many another Leskov character, she seems a potentially heroic figure somehow gone wrong. Fate may masquerade as society but really fools no one. In her energy, vitality, and sensuality, she is far more appealing than either her victims or her partner-in-crime; her obsession, her "possession," is an honest one, which she herself neither rationalizes nor justifies. The instincts which Sergey awakens in her are not all murderous—for the first time in her married life she really sees, hears, and smells the beauty around her. The very strength of her feeling leads to her downfall.

It is no accident that Sergey and Katerina's first bantering exchange is a challenge of strength. The old peasant weighing the flour says, "Our body... counts for nothing on the scales. It's our strength that weighs, not our body." In the end, it is Katerina's tragic strength, not inert weight, that pulls both herself and her rival beneath the waves.

Style and Technique

In "Lady Macbeth of the Mtsensk District," Leskov eschews his much-used *skaz* narrator—the chatty, distracted, half-educated storyteller who reveals more about himself than about his tale—in favor of a more detached voice. Although the narrator here is an insider, referring to the Mtsensk District as "our part of the country," he no longer seems a part of the life there. Far from making the story of Katerina Izmaylova a dry, judicial account of crime and punishment, this detachment gives it a straightforward, inexorable movement. Like any good storyteller, the narrator wants his listeners to pay attention, to wait for what happens next; in his very first paragraph, he promises a story and a character that none can remember "without an inward shudder." Thereafter, he ends each short chapter—there are fourteen—with either an obviously temporary resolution or a tantalizing hint at events to come: "This was what the old man decided to do; but he was not given the chance to carry out his decision"; "But time was passing not only for them: after his long absence, Zinovy, the wronged husband, was hurrying home."

The narrator's deliberate hints are not the only device that lends this tale its concentrated forward motion. Although Leskov's narrator avoids dialect and folksy locution, he still creates an air of folklore and myth. The young, beautiful wife kept under lock and key by an old, miserly husband and his tyrannical father, the saucy suitor with his swagger and his black curls—these are the stuff of folktale and magic. Magical, too, is Leskov's description of the lovers' night in the moonlit apple orchard, but the magic becomes more ominous in Katerina's vision of the snub-nosed cat in her bed—once there to wake her in place of her lover, once there to remind her of her sins.

The dreamlike, trancelike quality of Katerina's obsession leads her onward, hypnotizing both her and the reader. The dream turns into a nightmare on the march to Siberia, when Sergey's betrayals and mockeries come as fast as his flattery and blandishments came before. Animal imagery and prophetic vision come together at the end of the tale when Katerina, staring fixedly at the waves, sees the heads of her victims rising from the water, and when she herself rises up one last time to throw herself on her rival "like a strong pike on a soft little perch."

Jane Ann Miller

THE LADY OR THE TIGER?

Author: Frank R. Stockton (1834-1902)
Type of plot: Unresolved fairy tale
Time of plot: "The very olden time"
Locale: A semi-barbaric land
First published: 1882

Principal characters:
A SEMI-BARBARIC KING
HIS SEMI-BARBARIC YOUNG DAUGHTER, who is in love with a
young courtier at her father's court
A YOUNG COURTIER AT THE KING'S COURT, who is in love with
the princess

The Story

In "the very olden time," a half-barbaric king, who was also half-civilized because of the influence of his distant Latin neighbors, conceived a way of exercising justice upon offenders against his rule. He placed his suspect in a Roman-like arena and had him choose to open one of either of two doors which would open into the arena. Behind one of the identical doors lurked a ferocious tiger which would leap out and devour the accused; behind the other door awaited a lovely maid who would, if her door was the one opened, come forth and be married at once to the opener. (It mattered not that the man may be married or otherwise committed, for the whimsical king would have his justice.) The fate was to be decided by chance alone, and no one who knew of the placement behind the doors was allowed to inform him which to elect.

All of this was popular among the audience, and even their thinking members could not deny that it was a fair test. The public experienced pleasing suspense and an immediate resolution. Best of all, everyone knew that the accused person chose his own ending.

Now it happened that a handsome young courtier dared to love the king's daughter, who was lovely and very dear to her father. The man, however, though of the court, was of low station; His temerity was therefore an offense against decorum and the king. Such a thing had never happened in the kingdom before. The young lover had to be put into the arena to choose a door, a lady or a tiger. Yet the princess loved the young man; clearly and openly that was the case. She did not want to lose him to a ravenous tiger, but at the same time, could she bear to lose him to another woman in marriage?

The king searched the kingdom for the most savage of tigers. He also searched for the most beautiful maiden in all his land. No matter which door the young man selected, he would have the best that could be offered. The public could hardly wait, and as for the king, he reasoned that chance would have its way, and in any event the young man would be disposed of.

The princess achieved something no one had before: She knew which fate was behind each door. She worked hard to learn the secret, using the power of her will and gold to secure it. Moreover, the princess knew who the woman was, a lady who had directed amorous glances toward the young man at court, glances which—or so the princess fancied—he had sometimes returned. For her interest in the princess' lover, the princess hated the woman behind the door.

In the arena on the fatal day, the young man looked at the princess, expecting her to know which door hid what fate. The princess made an immediate and definite motion toward the right-hand door, and this door her lover opened directly.

Did the tiger or the lady come out of the doorway? The princess loved the young man, but she was also a barbarian and she was hot-blooded. She imagined the tiger in horror, but how much more often did she suffer at the thought of his joy at discovering the lady? In one fulfillment, she would be forced to see him torn to pieces before her very eyes; in the other, she would be forced to watch him marry and go off forever with a woman she hated. The story stops exactly at the point at which the young man opens the door. It does not tell his fate.

Themes and Meanings

Frank R. Stockton said of this story, "If you decide which it was—the lady or the tiger—you find out what kind of person you are yourself." He pretended that he himself did not know, that although he had planned a decided ending, he could not write one, "for I had not the advantage of being either semi-barbaric or a woman." Thus, interpretation of this story relies on each reader's decision, depending on how the reader views the world and human nature in it. The amount of faith the reader has in love and how much the reader believes that jealousy, hate, and pride may alter one's love will affect that decision. What the reader imagines "semi-barbarism" (that of the princess) to be, as well as its opposite, will also affect his or her own interpretation of the ending.

Yet certain points about the story are not open to interpretation. The princess does take the trouble, great trouble, to find out which door is hiding what. She is not her father's daughter; she does not leave things to chance, for her heart is engaged. She does not hesitate to give direction, nor does her lover hesitate to rely on her. If he trusts her so, would she trust him less? Still, this is a fairy tale, with a fairy-tale way of presentation. Are such complexities of motivation that would lead the princess to indicate the door to the tiger right for such a tale? One may answer no, yet the course of true love is here pointedly crowned with hate and jealousy. A possible theme of "The Lady or the Tiger?" is the necessity of trust in another person's humanity and love in a world where one never knows for certain what that person will do. The reader may wonder: "Which door would I have chosen?"

Style and Technique

This is a tale rather than a story. There is no dialogue; no one speaks to the reader but the narrator, who spins the yarn and asks the questions of interpretation at the end. He knows the story, but one senses that he does not have omniscience, that he is not there himself. He knows more than the populace and king, yet he does not know and will not reveal the outcome. That seems unfair—he leaves his readers dangling—but that is his purpose from the beginning. The story is a tour de force, hinging on a gimmick. What is annoying is that the narrator seems to know the ending but will not tell it.

Yet the tale may be saved for the reader by the distance the author keeps from his material and the atmosphere of mystery which he maintains. He has heard the story, and it has amazed him with its mixture of the humane and the barbaric. If the plot is a teaser, are its psychological concerns also? In not letting the characters speak, in not even naming them, and in having their motivations generalized, the author approaches allegory—the allegory of logical human emotions. He turns the tale into a matter of "what would you do?" He turns outward from the story to the reader directly, thus placing emphasis on theme rather than on plot.

In not deeply developing his characters, holding them at arm's length, he has made it impossible for one to know what they will do. One is told their motivations in general terms, but one does not experience the characters having them: One does not hear their words or glimpse their process of thought. Hence, the reader is not involved in the story. The characters in the tale are but once-upon-a-time people, representative but not real. When readers are asked at last to decide, on the basis of their personalities, what they will do, they are unable to respond but can say only what they would do or what people they have known would do. If the tale fails, it is in this aspect.

One can see that the king turned his fancies into facts, simplified them with his court of chance. He avoided the complexities of responsibility in the decisions by chance. His daughter turns facts into fancies (gold into information, and that information into what she fancies or wants—the right door). In other words, while the father simplifies, the daughter complicates, or takes on responsibility. With what ultimate intent does she do this? How cold or warm is she in her heart? One cannot know. The story lacks the nearness that readers require to answer the question Stockton asks them.

This story works the way a mystery story does, yet the necessary clues are not there. Hints are but hints, for they are canceled out: They do not add up or point in any direction. If "semi-barbarism" is to be looked to for a clue, it fails because one does not know what "semi-barbarism" means. Not only are explanations of motivations lacking, but also a corpse or an action which would shed light on the characters' motivations.

Without its brevity and fast pace, this story would have failed miserably. One moves directly from what the king is like to his testing procedure to the young couple's affair to preparations for the trial and finally to the critical—and incomplete—choosing of the door, all in eighteen medium-sized paragraphs. One remains on the surface of the story, which is really a summary of events and the reasons for them. In place of dramatization there are posturings, as if the story were a slide show with lecturer—except that the lecturer wants the listener to finish for him.

William E. Morris

THE LADY WITH THE DOG

Author: Anton Chekhov (1860-1904)
Type of plot: Psychological realism
Time of plot: The 1890's
Locale: Yalta and Moscow
First published: "Dama s sobachkoi," 1899 (English translation, 1917)

Principal characters:
DMITRII DMITRICH GUROV, a banker
ANNA SERGEEVNA VON DIEDERITZ, a married woman

The Story

The story begins with a description of a bored banker, Dmitrii Gurov, on vacation in the southern Russian city of Yalta. Idly attentive toward the other vacationers, Gurov takes special interest in a recent arrival to the resort town, a young woman named Anna Sergeevna von Diederitz, who strolls along the embankment with her little dog. Judging from her appearance, Gurov decides that she is a married woman alone and bored on her vacation. Although he too is married, he has had many affairs, and he becomes excited by the prospect of having a brief affair with this stranger. Beckoning her dog toward him, he uses the pet as an excuse to strike up a conversation with her, and within a short time they develop an easy air of companionship.

Chekhov next depicts the pair after a week has passed. It is a warm, windy day, and the two go down to the pier to watch a ship come in. As the crowd around the ship gradually dissipates, Gurov asks Anna Sergeevna if she wishes to go for a ride. Suddenly, on an impulse, he embraces her and kisses her. He then suggests that they go to her room. The next scene portrays Anna Sergeevna and Gurov in her room; they have just made love for the first time. She is distraught because she feels guilty, not only because she has deceived her husband, but also because she has discovered that she has been deceiving herself for a long time. She tells Gurov that she was twenty when she married her husband and has since realized that he is nothing but a flunky. Anna Sergeevna, on the other hand, wants to live, to experience life. Now she believes that her infidelity has proved her to be a petty, vulgar woman and that Gurov will not respect her. Gurov listens to this confession with an attitude of boredom and irritation. He feels that her repentance is unexpected and out of place. Nevertheless, he comforts her, and within a short time her gaiety returns.

They leave the hotel and drive to Oreanda, a scenic spot outside Yalta. There they gaze in silence at the sea and listen to its incessant, muffled sound. Chekhov writes that in the constancy of this noise and in the sea's calm indifference to human life and death there perhaps lies a pledge of eternal salvation, of uninterrupted perfection. Listening to this sound in the company of an attractive woman, Gurov gains a new insight into life. He perceives that everything in this world is beautiful except that which people themselves do when they forget about the highest goals of existence and their own human worth.

After this moment of transcendent reflection, the two return to Yalta, and for the next several days they spend all of their time together, indulging in the sensual pleasures of Yalta and the joys of their new relationship. At last, however, Anna Sergeevna receives a letter from her husband asking her to return home. After she bids Gurov farewell at the railroad station, presumably forever, he, too, thinks that it is time for him to return home to Moscow.

Back in Moscow, Gurov tries to return to his familiar routine of work, family life, and entertainment. He assumes that his memories of Anna Sergeevna will fade, just as the momories of his other lovers always have. He discovers, though, that he cannot stop thinking about Anna Sergeevna, and soon he begins to regard his present life as nonsensical, empty, and dull. Impulsively he decides to travel to Anna Sergeevna's hometown, hoping to see her and to arrange a meeting with her. After arriving in her town, he seeks out her house but does not enter it. Instead he decides to attend a premiere at the local theater that night in the hope of seeing her there. When he confronts her at the theater, she is shocked yet thrilled, and she agrees to meet with him in Moscow.

Now begins an agonizing time for Gurov. Meeting with Anna Sergeevna once every two or three months, he finds that he is living a double life. His everyday life is routine and conventional, but he regards it as being full of lies and deception. His other life, the one involving Anna Sergeevna, is of necessity kept secret, but it contains all that is important to him, and indeed it represents the core of his being. In the final scene of the story, Chekhov depicts the two lovers trying to come to terms with their difficult situation. Anna Sergeevna is in tears; she believes that their lives have been shattered by their love and the deceit that it requires to survive. He too recognizes that he cannot tear himself away from her, and he perceives a fearful irony in the fact that only now, when he has begun to turn gray and to lose his good looks, has he found true love. The anguished pair talk about the necessity of changing their lives, of breaking through the walls of deception around them, but they cannot see a solution to their dilemma. Chekhov concludes his tale with the comment that it seemed as though a solution would be found shortly and that a new, beautiful life would then begin, but that it was also clear to the couple that the end was still a long way off, and that the most complex and difficult part was just beginning. With this moment of unresolved uncertainty, Chekhov brings to a close his penetrating study of human love and human destiny.

Themes and Meanings

In "The Lady with the Dog," Chekhov provides a masterly portrayal of human psychology, demonstrating how one's expectations of life can be overturned by unpredictable reality. At the outset of the tale, Gurov is shown to be rather cynical and an egocentric opportunist in his attitude toward women. Coldly analytical about his own emotions and his numerous relationships, he has categorized his lovers into three types—the carefree, the intellectual, and the predatory. Yet he discovers in his relationship with Anna Sergeevna something new and unexpected. Love for the first time becomes an emotional experience that is deep, sincere, and touching. Significantly, the woman who created this effect on him is not depicted as being a dazzling beauty; he himself realizes how strange it is that this small woman, not distinguished in any way, has become the center of his life. Love, Chekhov suggests in this story, can transform even the most ordinary people and lives into something unique and extraordinary.

Chekhov's exploration of the process by which Gurov discovers that his preconceived notions about women are illusory illustrates one of the writer's broader concerns. Throughout his career, Chekhov emphasized the necessity of exposing falsehood or hypocrisy in society and of espousing the truth, honest and unconditional. Thus, he highlights Anna Sergeevna's despair over the hypocrisy of her marriage to her husband and Gurov's indignation over the falsehood permeating his regular existence in Moscow. Chekhov often articulated his belief in humanity's inalienable right to absolute freedom, and he has instilled this ideal into his two protagonists. In their longing to break free from the fetters of deceit marring their relationship, Chekhov's characters aspire to the kind of beauty and dignity glimpsed by Gurov as he sat with Anna Sergeevna by the sea outside Yalta. Chekhov's narrative illuminates both the value of this ideal and the difficulty of attaining it.

Style and Technique

Like most of Chekhov's late tales, "The Lady with the Dog" reveals the careful touch of a consummate craftsman. Constructing his story out of a small number of selected vignettes, Chekhov managed to evoke the full complexity of an intimate relationship between two sensitive human beings in a concise, almost laconic fashion. One technique that helped the writer achieve such conciseness is the use of minor yet significant detail to suggest emotional states. For example, as Gurov listens to Anna Sergeevna lament her situation when they first become lovers, Chekhov indicates the man's insensitivity to her agitation by depicting him slicing a watermelon and eating it without haste. Similarly, Chekhov's nature descriptions echo or shape a character's emotions: The sensuous sound of the Black Sea at night facilitates Gurov's recognition of the timeless beauty present in the world around him.

To underscore the subjective nature of his characters' perception of events, Chekhov often uses such passive and impersonal constructions as "it seemed" and "it appeared." Perhaps the most striking feature of the structure of "The Lady with the Dog" is the air of uncertainty with which it ends: Chekhov provides no definitive resolution to his lovers' problem. Such an inconclusive ending was not typical for nineteenth century Russian literature. Chekhov seems to imply here that life, unlike the tidy fiction that his predecessors liked to create, does not conform to neat patterns or boundaries, but rather continues in a way that defies human control or manipulation. Chekhov pioneered the use of this kind of "zero ending" in his fiction, and it has since become a staple of the modern short story.

Julian W. Connolly

THE LAGOON

Author: Joseph Conrad (Józef Teodor Konrad Korzeniowski, 1857-1924)
Type of plot: Symbolic realism
Time of plot: The late 1890's
Locale: Malaysia
First published: 1898

> *Principal characters:*
> TUAN, the white man
> ARSAT, the protagonist, a Malayan

The Story

Toward dusk in a tropical lagoon, a white man arrives by boat at the hut of Arsat, a Malayan whom he had befriended years earlier. Arsat greets him at the doorway with an anxious, fearful look and asks the white man, whom he calls "Tuan," if he has brought some medicine. Tuan asks who is sick, and Arsat brings him to the bedside of Diamelen, his woman. She has been stricken with fever and is seriously ill. Fearful that she will die, Arsat and Tuan keep watch by the fire outside the hut. As night arrives, plunging the lagoon into an unquiet darkness, Arsat begins to tell the white man the tale of how he and Diamelen came together, a story of love and betrayal.

Arsat and his brother were brave young warriors, sword bearers to the ruler, Si-Dendring. By chance Arsat met Diamelen one day, and from then on he could "see nothing but one face, hear nothing but one voice." By day he waited on the path to see her, and by night he crept along the hedges of the women's courtyard to steal a glance at her. Often they would whisper longingly to each other in the leafy shadows.

Yet Diamelen was forbidden fruit, the wife, or concubine, of Inchi-Midah, a noble chief. Nevertheless, Arsat longed for her all the more, and she for him. Baring his heart to his brother, Arsat was at first advised to wait. Patience, his brother told him, was wisdom. Yet as time passed, Arsat grew gloomy, and his warrior blood impatient.

One night, the tribe having gone down to the river to fish by torchlight, Arsat and his brother made their move. Courageously, they paddled their canoe past the tribesmen and waited quietly by the shore for Diamelen. She came running to them, and Arsat took her into his arms and swept her into the boat. Quickly, soundlessly, they made their way downriver, paddling through the night and arriving by afternoon of the next day at a little beach, close by the safety of the deep jungle. Here the men slept while Diamelen kept watch.

Suddenly Arsat and his brother awoke to Diamelen's cry of alarm. The ruler had sent a war party after them, and now the warriors were in sight, drawing toward them in a large boat. Escape by water was thus impossible, so Arsat's brother urged him to take Diamelen and run. The brother would hold off the party as long as he could and then catch up with them. Arsat and his woman ran, hearing the shots from the brother's gun. Making their escape, Arsat looked back and saw his brother surrounded by the enemy. He heard his brother's cries as the men fell upon him, but Arsat did not go back. Instead, he and Diamelen went on to safety and a new life together.

After his tale, Arsat rises from the dying fire and returns to the bedside of Diamelen. It is almost dawn. From the doorway, the white man hears a loud groan and sees Arsat stumbling out. "She burns no more," Arsat tells him.

The white man prepares to leave, urging Arsat to come with him, but the grieving lover refuses. He tells Tuan that since he has now lost his world, he is resolved to go back to his enemies. He will fight them on behalf of the brother whom he had deserted. As the white man pulls away from the hut, he sees Arsat standing motionless in the sunshine above the cloudy waters of the lagoon.

Themes and Meanings

"The Lagoon" is a story of love, courage, and cowardice and of their complex interweaving in the fabric of human behavior. Arsat is acknowledged a great warrior. The rank that he holds in the tribe attests his courage and skill; his daring first escape with Diamelen is further proof that he is a man unafraid to risk his life. Yet he is also a man capable of love.

The story he tells the white man is, on the surface, a tale of high romance and adventure, but, like the lagoon itself, it is deeper and more mysterious than it appears. The nature of his love is brought into question when he sees his brother fall amid the enemy. At that moment Arsat is faced with a choice. If he goes back to help his brother, he acts with the proper courage of a warrior and a man. Yet his courage would be purchased at the risk of losing what he most cherishes—not only his life but also his world, his Diamelen. He must therefore choose between love and honor, fidelity and betrayal. In effect, he can carry off his love only at the price of cowardice. In choosing love, that noblest attribute of man, he has paradoxically bought dishonor, and it is only at the end, when Diamelen dies, that Arsat decides to seek a form of redemption, to regain his honor and courage by returning to his enemies. The problem is that his resolution comes too late. With Diamelen dead, Arsat has nothing to lose. The choice now becomes irrelevant, for his return can be seen not as the pursuit of lost honor and bravery but as an expiation of guilt, an easing of the conscience, even a form of suicide—the ultimate cowardice.

Thus, at the very end of the story, Arsat is motionless, staring beyond the sunlight "into the darkness of a world of illusions." What is illusory is not love or courage or cowardice, but man's ability to act purely, to conduct his life without contradictory emotions or damnable choices. Significantly, Arsat's love of Diamelen allows him to see nothing but her face, hear nothing but her voice, and after her death he tells the white man that he can see nothing. "There is nothing," the white man responds—nothing but illusion, uncertainty, and the darkness of an impenetrable lagoon.

Style and Technique

The complexity of "The Lagoon" is heightened by Conrad's use of the frame narrative, the story-within-the-story. Arsat's tale of love and fraternal betrayal is framed by the arrival and departure of the white man, who is at once an observer and a participant. As in a later story, "Youth," in which the narrator provides a frame for Marlow's tale of adventure, this sort of double narrative and double point of view pushes Arsat's tale out of its personal focus and forces it to be seen in more cosmic terms. Arsat's tale has affected the white man, who understands that he, too, has become part of the world of illusions. He shares complicity in the love, bravery, and cowardice. (The brother's gun was a gift from the white man, for example.) Arsat's tale, like the lagoon itself, stirs ripples in the mind and experience of the white man and in the reader as well. The white man is the bridge between the personal agony of Arsat and the universal tragic experience of humanity, in which one's choices can lead to inescapable ruin.

Finally, the setting of the lagoon is the perfect embodiment of the illusory world of man's actions. As the dominant image, the lagoon exists on three levels of interpretation. Precisely and intensely described, the lagoon has literal, palpable reality. It is a place immersed in the sounds and dark shadows of the tropical wilderness.

On a second level, the lagoon is a symbol of evil, a malign force, aggressive and alive, like a predator. It is not a personal malignity, something that lies within the responsibility of Arsat or the white man, but a menace that exists independently of man's action—in the manner of an ancient Greek chorus chanting of fate and destiny.

Finally, the lagoon is a metaphor for the human condition, a symbol of the dark uncertainty of motive. It is a psychological entity, suggestive of a confused state of mind.

Edward Fiorelli

LAMB TO THE SLAUGHTER

Author: Roald Dahl (1916-   )
Type of plot: Suspense
Time of plot: The mid-twentieth century
Locale: A town or city, probably in England or the United States
First published: 1953

> *Principal characters:*
> MARY MALONEY, a devoted housewife
> PATRICK MALONEY, her husband, a police detective

The Story

This story begins with the most innocent of domestic scenes. Mary Maloney, a housewife in her sixth month of pregnancy, is waiting for her husband to return home. It is a Thursday night, and they usually eat out. When Patrick Maloney does come home, he is strangely moody and takes a stronger drink than usual. Mary tries to divert him with the usual domestic comforts, but to no avail. Patrick asks her to sit down, announcing that he has an important matter to discuss with her. Though the reader is never told, it is clear that Patrick is going to divorce Mary. He ends his speech by saying that he will see that she is provided for and that he hopes that there will be no fuss, since it might reflect badly on his position in the police department.

The announcement that she will lose the man around whom her world revolves puts Mary into a daze of unbelief. Instead of arguing with Patrick, she goes on as if nothing has happened, hoping that this will somehow cause her problem to go away. She prepares to make supper and goes down to the deep freezer. She chooses a frozen leg of lamb for the meal. Moving like a somnambulist, she walks into the living room. When Patrick tells her that he does not want dinner, Mary moves behind him and hits him over the head with the leg of lamb.

Patrick falls to the floor with a crash, and this brings Mary to her senses. Mary realizes that she has killed Patrick, and though she is willing to take the legal consequences, she fears for her unborn child, who might die if she is executed. Her mind is now working clearly, and she devises an elaborate deception for the police. She prepares the leg of lamb and puts it in the oven. She then goes to her room and gets ready to go out. As she does so, she rehearses the conversation that she will have with the grocer, trying to get the voice tones and facial expressions as close to normal as possible. This deception is put into operation. She goes to the grocery and uses the exact words that she has rehearsed, so that the whole scene at the grocery appears to be the everyday act of a wife picking up food for her husband's dinner and chatting with the grocer. She then returns home, telling herself that she must remain natural and to expect nothing out of the ordinary when she enters the house. Thus, when Mary does arrive, she calls out to Patrick as if he were still alive. Her shock at actually finding Patrick's body is almost completely unfeigned, as if she really did not know that she has already killed him.

Mary then calls the police and reports that Patrick Maloney has been killed. Two policemen, one of whom is Jack Noonan, arrive at the house. Both men are familiar to Mary, who knows most of Patrick's friends on the police force. They begin the investigation into Patrick's murder by recording Mrs. Maloney's story about going out to get food for supper and coming back to find Patrick's body. Noonan, completely taken in, comforts Mary, asking if she would rather go to her sister's house or stay with his wife. Mary, however, stays throughout the investigation. When a doctor and other specialists arrive to examine the body, the police conclude that Patrick was killed by a blow to the head with a blunt instrument, probably made of steel.

The police begin searching the house for the murder weapon but with no success. Mary asks Noonan for a drink, then invites him to have one himself. Soon all the police are having a drink, and the investigation has become a consolation scene. Finding that the lamb is now cooked, Mary asks the policemen to eat it, since she owes it to Patrick to extend the hospitality of his home to his friends. She finally persuades them to eat the meal as a favor to her. As they do so, they remark that the murder weapon would be very difficult to conceal. One man says to Noonan that the weapon is "probably right under our very noses," which causes Mary to giggle.

Themes and Meanings

The story of the woman who murders her husband with a frozen leg of lamb and then has the murder weapon eaten by the detectives is one of the most famous example of the "perfect crime" story. Yet this work's value lies, not simply in the originality of the murder method, but in the way that Dahl ties this to larger themes. The use of a leg of lamb as an instrument of death reveals the hidden and sinister meanings that lie in seemingly innocent objects. Dahl, like many modern suspense writers, weaves his stories around trivial, everyday events that suddenly take on frightening aspects revealing the danger and uncertainty that underlies modern life, rather than reviving medieval settings and horrors in the manner of the earlier gothic writers.

Mary Maloney lives the life of a devoted housewife almost until she actually murders her husband. The news of her divorce causes no outward change in her behavior. She goes on, as if pretending that nothing has happened will make it so. The murder seems almost an unconscious and unwilled act. Yet after the murder, Mary becomes a deliberate and clear thinker. She now artificially creates her alibi for the murder by consciously returning to her innocent state before Patrick's death. She practices her lines, voice tone, and facial expressions before she goes to the grocery so that they will appear perfectly natural and arouse no suspicions in the grocer's mind. When Mary arrives home, her shock at seeing Patrick's body is so spontaneous that she almost seems to have fooled herself. Mary's deception grows as she manipulates the police, reaching its peak when Patrick's friends destroy the evidence of his murder as a favor to his wife, who is his killer.

Dahl creates a series of bizarre metamorphoses in this story. A leg of lamb becomes a murder weapon. Mary Maloney, the victim of her husband's insensitivity, makes him her victim. Patrick, an investigator of crimes, becomes the subject of a criminal investigation. A dead man's friends console his murderer. The police destroy the evidence needed to trap the criminal. The best hiding place for the murder weapon turns out to be right under the policemen's noses. Dahl reveals how much of "normal" existence is actually a contrived appearance that can be easily manipulated. Mary moves outside the predictable by turning the lamb into a weapon, then overcomes the police by turning the weapon back into a lamb. Having experienced what lies beneath the surface, she can now arrange appearances to her own advantage.

Style and Technique

As befits a story dealing with appearances and reality, much of "Lamb to the Slaughter" is told through details that Dahl carefully selects and arranges into various patterns to cause the reader to go below the surface to find the meanings in the story. Reference is made to Mary's large, dark, placid eyes early in the story, indicating her harmless, domestic personality; they are referred to again when she persuades Patrick's friends to eat the leg of lamb, revealing this time how deceptive Mary's appearance is. Throughout the story, words such as "simple," "easy," "normal," and "natural" acquire an ironic overtone, for the reader perceives the complex, artificial, and abnormal state of the world. Patrick's announcement of divorce and the policemen's dismissal of Mary as a likely murder suspect are never actually depicted; the reader is left to deduce these events from snatches of dialogue.

Dahl's technique reaches a hilarious crescendo in the dinner scene, in which the policemen eat the leg of lamb and discuss the possibility of finding the blunt instrument used to kill Patrick. The policemen's complacence, their belief that as soon as they finish eating they will easily be able to track down the murder weapon, and their actual behavior as unwitting accessories to their friend's murder reveal the polarities upon which the story is built. On the surface, the story depicts a world that is orderly, rational, and easily understood, but beneath this world are strange forces which can invest even the most innocent and everyday scenes with grotesque meaning.

Anthony J. Bernardo, Jr.

THE LAST CLASS

Author: Alphonse Daudet (1840-1897)
Type of plot: Social realism
Time of plot: c. 1873, during the Franco-Prussian War
Locale: A town in Alsace, France
First published: "La Dernière Classe," 1873 (English translation, 1900)

> *Principal characters:*
> FRANZ, the young boy, the narrator
> MONSIEUR HAMEL, the teacher

The Story

"The Last Class" is the tender story of a young Alsatian boy and his last French lesson. The setting is an unnamed town in Alsace, and the story takes place near the beginning of the Prussian occupation of Alsace and Lorraine, about 1873. Little Franz is the narrator of the story. Having gotten a late start on this beautiful warm morning, Franz rushes to school. He is fearful that Monsieur Hamel will scold him because he is late and has not prepared his French lesson on participles.

On his way to school, Franz passes through the town square, and in front of the town hall he sees a small group of people reading notices posted on a grating. These are notices posted by the Prussians concerning orders issued from headquarters. While Franz is running across the square, Wachter, the blacksmith, calls to him that there is no need to hurry. Franz thinks that Wachter is teasing him.

Out of breath, he arrives at school. To his dismay, there is no noise or confusion to cover his entrance. Instead, this day, there is the silence and stillness of the Sabbath. Frightened and red-faced, he enters the classroom; instead of giving Franz a harsh scolding, however, Monsieur Hamel gently directs Franz to his seat.

Once settled in his seat, Franz begins to notice the differences that this day has brought. Monsieur Hamel is all dressed up in his Sunday best, the clothes that he wears when prizes are given or on inspection days. Franz's classmates are especially solemn this day. Then his attention is drawn to the back of the room, where villagers are seated, and to Hauser, there with his old primer spread across his knees. Everyone has an air of sadness and anticipation.

Monsieur Hamel gently announces that orders have come from Berlin that beginning tomorrow, German only will be the language of instruction. Today, he tells them, is the last lesson that they will receive in French. Franz regrets the time that he has wasted. The villagers are sorry that they have not visited more often and now wish to express their gratitude for Monsieur Hamel's forty years of service.

It is Franz's turn to recite, but, unprepared, he struggles to express himself and fails. Monsieur Hamel does not belittle or scold him. Instead he expresses the regret that Franz and all the children should have for not having learned when the time was at hand. He points out that it is not Franz who is chiefly at fault. He blames himself and the parents especially for not having been sufficiently concerned with their children's education.

With great patriotic fervor, Monsieur Hamel speaks of the French language as the best language in the world. He continues by reading their lesson to them. The grammar lesson is followed by the writing lesson, with the model provided by Monsieur Hamel's beautiful handwriting of "France, Alsace! France, Alsace." Every student in the class is intent on his work, and nothing but the scratching of pens can be heard.

From time to time, Franz observes Monsieur Hamel, who is studying every detail of the room in which he has taught for the past forty years, and sorrow for this man fills Franz's heart. The writing lesson is followed by history. Hauser joins with the little children to spell out the letters. Then the Angelus and a trumpet blast of the Prussians sound at the same moment. Monsieur Hamel rises from his chair and, in a choked voice, tries to address the class, but he cannot. Taking a piece of chalk, he writes on the blackboard in his largest hand, "Vive La France," and then dismisses them with a motion of his hand.

Themes and Meanings

Daudet expounds the themes of freedom and patriotism in his short story "The Last Class." Courage, the importance of education, and the preciousness of one's own language are interrelated themes.

The people of the town and of Alsace have already had their freedom taken from them. A reminder of this loss appears in the second paragraph, where mention is made of the Prussians drilling in Rippert Meadows. Another reminder is the posting of news on the grating in the town square in front of the town hall. Here the townspeople come to learn of any new regulations which are to be imposed on them. Even as Franz sees the people reading the notices, he expects more bad news, battles lost, requisitions made. There is an aura of helplessness which comes with this loss of freedom. The atmosphere of this day, however, is not like that of other days even under the Prussian occupation. The sadness, solemnity, and quietness of the classroom seem to forebode something worse to come. The gentle tone of Monsieur Hamel is not the usual voice that has instructed these young people. His is usually the confident, commanding voice of self-assurance, scolding, prodding, and encouraging his students to learn. Today the sense of defeat and loss of freedom is even greater than that usually evoked by the simple presence of the Prussians and their initial occupation of the country that Monsieur Hamel loves.

Monsieur Hamel announces that today will be his last day to teach. Tomorrow the students will have a new teacher, and tomorrow all instruction will be given in German. With that, he implores them to be especially attentive, because this will be the last lesson that they will have in French. Suddenly, Franz is struck with the realization that he is about to lose something priceless, a part of his life. At this moment too, he regrets the time that he has wasted, the classes that he has missed. The very things that the townspeople cherish, they have taken for granted; now the loss of freedom has robbed them of their precious language. The cut is even deeper when Franz's turn comes to recite, because he has not studied, he is unprepared. Yet Monsieur Hamel does not lay the blame on Franz. He states that he as well as the students' parents must be faulted for their indifference to their children's education. The language for which they have so much pride and feel such great love is to be taken from them. Language, the mark of one's heritage, is their key to personal freedom. By refusing to allow the Alsatians to teach in French, the Prussians have taken one more step to enslave them. The loss of national identity is especially cruel when one is denied expression in one's own language. This loss is driven home by the presence of old Hauser with his old primer, spelling out the letters with the children in the merging of generations with a common bond.

The proud Monsieur Hamel embodies at the same time the courage and frustration of a subjugated people. There is hope still in his demeanor, dressed as he is in his finest clothing on this sad day. His determination to teach once more comes as a rallying cry to those present not to forget who they are, not to give up their heritage and what they hold dear to them. In defiance, he has lifted the flag by writing in his finest hand, "France, Alsace! France, Alsace!" With one last courageous gesture, standing straight and tall, Monsieur Hamel assures his friends that freedom will be theirs once by boldly writing the words "Vive La France" on the blackboard.

Style and Technique

The language that Daudet uses in "The Last Class' is straightforward and earthy, depicting with poetic simplicity the setting of the story and the people who are the heart of it. The tone and mood blend into a tender sadness yet maintain the intensity of purpose intended by the author. The reader is immediately drawn into and made a part of the story through Daudet's skillful realism.

It is easy to visualize the scene and feel as Franz must feel on this beautiful, warm day. The temptation to enjoy the outdoors and the call to responsibility at school are so humanly portrayed that the reader can easily identify with Franz. The descriptions of the outdoors and of the interior of the school are indeed tableaux, but tableaux which radiate the warmth of the sun and encourage the reader to participate in the last lesson. One can share Franz's embarrassment at not knowing his lesson, and one can participate in the emotional distress which marks Monsieur Hamel's testimony to courage and patriotism. The reader is both an observer looking through the window and a student or villager sitting on a bench in the classroom.

An almost spiritual quality is felt when the Angelus rings—a sense of freedom. This is countered, however, by the trumpet blast of the Prussians— enforcing the realization that freedom must be won again.

David J. Quinn

THE LAST MOHICAN

Author: Bernard Malamud (1914-1986)
Type of plot: Quest narrative
Time of plot: The 1950's
Locale: Rome
First published: 1958

Principal characters:
ARTHUR FIDELMAN, an art scholar
SHIMON SUSSKIND, the beggar who pursues him

The Story

As the story opens, Arthur Fidelman, artist manqué, arrives at the Rome train depot for a stay of some weeks as part of his yearlong project to pursue research for a critical study of Giotto, only one chapter of which rests in his briefcase. Instead, he meets a refugee named Shimon Susskind, a beggar-peddler, who pursues Fidelman through a series of scenes. In the first scene, Fidelman, responding "Shalom" for the first time in his life, refuses to give Susskind a suit but grudgingly gives him a dollar. The next encounter takes place about a week later, after Fidelman has "organized" his life—working in libraries in the morning and studying in churches and museums in the after-noon. Returning to his hotel, he is surprised by a visit from Susskind, who again importunes him for the suit but settles for five dollars. The next day at lunch, Fidelman again glances up to see Susskind, who once more pleads for some investment money so that he can sell ladies' stockings, chestnuts, any-thing. Rebuffing Susskind, Fidelman continues his research, returning to his hotel late that night to discover that his briefcase is missing. The pursued now becomes the pursuer.

Yet before that event takes place, Fidelman dreams that he is pursuing Susskind through the Jewish catacombs under Rome, by the light of a seven-flamed candelabra. Elusive Susskind, who knows the ins and outs, escapes; the candles flicker; and in his dream Fidelman is left "sightless and alone."

Next Fidelman postpones his trip to Florence, reports the theft to the po-lice, and moves to a small pension, where he broods and attempts to write but feels lost without something solid—his first chapter—upon which to build. Then begins his search through the markets, through lanes and alleys of transient peddlers, throughout October and November, for Susskind. Although he truly knows Rome now, his "heart is burdened with rage for the refugee." One Friday night, Fidelman strays into a synagogue and hears about the tragic loss of life during the Holocaust, then wanders through the ghetto, tracking Susskind, who, he now knows, also makes money by saying prayers for the dead at the cemetery. Fidelman visits the cemetery the next day and sees grave markers lamenting those killed by the Nazis, but he does not find Susskind.

In mid-December, visiting St. Peter's to see the Giotto mosaic again, he sees Susskind selling black and white rosaries on the steps and confronts him, but is told nothing. Furtively, he follows Susskind to his "overgrown closet" in the ghetto but does not talk with him. In his dream that night, however, he does confront him, seeing him in the context of the Giotto painting which shows Saint Francis giving an old knight his gold cloak. The next day he hurries, bleary-eyed, to Susskind's room, taking a suit to him. Susskind admits that he burned the chapter because, although the "words were there . . . the spirit was missing." Fidelman experiences a triumphant insight and runs after the fleeing Susskind shouting, "All is forgiven," but the refugee is last seen still running.

Themes and Meanings

Arthur Fidelman, the Jew from the Bronx, makes a journey to Italy to discover its rich history and thus complete his study of Giotto. In a sense, what he actually does complete is the study of himself. His quest becomes transformed when he meets the mythic, archetypal trickster-beggar Shimon Susskind, who challenges Fidelman to recognize suffering—his own and that of the Jewish refugees of World War II—indeed, to recognize his own Jewishness and responsibility to his fellowman. In an early scene, Susskind asks, "You know what responsibility means?" Fidelman replies, "I think so." "Then you are responsible," says Susskind, "Because you are a man. Because you are a Jew, aren't you?" This exhortation comes to mind at the end of the story, when Fidelman achieves his revelation and willingly gives the suit to Susskind.

When Fidelman, after the theft of his briefcase, must stay in Rome to pursue Susskind, he immerses himself in the real life of Rome, casting off the veneer—replacing his oxblood gumsoles with light Italian shoes—burrowing beneath the surface of art in the churches and museums to the bedrock question posed in one of his dreams: "Why is art?" He begins to understand the real meaning of Giotto's work showing the saint bestowing a cloak on the old knight.

The scholar becomes a real human being rather than a superficial observer. As his dreams reveal, he begins to acknowledge his own Jewishness (the dream of the catacombs and candelabra) and his own larger humanity. The richness of his insight reverberates beyond simple statement, but one senses that in gaining understanding of the suffering of Susskind, he is beginning to understand the root of all suffering—his own included.

Style and Technique

Malamud's key framework involves the use of the journey-quest motif joined with pursuit and then reversal, so that Fidelman, initially the one hounded by Susskind, becomes the pursuer. The episodes consist of sharply focused encounters between the two key characters, though some critics find Susskind to be the central character of the story. In review, however, the reader will sense the balance between the mythic characterization of Susskind, the survivor, and Fidelman—the man who would have faith—learning through their interaction. When Fidelman begins the pursuit of Susskind, he enters Susskind's life, and Fidelman's quest for knowledge shifts from "static" words in the libraries and the scrutiny of the pictures on the walls to an awareness of the hidden life which generated Giotto's compassion. For Fidelman, this hidden life is found in the synagogue, in the reminders of Auschwitz, and in the freedom-seeking connivance of Susskind.

Within this journey-quest framework, Malamud sets dream sequences which show the reader the subconscious awareness growing in Fidelman. Susskind, the magical, appears and vanishes in dreams as he does in Fidelman's conscious life. In the dream of Jewish catacombs, Fidelman acknowledges his "sightlessness" without the seven-flamed candelabra. His final "vision" rests upon the last dream, which interprets the gift that Giotto portrays in the mosaic—the compassion, the awareness of suffering which can thus lead to Fidelman's final epiphany.

Content and construction blend in this story to make the conscious and subconscious accessible, to make Susskind at once a schnorrer and a savior, to render Fidelman capable of an act of faith, one which links him with humanity, not with mere scholarship.

Eileen Lothamer

LAURA

Author: Saki (Hector Hugh Munro, 1870-1916)
Type of plot: Comic fantasy
Time of plot: Early twentieth century
Locale: England and Cairo
First published: 1912

>Principal characters:
> LAURA, an English lady reincarnated successively as an otter
>   and a Nubian boy
> AMANDA, her confidante
> EGBERT, Amanda's irritating husband

The Story

"Laura" is a story in three parts. The first part consists entirely of a conversation between Laura and her friend (or possibly relation) Amanda, in which Laura expresses her belief that once she has died—which she expects to happen in about three days—she will be reincarnated in some shape appropriate to her nature and her behavior in previous lives. She thinks that her present life has probably earned for her demotion to the status of an animal, but an attractive animal, such as an otter; and that her behavior as an otter may earn for her promotion back to a "primitive" rank of humanity, such as being "a little, brown unclothed Nubian boy."

Amanda is reluctant to believe any of this, but the first part of Laura's prediction comes true, in that she dies on time, indeed slightly early. In the second stage of the story, Amanda is brought to complete belief in Laura's theory by the depredations of a marauding otter, which does exactly the kind of irritating things that Laura did when she was alive, and which seems to be conducting a vendetta against Amanda's husband, Egbert, with human skill and foreknowledge. This stage ends with the killing of the otter by an imported pack of hounds, and Amanda's collapse from nervous prostration—evidently caused by her guilt at having taken part in a kind of murder.

The third stage of the story functions almost as a coda. Amanda has been taken on a holiday to Egypt and has recovered, now dismissing the otter episode as mere coincidence. Then she hears her husband yelling in rage at some malignant prankster who, like Laura and the otter, knows exactly how to irritate him most. Who is the culprit? "A little beast of a naked brown Nubian boy." With that Amanda relapses, her worst fears confirmed.

In a sense, the center of the story is Amanda's growing conviction, which the reader is invited to share. She moves from utter doubt of Laura's theory (in itself mildly preposterous), to fear that it may be true, to total and crippling belief. Around this center, though, there are several unexpected questions. The reader is told that Laura's motivation in all of her shapes is dislike of Amanda's husband Egbert. Egbert, however, is never more than irritated by the killing of his hens or the spoiling of his shirts. Laura's true victim is Amanda, who appears to be, if not her friend, at least someone to whom she talks. Why is Amanda singled out? How are the two ladies connected? They do not seem to be related, for Amanda can ask cautiously if there is madness in Laura's family, like someone who does not know, but Laura certainly lives in Amanda's house. Conceivably they are relatives by marriage, in which case the animosity of Egbert and Laura could be familiar, familial, even that of brother and sister, while the handling of Amanda would contain a touch of scorn or contempt. This is left unexplained, however, like so much in the story—the nature of Laura's illness, the mechanics of the metamorphoses, and the source of Laura's insight.

Themes and Meanings

As a story, "Laura" functions mainly as an assault on the comfortable certainties of the English upper class in the last few years before World War I, which was to shatter that class's power and kill so many of its members (including the author, who was shot by a German sniper in 1916). The main vehicle of the assault is Laura, who projects from the start an air of total superiority. Her belief in the transmigration of souls most obviously contradicts central tenets of Christianity—Laura scornfully wonders if she could be imagined as an angel—but Laura also rises above fear (the thought of death causes her no emotion), above the doctor (whom she mentions only with sarcastic deference), and above all forms of social convention (even, in otter shape, exploiting the opportunities presented by her own funeral). Most of all, though, Laura rejects all forms of moral judgment. She does confess that "I haven't been very good," but immediately qualifies this by listing all of her failings without interest and then claiming that they are excused by circumstance. She furthermore goes on unrepentantly to repeat them all in future existences, and at all times takes a positive delight in mischief. The thoughts which she projects are that sin is fun, that virtue is so boring as to be provocative, and that dash and elegance are the most important qualities that a person can possess.

Amanda and Egbert function by contrast as images of sober rectitude and orthodoxy. Egbert's passions—such as they are—center on country hobbies and on keeping up a social front; there is a kind of significance at the very end in the disturbance of his highly imperial ritual of dressing for dinner. Amanda seems less hidebound but also views the death of her friend primarily as a nuisance, interrupting her plans for golf and fishing and preventing full enjoyment of her rhododendrons. In this she evidently represents her class. During a brief conversation, her uncle-in-law Sir Lulworth shows that he takes a similar view of Laura as "unaccountable" and "inconsiderate." The settled routine which all three of these characters imply is so rigid as to make every reader sympathize with Laura's defiance and disturbance of it.

Nevertheless, there is an ambiguity in Saki's story. For one thing, his original audience was drawn largely from the class which the story attacks. For another, Laura and Sir Lulworth at least share a quality of lordly open-mindedness, very much an upper-class quality. If "Laura" is a satire, it is an insider's satire which accepts much of what it pretends to reject. Possibly the key to its meaning lies in the fact that Amanda suffers so much more than the other characters in her social circle. The reason for this is, surely, that the others remain armored in certainty, like Egbert, or in self-confidence, like Sir Lulworth. Amanda, however, is fatally weak. At the very beginning she refuses to believe that Laura is dying. Once convinced, however, she wants Laura to take it more seriously. Then she rejects Laura's idea of reincarnation, apparently simply because it is unfamiliar, only to be talked into it later by Sir Lulworth. She continually oscillates between doubt and belief and is never capable of cool detachment. The narrator in fact passes judgment on her in a single sentence: "She was one of those who shape their opinions rather readily from the standpoint of those around them." In a word, she lacks individuality. She exists only as a member of society. To Saki this is an unforgivable flaw.

Style and Technique

Most of the force of "Laura" is generated by its style, and especially by the sardonic tone of its privileged speakers, Laura and the narrator. Both exploit a deliberately inappropriate ceremoniousness of phrase. "I have the doctor's permission to live till Tuesday," says Laura, implying that survival until Wednesday would be a breach of etiquette. "As a matter of fact Laura died on Monday," reports the narrator, with equal calm. Laura also repeatedly demonstrates a sort of literal-mindedness which challenges the unstated ethics of English conversation. "How could you?" asks Amanda when Laura confesses setting all of Egbert's hens loose—and by this Amanda means, evidently, "How could you be so irresponsible?" Laura, however, chooses to take the question as a mere "matter of fact," like her own death, and answers that it was easy. In the same way, when Amanda says "today is Saturday; this is serious," she clearly means, again implicitly, that what is serious is the fact that Laura has only three days to live. Yet Laura again takes the statement only at face value, as if what is serious is today being Saturday. Both exchanges, tiny in themselves, nevertheless reinforce the story's basic point that moral responsibility is no virtue and that being serious does no one any good.

Other devices within the story include the narrator's repeated indications that the moral attitudes of his orthodox characters are hypocritical, and the careful and studied use of verbs describing speech. It is noticeable that in the story's first section, Laura's speeches are followed by neutral or detached words, such as "said," "observed," and "admitted." Amanda, however, gasps, protests, exclaims, and sighs, though all this is created far less by grief than by indignation. Amanda, too, is almost the only character in the story incapable of using the highly dispassionate and class-bound English pronoun "one," so clearly demonstrated by Laura: "When one hasn't been very good in the life one has just lived, one reincarnates in some lower organism." Both Egbert and Sir Lulworth, however, use "one" at critical moments, to distance themselves or to indicate offense. The absence of this word from Amanda's armory is one more pointer to her vulnerable emotional status.

It is ironic that a woman so lacking in individuality should be unable to use a nonindividual form. Yet the truth behind the detail is that self-possession is necessary for detachment. In this as in other matters, Saki is remarkable for his close observation and for his power in packing complex satire into scenes of great brevity and simplicity.

T. A. Shippey

THE LEANING TOWER

Author: Katherine Anne Porter (1890-1980)
Type of plot: Initiation story
Time of plot: 1931
Locale: Berlin
First published: 1941

Principal characters:
> CHARLES UPTON, the protagonist, an American art student in Berlin
> KUNO HELLENTAFEL, his boyhood friend from Texas
> ROSA REICHL, Upton's landlady
> OTTO BUSSEN, a German mathematics student
> TADEUSZ MEY, a Polish music student
> HANS VON GEHRING, a young German student from Heidelberg suffering from a dueling wound

The Story

This lengthy story opens in Berlin in late December of 1931 as Charles Upton, a young, poor art student, the son of a farming family in Texas, is seeking new quarters because his hotel is unpleasant, oppressive, and expensive. On Christmas Eve his thoughts turn to Kuno Hallentafel, a childhood friend from Texas and the son of a prosperous merchant. Kuno, whose family came from Germany and later returned for visits, spoke so glowingly of the beauty and grandeur of Berlin that Charles decided to study art there. Charles "in his imagination saw it as a great shimmering city of castles towering in misty light."

Much of the rest of the plot is devoted to showing how Charles's early romantic perceptions of Berlin are contradicted by the reality of his life there. In this sense, it is an initiation story common in American literature, in which the protagonist, usually a young person, is disabused of earlier beliefs, or loses his innocence, as he comes to a sobering new awareness or understanding brought about by his travels or encounters with different types of people. Charles's disillusionment with Berlin comes most dramatically at the hands of the hotel owners and landlords he encounters, in general a base, grasping, and ill-tempered group who have little sympathy for the people who need to rent their ghastly and uncomfortable furnished rooms. When Charles tries to move earlier than expected, one landlady even summons a policeman, who treats him with disdain as she cheats him of some of his meager resources. The most important landlady is Rosa Reichl, a once-wealthy, affected, overbearing, and intrusive woman. During their first meeting Charles accidentally breaks a small plaster replica of the Leaning Tower of Pisa, a treasured memento of her honeymoon in Italy. In Rosa's furnished rooms, Charles comes to know three other young men who also are instrumental in his initiation.

The first of these young men is Otto Bussen, a very poor German mathematics student from Dalmatia. Bussen speaks Low German, an indication of his inferior social status. Under the guise of trying to improve him, Rosa continuously criticizes his manners and behavior. At one point he appears to try to commit suicide by poison, but he is saved by the efforts of Charles and the other boarders. The second boarder is Tadeusz Mey, a Polish student of music, also harassed by Rosa, who brings to Charles the perspective of an intelligent non-German who understands the larger cultural contexts of European history. The third boarder is Hans von Gehring, a student from Heidelberg who has come to Berlin for treatment of an infected dueling wound on his face, of which he is proud. Hans, at times a contemptuous and disdainful incipient Nazi, harbors notions of the superiority of the German race.

The last part of the story shifts from Rosa's rooms to a Berlin cabaret for a New Year's Eve celebration. Here again, the conflict between the three boarders is evident as they discuss women, social classes, racial distinctions, and World War I; for Charles, however, as the evening wears on and midnight approaches, the animosities dissolve into song and drunken camaraderie. The good will generated at the cabaret continues as the boarders return to their lodgings to find Rosa also happy from drinking champagne. At this point, Charles notices that the broken Leaning Tower of Pisa has been mended and is now behind glass in a corner cabinet. Charles's drunken jollity fades, however, as he begins to feel "an infernal desolation of the spirit." He expects that a good cry is all that is needed to complete the evening's adventure, but the concluding sentence indicates his deep and ultimate disillusionment: "No crying jag or any other kind of jag would ever, in this world, do anything at all for him."

Themes and Meanings

The principal theme of initiation already noted in Charles's disillusionment with Berlin through his encounter with landlords and through his association with Otto, Tadeusz, and Hans is reinforced by his perceptions of Berliners as surly, resentful, and hostile to outsiders. The lengthy December darkness of Berlin also increases his sense of alienation: "The long nights oppressed him with unreasonable premonitions of danger. The darkness closed over the strange city like the great fist of an enemy who had survived in full strength, a voiceless monster from a prehuman, older and colder and grimmer time of the world."

Charles's disillusionment extends beyond Berlin to Germany itself, a country still showing the effects of defeat in World War I, evidence of which he sees in the blinded and mutilated veterans on the street. The rise of Nazis to power and the coming of World War II is suggested by Hans's remark that Germany will win the next war. Charles, in other words, is coming to understand some important aspects of German culture in the 1930's.

Still another dimension of Charles's growing sensibility concerns Europe's relationship to the United States. He comes to understand through his conversations with his fellow roomers that the nations of Europe mistrust and stereotype one another. Tadeusz, the cosmopolitan Pole, who is Charles's mentor in these matters, tells him: "Europeans hate each other for everything and for nothing; they've been trying to destroy each other for two thousand years, why do you Americans expect us to like you?" Tadeusz's question points to still another aspect of Charles's education. Even though he is poor, he comes to realize that all consider him a rich American, regarding him with a mixture of scorn and envy.

Charles's trip to Europe is really, then, a journey into understanding. This innocent boy from Texas, with images of Berlin as a "shimmering city" dancing in his head, comes to know something about the dispiriting darker aspects of life. This disillusionment in the context of international travel has been a favorite theme in American literature, and it reflects the clash of cultures that accompanied America's rise to prominence as a world power in the early decades of the twentieth century.

Style and Technique

The dark and unpleasant atmosphere of Berlin and its impact on Charles is made vivid through Porter's use of animal imagery, which sometimes borders on caricature. Repeatedly, she turns to various animals to help her characterize the people of Berlin whom Charles finds so distasteful. They are often compared to pigs who waddle down the sidewalk or who have enormous rolls of fat across their backs. In one remarkable scene, porcine Berliners gather to gaze longingly at a shop window full of hams, sausages, and bacon, next to another window displaying various pigs made of candy, wood, or metal. Porter then describes these Berliners as "shameless mounds of fat" standing "in a trance of pig worship, gazing with eyes damp with admiration and appetite." A description of the landladies of the city brings forth a torrent of unpleasant animal comparisons: "They were smiling foxes, famished wolves, slovenly house cats, mere tigers, hyenas, furies. . . ." In addition to animals, Porter focuses on the furnishings of rooms and the decorations of Berlin to emphasize the essential grotesquerie of the city. Charles at one point closely examines a dozen repulsive pottery cupids on a steep roof and speculates on the unrefined taste of their owners.

The season of the year also helps to underscore symbolically Charles's psychological state. Besides the darkness of late December, the dying year is an appropriate time for the demise of Charles's illusions about Berlin, his dis-

appointment coming to a climax, ironically, after the New Year's Eve celebration. The one note of hope in this final scene can be inferred, again, from
the season. It is going to be a new year soon, and perhaps for Charles this
symbolizes a new beginning, free of previous misconceptions.

Another symbol, the most important one in the story, is the small replica
of the Leaning Tower of Pisa. It is not well integrated and clear, but it does
suggest several things important to the story. Its vulgarity is clearly associated
with that of its owner, Rosa, and with the German nation as a whole. Its
breaking by Charles, an American, brings to mind the chaos and breakdown
of German culture in the aftermath of the defeat of World War I. In this
connection, it is noteworthy that Rosa has put the repaired replica behind
glass, safe from Charles. In addition, Charles's final thoughts about the
tower suggest a personal symbolism for him, reflecting his state of mind at
the conclusion of the story: The precariousness of the leaning structure reminds him of threats and danger and, ultimately, death.

Finally, the intrinsic symbolism of the journey itself corresponds to the
main theme of initiation. Charles's travels to Berlin represent a journey into
awareness. The naïve boy from Texas has been initiated into knowledge
which leaves him sadder and more somber but also more sophisticated and
mature.

Walter Herrscher

LEAVES

Author: John Updike (1932-   )
Type of plot: Psychological sketch
Time of plot: The 1960's
Locale: New England
First published: 1964

> *Principal characters:*
> A WRITER, a man reflecting on his life
> HELEN, his ex-wife

The Story

Gazing out the window at grape leaves, a writer reflects upon their beauty, and upon the relation of the recent crises of his life to nature. The effortless creativity of nature and its freedom from guilt contrasts with the artifice of his writing and with his experiences of shame and fear. As he contemplates his natural surroundings, he is beginning to sort through the memories of his divorce, trying to make sense of his feelings of pain and love. He is also contemplating his own activity as a writer, drawing the reader into the processes of capturing the images of life on a leaf of paper:

> A blue jay lights on a twig outside my window. Momentarily sturdy, he stands astraddle, his dingy rump toward me, his head alertly frozen in silhouette, the predatory curve of his beak stamped on a sky almost white above the misting tawny marsh. See him? I do, and, snapping the chain of my thought, I have reached through glass and seized him and stamped him on this page. Now he is gone. And yet, there, a few lines above, he still is, "astraddle," his rump "dingy," his head "alertly frozen." A curious trick, possibly useless, but mine.

The writer of this passage continues to enter in and out of descriptions of the natural beauty around him, drawn back from entering fully into its profusion by images of his wife's departure. Sunlight playing through the grape leaves casts shadows in menacing shapes, yet the intricacy of the colors and patterns among the leaves suggests innocence, shelter, and openness as well. Drawn outward to the embracing leaves of surrounding trees, he is suddenly cast back inward to his sorrow.

Others have told him that he acted badly, but he is yet unable to feel the appropriate guilt. He is trapped between his inability to organize the events and tuck them safely into the past, and his inability to leap forward into his unforeseen future. When his wife left to get the divorce, the familiar patterns of their existence—searching for car keys, calling the baby-sitter—were broken along with their love. Driving along the familiar tree-lined streets became an act of moving back through the events of their life together, reinterpreting them in the light of their divorce. Meeting Helen in Boston, he sees her in her dual aspect of remembered "wife-to-be" and current ex-wife. He feels the darkness within him burst out and drown their love, and feels as if that world is now gone forever. "The natural world, where our love had existed, ceased to exist. My heart shied back; it shies back still. I retreated." Now he waits fearfully for each new stab of pain brought by letter or phone. Hidden away in a cottage to write, he discovers that he is unable to escape the past and sink into nature. The pages which he writes are no more able to join him and his guilt to nature than the dead leaves he has tracked into the cottage have the power to evoke the beauty of the living sunlit leaves.

Yet for the first time in a while, he is really able to see a low hill in the distance. Gazing at the lawn strewn with the fallen leaves of an elm, he recalls his first night at the cottage when he had gone to sleep reading Walt Whitman's *Leaves of Grass* (1855), certain that he was leaving his old life behind.

> And my sleep was a loop, so that in awaking I seemed still in the book, and the light-struck sky quivering through the stripped branches of the young elm seemed another page of Whitman, and I was entirely open, and lost, like a woman in passion, and free, and in love, without a shadow in any corner of my being.

After this awakening, he still must return home, but for him the shadows on the leaves have shifted with the changing light. "I imagine warmth leaning against the door, and open the door to let it in; sunlight falls flat at my feet like a penitent."

Themes and Meanings

Updike, in this brief but intricate story, evokes the complex tissue of relations and events which connect a person to others, to nature, and to the human spirit. Human beings find themselves in an awkward position between the natural world and their supernatural spirits, between earth and heaven. Nature itself exists without morality or guilt. It simply happens and need not search for meanings in all of its actions. Humans exist within nature yet they must struggle to find meanings and standards beyond nature in order to fulfill the urges of their spirits. They cannot act solely by nature, but must be responsible and self-conscious of their behavior. Thus, humans are in-between, drawn by the instincts of their natural bodies yet commanded by the rules of their supernatural spirits. Often, they are confused by this duality and torn between the two poles of their existence.

The writer in "Leaves" feels this split with painful clarity. He longs to be able to merge into nature in order to free himself from the agonies of guilt and sorrow which trouble his existence, yet he also desires to fulfill his ability to draw meaning out of events and shape his own future. He is able to capture in words enduring images of natural beauty, yet he feels unable to bring order out of the images of his own life. He wrestles to rediscover his place in the pattern of existence after the disaster of his divorce; his attempt to find meaning in his past actions still brings him great pain.

While his guilty humanity is the ultimate source of his discomfort, it is also the means through which he may begin to overcome his distress. Through the processes of writing and reflection, he begins to recognize his participation in both nature and humanity, and to realize the strength of the human spirit despite the fragility of the human situation. The mute pain of life can be lessened by the ability to give it words, to capture it and organize events into patterns which can be partly understood. The art of writing is a form of the spirit's struggle to harmonize itself with the natural world through which it lives. People are able to see events in new ways, turn them around, and partially rewrite the way these events affect the rest of their lives. This freedom of self-creation compensates for the spiritual pain and guilt which only humans suffer.

Style and Technique

Though written as prose, Updike's "Leaves" borders on poetry with its dense layering of meanings into a concise and rich imagery. The primary metaphor of leaves refers to the leaves of grape vines and trees, the pages on which the author writes, and the action of leaving each other. It brings together nature, spirit, and the events which bind them. The image also gradually draws the reader into the emotional process of a man taking leave of his past life and entering into the unknown patterns of a new stage of his existence.

The multiple meanings of this story's words and images suggest the inability of people to find clear and simple interpretations of their actions. Helen, the writer's wife, represents the naturalness their love once had, but as a participant in creating and maintaining the break in that love, she also represents the current pain and confusion of its loss. The sun shining on the leaves symbolizes life, love, and the guilt-free abandon of nature; it is also the image used for the guilt which casts shadows within the writer's soul and burns through his memories, changing them in the light of his sorrow. Updike's interweaving of this writer's reflections on nature, human nature, the art of writing, and his memories and emotions shows the complexity of the ways in which a person's life is shaped by, and shapes, the world around him.

This man is in the middle of his world in all ways. He is in the middle of sorting out his divorce which has broken his life into two parts, lost past and unattained future. He exists in the midst of his friends and family, bound to them by the ties of their mutual experiences, yet he is unable to see himself as they do: as unequivocally in the wrong. The writer's difficulty in understanding his own life and feelings is so realistic that it catches the reader up into the center of the story as well, uncertain of this man's past or future but sharing in his present pain. Finally, the writer also exists, along with all humanity, in the middle between heaven and earth, both of which offer him comfort and cause him pain. He can never exist solely in either but is always a participant in both, and this "in-between-ness" is his damnation as well as his salvation.

Mary J. Sturm

LEAVING THE YELLOW HOUSE

Author: Saul Bellow (1915-   )
Type of plot: Psychological realism
Time of plot: 1957
Locale: Sego Desert Lake in the American West, perhaps Utah
First published: 1958

Principal characters:
    HATTIE WAGGONER, the protagonist
    THE ROLFES, a retired couple
    THE PACES, the owners of a dude ranch
    DARLEY, the ranch foreman
    WICKS, Hattie's former lover
    INDIA, Hattie's dead friend

The Story

Hattie has lived in her yellow house at Sego Lake for twenty years. She arrived at the beginning of the Depression and lived a vagabond's life with a cowboy named Wicks. When Wicks left, she moved in with a woman of small but independent means named India, the original owner of the yellow house. As the story begins, Hattie is living alone in the small house, which was left to her by India. She has become something of a snob, preferring the society of the Rolfes and the Paces—who, like herself, are landowners and therefore worthy—to that of her former companions.

Into this fairly tranquil life, trouble intrudes. One evening, driving home drunk from the Rolfes, Hattie loses control of her car and ends up stuck on the railroad tracks. Darley, who works on the Paces' dude ranch, reluctantly agrees to tow Hattie's car, but he carelessly leaves the tow chain too long. Hattie, who is climbing over the chain as Darley jerks his truck into reverse, is knocked to the ground, her arm broken.

As she slowly recovers, Hattie wonders about the significance of her injury. Perhaps it is a judgment against her for her drunkenness, her laziness, her procrastinations. For the first time in her life she concerns herself with the past as fact, rather than as self-justifying fiction.

Yet admitting the truth has never been Hattie's style; about the accident, she always says she lost control because she sneezed, not because she was drunk. As Hattie proceeds in her quest for truth, her old self-deceiving patterns constantly impede her. While the old Hattie is bent on surviving, the new one is bent on knowing.

As a survivor, Hattie is a practical, social being. She must somehow pay her hospital bills, replace the blood she required during surgery, exercise her arm to regain its full use, keep the house in repair. Initially she assumes that her friends will be there to help her, as she would help them, but is the community really a safety net for the individual? Gradually she discovers that there are limits. The Rolfes are leaving for Seattle, the doctor will not buy her house, Amy (a neighboring miner and widow) will care for her only on condition of inheriting her house, and Pace offers a small monthly stipend if she will leave the house to him.

Growing confusion and isolation lead Hattie the survivor to yield more and more time to Hattie the seeker of truth. She scrupulously examines the past, focusing on her life with India, her life with Wicks, and the death of her dog, Ritchie.

An earlier version of Hattie's life with India casts her companion as an ill-tempered, foul-mouthed, helpless, drunken woman who ordered Hattie about and blamed her when things went wrong. Eventually, Hattie admits that she endured the abuse in order to inherit the house and concedes that India was basically kind and good to her.

Her memory of Wicks undergoes a similar revision. Earlier Wicks was the romantic cowboy who eventually drifted off into the sunset. Now she admits that she refused to marry him because she did not want to give up the distinguished Philadelphia name of her first husband. Among her recollections of their days as trappers is that of him kicking to death a beautiful white coyote. Their relationship ended prosaically at a remote hamburger stand they owned, when the lazy Wicks complained of the food. Hattie cooked a steak for him and threw him out. Now Hattie realizes that Wicks, like India, was a real friend.

Yet the vision of Wicks's killing the white coyote leads to another admission. Hattie has lamented the death of her dog, Ritchie, but at last she admits that it was she who killed Ritchie with an ax-blow to the head when he turned wild and sunk his teeth into her thigh. Her instincts for survival led her to shed blood; her guilt led her to blame her neighbor, Jacamares; her new commitment to truth leads her to confess the whole.

This confession of her own violent impulses intensifies her feeling of being alone, dependent now only on herself for survival. Her attention shifts away from reconstructing the past to planning for the future. She hurries out to her car to see if she is now able to drive, to maintain her independence, but she cannot shift or steer; her arm is all but useless.

Since she can no longer function in this life, she must prepare to leave it. She must make a will. A brief survey of her surviving relatives leaves only one likely heir: Joyce, the orphaned daughter of a cousin. Yet would leaving her the yellow house really be a kindness? Like Hattie, Joyce might become a lonely old drunk.

In a drunken blend of pain and joy, she decides to leave the yellow house to herself. Ironically, reconstructing the past has validated Hattie's sense of self and intensified her commitment to survival.

Themes and Meanings

Hattie discovers how to depend on herself when she is forced to depend on others. Like many aging people deprived of their former physical capabilities, Hattie begins to relive the past. She wants perspective on her life, an impartial view missing while she was actually caught up in events and in self-justification. This new vision helps Hattie accept herself as her own history, the sum total of her actions and her friendships. To some extent she acknowledges responsibility for her life, thus signaling a developing acceptance of death. She has come to understand that bodies, like houses, are "on loan."

Style and Technique

This story is remarkable for its unusual point of view, moving back and forth from a third-person central intelligence to a first-person confessional. The effect suggests that sometimes the author speaks and sometimes Hattie. The authorial voice, although sympathetic, tends to be more objective, whereas Hattie's voice is often lyric and subjective to the point of falsehood. Hence, the flickering point of view reflects Hattie's own vacillation between honesty and self-deception.

When readers are in Hattie's mind they find the world described in terms of simile and metaphor. For example, when Hattie is preoccupied with her dog Ritchie, the sofa cushions look like a dog's paws. Life itself is a "hereafter movie" recording a person from birth to the grave. The camera angle is always from behind, suggesting that one cannot falsify this record. As one lives, there is less and less film available, and as one prepares to die, one must watch the whole film.

The story's mixed chronology reflects Hattie's thoughts in like manner. One leaps back and forth among different layers of the past, then ahead to the future, the reader's confusion a strategic double to Hattie's own perplexity.

The symbol of the house unifies a fiction that might otherwise seem as disjointed as Hattie's mind. To Hattie the house symbolizes social position, achievement, and security. This meaning broadens when Hattie faces losing the yellow house, either by selling it to pay her medical bills or by dying and bequeathing it to someone. These are both ways in which she might have to "leave" the yellow house. In this sense, the material house becomes the outward sign of her tenuous hold on life.

Sheila Ortiz Taylor

LEFTY
Being the Tale of the Cross-eyed Lefty of Tula and the Steel Flea

Author: Nikolai Leskov (1831-1895)
Type of plot: Historical fantasy
Time of plot: 1815-1826
Locale: London, St. Petersburg, and Tula
First published: "Levsha (Skaz o tul'skom kosom levshe i o stal'noy blokhe),
1881 (English translation, 1906)

Principal characters:
> LEFTY, the protagonist, a gunsmith of folksy ways but
> consummate skill
> PLATOV, a Don Cossack of patriotic bent who accompanies
> Alexander I abroad
> TSAR ALEXANDER I, the ruler of Russia from 1801 to 1825
> TSAR NICHOLAS I, the ruler of Russia from 1825 to 1855

The Story

The Don Cossack Platov sets the tone for this whimsical tale by keeping the English off balance from the beginning. Alexander I's faithful but grumbling companion, in London with the tsar, refuses to acknowledge English superiority in anything. When the tsar exults over a gun in a museum, Platov pulls out a small tool, disassembles the gun, and proves that the mechanism was fashioned in Tula by a Russian craftsman. While the Englishmen stay up late endeavoring to come up with something the Russians cannot surpass, Platov sleeps soundly. In fact, each of the first two chapters ends with the Englishmen unable to sleep and Platov slumbering contentedly. When in need of guidance, the tsar's man quotes a Russian proverb, and when in need of sleep, he prays in the Orthodox manner, downs a shot of vodka, and drops off forthwith. Yet the result of his behavior is that the English hosts are frustrated, and the tsar is embarrassed. Thus, Alexander is pleased when the Englishmen present him with the gift of a miraculous steel flea. There could be nothing finer than this, he says; his own workmen could make nothing like it. The flea is wondrous in its workmanship, for, despite its exquisite daintiness, it has a key that winds up a motor within. Activated by the key, the mechanical insect executes kicks and dance steps and twitches its minuscule mustache. When Alexander praises the object lavishly, Platov must retreat for a time and accompanies the tsar home in obstinate silence.

In a short time, Alexander dies and is succeeded on the throne by his brother Nicholas I. After settling in to the job of being tsar, Nicholas one day notices the flea, which has been passed on to him, and wonders what it is.

None of his courtiers can tell him, but Platov soon appears and explains the matter to him. He also suggests to Nicholas that it would be a fine idea to allow the tsar's craftsmen in Tula to examine the piece and determine whether they might be able to design something better and outdo the English. Nicholas agrees, expressing faith in his men of Tula, and puts Platov in charge of the undertaking.

Wasting no time, Platov whirls into Tula with Cossack aides and negotiates with the workmen there, charging them with upholding the honor of Russia. Lefty and two other workmen promise to do their best but are vague about what they will do and how. As Platov's warnings not to bring shame to their native land still hover in the air, the three craftsmen set off for a nearby workshop. They take a few belongings with them, since they will be sequestered there for days on end. Once they are locked in and hard at work, their complete secrecy begins to intrigue those outside, who can hear them laboring but can see nothing. The townspeople even resort to trickery, shouting that the building is in danger because of a fire next door, but Lefty and the others inside ignore them and remain steadfast in their purpose, laboring feverishly up to the very moment of Platov's return.

Platov, who discerns no change in the flea, makes no effort to hide his chagrin, but pulls out some of Lefty's hair, expresses his outrage, and departs posthaste for St. Petersburg, dragging Lefty with him. When they arrive in the capital in two days, Platov leaves Lefty under guard and goes to report to the tsar. Nicholas asks expectantly what has been accomplished by his workmen and refuses to believe Platov's report that the men have done nothing. The flea, however, will not work when wound up by the tsar's daughter. Platov is furious and threatens to exact a dear price from the unfortunate Lefty. Nicholas still believes in his men, however, and asks that Lefty be brought in to explain, though he is shabbily dressed and knows no court manners. Lefty is unabashed in the tsar's presence and does proceed to explain the whole matter to him. Instructing the ruler to view one foot of the flea at a time under a powerful microscope, Lefty shows him that the Tula men have, indeed, done something even more remarkable than the Englishmen—they have put shoes on the flea. The tsar is delighted, and Platov asks Lefty's forgiveness. Lefty goes on to explain that each artisan has signed the pieces he has made, except that he himself has made the nails for the shoes, and the nails are too minute to be signed.

It remains for Lefty to act as the tsar's emissary and deliver the flea back to London, showing the foreigners what Russian craftsmen can do. Accompanied by an interpreter, Lefty speeds across Europe and to the English capital with the newly shod flea. When the Englishmen see what the Tula craftsmen have done, they are indeed impressed and give Lefty no respite from their questions. Since he has outdone their own workmen, they try to persuade him to wed an English lass and move to their country. Lefty, though not so blunt as Platov, is just as Russian and meets their suggestions with firm rebuttals, agreeing only to stay for a short visit. The English hosts reluctantly give in and shift their efforts to impressing Lefty with a round of visits to museums and factories, just as they had done with Alexander and Platov. Lefty takes in the sights with only mild interest—until he comes across a superior English method of cleaning rifle barrels. Immediately, the crafty Lefty recognizes this secret as something of potential military value to his country, and he demands to be taken home to St. Petersburg.

The English ship on which Lefty sails takes a long time to reach Russia, and to pass the time, Lefty engages in a drinking contest with an Englishman. As a result, he is in a deplorable condition upon reaching home shores, and he is taken to the police and finally to a lowly hospital. Although Lefty pulls himself together sufficiently to make his report, various petty officials fail to recognize him or his mission and eventually conspire to keep the report from the tsar. Lefty thus dies among the poor and insignificant in the hospital, a victim of ignorance, suspicion, and exceedingly rough treatment.

At the tale's end, the narrator observes that Lefty's real name is long since forgotten and that machines have taken over the work formerly done by such skilled artisans. There are no more master craftsmen such as Lefty, and therefore the legends that revolve around him continue to grow in the popular imagination.

Themes and Meanings

An abiding belief among the Russian folk of the nineteenth century was that the tsar was a benevolent man with their best interests at heart. It was believed that, although there were bureaucrats who came between the tsar and the people and intervened in the natural processes of trust and cooperation, if one could circumvent these petty officials and appeal directly to the tsar, everything would be fine. The narrative illustrates this idea well and shows it to be a two-way proposition, with Nicholas sticking firmly to his faith in the men of Tula, and Lefty, as their representative, feeling perfectly at his ease in the presence of the sovereign. Russian peasants referred to the tsar as "dear little father," and it is that feeling that is reflected in Lefty's behavior at court rather than any feeling of awe.

Russian nationalism and folk wisdom are blended in another theme in the text. Lefty and Platov are the chief fonts of the wisdom of the people, but Tsar Nicholas also plays a role therein, thus intertwining the ideas of nationalism and folk wisdom and the bond between tsar and folk. Platov, whose name probably alludes to Plato and thus to great wisdom, is the immediate reference point for the superiority and correctness of Russian ways. It is he who first deflates the English by behaving like the quintessential Russian nationalist while in London with Alexander. Platov is a Don Cossack, a fact that alone puts heavy stress on his Russianness. Beyond that, however, Platov considers Alexander too smitten with Western ways, so he does his best to steer the errant tsar back to his native roots and values. It is in this connection that Platov's Russian qualities are strengthened: He drinks Caucasian vodka, carries a folding icon with him and says his prayers before it, crosses himself in the Orthodox manner, quotes Russian proverbs, and points out that Russian soldiers defeated Napoleon without any of the fancy military paraphernalia that he views in the museums of London. Platov is also the one who suggests (later, when Nicholas is on the throne) that the matter of outdoing the steel flea be put in the hands of the craftsmen of Tula, a town much renowned for its master workmen, especially its metalworkers.

Lefty is much like Platov as a carrier of nationalism and folk wisdom. Both make a trip to London on behalf of the tsar, consume vodka, are connected with Russian icons, speak the folk idiom and make use of its rhyming aphorisms, and, most of all, prefer Russia to anywhere else. Defenders of Russian ways and of the Russian Orthodox faith both remain steadfast in their service of God, tsar, and country. Both shrewdly outwit the English. When Platov takes apart the marvelous gun in the English museum, demonstrating that its most intricate part was fashioned in Tula, it is a clear foreshadowing of the work that Lefty and his Tula brethren subsequently do, which is even more wondrous than the original work done by the English in creating the flea. Finally, both become homesick in England and long to go home to Russia.

Leskov's work, although highly nationalistic, is not without some barbs aimed at Russia as well. Foremost among these are two that are highly noticeable. The first is that, no matter how fine the quality of the Russian work on the flea, the fact remains that blind national pride and lack of technical knowledge have caused them to overtax the mechanism and partially disable the original creation. The second is that stupid bureaucrats not only prevent Lefty from getting his message to the tsar but also unnecessarily cause his death. Only in a backward nation could such things occur, and Leskov puts considerable stress on their happening in Russia. Lefty, after all, dies fruitlessly trying to reach Nicholas. The death, though, reminds one that it was this same Nicholas who was wonderfully constant in his faith that the men of Tula would not let him down—even when it appears that that is what they have done. Nicholas holds firm and gives orders that Lefty be allowed to explain in his own words. Thus is Lefty exonerated, and his passing marks the end of an era, enhancing the legends about him and bringing the story full circle, back to the wisdom of the Russian folk and their ways.

Style and Technique

The long, convoluted title of Leskov's work serves a dual function. It gives the tale a comic tinge at the outset, causing the reader to chuckle and to suspect that the narrative will be colored by fantasy. At the same time, its inclusion of such a detail as the protagonist's left-handedness is an indication of the humorous but intense nationalism of the story. Both expectations— the fantastic and the nationalistic—are realized during the unfolding of the plot. It would be impossible for Lefty and his coworkers, merely by "sharpening" their eyesight, to see details with the naked eye that ordinary mortals are able to view only through a powerful microscope. Yet one accepts this miraculous incongruity in the spirit of the work, an air of purest whimsy despite the historical background. Similarly, the fact that the hero is left-handed adds much to the story's effect. Indeed, Russians emphasize this aspect by commonly referring to the tale simply as "Lefty." The author's purpose is well served, since the resultant feeling on the part of Russians is that even a left-handed, scruffy, admittedly uneducated Russian can surpass anything that the supposedly civilized, urbane English can do. Prejudice about left-handers being what it is, this seemingly insignificant characterization becomes a vital symbol at work for the author, and the fact that Lefty has no other name known to the reader underscores its importance.

Much of the humor inherent in the work derives from the author's remarkably creative use of language. Using a device known as *skaz*, from the Russian for "tell," or "narrate," Leskov painted such a deceptive verbal landscape that one must read it very carefully for full appreciation of its merits. *Skaz* involves the use of fictitious narrators with highly original peculiarities of language, and the linguistic distortions, puns, and malapropisms of the tale, particularly those uttered by Lefty and Platov, are virtually untranslatable. The story's enjoyableness even in translation is the result in large part of its fancifulness and cleverness.

Edgar Frost

LEGAL AID

Author: Frank O'Connor (Michael Francis O'Donovan, 1903-1966)
Type of plot: Psychological realism
Time of plot: The 1940's
Locale: A provincial town in County Cork, Ireland
First published: 1946

Principal characters:
DELIA CARTY, a nineteen-year-old, working-class girl
TOM FLYNN, her young lover, a farmer's son
NED FLYNN, his father
FATHER CORCORAN, their parish priest
JACKIE CANTY, the Cartys' solicitor
MICHAEL IVERS, the Cartys' council
PETER HUMPHREYS, the Flynns' solicitor
DAN "ROARER" COOPER, the Flynns' council

The Story

Delia Carty, until the age of nineteen, had always been a "respectable" girl, but working as a maid for the O'Gradys proved to be her ruin, mainly because of the bad example they set for her. Within six months she was smoking and within a year she acquired a young lover named Tom Flynn, the son of farmer Ned Flynn. The narrator says that Tom is no great catch, being a big, uncouth galoot who loves to drink and chase the girls. After a two-year love affair, Delia becomes pregnant.

This is very bad news for Tom, who knows that his father "would first beat hell out of him and then throw him out and leave the farm to his nephews"; in this section of Ireland, no laborer's daughter is considered suitable for a farmer's son. Delia has to tell her mother, who persuades their parish priest, Father Corcoran, to talk to Tom's father about a possible marriage. As expected, however, Ned Flynn will not hear of it; in fact, he will not even agree to a small financial arrangement. This leads the narrator to remark, "Then, of course, the fun began."

When Delia Carty's father is told, he beats his daughter. Then he broods and grows angry about this blemish to his family name. He says, "Justice is what I want," so he brings Delia to Jackie Canty, the solicitor in town. Delia, although reluctant about bringing any kind of legal action against the man she loves, tells Canty that she has nothing in writing from Tom. She is upset when Canty informs her that Tom and his father will certainly claim that someone else is the father. Delia maintains that "Tom could never say that," but she is wrong. This is exactly the charge that Tom and his father decide to levy during the court case.

After Delia's baby is born, the court action begins. The Flynns' solicitor, Peter Humphreys, does not like the case at all, remembering "when law was about land, not love." He arranges for the Flynns to have as their council "Roarer" Cooper, a man who would normally rather fight than settle and one who has the reputation of always commanding attention—even as a first-class variety act.

On the day of the hearing, the court is crowded in order that the townspeople might hear whatever gossip is to be gained. Delia's council, Michael Ivers, approaches Roarer Cooper, asking for a settlement. Although Cooper is prepared to decline, he is sympathetic to the plight of poor Delia. After all, as Ivers knows, Cooper has daughters of his own. Ivers assures Cooper that Delia has never slept with anyone else because she was too much in love with Tom. Ivers also tells Cooper that it is the two respectable fathers that are behind this court action, not Delia. As Ivers says, "The trouble about marriage in this country, Dan Cooper, is that the fathers always insist on doing the courting." Cooper then asks why the priest did not make Flynn marry Delia. Ivers responds, "When the Catholic Church can make a farmer marry a laborer's daughter the Kingdom of God will be at hand."

Ivers is asking for a high cash settlement: £250. Cooper agrees to tell the Flynns to settle that amount on Delia, hoping that when she has that much money Ned Flynn will agree to Tom's marrying her. After lying about the judge, Cooper persuades Flynn to settle. He then acts as marriage broker, telling Ned Flynn that he would be a fool to let all that money get out of the family. When asked by Cooper, Tom says of Delia, "Oh, begod, the girl is all right." Making his way over to Delia, Cooper learns that she still loves Tom and asks her if she wants to marry him. With tears in her eyes, "as she thought of the poor broken china of an idol that was being offered her now," Delia says yes. Cooper tells her she "might make a man of him yet."

The two lawyers, Cooper and Ivers, make the match themselves in Johnny Desmond's pub; Desmond later remarks that the proceedings resembled a church mission, with Cooper threatening hellfire on everyone concerned and Ivers "piping away about the joys of Heaven." So the marriage is settled. The narrator, however, humorously observes, "Of course it was a terrible comedown for a true Roarer, and Cooper's reputation has never been the same since then."

Themes and Meanings

One of the main ideas in "Legal Aid" is that mature, reasonable adults can correct the serious errors that other adults commit out of silliness, prejudice, or plain stubbornness. As O'Connor often does in his stories, he shows that social prejudice can cause serious personal problems for everyone, especially, in this case, for the young. Delia Carty and Tom Flynn would have married happily early in the story except for the prejudice his father Ned has against allowing Tom to marry beneath his station in life. Fortunately, the social prejudice that prevents the marriage is overcome by the cleverness of the two lawyers.

A second theme closely accompanying the first is that people need to understand others—particularly the young—and treat them with the kindness they would like shown to themselves. Certainly Roarer Cooper realizes that Delia Carty is a nice young girl, not much different from his own daughters. Delia may have been led astray, but her truthfulness and her obvious love for Tom persuade Cooper that he should work on her behalf. This, then, is one of O'Connor's optimistic stories, for in it he shows that human experience and humanity can lead responsible people to do the right thing and to help others who are in need.

Style and Technique

"Legal Aid" is precisely what this story is about. In keeping with O'Connor's use of humor throughout the story, it is Roarer Cooper, the council for the Flynns, who works hardest to help Delia Carty and to arrange her marriage with Tom Flynn. One would expect the parents to work out the marriage, or the parish priest, but when all else fails, it is the legal profession which straightens out this matter. O'Connor uses his frequent humor to remind readers that the human situation indeed is often comic. Delia might never have gotten into trouble if she had not been exposed to the O'Gradys, for, as the narrator comments: "The whole family was slightly touched." Of Tom Flynn's attempts to justify himself to God, the narrator says: "Between lipstick, sofas, and tay in the parlor, Tom put it up to God that it was a great wonder she hadn't got him into worse trouble."

As he often does, O'Connor makes skillful use of dialogue to convey the action and the characterization in the story. Readers are allowed to sit in on a variety of revealing conversations among each of the principal characters. Delivered in the charming, everyday speech of the Irish countryside, these conversations reveal all the key points of the story. Arranged in simple, chronological order, the story proceeds swiftly to the courtroom scene, followed by only one brief paragraph of epilogue. It is because O'Connor has characterized his people so clearly that the reader can accept the happy ending without finding it implausible.

A. Bruce Dean

THE LEGEND OF ST. JULIAN, HOSPITALER

Author: Gustave Flaubert (1821-1880)
Type of plot: Morality tale
Time of plot: Early Middle Ages
Locale: Medieval Europe
First published: "La Légende de Saint Julien l'Hospitalier," 1877 (English translation, 1903)

> *Principal characters:*
> JULIAN, the protagonist, the only son of a noble couple, an adventurer and hermit
> JULIAN'S PARENTS, a prototypical lord and lady
> JULIAN'S WIFE, the daughter of the Emperor of Occitania
> THE LEPER, an incarnation of Jesus

The Story

In this tale, Gustave Flaubert chooses to re-create the vision of the world of medieval faith, and tells a venerable story as seen through the eyes of the twelfth century, even as such a story might be told in stained glass. The hero is followed through the twists of a plot where his predestined place as a saint is proven through the testings of life and sin, repentance and redemption. The world of Julian's birth is a perfect realization of the ideal manor life. Julian himself is the answer to his mother's prayers, and his christening is attended by the appearance of two divine messengers, each with a different prophecy. To Julian's mother appears the shadow of a holy hermit, predicting that her son will be a saint; to his father comes a Bohemian mendicant who predicts military glory, much blood, and an emperor's family. Both parents keep their visions secret and Julian grows surrounded by every fond hope. His underlying fault, an unconquerable lust for killing, is unleashed by his trapping of a white mouse which has disturbed him at Mass. From this point, at first encouraged by his parents in the medieval art of venery, Julian pursues a path which reduces him to the most savage of beasts, killing for the sake of killing, returning home matted with gore. One day, after a hallucinatory sequence of killings, Julian mortally wounds a great stag which turns and curses him in a human voice, predicting that he will kill his own parents. Again, the prophecy is kept as a secret, but Julian's fears make life at home impossible and he must forsake the world of his childhood. Thus ends the first segment.

The second part of the tale sees Julian as a mercenary soldier, killing in battle rather than in the hunt, as he gathers an army and reputation about him, finally saving the Emperor of Occitania from the Caliph of Cordova. The Emperor rewards this fairy tale hero and slayer of dragons with the hand of his daughter in marriage. A true Arabian Nights princess, she brings a handsome dowry and castle with her. Julian attempts to adopt domestic happiness, but his blood lust and his fear of killing his parents torment him, and one night he runs out of the palace to hunt, pursuing a host of animals which he cannot wound, until they surround him and through the pressure of their bodies force him to return to his castle. In his absence, his wife welcomes a pair of aged pilgrims who prove to be Julian's parents. She gives them her own bed, and Julian, returning in the dark, supposes them to be his wife and a lover and slaughters them, thus fulfilling the second of the prophecies. There remains only the third, of sainthood, to be realized as this second part of the tale ends.

Julian, having forsaken his wife and lands, becomes a wandering mendicant, forced by guilt to recount his sin of patricide and cast out by all men. He fears scenes of domestic happiness, the crowds in towns frighten him, and at the end of many wanderings he settles as a ferryman on the bank of a wide river. Profoundly repentant, he accepts the poor treatment accorded him by his passengers, lives on the most meager fare in a small hut, and attempts to atone for his sin by service to humanity. One stormy night, he ferries a hideous leper across the river. The leper demands shelter, food, Julian's bed, and eventually the very warmth of his body. When Julian has given all these things, without shrinking, the leper is transformed into the radiant Lord, Jesus, and rises to Paradise, bearing the transfigured saint with him. This, the author tells the reader, is more or less the story of Saint Julian, Hospitaler, as it was told in the stained glass windows of a church in his home region.

Themes and Meanings

Flaubert exploits a seemingly naïve tale to explore his own concerns of meticulous artistry and individual faith. The great lines of the story are determined for the writer even as Julian's life is prescribed for him in the prophecies of his youth. It is how the individual moves within the preordained limits of his fate that determines his final triumph. Julian is not a man of doubts, and in all of his actions he is shown as the perfect type of whatever role he fills: the perfect son, the consummate huntsman, a general and soldier without peer. His fault is imposed from without, yet it is wholly his own, and he both recognizes it, under the fear of the stag's prophecy, and agonizes under his inability to completely control it. Yet he does not question the right of God to impose such suffering on him. He combats his fate by what means he can command; abandoning hunting for warfare, yet obeying the strictest rules of chivalry, giving up both warfare and hunting as a kind of penance to avoid killing his parents. Yet when the actual deed is done, Julian's sorrow and repentance drive him into penitence, not rebellion. The omniscient narrator of "The Legend of St. Julian, Hospitaler" tells the state of Julian's mind, his agonies and angers, and it is through the narrator's posing of Julian's story that the reader himself may question the justice of a divine predestination that forces the individual to such glory through such suffering. While Julian is given a name by the narrator, the other characters remain at the level of their narrative function: mother, father, wife, old monk. The only other named character is Jesus, in His apotheosis at the culmination of the story. Thus, each mark of individuality, each change in Julian's motivations is set in relief by the nameless, static quality of his companions. The continuity of the name is needed to preserve the continuity of this individual who is in turn a model child, enraged huntsman, warrior, fairy-tale prince, murderer, penitent, and saint.

Style and Technique

Flaubert is generally recognized as one of the greatest stylists of the nineteenth century. In "The Legend of St. Julian, Hospitaler," he deliberately adopts the naïve colors and simplistic story line of a twelfth century stained glass window, a tour de force of hidden effort and sophistication. Perhaps his greatest accomplishment lies in his transposition through words of the visual imagery of his supposed model. The tableaux emblematic of the stages of Julian's life are set within the narrative frame of the story as glass medallions are set within their lead strips. In the opening pages, the reader sees Julian's parental estate, serene and perfect in its sunny beauty, complete even to the pots of heliotrope and basil on the windowsills. The prophets appear before Julian's parents in carefully set-off scenes, parallel and balanced, as if two medallions were set side by side. Julian's hunting days bring careful presentations of emblematic animals, beavers, and stags. His battles are shown with red donkeys and golden Indians, colorful combatants drawn from exotic lands. Even his princess and her fairy-tale castle are drawn with the same brilliant colors and endowed with the same clearly defined static unity. The reader feels the effect of these visually composed scenes long before the final paragraph explains them in its identification of story and church window. It is Flaubert's triumph to unite the themes of faith and redemption with a narrative technique capable of bringing his scenes clearly before the eye, to enable his reader for a short time to walk with Julian in the sunlit Age of Faith.

Anne W. Sienkewicz

THE LEGEND OF SLEEPY HOLLOW

Author: Washington Irving (1783-1859)
Type of plot: American folktale
Time of plot: Early nineteenth century
Locale: A Dutch village in the Hudson Valley, near Tarrytown, New York
First published: 1819

Principal characters:

ICHABOD CRANE, the protagonist, a ragged, impoverished
  schoolteacher of Connecticut Yankee stock
KATRINA VAN TASSEL, the daughter of a prosperous Dutch
  farmer, Ichabod's desired bride
ABRAHAM "BROM BONES" BRUNT, a strong, handsome local
  boy, Katrina's suitor

The Story

Ichabod Crane is a newcomer to the Hudson Valley; unlike the generations of Dutch settlers that have preceded him, he has neither the strength nor the means to become a farmer and landowner. His single marketable skill is teaching, and in the isolated hamlet of Sleepy Hollow this pays meager rewards. His schoolhouse is decrepit, one large room constructed of logs; its broken windows have been patched with the leaves of old copybooks. Ichabod's quarters are whatever rooms the neighboring Dutch farmers who board him for a week at a time are willing to provide. Ichabod thus makes the rounds of the neighborhood, and his small salary, combined with his constantly changing address, allows him to store all of his personal possessions in a cotton handkerchief.

Since he comes from Connecticut, a state whose major product is country schoolmasters, Ichabod feels both superior to the old Dutch stock of the valley and frustrated by his perpetual state of poverty. He compensates for the former by regularly caning the more obstinate of his little charges and for the latter by doing light work on the neighboring farms. He further supplements his income by serving as the local singing master, instructing the farm children in the singing of psalms. Never missing a chance to curry favor with the local mothers, Ichabod always pets the youngest children "like the lion bold" holding the lamb. In short, his single goal is self-advancement, and though he has merely "tarried" in Sleepy Hollow, he clearly will remain if his prospects improve.

Ichabod cannot rely on his looks or strength to advance him, so he cultivates a circle of farmers' daughters, particularly those from the more prosperous families, and impresses them with his erudition and vastly superior tastes. He has, indeed, "read several books quite through," among them Cotton Mather's account of witchcraft in New England. He believes even the strangest of these tales; indeed, he frightens himself so much when he reads them that he is startled when he hears a bird or sees a firefly. He is, in other words, completely naïve and suggestible. The local tale of the Galloping Hessian who rides headless through the woods of Sleepy Hollow particularly alarms him. A snow-covered bush in the half-light is enough to convince Ichabod that he has seen the headless horseman.

One of Ichabod's music students is Katrina Van Tassel, the eighteen-year-old daughter of a prosperous Dutch farmer. She is "plump as a partridge; ripe and melting and rosy-cheeked as one of her father's peaches." She also, as her father's only daughter, has "vast expectations." Though she is also something of a coquette, the prospect of her inheritance makes her seem to Ichabod a desirable bride, and he determines to win her.

Ichabod's mouth waters when he contemplates the fruits of old Baltus Van Tassel's land. He dreams of the fat meadowlands, the rich wheatfields, and the rye, buckwheat, fruit, and Indian corn that will be his if he can win Katrina's hand. Once married to Katrina, he could invest in large tracts of land. He can even imagine Katrina with a whole family of children, setting out with him for promising new territories in Kentucky or Tennessee. It is, however, the sumptuous comfort of the Van Tassel home that makes him realize that he must have Katrina.

Winning Katrina, however, presents a problem in the person of her rugged, rough-edged Dutch boyfriend, Abraham Brunt, nicknamed "Brom Bones" because of his Herculean size and strength. Brom, who has long considered Katrina his, immediately recognizes Ichabod as his rival, and with his gang of roughriders plays a series of practical jokes on the Yankee schoolmaster. Yet his pranks—stopping up the singing-school chimney, upsetting the schoolhouse, even training his dog to whine whenever Ichabod sings— do little to thwart the progress that Ichabod believes he is making in his campaign to win Katrina's hand. Indeed, Ichabod is encouraged when he receives an invitation to a "quilting frolic" at the Van Tassel home.

Ichabod spends extra time dressing and even borrows a horse so that he can arrive in style. The horse, somewhat inappropriately named Gunpowder, is as gaunt and shabby as Ichabod, but this does not prevent him from thinking that Katrina will be impressed. Ichabod continues to imagine the Van Tassel wealth that he will have if he can make Katrina his, and he quickly becomes the center of attention when Katrina dances with him. Brom, meanwhile, looks on with helpless jealousy. Brom enjoys himself only when telling of his close encounter with the headless horseman. Ichabod counters with extracts from Cotton Mather and stories of his own close calls with Connecticut and local ghosts.

An interview between Ichabod and Katrina follows the party, and Ichabod leaves, crestfallen. Could Katrina merely have been trying to make Brom jealous? Ichabod's anger, frustration, and sudden obliviousness to the rich Van Tassel lands seem to answer this question.

The midnight quiet of the countryside, the gathering clouds, and the ghost stories that Ichabod has heard do not improve Ichabod's mood. Indeed, he becomes increasingly uneasy as he approaches the tree from which Major André had been hanged. Ichabod knows that he will be safe if only he can cross the church bridge, but just then the goblin rider appears on his black horse, closing in fast behind him. Instead of disappearing in a burst of fire and brimstone as he has always been said to do, the rider throws his head at Ichabod. It strikes Ichabod's own cranium, and the rider passes on like a whirlwind.

Though Ichabod's borrowed horse reappears the next morning, Ichabod does not. The executor of his estate, Hans Van Ripper, burns Ichabod's copy of Cotton Mather and the scrawled fragments of a few love poems to Katrina. Ichabod himself becomes part of Sleepy Hollow's folklore. Some say that he was snatched by the Galloping Hessian, but others say that Ichabod is still alive, that he was afraid to return from fear of the goblin and Hans Van Ripper (from whom he had borrowed the horse) and was mortified by Katrina's refusal. Brom Bones appears soon after such discussions, always wearing a knowing smile whenever the goblin's pumpkin head is mentioned.

Themes and Meanings

In a postscript appended to the story in the handwriting of Diedrich Knickerbocker (Irving's gentle burlesque on old Dutch New Yorkers and the fictive annotator of *The Sketch Book of Geoffrey Crayon, Gent.*, 1819-1820, in which this tale was published), the Dutchman records his having heard this story from an old, "dry-looking" gentleman described as possessing features strikingly like those of Ichabod Crane. When pressed for a moral, the storyteller replies: " . . . he that runs races with goblin troopers is likely to have rough riding of it." This, indeed, sums up a recurring theme in Irving's sketches: the results of the culture clash between industrious and poor but to some degree unscrupulous Yankees and the hardheaded and prosperous but also wily Dutch.

Neither the Dutch nor the Yankee newcomers possess a clear moral superiority. Here, for example, Ichabod has only a slightly better education than the Dutch children he teaches, and he would marry Katrina not from love but for her father's wealth. Similarly, Brom recognizes the threat to his interests and in his own rough way thwarts his Yankee opponent. Since Katrina does not appear especially attractive or faithful, Brom's motives hardly seem purer than those of Ichabod.

Style and Technique

Irving's version of this folktale features an effective series of starvation images that begins with his lengthy description of the gaunt, cadaverous Ichabod and extends to the almost physical hunger that his protagonist feels when he sees the rich produce of Van Tassel's land. Indeed, Ichabod's mouth waters as he contemplates this wealth and dreams that it might be his.

Complementing the starvation imagery is Irving's choice of names. Ichabod is tall and as gaunt as the crane whose name he shares. Like the biblical Ichabod, Irving's protagonist is as much an outcast as is his Old Testament namesake. Similarly, Brom, whose given name is Abraham, is as much a patriarch of his people as is the father of the tribes of Judah.

Robert J. Forman

LENZ

Author: Georg Büchner (1813-1837)
Type of plot: Biographical fragment
Time of plot: Late January and early February, 1778
Locale: The Vosges Mountains southwest of Strasbourg, France
First published: "Lenz: Eine Reliquie von Georg Büchner," 1839 (English translation, 1960)

> *Principal personages:*
> JAKOB MICHAEL REINHOLD LENZ, one of the principal dramatic writers of the German *Sturm und Drang* period
> JOHANN FRIEDRICH OBERLIN, a philanthropist and social reformer, the pastor in Waldbach, and Lenz's host for a brief period

The Story

"Lenz" is a fictionalized account of an episode in the life of the troubled dramatist Jakob Michael Reinhold Lenz (1751-1792) which was recorded by Johann Friedrich Oberlin, a pastor in whose care Lenz was placed when he began showing increasing signs of mental disturbance in 1778.

The beginning of Büchner's account finds Lenz traveling on foot across the hills and valleys of the Vosges Mountains toward the village of Waldbach. As he walks, he passes in and out of a state of anxiety. He sees fantastic images in the wet, snowy landscape, in the cloud formations, and in the shifting sunlight. Like one hallucinating, he imagines that he must absorb the whole of creation, and he throws himself to the ground; "it was an ecstasy that hurt him. . . ." At other times, he feels very much alone and pursued by some unbearable thing, "seized with a nameless terror in this nothingness: he was in the void!" Then, each time, the terrifying attack passes, and he regains his calm and continues on his way. When he finally arrives at the vicarage in Waldbach—where he is quite unexpected but is hospitably received by Oberlin and his family—the domestic serenity of the place calms Lenz and recalls to him familiar images of contentment from earlier times at home.

He is given lodging in an upstairs room of the village schoolhouse, but before he can sleep, the anxiety of being alone and in darkness returns. Lenz rushes downstairs and into the street, bruising and cutting himself on the stone walls. He leaps into the water of the fountain and soon comes to his senses. Oberlin and other villagers come to his aid, and Lenz is ashamed of his bizarre behavior. Exhausted, he is finally able to sleep.

In the days following, he accompanies Oberlin on his pastoral rounds through the valley and is comforted by the man's acts of charity and sensible practicality, as well as by the affection that the rural people feel toward their benefactor. With nightfall Lenz's anxiety returns, however, and he continues his nocturnal baths in the village fountain, though more quietly, so as not to alarm his hosts and the other residents.

One day, after a solitary walk in new-fallen snow, he tells Oberlin that perhaps he might deliver a sermon in the church. Oberlin asks him if he is a theologian, and Lenz answers that he is. His request is granted for the next Sunday. Lenz preaches the sermon, and its effect on him is euphoric. With a sense of cosmic communion and self-pity, a "voluptuous crisis" suggestive of the late-medieval mystics, he passes the night in profound sleep. The following morning, he tells Oberlin of having dreamed of his mother's death, and their conversation turns to reports and experiences of clairvoyance and premonitions.

A man, Christoph Kaufmann, with whom Lenz is already acquainted, comes with his fiancée to visit Oberlin and his family. Lenz is troubled by this intrusion into his relatively anonymous life in Waldbach. At a dinner conversation about literature, Lenz argues for the honest, simple representation of life, and against the artificial idealism currently becoming fashionable. Kaufmann tells him that he has received letters from Lenz's father and tries to persuade him to return home, but Lenz is angered by the suggestion that he should leave the place where he has found peace.

When Kaufmann departs, Oberlin goes with him to visit a colleague in nearby Switzerland. Lenz is apprehensive about the separation and accompanies the pastor for a part of the way. On his way back to Waldbach he comes to the cottage of an old woman and a girl who is subject to mysterious convulsions and appears to possess visionary powers. He passes a strangely restless night there. During the days that he spends with Oberlin's family in the pastor's absence, Lenz's religious and emotional torments become more intense again. He hears of a young girl who has died in another village, and he decides to go to the place in sackcloth and ashes. He prays over the corpse and implores God to revive the child by a miracle. When no miracle occurs he flees in terror. He is seized with a fit of blasphemous anger.

Oberlin returns from his trip and tries to restore Lenz's faith in Christ's redeeming love, but Lenz is convinced of his irreparable sinfulness and falls once again into the pattern of violent nighttime seizures and garbled discourses during the day. He attempts suicide. He wanders off, insisting that he be arrested as a murderer, and is brought back by two shopkeepers. His behavior, even in Oberlin's presence, becomes more and more irrational, and his speech becomes more and more fitful and incoherent. The attacks which he formerly suffered only at night now occur during the day as well. Lenz struggles with himself, complains that the silence of the valley is unbearably loud, seeks physical pain to deny the emptiness that he feels, and again throws himself into the street from an upstairs window. Finally even Oberlin's patient faith in a recovery is exhausted, and he has Lenz taken under close surveillance to Strasbourg for his eventual return to the care of friends in Germany. The account breaks off with a terse description of the momentarily subdued but empty man.

Themes and Meanings

The Lenz whose twenty or so days in the village of Waldsbach are depicted in this story interests Büchner in at least two ways: as a fellow literary artist and as an intensely sensitive fellow human being. His personal sufferings are clearly the more important of the two concerns. While madness and art may go hand in hand, "Lenz" is not a very strong example of the artist-novella, for it does not speculate on the nature of artistic creativity or the social role of the artist. Even though Lenz holds forth on the subject of literature in his conversation with Kaufmann, his discourse stands in isolation and only recalls—somewhat poignantly—his earlier literary successes. It is part of the story's realism, not a true theoretical digression.

Lenz's humanity, the subject of greater interest for Büchner and his readers, has several facets. At the center of Lenz's story is his struggle with himself, the schizophrenia in which "he seemed to be split in two, with one part of him trying to save the other and calling out to itself." Self-destructive and self-preserving instincts conflict within him. At the level of the individual, Büchner is crucially concerned with this kind of derangement, one perhaps common to all humankind, but visible only in the intensified form called insanity.

Lenz turns to the hope that religious faith seems to offer him, but his faith, like his instincts, oscillates between visions of preservation and destruction, salvation and damnation. He imagines himself alternately as his own prophet-savior and as the sinner rejected by God. He tries to appropriate a religious faith like Oberlin's, but it becomes distorted and threatening in his mind. Lenz encounters the traditional, integral Protestant faith of the age before Europe's great revolutionary upheavals, but as interpreted by the politically radical Büchner of the postrevolutionary 1830's.

Style and Technique

As noted above, the principal basis for the story was the account which Pastor Oberlin gave in his journal entries from January 20 to February 8, 1778. Büchner's version does not correspond strictly to Oberlin's inclusions and emphases by any means, although there are sections in which the pastor's careful observations are clearly reflected in the language of Büchner's text. Private journals and creative narrative are two different things, however, and the modernity of "Lenz" lies in its emergence from personal observations into a psychological portrait conceived as literature. In the twentieth century (which saw the first appreciation of Büchner), such psychological realism would not be considered unusual, but in 1839 it surely was.

The persuasiveness of Büchner's realism in "Lenz" owes much to his combination of narrative points of view, especially the alternation between the third-person narrative, in which Lenz's visible actions and audible words are recorded, and the indirect interior monologue, through which his states of mind are conveyed (a style of narration rarely exploited in German literature for another half-century). The latter mode especially does what no journal entry could, and it has a frightening power that marks "Lenz" as a revolutionary work. The hallucinatory visions of this tormented man are gigantic and violent, even cosmic in their size and force. Thus too, through the drastic imagery, language, and gesture for which the literature of *Sturm und Drang* was known in the 1770's, Büchner has re-created the mind of one of its chief exponents.

Michael Ritterson

THE LESSON OF THE MASTER

Author: Henry James (1843-1916)
Type of plot: Social realism
Time of plot: The 1880's
Locale: London, English countryside near London, and Switzerland
First published: 1888

Principal characters:
PAUL OVERT, the protagonist, a young novelist
HENRY ST. GEORGE, the Master, a famous, elderly novelist
MRS. ST. GEORGE, his first wife
MARIAN FANCOURT, the love interest of Overt and the second wife of St. George
GENERAL FANCOURT, her father

The Story

Henry James's "The Lesson of the Master" focuses on Paul Overt, a young novelist with three or four novels to his credit, who is caught up in the dilemma of choosing the time-absorbing business of living or the isolation of art. Henry St. George, whose reputation as an artist remains high though his later work is inferior, is the master of the title, with Overt his pupil.

The tale begins with Overt arriving at Summersoft, an old country house near London, to find, to his delight, that St. George, whose early works played an important part in forming Overt as a novelist, is a member of the party. Before meeting St. George and within minutes after meeting Mrs. St. George, Overt determines that the cause of the decline of St. George's work is without doubt Mrs. St. George. She is, in his opinion, more suitable a wife for a keeper of books than for a literary master.

St. George joins the party but is preoccupied with the beautiful young Marian Fancourt, who has recently arrived in England from India and is very fond of literature and writers. From Marian, Overt learns all that he can about St. George. He tells her that if he were to be brought together with his idol he would be prostrate.

Prostrate is what Overt is when St. George expresses admiration for his work and special esteem for Overt's latest novel, *Ginistrella*. St. George advises Overt to learn from the example of the failure of his later works and not let his old age become a "deplorable illustration of the worship of false gods." The false gods are, in St. George's view, all that is associated with having an active social life, "the idols of the market—money and luxury and 'the world,' placing one's children and dressing one's wife—everything that drives one to the short and easy way."

Back in London, Overt is tempted by one of St. George's false gods in the form of Marian Fancourt. As Overt and Marian's relationship becomes serious, St. George sends for Overt to come to him. St. George says that his life is that of the successful charlatan who, having everything for personal happiness, has missed the real thing. He has missed "the sense of having done the best—the sense, which is the real life of the artist and the absence of which is his death, of having drawn from his intellectual instrument the finest music that nature has hidden in it, of having played it as it should be played." The master's confession of his mistake and his desire to save Overt from making the same one overwhelm the younger man, and he agrees to give up Marian and all pursuit of personal happiness.

The converted Overt exiles himself to Switzerland, where he learns from Marian by letter that St. George's wife is dead. When Overt writes in sympathy to St. George, he receives a bewildering reply: Earlier St. George had told Overt not to marry, but now he writes that he would not be at the head of his profession if it had not been for his wife. All that St. George has advocated seems a bad joke, and Overt thinks of returning to London, giving up his ambitions; instead, however, he recommits himself to his art.

After two years in Switzerland, Overt returns to London, where he is told by Marian's father that St. George is engaged to marry Marian. Overt feels betrayed and confronts St. George, who assures him that he was always sincere; the knowledge that he is saving Overt as an artist adds greatly to the pleasure of marrying Marian. He also informs Overt that he is through as an artist and will not write again.

Later in the year, Overt's new book is published and considered "really magnificent" by the St. Georges; the narrator of the tale adds that Overt is "doing his best but . . . it is too soon to say." The narrator goes on to say that the proof that Overt is dedicated to his art and not to personal happiness is that he would be the first to appreciate a new work by St. George should there be one.

Themes and Meanings

Henry James wrote many times, as he does here, about the relationship of the artist to the social world and the conflicting obligations of life and art. "The Lesson of the Master" is one of the stories that James wrote during his middle years about the artist's relationship to the world. James struggled for three decades with the theme, from "Benvolio" (1875) to "The Great Good Place" (1900).

The conflict between life and art was central to James's own experience, as is clear in Leon Edel's five-volume biography *Henry James* (1953-1972). James himself chose a life wholly dedicated to his art, the life that St. George advocates and Overt comes to live.

The other characters in the tale seem intended only to bring Overt to terms with the realization that art is the only life for him. Yet James's treatment of this decision is not unambiguous: The reader is not sure if James agrees entirely with St. George's lesson, Overt's decision, or the narrative voice when it says, "St. George was essentially right and. . . . Nature dedicated him [Overt] to intellectual, not to personal passion."

Style and Technique

"The Lesson of the Master" is told in the characteristic manner of James's middle years, without the notorious complexity of his late style. The sentences are relatively short, and the plot, on the surface, is easy to follow. Yet nothing is straightforward in James. Indeed, the tale is steeped in irony and ambiguity; one might apply a statement that Overt makes about St. George's work to James and this tale: "For one who looks at it from the artistic point of view it contains a bottomless ambiguity."

The point of view is that of a third-person, omniscient narrator who concentrates on Overt's thoughts and actions. The use of the narrator allows James to explore the relationship between the artist and an active social life without passing judgment on any of the primary or secondary characters. This technique alone casts a shadow of ambiguity over every aspect of the tale.

The plot is ironic and ambiguous in that St. George tells Overt not to marry Marian because it is clear that his decline is attributed to his marriage; then St. George, upon the death of his first wife, marries Marian himself. The twist is that while St. George seems to have betrayed Overt, he has, in effect, sealed Overt's future. Point of view is all-important here; it is not the events themselves that are important but how they are perceived.

Brenda B. Adams

THE LIBRARY OF BABEL

Author: Jorge Luis Borges (1899-1986)
Type of plot: Fantasy
Time of plot: Unspecified
Locale: An imaginary library
First published: "La biblioteca de Babel," 1942 (English translation, 1962)

Principal character:
THE NARRATOR, unnamed

The Story

The setting of "The Library of Babel" is not only the story's most important characteristic, it is, in a way, everything. Much of the narrative consists of descriptions of an imaginary library which is so large that no one has seen the top, bottom, or end of it. It is so old that the recorded history of its librarians stretches back for many centuries and still one cannot account for the library itself or for its architects. It houses so many books that the most accepted explanation for its collection is that it contains all possible books; that is, it contains all the infinite variations on every book whose pages could be generated by random strings of letters, words, or phrases without duplication. The narrator of the story asserts that, "like all men of the Library," he traveled in his youth, journeying from cubicle to cubicle searching for a book or "a catalogue of catalogues" which might explain where he was and why he was there. He anticipates dying without finding that knowledge, only "a few leagues from" the bookshelves by "which I was born." "Once dead there will not lack pious hands to hurl me over the central banister of the vast building," he claims, "my sepulchre shall be the unfathomable air. . . . My body will sink lengthily and will corrupt and dissolve in the wind engendered by the fall, which is infinite."

The story turns on the narrator's and the librarians' attempts to make sense of the infinite building in which they find themselves, a building which has been neatly divided into hexagonal rooms which open on to one another while surrounding a grand central staircase. Generations are born and die within these rooms without understanding the mysteries of their universe or their place in it. Apparently, an increasing number seem to resolve such questions by committing suicide.

The theories that others concoct to explain their situation are like the theories men have traditionally concocted to fathom their own sense of the infinitude of the world. Some believe it their duty to eliminate useless books, books filled with nonsense syllables or unknown languages. Others believe that it is useless to read or write or study in such an environment. Knowledge, they claim, will be more likely produced by chance. They roll dice.

Some believe in the superstition of "the Man of the Book." They argue that since there must be some one book on some one shelf somewhere which is the "perfect compendium to all the rest," at least one person must have read it. Such a librarian, they hope, has found the knowledge which would make him "analogous to a god." They search for him. Others search for books which foretell their own futures. The librarians spend their lives looking for such volumes, never knowing whether they have found a meaningful fiction or an absolute fact.

The history of their theories, discoveries, and disappointments, as summarized and evaluated by the narrator, moves the plot along. Like many of Borges' narrators, however, this one claims that no one theory seems persuasively better than the others. The story ends without accounting for the mysteries it has raised, the narrator himself claiming to have settled upon his own solution to the nature of his universe: The library is "limitless and periodic." The same volumes repeat themselves "in the same disorder (which repeated, would constitute an order: Order itself). My solitude rejoices in this elegant hope." Yet his hope is a purely personal one. When confronted with a world too big and too complex to explain, men must settle on an idea which satisfies their own personal natures and which plausibly explains what data they have. In "The Library of Babel," this seems to be the closest the inhabitants will come to achieving absolute truth.

Themes and Meanings

Most stories by Jorge Luis Borges do not "mean" something in the sense that this word is usually used. The narrator of "The Library of Babel" reminds his readers that even the word "library," which to him means "ubiquitous and everlasting system of hexagonal galleries," also means many other things in many other languages. It can mean "bread" or "pyramid" or "almost anything else." "You who read me," he addresses his audience directly, "are you sure you understand my language?" With such warnings, it is often foolhardy to close too quickly on one explanation of a Borges story and claim that it "means" one thing. He conceives of his stories more playfully and, often, more seriously than the quick application of a "meaning" would allow. "The Library of Babel" summarizes many different solutions to one intellectual puzzle: How do small, autonomous, and thinking men coexist with a world that is unimaginably large and complex? Where is their significance in such a world?

While "The Library of Babel" clearly raises this question, it does not clearly resolve it. The story offers not one but a variety of hypothetical answers. Borges' theme seemingly has more to do with how all men address such problems than with recommending one or the other of their solutions as the correct idea or meaning. He explores the variety of ways in which men grapple with understanding themselves and their world, fascinated by the "fiction" they are forced to create to survive. If the story does not have simply one meaning, it does, like many of his narratives, resonate on different levels of associations. It places imaginary characters in a fictive world as large and as mysterious as the world usually posited by twentieth century science, and it provides a structure or a pattern which can be used to apprehend both the marvels of modern astrophysics and the troubling psychological problems which contemporary cosmology often raises. Like many of Borges' stories, this one duplicates the familiar in an unfamiliar way, playing tricks with readers' normal or expected patterns of perceptions to expand their frames of reference so that the familiar is seen in an unexpected, but more comprehensive way.

Style and Technique

"The Library of Babel" is typical of Borges' style. It has little plot, little characterization, and little conflict. It presents, rather, an intellectual challenge or puzzle to the reader. Borges often aims at getting his readers curious about a novel idea and then urging them to reevaluate their own experiences and conceptions with a fresh new perspective. Frequently, he avoids complex characterizations and plots to put more emphasis on these new ideas, moving his stories along with a prose style borrowed from the essay form. He takes his bizarre ideas and then underplays them with a spare, matter-of-fact style which makes them seem more plausible. Like many of his stories, "The Library of Babel" has a mock scholarly tone which belies its sensational and fantastic conceptions. The narrator uses a calm, dispassionate voice, which is dry, but occasionally witty. Such a tone creates the impression of a monograph hidden in some obscure scholarly journal. The narrator summarizes the second axiom of what is known about the library, saying "the number of orthographic symbols is twenty-five. . . . This bit of evidence permitted the formulation, three hundred years ago, of a general theory of the Library." The passage even includes a mock footnote which purports to theorize about why precisely twenty-five letters were enough to form all the different words in the library's infinite collection of books.

This essay style, stripped of vivid description and running commentaries about the interior states of characters' minds, lets Borges cover a wide range of ideas quickly. It also jostles many readers' prior experiences with reading literature: Most readers do not anticipate that fiction will be presented as fact.

Philip Woodard

LIFEGUARD

Author: John Updike (1932-   )
Type of plot: Stream-of-consciousness
Time of plot: The early 1960's
Locale: An American beach
First published: 1961

> *Principal characters:*
> THE LIFEGUARD, the narrator and a seminarian
> THE CROWD AT THE BEACH

The Story

No action takes place in this short story, only the musings of a divinity student pondering the purpose of life while gazing upon swimmers and sun worshipers at the beach. A summer lifeguard, he is proud of his tanned, "edible" body. Transformed from the pallid seminarian who for the past nine months has pored confusedly over "handbooks of liturgy and histories of dogma," he mounts his white wooden throne (with a red cross painted on the back) as though he were climbing into "a vestment."

There is no contradiction, the lifeguard asserts, between the desires of the spirit and those of the flesh. To shine in the sun is man's goal. Love is like the ministry, the lifeguard ruminates, like being rescued. Beauty is personified in the curvature of a nymph's spine, the "arabesque" between back and buttocks.

Sunday mornings on the beach depress the young lifeguard because so few people are in church. No longer do the masses have a palpable terror of the unknown; people "seek God in flowers and good deeds." The sea seems more a "misty old gentleman" than an ominous "divine metaphor." Yet it has meaning for the lifeguard. In the water, he believes, "we struggle and thrash and drown; we succumb, even in despair, and float, and are saved."

The day unfolds like a backward cinema. First come the elderly, who "have lost the gift of sleep." The women smile and search for shells; their mates, whose "withered white legs" support "brazen barrel chests, absurdly potent," swim parallel to the shore at a depth "no greater than their height." Next come middle-aged couples burdened with "odious" children and aluminum chairs. Bored women gossip and smoke incessantly. Finally come young people, maidens and boys, infants in arms and toddlers "who gobble the sand like sugar" and "wade unafraid into the surf."

Assaying this immense "clot" swarming around him, the lifeguard believes them unworthy of redemption. They are "Protestantism's errant herd," a "plague" deserving of oblivion. He is different, both a seducer and a savior, capable of providing rapture and grace. Absurdly, he speculates whether women will be eternalized "as maiden, matron and crone" and "what will they do [in Paradise] without children to watch or gossip to exchange."

On Sunday afternoon, the lifeguard experiences an Edenic vision of the beach, cast back in time just prior to "the gesture that split the firmament." A revelation comes to him, a commandment to be joyful, to "romp; eat the froth; be children." Atop his station, alertly awaiting his calling; the lifeguard listens for a cry for help. So far, he has not heard one.

Themes and Meanings

Critics have hailed Updike as a magician with words, but he has been criticized, perhaps unfairly, for shallowness of theme. Here, without frills, he tackles important issues. In this meditation, the central question is not "What happens?" but "What is felt?" As Arthur Mizener concluded about *Pigeon Feathers and Other Stories* (1962), the collection which contains "Lifeguard," Updike's "fine verbal talent is no longer pirouetting, however gracefully, out of a simple delight in motion, but is beginning to serve his deepest insights." There are interesting similarities between "Lifeguard" and two other stories in this collection, "A & P" and the title story, "Pigeon Feathers." In the former, the fascination is with three girls, including one described as a queen. In the latter, the fascination is with death and immortality. Compared to "Lifeguard," the other two stories are more situational and the characters less passive. In "Pigeon Feathers," a fifteen-year-old shoots a half-dozen birds; in "A & P" a nineteen-year-old quits his job at the supermarket when his boss insults three barefoot female customers.

The lifeguard is fascinated not only with religion and sex but also with aging, not unlike Harry Angstrom in Updike's Rabbit trilogy and Piet Hanema in *Couples* (1968). As in many of the other short stories contained in *Pigeon Feathers and Other Stories*, the Protestant ethic of individual responsibility is quite pronounced, and the lifeguard suffers spiritual tensions of a neo-Calvinist nature. Seeking atonement in an unfathomable world, he believes that expiation comes through love. He has studied "with burning eyes" the bewildering, terrifying attempts of theologians to "scourge God into being"—only to "sway appalled on the ladder of minus signs" by which others "would surmount the void."

Clearly, for the seminarian, the beach is a more palatable environment for celebrating life and seeking ontological assurance than dusty library shelves. The insight provided by the sea (and the crowd) is that "the tides of time have treacherous undercurrents." While one should seek the joy of the moment, the current of life inevitably pulls toward death's horizon.

Turning the concept of original sin on its head, the lifeguard-seminarian's philosophy implies that man is never so innocent as at birth. Only children and eunuchs truly love, he quips; virtue is otherwise corrupted by an "encumbering biological armor." Like the characters in tawdry biblical films, "we are all Solomons lusting for Sheba's salvation." Withdrawal from the world is no solace, for "the stony chambers need jewels, furs, tints of cloth and flesh, even though, as in Samson's case, the temple comes tumbling."

The lifeguard's references to women, even from the perspective of the early 1960's, are hostile and condescending. Women are stereotyped as old crones, bored matrons, and sexy maidens whose function is to rear children and fulfill men. While little is revealed about the lifeguard's past, the strong implication is that he is a lonely virgin casting envious eyes around him for a meaningful relationship.

Alone and somewhat alienated, the lifeguard pontificates about the "hollow heads" below him, but he is not a particularly somber fellow—more like a bored adolescent daydreaming during an interminable church service. His eyes are open, his mind alert, but despite his preparation and sacrifice, nobody needs him.

Thus, Updike ends on a note of ambiguity. Is the lifeguard heroic or merely pompous, a callow fool or a sincere pilgrim, worthy of grace or a deluded egotist? Is his summer raiment ludicrous or compatible with his spiritual yearnings? The enigma is distinctly existential, reminiscent of Søren Kierkegaard's concept of the crowd as collective anonymity. Against a blackened beach, the individual must set himself apart, venture forth from the shallow waters and, risking everything, cry for help. That "unheard cry" is what haunts "Lifeguard."

Style and Technique

In contrast to some of the other stories in *Pigeon Feathers and Other Stories*, this narrative essay is bereft of any real plot, action, or dialogue. The technique is well suited to Updike's tone and accentuates the protagonist's dualistic nature. The diction of the story runs the gamut from stilted and monastic to lusty and sensuous; some antiquated phrases (*memento mori*) suggest the pedantic seminarian, others the efficient healer armed with "splints, unguents and spirits of ammonia." Then there are phrases descriptive of his temporal side, as when he observes the "dimpled blonde in the bib and diapers of her Bikini, the lambent fuzz of her midriff shimmering like a cat's belly."

First published in *The New Yorker* magazine, "Lifeguard" is almost a parody of a sermon—sensitive and urbane, short and bittersweet, a parable about balancing piety and spirituality. For Updike it was a tour de force, demonstrating a continued mastery of style while expanding his thematic horizons. It is clever, if not hilarious, and thought-provoking without being overly ponderous.

James B. Lane

LIFE-STORY

Author: John Barth (1930-   )
Type of plot: Absurdism
Time of plot: 1966
Locale: Anywhere in the United States
First published: 1968

Principal characters:
THE NARRATOR, an unnamed writer of stories and novels
THE NARRATOR'S WIFE
AN IMAGINARY MISTRESS, who may be real
THE READER

The Story

The narrator of "Life-Story" says that his greatest desire is to be "unself-conscious" as a writer. The irony is that his every comment, including this initial one, points to exactly the opposite. He worries in an acutely conscious way, for example, that his story contains no "ground situation" (a coherent, trenchant plot and conflict), and he agonizes over a prose style that he fears is "fashionably solipsistic" and unoriginal. What is even more frustrating to the narrator is that his artistic impulses are directly contradictory; he prefers "straight-forward tales of adventure" to the "experimental, self-despising, or overtly metaphysical characters of Samuel Beckett's or Jorge Borges's," but he can muster only self-conscious, solipsistic stories in which the story's artistic processes are conspicuous and cumbersome—such as in the "theatre of absurdity, black humor or allegory." He thus prefers, like his wife and adolescent daughters, real life to literature, and he reads only for entertainment. He concludes that the medium in which he desires to write is "moribund if not already dead . . . along with society."

He even suggests that his increasing preoccupation or obsession with pattern and design for their own sakes is a manifestation of schizophrenia. Later, one of his literary characters, whom the reader can see is merely a replica of the narrator (a writer writing a story about a writer writing a story), worries that he can produce no stories of "passion and bravura action," detailing further the traditional elements of fiction which seem to elude him, such as "heroes they can admire, heroines they can love, memorable speeches, colorful accessory characters, and poetical language." At one point, the writer in the narrator's story asks gloomily, "Why must writers choose to write such stuff (self-conscious introspection) when life is so full of people and places and situations to write about?"

The narrator then begins to develop his proposition that his own life might be a fiction in which he is the leading character, whereupon he decides to write about just such a phenomenon. In a sense he makes this proposition come true by writing a story about a man writing a story about a man writing a story, *ad infinitum*, all of whose existences are indisputably fictional. Adding to his frustration, the narrator suspects not only that he is a fictional character but also that the fiction that he is in is the sort that he least prefers. Following this line of thought, one of the narrator's fictional narrator-authors, identified as "C," suggests that to get his story moving, he must expunge the writing of "overt and self-conscious discussion of the narrative process," which is exactly what the original narrator is doing, or rather, trying to do. The original narrator says that he would like to write a story leading to an exciting climax and denouement, if he could. He is, after all, dependent upon his reader for his existence.

Following up the premise that his own life is a fiction like the ones that he detests, written by an author who might resemble himself, the narrator wonders if he could not appeal to his own author to change the tone and style of his boring and colorless tale to one in which "the outmoded virtues of courage, fidelity, tact, restraint, self-discipline, amiability, et cetera" would occur. He wonders too if he could not make his own life apart from the design of his author—"to achieve factuality" or at least to be a more positive hero, but he admits the futility of such a proposal. Yet, ironically, the narrator's mistress, real or imagined, shows her contempt for the dullness and passionlessness of her life with the narrator by withdrawing from his life—or story. He then confesses feelings of creative and sexual impotence—the very substance of his fiction. Only the need to move his story along—paying attention to the needs of the immediate sentence before him—keeps him going.

Additional problems occur when the narrator wonders whether the story he is in might be "a *roman à clef*," whether it might not be a film or theater piece rather than a novel, or whether, in fact, his story might not focus on someone other than himself—his wife, for example, or his daughter, or his mistress, or even the man who once cleaned his chimney. He speculates that his childhood might not even have been real—that the part of the story that he is in might be mere background, mere forced exposition. He concludes that at this advanced stage of his story, the absence of a ground situation means that his story is "dramatically meaningless." Is that, then, he inquires, the meaning of his life as well?

The narrator brings his story to a close by arguing that in a sense he is his own author and that therefore his life is in his own hands. The old analogy between Author and God, novel and world, has broken down. Reality and creative illusion are one. Rather than being bound to and directed by an omniscient Lord or Author, one's existence as author-character necessitates the authoring of one's own life-story. At this point, the narrator's "real wife and imaginary mistresses" enter his study unannounced and unsummoned by him, confirming the notion that people as fictional beings are free from an author's dictates.

Themes and Meanings

The major technical development in early twentieth century fiction was the artist's attempt to objectify his material—to get as much distance between himself and the work of art as possible, to refine himself out of existence, as James Joyce said. Henry James said that the author's voice should never be heard lest the illusion of real life be disturbed. Yet in Barth's "Life-Story," the narrator intrudes himself conspicuously between the reader and the work of art, writing about the writing process itself. It is not verisimilitude but the very artificiality of fiction that Barth wishes to convey.

On the one hand, Barth's narrator appears to sympathize with the elements of traditional fiction and to eschew the artistic tendencies of postmodern literature. Getting inside the artistic consciousness of the narrator, one sees that his sense that traditional fiction has run its course prevents him from emulating the literary forms of his predecessors: the well-made novel with a bold story line and characters who are interesting and powerful. Instead, he writes just like those contemporary authors he supposedly dislikes, such as Samuel Beckett and Jorge Luis Borges. He has no use, he says, for the Absurdist fiction of these writers—metaphysical, solipsistic, antiheroic, and radically experimental.

If not before, the narrator's sarcasm (Barth's, certainly) becomes clear when he aligns his literary tastes with those of his wife and adolescent daughters, who prefer sentimental romances and read, when at all, strictly for entertainment. He is making fun of such escapist, fraudulent drool and is drawn to fiction of the Absurd because it represents the world that makes the most sense to him, a world without cause, direction, or coherence. He bodies forth the Absurd in a story that is relatively plotless, fragmented, and incoherent—devoid of essential meaning or action—because these are the forms that most honestly portray his own life-story. Traditional artistic conventions would be contradictory to Barth's and his narrator's true vision. It is from this understanding that the narrator concludes that his story is "dramatically meaningless," and that the absence of a ground situation is in fact the proper ground situation of his tale. The meaninglessness becomes the drama—whether the narrator will kill himself in despair or find sufficient purpose in the act of creativity to continue his story, his life-story.

Herein lies the essential affirmation of a story that could easily be read as pessimistic. At the heart of the Absurdist vision is the absence of an all-knowing, caring God whose design gives purpose and direction to existence. The narrator would seem to believe that without such a God to whom to appeal for assistance, his life is fated to be barren and insignificant. At best, the Creator is an Author like himself who is relatively helpless in controlling and directing his creation. Yet if this is true—if the relationship of God to mankind is analogous to that of author to novel—then, just as the narrator's characters come and go as they please in his story, so he, too, may be free to direct—to author—his own existence. Life is a fictional narrative, a work-in-progress whose only meaning is that which the author-character has the courage and imagination to provide.

Style and Technique

As seen from the previous discussion of theme, it is impossible to discuss theme apart from style and technique in the case of Absurdist fiction. The vehicle becomes the message. In short, the view that life is essentially meaningless and incoherent is dramatized by a plot, characters, and actions that embody that vision. There is no gradually ascending series of events that leads to "an exciting climax and denouement," but is instead a kind of interior monologue that seems to end where it begins, static or circular in its movement. Even the tone of the story is mechanical and sterile, capturing the narrator's announced feelings of sexual and creative impotence. The repetition of "et cetera" and the use of multiple narrators and stories within stories, all of which are replicas of the initial narrator and story, suggest life without variation, life that is dull, monotonous, and endlessly repetitious.

The essential technique of the story is the purposeful attack upon traditional mimesis. The narrator's cumbersome and painfully self-conscious manipulation of text focuses the reader's attention upon fiction as artifice, not as a reality fixed and determined by a Supreme Creator. Similarly, by establishing parallels between life and art as similar creative ventures, the narrator leads the reader to see, as he says, that "I'm an artifice," author of his own life-story. By addressing the reader at numerous points, the narrator forces readers to become cocreators of his story, even further establishing the oneness of life and fiction.

Lawrence Broer

LIGEIA

Author: Edgar Allan Poe (1809-1849)
Type of plot: Supernatural fantasy
Time of plot: The indefinite past
Locale: A castle on the Rhine and an abbey in a remote area of England
First published: 1838

Principal characters:
THE PROTAGONIST, an unnamed first-person narrator
LIGEIA, the narrator's strangely beautiful first wife
LADY ROWENA TREVANION OF TREMAINE, his unloved and
    loathed second wife

The Story

The narrator-protagonist recalls with obsessive longing the nature of the love that he felt for Ligeia, his first wife, who has died. Her beauty had about it the strange attractiveness of antiquity. She had the radiance of a Delian Muse; her hair was Homerically "hyacinthine" in color, her nose Hebraically aquiline. Her eyes were those of the black-eyed houri, nymphs of the Muslim paradise; they were the twin stars Castor and Pollux and shone like the truth at the bottom of Democritus' proverbial well. They recalled the timeless change found in the contemplation of a moth, a butterfly, a chrysalis, running water.

Ligeia's physical presence had an equally strange beauty. Her outward calm complemented an inner intensity in thought, action, and volition. Her intellect was as profound as her beauty. She knew well all the physical and mathematical sciences, was gifted in the classical and the modern languages. Still, Ligeia's immense and varied gifts could not vanquish death, the "Conqueror Worm" whose arrival Ligeia anticipated in the poem she had written shortly before her death.

The narrator records his lonely destitution of spirit after Ligeia's death. In an attempt to forget, he changes his castle on the Rhine for an equally desolate abbey in a remote and unpopulated area of England. He takes a new bride, the fair-haired, blue-eyed Rowena, a woman of a noble but haughty family; their bridal chamber is an elaborate, octagonal turret of the abbey, semi-Gothic and semi-Druidical. Its furniture is massive, and the heavy canopy over the bridal couch seems to emphasize the pall cast over the marriage from its outset.

Indeed, after a month, the narrator becomes moody and sullen. He begins to loathe Rowena, for his memory flies back to the dead Ligeia. He wonders if the force of memory, directed by a strong enough will, might restore her. The narrator pursues these fancies even as Rowena is suddenly taken ill.

Though she recovers briefly, Rowena's relapses are periodic and increasingly serious. She speaks with increasing frequency of the slight sounds and motions that she believes come from behind the tapestries of the bridal chamber. Though the narrator at first attempts to convince Rowena that the wind has caused these, he himself realizes that some invisible object has passed him; then he notices a faint "angelic" shadow on the golden carpet beneath the censer. He wonders whether these are opium-induced hallucinations, and does not mention them to Rowena. Then he hears light footsteps and believes that he sees several ruby-colored droplets fall into the goblet of wine that he gives the dying Rowena.

Four nights after this, the narrator is sitting beside the shrouded body of the dead Rowena. He notes his recollection of the angelic form, looks at the dead Rowena, and remembers Ligeia with all the intensity that his willed concentration can muster. By midnight, he believes that he "felt" a sound coming from the ebony bed on which Rowena's corpse lies. As he directs every ounce of psychic energy that he can on the corpse, he perceives the slightest tinge of color come to its cheeks. He believes Rowena still lives and continues his conjurings, but he can think only of Ligeia. The corpse's lips seem to part for a moment, then relax in death. No conventional procedures reverse the condition, but when the narrator returns to his thoughts of Ligeia, he hears a sob come from the bed.

By dawn, the figure stirs, and the narrator wonders whether Rowena could actually have returned from the dead. He notices that the figure is suddenly taller than before. When the narrator loosens the cerements which cover the head, he finds huge masses of black hair, long and disheveled. It is only when the wild black eyes open that the narrator knows. His first love, his dear Ligeia, has returned to the world of the living.

Themes and Meanings

Edgar Allan Poe filled this story with allusions that he could hardly have expected the average reader to recognize. The story's primary theme, the incalculable potency of the directed will, derives from Joseph Glanvill (1636-1680), the English philosopher and clergyman. Glanvill held that will could survive body if determined to do so, that God's immortality proceeded from the perfection of volition, and that humanity yielded itself to the angel of death only when weakness of will could no longer sustain life.

Ligeia has all the prerequisites to test Glanvill's thesis. Poe's detailed character sketch gives her the timeless, strange, and ancient beauty of Egypt, Greece, and Israel. Her eyes, which Poe describes in vivid detail at the beginning and end of his story, combine the immortality of the twin stars Castor and Pollux and that of the Turkish houri, nymphs of the Muslim paradise. Ligeia remains unchanged change and recalls moth, butterfly, chrysalis, and running water. She is universal intellect, Psyche, and a true child of

Apollo, and her broad and deep erudition implies her privileged place in the order of creation.

Rowena is, by contrast, mediocre. Her beauty, though genuine, is conventional and superficial compared to that of Ligeia. It is this mediocrity, not Rowena herself, which the narrator loathes. Correspondingly, it is the force of Ligeia's will, still alive after her death, which directs the narrator's own volition to Ligeia's rebirth in Rowena's body. Poe has, therefore, elaborated on a traditional love-death theme to make a statement on the regenerative nature of the human spirit and the indomitable, irrepressible nature of the intellect.

Style and Technique

Ligeia is a woman whom Poe's readers have often encountered; she is Lenore, whose spirit hovers behind "the silken, sad, uncertain rustling" of the purple curtains in "The Raven"; she is Ulalume, whose spirit calls the narrator to her tomb to live in love-death; she is Annabel Lee in her "sepulchre . . . by the sea"; she is Annie, who has conquered "the fever called 'living.'" She is, just as likely, Poe's own mother, whose slow death from tuberculosis remained always in the poet's memory, or Virginia Clemm, Poe's child bride who died at the age of twenty-three.

Poe's special gift, which "Ligeia" well illustrates, is his ability to combine these intensely personal motifs with gaudy, arcane, and intentionally cryptic imagery, which he does not require his readers to unravel. To do so, however, is to appreciate the care with which Poe fashioned his works and to see that he did not strive merely for the sensational and the strange.

Robert J. Forman

LIGHTNING

Author: Donald Barthelme (1931-   )
Type of plot: Psychological realism
Time of plot: Unspecified
Locale: New York City
First published: 1982

> *Principal characters:*
> EDWARD CONNORS, a free-lance writer for magazines and
>   newspapers
> EDWINA RAWSON, a black fashion model, part-time student,
>   and mother of a two-year-old boy
> PENFIELD, an editor of *Folks* magazine

The Story

The protagonist of "Lightning," Edward Connors, is introduced as he begins to interview people who have been struck by lightning, an assignment given him by Penfield, an editor of *Folks*. He instructs Connors to interview at least nine people, including one "slightly wonderful" person to be featured in the article.

Connors begins his research by advertising in *The Village Voice*. From the many responses he learns that many people have great-grandfathers or great-grandmothers who were struck by lightning in 1910. (Variations on this factual detail, as on others, will recur later in the story.)

Before the interviews begin, the reader learns of Connors' past, especially his earlier jobs. He was "a reporter for ten years and a freelancer for five, with six years in between as a PR man for Topsy Oil in Midland-Odessa." As a reporter, he covered business news, so his moving on to public relations with an oil firm was a logical change (urged on him by his wife, for financial reasons). He had been "in love with his work" as a reporter. The PR job paid three times as much but was dull, so when his wife left him for a racquetball pro at a country club, he left Topsy Oil and Texas for New York City and free-lance work: "To each assignment he brought a good brain, a good eye, a tenacious thoroughness, gusto."

The first man interviewed, Burch, reports that being struck by lightning was the best thing that ever happened to him. After the event he became a Jehovah's Witness, and he describes his life since then as "*Serene*. Truly serene." Connors is impressed. The next interviewee, a woman named Mac-Gregor, reports that being struck led to "some important changes" in her life: She married the man she had been seeing and quit her job, which had necessitated tiring commuting.

Still seeking a feature subject for his article, Connors then arranges to interview Edwina Rawson. She is reluctant but consents, and she turns out to be young, black, lovely, and charming, "not only slightly wonderful but also mildly superb." The reader watches Connors fall in love with her. The reader also learns much about her life, including her two-year-old son Zachary and her departed husband Marty, who gave her mouth-to-mouth resuscitation when she was struck by lightning. (She connects his ability to do so with "his cautious, be-prepared, white-folks' attitude toward life.")

Edwina is unsure about the effect of being struck by lightning. When Connors, who has fallen for her, asks if it changed her life, she says, "yes and no." It removed her eyebrows and "got rid of Marty," she says. Now she models to support Zachary and herself.

Hearing her story, Connors reacts unexpectedly. He thinks that the soul burns when struck by lightning, he connects lightning with music—"Lightning an attempt at music on the part of God?"—and he wishes that he had a song to sing to Edwina. Having none, he tells her odd facts about armadillos, facts more and more fanciful. Calling him "sentimental" and "crazy," Edwina goes to the movies with him.

The story shifts abruptly to Connors' next interviewee, a man named Stupple, who after being struck by lightning joined the American Nazi Party in Newark, New Jersey, and who passes on to Connors "pages of viciousness having to do with the Protocols of Zion and the alleged genetic inferiority of blacks."

Returning from that interview, turned down by Edwina for a dinner date, and "vexed by his inability to get a handle on the story," Connors talks to Penfield, the editor. He tells Penfield that he does not yet understand how being struck by lightning changes people. Penfield is not interested, but he is pleased to hear that Edwina is beautiful and will provide him with a good illustration for the cover of *Folks*.

The next day Connors interviews a Trappist monk in Piffard, New York, who received a Sony Walkman tape player from his community after he was struck and who listens to rock music on it. Connors is moved by the monk's happiness. Dining with Edwina and Zachary that night, Connors raises yet another question about the experience: "What effects the change . . . ?" Edwina is not interested, but she offers to give him a back rub.

The last paragraph of the story summarizes Connors' interviews with five more people. One of them, dumb from birth, speaks perfect French after being struck. Connors' finished article is reported as containing a passage on the religious quality of the experience, which Penfield properly deleted, and as having devoted extra space to Edwina, who looked "approximately fantastic."

Themes and Meanings

Donald Barthelme's stories recurrently take up the theme of the incomplete life. Usually the life is incomplete because the protagonist lacks someone to love and be loved by. The story either develops that kind of life or, as in "Lightning," finds for the protagonist the woman he has sought. Barthelme, however, seldom has in mind a long-term relationship. The emphasis is put, rather, on the excitement, the novelty, and the anticipation evoked by awakened desire and the sense of unspecified possibilities.

Connors is characterized as deserving and ripe for such a discovery. He is enthusiastic, hardworking, and open to change. He was a good reporter in the old days and brought those qualities even to the reporting of business news. Though the public relations job dampened his enthusiasm, he was still "very fond" of the company's amiable chief executive officer. The reader sees him eagerly doing research on his struck-by-lightning project and sympathetic to the kindly people he encounters, but not to the Nazi bigot.

Edwina is presented as Connors' ideal woman. Of his wife, the reader learns only that she complained about the low pay of his reporter's job and that the public relations salary permitted him to enjoy "briefly" his wife's "esteem." On the other hand, Edwina is beautiful and amusing and undemanding. Her first name suggests that she is Edward Connors' counterpart, while her black femininity complements his white masculinity. Best of all, perhaps, their relationship has progressed only to the hopeful moment of the offered back rub when the story ends; there is no suggestion of any letdown or boredom to come.

Style and Technique

Barthelme prefers a mixed mode to pure comedy or tragedy, admitting that he thereby sacrifices the opportunity to move his readers' emotions. He keeps his readers intelligently alert by shifting from level to level of diction, by finding colloquialisms and clichés to which an odd twist or application can be given, and by including unexpected topics and concerns. In a brief speculation about lightning, for example, Connors thinks: "Lightning at once a *coup de théâtre* and career counseling?" Here the comic juxtaposition of two very different interpretations is reinforced by the dramatic and sociological jargon. When Edwina generalizes from her marriage to a white man, one reads, "She had nothing against white folks, Edwina said with a warm smile, or rabbits, as black folks sometimes termed them, but you had to admit that, qua folks, they sucked." The sentence is a comic hash of mixed terms where "white folks" and "warm smile" suggest geniality that is cooled by the amusingly denigrating term "rabbits," is then altered completely by the mixture of a bookish Latin word and the colloquial in "qua folks" (which sounds silly), and is brought to a sharp ending with an insulting slang verb. (The thrice-repeated "folks" is a reminder that Connors is writing for the magazine *Folks*.)

The most obvious comic device is the story itself. This odd exploration of an odd subject, being hit by lightning, is a typical Barthelme literalization of a common notion. As his story "Falling Dog" acts out the common phrase "struck by a new idea," so "Lightning" develops the common image of a life-changing event as "like being struck by lightning."

Since Barthelme likes to surround any positive idea with ironic alternatives and doubts, several of the characters struck by lightning experience negative or less than profound results—adherence to Nazi ideas, ability to speak French, the end of a tiring job. On the other hand, two of them achieve serenity and happiness. Yet the central experience of being "struck by lightning" is Connors', and it takes place when he meets and falls in love with Edwina. For her, the results of an actual bolt of lightning were ambivalent ("yes and no"), and the story ends so quickly that one is left to wonder which of these terms will apply to Connors' new love—perhaps both.

J. D. O'Hara

LIKE THE NIGHT

Author: Alejo Carpentier (1904-1980)
Type of plot: Magical realism
Time of plot: From the Trojan War through World War II
Locale: Greece, Spain, and France
First published: "Semejante a la noche," 1958 (English translation, 1970)

> *Principal characters:*
> THE NARRATOR, the unnamed protagonist, a young soldier
>   about to leave by ship for warfare
> HIS FIANCÉE, unnamed

The Story

The events of the story occur in a single day, but it is a day that takes more than two thousand years to be completed. The main character, who is also the narrator, is going through an ancient ritual for young men: leaving his homeland for war and conquest. In this traditional situation, the narrator undergoes several obligatory encounters. He says farewell to each of his parents, his fiancée and friends, gets drunk on his final evening at home, then boards the boat in the cold light of day to leave his country.

Alejo Carpentier divides the story into five numbered sections, each of which advances the action while transposing it to a different place and time. The movement of the story is circular, however, beginning with the preparations for the Trojan War in section 1, moving to phases of the Spanish exploration and conquest of the New World in sections 2 and 3, to a sort of hybrid of World War I and World War II in sections 4, and in section 5 returning to the initial scene.

A note blown on a conch announces the arrival of King Agamemnon's fifty black ships, come to take the Achaean troops to Troy. Instantly, as if that note were the beginning of a vast symphony, the scene comes noisily to life. Those who had been waiting for many days begin to carry the wheat toward the ships, the ships scrape the sand with their keels, the Mycenaean sailors try to keep the Achaeans away from the ships with poles, and children run about, hindering the soldiers' movements and stealing nuts from under the oarsmen's benches.

The narrator finds the scene disillusioning. He expected a solemn ceremony celebrating the meeting of two groups of warriors, not this pandemonium in which the leading citizens could not make their speeches of welcome. He withdraws from the beach and sits astride a tree branch because it reminds him of a woman's body. The sexual theme, here a consolation for his vague sense of disappointment, will later become a source of frustration for him. The suggestion of disappointment is readily dispelled, however, by attributing it both to fatigue from waiting all night and to a hangover. His pride and sense of superiority return when he reflects that he and the other soldiers are the occasion of all this activity. He scorns the peasants for spending the day looking "at the earth over the sweating backs of their animals," or working the earth hunched over like cattle themselves. He tells himself that they will never see Troy, the city he and his comrades are about to "surround, attack, and destroy."

His ferocity is fueled by messages—which will ultimately be revealed as lies and propaganda—sent by Agamemnon about the Trojan King Priam's "insolence," the taunts that the Trojans have made against the Achaeans' "manly way of life," and the cruelties that the abducted Helen of Sparta suffered in Troy. He believes that to rescue Helen will be a "manly undertaking and the supreme triumph of a war that would give us prosperity, happiness, and pride in ourselves forever." His optimism is tempered only by the thought of giving grief to his mother and father.

In section 2, the noise about the ships changes to music from guitars and cymbals, and the sound of people dancing the zarambeque and singing coplas. The wheat being loaded in the previous section is now accompanied by wine, oil, and a wooden pipe organ to help convert the Indians of the New World. The narrator is about to depart to conquer a new empire for Spain, and the soldiers' arrogance infects him as it did previously. He feels that he and his fellows are men different from ordinary men by nature and capable of deeds unimaginable to them. His father's praise of a peaceful and prosperous life, then, is to no avail, and though he again feels a sense of disillusionment when his father warns him that such expeditions were the "madness of many for the gain of a few," he takes leave of his father and mother with the buoyant promise that, by freeing the Indians "from their barbarous superstitions our nation would win imperishable glory and greater happiness, prosperity, and power than all the Kingdoms of Europe." His idealism is undercut, however, in the scene with his mother, in which she warns him to have no sinful dealings with the Indian women but then realizes that her son is already dreaming of trying what she has warned him against. The base motives for his adventure give the lie to the narrator's idealism even before he articulates it.

Ultimately he sees through the propaganda, his own false idealism and sexual bravado. That disillusionment takes place in the final three sections of the story, in which he argues with his fiancée (section 3), angrily leaves her to visit his mistress (section 4), and returns to his fiancée, who is ready to give herself to him (section 5). By then he is sexually exhausted and filled with a tremendous fear of failure. Insulted by his weak refusal of her body, she flees. He is left emasculated and demoralized, his soldier's pride changed to self-reproach and disgust. His motive for heroism is debased. He is in the end merely a foot soldier, traveling on a slow, overloaded boat, and he will not see his loved ones for many years, if ever.

Themes and Meanings

Carpentier's work frequently expresses an incisive criticism of modern society. His best-known novel, *Los pasos perdidos* (1953; *The Lost Steps*, 1956, 1967), chronicles the efforts of a man to rediscover his humanity after being alienated from a society devoted to ambition and greed. A Cuban writer, Carpentier criticizes postcolonial and capitalist society not through preaching but through storytelling, allowing his Everyman characters to experience the depths of their victimhood and discontent in order to find a way out.

The narrator of "Like the Night" is at such a crucial point. He is about to take on warriorhood for the good of his society, but beneath the public promises lies economic self-interest, such as the possibility of a better trade with Asia after the Trojans are eliminated as competition. For the narrator, his adventuring involves more than merely expending his youthful energy. It has consequences for his parents, of whom he begins to be mindful, and for his fiancée, whose real passion exposes the confusion and doubt beneath his bravado. The narrator's relations with women—with his mother, fiancée, and mistress—are determined by the same false idealism and baseness that have moved him to go to war. He departs at exactly the wrong moment, when he begins to realize his victimhood and loses all heart for the ordeal he has chosen.

Style and Technique

The narrator is not the victim of a single ideology or historical movement, but is a kind of Everyman (hence his namelessness) leaving for war, as it were, simultaneously from several countries thousands of years apart. The significance of the departure is deepened by the layering of history. The falsehoods stretch thinner and thinner until they can no longer provide supportive ideology for the narrator. The Trojan War is a matter of honor and manhood, the Spanish conquest begins in order to win souls, and modern war promises eternal brotherhood. None of those promises is kept, as history has proved, but in the story they keep reappearing as new heads on an old monster.

While it debunks the narrator's idealism, Carpentier's technique of movement through time also magnifies the human pain his folly causes those who love him. His parents suffer, certainly, though the main focus is on his fiancée being left unfulfilled, the promise of their future together hopelessly ruined. The central section is given to their argument about his enterprise in the West Indies among the native people. She has no faith in the European claims of uplifting the Indians, who, according to Michel de Montaigne (whose *Essais*, 1580, 1588, she is reading), have been corrupted by the example shown them in the behavior of the explorers. The duplicitous European treatment of the Indians is but one example of a cyclic historical process, a pattern of exploitation that has been repeated for thousands of years.

Robert Bensen

LIONS, HARTS, LEAPING DOES

Author: J. F. Powers (1917-   )
Type of plot: Theological allegory
Time of plot: Probably the mid-twentieth century
Locale: A Franciscan monastery in the northern United States
First published: 1943

Principal characters:
FATHER DIDYMUS, an aging Franciscan friar
BROTHER TITUS, Didymus' devoted companion

The Story

The striking title, "Lions, Harts, Leaping Does," is from a passage in Saint John of the Cross: "Birds of swift wing, lions, harts, leaping does, mountains, valleys, banks, waters, breezes, heats and terrors that keep watch by night, by the pleasant lyres and by the siren's song, I conjure you, cease your wrath and touch not the wall. . . ." Titus, who is a devoted but slow-witted Franciscan brother, reads this lovely prose to the companion whom he attends in the monastery, the octogenarian priest Didymus. The lines well suggest the plangent lyrical tone of this narrative of the aged Didymus' struggle to find grace.

When the story opens, Titus is reading to Didymus from Bishop John Bale's *Pageant of Popes' Contayninge the Lyves of all the Bishops of Rome, from the Beginninge of them to the Year of Grace 1555* (1574), an idiosyncratic and splenetic chronicle to which Didymus refers as "Bishop Bale's funny book." Titus also quotes from memory fragments from Thomas à Kempis' *The Imitation of Christ* (fifteenth century), silently challenging Didymus to identify the source in an "unconfessed contest." This introductory scene fixes the characters of the two Franciscans and reveals their warm relationship. Titus is a saintly innocent, full of childlike glee as he spars mildly with Didymus in an attempt to please. Didymus is a geometry teacher who is always alert to impulses of spiritual pride in himself and feels ashamed at impatiently patronizing Titus.

As they walk the monastery grounds together at the close of a frigid day, Didymus ruminates on the life of poverty, chastity, and obedience that he has led. He concludes that "it was the spirit of the vows which opened the way and revealed to the soul, no matter the flux of circumstance, the means of salvation," and this realization saddens him with a sense of having sinned against his older brother, Seraphin. The dying Seraphin, also a priest, had asked Didymus to visit him in St. Louis, but Didymus had refused out of what he now judges to have been a false interpretation of his duty to obey

God. Didymus ruefully admits that "he had used his brother for a hair shirt," an admission that sets up the crucial question of Didymus' grace, around which the story revolves.

As the two return to the monastery, they meet the rector, who speaks to Didymus of a telegram for him, and it turns out that Titus has forgotten to give the message to Didymus. The abashed Titus produces the telegram, which announces the death of Seraphin.

In the short second section, Didymus falls asleep in the chapel and dreams of himself and Seraphin walking on a serpentine river. The two brothers talk of their parents and of their own lives until two crayfish surface and grab Didymus, who then awakens to find himself prone on the floor. Didymus is helped to his feet by Titus and starts to walk away, only to collapse from an apparent stroke.

The next day Didymus sits in a wheelchair, bundled in blankets and struggling to focus on the cold, inert landscape visible through his window. He hears Titus enter the room and move around mysteriously, gradually learning that the quietly gleeful Titus has brought him a canary in a cage: "one of the Saint's own birds," as Titus puts it. Didymus spends his long days at the window, the canary his silent companion, with Titus reading to him on occasion. His life is dreary. "They were captives, he and the canary, and the only thing they craved was escape."

In his meditations on his condition, Didymus wonders if his incapacitation is God's punishment of him for not having "gloried too much in having it in him to turn down Seraphin's request to come to St. Louis." He cannot decide if he has erred, and his uncertainty puts him in a moral predicament. If he is being punished, then praying for recovery would suggest that he has missed "the divine point." Didymus finally concludes he is not man enough to see "the greatest significance in his affliction," and wants only to walk again and eventually die a normal death. So, he copes with his situation, prays for good health, and watches the canary, identifying in his misery with the forlorn bird trapped in the cage.

One day Didymus sends Titus on an errand, and with an exhausting effort he reaches up and opens the canary's cage, then falls face down on the floor. That night in his room, having received the last sacrament, Didymus waits for death, free from desire but "beset by the grossest distractions." After Titus reads to him from St. John of the Cross, Didymus has a vision of his life as "tied down, caged, stunted in his apostolate, seeking the crumbs. . . ." At this moment he asks Titus to open the window, and as Didymus prays to lose himself in God the canary flutters through the open window into the snowy night outside. As Titus stares out the window seeking the lost bird, "the snowflakes whirled at the window, for a moment for all their bright blue beauty as though struck still be lightning, and Didymus closed his eyes, only to find them there also, but darkly falling."

Themes and Meanings

Critics disagree over the question of whether Didymus achieves grace, and each reader will have to decide the state of Didymus' soul in the light of his own interpretation of the way to religious salvation. Didymus himself is in doubt, and just before the end can find no "divine sign within himself." His own evaluation of his condition cannot be taken as definitive, however, even if his judgment of his sin against Seraphin is accepted as accurate—as it probably should be. His faults proceed not from desire but from an earnest desire to follow the will of God, and the genuine human anguish he suffers must count in his favor.

Perhaps most significant of all the evidence is the moving *nunc dimittis* with which the story ends, contributing significantly to the compassionate tone that suffuses the story of Didymus' tormented self-questioning and death. Didymus dies as the canary flees to "the snowy arms of God," and it is difficult to believe that the two of them, who want most of all to escape, do not come to the same resting place. If not, the canary is reduced in meaning to a symbol of the peace that comes in the annihilation of death, and if that is J. F. Powers' intent, then Didymus' ordeal seems greatly diminished and the allegorical elements emerge as little more than literary ornamentation.

Style and Technique

The two most salient features of Powers' direct, simple style in "Lions, Harts, Leaping Does" are his effective use of weather and landscape and the development of the allegory represented by the bird in the cage. The "angular winter daylight" proves to be a pathetic fallacy that complements the somber spiritual considerations of Didymus' inner life: The first scene, with Titus reading from "Bishop Bale's funny book," is bathed by the dying light of a cold winter day, and as they emerge from the buildings into the outdoors, the "freezing air" bites into their bodies and they pace a walkway littered with shards of ice. Didymus' face becomes "a slab of pasteboard" and his eyes water. Such imagery suits the climate of Didymus' soul as he pursues his solitary quest for an answer to his spiritual fate. Nowhere is there any greenness, any fullness of life. Even the canary is mute and joyless, enduring its alien habitat with resignation and longing for freedom.

When Titus first brings the canary to Didymus' room, the bird chirps cheerfully, and for a while it enjoys the swing that Titus provides for it. Gradually, though, the creature tires of looking out the window on the bleak snowscape, and its sadness reflects the weariness in Didymus' heart. The two of them share a tacit fellowship: "Nothing was lost of the communion he kept with the canary." As a symbol of Didymus' soul, the canary matches its moods to the priest's. As Didymus lies dying, "the canary perched in the dark atop the cage, head warm under wing, already, it seemed to Didymus, without memory of its captivity, dreaming of a former freedom, an ancestral summer day with flowers and trees." When the bird flies to freedom, the soul of Didymus makes good its escape as well.

Frank Day

LISPETH

Author: Rudyard Kipling (1865-1936)
Type of plot: Social satire
Time of plot: The nineteenth century
Locale: Northern India
First published: 1886

> *Principal characters:*
> LISPETH, the protagonist, a Hill-girl
> THE CHAPLAIN OF KOTGARH, Lispeth's guardian
> THE CHAPLAIN'S WIFE
> THE ENGLISHMAN, the man Lispeth wants to marry

The Story

A Hill-girl christened Elizabeth, but known as Lispeth according to local pronunciation, grows up in the Kotgarh valley in Northern India. Her parents, having become Christians out of destitute poverty, bring their baby daughter to the Kotgarh Chaplain to be baptized. When both her parents die of cholera, Lispeth becomes half servant, half companion to the wife of the Chaplain then residing in Kotgarh. She grows tall, vigorous, and as lovely as a Greek goddess. Unlike other Hill-girls, when she reaches womanhood she does not give up the Christianity she has accepted. She is happy playing with the Chaplain's children, taking Sunday School classes, reading all the books in the house, and taking long walks in the hills. When she is seventeen, however, an event takes place that completely changes her attitude toward the English. Interaction with them at a deeper level reveals to her that the ways of her people are more congenial and acceptable to her than the supposedly superior culture represented by the Chaplain of Kotgarh, his wife, and an Englishman.

One day at dusk, Lispeth returns home from her long walk in the hills carrying a heavy burden: a young Englishman who is unconscious from a cut on the head. She falls in love with him and announces that she intends to marry him when he is well again. Horrified, the Chaplain and his wife rebuke her for the impropriety of her feelings, but she is firm in her resolve.

The Englishman is a traveler in the East who lost his footing and fell while hunting for butterflies and plants in the Simla hills. Lispeth discovered and saved him. Recovering coherence after two weeks, he spends two more leisurely weeks regaining his strength. While doing so, even though he is engaged to a girl in England, he finds it very pleasant to walk and talk with Lispeth and say sweet, endearing words to her. All this means everything to her but nothing to him, for he finds Lispeth's love for himself merely amusing and romantic.

Even when he takes leave of her, he puts his arm around her waist and repeatedly promises to return, knowing all the time that his promises are false. He acts, in fact, according to the advice of the Chaplain's wife, who wants to avoid a scandal. After Lispeth waits in vain for three months, the Chaplain's wife tells her the truth. Lispeth is incredulous, for the Englishman had professed love and the Chaplain's wife had assured her of his return. She wants to know how what they told her could be untrue. When the Chaplain's wife self-righteously explains their strategy to keep her quiet, Lispeth realizes that they lied to her deliberately. She leaves in silent indignation, and comes back in the garb of a Hill-girl with braided hair to make a twofold announcement: that she is returning to her people as a devotee of Tarka Devi, and that she thinks the English are all liars.

Thereafter, Lispeth takes to her people with great ardor and soon marries a woodcutter who beats her in the manner of the Hill-people. Her beauty fades, and she grows very old. Yet she may be persuaded, when drunk, to recount in perfect English the romance of her first love affair. It is hard to believe that this very old, wrinkled, and withered woman is the formerly beautiful Lispeth.

Themes and Meanings

The satiric purpose of the author is achieved by an accumulation of ironies. The epigram at the head of this story begins, "Look, you have cast out love! What Gods are these you bid me please?" Since the central ethical value of Christianity is love, casting out love is the most unchristian of acts. This is exactly what Christian missionaries and imperialists do. In the name of superior faith and breeding, they substitute deceit and untruth where all-embracing love should be. As a result, the gods that the Englishman, the Chaplain, and the Chaplain's wife worship become questionable, a "tangled Trinity" to a simple Hill-girl.

Ironies abound. Not only are Christians and imperialists unchristian and ordinary, but it is Lispeth—the heathen, the savage, the one guilty, according to the English, of shameless folly—who demonstrates a love that is unalloyed devotion and trust.

By baptizing Lispeth, the missionaries hold out the promise of a new and better life of the spirit. Instead of keeping that promise, they kill her, as she declares; they kill her faith in their God; they kill her trust in their way of life; they abandon her to social evils; and indirectly they ruin her unspoiled beauty. They try to put a free and innocent Hill-girl with the beauty and poise of Diana, a pagan goddess, into their own kind of garb—gaudy floral prints—that in this context may well be a metaphor for ostentation and lack of sensitivity.

When Lispeth returns to her people, the Chaplain's wife is shocked at her conversion, as though it were an unnatural act. She attributes it to the innate savagery of the girl's race and finds no blame whatsoever in the deceit of the Englishman or herself. In the presence of such self-righteous superiority, no true human relationship can flourish.

When Lispeth returns to her people's way and marries, she has to endure the beatings of her husband. Her faith is strong, though, for she thinks of herself as the servant of Tarka Devi, the Goddess who saves. As for her first romance, the memory of it is hers for life, clean, uninhibited, and unshackled by falsehood.

"Lispeth" is an unequivocal indictment of racist, religious, and imperialist attitudes of superiority. Kipling shows how absurd and inhumane the outcome is when people who lack integrity and sensitivity take it upon themselves in their self-satisfied stance to improve others whom they have not even tried to understand, let alone appreciate.

Style and Technique

For success at satire, the writer must engage the interest of the reader in the narration itself, and then almost imperceptibly make an about-face from lightness to depth, from pleasant entertainment to pungent import. This is exactly Kipling's technique; he tells a romantic tale set in the hills of Northern India which has the allure of distance and strangeness. Even a familiar name such as Elizabeth is changed to Lispeth in the hills, and names of places—Simla, Kotgarh, Narkunda—add to the romance. Kipling's narrator takes on the easy, purposeful tone of the fireside storyteller, step by step piling irony upon irony, up to the climax, when the reader feels the full thrust of the satire.

Apart from the skillful management of content and style, Kipling uses the two notable techniques of contrast and irony. Lispeth is the only character who is individualized. She is, therefore, the only one of the principal characters who is mentioned by name—and a distinctive one at that—to show how extraordinary she is in beauty and character. In contrast, none of the English characters is mentioned by name, and they accordingly share a stereotyped attitude of superiority. Lispeth's depth of feeling, her forthright character and conduct, stand in ironic contrast to the superficial proprieties and deviousness of those who pride themselves on being her betters. The contrast helps pinpoint the irony that assumed superiority is pathetically hollow, altogether incapable of uplifting the so-called "savage," who in this story is the only one possessed of redeeming nobility. Instead of helping to save her soul, her would-be benefactors reduce her to poignant misery.

Contrasts work throughout in subtle as well as obvious ways. When Lispeth comes down the hill carrying the Englishman, her burden is both literally and symbolically heavy, and unconscious of her vigor and purity. Lispeth's strenuous effort and devotion contrast with the Chaplain's wife's indolence of body and spirit, for when Lispeth comes in exhausted from her tremendous lifesaving effort, the Chaplain's wife has been dozing in the living room. Lispeth saves by her own effort; the English promise to save by conversion to the Church of England. Lispeth walks twenty or thirty miles; English ladies walk a mile and a half into the hills and return by carriage. Lispeth is referred to as a child, and she has a child's innocence and lack of knowledge of the world; she cries and tries to see in a jigsaw-puzzle map where her beloved might be. The Englishman, on the other hand, much traveled and educated, forgets the girl who loves him and to whom he owes his life. In a book he writes on the East, her name does not appear. The contrast of devotion and opportunism, of innocence and manipulation, highlights the irony of the white man's "burden," which consists not of improving but of exploiting other people. Contrasting perceptions reveal the gap that separates the characters. What is honorable passion in Lispeth's eyes is shameless folly according to the English. The relationship between them remains within the confines of racial and religious prejudice instead of growing into a richly human interaction.

Among the many ironies strung into the narrative, Kipling includes the Englishman's pledge of discretion, which is nothing short of irresponsibility, and the Chaplain's wife's concern for morality, which is little more than an effort to avoid scandal. Christians in the story lack charity, and the savage displays sensitivity. Through a maze of paradoxes, the reader finally arrives at a point where both sides reveal their generalized prejudice. Lispeth concludes that all the English are liars. The Chaplain's wife declares that no law can explain the vagaries of the savage. Lispeth's perfect English is no passport to communication; the distance between her and the English increases. Her beauty fades and her one-sided romance is only a memory.

Kipling observes the misery which those human beings in power inflict upon other human beings, and writes about it in "Lispeth," a very moving satire.

Sita Kapadia

A LITTLE CLOUD

Author: James Joyce (1882-1941)
Type of plot: Symbolic realism
Time of plot: c. 1900
Locale: Dublin
First published: 1914

Principal characters:
THOMAS MALONE ("LITTLE") CHANDLER, a thirty-two-year-old law clerk
IGNATIUS GALLAHER, a Dublin-born London journalist

The Story

Thomas Malone Chandler, known as "Little Chandler" because of his boyish appearance and delicate manner, works as a legal clerk. On this particular fall evening, he has an appointment with an old friend named Ignatius Gallaher. After eight years abroad, during which time he has become a self-confident and successful journalist, Gallaher has returned to visit his native Dublin.

The prospect of an evening with Gallaher arouses certain conflicts in Little Chandler. On the one hand, he is proud to have a talented and successful friend; on the other hand, he is reminded of the drudgery of his own work, which he associates with the drabness of his native city. When such melancholy moods strike him, he thinks of the books of poetry that he bought before his marriage. Remembering some of their lines, he is often consoled.

When his work day ends, he sets out for his appointment. His anticipation of the evening out causes him to ignore the squalor of the city slums. His rendezvous with Gallaher is to be at Corless's, a fashionable restaurant patronized by the upper classes. He has always viewed their lives from a distance, with envy and apprehension. Yet thoughts of Gallaher's dash, talent, and resources buoy him up and make him feel equal to the occasion. He reflects that the contrast between the brilliance of Gallaher's career and his own prosaic job is explained by the lack of opportunity in Dublin.

He considers himself a poet of moods, now perhaps reaching emotional maturity. His melancholic temperament, he believes, would be seen by outsiders as typical of the work of the Celtic Twilight, the Irish literary movement led by William Butler Yeats. He conjectures that Gallaher may be able to advise him on publication strategies.

In Corless's bar, Gallaher greets him jovially, joking about the signs of his approaching middle age. As they order drinks and reminisce, however, Chandler begins to recognize Gallaher's crude and patronizing manner as he boasts of the pressures and prestige of his job, his adventures in "immoral"

Paris, his taste for neat whiskey, and his acquaintance with the corruption of the religious orders and the aristocracy of the Continent.

Then Little Chandler tells Gallaher of his marriage and baby son and invites him to visit. Gallaher declines, however, and as they drink their final whiskeys, Chandler's resentment against his own humble life and Gallaher's condescension begins to grow stronger. Emboldened by the effects of the alcohol, he predicts Gallaher's own marriage. Gallaher insists that he is liberated from all romantic illusions about women: He is too worldly-wise for that.

When Little Chandler gets home late for tea, he has an argument with his wife. She goes out on an errand, leaving him in charge of their sleeping infant. As he awaits her return, he reflects on their dull marriage, his timidity, and his mean and domineering wife. From these doleful reflections on his domestication, he turns again to thoughts of poetry. Yet when he opens his volume of Lord Byron's poems, the first verse that he reads sends him into another melancholic reverie.

This is broken by his child, who wakes and begins to cry. As he tries to read while rocking the child, a resentment against all the circumstances of his life wells up in him. He shouts at the child, driving it into hysterics. His wife rushes in upon the scene, snatches the child from him, and soothes it. Little Chandler stands by, helpless before her hatred and conscience-stricken by his outburst.

Themes and Meanings

Like each of the *Dubliners* (1914) stories (this is the eighth of fifteen), "A Little Cloud" develops the theme of the paralysis of intellect and spirit in Dublin. In this story there are two specimens: Little Chandler the legal clerk and Gallaher the journalist. Through their occupations, they share a common professional interest in language as well as a Dublin background. Further, Gallaher has the reputation of success, and Little Chandler has ambitions as a poet. Yet it is clear from the story that Chandler is emotionally limited. Gallaher is unsympathetic and crude, and each is self-deceived about his talents. Chandler's thoughts and Gallaher's conversation betray conventional attitudes in derivative, cliché-ridden language that belies their individual pretensions.

From the very outset, the story establishes Little Chandler's physical, emotional, and social immaturity. He has the appearance of a child, takes his own fantasies much too seriously, shows no capacity for original thought or expression, and views the social and artistic life of Dublin from a private distance. At the same time, he pins some hopes on his reunion with Gallaher to help him break out of this condition, as Gallaher's reputation and his invitation to Corless's seem to promise. Yet, as their conversation progresses, it is clear—clearer to the reader than to Chandler—that these expectations are not to be fulfilled. Despite his disappointment, Chandler is inclined to ignore Gallaher's insulting behavior, and he allows the gaudy images of Gallaher's life abroad to disconcert his own fragile self-image. Thus, at the conclusion of the story, Chandler's rebellion against his domestic responsibilities is no wiser than was his vague discontent at the beginning.

The main focus of the story is Chandler: His life is circumscribed by his dull job, his passionless marriage, and his general insularity. The secondary focus is on Gallaher, who, for all of his vaunted talents and experience of the world, brings home nothing more than vulgarity and materialism. He makes no effort to understand or sympathize with Chandler, and finally has nothing to offer him but further reason to doubt himself. It is a measure of Little Chandler's lack of perspective that he allows the conversation to disconcert him: Another person might just as easily have found in the example of Gallaher's manner and values good reason to restore his faith in his workaday Dublin life.

Noting that both Little Chandler and Gallaher are significantly lacking in powers of observation, given to trite expression, yet claim to have linguistic talent, another theme of "A Little Cloud" may be observed. Each of them is more interested in the effect that he might have on others than in developing an individual perception of the world around him and a respect for language to represent that world. Moreover, the impression of Chandler's mental life does not lead to any degree of confidence in his spiritual powers. Nevertheless, because of the moody, impressionistic, and allusive poetry that he thinks he might write, Chandler considers himself as a potential member of the Irish Literary Revival. Without explicitly admitting it, therefore, he imagines himself as a follower of William Butler Yeats, whose poetry of the 1890's was marked by similar qualities and was at the turn of the century much imitated by Irish writers of meager talent. From this historical perspective, then, like Yeats's poem "A Coat," "A Little Cloud" is Joyce's satire on these writers.

Style and Technique

This story, like all those in *Dubliners*, displays a high degree of realistic exactitude while at the same time maintaining a firmly controlled sense of design and symbol. The narrator's point of view, moreover, is nicely poised between the idiom of the characters—which verges on caricature—and the language of subtle irony.

First, it reports accurately the geography, architecture, and atmosphere of turn-of-the-century Dublin: the details of Chandler's route to his meeting with Gallaher (he is, in fact, literally drawing nearer to London), the townhouses of the former aristocracy that have become shabby tenements, and the exclusive reputation of Corless's. On this level alone, Joyce's and Little Chandler's notions of artistic integrity are a world apart.

Second, the story is told in a dialectical progression of three scenes: the first, presenting Chandler's eager anticipation of Gallaher; the second, the unhappy reality revealed at Corless's; and the third, the conflict in Chandler's feelings set up by the contrast between these perspectives. Each of these scenes follows a consistent progression in subject: from particular considerations of Gallaher, to Chandler himself, to general reflections on "life," ending with a retreat to "art." The rhythm of this development suggests Chandler's inability to draw any coherent or expressible conclusion from his actual experience.

Third, the language and symbology of the story suggest the theme of false feeling and forced manner. Both characters think and speak in clichés, as can be seen, for example, in the quality of mind attributed to Chandler in the opening paragraph and in the way in which Gallaher, in the middle scene, greets the news of his friend's marriage. A pattern of symbols and allusions suggests Gallaher's exaggeration and vulgarity: his orange tie, his ordering "whisky," and his ostentatious use of Gaelic and French expressions. Finally, these images are complemented in the concluding paragraphs as Little Chandler hears his wife's soothing words to their child: They remind him that he is a man of little consequence.

Cóilín Owens

LITTLE HERR FRIEDEMANN

Author: Thomas Mann (1875-1955)
Type of plot: Symbolic realism
Time of plot: The 1890's
Locale: Lübeck, Germany
First published: "Der kleine Herr Friedemann," 1897 (English translation, 1936)

Principal characters:
JOHANNES FRIEDEMANN, the protagonist, a hunchback and dwarf
FRAU GERDA VON RINNLINGEN, a femme fatale, both beautiful and cruel
FRIEDERIKE,
HENRIETTE, and
PFIFFI FRIEDEMANN, Johannes' unmarried sisters
COLONEL VON RINNLINGEN, Gerda's husband and the district commander

The Story

Johannes Friedemann, as a month-old infant in Lübeck, had taken a bad fall while in the care of his drunken nurse. As a result, he is destined to live out his life as a hunchback and a dwarf. Remarkably so, Friedemann as a young adult has made an accommodation with his plight. At sixteen he had fallen in love with a blonde girl his age, but one summer afternoon he saw her embracing and kissing a boy while hiding behind a jasmine bush. Friedemann made an instant vow: "Never again will I let myself in for any of it. To the others it brings joy and happiness, for me it can only mean sadness and pain. I am done with it." As a consequence, the dwarf teaches himself to revel in the changing splendors of the natural world: He learns to love music (in fact, he plays the violin passably), literature, and especially the theater, his real passion. In a substantive way, then, he has made his private peace with the world. Indeed, his surname in translation can mean "the man who seeks or finds peace."

In June of his fateful year, Friedemann happily celebrates his thirtieth birthday. Taking inventory of his life, Friedemann considers that he has boldly renounced that which he will never have, has successfully established himself in business, lives happily in the family home with his three unmarried sisters (Friederike, Henriette, and Pfiffi), and can optimistically anticipate ten or twenty more years of the good life: "And I look forward to them with peace in my heart."

In July, little Friedemann has five encounters with a voluptuous married woman, Frau Gerda von Rinnlingen. Her husband, who is forty years old (Gerda is sixteen years his junior), is a military officer (Colonel von Rinnlingen) and is the newly appointed district commander of the Lübeck area. Strangely enough, almost from his first sight of her, Friedemann instinctively recognizes and accepts Gerda as the agent of his doom; that is, she will bring about his death in a most direct way.

On a Tuesday noon, Friedemann has his first glimpse of her. While he is strolling with a business acquaintance, they see her in a yellow car being drawn by a pair of thoroughbreds. In a few words Mann describes her. Gerda's hair is red-blonde; her face is "oval, with a dead-white skin and faint bluish shadows lurking under the close-set eyes." Friedemann fixes his gaze on her as she goes by. She in turn nods at him. While his companion chatters on, Friedemann stares stonily at the pavement.

Three days later he comes home for lunch and is informed that the district commander and his wife have arrived for a courtesy visit. Ignoring protocol, Friedemann without explanation retreats to his room and refuses to meet them. When his sisters announce to him that they will be returning the visit on Sunday, Friedemann says nothing: "He was eating his soup with a hushed and troubled air. It was as though he were listening to some strange noise he heard."

The dwarf's third encounter with Gerda, on the following night, is a most unsettling one. Attending the opera, he finds that he is seated next to her. His inner turmoil now begins in earnest. Little Friedemann is overwhelmed by the physical presence of the woman: her imposing height, her striking red-blonde hair, her low-cut gown and full bosom, and the warm, alluring scent of her body. They do not speak, but after intermission his eyes become locked with hers. She continues to stare until he turns away. Friedemann is humiliated because he thinks that she has compelled him to cast his eyes down before her steadfast gaze.

Toward the end of the opera, Gerda drops her fan in what he interprets as a coquettish ruse. They both bend to retrieve it and their heads momentarily touch. Without a word he flees the theater and heads home, absolutely convinced that her eyes glittered at him with "unholy joy." Once he calls out her name; twice he murmurs, "My God, my God!"

Friedemann is ill the next day as his sisters go off early on their visit to the von Rinnlingens. Late that morning he finds a reservoir of strength and impulsively decides to seek out Gerda at her home. Ushered into a half-darkened room, he converses rather pleasantly with her about their mutual health and about his violin playing. Suddenly, without warning, her expression changes from one of real concern about him to one of genuine cruelty. Again she stares at him until he submits and begins to look at the floor. As he prepares to leave, she invites him and his sisters to her home the next week for an informal dance.

Friedemann goes home by way of the river, which is adjacent to her property. He knows now that his fate is in her hands. There is a scenario to be acted out, and he will submit to his role. Even though he has always yearned for peace, it cannot be his until she has had her way with him, whatever that might be. Prior to her arrival in Lübeck, he had held the sensual world at bay with his formidable gift for sublimating his sexual drive. Her presence has changed all that now. She is simply too powerful a force for him to resist.

The final episode with Gerda is an obligatory scene. Little Friedemann is prepared for the end. At her home that Sunday night the guests have gathered. A resigned Friedemann quietly sits and looks at Gerda with a gaze of unwilling adoration. In time she invites him into her garden. A subservient Friedemann follows her beyond the garden into a little park by the river's edge, leaving all the other guests behind. Seated on a bench they chat once more about their health. He admits to her that those years of sublimation had been unhappy ones. The kindness in her tone apparently causes him to stand up abruptly, to emit a loud wail, and then to take her hands in his as he kneels before her with his face buried in her lap. With his diminutive body trembling, he gasps: "You know, you understand . . . let me . . . I can no longer . . . my God, oh my God! "

Scornfully laughing at him, Gerda pushes him away and then flings him to the grass. In supreme disgust at having lost control of himself, the self-absorbed hunchback drags his body to the water's edge as she runs up the path to her husband and the other guests. Little Friedemann lets his upper torso immerse itself in the river.

Themes and Meanings

Two of Mann's themes are to be found in this story: the fate of the unhealthy artist and the destructive power of the femme fatale. The former theme is often found in his early fiction; the latter is not so prevalent. When Mann incorporates them into one tale such as "Little Herr Friedemann," the result is a work of rather unsettling power. Few Mann stories from the 1890's achieve the weight and dramatic thrust of this one.

As a typically doomed Mann male, Friedemann is one who is "marked out" from society by his deformity. Despite whatever derision he must endure because of his boy-man appearance, Friedemann has become part of the mainstream of Lübeck society: He is an entrepreneur; he leads a gainful, productive life; he is a member of a respected Lübeck family; and he is a rather visible member of the local artistic scene in that he plays the violin and is an avid patron of the arts.

Counterbalanced against all these achievements, however, is the fact that Friedemann has deliberately renounced the sensual life (love, passion, and sex). For Mann, that is unhealthy; in fact, it is for him a form of decadence in its own way. Thus, as an artist of sorts, Friedemann is considered by Mann to be typical of that class. That is, notwithstanding Friedemann's relative bourgeois stability, he leads an unhealthy and by extension an unhappy life. His fate in the river, Mann suggests, is the culmination of such a life.

The other theme has to do with Gerda as femme fatale and the deadliness of her relationship with the harmless cripple. Her motivation may be beyond the reader's understanding given that Mann does not go into her mind. Friedemann, however, most assuredly sees her as one whose actions cannot be misinterpreted: She is determined to be the cause of his destruction, as she is. He is positive that she has with great calculation brought him to the point in his life at which he must take his own life. After all, she is the one who invites him to her party. She is the one who entices him to the isolated bench by the river's edge. And Gerda, finally, is the one who seduces him into passionately confessing his desire for her—and then physically rejects him. Her mocking laughter on the way back to her guests is the last sound little Herr Friedemann hears, along with the chirping of the crickets.

Style and Technique

One of the primary characteristics of Mann's style is his frequent use of leitmotifs. The particular images and verbal patterns which recur throughout "Little Herr Friedemann" serve as reinforcement of Mann's emphasis on the vulnerability of Friedemann and the strength of Gerda. For example, there are numerous references to small birds and bird sounds. Several times Friedemann is described as being pigeon breasted. Taken all together, they remind one that Friedemann is much like a frail bird, the prey of a far larger, predatory creature.

The numerous references to Gerda having a dead-white face and arms and skin not only stress the connection she has with the femme fatale (who is almost always described in those ways), but also portray her as an emissary of death itself. Further, the motif of the jasmine bush recurs at critical points in the narrative: when Friedemann at sixteen sees his first love embracing behind that bush; when he sits on a bench near a blossoming jasmine by the river as he tries to make sense of Gerda's ambiguous attitude toward him when he visited her at home; and, finally, again on that last night on the bench as he pours out his stumbling protestations of desire to her. The jasmine is white and is heavily scented. Clearly Mann wants it to be identified with Friedemann's youthful sexual awakening and later with his several tormenting encounters with the only woman in Friedemann's adult life, Frau von Rinnlingen.

Gerald R. Griffin

A LIVING RELIC

Author: Ivan Turgenev (1818-1883)
Type of plot: Social realism
Time of plot: The 1850's
Locale: The village of Alekseyevka, in Belyov province, Russia
First published: "Zhivye Moshchi," 1874 (English translation, 1895)

> *Principal characters:*
> PYOTR PETROVICH, the narrator, a landowner and hunter
> ERMOLAY, a serf, Pyotr's companion and guide
> LUKERYA, the protagonist, a paralyzed twenty-nine-year-old
> serf girl
> VASILY POLYAKOV, a freed serf and bailiff
> AGRAFENA, Vasily's wife
> FATHER ALEKSEY, a priest

The Story

The title, "A Living Relic," refers to a paralyzed serf girl, Lukerya, whom the narrator, Pyotr Petrovich, unexpectedly encounters lying alone and abandoned in a small shed on one of his mother's farms. Pyotr is stunned by the sight of the immobile, mummylike body that lies before him and cannot believe that the half-dead creature is the same lively, beautiful, robust young girl who loved to sing and dance a mere six years ago, when she lived in his mother's manor house as one of her household serfs.

Pyotr's compassion for the girl grows as he questions her about her misfortunes and learns that she fell, injured herself internally, and gradually lost the use of her legs. Since the doctors were unable to diagnose her illness and the gentry considered it inconvenient to keep cripples in the manor house, she was sent to the village of Alekseyevka. Her affliction caused her great grief because it separated her from the young peasant lad, Vasily Polyakov, whom she loved and to whom she had been betrothed. Vasily also grieved but eventually married another girl, named Agrafena. As Lukerya relates her misfortune, the narrator is astonished to learn that she harbors no resentment. She is grateful knowing that Vasily has found a good wife who has provided him with children. She weeps only after Vasily's visits, when she recalls the happy times that they shared together. For the most part she endures her suffering quietly and patiently, without dwelling on her affliction. She explains that as long as she still breathes, she is alive and she values that life. She takes delight in the beauty of the natural world around her: the aroma of wild flowers; the sounds of insects; the activities of birds, fowl, and other small woodland creatures which creep into her shed. Although it is with great effort, she continues to sing and even teaches the songs she remembers to an orphan girl. Pyotr is overwhelmed by the scarcely audible but pure sound which she emits from her trembling lips.

Deeply moved by the condition of the unfortunate Lukerya, he offers to transfer her to a hospital, but she declines, remembering the painful medical treatment she received. She asks only that he try to obtain for her more opium to help relieve her sleeplessness. Then, in a supreme expression of compassion and concern for others, she asks Pyotr to persuade his mother to reduce the quit-rent for the peasants, since they are poor and do not have enough land. Pyotr agrees and departs. As he leaves, the foreman on the farm tells him that the local peasants call Lukerya "Living Relic," since she never complains and is grateful for everything. A few weeks later, Pyotr learns that Lukerya has died as she had foreseen in one of her dreams.

Themes and Meanings

Turgenev's story may be viewed as an allegory on the spiritual beauty of the Russian people symbolized by Lukerya, who personifies their longtime suffering and endurance. The story was written for a literary symposium that was published in 1874 to aid the victims of a famine. It was also included in the 1874 edition of Turgenev's *Zapiski okhotnika* (*A Sportsman's Sketches*, 1932), originally published by Turgenev in 1852 as an exposé on the evils of serfdom.

Thematically, "A Living Relic" stresses the dignity and moral worth of the peasantry and reflects Turgenev's humanitarian concern and compassion for suffering. He calls the reader's attention to the theme of suffering by introducing his story with a two-line epigraph from a poem by the Russian poet Fyodor Tyutchev (1803-1873): "Native land of long endurance, Thou land of the Russian people!" Lukerya becomes the major symbol of that endurance in the story. She accepts her suffering with patience and dignity approaching sainthood; she does not complain, and she makes no demands on others. Her needs are modest. She eats nothing and subsists only on the water contained in a jug at her side, which she can still reach herself with her one unparalyzed arm. She accepts her affliction, pointing out that others are more unfortunate than she, for they have no shelter or are blind or deaf. Furthermore, she considers her physical affliction a spiritual advantage, since it relieves her of the temptation to sin which burdens healthy people. She has even managed to overcome the sin of thought by training herself not to think. She interprets her suffering as a sign that God has sent her a cross to bear, which means that He loves her. She regards her solitude as an opportunity to become more spiritually aware, maintaining that this spiritual awareness would not be as highly developed if she were surrounded by people. She accepts her own misfortunes without malice and selflessly shows concern for the suffering of others when she pleads with Pyotr to request his mother to lower the quit-rent of the peasants to alleviate their plight.

While Lukerya emerges as noble and compassionate, Turgenev depicts the members of the upper classes in a less positive manner, emphasizing their insensitivity. Unable to cure Lukerya, the doctors who treat her abandon her. Pyotr's mother, finding it inconvenient to keep cripples in the manor house, sends Lukerya to another village so she will not be in the way. Another doctor comes to examine Lukerya, not for the sake of helping a suffering human being but merely to satisfy his scientific curiosity. The doctor disdainfully refers to her and the other peasants he treats as fools.

Through his sympathetic portrayal of Lukerya, Turgenev suggests her moral superiority to those surrounding her. She emerges as a powerful symbol of the masses of the Russian peasantry, paralyzed, unable to help themselves, enduring misfortune and mistreatment, and regarded with disdain or indifference by the upper classes. Despite their suffering, however, the peasants, like Lukerya, persevere through patience, quiet humility, and resignation.

Style and Technique

Turgenev emphasizes the spiritual significance of Lukerya's suffering through a series of Christian symbols. Symbolically, Lukerya is given the name "Living Relic" by the peasants, who recognize her patience, meekness, and gentleness. The term "relic" has obvious religious overtones, associating her with sainthood or martyrdom. This religious symbolism is reinforced when Pyotr first encounters Lukerya and describes her face as "all of one color, bronze, for all the world like an icon painted in the old style; the nose narrow like the blade of a knife." The religious symbolism of her suffering is repeated in three of Lukerya's dreams. In the first dream, her parents appear to her and thank her for making it easier for them in the other world by suffering for their sins, asserting that she has already atoned for her own sins by her prolonged suffering and that she has now started to atone for the sins of others. In the second dream, Lukerya sees herself standing in a field of golden rye and placing a moon on her head like a festive headdress. The circular shape of the moon suggests a halo. She begins to shine and light up the field around her as a beardless, tall, young man in white, whom she identifies as Christ, approaches her and soars with her to Heaven, leaving behind a vicious dog that keeps biting at her legs and which symbolizes her illness. The dream reveals to Lukerya that her suffering will cease only at her death, for the dog which is her illness will have no place in the Kingdom of Heaven. Her third and final dream both foreshadows her death and suggests her sainthood by associating her death with a religious holy day. Lukerya encounters a tall woman with large, yellow, falconlike eyes who announces to her that she represents death, which will come for Lukerya after the fast for Saint Peter's day. Lukerya dies as predicted, after Saint Peter's day, and on the day of her death, she reports hearing the sound of church bells "from above"—which the narrator, Pyotr, interprets as "from Heaven," thus acknowledging her saintliness and affirming her spiritual beauty, which is the major theme of the story.

Jerome J. Rinkus

LIVINGSTONE'S COMPANIONS

Author: Nadine Gordimer (1923-   )
Type of plot: Social realism
Time of plot: c. 1970
Locale: Africa
First published: 1971

> *Principal characters:*
> CARL CHURCH, the protagonist, a British newspaper
> correspondent
> MRS. PALMER, the owner of a hotel where Church takes a
> break from an assignment
> DICK PALMER, her son, manager of the hotel, who wants to be
> a pop musician
> ZELIDE, the secretary-receptionist at the hotel, with whom
> Dick is having an affair

The Story

"Livingstone's Companions" is a somewhat indeterminate story, for it combines two tangential but still related plot interests: Carl Church and his fascination with the lake near the hotel where he is staying, and Dick Palmer's attempt to break the bonds of his domineering mother. Both these stories are undergirded by Church's reading the journals of the famous African explorer David Livingstone. Moreover, providing a social background (typical of Nadine Gordimer's fiction) is the story of the complex relationship between white colonials and black natives in Africa.

The story begins with Church's bored response to the petty political posturing of the Minister of Foreign Affairs in an anonymous African country, a country, like many in modern Africa, which is newly independent. Church's story begins with an assignment from his British editor to do a piece on the one hundredth anniversary of the Royal Geographic Society sending a party to search for the famous explorer David Livingstone. Church is told to retrace the steps of Livingstone's last journey. With this assignment, the central metaphor of the story is established, for although Church—less than delighted with what he considers to be the triviality of such a task—does not retrace Livingstone's steps literally, he does so psychologically and symbolically.

Church's journey begins in the airport with a chance meeting with a blonde woman who runs a hotel in a neighboring country near the graves of Livingstone's companions, graves which the woman proprietorially calls "my graves." The central theme of the story, and that which connects the story of Church with the story of Mrs. Palmer (the hotel proprietor) and her son, is indicated when Church reads from Livingstone's journal about how a community of interests and perils makes everyone friends. Church says, as though referring to "Livingstone's Companions," that such an idea could be the lead for his own story. Indeed, it is the community of interests and perils that connects Church with Dick Palmer and thus with the story of Africa itself.

Church's involvement with the Palmers begins when he gets lost looking for Livingstone's trail, stumbles upon Mrs. Palmer's hotel, and meets Dick and Zelide—he wearing diving fins and she dressed in a bikini, as if they were the inhabitants of an ocean world right in the middle of the African bush. Although it is getting lost which leads Church to the hotel, it is the lake that keeps him, for it is the lake which serves as Nadine Gordimer's central metaphor of irresistible allure, as the Livingstone journals (particularly Livingstone's account of the death of one of his companions) serve as a reccuring motif of interest. Church, in this hiatus in his journalistic tours, responds to the journals in place of the usual Gideon Bible he might find in a hotel. Although he plans to seek out the graves of Livingstone's companions, he has difficulty finding them, and thus discovers them more significantly in the journals themselves.

Dick's story is one of being dominated by his mother; even as she urges him to grow up, she tries to keep him from making decisions of his own. Dick tells Church about having his own band, about playing the guitar, about composing his own material, but when he cannot agree with his mother, he, like Church, heads for the lake and skin-dives. Church sees in him the image of a homosexual boy in the Berlin 1920's, the master-race face of a George Grosz drawing. It is this decadent sense that takes hold of Church, for he feels that such a pause or break as this is difficult for him: If he is not focused on what he will do next he knows not what to do. His mind turns to death, and he goes back to the lake.

In fishing with a spear under the lake surface, Church discovers the miracle of an unself-conscious technique of the hunt: the miracle of hitting the fish without thinking of it, a kind of magic typical of primitive intuitiveness. When the miracle occurs and he does spear a large fish, however, it twirls about so vigorously on the spear that it unscrews itself from the shaft and disappears with the harpoon point sticking out of its belly and its entrails floating out. At this point in the story, Church no longer remembers the error that brought him to this place; he simply accepts himself as "here"—an experience not common to him, for he is not accustomed to being present in the places and situations in which he now finds himself, and he identifies with the first travelers in Africa, who must have experienced each day as detached from the last and next.

The conflict between blacks and whites in Africa with which Gordimer is often concerned is embodied in Mrs. Palmer, who says that blacks simply do not know how to look after anything—a comment which Church ironically sees as the enlightenment the white man has brought to the natives. She treats her son the same way. When Dick tells Church that he has just received a phone call from his fiancée in another city and that someone has told her that he is having an affair with the secretary-receptionist, the reader knows that the mother is the guilty party. When Dick disappears, the mother worries that he will "do away with himself" as his father did.

Such confessions prompt in Church a desire to go to the lake, to feel the cool mouth of waters close over him. Yet he does not go back to the lake. As Church is leaving he finds the path to the graves of Livingstone's companions, the graves he was originally seeking. Among the five graves is that of Dick's father—a sixth companion to Livingstone. All of them look toward the lake, a lake that stretches as far as one can see.

Themes and Meanings

This is one of those stories which is so slight in plot that the reader is left with a feeling that it is not a story at all. It manifests a technique of inconclusiveness that Gordimer learned from the great modern, Anton Chekhov, for the story does not present its theme by means of plot or character dialogue, but rather by implication and understatement. Carl Church is the central character, but he is less a character than a convention: the convention of the bored and jaded newspaperman who remains objective, aloof, and uninvolved with the lives of others, one who is usually not really "there," but who, because of the influence of the lake, now seems actually "here," who seems most alive when he is under the influence of the lake itself. Although he does not have any interest in Dick's dilemma, nor any sympathy for Dick's mother, he still somehow sees a relationship (though he never explicitly mentions it) between the experience of Livingstone and his own experience.

Thus, ironically, he does not write his newspaper story about following in the footsteps of Livingstone, and yet in a strange way he does, for this very story entitled "Livingstone's Companions" is an artistic version of that story he was assigned. Church somehow believes that he is following in the footsteps of Livingstone, exploring the mysteries of Africa; here, the mysteries of Africa are those of the proprietorial and paternalistic attitude of the white toward the black, reflected by the fact that Dick is an employee of his mother, who believes that neither her son nor the blacks can take care of anything. Thus, the story is really about the fact that all whites in Africa are Livingstone's companions, following in his footsteps, leaving graves in their wake. Yet none of this is made explicit; all is suggested indirectly.

Style and Technique

The technique which Gordimer uses here is typical of her stories. The style is fairly straightforward and realistic, focusing on trivial events and only gradually revealing that there is a story at all, that there is indeed a conflict. Juxtaposition is the technique Gordimer uses to reveal the theme: juxtaposition of the story of Church with that of Dick, and juxtaposition of both of their stories with the journals of Livingstone. Moreover, Gordimer makes use of a central metaphor, the lake, to indicate the cool and mysterious submerged nature of Africa, where true reality is to be found, in contrast to the hot and complicated world of surface human interaction. Gordimer is a realist, but only if that term is understood as referring to the symbolic realism of Chekhov, Katherine Mansfield, James Joyce, and Sherwood Anderson. Her stories seem realistic in the sense of being detailed small slices of life, but they always carry more meaning beneath the surface than may at first appear.

Charles E. May

A LODGING FOR THE NIGHT

Author: Robert Louis Stevenson (1850-1894)
Type of plot: Historical realism
Time of plot: 1456
Locale: Paris
First published: 1877

> *Principal characters:*
> FRANCIS VILLON, a poet and thief
> DOM NICOLAS, a Picardy monk, one of the band of thieves
> GUY TABARY, another thief
> REGNIER DE MONTIGNY, a thief and murderer
> THEVENIN PENSETE, another thief, who is murdered by
>   Montigny
> ENGUERRAND DE LA FEUILLÉE, a lord and veteran of the wars,
>   who gives Villon shelter and hospitality

The Story

On a bitterly cold winter's night in 1456, Francis Villon, the greatest poet of medieval France, is huddled in a small house by the cemetery of St. John, trying to write "The Ballade of Roast Fish" while Guy Tabary slobbers over his shoulder, Regnier de Montigny and Thevenin Pensete play a game of chance, and the renegade monk Dom Nicolas watches. All of them are thieves, among whom there is no honor. Hearing the wind rattling the rafters, Villon reminds the others of hanged men dangling on the gibbet at nearby Montfaucon. Despite this *memento mori*, Montigny leaps up and stabs Thevenin to death after losing to him. The thieves divide the dead man's money, but then the others steal Villon's purse before they all flee into the night.

The snow has ceased, and Villon fears that his footprints will lead the authorities to him. Trying to elude a patrol, he takes refuge on the porch of a ruined house, where he finds the body of a woman frozen to death and steals two small coins from her stocking. Then, discovering his purse to be missing, he wanders in search of it, to no avail. Fearing that he, too, will freeze before morning, he seeks shelter from his adopted father, the chaplain of St. Benoit, but is turned away. Wandering once more, he recalls that wolves devoured a woman and child nearby. When he begs shelter from former friends whom he has lampooned, they drench him with a slop bucket, and his legs begin to freeze.

In desperation, he knocks at the door of a strange house in which he sees a light. The door opens, and an elderly gentleman invites him in. While his host goes for food and drink, Villon surveys the riches of the apartment and considers stealing the golden plate but thinks better of it. When his host returns, they strike up a conversation, and Villon learns that the master of the house is Enguerrand de la Feuillée, a great lord and a veteran of the king's wars. Villon confesses himself a poet and thief. They engage in a dialogue over the nature of honor, Villon claiming that the soldier is a greater thief than himself and that their different status is merely a matter of birth, the lord maintaining the traditional view of honor. When the host condemns Villon's rascality, the poet defends himself by claiming that he too has honor, which has kept him from stabbing Enguerrand and robbing him. By then, morning has broken, and the enraged host orders his unwanted guest to leave.

Themes and Meanings

"A Lodging for the Night," Robert Louis Stevenson's first published fiction, was also the first fictional treatment in English of François Villon (1431-1463?), the greatest poet of medieval France. Born as François de Montcorbier, Villon, author of *Le Petit Testament* (1456) and *Le Grand Testament* (1461), was neglected in subsequent centuries but rediscovered in the nineteenth century, when his bohemianism struck a kindred chord and his writing contributed to the romanticizing of the Middle Ages. In the 1860's, Dante Gabriel Rossetti (1828-1882) did three notable translations of Villon, and soon several other poets, including Algernon Charles Swinburne (1837-1909), did some translations and imitations of the French poet. The first complete translation into English did not appear until 1878, the year after Stevenson's story, and it may well be that "A Lodging for the Night" was the catalyst for the project. Just before writing the story, Stevenson wrote in 1877 an article entitled "François Villon, Student, Poet, and Housebreaker."

In it, Stevenson, an advocate of the heroic, stoic, and active life, condemned Villon as a whining, cowardly knave and used this portrait to attack the aesthetes and bohemians of his own day. Stevenson was both drawn to and contemptuous of Villon; he preferred the vigor and sometimes brutal realism of Villon to the work of more effete and languid poets of his own day, but he also disliked the extreme realism of the rising naturalist writers, of whom he saw Villon as an ancestor. "Not only his style, but his callous pertinent way of looking upon the sordid and ugly aspects of life, becomes every day a more specific feature in the literature of France," Stevenson complained. Nevertheless, Stevenson was fascinated by the vitality of evil, a subject that he explored in "Markheim," *The Strange Case of Dr. Jekyll and Mr. Hyde* (1886), *The Master of Ballantrae* (1888), and elsewhere, and he was drawn to Villon's vivid picture of the Parisian underworld. He envied Villon an artistic freedom denied the Victorians: "No thought that occurred to him would need to be dismissed without expression; and he could draw at full length the portrait of his own bedevilled soul, and of the bleak and blackguardly world which was the theater of his exploits and sufferings."

Later authors were to transform Villon into a romantic hero. In *If I Were King* (1901), Justin Huntly McCarthy (1860-1936) makes Villon not merely a thief but also a king of vagabonds, whom Louis XI then makes Grand Constable of France for a week, during which Villon saves Paris from the Burgundians and wins the love of a highborn lady. This version of Villon, and variations on it, flourished in the operetta *The Vagabond King* (1925) and in several films, in which Villon is portrayed by Dustin Farnum, John Barrymore, and Ronald Colman. Stevenson's biographer J. C. Furnas observed that "Louis would probably have been genuinely shocked by the distortions of *If I Were King.*" According to Stevenson, the poor should bear their burdens with stoic fortitude and "smile with the fox burrowing in their vitals. But Villon, who had not the courage to be poor with honesty, now whiningly implores our sympathy, now shows his teeth upon the dungheap with an ugly snarl."

"A Lodging for the Night" shows Villon doing both. He is so ineffective even in crime that his colleagues pick his pocket and call him a crybaby while he stands limp and trembling after the murder. During his dialogue with Enguerrand de la Feuillée, he is alternately swaggering and servile, justifying his unsavory life by blaming it on the poverty into which he was born. The snarl comes when he challenges the lord's claim to honor; Villon observes with bitter truth that the honor of a conquering army is that of plunder and rapine, that his own petty crimes are trivial compared to those committed by royalty and their troops. Villon says that his own honor consists in not cutting his host's throat and stealing his golden goblets; that is his thanks for the night's hospitality. He leaves with his neck still unstretched and his impudence intact.

Style and Technique

Like all of Stevenson's writing, "A Lodging for the Night" is notable for a clear, well-crafted style. There is nothing complicated about the construction of the story; it moves in a linear manner from beginning to end. Stevenson made his moralizing dramatic by couching it in the form of a dialogue between Villon and his host, and the argument between them is fairly well balanced, with Villon getting the last word. The genesis of the story can be found in Stevenson's earlier article about Villon, where he briefly recounted the murder of Thevenin and commented, "If time had only spared us some particulars, might not this last have furnished us with the matter of a grisly winter's tale?" Upon further reflection, he fashioned just such a tale out of the incident. The story contains a marvelous evocation of medieval Paris on a wintry night, when people were frozen to death on the streets and wolves were prowling over the snow. Furnas writes, " 'A Lodging for the Night' has a high and valuable flavor of Balzac—the harsh little literary curiosity is still shapelessly cunning, and, for all its didactic dialogue, strangely alive."

As a novelist, Stevenson was to make his mark with vigorous historical romances, and "A Lodging for the Night" was his first work in that genre.

Robert E. Morsberger